About the Author

Photograph by Carmen Ronan.

Jerome Clark is a prize-winning author of the multi-volume *UFO Encyclopedia* (1990–1998) and other books, including *Unnatural Phenomena* (2005) and *Hidden Realms, Lost Civilizations, and Beings from Other Worlds* (Visible Ink Press, 2010). A former editor of *Fate* magazine, he serves on the board of the J. Allen Hynek Center for UFO Studies. In June 2008 the Society for Scientific Exploration, an organization of professionals in the physical and social sciences, gave him its Dinsdale Award for "significant contributions to the expansion of human understanding through the study of unexplained phenomena … which have brought to the general public comprehensive and trustworthy information presented from a sophisticated perspective."

Clark is also a songwriter (Emmylou Harris, Mary Chapin Carpenter, Tom T. Hall, Seldom Scene, Mary Black, and others) and a prolific writer on folk and roots music. He pursues a wide range of interests—political, historical, and literary—from his home in Minnesota.

ALSO FROM VISIBLE INK PRESS

Armageddon Now: The End of the World A to Z
by Jim Willis and Barbara Willis
ISBN: 978-1-57859-168-8

The Astrology Book: The Encyclopedia of Heavenly Influences, 2nd Edition
by James R Lewis
ISBN: 978-1-57859-144-2

Conspiracies and Secret Societies: The Complete Dossier, 2nd Edition
by Brad Steiger and Sherry Hansen Steiger
ISBN: 978-1-57859-368-2

The Dream Encyclopedia, 2nd Edition
by James R Lewis and Evelyn Dorothy Oliver
ISBN: 978-1-57859-216-6

The Encyclopedia of Religious Phenomena
by J. Gordon Melton
ISBN: 978-1-57859-209-8

The Fortune-telling Book: The Encyclopedia of Divination and Soothsaying
by Raymond Buckland
ISBN: 978-1-57859-147-3

Hidden Realms, Lost Civilizations, and Beings from Other Worlds
by Jerome Clark
ISBN: 978-1-57859-175-6

Real Aliens, Space Beings, and Creatures from Other Worlds
by Brad Steiger and Sherry Steiger
ISBN: 978-1-57859-333-0

Real Ghosts, Restless Spirits, and Haunted Places, 2nd Edition
by Brad Steiger
ISBN: 978-1-57859-401-4

Real Miracles, Divine Intervention, and Feats of Incredible Survival
by Brad Steiger and Sherry Steiger
ISBN: 978-1-57859-214-2

Real Monsters, Gruesome Critters, and Beasts from the Darkside
by Brad Steiger
ISBN: 978-1-57859-220-3

Real Vampires, Night Stalkers, and Creatures from the Darkside
by Brad Steiger
ISBN: 978-1-57859-255-5

Real Zombies, the Living Dead, and Creatures of the Apocalypse
by Brad Steiger
ISBN: 978-1-57859-296-8

The Spirit Book: The Encyclopedia of Clairvoyance, Channeling, and Spirit Communication
by Raymond Buckland
ISBN: 978-1-57859-172-5

The Vampire Book: The Encyclopedia of the Undead, 3rd Edition
by J. Gordon Melton
ISBN: 978-1-57859-281-4

The Werewolf Book: The Encyclopedia of Shape-shifting Beings, 2nd Edition
by Brad Steiger
ISBN: 978-1-57859-367-5

The Witch Book: The Encyclopedia of Witchcraft, Wicca, and Neo-Paganism
by Raymond Buckland
ISBN: 978-1-57859-114-5

Real Nightmares ebook series volumes 1–12
by Brad Steiger
ISBN: various

Please visit us at visibleinkpress.com.

UNEXPLAINED!

Strange Sightings, Incredible Occurrences, and Puzzling Physical Phenomena

THIRD EDITION

Jerome Clark

VISIBLE
INK

Detroit

UNEXPLAINED!
Strange
Sightings,
Incredible
Occurrences,
and Puzzling
Physical
Phenomena
3rd Edition

Visible Ink Press®
43311 Joy Rd., #414
Canton, MI 48187-2075

Visible Ink Press is a registered trademark of Visible Ink Press LLC.

Most Visible Ink Press books are available at special quantity discounts when purchased in bulk by corporations, organizations, or groups. Customized printings, special imprints, messages, and excerpts can be produced to meet your needs. For more information, contact Special Markets Director, Visible Ink Press, www.visibleinkpress.com, or 734-667-3211.

Managing Editor: Kevin S. Hile
Art Director: Mary Claire Krzewinski
Typesetting: Marco Di Vita
Proofreader: Chrystal Rosza
Indexing: Shoshana Hurwitz

ISBN 978-1-57859-573-0

Cover image: Shutterstock.com.

Printed in the United States of America

Cataloging-in-Publication data is on file at the Library of Congress.

10 9 8 7 6 5 4 3 2 1

CONTENTS

Fables ... 367

FOREWORD

The first edition of this book appeared in 1993, the second in 1999. With this edition the book enters the twenty-first century in considerably revised, much expanded form. The mass of fresh material that had accumulated over a dozen years rendered the new volume something worth doing. A good deal of what you will read has never appeared between book covers. Some subjects—for example the curious affair of the Belled Buzzard—have not, as far as I know, been examined comprehensively until now.

This is not an attempt, let me be clear, to represent the broad spectrum of anomalies and other allegedly unexplained events and experiences. Such an effort would require many fat volumes, and it would also cover paranormal phenomena—ESP and psychokinesis, apparitions, out-of-body and near-death experiences—which are, frankly, outside my area of expertise (to the extent that anyone can pretend to have "expertise" in anomalous matters). Nor does the present volume carry over everything from its previous incarnation. Some things simply didn't seem worth revisiting because I felt I had said all I had to say about them and there were no interesting new developments. Ultimately, what I have kept and what I have added have one element in common: they interest me.

A few chapters and sidebars return more or less intact because I thought they needed to be there to serve as a corrective to persistent misinformation regularly peddled by cable television's snake-oilish "true mystery" shows. (My inclination is to think of these as the television equivalent of those ubiquitous unsourced email forwards that peddle bald-faced lies and shameless distortions for the edification of the naïve and otherwise readily bamboozled.) In fact, this book is intended, in part anyway, for intelligent persons who have seen those programs—a few of which, fairness compels me to state, rise above the generally abysmal level—and who may be looking for something more accurate and substantive. Veterans of anomalies literature, however, will also be exposed to information they haven't seen until now.

In that regard, this third edition, in contrast to its predecessors, does not include chapters on UFOs, Sasquatch, and the Loch Ness Monster. Information on these, the most celebrated of all anomalies, exists in abundance, by which I mean one could fill the shelves of a small library with books devoted solely to each. Those who don't know that literature may easily seek it elsewhere. Mostly, I have preferred to concentrate on lesser-known, sometimes entirely obscure, mysteries and curiosities. UFOs show up only in a very few cases exemplifying the most extreme claims associated with the idea of alien visitors (as opposed to the hard evidence of radar/visual cases, physical traces, and the like). Sasquatch's alter ego, the Hairy Biped, to which resemblances to the hirsute giants of the Pacific Northwest seem more apparent than real, figures in a long, detailed chapter. The Loch Ness Monster is treated in succinct fashion in the chapter on Lake Monsters.

Another decision I made as I selected material was to confine it to two categories of interpretation: first, testimony that to every indication is sincerely related and apparently truly puzzling, and two, stories that are certainly or probably somebody's invention. The pages that follow contain plenty of examples of both. A third category, the one that has sparked a massive, often eye-glazing literature, concerns instances where witness misperception or other error is certain, or at least, at varying degrees of plausibility, arguable. In other words, instances in which someone relates an encounter under uncertain viewing conditions in which the object of attention may or may not be what the witness infers it may have been. In these pages, the choices are starker: it almost surely happened (however one defines "happened"), or it almost surely didn't.

On his late-night CBS television program, comedian David Letterman runs an occasional feature in which some unfamiliar, baffling-looking activity is presented, accompanied by the question, "Is this something?" In other words, does the activity have purpose and meaning, or is it only some sort of goofy exhibition? From our side, we may well ask ourselves, are anomalous experiences significant, or are they just some form of absurd, empty display?

I don't know. Neither do you. Maybe one day we'll find out.

* * *

Thank you, as always, to my ever patient and supportive publisher Roger Jänecke, and love, as always, to Helene Henderson, who was my editor before she was my wife and who became my editor again on the first draft of a fat and complicated manuscript. Less happily: When I was a day from completing the manuscript, I received the sad news that my friend and colleague W. Ritchie Benedict had died. Ritchie, who lived in Calgary, Alberta, was an energetic, conscientious inquirer who spent decades scouring old newspapers and journals in search of accounts of anomalous occurrences. Few could match Ritchie's knowledge of Canada's arcane legends and mysteries. The bulk of the North Country material in the pages that follow came to me via Ritchie's labors and generosity. Beyond that, he was a good guy, and I will miss him.

Some additional words of gratitude to the kind souls who, through their good efforts and intellectual curiosity, helped me bring this book to be: Chris Aubeck, Evan Clark, Loren Coleman, Fred Davis, Gary Davis, the late Lucius Farish, Alex French, J. Gordon Melton, Theo Paijmans, Fabio Picasso, and Nick Sucik. Also, all those splendidly philosophical minds who over the years, against all my lazy and complacent instincts, forced me to think harder and smarter about anomalies: Henry H. Bauer, Thomas E. Bullard, the late Hilary Evans, David J. Hufford, Michael D. Swords, the late Marcello Truzzi, Jacques Vallee, and Ron Westrum. It goes without saying that none of them is to be held accountable for what I have made of those lessons.

INTRODUCTION

Grappling with the Anomalous

The three hardest words for human beings to utter are "I don't know." We demand an accounting for every claim or experience, and when no accounting is available, someone will invent one for us.

Thus, a New Hampshire man, a veteran outdoorsman considered reliable by those who knew him, reports a daylight encounter with a nine-foot-tall apelike creature. A game warden explains it, with neither investigation nor specific cause, as a moose. Or when a number of West Texas motorists, over a period of hours, independently tell of close-range sightings of a 200-foot-long, egg-shaped, brilliantly luminous structure, U.S. Air Force personnel conduct a brief inquiry and identify the phenomenon as ball lightning, an allegation the national press happily endorsed soon afterwards. In fact, what the witnesses had described bore no resemblance to this rare aerial phenomenon, and the electrical storm that, according to the Air Force, had given rise to it did not exist according to weather records.

In both of these cases, the proposed solutions are so flimsy that one thinks it would have been easier to charge the witnesses with bald-faced lies and be done with it. Either that, or diagnose them as dangerous lunatics whose vivid hallucinations call for their immediate sedation and hospitalization.

Of course, if these were isolated episodes, the sorts of stories told and heard rarely, and then usually from excitable or gullible souls, we could probably tell ourselves, "Yes, I suppose it is possible, once in a great while, for someone to see a moose and mistake it for a nine-foot-tall bipedal anthropoid, or for a person to have a close-up view of a globe of ball lightning, ordinarily the size of a basketball or smaller, and judge it to be 200 feet in diameter." After all, where human behavior is concerned, just about anything that could happen has happened at some time or another.

It's just that the sorts of colossal perceptual breakdowns being proposed here run as counter to the experience of most human beings as do encounters with hairy giants in New England woods. Suppose the New Hampshire witness had seen something else, say a fugitive on the lam, and reported it to the sheriff. We may safely assume that the latter would not have said—at least without serious inquiry and specific cause—that the witness had mistaken a moose for a man. Far more likely, the sheriff and his deputies would have raced to the scene in anticipation of an arrest.

Yet if we allow ourselves to believe (still in the absence of specific evidence to the effect) that at times, even under what are thought of as good viewing conditions, a moose can look like an ape, we will only be stymied if we try to employ this identification in the many places where similar "apes" have been reported and where moose (or, in many cases, any wild mammals larger than deer) do not exist.

It will not help us, either, to level indiscriminant charges of dishonesty against all witnesses wherever we find them—whether in New Hampshire or Indiana or Pennsylvania or South Dakota or Texas or British Columbia or Labrador, or just about any state or province you can name—and off-the-cuff speculations about perceptual disorders of so radical a character as to suggest mental illness and social dysfunction take us only so far. At some point we are going to have to listen to what the witnesses say.

Hagged

Let us consider the case of the Old Hag.

The victim wakes up unable to move. As he lies there helpless, he hears footsteps and sees a horrifying form. An invisible force presses on his chest, and he thinks he is going to die. At last he is able to shake off his paralysis, and the eerie attack ends.

Chances are you have never heard of an incident like this—unless it has happened to you. And if it has happened to you, you are not alone. There is reason to believe that one American in six has had this kind of experience; yet it is so little discussed in our culture that it has no name.

But in other cultures the same experience is the subject of a rich folk tradition. Newfoundlanders, for example, call it the "Old Hag," "The Hags," or "Hagging." When it was first used in connection with these experiences, the word "hag" referred to "witch," and a victim of hagging was thought to be hag- or witch-ridden. In fact, the most common expression for the experience in English is "riding." Interestingly enough, the original name is one with which we are all familiar: nightmare. Nightmare, which to us means simply "bad dream," once had a far more specific definition; it referred to an incubus or succubus that came in the night to put a crushing weight on a victim's chest.

The importance of testimony

In a remarkable book, *The Terror That Comes in the Night* (published by University of Pennsylvania Press in 1982), Penn State folklorist and behavioral scientist David J. Hufford used the Old Hag to address a crucial question: Do persons reporting firsthand encounters with anomalous and paranormal phenomena know what they are talking about?

Standard wisdom holds, as we have already noted, that such experiences are the product of perceptual errors, faulty memories, lies, psychotic episodes, and hallucinations shaped by ideas in the claimants' cultural environment. Through the example of the Old Hag, Hufford tested this hypothesis, which—except in cases where consciously false testimony is alleged—might be phrased as the "believing is seeing" theory. This theory proposes that individuals believe they have seen something extraordinary because society has provided them with the images that shape their imaginings.

After an in-depth examination of Old Hag accounts both in cultures in which such beliefs are widely known and in others (ours, for instance) in which they are all but unspoken of, Hufford learned that descriptions of the core experience, by those who say they have had it, are strikingly consistent wherever they occur. Such experiences are not culturally determined. "Recognizable Old Hag attacks of great complexity can and do occur in the absence of explicit models," Hufford wrote.

He then considered psychologists' efforts to account for the phenomenon and found them hopelessly muddled. Of one famous psychoanalytic study, Hufford said that "one can hardly distinguish the experiences themselves from their interpretations. The lack of scientific precision attributed to popular thought is found here in academic disguise." The consistent unwillingness of psychologists and other professionals to listen to those persons who have had these experiences has led them to engage in freewheeling speculation devoid of empirical justification. "The subject of supernatural belief somehow leads to a lot of forgetting about what constitutes serious scholarship," Hufford observed.

"It was just such rejection of untutored observation that delayed for so long the 'scientific' discovery of giant squid, gorillas, meteors and any number of other wild and wonderful (but apparently unlikely) facts of this world. In those cases *post hoc* scientific rationalization was used to explain how people came to believe in such things. Seasoned fishermen were said to mistake floating trees with large root systems for huge animals attacking their boats; farmers were said to have overlooked iron-bearing rocks in the midst of their fields until they were pointed out by lightning; and in this case [the Old Hag experience] 'children and savages' were said to have difficulty knowing when they were awake and when they were asleep"—even though the victims, persons of all ages, cultures, and education levels, insist they were not "dreaming," that they were fully conscious when they heard and saw weird things.

Hufford argued that we must take seriously "an experience with stable contents which is widespread, dramatic, realistic and bizarre" and which has been repeatedly reported "by large numbers of our fellow humans."

Nor did Hufford hesitate to consider the implications of his Old Hag research for other claims of strange experiences. "I think the present study has amply demonstrated that at least some apparently fantastic beliefs are in fact empirically grounded," he wrote, noting that nonetheless most scholars have acted more interested in explaining troublesome claims "out of existence" than in investigating them. The farther they remove themselves from the data (the accounts of those who have had the experiences), the more exotic, facile, and irrelevant their theories become. In Hufford's blunt assessment this practice amounts to "careless thinking retroactively applied with little regard for evidence."

An empirically based "experience-centered" approach such as the one Hufford employed would show, he contended, that phenomena like the Old Hag are believed in because they really happen; they are not simply imagined by people who are so stupid, crazy, or credulous that they cannot tell the difference between a popular superstition and a personal experience. Inquirers would learn not to confuse "folk explanation"—for example the notion that witches cause Old Hag attacks—with "folk observation"—which, as Hufford demonstrated, can be quite accurate, consistent, and scientifically valuable.

Hufford's argument brings revolutionary implications in its assertion that rational persons are accurately reporting experiences that at least appear to be extraordinary, and that those who have attempted to explain away such accounts have failed to make their case and or even understood what they are trying to explain. As a consequence scholars have failed to come to grips with a significant part of human experience.

Can the Old Hag experience be accounted for in non-paranormal terms? Drawing on findings from sleep research conducted in later years, Hufford concluded that the "state in which this experience occurs is probably best described as sleep paralysis with a particular kind of hypnagogic hallucination." In other words, science can explain how someone could wake from sleep, be unable to move, and have a frightening experience. But it cannot explain the fact that the contents of the experience are consistent no matter to whom or in what cultural environment they occur. This mystery cannot be solved, in Hufford's informed estimation, "on the basis of current knowledge."

Seeing is believing

When the experience of hairy bipeds, UFOs, lake monsters, or other anomalous entities or objects is concerned, one need not believe in, or even have heard of such, to see one. The isolated folk of early twentieth-century Newfoundland had never heard of "Sasquatch" or "Bigfoot"—names that did not come into popular currency until decades later, and on the other side of the continent. Even so, they reported seeing manlike entities they called "Indians." Few of the Newfoundlanders knew what a real Indian looked like, but that was the name they attached to creatures whom other North Americans, who had never heard of Bigfoot or Sasquatch either, were calling "wild men" or "gorillas."

In our time, even when such phenomena are staples of popular culture, it is still possible to find occasional individuals who have never heard, for example, of UFOs; yet they report unusual experiences with what they may interpret as everything from "secret airplanes" to "demons." Their interpretations aside, they relate sights or occurrences that are in every way congruent with those experienced by more culturally sophisticated observers. Witnesses often say, "I wouldn't have believed if I hadn't seen it myself"—a statement that resonates with meaning.

There are some things people believe in not because they are ignorant, credulous, or crazy, but because either they or persons they trust see them. Seeing is believing, indeed.

Bogus photographs and pseudomysteries

Historically, photographs alleged to be of extraordinary anomalies are more likely than not to be bogus or at least suspect. Serious Sasquatch researchers reject as inauthentic most—albeit not all—photographs and films said to depict the creature. Probably more than 90 percent of all "UFO" photographs are of dubious provenance, and some of the most spectacular footage of Loch Ness monsters is known or suspected to be fake. The debate about photographic evidence of these kinds of phenomena centers on a surprisingly small number of recorded images.

Sometimes, in fact, critics act as if the paucity of arguably authentic photographs amounts to evidence against the reality of these sorts of anomalies. This argument, however, is not particularly compelling when one considers that nearly all anomalous encounters occur abruptly and occasion emotions ranging from deep shock to sheer terror. Usually, too, the duration of most such experiences can be measured in seconds. These are not conditions conducive to the accumulation of a large body of photographs and video images. And that is why there are so few reputable pictures of ball lightning, a strange natural phenomenon whose reality most physicists and meteorologists no longer dispute.

It is one of the perversities of anomalies research that the fuzzier the image, the more likely it represents something real, inasmuch as the circumstances that cause photographs to be rare are the same ones that are likely to cause them to be unclear. Pictures taken hastily by individuals with shaking hands do not produce sharp images, and hoaxers who seek attention or profit know that photographs like these won't get them anywhere. Fuzzy images are such a feeble variety of evidence that witnesses who trumpet them are only asking for yet more ridicule to be heaped upon their heads.

Some tales marketed as "true mysteries" began less as hoaxes than as jokes or science fiction—in other words, as tales that, though they may not have been intended to be taken seriously, took on lives of their own and over the decades reincarnated in print as records of events that, it was assumed, someone somewhere had validated. Two of the most notorious "mysterious disappearance" cases feature victims usually identified as David Lang in one and as Oliver Lerch in the other. Like true folktales names and details sometimes changed in the telling. While by now their origins either are known (Lang) or murky (Lerch), it is certain that neither man ever lived, much less left the planet in such singular fashion.

Other "mysteries" arise from imaginative interpretations of events that, if unusual, are not so bizarre as they are made to seem. These sorts of pseudomysteries flourish in part, of course, because people are drawn to exotic novelties and, moreover, enjoy being scared in comfort and safety. The many, mostly trashy pseudodocumentaries that play in endless rotation on cable television cater to these familiar human sentiments. Few people possess the specialized knowledge that would expose the foolish or careless assertions of the mystery-mongers.

Beyond the hoaxes and the legends are the occasional misperceptions and the honest mistakes. No conscientious investigator embarks on his or her labors without considering these possibilities and pursuing them actively. (Neither, however, will he or she force them on the data if they manifestly fail to fit.) Some witnesses, though not so many as popular lore would lead one to think, are mentally unwell.

Cautiously open minds

A deeper reason for skepticism has to do with the nature of the more fantastic claims. Many reports attest to beings, creatures, and occurrences that, if established as real, would rewrite science's map of reality. Some would shake the foundations of consensus reality. In short, what is being alleged here is nothing to be taken lightly. The implications are enormous.

Because the stakes are high, we would do well to be very cautious. Very cautious. After all, one does not redefine the world on no more than the word—however sincere it may appear to be—of sailors and shore-dwellers who swear they have seen merbeings. No biological principle, or even conceivable biological principle, allows us to believe in beings or animals that are half fish and half human, or even in creatures that look as if they could be half fish and half human.

Just as unlikely are fairies, though first-person sighting reports in no small number have been logged over the centuries. (Experiences of the fairy realm are discussed in my previous Visible Ink Press book, *Hidden Realms, Lost Civilizations, and Beings from Other Worlds*, 2010; see pages 193–211.) In a handful of cases they are preserved in affidavits sworn by presumably reputable and sober members of the clergy. Practically nobody except folklorists collects these reports anymore. Folklorists are interested in them because they represent survivals of older traditional beliefs; as to their status as descriptions of real events, most shrug and say this is a question for scholars of abnormal psychology or, perhaps, parapsychologists. Parapsychologists, for their part, say fairy sightings are of interest only to folklorists and psychologists.

Who can blame anyone here? Even to raise the question of fairy (or merbeing) sightings is to raise multitudes of eyebrows. For any number of reasons no rational person can fail to think of, fairies cannot exist, and the descriptions of fairy realms and life preserved in traditional narratives are clearly fabulous; not only that, they are so at variance that even a committed supernaturalist would be hard-pressed to fashion a geography of fairyland from such accounts. But could it be that fabulous elements attached themselves to experiences at least perceived as real, much in the way those who experienced Old Hag attacks, which really happened, attributed a folk cause (witch assaults) to them? In their *Scottish Fairy Belief* (2001), two wise folklorists, Lizanne Henderson and Edward J. Cowan, remark, "It should be possible to believe one's informants without believing their explanations."

It has to be conceded that the Old Hag experience is at least partially explainable by known physiological mechanisms, which is to say its degree of strangeness in some ways may be more apparent than real. These are also, virtually always, single-person experiences. If you were in a bedroom with someone who was undergoing an Old Hag attack, you would be unlikely to see the approaching apparition; you would see no more than the victim lying motionless and staring with a fearful expression. (Several years ago, as I lay in bed one morning not quite fully awake, I had what I recognized as an Old Hag experience. In my case the fearsome entity resembled the traditional vampire—a horrifying, decaying monster—not to be confused with its suave equivalent in Hollywood movies.)

Sightings of fairies and merbeings, on the other hand, typically are said to occur in settings where hallucinations tied to sleep are not an issue. The witnesses are usually individuals otherwise deemed sane and well, and consequently not susceptible to dramatic delusions. ("In our society," Graham Reed writes in *The Psychology of Anomalous Experience* [1988]), "hallucinatory content is usually concerned with the fears and conflicts which would be expected from people who are suffering from mental disorder or delirium due to physical health.") A number of these sightings, moreover, involve multiple witnesses.

That just about sums up the case for high-strangeness anomalies: credible persons reporting incredible things, and little but sincerity to show for it. This is not, in short, the stuff of a scientific revolution. Neither is it, however, occasion to rush into the vacuum with a naïvely reductionist explanation that renders the anomalous claim harmless by covering it with a "prosaic" cause pulled out of a hat—an approach that amounts to the fetishization of current knowledge, an expression of faith in the ahistorical proposition that what we know at the moment is all that we need to know. At the same time, it is just as unwise to fill the explanatory hole with scientifically meaningless or overtly supernatural guesswork based on a host of unprovable assumptions about ultimate reality.

It ought to be clear—though the literature on anomalous phenomena (whether written by proponents or debunkers) shows it is everything but that— that we do not know why honest individuals, in all times and places, claim to see things that all evidence and logic tell us do not and cannot exist. Nearly everybody who pays attention to such anomalous testimony can get him- or herself worked into an intellectual and emotional knot over it. Human nature abhors an explanatory vacuum; thus in the rhetoric of the debate that has raged in one form or another over the centuries, a strange entity or beast gets transformed either into a conventional object or animal to which it bears no appreciable resemblance or into an intruder from some magical dimension.

If neither explanation seems especially helpful, it is because the question has been framed wrongly. The question ought not to be, though it always is, "Do bizarre beasts and entities exist?" No sensible, all-encompassing answer is possible, and it is futile to pretend otherwise. The question really is this: "Is it possible to have the experience of encountering bizarre beasts and entities?" And the answer to that is yes.

To respond affirmatively is only to acknowledge modestly the obvious, which is, as folklorist Bill Ellis puts it, "Weird stuff happens." We are in no way conceding anything about what all this weird stuff means. We can grant that people "see" fairies or merbeings without for a moment proposing that such creatures are part of the planet's ecology. We simply acknowledge that such sightings are an experience it is possible to have, even while the actual dynamics of the experience remain unknown so far. Consequently, science as currently constructed has little to offer in the way of elucidation, and occultism has only obfuscation to offer. The nature of these experiences need not remain forever inexplicable. With the ever accelerating accumulation of knowledge in all areas it will be possible sooner or later to place these experiences in a rational perspective, as either heretofore-unsuspected perceptual anomalies, or dramatic glitches in consciousness, or glimpses of an otherwise-undetected larger reality (in which we are likely to encounter the phrase "multiverse"). Whether the solution comes from the micro (subjective) or macro (objective) side of the existential ledger, it is sure to teach us something new and fascinating.

Until then, these encounters should be regarded simply as curiosities that represent some of human experience's more peculiar and unclassifiable aspects and about which it is difficult to say more. In other words, they should not be seen as the foundation of a new science or a new religion, and they ought not to threaten anyone who does not need to believe early twenty-first century science has accounted for all the interesting phenomena of mind and nature.

Phenomena that stir but do not shake

Not all, or even most, anomalous claims are of such an extreme variety. On the lower side of the strangeness scale, we find ball lightning, ice falls, possibly surviving thylacines, that—while undeniably intriguing mysteries—seem unlikely to shake the world, even if answered affirmatively. Physicists, meteorologists, wildlife specialists, and others will solve these puzzles one day. Newspapers, television, Internet, and radio will take notice for a few days, and the phenomena will then sink from popular view, to be revived occasionally on cable TV's ubiquitous nature-themed programs.

But if cryptozoologists were to produce a specimen or body of a Sasquatch or a mokele-mbembe (an ostensible sauropod dinosaur alleged to survive in the remote regions of the Congo), the consequences for anthropology, paleontology, and evolutionary theory would be immense, if only because their presence (while improbable, not impossible) is so unexpected—not just by scientists but by almost everybody else. It is hard to imagine anybody who would not be excited. On the other hand, once the serious research—on these animals' physiology, diet, and behavior—began, popular interest would slacken, and in time Sasquatch and mokele-mbembe would be just more fodder for wild-animal documentaries. The same can be said of lake monsters, sea serpents, and the like.

Shaken, not stirred

On the other hand—and discussions of anomalies are nothing if not a long series of "on the other hands"—cryptozoologists deal with questions that seem straightforward enough but become complicated by unwelcome intrusions of high-strangeness manifestations. Confronted with such reports (recorded even at Loch

Ness), most of them related by persons seemingly no less sane or sincere than those whose accounts of encounters with less exotic, more zoologically imaginable specimens, cryptozoologists may resort to the same rationalizations they complain about in their critics. Even the ordinarily judicious Roy P. Mackal, a highly intelligent and informed academic who wrote one of the essential books on the Loch Ness questions, dismissed one bizarre land sighting as an encounter with what he speculated was a "congenitally deformed specimen of the highland cattle common in the area." (Another academic, this one dealing with fairy traditions, dismissed sightings of such entities as having arisen from "congenitally deformed" humans.)

Scientific proponents of the Northwest's Bigfoot/Sasquatch are often reluctant to discuss or even acknowledge hairy-biped reports in Eastern, Southern, and Midwestern states. The presence of such creatures in these places is all but indefensible on biological or logical grounds. Even worse, some aspects of their appearance verge on the apparitional, and a few instances hint at an association with UFOs. Some wildlife biologists believe, not unreasonably, that cougars, once thought extinct everywhere east of the Mississippi River except in the Florida Everglades, have reestablished a small foothold in the Northeastern wilds. They do not know what to do with uncountable reports, some of them in excellent viewing conditions, of "black panthers" and comparably anomalous felines (including maned African lions) all across the continent, not to mention the British Isles and Australia.

Ambiguity and high strangeness

It seems in the nature of things, in short, for something thought of as a single anomalous phenomenon to look like two phenomena, one merely fantastic, the other utterly incredible. One seems potentially explainable, more or less, by current (or near-future) science; the other is absurd or inexplicable, or both. This peculiar duality is apparent even in such relatively sedate manifestations of nature as ball lightning. Small luminous spheres that in other contexts would be labeled ball lightning demonstrate, in the testimonies of not a few witnesses, a bewildering purposefulness and intelligence. In his *Deviant Science* (1984) sociologist of science James McClenon remarks on an interview with a man who swore he had seen a small ball of light enter his bedroom after the closed window magically rose. After sailing about the house, it departed via the front door, which obligingly opened to permit it to escape.

What all this means, of course, is hard—really, impossible—to say. We can be assured, however, that this small consideration will stop no committed debunker or believer from saying it anyway. The temptation to reductionism (the witness was dreaming it) or occultism (it was a paranormal being from the etheric realm) is difficult to resist. Again, human nature abhors an explanatory vacuum. Real understanding demands intellectual modesty and patience, not to mention a huge tolerance for ambiguity. Where the most extreme sorts of claims—excepting those that are demonstrably bogus or otherwise suspect, naturally—are concerned, we are required neither to believe nor to disbelieve, and absolutely nothing calls for us to pursue explanations that defy reason and experience.

Common decency and common sense compel us to be courteous to witnesses and to hear them out. They, after all, were there; we weren't. If we can provide a reasonable unextraordinary explanation for what they tell us they have seen, fine. If not, we need not insult them by reinventing their sightings so as to trivialize them into crude misperceptions of ordinary stimuli. We need not ridicule them or call them, without evidence to the effect, liars. Yet the sincerest testimony to the most fantastic event or entity, even if we deem it accurately rendered, is not enough to remake the world on its own, in the absence of other, more compelling evidence. Of sightings of merbeings, fairies, hairy bipeds, thunderbirds, and the rest, all we can say is that these comprise some people's experience of the world.

Science will explain what it can explain, and the more science learns, the more it will be able to explain. If there are large, uncatalogued animals living in the planet's oceans and lakes, if Gigantopithecus lives on in the northwestern American wilderness, if extraterrestrial visitors are streaking through our air space, or if sauropods and thylacines are not truly extinct, we will know about them, once we bring the appropriate attention and resources to a serious effort to answer these questions. Presumably, the answers will come in the form of physical specimens.

But where high-strangeness claims are concerned, probably no amount of funding and expertise will do much more than produce still more sighting reports. Funding will permit analyses of the few (often literal) threads of physical evidence (hairy-biped hair, for example), with results that will either disappoint (it was dog hair) or frustrate (sort of like dog hair but also sort of like human hair, not quite either). Psychologists who are participating in the investigation will develop psychological profiles of the witnesses and will find their subjects to be essentially indistinguishable from nonwitnesses. To wit: ordinary people reporting extraordinary experiences—something we already knew. In other words, the end of the investigation takes us back to its beginning. Present knowledge is an unhelpful guide through the thickets of extreme anomalous experience.

That makes such experience no less interesting, of course. Whether taken as wonderfully strange stories, the makings of a future science, or intimations of hidden dimensions of matter or spirit, these accounts tell us, at the very least, that the possibilities of experience are far more various than we are led to believe. No amount of rationalization can alter the simple truth that—whatever their ultimate nature—all sorts of incredibly odd things can be experienced. If that fact does nothing else, it should alert us to the folly of ridicule. After all, if sober and sane Joe Smith can encounter something weird, presumably so can you and I. (And, in full disclosure, I already have.) If it happened to us, we would expect a courteous reception and be outraged if we received anything else—as we almost certainly would.

Weird stuff happening

In this book about weird stuff that happens to people, we hear the witnesses out. And why not? All other approaches, after all, have proven unhelpful and have done nothing but conceal, thinly, our ignorance. A radically objective approach that respects the testimony that deserves respect, even when it speaks of the incredible, is all that is left to us. This testimony may or may not tell us extraordinary truths about the world, but it does tell us something about the peculiar things people can experience in the world.

The causes more than the occurrences, the details of which may be only incidental, ought ultimately to comprise the focus of investigation, reflection, and debate. It is surely futile by now to argue that all anomalous experiences must fall to conventional causes; yet we cannot justify broad extrapolations from such experiences—which may not mean at all what they appear to mean—to invent, on no other basis than a witness' account, an extraordinary phenomenological context in which the reported phenomenon is said to make sense. What we experience anomalously may not "exist" in the literal sense in which that verb is ordinarily understood. We must proceed very cautiously, all the while keeping in mind what we do not know and cannot demonstrate.

Anomalies of the highest strangeness dwell in a twilight zone of ambiguity. To say that you have "seen" one is not necessarily to state that anomaly lives on in the world when it is not briefly occupying your vision and scaring the daylights out of you. We may experience unbelievable things, but our experiences of them may tell us nothing about them except that they can be experienced. You can "see" a merbeing or something else comparably outlandish; but however vivid the experience may be to you, the rest of us cannot infer from that that merbeings and other outlandish entities are "real." In fact, we can be certain that they are not. And that is all we can be certain of, because all we have done is to remove one explanation (that mermaids and outlandish entities live in the world) from consideration while failing to put another in its place.

Here at the fringes of reason and experience, we can only marvel and feel humble. For now, that should be enough.

—Jerome Clark
Minnesota
May 20, 2012

Dedication
In memory of my friend Budd Hopkins (1931–2011)

Photo Credits

MYSTERIES

Anomalous Clouds

 One pleasant summer morning in 1975, an Oyster Bay, New York, science teacher named Tom D'Ercole was in his driveway about to enter his car when he glanced up at the sky. There, hovering above the roof of his house, he saw a small dark cloud unlike the occasional cumulocirrus clouds that were floating by at a much higher altitude.

"The 'cloud' seemed to move and slightly enlarge as I watched it," D'Ercole related. "This basketball-sized 'cloud' floated back and forth across the peak of the roof, changing in shape from a small globular mass to a larger ovoid and finally becoming an abstract, multicurved, dark, vaporous 'something.' It finally measured about six feet in height and 1.5 feet in width."

Stunned and unable to think of a rational explanation, he continued to watch it in disbelief as events took an even stranger turn. The cloud seemed to inhale, purse its "lips," and direct a stream of water toward him and the car, soaking both. After a minute the spray stopped, and the cloud vanished instantly.

After changing his clothes, D'Ercole took his wet shirt to Garden City Junior High School, where he worked, and ran a pH test on it. The precipitation was simply water.

This event, which sounds like nature's idea of a prank, may or may not be beyond current science's ability to explain. Clouds *are* capable of peculiar appearance and behavior. In his *Tornados, Dark Days, Anomalous Precipitation, and Related Weather Phenomena* (1983) the late William R. Corliss culled from the scientific literature reports of cloud arches, luminous clouds, rumbling clouds, clouds with holes in them, and more. Though unusual, these are, no doubt, mostly or entirely of interest to meteorologists, rather than to those seeking evidence of truly inexplicable events in the atmosphere. In what follows, we concern ourselves with the latter: instances of clouds so out of the ordinary that some of them, in fact, may not have been clouds at all.

Falls from clouds

Falls from the sky of organic or inorganic materials are sometimes associated with extraordinary clouds.

One interesting case, reported in scientific journals of the period, concerned a small, slow-moving, perfectly spherical white cloud that suddenly appeared in an otherwise clear sky northwest of Agen, France, at 11 A.M. on September 5, 1814. Within a few minutes it stopped and remained motionless for a period of time, then abruptly sped southward, all the while revolving on its own axis and emitting ear-shattering rumbling noises. These climaxed with an explosion and the expulsion of a variety of stones, some of them of impressive dimensions. The cloud then ceased its movement and faded slowly away.

Comparable events are recorded at Sienna, Italy (1794), Chassigny, France (1815), Noblesville, Indiana (1823), and elsewhere.

This item appeared in an Adelaide newspaper, *South Australian Register*, on December 11, 1844, reprinted from Ireland's *Derry Standard*:

> An esteemed correspondent informs us, that on June 29, distant thunder was heard in the neighborhood of Killeter, at a quarter-past five in the afternoon. About four minutes after this, a strange looking small cloud was seen to sail along from the south-east, which attracted great attention from its unusual appearance. In a moment it seemed to burst, and volumes of smoke to issue from it, followed instantaneously by a very extraordinary noise, somewhat resembling the rattling of carts on a newly made road. It was soon ascertained that a number of aerolites, or hair-stones, were discharged from the cloud, which came to the ground with great violence, but providentially without doing any harm. One small stone was picked up about two hundred yards to the south of Derg-Lodge, the property of Sir Robert A. Ferguson, Bart. M.P., four miles from Castlederg. Another, that could not be less than ten or twelve inches in diameter, had it remained whole, was found about a quarter of a mile in the south of the same place, within a very short distance of men engaged in field labor. It is believed, also, that many fell in the newly turned up ground, which have not yet been found. The surface of these stones is black, evidently the effect of fire, and resembling the dross of a forge; the interior is light and porous, and very like pale pumy stone or cassub.

In a letter published in a 1932 issue of *Science*, John Zeleny recalled a strange sight he had witnessed "on a clear summer night at Hutchinson, Minnesota, some 35 years ago." A solitary, brilliantly luminous cumulus cloud "rose majestically from the eastern horizon," he wrote, "shone with a uniform, steady, vivid, whitish light and passed directly over the town. When the cloud was overhead a great shower of insects descended to earth covering the ground all around to the number of about 50 to 100 per square foot. These insects proved to be a species of hemiptera and were nonluminous."

That same summer (if Zeleny was correct in thinking the episode to have taken place in 1897) numerous small, blood-colored clouds filled the sky over Macerata, Italy. An hour later a storm broke, during which thousands of seeds fell. Unfamiliar to local people, they were eventually identified as being those of a kind of tree found only in central Africa and the Antilles.

Cigars in clouds

"Although I have studied the skies for many years," Charles Tilden Smith wrote in the British scientific journal *Nature*, "I have never seen anything like it before." "It" was two triangle-shaped shadows in the clouds. These dark patches maintained their stationary position even as the clouds rolled on. To all appearances, he said, each was a "heavy shadow cast upon a thin veil of clouds by some unseen object."

This sighting occurred on April 18, 1912, at Chisbury, Wiltshire. After the commencement of the flying-saucer era thirty-five years later, it would have been noted in the UFO literature as yet another instance in which UFOs had hidden themselves in clouds. As early as 1919, in *Book of the Damned*, anomalies chronicler Charles Fort was speculating, "If a large substantial mass, or super-construction, should enter this earth's atmosphere, it is our acceptance that it would sometimes … look like a cloud."

Lenticular clouds such as this one have occasionally been mistaken for UFOs.

Fort's prescient remark anticipated a later phenomenon that would be dubbed the "cloud cigar." Cloud cigars figured in a number of UFO reports from the late 1940s (what may have been the first was reported in Toronto in November 1947) into the present. Usually, such objects have been associated with smaller disc-shaped structures; thus cloud cigars have sometimes been known as "motherships."

Just before the onset of the great autumn of 1954 UFO wave in France, several witnesses, among them a businessman, two police officers, and an Army engineer, recounted a spectacular observation of an extraordinary object over the town of Vernon. Merchant Bernard Miserey, who watched it from his driveway at 1 A.M. on August 23, described it as an enormous vertical cigar, 300 feet long, hovering above the north bank of the Seine River, 1,000 feet away. According to his testimony, "Suddenly from the bottom of the cigar came an object like a horizontal disc, which dropped at first in free fall, then slowed, and suddenly swayed and dived horizontally across the river toward me, becoming very luminous" before vanishing in the southwest. Over the next forty-five minutes other, similar discs dropped out of the cigar. By this time the mother craft had lost its luminosity and disappeared into the darkness.

Though no clouds are mentioned in connection with this sighting, it set the scene for an even more spectacular event. This one, with hundreds of witnesses, took place three weeks later on September 14, in the southwest of France along the Atlantic coast. At 5 P.M., while working with his men in a field, a wealthy farmer who lived near St. Prouant saw a "regular shape something like a cigar or a carrot" drop rapidly out of a thick bank of clouds. The object, essentially horizontal though tipped slightly toward the earth, was luminous and rigid, and its movements did not correlate with the clouds just above it. It looked, Georges Fortin said, like a "gigantic machine surrounded by mists." It ceased its descent, then moved into a vertical position and became motionless.

By now, citizens of half a dozen local villages, as well as farmers living in the region, were watching in awe. White smoke like a vapor trail began to pour out of the bottom of the object and head straight down before slowing and ascending to circle the cigar in ascending spirals. By the time it got to the top, the wind had blown away all the smoke or vapor, revealing its source: a small metallic disc which shone like a mirror and reflected light from the larger object. The disc darted about the area, sometimes moving with great speed, sometimes stopping abruptly, before finally streaking toward the cigar and disappearing into its lower part.

> **"Perhaps a minute later, the 'carrot' leaned over as it began to move, accelerated, and disappeared into the clouds in the distance...."**

"Perhaps a minute later, the 'carrot' leaned over as it began to move, accelerated, and disappeared into the clouds in the distance," Fortin told investigators, "having resumed its original position, point forward. The whole thing had lasted about half an hour." Other witnesses up and down the valley confirmed this account. Meteorologists confirmed that no tornado or other unusual meteorological activity was occurring at the time of the sighting—though it is hard to imagine how, even if it was, it could account for what the observers reported.

A 300-foot-long, dull-gray, cigar-shaped machine emerged from a cloud during a rainstorm over Cressy, Tasmania, on October 4, 1960. Among those who saw it was the Rev. Lionel Browning, an Anglican minister and Tasmanian Secretary of the World Council of Churches. As he and his wife watched this astonishing sight—they estimated the object to be four miles away and 300 feet off the ground—five or six domed discs, approximately thirty feet in diameter, shot out of the clouds just above and behind the cigar. They headed toward it "like flat stones skipping along water"—exactly how Kenneth Arnold described the motion of the discs he saw over Mount Rainier, Washington, on June 24, 1947, in the sighting that ushered in the UFO age.

"After several seconds the ship, accompanied by the saucers, reversed the way it came," Browning reported. "It ... was gone from sight after 30 seconds.... It appears the ship sailed on for some seconds unaware that it had shed its protection. Possibly when this was discovered, the saucers were called to the mother ship. The objects then moved back into the cover of the rain storm."

UFO-like clouds

This incident, which took place on the Atlantic Ocean, off the coast of West Africa, south of Cape Verde, on March 22, 1870, is from the log of the barque *Lady of the Lake*:

> At from 6.30 to 7 P.M. a curious-shaped cloud appeared in the S.S.E. quarter, first appearing distinct at about 25 degrees from the horizon, from where it moved steadily forward, or rather upward, to about 80 degrees, when it settled down bodily to the N.E. Its form was circular, with a semicircle to the northern face near its center, and with four rays or arms extending from center to edge of circle. From the center to about six degrees beyond the circle was a fifth ray broader and more distinct than the others, with a curved end—diameter of circle 11 degrees, and of semicircle 2 ½ degrees. The weather was fine, and the atmosphere remarkably clear, with the usual Trade sky. It was of a light grey color, and though distinctly defined in shape, the patches of cirro-cumulus at the back could be clearly seen through. It was very much lower than the other clouds; the shape was plainest seen when about 55 degrees to 60 degrees high. The wind at the time was N.N.E., so that it came up obliquely against the wind, and finally settled down right in the wind's eye; finally lost sight of it through darkness, about 30 degrees from the horizon at about 7.20 P.M. Its tail was very similar to that of a comet. The men forward saw it nearly 10 minutes before I [Capt. F. W. Banner] did, and came aft to tell me of it.... Its general appearance was similar to that of a halo around the sun or moon.

A pair of clouds resembling "puffy-like daubs of cotton" passed in an eastward direction over Sunset, Utah, late on the afternoon of October 4, 1961. The clouds were linked by a cord of long, stringy material. Immediately behind them were two smooth, metallic, disc-shaped structures. All four objects disappeared over the horizon. The next day Ronald Miskin, an investigator for the Aerial Phenomena Research Organization, interviewed the witnesses. One was Sunset's mayor, who was pointing upward and illustrating the objects' trajectory when suddenly a "puffy" white object flew overhead, joined soon afterward by another, and the two proceeded to streak across the sky in the same direction as the objects of the previous day.

Aliens and clouds

Looking out the window of a cliff-top house along the seashore at Sydney, Australia, late one afternoon in the spring of 1965, a tourist noticed a beautiful, stationary pink cloud. An hour later, when she looked again, the cloud was moving in her direction and soon was actually below her eye level, enabling her to look down on it and see, to her amazement, a round, white object. Vents along the object's side emitted gray steam that, as it enveloped all but the top portion of the object, turned pink. The "cloud," in short, was an artificial creation.

As if this were not mind-boggling enough, an engine sound came from the still descending object. A luminous ladder was lowered from the underside, and a human-like figure climbed down to a lower rung. There he sat down and directed a searchlight toward the sea below. Some distance out on the water a pink flare shot into the air. Immediately the ladder retracted, and the object shot off in the direction of the flare. The witness then noticed a long but clearly visible shape in the water from which the flare had ascended. Both the UFO and the underwater shape vanished in a "vivid pink flash."

On the afternoon of January 7, 1970, two Finnish ski enthusiasts reportedly encountered a mysterious luminous red "cloud" that, when it got within fifty feet of them, turned out to contain a smoke-spewing domed disc at its center. The object hovered over them, and in the light it cast they could see a three-foot-tall humanoid with a waxy, pale face and a hook-like nose, but no visible eyes. The creature was standing on the ground just under the UFO. After about twenty seconds the red fog reappeared suddenly, and by the time it disappeared, both the object and the being were gone.

Phantom planes and vanishing clouds

A drought that began in 1973 and continued for more than a decade gave rise to a curious episode that, though the details are different, nonetheless is reminiscent in its effect of stories of "mad gassers." In other words, a person or persons unknown are said to be effecting weird havoc on a community; yet the assailants' existence cannot be proved, and neither can their nonexistence.

In the early 1980s farmers in three southern Spanish provinces that drought had reduced to almost a desert landscape began charging that the absence of rainfall was not a sorry condition of nature but a sinister conspiracy. The principal, though not the only, suspects were big tomato growers, who small farmers asserted (without discernible logic) did not want precipitation to fall on their crops. Farmers charged, moreover, that the conspirators had hired pilots to destroy rain clouds.

If there is a technology that can break up rain clouds no meteorologist is aware of it. In spite of repeated denials by atmospheric scientists, legal authorities, and aviation experts (who swore that small planes could not fly into storm clouds without serious risk of crashing), the farmers refused to back down. They said they had seen, on quite a number of occasions, the appearance of a thunderhead on the western horizon, followed within minutes by the appearance of an unmarked aircraft. The aircraft would fly into the cloud, spew out chemicals, and reduce it to mere wisps.

A drought in southwestern France in 1986 produced identical claims. This time the villains were said to be corporate interests financing anti-hail seeding experiments. It did no good for the experts to retort that nothing can be done to prevent hail. Again, some farmers insisted that they had seen, or at least heard, the mysterious aircraft. The affair ended when heavy rain fell that summer.

Social scientists attributed the episode to mass hysteria. Even some individuals not directly affected by the drought, though, said they had seen the planes in action. One of them, Agriculture Minister and engineer Francisco Moreno Sastre, asserted, "It's not just the collective imagination." He told *Wall Street Journal* reporters that witnesses numbered in the "thousands." A priest, Father Manuel Prados Muñoz, of the mountain village of Maria, reported repeated sightings, sometimes as many as a dozen a month. He said the planes would show up whenever his desktop barometer, and his eyes, indicated an impending storm. After local people began to report their sightings to him, he learned of hundreds of other such episodes.

In cases such as these, no explanation really makes sense, and any speculation brought to bear on the episode is simply guesswork. No one suggested another possibility—for which no evidence exists either—that a supersecret military or intelligence weather-control operation was responsible. One suspects that had these events occurred in the United States, where paranoia about such things is always intense, this would have been the (non)explanation of choice. Fortunately for all concerned, except those who wanted answers, the drought's passing put the mystery planes, real or imagined, out of sight and soon out of mind.

Further Reading:

Banner, Frederick William. "Extract from Log of Barque 'Lady of the Lake.'" *Quarterly Journal of the Royal Meteorological Society* 1 (1873): 157.

Bowers, Brent, and Ana Westley. "Spanish Farmers Say Barren Land Victim of Buzz of Darkling Planes." *Wall Street Journal* (August 6, 1985).

Brodu, Jean-Louis. "Cloud-Chasing Planes." *Fortean Times* 24 (1978): 42–46.

Corliss, William R., ed. *Handbook of Unusual Natural Phenomena.* Glen Arm, MD: Sourcebook Project, 1977.

———, ed. *Tornados, Dark Days, Anomalous Precipitation, and Related Phenomena: A Catalog of Geophysical Anomalies.* Glen Arm, MD: Sourcebook Project, 1983.

Delair, J. B. "UFOs, Clouds and Pseudo-Planes." *Fortean Times* 24 (1978): 42–46.

D'Ercole, Tom, as told to Rene Decker. "True Mystic Experiences: My Own Little Cloud." *Fate* 32,2 (February 1979): 54–55.

"Flying Saucers over Tasmania." *Flying Saucer Review* 7,2 (March/April 1961): 27–28.

Fort, Charles. *The Books of Charles Fort.* New York: Henry Holt and Company, 1941.

Jessup, M. K. *The Case for the UFO.* New York: Citadel Press, 1955.

Lorenzen, Coral, and Jim Lorenzen. *UFOs: The Whole Story.* New York: Signet, 1969.

———. *Encounters with UFO Occupants.* New York: Berkley Medallion, 1976.

"Meteorological Curiosities." *Fortean Times* 8 (1975): 6–8,20.

Michel, Aimé. *The Truth about Flying Saucers.* New York: Criterion Books, 1956.

———. *Flying Saucers and the Straight-Line Mystery.* New York: Criterion Books, 1958.

Michell, John, and Robert J. M. Rickard. *Phenomena: A Book of Wonders.* New York: Pantheon Books, 1977.

Smith, Charles Tilden. "Clouds and Shadows." *Nature* 89 (1912): 168.

Vallee, Jacques. *Anatomy of a Phenomenon: Unidentified Objects in Space—A Scientific Appraisal.* Chicago: Henry Regnery Company, 1965.

Zeleny, John. "Rumbling Clouds and Luminous Clouds." *Science* 75 (1932): 80–81.

Black Dogs

As he approached a crossroads on an autumn night in 1984, a Devonshire, England, man saw "this bloomin' great black thing.... I put on my anchors [brakes] and in the headlights it slowed down and walked right up to the car. I could see its eyes as plain as day, green and glassy they were, and he looked right over the bonnet [hood] at me, he was that tall, and then he went! ... like a light going out. I just couldn't see it anymore. It isn't real like an ordinary dog. I could feel the hairs of my neck standing up."

This story was told to local naturalist Trevor Beer, who was investigating reports of large, livestock-killing cats in the area. Beer apparently saw no reason to disbelieve the account, even when he was told the encounter took place on October 31. To every appearance the story is a fabrication consciously based on a worldwide folklore, known from England's West Country to the American South, about supernatural black dogs that appear at crossroads and that are associated with the underworld.

In rural Mississippi in the early part of the twentieth century, African Americans told folklorist N. N. Puckett of huge black dogs with "big red eyes glowing like chunks of fire." In the 1930s Mississippian Robert Johnson, the much-celebrated folk-blues singer and guitarist, did not deny rumors—spread by both those who resented his talents and those who held them in awe—that he had acquired his considerable musical skills in a midnight deal with a man in black (the devil) whom he met at a crossroads, an event hinted at in his 1936 recording "Cross Road Blues." (Comparable rumors surrounded Tommy Johnson, Robert Johnson's contemporary but not a relative.) He reported on the consequences of this pact the next year in another scary blues lyric: "I've got to keep movin' .../ There's a hellhound on my trail."

Theo Brown, a leading authority on black dog lore, has written, "Oral tradition sometimes gives us a legend, but this has probably been invented to explain the ghost." In other worlds, black dogs exist not just in thricetold tales but also in firsthand reports, at least some of them from individuals meriting greater credence than Beer's informant. Brown adds that the black dog "if regarded purely as a symbol must represent some universal guardian of the threshold personified to various cultures."

A large and complex lore surrounds black dogs. ("Black dog" is in some senses a generic term, meaning supernatural canine. Most tales and reports of such crea-

UNEXPLAINED! Strange Sightings, Incredible Occurrences, and Puzzling Physical Phenomena

tures described them as black, but white, gray, and yellow "black dogs" figure in some stories.) Brown believes the legend is rooted in prehistory but acknowledges this conclusion is necessarily speculative. In historical time, especially in Britain, where the tradition is most fully documented, black dogs may encounter travelers on a dark road and either guide them to safety or menace them, or their appearance may presage the death of the witness. They may also attach themselves to families—such a real-life family inspired Sir Arthur Conan Doyle to write the most celebrated of his Sherlock Holmes novels, *The Hound of the Baskervilles*. Black dogs are said to have glowing eyes and often to vanish in an instant, as did Devonshire's Halloween apparition. Sometimes, especially in medieval and post-medieval chronicles of manifestations associated with witchcraft, the black dog is a shape-shifter, at some point revealing his true identity as the devil.

The generic term of "black dog" can be applied to any supernatural canine encounter.

Sightings

Traditional beliefs are one thing, actual (or alleged) experiences another, and it is the latter that are discussed here.

The first known example of a sighting claim survives in a French manuscript, *Annales Franorum Regnum* (856 C.E.), wherein a chronicler records what happened after sudden darkness enveloped a provincial church midway through a service. A large black dog with fiercely glowing eyes appeared, dashed about as if searching for something and vanished abruptly. On August 4, 1577, in Bungay, ten miles from Norwich, England, a black dog showed up inside a church during a violent storm, ran through the aisle, and killed two worshippers. The same day a similar attack occurred inside Holy Trinity Church in Blythburg seven miles away; this time two men and a boy were slain. So wrote the Rev. Abraham Fleming in a broadside titled *A Straunge and Terrible Wunder*, published not long afterwards. Fleming claimed to have been inside the Bungay church when the apparition went on its rampage. His account, he acknowledged, "to some will seem absurd."

In July 1889 the *Philadelphia Inquirer* reported on mysterious nocturnal goings-on in a mountainous area four miles south of the city:

It appears that a large black dog makes his appearance at a certain point along the turnpike and walks with the traveler until a well-known mark,

(Continued on page 14)

Beast of Exmoor

The name "Beast of Exmoor" was coined in the spring of 1983, after a marauding predator killed a ewe belonging to Eric Ley of South Molton, Devonshire. In the next two and a half months Ley lost 100 of his sheep. The killer did not attack its prey at the hindquarters, as would a dog or fox, but instead ripped out their throats.

The Beast of Exmoor is described by many people who say they have seen it as a huge, jet-black cat, eight feet long from nose to tail. Other witnesses—about one in five—report a tan- or fawn-colored puma-like feline. In a few instances two giant felines, one black and one tan, have been seen in each other's company. A small number of witnesses recount sightings of large animals that look like unusual dogs.

Sightings of the "Beast" go back at least to the early 1970s, but they made no impact on popular attention until the depredations occurred at the Ley farm. In early May Britain's Royal Marines descended on the area, and London's *Daily Express* offered a monetary reward of £1000. Marine sharpshooters hid in the hills, and some even said they saw a "black and powerful animal," but were unable to get a clear shot at it. The beast or beasts mostly lay low, but as soon as the soldiers were withdrawn, the attacks started again.

One witness, local naturalist Trevor Beer, reported that he saw a beast in the summer of 1984, while watching birds in an area where deer carcasses had been found. "I saw the head and shoulders of a large animal appear out of the bushes," he wrote. "It looked black and rather otter-like, a first impression I shall always remember for the head was broad and sleek with small ears. The animal's eyes were clearly greeny yellow.... As it stared back at me I could clearly make out the thickish neck, the powerful looking forelegs and deep chest, and then without a sound it turned and moved swiftly away through the trees. That it was jet black I was sure, and long in the body and tail. I guessed at four and a half feet in body length, and about two feet at the shoulders."

Beer chased it to the edge of the woods. He recalled, "It ran like a greyhound, its forelegs pushing through the hind legs and they seeming to go forward in front of its round head as it raced away, then forcing back as the forelegs came forward to hit the ground together, a beautiful, very large black panther was my immediate thought."

In 1988 an area farmer reported he saw a "fantastic cat going at a hell of a speed. Every time it moved you could see the lights shine back across its ribs." Another time he saw a huge cat "jump a hedge, 15 feet from standing, with a fair-sized lamb in its mouth." Late one night in December 1991, a rural family watched a large panther-like animal for some minutes as it prowled near their house. Several weeks earlier the thirteen-year-old son had seen it or a similar animal climbing a tree.

Felis silvestris grampia is a small wild cat that lives in the rugged regions of northern England and Scotland. Might some people have mistaken it for the Beast of Exmoor?

By now, a January 1992 article in London's *Daily Telegraph* remarked, a significant number of persons who lived in the wild countryside of southwestern England allegedly had seen the beast or beasts.

Theories about the beasts range from misidentification (the cats are really dogs) to the paranormal (the creatures are intruders from a parallel universe). The former view is the official position of the Ministry of Agriculture. Another favorite conservative explanation is that witnesses have overestimated the sizes of the animals, which are domestic cats

small breeding population of pumas, let loose by persons who once kept them as pets, populates England's wild West Country. A more extreme hypothesis, advanced by Di Francis but nearly universally rejected by zoologists, holds that large felines have secretly inhabited Britain since prehistoric times.

Complicating matters is the curious fact that giant cats have been reported all over the British Isles. Officially, the only recognized nondomestic feline is *Felis silvestris grampia*, a small wild cat that lives in the rugged regions of northern England

(Continued from previous page)

Further Reading:

"The Beast of Exmoor." *The ISC Newletter* 2,3 (Fall 1983): 7–8.

Beer, Trevor. *The Beast of Exmoor: Fact or Legend?* Barnstaple, Devonshire, England: Countryside Productions, 1985.

Martin, Andrew. "In the Grip of the Beast." *London Daily Telegraph* (January 4, 1992).

"Mystery Moggies." *Fortean Times* 59 (1991): 18–20.

Rickard, Bob. "The Exmoor Beast and Others." *Fortean Times* 40 (1983): 52–61.

———. "Out of Place: The Exmoor Beast, Continued." *Fortean Times* 42 (1984): 40–41.

(Continued from page 11)

still further up the mountain, is reached, when he suddenly disappears as he came. The dog utters no sound and betrays not the least show of either friendship or violence…. There are a dozen men who claim to have encountered the dog at that exact spot, some of them more than once.

Twentieth-century reports of black dogs sometimes share the extravagant character of the older stories. Many seem simply to be a variety of ghost story. Typical of these is the account Theodore Ebert of Pottsville, Pennsylvania, gave to folklorist George Korson in the 1950s: "One night when I was a boy walking with friends along Seven Stars Road, a big black dog appeared from nowhere and came between me and one of my pals. And I went to pet the dog, but it disappeared from right under me. Just like the snap of a finger it disappeared."

Hopkinsville's *Kentucky New Era* (January 30, 1903) reported the experience of John Wigham on a lonely road in the western part of Mercer County. Riding home on horseback, he heard a dog yelping behind him. When he looked, he was startled to observe a large dog, bigger than a calf, bearing down on him, its eyes glowing like balls of fire. Terrified, he lashed his horse and galloped away as the strange creature pursued him. As he neared his hometown of Nevada, the beast ceased the chase and disappeared into the night. It "has for some time been terrifying the people of the neighborhood," the paper stated. It is the glowing red eyes and the size that link this canine to the black-dog tradition.

In the early 1920s young Delmer Clark—who would grow up to be, among other things, the father of the author of this book—of La Crosse, Wisconsin, saw "something … with shining eyes, with the face of a dog." In the darkness he thought he could make out vaguely a "dark black body." When he saw it again a week later in the same location near his home, he kicked at it, only to find his foot inside its mouth as if it had been anticipating his action. At that moment it vanished. The experience remained vivid in his memory for the rest of his life.

There is no shortage of modern black dog sightings. Ethel H. Rudkin collected a number of reports from her native Lincolnshire and published them in a

1938 paper in *Folklore*. "I have never yet had a Black Dog story from anyone who was weak either in body or mind," she wrote. "Perhaps it is because I have seen the Black Dog, and can therefore believe that the narrator has also seen him, that I have been able to get such good first-hand stories." Unfortunately, Rudkin provided no details of her own encounter with this ghostly canine that, unlike its counterparts elsewhere, was of a gentle nature. According to her:

> The spectator may be startled or annoyed, at first, by finding the huge creature trotting alongside, but fear of the Dog never enters into it, once he is recognized for what he is. He is always "table high," sometimes spoken of as being "as big as a calf" which often produces a muddled idea as to whether he is a calf or a dog. In the story he is often associated with a woman. No matter how dark the night the Dog can be seen because he is so much blacker. He seems to have a tendency to appear on the left side of the spectator; he crosses the road from left to right, and he is definitely looked on as a spirit of protection.... He is often heard, for when he disappears into a hedge the leaves rustle loudly.... In one description, his coat is wiry "like pig bristles"—in another he is "tall and thin and with a long neck and pointed nose."

Something that looked like a "Great Dane" reportedly stepped in front of a moving car on Exeter Road in Okehampton, England, on October 25, 1969. Before the driver could stop, the car passed *through* the animal, which then disappeared. In April 1972 a member of Britain's Coastguard saw a "large, black hound-type dog on the beach" at Great Yarmouth. "It was about a quarter of a mile from me," he told the *London Evening News* (April 27, 1972). "What made me watch it was that it was running, then stopping, as if looking for someone. As I watched, it vanished before my eyes."

Black dogs, or creatures much like them, occasionally are reported during mystery-cat scares. In the spring of 1974 some residents of the English counties of Hampshire and Cheshire halved the difference; they said the creature looked "half cat, half dog."

In the curious (or inevitable) way in which seemingly separate categories of anomalous phenomena have of overlapping at the edges, the UFO literature contains a small number of reports in which black dogs are linked, directly or circumstantially,

Before the driver could stop, the car passed *through* the animal, which then disappeared.

with flying saucers. None of these cases, it should be noted, is especially compelling or notably documented, but they do tell us something about the persistence of the black-dog image.

Among the circumstantial-link cases is one reported from South Africa in 1963. Two men driving at night on the Potchefstroom/Vereeniging road observed a large, doglike animal crossing the highway in front of them. Moments later a UFO showed up to buzz their vehicle several times, sending them on a frantic flight from the scene. Probably this *was* a large dog, and only coincidence tied it to the UFO. Several Georgia youths asserted a more direct association a decade later, when they claimed to have spotted "10 big, black, hairy dogs" running from a landed UFO and through a cemetery in Savannah.

My own phantom dog, my own quandary

Throughout this book I have refrained from using first-person pronouns. The accounts represented here, after all, are not my stories. I am able to stand outside them and view them coolly. But what follows *is* my story, my own repeated encounters with something like a black dog, or at least a quadrupedal apparition with broadly canine characteristics. Besides being a direct experience of an unexplained phenomenon, it was a lesson in how difficult it is for even an open-minded witness to process the full implications of an unorthodox, uncategorizable sighting.

It occurred in the summer of 2000, and it began late on a pleasant summer evening as I pulled my car up in front of our house in a small rural Minnesota town. I had been working late at the office I then rented for my writing projects. Till then, everything about the day had been ordinary.

As I started toward the house, I was taken aback to see something lying on the landing at the top of the front steps. My immediate instinct was to think it was our dog. Then I realized how unlikely that was; Misha's domain was our fenced-in backyard. If she had somehow managed to get into the front, she would have strayed away, as she was wont to do, following her nose wherever it took her. In other words, she would not have contented herself to rest by the door. Nor would I have had a particularly difficult time recognizing her because she was big and covered in white hair.

At that point I wasn't entirely sure it was a dog at all. It *was* an animate object, and it was, so I dimly discerned, a quadruped too big to be a domestic cat. Darkness concealed it so that I could see nothing but an outline, a shadowy form that somehow managed to evade any streak of streetlight or moonlight that could have fallen on it and rendered it identifiable. I began to stride quickly in its direction, on the reasonable supposition that if I got close enough, I would see what it was.

A mere fifteen footsteps separated the curb from the house, and I was moving at a brisk pace. But the thing was faster. I couldn't have propelled myself more than three or four steps forward before it was coming off the porch, passing at an angle to my left (more or less southwestward). From the streetlight on the corner, a bright yard light across the street, and the moonlight, the view immediately ahead should have afforded sufficient illumination for me to identify the animal. Yet, curiously, it always remained in shadow.

And then it was no longer there. It didn't run into a bush or onto a sidewalk or behind a building. In fact, as far as I could tell, it was not especially close to our neighbors' house when it was … well … gone. All the while, as this played out, I was listening for a sound associated with the thing. I heard nothing: no breathing, no cries, meows, yowls, or barks, no scurrying sounds as it passed over cement or grass.

Black dog appearances have at times been connected to UFO sightings.

I followed in the direction the thing had passed, but saw and heard nothing out of the ordinary. After a few moments I shrugged and went inside. When I mentioned the curious experience to my wife, Helene, I asked if Misha had acted up. Misha was usually sensitive to—in other words, she barked at—passing or intruding animals (mostly dogs, sometimes rabbits) she tracked from her perch on the couch by the front window. I know the wild mammal population of this area fairly well, and I ruled out the possibility—unlikely for a host of reasons—that what I had seen was a deer, coyote, or fox.

Puzzled, over the next days I took some wildlife reference books off the shelves and studied them as time permitted. I supplemented this research with some Internet searches. No identification leaped out at me.

A week or two later, at 10:30 one night I arrived home from the office. There it was: same spot, same shadowy shape. The same sequence of events ensued. It was almost as if I had entered a rerun of a movie scene, or as if I had stepped into a dream. At that point I was getting a sense that all this just *felt* peculiar.

I returned to the wildlife texts and the web searches. I expanded my inquiry to unusual breeds of dogs and cats. I cautiously asked neighbors if they had seen any strange—as in not ordinarily around—animals lately. At this stage the phrase "anomalous phenomenon" had not, to the best of my recollection, crossed my mind, mystified as I was by an experience unlike any other. No animal I considered plausibly matched what I had seen. On the other hand, "seen" may have been stretching the point. The mystery nagged at me. I had no doubt of a conventional answer to it, but this answer eluded and frustrated me.

Some days passed. Then a ringing phone shook us out of our 3 A.M. slumbers. A relative (since deceased) suffering from a crippling illness had fallen out of bed and needed urgent assistance. We rushed over and lifted her back on to the mattress and under the covers, then returned home. On our arrival we happened to notice a light flickering in the upstairs front bedroom of a house that borders ours on the east. We knew that the neighbor, an elderly woman, was out of town and would not be back for another week or two. The longer we studied it, the more uneasy we became. Was it a burglar? The earliest stage of an electrical fire? We decided to call the police.

The officer who arrived was as mystified as we were. He alerted the owner's son-in-law, who showed up with a key. The two entered the house to discover a malfunctioning night light which could easily have sparked a fire. Through the accidental circumstance of our being awake and outside at an unlikely hour, we had probably saved our neighbor's house.

As the policeman and the son-in-law departed, Helene and I turned to go home. By now the time was around 3:45 A.M. As soon as my eyes fell on our front porch, I gasped. A moment later I managed to shout, "There it is!" I could see—or thought I could see—it watching us. I broke into a run, knowing by now how fast it moved and how fleeting my chance of identifying it would be. Helene was right behind me. The thing was down the steps, crossing the western edge of our lawn at the usual southwestern angle, keeping to the shadows, and then, metaphorically or literally, fading into the ether.

It eventually came to me, of course, that my experience—and in the last instance, Helene's experience as well (her perceptions were identical to my own)—were pretty strange and not easily explainable. Even, yes, anomalous. This was a conclusion I resisted, mostly unconsciously because it seldom rose to a place in awareness where I would be forced to notice its presence. For some time, in fact, I did not allow myself to entertain the possibility, and any contrary thought amounted to barely a ripple in the stream of consciousness.

I never identified the animal (if that's what it was) or found an explanation that satisfied me—not for lack of trying. It took months for me to acknowledge the anomalous, even dreamlike, quality of the encounters. By then, I suspected my own memories—conveniently, I reflected ruefully. My resistance to the notion of a personal anomalous experience had given me an out; all else having failed, now I could transform discordant, heterodox details into mere mind tricks. I knew better—for one thing, Helene finally had seen the thing, too—but in idle moments I sought comfort in the thought that I could accept other people's strange experiences, but to have one of my own … well, it seemed like a confession of failure. *I couldn't be stumped.*

Without realizing it, I had internalized society's compulsion to rationalize away troubling anomalies. Even after spending most of my life studying accounts of the unexplained and interacting with witnesses, having no conscious problem with the abstract principle that the world hosts peculiar things, somehow I couldn't credit the notion that any such phenomena could ever intersect with my life. Worse, the experience itself was ambiguous, nebulous, downright pointless, perhaps inherently unresolvable. The only certainty was that it had happened. Beyond that, what? I had both seen and not seen something. It moved, always, in shadows. It felt less like a thing than the *idea* of a thing. There—at least in metaphor—it remains, never seen again.

Further Reading:

Beer, Trevor. *The Beast of Exmoor: Fact or Legend?* Barnstaple, Devonshire, England: Countryside Productions, 1985.

"The Black Dog of Bungay." *Notes and Queries* 4, 2nd series 94 (October 17, 1857): 314.

Bord, Janet, and Colin Bord. *Alien Animals.* Harrisburg, PA: Stackpole Books, 1981.

Brown, Theo. "The Black Dog in English Folklore." In J. R. Porter and W.M.S. Russell, eds. *Animals in Folklore*, 45–58. Totowa, NJ: Rowman and Littlefield, 1978.

Bunn, Ivan. "Black Dogs and Water." *The News* 17 (1976): 12–13.

Clark, Jerome. "Among the Anomalies." *Journal of Scientific Exploration* 19,4 (Winter 2005): 515–29.

Gordon, Stan. "UFOs in Relation to Creature Sightings in Pennsylvania." In Walter H. Andrus, Jr., ed. *MUFON 1974 UFO Symposium Proceedings*, 132–54. Quincy, IL: Mutual UFO Network, 1974.

Gurdon, Lady Eveline Camilla, ed. *County Folk-Lore: Suffolk.* Ipswich, England: 1893.

Johnson, Robert. *The Complete Recordings.* Columbia Records, 1990.

Keel, John A. *Strange Creatures from Time and Space.* Greenwich, CT: Fawcett Gold Medal Books, 1970.

Korson, George. *Black Rock: Mining Folklore of the Pennsylvania Dutch.* Baltimore: Johns Hopkins University Press, 1960.

Rudkin, Ethel H. "The Black Dog." *Folklore* 49 (June 1938): 111–31.

Saunders, Christian. "Of Hags and Hellhounds." *Fortean Times* 159 (2002): 28–32.

Stein, Gordon. "Black Dogs: Fact or Fancy?" *Fate* 43,6 (June 1990): 65–73.

Stubbs, Claire. "A Straunge and Terrible Wunder." *Fortean Times* 195 (2005): 30–32, 34–35.

Sutton, David. "Black Dogs: A Fancier's Guide." *Fortean Times* 195 (2005): 33.

Tebbult, L. F. "A Buckinghamshire Black Dog." *Folklore* 56 (March 1945): 222.

W.C.B. "Black Dogs: Gabriel Hounds." *Notes and Queries* 11,5 (March 9, 1912): 185–86.

Watson, Nigel. "Notes on Lincolnshire Ghost Phenomena—1." *The News* 1,6 (September 1974): 18–19.

Webb, David, with Mimi Hynek, ed. *1973—Year of the Humanoids: An Analysis of the Fall 1973 UFO/Humanoid Wave.* Evanston, IL: Center for UFO Studies, 1976.

Woods, Barbara Allen. "The Devil in Dog Form." *Western Folklore* 13,4 (October 1954): 229–35.

Falls from the Sky (Inorganic Matter)

For as long as human beings have been keeping historical records, all kinds of objects, living and otherwise, have been reported to fall out of the sky. Usually, though not always, these falls take place in the midst of a furious storm. On occasion, however, a fall may occur out of a clear sky.

The first skeptics "explained" falls as a misunderstanding of a fundamental process of nature, which was that rain triggered the spontaneous generation, out of mud, slime, and dust, of things (especially living things) already on the ground. This view, held for example by Pliny (who proposed it in *Natural History* [77 C.E.]), eventually evolved into a more realistic hypothesis, namely that naïve witnesses falsely associated the fall of rain with the appearances of animals, vegetable matter, artifacts, or other inorganic materials in the rain's aftermath. These things had been there all along, but the rain had driven or washed them into view.

In due course, after it finally proved futile to dispute reliable observations (some by scientists) of objects falling, conventional opinion bowed to the superiority of eyewitness testimony over armchair dismissal. But conventionalists were ready with another explanation. This one held that waterspouts, tornadoes, and whirlwinds pick up materials and deposit them somewhere else; consequently, though falls are real enough, they are merely curious, not extraordinary.

That strong winds rip objects off the ground and drop them somewhere else is, of course, beyond dispute. That such weather phenomena account for the most anomalous falls, on the other hand, is decidedly less certain. What makes anomalous falls so puzzling is their strange selectivity. Violent storms drop everything they pick up; most anomalous falls drop only one thing and the rest a very few things. Often, too, the volume of material is so staggering that its disappearance from one place, even if a place could be found where much of it was held, would not go unnoticed. Some falls go on for hours, with the material falling in a steady stream over a significant area of ground.

Of the two types of falls (inorganic and organic; the latter is discussed in the next chapter), however, those involving inorganic matter, especially if that matter consists of dust or ash, are the more amenable to mundane accounting.

✳
Fire in the sky

Though many falls of "sulphur" turn out to be of pollen, a few reports, if they are to be believed, cannot be so explained. In other words, they really may be of sulphur or a sulphur compound. William R. Corliss, of the multivolume Sourcebook Project, remarks that a storm-driven fall of sulphur, a substance "rarely found in surface deposits where winds could pick it up, would seem to be very unlikely although not impossible"; yet "tales of burning sulphur," if true, post a "significant anomaly." One such case was reported in *American Journal of Science*:

> In March last [1832], there fell in the fields of the village of Kourianof [Russia] ... a combustible substance of a yellowish color, at least two inches thick, and covering a superficies of between six and seven hundred square feet. The inhabitants, at first, thought it was snow, but on examination, it appeared to have the properties of cotton, having, on being torn, the same tenacity; but, on being put into a vessel full of water, it assumed the consistency of rosin. On being put into the fire, in its primitive state, it burnt and sent forth a flame like spirits of wine; but in its resinous state, it boiled on the fire, without becoming inflamed, probably because it was mixed with some portion of snow, from which it had been taken. After a more minute examination, the rosin had the color of amber, was elastic like indian rubber, and smelt like prepared oil, mixed with wax.

The Roman philosopher and naturalist Pliny the Elder (23–79 C.E.) held that rain could cause the spontaneous generation of certain living things.

An even stranger event took place on October 18, 1867, when residents of Thames Ditton, Surrey, England, were startled by the appearance of a "shower of fire" in the evening sky. The light it cast was "brilliant" for the ten minutes it lasted. "Next morning it was found that the waterbutts and puddles in the upper part of the village were thickly covered with a deposit of sulphur," *Symons's Monthly Meteorological Magazine* recounted.

On the evening of April 13, 1879, snow fell on the eastern Pennsylvania cities of Allentown, Easton, and Reading. Interspersed with the ordinary flakes was a large amount of a substance that looked and smelled like sulphur, half an inch deep in some places. Contemporary press accounts noted that "small quantities that were scraped together and set on fire burned as readily as [sulphur] and emitted the same fumes."

Stones falling and tossed

A larger, more significant category of anomalous falls of inorganic materials concerns non-meteoritic rocks and stones.

One dramatic instance took place in Hungary in 1841, according to contemporary press reports. "The shower fell so thick and over so large a tract," according to the *Augsburg Gazette,* which had dispatched a scientific correspondent from Vienna to the site, "that the number of stones which fell are computed at 350,000 million"—surely a considerable exaggeration for what must, in any event, have been an impressive abundance of stones. The account continued, "They varied in size from a hazelnut down to a poppy seed, but most of them were about the size of a pea—the composition of stones, besides flint, lime, and clay earth, containing oxydate [sic; oxidant] of iron.... The stones were quite cold, and though the night was very calm, fell almost at an angle of 45 degs., so that some other power than gravity must have been working on them as well as their gravity."

> Vast numbers of small black stones are said to have fallen on Birmingham, England, in August 1858, and again at Wolverhampton in June 1860.

A similar phenomenon occurred near Utica, New York, in the late spring and early summer of 1921. "For several weeks," the press wires reported, "stones as large as billiard balls have been dropping on the house, apparently out of a clear sky. They fall perpendicularly, as if dropped, not thrown. All efforts to explain their source have been in vain."

In June 1870, stones are said to have fallen from 2 P.M. till sundown on a district of Argentina. Vast numbers of small black stones are said to have fallen on Birmingham, England, in August 1858, and again at Wolverhampton in June 1860. Both incidents took place during violent storms, though the source and sheer quantity of the material remained a mystery.

Anomalous stone falls—throwings is perhaps the more accurate term—are often associated with poltergeist manifestations. In a number of cases, the unexplained movement of stones, pebbles, and rocks comprises the bulk or even entirety of the phenomenon. As the late parapsychologist D. Scott Rogo remarked, "Rock-throwing poltergeists represent a specific type of spookery.... They can make the stones shower from the sky ... or they will simply pelt the building. The rocks will even fall inside the home.... It is not odd for the rocks to fly abnormally slow, zigzag in flight, or even make ninety-degree turns in the air."

Thanks to Charles Fort, who chronicled it in his widely read *New Lands* (1923), the most famous instance is one that happened in Chico, California, in the early 1920s.

In November 1921, J. W. Charge, the owner of a grain warehouse along the Southern Pacific railroad tracks in Chico, complained to City Marshal J. A. (Ted) Peck that an unseen someone was daily hurling rocks at the building. Taking this to be a harmless prank, Peck paid no attention—until March 9, 1922, when stones and rocks ranging in size from peas to baseballs came down on the warehouse. The fall continued intermittently all day. The rocks struck the roofs of warehouses belonging to Charge and J. H. Priel. At one point a man named Frank Lyons climbed up to a roof but had to retreat under merciless pelting. Charge, on the ground, was struck on the leg.

According to the *Chico Record*:

Fire Chief C. E. Tovee and Traffic Officer J. J. Corbett had the scare of their lives while prowling about the Charge warehouse in an endeavor to sight the direction from which the rocks came. They had just approached the sound end of the warehouse and were looking skyward when a fair-sized boulder struck the wooden wall above them with a mighty force and rebounded to the ground at their feet, leaving a dent where it had struck the timber.

A dragnet through several surrounding blocks failed to flush out the rock-thrower.

After effecting considerable destruction to its original targets, the two ware-houses, the stone attacks expanded to nearby buildings in a cluster of houses alongside the tracks. Meantime, on March 23, an anonymous letter to Marshal Peck, allegedly from the culprit, boasted that he had invented the device responsible and now would cease tormenting fellow citizens with it. Nonetheless, the incidents continued into April amid frantic efforts by police and others to catch the individual or individuals presumed responsible. At one point three airplanes flew over the site in search of the elusive man with a catapult.

Among the outsiders who arrived to probe the events was Vincent Jones, vice president of the California Society for Psychical Research. He reported, "Witnesses who have seen the missiles before they hit the building testify that they seemed to come perpendicularly from above, and were first discerned at a distance of some 40 feet away." Fort asked a friend, San Francisco-based writer Miriam Allen deFord, to go to Chico to look into the matter personally. There she, in her words, "saw a stone fall from some invisible point in the sky, and land gently at my feet."

However enigmatic their behavior may have been, their place of origin was known. The stones were local, or so judged geologist C. K. Studley, who deduced they were from either Chico Creek or Little Chico Creek.

Subsequently, the writer and critic Anthony Boucher would note that he met deFord "when I investigated a similar stone-fall case in Oakland, California, in 1943. We compared our notes and found our experiences almost identical." That's not surprising.

Except for catching Fort's attention and thereby entering anomaly immortality, the Chico episode was a fairly ordinary instance of what some call a rock-throwing poltergeist, an international phenomenon with a long history. Some other examples recorded in the American press:

Iredell County, North Carolina, 1842: Rocks started falling on a rural residence owned by Louis Day, though they were never seen until just before they struck. Sometimes they came down inside the house. The stones destroyed windows and the glass covering a clock face. The rocks apparently emanated from an area of the property where the owner slaughtered hogs. Other poltergeist manifestations, notably the mysterious disappearance and subsequent reappearance of household items, plagued the family (*Statesville Landmark*, reprinted in *The Robesonian*, Lumberton, North Carolina, June 6, 1905).

Near Port Republic, Virginia, May 9–10, 1865: As family members were eating their evening meal, a servant girl rushed in to report that someone unseen was throwing stones at her. A search for the culprit was unsuccessful, but soon (starting that evening and concluding at 10 P.M., only to resume at sunrise the next day) stones and rocks flew outside and inside the house, breaking windows. "None of them could be seen until they had struck. One of them was very wet, and Mrs. Ergenbright held it to see if water would drip from it, but it did not." Tables and other household items were tossed about. The infestation ended at around 4 P.M. (*Staunton Spectator*, reprinted in *The Alleganian*, Cumberland, Maryland, August 16).

Akron, Ohio, October 1878: While husking corn in a field, a woman identified as Mrs. Michael Metzler was hit by stones of undetermined origin. Soon afterwards, her children had the same experience and fled to the house. The next evening, as she worked in the same field, stones and clumps of earth again struck Mrs. Metzler. The next morning she and her young daughter were standing near an open cellar door when a large pebble arose from the cellar and hit the girl in the face. Later, "a party of eight gathered in the main room, which consists of two windows and two doors. Father Brown ... was present, and about ten o'clock offered a prayer. Hardly had he finished, however, before two large-sized stones fell at his feet, followed by a dozen more pebbles, which came from the ceiling and walls, striking the persons who were in the room." A newspaper reporter who came to investigate witnessed the phenomena and had a pebble strike him on the shoulder (*Akron Leader*, reprinted in *The Weekly Republican*, Elyria, Ohio, October 17).

Baltimore, Maryland, September 1881: At 10 A.M., in the yard of a saloon near the corner of Fredrick and Fayette Streets, stones and coal began sailing through the air minus any visible thrower. After an hour they stopped, only to resume after 3 P.M. and continue unabated until 1 A.M. In daylight, the next day, a rock struck a servant girl causing severe injury. Other rocks smashed windows in nearby shops and businesses. Firemen and police set up observation posts, "but still the stones fell and the thrower could not be discovered" (*Fort Wayne Daily Gazette*, September 13, and other newspapers).

Near Bedford, Indiana, early June 1882: "The storm ... on a recent night was a strange one. The strangest thing that took place was at the farm of Abraham Smith, who lives four miles south of Bedford, where a real, genuine shower of stones fell, mixed with what seems to be plastering. The stones are of various sizes, some really as large as a man's fist, while others are quite small. The most of them are white flint, a stone that is not found in that part of Indiana. Many of Mr. Smith's windows were broken and several shingles knocked off his roof. In the immediate vicinity of the house more than a barrel of these stones could be gathered. A great many persons have visited the Smith farm to satisfy themselves in regard to the matter" (*Indiana Democrat*, Pennsylvania, June 8).

Jordan, New York, December 1883: At the farm of a well-to-do family, the Stevenses, "a strange fall of stones occurred, and at night more than 150 were picked up." The following Sunday, as they stood singing at church, the two daughters saw three stones fall at their feet. "People are flocking there from all parts of the country to see the stones fall. The latter are small, varying from the size of a pebble to half the size of one's fist." The strain was said to have hastened the death of the already ill Mrs. Stevens (*Iowa State Reporter*, Waterloo, January 3, 1884, and other newspapers).

Cory, Indiana, July 1898: "A little girl named Miller" found herself the focus of a shower of stones every time she stepped outside. None hit her, as there were persons standing near her; the stones did break nearby windows. "On one occasion it is said stones fell back of her bed" (*Fort Wayne Sentinel*, July 29).

Phoenix, Arizona Territory, summer 1898: Josefa Núñez, an elderly woman, and her family reported episodes of stone throwing about their residence on the east end of the city. "Small stones hurled from an invisible source broke the window of the house or rattled against the outer wall. Though they landed sharply they brought no other pain than a scorching sensation. She picked the stones from the ground and found some warm and others almost ice cold." When the attacks didn't stop, she moved to another house in the area, to no avail. She complained to the police, who investigated on the presumption that a prankster was responsible, but no perpetrator was detected. One night, Officer George McClarty and a newspaper reporter "saw a stone dropping on the old woman's shoulder and fall thence to the ground." It was warm to the touch. Curiosity-seekers who flocked to the scene claimed to have seen flying stones on various occasions (*Arizona Republican*, Phoenix, September 23).

> **V**ast numbers of small black stones are said to have fallen on Birmingham, England, in August 1858, and again at Wolverhampton in June 1860.

Near Mansfield, Ohio, September 1915: "A resident of the city was out in the country and while passing the farm noticed some stones dropping from a hedge. He made a startling discovery that the stones came from apparently nowhere out of the air and had the appearance of falling from the hedge. He took members of his family to the scene and they also saw the phenomenon and brought specimens of the stones back to the city. The story was spread … and the farm has since been visited by hundreds of people. Stories differ, however, as to what occurs, but many insist that the stones fall from the hedge and at times they gush forth from the ground in a veritable shower" (*Mansfield News*, September 24).

Spokane, Washington, late summer 1977: Stones the size of golf balls, and of no apparent origin, fell on the front lawn and through the front windows of a family residence. Some of the stones came down at relatively low speeds, while others traveled at high velocity. When Police Capt. Charles Crabtree climbed to the roof for a better view, two stones landed near him. With a fifteen-foot overhang protecting the porch and fifty-foot-tall trees in the lawn, the police could only deduce that a launching device was hurling the rocks; but surveillance from ground and air failed to detect anyone or anything responsible. "We're still baffled," said a police spokesman (*Victoria Colonist,* British Columbia, September 4; *Vancouver Province,* September 6).

Stone-throwing poltergeist in Tucson

In mid-1982 Richard and Mary Berkbigler began building a 4,400-square-foot house, surrounded by hundreds of square yards of bush, cactus, and underbrush, on the rural northern outskirts of Tucson, Arizona. With three of their children (ages between fifteen and twenty) they moved out to a trailer house on the property, living there until September 1983, when they took up residence in the still-uncompleted house. Within days odd events were taking place, starting with knockings on the front door. No knocker was ever spotted, though the Berkbiglers sped to the door and even searched for one outside. Still, they assumed that a vagrant was playing tricks on them.

> "It was just like the bush was throwing rocks with its branches," Rick Berkbigler said later.

Soon the weirdness escalated. Late one afternoon a flurry of five stones, of no visible origin, hit the house and a van parked in the adjoining driveway. After that, in the coming days and weeks, attacks resumed at five- to fifteen-minute intervals, sometimes continuing for as long as two or three hours. Often, they would stop only when the family turned out all the lights and retired for the night.

In early November, after repeated searches by family and friends failed to uncover the guilty individual or individuals, the sheriff's department entered the investigation. Deputies and a helicopter patrolled the site repeatedly, again without solving the mystery. The attacks only grew more intense. On Sunday, November 27, after especially relentless bombardment, family and friends broke into two teams, one (led by son Rick) to search the northern end of the property, the other (led by an uncle) the southern. In the darkness of mid-evening they set out armed with flashlights. In short order, one of the team members on the latter front was struck on the jaw.

When the group fled to take shelter behind the house, the uncle called to them that he and his fellows had trapped the prowler in some bushes twenty-five feet away. Rick and his friends rushed to the site. When beams of light were directed into the bushes, there was nothing to be seen, though onlookers could hear rustling sounds. Suddenly, eight rocks sailed out of the bush. One struck the uncle and knocked him unconscious. Some of the group picked up their own stones and rocks and threw them back at full speed. Nobody escaped from the bushes. Then the searchers, carrying the dazed uncle, returned to find shelter in the house.

"It was just like the bush was throwing rocks with its branches," Rick Berkbigler said later. Investigator Scott Rogo would observe, "The clump of brush actually grew out of a small knoll above the little trail Rick's uncle was following. I conducted several experiments there and was able to determine that rocks could not be thrown *through* the brush. You had to stand up and throw the rocks *over* the brush. Since both Rick and his uncle were focusing their flashlights on the brush, they certainly could have seen anyone cavorting about in this way."

After press accounts alerted parapsychologists to the ongoing phenomena (which the Berkbiglers still ascribed to a seemingly uncatchable prankster), poltergeist authority W. G. Roll, of the Psychical Research Foundation in North Carolina, sent Los Angeles-based researcher Rogo to the site on December 6. Rogo soon learned that two days earlier, when the family's married daughter, husband, and little daughter had visited, a rock had struck the child on the arm, initiating a late-morning barrage. Fortunately, the girl was not seriously hurt, but the outraged family called the sheriff's department, and the biggest search yet, complete with helicopter, ensued—again without results.

The next day reporters arrived in the late afternoon, to be greeted by the two Berkbigler sons. Soon, they heard a rock hit a side door, and just after 6 P.M., when the parents arrived, the attacks commenced in earnest. The journalists were pinned inside the house until 7:45, when law-enforcement personnel arrived to usher them out. A stone hit a deputy as he walked to the house. Meantime, a friend of the family, a private detective, was secretly prowling the site when, as he approached the garage, he was hit on the head. He was wearing a helmet, possibly preventing more serious damage to his health. He later found that a rock had also hit and damaged his motorcycle.

Rogo himself witnessed rock throwings. Like everyone else, in spite of his most determined efforts, he could not find a thrower. He did note that in the face of serious physical obstacles such as buildings and vehicles, the stones and rocks were thrown with ever more astounding accuracy at individuals. With the exception of the uncle's unfortunate experience, however, the missiles—whatever the velocity which they sailed through the air—only gently tapped victims on impact, as is characteristic in poltergeist-related stone throwings.

Observers of the phenomenon included all—family, friends, police, reporters, professional trackers, curiosity-seekers—who came to the spot in the late afternoon to early evening. The infestation ended later that month, as suddenly as it had begun. The police never solved the case. For his part Rogo offered the speculation (not provable, of course) that fifteen-year-old David Berkbigler was the poltergeist agent, unconsciously unleashing the attacks via psychokinesis linked to "abnormal neuronal 'firing' in his brain."

Falls of artifacts

The most fantastic claims, those concerning falls of manufactured objects—most famously thunderstones, the subject of a worldwide folklore that alleges that shaped stones (ax heads, for example) sometimes come down during storms, and especially in the wake of a spectacular roar of thunder—are all but forgotten. Instances of supposed thunderstones, however, continued into the latter nineteenth century. There may be some factual basis to the stories, which probably take their inspiration from the fall of meteorites during rainstorms.

A handful of reports seem at least curious, however. One took place in Wolverhampton, England, in the fall of 1876, after the fall of "a huge ball of what appeared to be green fire ... during a severe windstorm, otherwise unaccompanied by lightning," the *Times of London* related. Witnesses who went to the spot found a "highly polished stone, totally different from any mineral deposits in the vicinity and equally different from any meteorite in existence." Critics argued that the stone could have been there all along, and since there was no way to disprove the assertion, the episode was left in limbo, where it still lies. As do a number of comparable cases.

According to a newspaper story filed on November 28, 1909, farmers near Kankakee, Illinois, reported that a strange "whizzing" noise was heard in the midmorning. At the same time showers of pennies, nickels, and dimes rained to the ground. "One of the coins was shown to your correspondent," the dispatch stated. "It was still warm to the touch." It went on, "As this rain of money occurred in the same district where the showers of fish and frogs are observed occasionally ... little credence is placed in the story."

On the morning of May 28, 1982, a young girl was walking through the yard of St. Elisabeth's Church in Redding, a small town near Manchester, England, when—or so she would later tell the Rev. Graham Marshall—she spotted a fifty-pence coin fall "from nowhere." As the day went on, children discovered numerous other coins at the same spot. Finally, the owner of a local candy store, concerned that the children were stealing from the poor box, informed the clergyman of the sudden rush in business at his establishment. No money was missing, but the children all swore, when Marshall interviewed them, that the coins seemed to be coming from the sky. Or so they inferred from the fact that they would hear a tinkling sound on the sidewalk and, on looking, see a coin.

Marshall conducted his own investigation and eliminated some obvious explanations, such as that a prankster was tossing coins over the church wall (the wall was too high and bare for a coin-tosser not to be easily visible to passersby) or that birds were dropping them (too many coins clustered together and no nests overhead). Some of the coins were embedded edgewise into the ground, suggesting a fall from some height. Marshall experimented by hurling a handful of coins to earth; they made no impression.

An incident like this is insufficient to prove anything one way or another, but as already noted, it is not unprecedented. One day, in December 1968, shoppers in another English town, Ramsgate, Kent, heard pennies bouncing off the pavement. "Between 40 and 50 of them came down in short scattered bursts for about 15 minutes," one witness, Jean Clements, told the *London Daily Mirror*. "You could not see them falling—all you heard was the sound of them hitting the ground." They hit hard enough so that dents registered on them. There were "no tall buildings nearby," Clements said, "and no one heard a plane go overhead." Among other coin falls are those said to have happened in Meshehera, Russia, summer 1940 (during a storm); Bristol, England, in September 1956; Bourges, France, April 15, 1957 ("thousands" of 1,000-franc notes, never claimed); and Limburg, West Germany, January 1976 (2,000 marks, seen falling by two clergymen).

> "You could not see them falling—all you heard was the sound of them hitting the ground."

Usually artifacts (including, legend has it, thunderstones) fall not in clusters but by themselves. On April 17, 1969, the *New York Times* reported the bizarre experience of a California woman, Ruth Stevens, who was driving in Palm Springs when a wheel sailed out of the sky and onto her car's hood, where it left a one-foot dent. The account does not tell us what kind of wheel it was, but it does note that no local airport received a report of a missing wheel from any pilot.

Such instances of artifact falls are poorly documented on the whole, and only the foolhardy would rush in to wave wild paranormal "theories" on the assumption that no other explanation is possible. Without real investigations and firm reasons to dismiss prosaic alternatives, these events should be viewed cautiously.

Further Reading:

Aldrich, Hal R. "Rainbows Keep Falling on My Head." *INFO Journal* 6,2 (July/August 1977): 3–6.

———. "Fireballs and Rockfalls." *INFO Journal* 8,4 (January/February 1981): 4–5.

Arnold, Larry E. "Money from Heaven." *Fate* 31,12 (December 1978): 65–71.

"Chico's 1920s Mystery of Falling Rocks Remains Unsolved." *San Jose Mercury News* (October 27, 1985).

Chorvinsky, Mark. "Our Strange World: It Came from the Skies." *Fate* 45,9 (September 1992): 31–35.

Corliss, William R., ed. *Handbook of Unusual Natural Phenomena.* Glen Arm, MD: Sourcebook Project, 1977.

———, ed. *Tornados, Dark Days, Anomalous Precipitation, and Related Weather Phenomena: A Catalog of Geophysical Anomalies.* Glen Arm, MD: Sourcebook Project, 1983.

"Fall of Stones." *Res Bureaux Bulletin* 24 (October 6, 1977): 2–3.

"Falls!" *INFO Journal* 4,2 (November 1974): 22–30.

Fort, Charles. *The Books of Charles Fort.* Henry Holt and Company, 1941.

Knight, Damon. *Charles Fort: Prophet of the Unexplained.* Garden City, NY: Doubleday and Company, 1970.

Koening, Vernon E. "Glob of Glass from the Sky." *Fate* 34,2 (February 1981): 81–83.

Magin, Ulrich. "Fortean Falls in Germany, Austria and Switzerland." *INFO Journal* 13,3 (March 1990): 12–14, iii.

Michell, John, and Robert J. M. Rickard. *Phenomena: A Book of Wonders.* New York: Pantheon Books, 1977.

Quast, Thelma Hall. "Rocks Rain on Chico, California." *Fate* 29,1 (January 1976): 73–81.

Rickard, Robert J. M. "Falls." *Fortean Times* 36 (Winter 1982): 26–27,41.

Rogo, D. Scott. *On the Track of the Poltergeist.* Englewood Cliffs, NJ: Prentice-Hall, 1986.

"Shower of Stones." *Symons's Monthly Meteorological Magazine* 2 (1867): 130.

Splitter, Henry Winfred. "Wonders from the Sky." *Fate* 6,10 (October 1953): 33–40.

Thomas, John. "Do Thunderstones Fall from the Sky?" *Fate* 5,8 (November 1952): 20–26.

Vambos, Thanassis. "Some Accounts of Fortean Falls in Greece." *Strange Magazine* 4 (1989): 20–22.

Whitley, Gilbert. "Falls: Fishes, Ice, Straw." *INFO Journal* 3,2 (Spring 1973): 22–25.

Falls from the Sky (Organic Matter)

As a heavy rain fell and a strong wind blew, a curious event took place at Mountain Ash, Glamorganshire, Wales, late on the morning of February 9, 1859. Numerous residents, including members of the clergy, witnessed it. One observer, John Lewis, provided this account not long afterwards, to a correspondent for the *Annual Register*:

> I was getting out a piece of timber, for the purpose of setting it for the saw, when I was startled by something falling all over me—down my neck, on my head, and on my back. On putting my hand down my neck, I was surprised to find they were little fish. By this time I saw the whole ground covered with them. I took off my hat, the brim of which was full of them. They were jumping all about. They covered the ground in a long strip of about 80 yards by 12, as we measured afterwards. [The] shed was covered with them, and the shoots were quite full of them. My mates and I might have gathered bucketsful of them, scraping with our hands. We did gather a great many, about a bucketful, and threw them into the rain pool, where some of them now are. There were two showers, with an interval of about 10 minutes, and each shower lasted about two minutes or thereabouts. The time was 11 A.M. The morning up-train to Aberdare was just then passing. It was not blowing very hard, but uncommon wet.... They came down with the rain [as if] in a body.

Another witness, the Rev. John Griffith, collected some specimens, the largest of which was five inches long.

Falls of fish—and, as we shall see, of other animals, as well as organic matter generally—have been remarked on for many centuries. The first known printed reference appears in Pliny's *Natural History* (77 C.E.). In common with some subsequent would-be explainers, he doubted that living things actually fell, presumably reasoning that since fish do not live in the sky, fish cannot fall from the sky. In his view the creatures were already present, on the ground—where, in point of fact, they do not live either—as dust and slime that, when exposed to a vigorous spring rain, sprouted into animals (which then returned to dust and slime with the onset of winter). In recent centuries, some theorists have held that a hard rain drives small animals from their usual hiding places; thus the impression that the animals fell in the rain is a delusion. No doubt that happens sometimes, and that is why we here concern ourselves mostly with witnessed falls. Other "explanations" need not concern the serious inquirer. A particularly notorious example is a British Museum scientist's suggestion that the Mountain Ash fall recounted above resulted from the dumping of a pail of fish on someone's head. A mass fall of crabs and periwinkles near Worcester, England, in 1881 was attributed to a crazed, though untraceable, fishmonger.

Today hardly anyone disputes the occurrence of falls. The debate instead centers on how anomalous their causes are. For those to whom falls are a mere curiosity of nature, such events happen when waterspouts or tornadoes carry animals from a nearby body of water and dump them on land. While superficially plausible, this explanation does not begin to deal with some of the central and thoroughly bizarre aspects of the phenomenon. With his characteristic succinct wit, Charles Fort defined the shortcomings of this view:

> Coffins have come down from the sky; also, as everybody knows, silk hats and horse collars and pajamas. But these things have come down at the time of a whirlwind. The two statements that I start with are that no shower exclusively of coffins, nor of marriage certificates, nor of alarm clocks has been recorded; but that showers exclusively of living things are common. And yet the explanations by orthodox scientists who accept that showers of living things have occurred is that the creatures were the products of whirlwinds. The explanation is that little frogs, for instance, fall from the sky unmixed with anything else, because, in a whirlwind, the creatures were segregated, by differences in specific gravity. But when a whirlwind strikes a town, away go detachables in a monstrous mixture, and there's no findable record of washtubs coming down in one place, all the town's cats in one falling battle that lumps its infelicities in one place, and all the kittens coming down together somewhere else, in a distant bunch that meows for its lump of mothers.

The truly anomalous falls usually consist of one species of animal or organic material. In other words, other species of animals do not rain down with fish or frogs (and if they do, it is only a very small number of other species); mud, sand, plant life, and debris such as a whirlwind picks up as it passes over a lake, creek, river, or sea are not to be found. The selectivity is such that often the falling animals are not only of the same species but of the same age.

In many cases, moreover, there are vast numbers of them. On September 23, 1973, for example, *tens of thousands* of toads fell on Brignoles, France, during what was described as a "freak storm." And they were all *young* toads. In September 1922 young toads fell for *two days* on another French village, Chalon-sur-Saone. Between 7 and 8 A.M. on October 23, 1947, wildlife biologist A. D. Bajkov and residents of Marksville, Louisiana, witnessed the fall of many thousands of fish, which landed—cold and even frozen in some cases—on a strip seventy-five feet wide and 1,000 feet long. Weather conditions were foggy but otherwise calm, which makes this episode unusual but not unprecedented; most falls take place during storms. (Another fall of a frozen fish occurred on December 22, 1955, when one smashed through the windshield of a car occupied by two men driving to work near Alexandria, Virginia. Traffic was light, and they were nowhere near an underpass. From the damage done—a photograph appears in the same day's *Washington Evening Star*—the fish, apparently a large carp, fell from some considerable height.)

The animals that fall may or may not be known to the area. The Marksville fish were, according to Bajkov, identical to those found in local waters. In *Science*, J. Hedgepath recorded a brief fall he had witnessed in Guam in 1936, noting that "one of the specimens ... was identified as the tench ... which, to my knowledge, is common only to the fresh waters of Europe. The presence of this species at a locale so remote from its normal habitat is worthy of note." Sometimes the animals cannot be identified. When fish fell on Montgomery County, California, in February 1890, they proved to be of, according to one who saw them and wrote up the event, "a species altogether unknown here" (*Philadelphia Public Ledger*, February 6). The people of Clifton, Indiana, did not recognize the brown worms that fell on them one day in February 1892, and neither did the editor of *Insect Life*.

A 1958 issue of *Fate* magazine included a story about raining frogs.

On occasion the falling animals arrive in a peculiar condition. At Nokulhatty Factory, India, on February 19, 1830, a great quantity of fish descended from the sky. Writing in *American Journal of Science*, M. Prinsep reported, "The fish were all dead; most of them were large; some were fresh, others rotted and mutilated. They were seen at first in the sky like a flock of birds descending rapidly to the ground. There was rain drizzling at the time but no storm." Some of the fish had no heads. Thousands of dead and dry fish landed on Futtehpur, India, in mid-May 1831. In a fall that lasted 10 minutes, sand-eels—stiff, hard, and dead—plummeted to earth near Hendon, England, on August 24, 1918, and some even broke when they hit the ground.

Fort, who found the phenomenon endlessly fascinating, collected some 294 accounts of falls of organic materials. Since his death in 1932, of course, many more have occurred, and other instances that took place before then have also come to light. What follow are examples of the kinds of things and materials that figure in fall reports.

Fish

Norfolk, Virginia, May 17, 1853: During an evening hailstorm numerous "catfish, some measuring a foot in length, fell in different sections of the city, and some of the fields were literally strewed with them. Hundreds were picked up in the morning" (*Gettysburg Star and Banner*, Pennsylvania, May 20, citing *Norfolk Argus*).

Carroll Parish, Louisiana, mid-May 1872: "A heavy storm visited that parish … and during the storm fish bones fell to the ground by the million. These bones seemed to come from an exceedingly large black cloud.… The shower of bones was attended by a very heavy fall of rain.… This strange phenomenon extended over a belt of country ten miles in width by many miles in length.… Specimens have been shown to experienced coast fishermen, and also to learned ichthyologists, but they are not able to ascertain to what particular kind of fish the bones belonged" (*Little Rock Daily Republican*, Arkansas, June 28, citing *New York Journal of Commerce*, whose Louisiana correspondent "is vouched for by the editor of that paper").

Near Union Springs, Alabama, October 12, 1882: "S. P. Thomson, one of our leading prairie planters, assures us that … he saw three fish of the perch variety fall into his front yard during a shower of rain. Mr. T. gathered up the fish, which were still alive, notwithstanding their long and rapid journey through space toward the center of gravity, and, after satisfying himself that they were only ordinary perch, placed them in an adjacent stream, where they swam off.… Mr. Thomson says he is not natural philosopher enough to explain this strange occurrence, but he is absolutely certain that the fish did fall from the clouds" (*Atchison Globe*, Kansas, November 16, reprinting article from *Union Springs Herald*).

Seymour, Indiana, August 1, 1888: "During a heavy storm Wednesday night a large number of fish, of a variety unknown here, some of them four inches in length, fell in this neighborhood. The occurrence excited a good deal of curiosity, but no one has been able to explain the phenomenon" (*Newark Daily Advocate*, Ohio, August 4).

Nashville, Tennessee, late January 1891: "A singular phenomenon was observed in connection with a heavy fall of snow.… Large quantities of small fishes came down with the snow, and in many localities the ground was literally covered with them. The largest were nearly two inches in length" (*Indiana County Gazette*, Pennsylvania, January 29).

Emporia, Kansas, June 30, 1893: "A very heavy fall of rain … occurred here.… Small fish fell in the midst of the heaviest showers. One of the largest, picked up by E. A. Tobias in his front yard, was a well developed black bass about three inches in length, which, though at first [it] showed but little life, once placed in a jar of water soon recovered and is now as lively as any of his companions in an aquarium of goldfish at the residence of ex-Governor C. V. Eskridge" (*Cedar Rapids Evening Gazette*, Iowa, July 1).

Queensland, Australia, late April 1906: "During the remarkable thunderstorms … last week an extraordinary phenomenon at a place called Cooper's Plains, near Brisbane [took place]. In the midst of the rain there suddenly fell from the skies a large number of young fish. The fish fell at first in twos and threes, but subsequently came in dozens, until a large area of ground was strewn with live fish measuring from one and a half inches to three inches. Experts in the district described the fish as of a fresh-water variety never before seen near Brisbane" (*Washington Times*, April 30).

Theresa, New York, July 16, 1913: "A peculiar phenomenon occurred during the electrical storm … Wednesday evening. Hundreds of small fish, mostly shiners, were picked up by the villagers after the storm had passed.… The water fell in torrents, the storm resembling a cloudburst. One person picked up seven of the little fish in his dooryard" (*Lowville Journal and Republican*, New York, July 17).

Klamath Falls, Oregon, mid-July 1938: "What is believed to have been at least a 10-pound fish hurtled down through a tree and struck the rear trunk of Francis McCarthy's automobile, inflicting a large dent" (*United Press*, July 21).

Fort Worth, Texas, May 8, 1985: As he was working in his back yard, three or four fish, each two inches long, dropped at Louis Castorano's feet. More followed—thirty-four in all. The fall occurred after a dark cloud passed overhead (*United Press International*, May 9).

THE RAIN OF FISH

There are hundreds of instances on record of a rain of fish from the sky. Many of them cannot be explained away in any logical manner. Details of this mystery appear on page 175

A Welsh village experienced a rain of fish, according to this late 1940s issue of *Fate*.

Fish and frogs

Collin County, Texas, May 1899: "A peculiar phenomenon occurred west and northwest of McKinney.… Fish and frogs fell from the sky, and in some places, almost covered the ground. This occurred in the afternoon when a heavy thunderstorm drenched the county. After it had passed the ground was strewn with thousands of small fish, an inch or less long, and countless numbers of very small frogs. The most peculiar thing about this was that the fish were unknown here and the frogs, all alive, were coal black and were also unknown" (*Paris News*, Texas, April 30, 1951).

Frogs

Artafelle, Scotland, August 10, 1856: "The post-runner between Redcastle and Kessock … was suddenly enveloped in what appeared to be a shower of frogs. They fell fast upon his hat and shoulders, and dozens of them found an easy resting-place in his coat-pockets. The air was quite darkened with them for about 30 yards by 14 or 15 yards, and the road was so densely covered with the dingy little creatures that it was impossible to walk without treading on them. They were about the size of a bee, and were quite lively when they found themselves on the road" (*British Banner*, London, August 15, quoting *Inverness Courier*).

Cairo, Illinois, August 2, 1883: "Early [in the] morning the decks of the steamers *Success* and *Elliott*, moored at the Mississippi levee, were observed to be literally covered with small green frogs about an inch in length, which came down with a drenching rain which prevailed during the night. Spars, lines, trees and fences were literally alive with the slimy things, while the lights from the watchmen's lanterns were obscured by the singular visitation" (*Decatur Daily Republican*, Illinois, August 3).

Big Flat and Cecilville, California, July 16, 1886: "A curious phenomenon occurred ... at Big Flat ... during a heavy shower of rain. The ground became literally covered with frogs for many hundreds of acres, extending fully three miles in one direction. On the same day, a similar shower fell ... below Cecilville, though on a smaller scale. In both cases the frogs were small, being about the size of crickets, and very lively" (*Fresno Republican*, California, August 5).

Mexico, Missouri, May 19, 1892: "A heavy rainfall of frogs took place five miles from Mexico last night. The largest fall was on the farm of Philip Shearer, who estimated the number at 800 or 1,000. The frogs were of all sizes and alive" (*Galveston Daily News*, Texas, May 20).

Moseley, England, June 30, 1892: "During the storm that raged with considerable fury ... on Wednesday morning ... a shower of frogs fell in the [Birmingham] suburb.... They were found scattered about several gardens. [They were] almost white in color" (quote cited in *Danville Bee*, Virginia, June 29, 1926).

Near Muncie, Indiana, August 10, 1894: "Shortly after 3 o'clock a shower of living things began falling. The shower of living creatures continued for five minutes and covered a ten-acre field on the farm of Ezra Willburn. The frogs fell only on Mr. Willburn's farm and at the time they fell the sky was cloudless. Mr. Willburn's small son was the only person who witnessed the shower, and after recovering from his surprise at such a strange occurrence, he informed his father of the affair. The Willburns at once began catching the largest of the frogs and enjoyed a regal repast of delicious hams for supper. The neighbors were also liberally supplied" (*Fort Wayne Sentinel*, Indiana, August 13).

Greencastle, Indiana, May 18, 1896: "In the frequent heavy rains that visited this section Monday night ... thousands of small frogs fell from the clouds, the southern part of the city being alive with them" (*Delphos Herald*, Ohio, May 21).

Near Red Hills, Maryland, June 8, 1901: "The phenomenon lasted only a few minutes, but it is estimated that nearly 500 small frogs fell to the ground. The curious sight was witnessed by several people. Several years ago a similar shower was witnessed in the same vicinity" (*New Oxford Item*, Gettysburg, Pennsylvania, June 14).

Bath, New York, mid-July, 1901: "Morris street ... was almost covered with frogs immediately after a heavy shower. Some of them were scarcely half an inch long, but all were lively. There were so many frogs in the roadway that bicyclists found riding difficult" (*Fort Covington Sun*, New York, August 1).

Lockport, New York, late March 1902: "Wherever they came from, the sidewalks and streets abounded in frogs.... There were clouds and showers this morning and after them a deluge of frogs.... They were not the bull frog, but the marsh frog.... This variety clings especially close to vegetation, but hundreds of specimens were found on the hard pavement this morning, blocks away from a spear of grass" (*Niagara Falls Gazette*, New York, March 31, quoting the *Lockport Union-Sun*).

Chester, Pennsylvania, late September 1903: "While spinning in from the suburbs of this city[,] the trolley car on which Amos Kennard was motorman was caught in a thunder storm. The man at the comptroller was pelted with rain, then with hail, and next, he says, it began to rain frogs. The passengers on the car were skeptical, but Kennard exhibited a small frog which, he says, he caught in his hand" (*Bluefield Daily Telegraph*, West Virginia, October 1).

Frackville, Pennsylvania, June 16, 1937: "Astonished householders of this little mining town, ten miles north of Pottsville, went out with brooms and swept bullfrogs off their open porches after a thunderstorm today. The tiny frogs sounded like the thudding of hailstones as they dropped by hundreds of tin roofs" (*New York Times*, June 17).

Near Clarendon, New York, October 5, 1937: While driving to a friend's farm, Mr. and Mrs. James P. O'Donnell observed tiny frogs falling in a storm. "I thought there were leaves coming down with the rain at first," Mr. O'Donnell said. "Then I could see the frogs hopping around on the road." His wife added, "Neither one of us said anything about frogs until we got to the farm and [farmer Anthony Sabo] ... asked us if we had ever seen it rain frogs before" (*Batavia Daily News*, New York, October 6).

Near Ewingdale, New South Wales, Australia, early July 1947: "Hundreds of inch-long black and cream [colored] frogs fell from the sky, some landing on motor cars, the roofs of houses, and on the hard roads" (*Adelaide Advertiser*, July 9).

Toads

Haverstraw, New York, July 3, 1877: "On Tuesday night there was a shower of toads in this village. The shower was very heavy and accompanied by a high wind. The toads, [of which] there were millions, ... were of a dark color and all of uniformly small size. Before the shower not one was to be seen—some still may be seen—if any one doubts the fact" (*Port Jervis Evening Gazette*, New York, July 10, quoting *Haverstraw Messenger*).

Harlan, Iowa, July 1881: "During a recent rain storm ... a number of live toads fell. In places they were so numerous that they might have been scraped up by the peck. They were lively, and showed no bad effects from the fall" (*Waterloo Courier*, Iowa, July 13, citing *Allison Tribune*).

Millbrook, Ontario, late September 1881: "During a heavy shower … countless myriads of small black toads fell with the rain. Shortly after the rain, and next day, in some places it was almost impossible to step on the sidewalk without crushing some of these little hoppers" (*Indiana Democrat*, Pennsylvania, September 29).

Near Spring Grove, Pennsylvania, early July 1887: "A shower of toads fell.… Parts of the farms of Peter H. Souder and Christian Weaver were covered with millions of little toads as big as a man's thumb nail" (*Tyrone Daily Herald*, Pennsylvania, July 14).

Central Maine, July 1893: "A remarkable shower of live toads fell between Olamon, this county, and Grand Falls. Millions of them half an inch long were seen hopping in all directions" (*Middletown Daily Times*, New York, July 13).

Dunkle, New York, June 7, 1895: "During a heavy shower … thousands of little toads seemed to fall from the clouds, until they nearly covered the ground. They were very frisky and remained hopping about for some time after the shower was over, when they disappeared about as mysteriously as they came" (*Olean Democrat*, New York, June 14, quoting *Kane Republican*, New York).

"A shower of toads fell.… Parts of the farms of Peter H. Souder and Christian Weaver were covered with millions of little toads as big as a man's thumb nail."

Near Delphos, Ohio, June 7, 1896: "During a rain a shower of toads fell about a half mile west of town. Our informant says there were myriads of them and very small" (*Delphos Daily Herald*, June 9).

Leeds, New York, mid-July 1897: "During a heavy rainfall … there was a shower of toads. The toads fell in a limited area, perhaps 100 square feet. Within that space the earth was literally covered with perfectly formed but diminutive toads. The creatures were uniformly of the size of common white beans of a translucent white color" (*Trenton Evening Times*, New Jersey, July 16).

Near Ogden, Utah, late August 1903: "During a heavy thunderstorm a remarkable phenomenon occurred a few miles northwest of that city. People driving to town after the storm encountered an army of small toads. There were millions of them and the wagon wheels crushed them by the thousands all along the roads. Where they came from is a mystery, but it is the general opinion that they fell from the skies" (*San Francisco Call*, August 24).

✳

Crabs

San Francisco, California, December 18, 1889: "A peculiar phenomenon was witnessed just off Kearny early this morning, it being nothing more nor less than a shower of small crabs. A light shower was falling, and accompanying it were crabs by hundreds, ranging in size from that of a dime up to that of a good-sized oyster. A similar visitation occurred at about the same hour on California street, between Sansome and Battery, but the crabs which fell there were few in number, while here they covered the sidewalk and gutter for a space at least twenty feet in length" (*Morning Oregonian*, Portland, December 19).

Snails

Tiffin, Ohio, April 21, 1889: "A strange phenomenon … took place there last night. It was no more nor less than a heavy shower of snails, from a pin head in size to some as large as a half dollar. The ground on Highland addition, a suburb of the town, was covered with them, and the noise made in their descent was like the falling of hail. In the eastern part of the city snails literally covered the sidewalks … although it only sprinkled slightly" (*Newark Daily Advocate*, Ohio, April 22).

Crawford County, Ohio, September 21, 1903: "During the night millions of diminutive snails fell and in the morning the earth was slimy with the little specimens of the gastropod. Handfuls of the snails were gathered up and examined under the microscopes and proved to be perfect specimens. The rain of snails does not seem to have been general, but it was noticed by several sections south and west of Bucyrus" (*Logansport Reporter,* Indiana, September 21).

Mercedes, Texas, October 2, 1931: "During a light shower [in the evening] Misses Marjorie and Bettie Welch were riding along this highway, and they came to a spot in the road where hail appeared to be falling. The highway was literally covered with an inch or so of some white objects appearing to be hail. The girls got out with their escorts and examined the highway, and found it covered with thousands and thousands of tiny snails. The pavement could not be seen through the snails, they said…. Other residents on the Progreso highway today reported they had also seen the snails in large numbers" (*Brownsville Herald,* Texas, October 4).

Worms, caterpillars, creepy-crawlies

Danville, Pennsylvania, February 2, 1849: "A young gentleman showed us … some small black looking caterpillars, about a half inch in length, which he had picked up on the top of the snow, near the woolen factory a short distance above town. It was snowing at the time he found them, and there were large quantities of the same sort promiscuously scattered over a large space, all alive" (*Danville Democrat*, February 9).

Lyndon, New York, mid-January 1891: "A curious sight that may be worthy of mention was seen by several persons one morning last week. A large number of worms, yellow in color, flat in shape, from a third of an inch to an inch in length, and forked at one extremity, were seen mingled with and crawling over the freshly fallen snow" (*Olean Democrat*, January 29).

Near Clifton, Indiana, January 27, 1892: "A very strange occurrence was reported … by Ben Snyder, correspondent for the statistic bureau in Washington. Upon investigation it was proven a fact by other reliable men from the same place, near Clifton in this county. Wednesday there came a cold, sleety rain, and with it came a shower of worms which were curiosities, for nothing like them has ever been seen in this part of the country. They were about an inch in length, of a dark brown color and had six legs, which were well to the front of the body, the body being as large around as a ten-penny wire nail. Under the microscope it was found that the body of the worm was covered with very fine hair, and had eyes similar to a fly, so numerous that it was impossible to count them. The shower covered an area of five miles" (*Hamilton Daily Democrat*, Ohio, February 1).

> **W**ednesday there came a cold, sleety rain, and with it came a shower of worms which were curiosities, for nothing like them has ever been seen in this part of the country.

Winsted, Connecticut, early March 1911: "Abram C. Shelly … while walking along Torrington street the other morning during a snowstorm, perceived hundreds of live grub worms on top of the snow. He gathered a handful of them and brought them to Winsted to corroborate his statement. In a warm room the worms appeared as lively as in the summer. Shelly is certain the worms did not crawl up through five inches of snow, and the only way he can account for their presence on the snow is that the winds picked them up in the South and they came down in Winsted with the snowstorm" (*Sheboygan Press*, Wisconsin, March 9).

Near Grass Valley, California, early July 1913: "A strange phenomenon of nature was reported by Rural Carrier John F. Carey of the post office of [Grass Valley] during the recent rain. For a distance of a hundred yards in the vicinity of Kreiss Summit, near the narrow gauge tracks, there were thousands of small worms on the ground, all apparently dead. One … who lives in that section was spoken to concerning it and he stated that for a short time during the heavy showers the worms appeared to come from the heavens. The sight was so unusual that it impressed the mail carrier and he reported the incident upon his arrival in town" (*Indianapolis Star*, July 6).

Flesh and blood

Wilson County, Tennessee, August 6, 1841: "A shower, *apparently of flesh and blood* [italics in original], [has] fallen … near Lebanon … The fields were covered to a considerable extent. The account staggered our belief, but, strange as it may appear, it has been confirmed by the statement of several gentlemen of high character, who have personally examined the scene of this phenomenon. They state that the space covered by this extraordinary shower is half a mile in length and about seventy-five yards in width. In addition to the information just received, we

In this 1608 engraving, scientists and the religious try to explain a rain of blood in Aix-en-Provence, France.

have been favored by Dr. Troost, professor of chemistry in the University of Nashville, with the following letter from a highly respectable physician in Lebanon. We have also seen the specimens sent to him for examination. *To us they appear to be animal matter, and the odor is that of putrid flesh.* [Letter to Dr. Troost from W. P. Sayle:] 'With me there can be no doubt of its being animal matter—blood, muscular fibre.... The particles I send you I gathered with my own hands. From the extent of surface over which it has spread, and the regular manner on some green tobacco leaves, leaves very little doubt of its having fallen like a shower of rain; and it is stated ... to have fallen from a small red cloud; no other clouds visible in the heavens at the time. It took place on Friday last, between eleven and twelve o'clock, about five miles northeast of Lebanon'" (*Ohio Repository*, Canton, September 9, 1841, reprinted from *Nashville Banner*).

Sampson County, North Carolina, February 15, 1850: "We received ... the following communication from Mr. Clarkson [writing in the third person], through Mr. Holland, of Clinton: 'There fell within 100 yards of the residence of Thos. M.

Clarkson … a shower of Flesh and Blood, about 30 feet wide, and as far as it was traced, about 250 or 300 yards in length. The pieces appeared to be flesh, liver, lights [?], brains and blood. Some of the blood ran on the leaves, apparently very fresh. Three of his (T.M.C.'s) children were in it and ran to their mother, exclaiming "Mother there is meat falling!" Their mother went immediately to see, but the shower was over, but there lay the flesh, etc. Neill Campbell, Esq., living close by, was on the spot shortly after it fell, and pronounced it as above. One of his children was about 150 yards from the shower, and came running to the rest saying he smelt something like blood. During the time it was falling there was a cloud overheard, having a red appearance like a wind cloud. There was no rain'.… The piece which was left with us, has been examined with two of the best microscopes in the place; and the existence of blood [is] well established; but nothing was shown giving any indication of the character of the matter. It has the smell, both in its dry state, and when macerated in water, of putrid flesh; and there can be scarcely a doubt that it is such" (*Fayetteville Carolinian*, March 9).

Near Los Angeles, California, July 1869: As mourners gathered for a funeral at a farm, blood and meat rained out of a clear sky for three minutes. The substances blanketed two acres of a corn field. On examination the blood was found to be mixed with what looked like hairs from animal fur. The flesh ranged in size from small particles to six- and eight-inch strips and included what witnesses took to be pieces of kidney, liver, and heart. One witness brought samples to a local newspaper, whose editor subsequently declared, "That the meat fell, we cannot doubt. Even the persons in the neighborhood are willing to vouch for that. Where it came from, we cannot even conjecture" (*Los Angeles News*, August 3).

Gastonia County, North Carolina, November 25, 1876: "A gentleman writing from Gastonia … gives an account of a truly wonderful occurrence. He states that the shower of flesh—genuine, unmistakable flesh—fell … on the farm of Mr. James M. Hanna. The circumstances so far as they can be gathered from the letter alluded to, and from the statement of Mr. G. W. Chalk, of the city [Charlotte], who visited the spot and heard the statements of those who witnessed the phenomenon, are as follows: Saturday afternoon, about 3 o'clock, while Mr. James M. Hanna and some of his little grandchildren were picking cotton in a field near his house, they were astonished at the sight of small pieces of flesh falling all around them. The shower continued for some time, and when it ceased it was discovered that the flesh was scattered over an area of about half an acre of ground. The pieces varied from a half ounce to an ounce in weight. In the words of our correspondent, 'the ground was not covered, but the flesh fell like light hail.' In appearance it is described as resembling beef, part of it being filled with small sinews, but in no piece were bones or fatty matter found. When it fell it had the appearance and odor of fresh meat, but the pieces sent us for inspection are almost entirely odorless and resemble dried beef. It may be added that the weather was perfectly calm at the time of the shower, and that there has been no storm and no heavy wind in that section in several weeks" (*Newark Advocate*, Ohio, December 1, quoting *Charlotte Observer*).

Reptiles

Near Taylorville, Illinois, August 20, 1869: "The great storm of last Friday night … burst in its full fury … about dark, and the rain fell in torrents. The electric storm presented the same features as here.… But the most singular phenomenon … was a shower of snakes.… On Saturday and Sunday last [August 21–22], every ditch, brook and pool on the prairie north of Taylorville was alive with nondescript creatures, which have been described to us as being from one-and-a-half to two feet long, and three-fourths of an inch to an inch in diameter. This diameter is very slightly lessened at the head and tail. The tail is flat, like that of an eel, but has no caudal fin. Indeed, there is no fin at all. The head is in shape that of an eel, but the mouth is that of a sucker. The eyes are small, and the ears are simply orifices. Immediately behind the head, on each side, is a flipper, like that of a turtle, say three-fourths of an inch to an inch in length, including the limb, which has a perfectly developed joint. In color, these snakes, or whatever they are, are of a dark hue. The number of these creatures is beyond all estimate. They swim in every branch and puddle of water" (*Illinois Daily Register,* August 27).

> The meadow … was thickly strewn with the bodies of the strange creatures, none of which were discovered alive.

Near Elk River, Minnesota, July 3, 1873: "A shower of reptiles … fell upon a meadow on the farm of Edward Upham … [in] the morning … during a heavy rain and wind storm. The meadow, he says, was thickly strewn with the bodies of the strange creatures, none of which were discovered alive. They are described as about six inches long, having gills and fins like fish, but having also four legs about two inches long and terminating in claws" (*Port Jervis Evening Gazette,* New York, July 19).

Silverton Township, South Carolina, December 1877: "Dr. J. L. Smith … while opening up a new turpentine farm, noticed something fall to the ground and commence to crawl toward the tent where he was sitting. On examining the object he found it to be an alligator. In the course of a few moments a second one made its appearance. This so excited the curiosity of the Doctor that he looked around to see if he could discover any more, and found six others within a space of 200 yards. The animals were all quite lively, and about 12 inches in length" (*New York Times,* December 26).

Canton, South Dakota, August 14, 1901: "Conductor Paddy Moran, of the Canton cannonball, is authority for the following snake story. He says: 'I hope to die if the railroad yards at Canton this morning when I arrived at 6 o'clock were not covered with snakes. The people called them hair snakes and they were so numerous and their actions so lively as to make one dizzy to cast one's eyes upon the ground. They were everywhere and wriggling to beat the band. They were from four to twelve inches in length and the largest were about as large as a match in circumference.… The common opinion was that they came down in the big rain storm of the night before. The head of one was cut off and placed under a microscope and it looked like that of a fish'" (*Minneapolis Journal*, August 15).

Seeds, leaves, flakes

Rockdale, Texas, mid-March 1878: "Rockdale ... witnessed a strange phenomenon. It was a shower of leaves. As far as the eye could reach[,] the heavens above were filled with them.... There was no commotion of the atmosphere to be observed in any direction on the horizon.... They were falling all day along" (*Atlanta Daily Constitution*, March 19, quoting *Rockdale Messenger*).

Boonville, North Carolina, September 20, 1897: "Last Monday morning while the sun was shining brightly the air suddenly became filled with falling flakes like snow, except they were not cold, but were of a greasy nature and many were much larger than snowflakes, being two inches long in some instances. The people became greatly interested and some of them very much alarmed. The school children all left school to witness the strange sight and business for the time being was suspended. No one is able to give any explanation of the phenomenon" (*Winston Journal*, September 27).

Winchester, Virginia, April 22, 1904: "A curious phenomenon was witnessed ... when a heavy downfall of dry leaves from the sky occurred.... The leaves for several hours fell thick and fast, and were principally oak" (*Bluefield Daily Telegraph*, West Virginia, April 28).

Wichita, Kansas, August 3, 2001: "People in homes near 13th and Woodlawn reported seeing what looked like extraordinarily large, dried corn husks spiraling down from the sky about 6 P.M.... 'They just kept coming down,' [a witness] said. 'There had to be, I don't know, a thousand of these things' .... There is no telling how many of these leaves fell.... Our region—in fact, the whole country—was tornado-free on Friday. It wasn't even particularly windy, [meteorologist Jeff] House said" (*Wichita Eagle*, August 6).

Theories

If we eliminate waterspouts, whirlwinds, and earthbound animals and plants mistakenly assumed to have fallen as adequate explanations for the most anomalous falls, we are left with a mystery with no plausible answers. That, of course, has not discouraged some writers from proposing their own rather implausible answers.

Fort at least had his tongue in his cheek when he put forth his own explanation. His favorite "theory," which he cheerfully acknowledged to be preposterous and outrageously pseudoscientific, was that giant land masses float above the world. Tornadoes, hurricanes, and cyclones on the earth's surface carry all sorts of items upward and dump them on these lands. Some fall into the "Super-Sargasso

A waterspout in Mobile Bay, Alabama. One theory about falling fish is that waterspouts such as this one pull fish up into the air.

Sea," to join other junk from other times and even of other worlds. In that vast atmospheric ocean can be found almost anything conceivable:

> Derelicts, rubbish, old cargoes from inter-planetary wrecks, things cast out into what is called space by convulsions of other planets, things from the times of the Alexanders, Caesars, and Napoleons of Mars and Jupiter and Neptune; things raised by this earth's cyclones; horses and barns and elephants and flies and dodoes, moas, and pterodactyls; leaves from modern trees and leaves of the Carboniferous era—all, however, tending to disintegrate into homogeneous-looking muds or dusts, red or black or yellow—treasure troves for the palaeontologists and for the archaeologists—accumulations of centuries—cyclones of Egypt, Greece, and Assyria—fishes dried and hard, there a short time; others there long enough to putrefy … or living fishes, also—ponds of fresh water, oceans of salt water.

Violent terrestrial storms not only dump things into the Super-Sargasso Sea but cause disturbances there so that sometimes things drop from it—thus falls of all sorts of organic and inorganic matter.

Unlike Fort, John Philip Bessor actually *meant* his alarming theory. According to Bessor, the "many falls of flesh and blood from the sky in times past" constitute evidence that UFOs are carnivorous atmospheric life forms, otherwise known as "space animals"; how else to explain mysterious disappearances of people? Relatively more prosaically, another 1950s UFO writer, Morris K. Jessup, thought the answer fairly obvious. The live things that have fallen from the sky are

> the inhabitants of celestial hydroponic tanks and ... their falls come from one of two things: (1) when the tanks are dumped and cleared for refilling, for whatever reason there might be, (2) that the falls may be the residue from the collection from earth while the monitors of the tanks are replenishing their supplies.

In other efforts to make sense of falls, writers of a Fortean disposition are inclined to draw on the concept of teleportation—the paranormal transportation of an object from one place to another—as a sort of blanket explanation. But even if teleportation is a real phenomenon in nature, which is by no means certain (to put it mildly), it begs the same sorts of questions more conventional approaches do. In other words, it does not address the selectivity of falls and the staggering volume that falls in a number of the cases.

The late Damon Knight formulated what amounts to a nonsatirical reworking of Fort's satirical hypothesis. A sober, scientifically sophisticated man, a highly regarded science fiction writer (and biographer of Fort), Knight charted weather records and matched them against reports of falls and unusual space and aerial phenomena in Fort's books. From 1877 through 1892, a period of unusually intense anomalous activity, he found what seem to be striking correlations. He reviewed other kinds of evidence from physics and astronomy on the effects of extraterrestrial energies on everything from weather to behavior, as well as scientific theories about parallel universes. These led him to suggest that

> under certain conditions of gravidic and electromagnetic strain in the solar system, channels open through which material objects can reach the earth from parts unknown, or can be transferred from one part of the earth's surface to another.... Let us suppose that a channel opens between this earth and another, where the surface is a few hundred feet, or a few thousand feet, higher. Then things fall, from that earth to this. Frogs, minding their own affairs in a pond, feel the bottom drop out....

Falls certainly seem a sufficiently extraordinary phenomenon to require an explanation like this, but the problem here is, ironically, the same one that makes the waterspout hypothesis unsatisfactory: the selectivity and the volume. Knight did make some slight effort to deal with at least the first issue: "If these channels are electromagnetic in nature, we may approach an answer to the puzzling question of selectivity.... All living things have electric charges, and it is possible to imagine that an electromagnetic field would discriminate between them." Perhaps wisely, he took this vague idea no further.

Further Reading:

Bajkov, A. D. "Do Fish Fall from the Sky?" *Science* 109 (1949): 402.

Bessor, John Philip. "Are the Saucers Space Animals?" *Fate* 8,12 (December 1955): 6–12.

"Black Worms Fall from the Sky." *Nature* 6 (1872): 356.

Corliss, William R., ed. *Handbook of Unusual Natural Phenomena.* Glen Arm, MD: Sourcebook Project, 1977.

———, ed. *Tornados, Dark Days, Anomalous Precipitation, and Related Weather Phenomena: A Catalog of Geophysical Anomalies.* Glen Arm, MD: Sourcebook Project, 1983.

Dennis, Jerry. *It's Raining Frogs and Fishes: Four Seasons of Natural Phenomena and Oddities of the Sky.* New York: HarperCollins, 1992.

Dobbins, Ron. "The 'Fish Falls' of Yoro, Honduras." *Pursuit* 8,4 (October 1975): 93–95.

"A Fall of Green Slime." *Journal of Meteorology* 4 (1979): 312.

Fort, Charles. *The Books of Charles Fort.* New York: Henry Holt and Company, 1941.

"Frozen Flying Fish Sails Out of Sky to Smack Car." *Washington Evening Star* (December 22, 1955).

Hedgepath, I. "Rainfall of Fish." *Science* 110 (1949): 482.

Jessup, M. K. *The Case for the UFO.* New York: Citadel Press, 1955.

Knight, Damon. *Charles Fort: Prophet of the Unexplained.* Garden City, NY: Doubleday and Company, 1970.

Little, Gregory L. "Snakes Fell on Memphis." *Fate* 38,2 (February 1985): 74–77.

Meyer, Arlene O. "Report from the Readers: Raining Dogs." *Fate* 21,12 (December 1968): 131–32.

Michell, John, and Robert J. M. Rickard. *Phenomena: A Book of Wonders.* New York: Pantheon Books, 1977.

———. *Living Wonders: Mysteries and Curiosities of the Animal World.* New York: Thames and Hudson, 1982.

Pim, Arthur. "A Shower of Hazel Nuts." *Symons's Monthly Meteorological Magazine* 2 (1867): 59.

Prinsep, M. "Fall of Fishes from the Atmosphere in India." *American Journal of Science* 1,32 (1837): 199.

"Remarkable Hail." *Monthly Weather Review* 22 (1894): 215.

Sanderson, Ivan T. *Uninvited Visitors: A Biologist Looks at UFOs.* New York: Cowles, 1967.

Schadewald, Robert. "The Great Fish Fall of 1859." *Fortean Times* 30 (1979): 38–42.

Shoemaker, Michael T. "Back from Limbo: The California Candy Falls." *Strange Magazine* 4 (1989): 23.

"Shower of Grain." *American Journal of Science* 1,41 (1841): 40.

Splitter, Henry Winfred. "Wonders from the Sky." *Fate* 6,10 (October 1953): 33–40.

Vembos, Thanassis. "Some Accounts of Fortean Falls in Greece." *Strange Magazine* 4 (1989): 20–22.

Wallace, R. Hedger. "A Marvelous 'Rainfall' of Seeds." *Notes and Queries* 8,12 (1897): 228.

Whalen, Dwight. "Niagara Fishfalls." *Pursuit* 16,2 (Second Quarter 1983): 64–67.

Whitley, Gilbert. "Falls: Fishes, Ice, Straw." *INFO Journal* 3,2 (Spring 1973): 22–25.

Flying Humanoids

When a mysterious object passed over Mount Vernon, Illinois, on the evening of April 14, 1897, a hundred citizens, including Mayor B. C. Wells, saw something that, so press accounts had it, "resembled the body of a huge man swimming through the air with an electric light on his back."

The alleged sighting took place in the midst of a nationwide wave of mystery-airship reports, and it received little attention then or later. It is not clear, moreover, if the resemblance to a flying man was literal or metaphorical, though if the former it joined a host of comparable sighting stories from around the world, such as this one, recalled in a 1980 letter to the Center for UFO Studies, from an experience four children allegedly had in Silver City, New Mexico, at the twilight of a summer day in 1938:

> We all saw him. He was dressed all in gray and *he* even seemed gray; he was drifting or floating at tree-top level. The thing I remember the most about him was that he seemed to be wearing a belt which was wide and had points sticking out of it. He also seemed to be wearing a cape (a la Flash Gordon).

> He drifted across the sky above us and we all stood and stared, speechless. It did not occur to us to question this phenomena [sic]; as children we accepted it....

> About fifteen years ago I was telling my husband about it. When I did, I questioned myself—perhaps I had had a dream. But just in case, I called my brother. By now I was about thirty-five and he about thirty-two. I prefaced my conversation by telling him that I had a strange story to tell and that perhaps it had all been a dream, but that I thought that in about 1938 I had seen a man fly over our heads. He stopped me and said, "It wasn't a dream." He went on to describe everything as I have described it here, including the belt and the cape.

One night, in 1952, U.S. Air Force Pvt. Sinclair Taylor, on guard duty at Camp Okubo, Kyoto, Japan, reportedly heard a loud flapping noise. Looking up, he saw an enormous "bird" in the moonlight. When it approached, he got frightened and put a round into the chamber of his carbine. The "bird" now had stopped its flight and was hovering not far away, staring at the soldier.

"That thing, which now had started slowly to descend again, had the body of a man," Taylor recalled. "It was well over seven feet from head to feet, and its wingspread was almost equal to its height. I started to fire and emptied my carbine where the thing hit the ground. But when I looked up to see if my bullets had found home there was nothing there." When the sergeant of the guard came to investigate and heard the story, he told Taylor that he believed him because a year earlier another guard had seen the same thing.

An even more disturbing incident allegedly occurred in Falls City, Nebraska, one fall afternoon in 1956. The Hanks family (a pseudonym; the witness did not want his real name known) had just returned home from an outing, and all but John, the husband/father, had gone into the house. John Hanks was loading work equipment into the back of his pickup when a casual glance caught something in the air three blocks away. As it got closer, what Hanks had first taken to be a kite began to look more and more like something unimaginable: a large, winged human form. Soon he could see its "very frightening, almost demonic" face.

"We saw what looked like wings, like a bat's, only it was gigantic compared to what a regular bat would be."

Years later, speaking with investigator Ray Boeche, he remembered its eyes as "very large, blue in color. They were shaped on his face almost like horse's eyes. The skin on his face was like tan leather. It was very wrinkled and seemed to overlap in folds. I had a good look at his face—he was only about 25 feet away, and hovering maybe 15 feet above the ground. He was between eight and nine feet tall."

At that point the figure wobbled and plummeted to the ground, stopping just before it hit the pavement. It resumed its flight toward Hanks, who wanted to flee but felt paralyzed. As it flew over him, he could see that the wings stretched fifteen feet from tip to tip, two feet wide at the closest points to the body, and three feet wide at the outer extremities. They resembled polished aluminum, with grids on their upper surfaces. Four- to five-inch colored lights, moving outward from blue to yellow, orange, and red at the tip, ran along each underside. The wing, according to Hanks, "was fastened to him by a shoulder harness, which seemed to have a breast plate of some sort with dials on it. He seemed to touch and move these dials, but his hands, if that's what they were, looked more like a white dove's wings, all opened up." A hissing sound came from the back of the wings.

Only after the figure vanished behind trees two blocks away did Hanks recover his mobility. But it took much longer than that to regain his peace of mind. For the next two decades he suffered terrifying nightmares concerning the figure, and its image haunted him even during his waking hours. In the late 1970s, through a conscious act of will, he finally succeeded in putting the memory behind him. In the mid–1980s he told Boeche, "It doesn't matter anymore."

Another tale of a flying humanoid came to ufologist Don Worley from Earl Morrison, who served with the First Marine Division in Vietnam. While stationed

(Continued on page 51)

Hairy Dwarves

The dwarves in Snow White and the Seven Dwarves were nothing like the sinister, hairy, alien dwarves described by a number of witnesses.

During the fall of 1954, a worldwide UFO wave erupted. Among the many reports were a striking number involving humanoid occupants, sometimes described as hairy dwarves. On October 9, for example, three rural French children out roller-skating reported that a "round shiny machine came down very close to us. Out of it came a kind of man, four feet tall, dressed in a black sack like the cassock M. le Cure wears. His head was hairy, and he had big eyes. He said things to us that we couldn't understand, and we ran away. When we stopped and looked back, the machine was going up into the sky very fast." Five days later a French miner encountered a humanoid with a squat, furry body and oversized, slanted, protruding eyes. It was wearing a skull cap and had a flat nose and thick lips.

In Venezuela, in early December, several reports recounted nocturnal encounters with three-foot-tall hairy dwarves of aggressive disposition. In one instance, said to have taken place on December 10, four such beings stepped out of a hovering UFO and attempted to abduct a young man. His companion, who happened to be armed because the two were hunting at the time of the encounter, struck one of the entities on the head with his gun butt. The butt splintered as if it had collided with solid rock. The two men, bruised, cut, and clearly terrified, told their story to the police soon afterwards. Nine days later, at Valencia, a jockey on a late-night training ride said he saw six hairy dwarves hauling rocks into a nearby UFO. When they noticed him, one fired a beam of violet light and paralyzed him, even though he had been trying to flee. Police found footprints on the scene. They looked, they said, "neither human nor animal."

Though accounts of encounters with UFO occupants continue to the present, hairy dwarves faded from the scene by the end of 1954 and were seen, or at least reported, no more.

Further Reading:

Bowen, Charles, ed. *The Humanoids: A Survey of Worldwide Reports of Landings of Unconventional Aerial Objects and Their Alleged Occupants.* Chicago: Henry Regnery Company, 1969.

Keyhoe, Donald E. *The Flying Saucer Conspiracy.* New York: Henry Holt and Company, 1955.

Lorenzen, Coral, and Jim Lorenzen. *Encounters with UFO Occupants.* New York: Berkley Publishing, 1976.

Michel, Aimé. *Flying Saucers and the Straight-Line Mystery.* New York: Criterion Books, 1958.

(*Continued from page 49*)

near Da Nang in August 1969, he and two other guards reportedly saw an extraordinary sight, just after one o'clock in the morning. They were sitting atop a bunker and talking when they noticed something approaching them in the sky. Morrison told Worley:

> We saw what looked like wings, like a bat's, only it was gigantic compared to what a regular bat would be. After it got close enough so we could see what it was, it looked like a woman. A naked woman. She was black. Her skin was black, her body was black, the wings were black, everything was black. But it glowed. It glowed in the night—kind of a greenish cast to it.... She started going over us, and we still didn't hear anything. She was right above us, and when she got over the top of our heads, she was maybe six or seven feet up.... We watched her go straight over the top of us, and still she didn't make any noise flapping her wings. She blotted out the moon once—that's how close she was to us. And dark—looked like pitch black then, but we could still define her because she just glowed. Real bright like. And she started going past us straight towards our encampment. And we watched her—she had got about 10 feet or so away from us—we started hearing her wings flap. And it sounded, you know, like regular wings flapping. And she just started flying off and we watched her for quite a while.

Morrison thought the covering on her skin was more like fur than feathers. "The skin of her wings looked like it was molded on to her hands," he said, and the movement of her arms suggested they had no bones in them.

On the Indonesian island of Seram, residents speak fearfully of the *orang bati* (flying men), nocturnal, winged, human-like creatures who live inside dead volcanoes. At night, it is claimed, they fly from the mountains to the coastal villages, where sometimes they snatch small children, who are never seen again. These creatures, said to be four or five feet tall, resemble the one Morrison supposedly saw (including the skin color) except for their long, thin tails. Those inclined to the view that the *orang bati* tradition grows out of exaggerated sightings of monkeys should know that no monkeys exist on Seram. In the mid–1980s a Western agriculture specialist named Tyson Hughes, who lived on the island, was taken to a thick jungle area where *orang bati* supposedly lived. He saw nothing out of the ordinary, but the terror his native informants expressed when speaking of the creature left an impression on him.

Sky people

Stories like these tend to get reported in UFO literature, even in the absence of UFOs. Perhaps the earliest such report from the age of flying saucers—which begins in late June 1947—dates to January 6, 1948, when an elderly woman and a group of children told of seeing a man with long mechanical wings that he manipulated with instruments on his chest as he flew in an upright position. In a handful of close encounters of the third kind, occupants are described as floating just above the ground near landed craft. These kinds of reports may or may not be related to traditions of flying humanoids.

In the nineteenth century and before, witnesses often presumed such presences to be angels. Eli Curtis's religious tract *Wonderful Phenomena* (1850) recounts an incident told by farmer Charles Cooper of Warwick, Ontario, on October 3, 1843. Cooper said that the incident took place in the wake of a brief rain shower, followed by the appearance of a vividly colored rainbow. As the sky cleared, Cooper heard a distant sound to the west. Taking it to be thunder, he gazed toward the west. While he was gazing in that direction, the sound seemed to grow louder and closer. Soon:

> I beheld a cloud of very remarkable appearance approaching, and underneath it, the appearance of three men, perfectly white, sailing through the air, one following the other, the foremost one appearing a little the latest.

> My surprise was great, and concluding I was deceived, I watched them carefully. They still approached me underneath the cloud, and came directly over my head, a little higher up than the tops of the trees, so that I could view every feature as perfectly as of one standing directly before me. I could see nothing but a milky-white body, with extended arms, destitute of motion, while they continued to utter doleful moans, which, I found as they approached, to be the distant roar that first attracted my attention. These moans sounded much like Wo-Wo-Wo.

> I watched them until they passed out of sight. The effect can be better imagined than described. Two men were laboring at a distance, to whom I called to see the men in the air, but they say they did not see them.

> I never believed in such appearances until that time.

William H. Smith of Brooklyn wrote this letter to the *New York Sun* (September 21, 1877):

> On Tuesday afternoon [September 18] of this week, a few minutes after 6 o'clock, I noticed from my window a very peculiar, solitary, vapory object in the heavens. Its position was about where the constellation of the Dipper would be at that hour, viz., due north, and thirty-five degrees above

the horizon. In magnitude and contour it in a marked degree resembled a human form, head, body, and nether limbs, the body and limbs robed in shadowy drapery. The head, which was of brighter luminosity on the crown and forehead, had thick flowing hair, and the whole figure was extended horizontally, with the head eastward and the front downward. But there was another feature quite as marked, and that was an appearance as of wings projecting upward and backward from the shoulders, and these in due proportional extent to the body and limbs. The last named feature gave the entirety the appearance of an angel, flying in mid-heaven, considered as a cloud. It was remarkable that it kept the same outline continuously, which is uncommon in these vapory [illegible], while I had it in view for a considerable time, as it progressed swiftly toward the east. The luminosity of the shadowy angel was of a golden white, and it presented a very beautiful appearance against the blue background of the sky. In addition to the startling outline of the object, the interest in it was greatly increased by its being at the time the only one visible in the whole northern heavens, except some low-lying black clouds on the horizon. I called the attention of several persons to it, one of whom discovered himself the resemblance I did.

> "**The luminosity of the shadowy angel was of a golden white, and it presented a very beautiful appearance against the blue background of the sky.**"

If Smith's words alone don't make it entirely clear that this wasn't just an unusually interesting, imagination-inspiring cloud, the entity that appeared over three Wayne County, New York, villages on the afternoon of November 2, 1896, is said to have manifested "in broad daylight in a clear sky," according to a local newspaper, the *Olean Democrat* (November 20), which added that "there appears to be no possible hypothesis except a spiritual one."

At least twenty residents—four of whom the *Democrat* names—of South Butler, Butler Center, and Slyburg reported sighting a figure in the air around 3 P.M. Butler Center schoolteacher D. F. Everhart provided this account:

I was returning from Wolcott … when I noticed an object floating in the air about 100 yards away and nearly over my head. Its appearance was that of a girl about 20 years of age, clad in a long white robe with the arms bare. On its shoulders was a pair of long white wings which were nearly motionless. At first the features were clearly visible, but as the object floated higher, they gradually became indistinct. The day was clear, not a cloud in sight. I saw it for fully twenty minutes. To be convinced that I was awake and not dreaming, I even pinched myself. I said nothing for several days, fearing ridicule, till I heard others speaking of similar occurrences.

The figure's motionlessness leaves open one non-spiritual possibility: that this may have been a kite. Of course, at this late date—as with so many late dates—the reality will likely remain forever muddled. Hoaxes (themselves a popular pastime in an era when mass entertainment was not as close as a computer or a television set) involving kites, however, were hardly an unknown feature of nineteenth-century small-town life.

On the other hand were some accounts which apparently defy any conceivable explanation. One is set in rural Sussex County, New Jersey, and is said to have taken place on the evening of August 21, 1818. Described as "persons of integrity," the witnesses, who provided sworn affidavits to local legal authorities, claimed to have seen whole armies of white-clad angelic figures, first on the ground, then ascending into the sky. (See my *Hidden Realms, Lost Civilizations, and Beings from Other Worlds*, Visible Ink Press, 2010, pp. 213–14. The chapter "Ghost Riders in the Sky: Spectral Armies on the March," in which the Sussex County story is told in detail, recounts comparable stories of apparitional aerial phenomena, often with martial imagery.)

More mirth than menace

A story often retold in true-mysteries literature first saw print in the September 12, 1880, issue of the *New York Times*. The piece told of a sighting by Coney Island residents of a winged flying man with "improved frog's legs," sailing in the direction of the New Jersey coast. His arms were making flapping motions while his legs moved as if swimming. The figure was all black, and though estimated to be a thousand feet in the air, he wore a "cruel and determined expression," according to the alleged witnesses, who either had unusually acute eyesight or were letting their imaginations supply the details.

A search through contemporary New York City press accounts by researcher and writer Theo Paijmans suggests that the story was intended to satirize a then-prominent social reformer. Its inspiration was a spate of rumors about a flying machine propelled by a single visible pilot. The aerial device did exist. When it came to earth, however, it was a balloon or kite (the accounts are ambiguous on that detail), and its occupant proved imaginary.

Further Reading:

Curtis, Eli. *Wonderful Phenomena, Wonder of the Ages*. New York: The Author, 1850.

Fort, Charles. *The Books of Charles Fort*. New York: Henry Holt and Company, 1941.

Keel, John A. *Strange Creatures from Time and Space*. Greenwich, CT: Fawcett Gold Medal, 1970.

Shuker, Karl. *Alien Zoo*. Bideford, North Devonshire, England: CFZ Press, 2010.

Taylor, Sinclair. "True Mystic Experiences: The Bird Thing." *Fate* 13,12 (December 1960): 53–54.

"Winged Wonder Over Falls City?" *Journal of the Fortean Research Center* 1 (April 1986): 3–4.

Worley, Don. "The Winged Lady in Black." *Flying Saucer Review Case Histories* 10 (June 1972): 14–16.

Ghost Lights

host lights are luminous phenomena, usually either points of light or spheres, whose appearance, behavior, location, or regular manifestation puts them, at least ostensibly, into a separate category from ball lightning or UFOs. Ghost lights are often taken to be supernatural or otherworldly, and in many cases, especially those in which they appear regularly over a period of time in one place (as with the famous Brown Mountain lights and the Marfa lights), legends have grown around them, often associating the lights with apparitions of the dead.

Lights in folk tradition

More than 300 years ago, Nathaniel Crouch wrote in *The English Empire in America* (1685) that the Indians "have a remarkable observation of a flame that appears before the death of an Indian or English upon their wigwams in the dead of night; I was called out once about twelve a clock … and plainly perceived it mounting into the air over a church…. You may certainly expect a dead corpse in two or three days."

Three decades earlier, in fact, John Davis, vicar of Geneu'r Glyn, Cardiganshire, Wales, recorded his and others' observations of varyingly colored lights that foretold deaths. These lights could be encountered anywhere: in the open air, on their way through a door, or inside a house. A small light presaged the death of a child, a bigger light that of an adult. Several lights together meant as many deaths. His wife's sister, Davis said, had observed five lights in a room; that night, in that very room, five servants suffocated to death in a freak accident.

In 1897 R. C. Maclagan published a long survey of ghost-light traditions, stories, and reports from Scotland's West Highlands. Typical of them are tales told by an Islay man:

One time lights were seen moving about at night on the rocks on the shore near Kilchearan. Shortly after that, a vessel was wrecked there, and the body of a man was washed ashore at the spot where the lights had been seen. One time lights were seen on Lochandaal, between Bowmore and Blackrock. Not long after that, two young men were crossing the loch

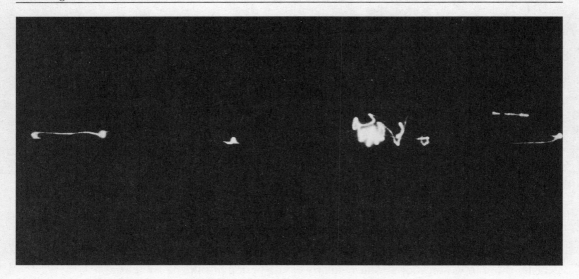

Marfa lights photographed by James Crocker in Texas, September 1986.

on a small boat, and at the place at which the lights had been seen the boat was capsized and the two lads drowned.

Such widespread traditions of "corpse candles" continued into the twentieth century. As a Welsh informant told W. Y. Evans-Wentz early in the century, "The death-candle appears like a patch of bright light; and no matter how dark the room or place is, everything in it is as clear as day. The candle is not a flame, but a luminous mass, lightish blue in color, which dances as though borne by an invisible agency, and sometimes it rolls over and over. If you go up to the light, it is nothing, for it is a spirit."

In February 1909, for example, newspaper accounts told of the excitement generated in Stockton, Pennsylvania, over the "appearance at night of an arrow of flame, which hovers over the spot on the mountain where the dismembered body of a woman was found in a barrel two years ago.... The light appears every night at about 9 o'clock, and hovers over the spot until midnight, but it disappears when anyone approaches the spot to investigate. The superstitious villagers say it is the avenging spirit of the slain woman come back to keep alive the history of the crime so that the murderers may some day be apprehended."

Writing from Willoughton, Lincolnshire, folklorist Ethel H. Rudkin related sightings of ghost lights in the years between the world wars:

Night after night in winter-time the light could be seen; usually between the cross roads on Ermine Street and nearby to the gate leading to Old Leys Manor, always on the road. It looked like a bicycle lamp and was about the same distance from the ground and the same color. A. B.'s daughter has seen it often between eight and ten o'clock at night when she has been coming home, so also has her son. A man from Atterby used to come courting to Willoughton and he was so scared by this light that he used to go another way, many miles round. One of our policemen was at the cross roads late one night, and saw a bicycle light coming up Atterby Lane. Though it was time to go off his beat he thought he would stay and see who it was; so he waited until the light got level with him—and then there was nothing! This light does not "dance," it moves in a steady way, three feet or so from the ground.

Ghost lights in the historic American press

Along with other kinds of weirdness of varying levels of credibility, the occurrence of ghost lights and comparable anomalous luminosities was often noted in period American newspapers, demonstrating the ubiquity of such phenomena. Some examples:

Greenville, Tennessee, April 8, 1843: "On Sunday night last, about eight o'clock, there was seen in the south-western sky a luminous ball, to appearance two feet in circumference, constantly emitting small meteors from one or the other side of it. It appeared in brightness to outrival the great luminary of day. On its first appearance it was stationary one or two minutes; then, as quick as thought, it rose apparently thirty feet, and paused—then fell to the point from whence it started, and continued to perform this motion for almost fifteen times. Then it moved horizontally about the same distance, and for nearly the same space of time. At length, it assumed its first position; then rose again perpendicularly about twelve feet, and remained somewhat stationary, continuing to grow less for an hour and a quarter, when it entirely disappeared" (*Boston Daily Atlas*, May 9, reprinted from *Greenville Miscellany*, April 12).

Adamstown, Pennsylvania, August 7, 1869: "About 200 yards north of the village is an open lot and at 12 o'clock, while the villagers were taking dinner, a luminous body was seen to settle near the center of the lot. It is represented by 4 or 5 different parties, who witnessed it from several points, to have assumed a square shape and shooting up in a column about 3 or 4 feet in height and about 2 feet in thickness. The sun was shining brightly at the time and under its rays, the object glittered like a column of burnished silver. The presence, after reaching its full effulgence, gradually faded away and in 10 minutes time it had entirely disappeared. Those who saw it were unable to tell what it was. It seemed to inspire terror rather than admiration. After it had disappeared a number of persons visited the spot but not a trace of anything unusual could be found. Similar objects have been seen in the neighborhood on several occasions during the nighttime but none before in the daytime or so bright as this. The land in the immediate vicinity is dry, there being no swamp about, otherwise the phenomenon might be accounted for" (*Reading Daily Eagle*, August 14).

> On its first appearance it was stationary one or two minutes; then, as quick as thought, it rose apparently thirty feet, and paused....

Granville County, North Carolina, circa early January 1875: "Wilson Hicks, a young man, was returning home from a party about 12 o'clock at night, and was in company with four ladies.... As he started around the corner to open the back of the house and let the ladies in, a piercing bright light seemed ... to fall on top of him, and the young man fell stretched to the ground, and lay for some moments stunned and insensible. The ladies all saw the light, but was [sic] not affected by it. Miss Vick Bridgers, who is partially blind, was peculiarly affected by it. Young Hicks did not fully recover from the sensation all the next day" (*Petersburg Index and Appeal*, Virginia, January 9, reprinted from *Raleigh Standard*).

Osceola Township, Iowa, late January 1878: "A young man[,] well known in the community and regarded of undoubted veracity, relates that he was going home across the fields from a neighbor's when his attention was attracted by a light moving along the road at some distance from him. He thought at first that the light proceeded from a lantern, carried by some one traveling the highway, but as it approached nearer he noticed that it was much larger than a lantern. When the light reached a point in the road nearly opposite him it stopped and came directly toward him with great velocity, until it was within a few feet of him when it stopped. The observer describes it as about the size of a half bushel and of intense brightness. It then rose in the air a distance of several rods and then began to descend where the gentleman stood. He says that he is not usually easily frightened, but he could not account for the strange sight and he retraced his steps to the house he had just left. The light followed him until he reached the house when it went off a short distance and he lost sight of it. He told the people what he had seen and asked a couple of young men who were there to accompany him home. They started, but could see nothing of the phenomenon described, for a few moments, when it again made its appearance and was distinctly seen by all three. It did not come so close as before but would suddenly disappear and soon come in sight again in an entirely different direction and at a considerable distance from where it was last seen. The light was also seen by the people at a number of houses in the neighborhood. None ... are able to give any explanation of the phenomenon" (*Ackley Enterprise*, February 8, reprinted from *Hampton Chronicle*).

Algona, Iowa, September 29–October 1, 1879: "An unexplained phenomenon was witnessed several evenings last week by a number of people living in the vicinity of Woodward hill, nearly opposite the Park Hotel. John Hyman, the depot master, first noticed it on Monday evening and has been trying to solve the mystery ever since. The object ... is, or was, apparently a large ball of fire, which, for three successive evenings[,] made its appearance over the brow of the hill, and after floating about in the air for some minutes would burst and form into smaller balls, which in turn would also seemingly explode, and gradually become reduced in size until they were finally invisible.... On the second night he called the attention of the hotel guests to it, but they were equally at fault to explain it satisfactorily. On Wednesday evening the excitement had reached a fever heat.... It did not make its appearance until about 9 o'clock, and then ... it suddenly came in sight and rolled along the brow of the hill. In size it was as large as a cartwheel and glowed like a live coal, emitting every minute sparks similar to those sometimes seen flying from the armature of an electric battery. It seemed to be pliable and elastic, for on striking an obstacle it would bound up in the air and then continue on its singular journey. At a certain point about two-thirds of the way across the hill it suddenly arose to a height of nearly 50 feet, and with a report plainly audible flew into a hundred pieces. The sight now looked like a beautiful pyrotechnic display.... Presently, as on former evenings, the particles formed into smaller balls, some of which had been thrown nearly half way down the hill, but, after hovering about for a few seconds, returned to the crest and formed a circle, only to be broken when the succeeding explosions took place. Several gentlemen crossed the field which intervened and started up the hill, determined to solve the mystery, but the ball receded at their approach, and they could get no nearer than at first.... The peculiar object was supposed to be a will-o'-the-wisp, but as there are no swamps or low lands anywhere in the vicinity, this theory was soon abandoned" (*Algona Upper Des Moines*, October 8).

Between Corfu and Indian Falls, Wisconsin, March 1888: "People residing near the Peanut Railroad ... are very much disturbed over the appearance of supernatural lights on the railroad in their vicinity. As the story is told, several times within the past week lights resembling the flames of a large lamp have been seen dancing about on the track within a few feet from the ground on both sides of the road. It was thought at first that there were men on the track carrying lanterns, but on account of the unusual activity displayed by these supposed men, an investigation was made by persons who had witnessed the sight, and it was ascertained that the lights were not from lanterns and there were no human beings in sight. It is reported that one person of an inquisitive nature attempted to approach one of the flames, but it suddenly disappeared from view. The lights are said to be very brilliant. They are seen between the hours of 8 o'clock and midnight. Sometimes there are but three and at other times there are fifteen or twenty. One person who has witnessed the phenomena says that frequently one of the flames will burst, shooting forth a number of smaller flames, which instantly disappear. On both sides of the railroad is a large swamp, but the lights are seen only over the track" (*Weekly Wisconsin*, Milwaukee, March 17).

> One person who has witnessed the phenomena says that frequently one of the flames will burst, shooting forth a number of smaller flames, which instantly disappear.

Near Waterford, Indiana, October 1889 and March 1890: "A strange apparition in the shape of a remarkable light has been seen a number of times.... Six months ago Charles and Henry Powell were walking along the roadway in the vicinity of Waterford and were the first to see it. The light seemed to flit along the road and rise high in the air, and although the men tried to overtake it[,] they were unsuccessful. A few nights ago the light appeared near John Pattee's house, and when Mrs. Pattee looked out of the window she was startled by its appearance but a few yards away. The lady called for her husband, and for half an hour they watched its movements. When near[,] it had the appearance of a locomotive headlight. At times it would be near the ground, then suddenly shoot upward higher than the tree-tops, and sail over the fields in a circular manner. Although the parties who have seen the lights are not superstitious, its appearance is a mystery which they cannot solve" (*Weekly Messenger*, Milwaukee, March 8).

Oneida Lake, New York, 1891 and before: "Along the shore ... there is an Indian's grave where, at times, a weird and supernatural light makes its appearance. It is described as a ball of fire about the size of a large orange, and always swaying to and fro in the air about twenty feet from the ground, confining its irregular movements within a space about 100 feet square" (*Gogebic Advocate*, Ironwood, Michigan, May 23, 1891).

Gulf of Mexico, off Florida's west coast, circa early February 1894: "Captain Corning of the British schooner *W. and H. Witherspoon*, from Porto Cabello, reports a peculiar phenomenon.... The captain says he saw strange lights which apparently would rise from the water and ascend to a height of about 25 feet and then, after a report similar to an explosion, would go out. Captain Corning has no explanation to make of this strange phenomenon, but is positive that he did see the lights" (*Lowell Daily Sun*, Massachusetts, February 8).

East Macon, Georgia, mid-summer 1894: "The negroes ... are very much worked up over a strange phenomenon that they claim made its appearance on Fort Hill.... They spent nearly the whole night hunting and were returning home ... when, just as they reached the Indian mound beyond the railroad, a large, faint light was seen on the summit of the hand-made mountain. It would move about as if carried by some one and passed from one side of the mound to the other, going each time to the edge and at times appearing to swing some distance down the side. It was too large and too faint for a lantern. It is described as being the size of a Japanese lantern, though the light was red, rather than yellow.... They say that when they approached near enough to the top to get a view all over its surface the mysterious light was seen half hidden behind a clump of bushes on the opposite side from which they approached. It was as large as a water bucket and was so dim as not to throw any noticeable light upon the ground around it. The [three] men ... as soon as they reached the top made a bold rush toward the 'thing.' It was too quick for them, however, and, seeming to divine their purpose, rose up with a weird, hissing noise and floated heavenward.... They stood there watching it until from the diminished size of a baseball it passed out of view" (*Macon Telegraph*, August 9).

Fincastle, Virginia, May 5, 1895: "On last Sunday morning about 7 o'clock a number of citizens ... witnessed a most remarkable solar display. At the hour mentioned Mr. S. B. Smith, deputy postmaster, noticed at home, on Roanoke street, what appeared to be balls of different colors, about the size of a man's head, falling about his garden, coming from the direction of the sun, and some falling straight to the ground. They seemed to fall in clusters of about 15 ... some of brilliant hue, others pale and black, and in a brief time would dissolve into smoke. Others would seem to sparkle brilliantly and disappear. This unusual sight continued 15 minutes. At times the cluster of balls was in the shape of pyramids and other shapes. This phenomenon was seen by a number of residents of Roanoke street … who are worthy of belief" (*Olean Democrat*, May 10, New York, reprinted from *Richmond Dispatch*).

Green Bay, Wisconsin, December 16, 1895: "A large number of Green Bay citizens observed, some of them with not a little awe, a peculiar phenomenon high in the eastern sky. It was seen first at 7 o'clock in the evening and was visible for about ten minutes, when it disappeared. Those who saw it unite in describing its appearance as a ball of fire. It was perfectly round, about ten feet in diameter, and of a dark red color. The entire heavens elsewhere were dark" (*Stevens Point Daily Journal*, December 17).

It seemed to come out of the ground at his feet. It rose up, went over his head and disappeared in the earth behind him.

Madison, Indiana, February 1896 and before: "'The light' … has reappeared. It appeared some years ago and frightened a number, then it died away and was forgotten. Recently a young man named George Phillips was walking near the cemetery on Riker's ridge when, he claims, the light reappeared. It seemed to come out of the ground at his feet. It rose up, went over his head and disappeared in the earth behind him. Phillips fainted and had to be carried home. Since that time it is claimed that it has been seen at ex-Sheriff Hogland's place, on the Canaan road, and a man named Brown, who saw it on his farm near the toll gate at Riker's ridge, got a gun and shot at it. It remained stationary and the shot seemed to have no effect. The light is described … as a globe of fire, steady and not flickering. It never remains still long enough for people to get close to it" (*Galveston Daily News*, Texas, March 1, reprinted from *Chicago Record*).

Near McGregor, Iowa, 1904: "Railroad men on the Milwaukee here have revived the mysterious light which bobs up every spring and then as suddenly ceases to play its pranks. It is the famous mysterious light at Beulah, a little station on this division of the Milwaukee road.… It seems to be about as large as an engine headlight, red in the middle and blue on the outer edges. It has been seen at intervals ever since the country was settled and no man has found out yet what it is. It starts somewhere near bridge 1068 … and would long ago have been put down as a headlight, but it does not stick to the railroad, but takes the highway and gallops across the fields in the direction of the Schneider school house at a pace seemingly of thirty or forty miles an hour.… At the speed it travels it is mysterious that it never collides with any traveler but it generally keeps well above the earth.… No one has ever been able to investigate the stranger closely and no one knows what it is" (*Semi-Weekly Iowa State Reporter*, Waterloo, April 22).

✳

The Welsh lights

In early December 1904, a thirty-eight-year-old Welsh housewife, Mary Jones of Egryn, Merionethshire, allegedly experienced a vision of Jesus, and in short order she became the leading figure in a Christian revival that in the weeks and months ahead attracted international attention—not because of her message, which was simply the tried and true one, but because of the peculiar phenomena that accompanied it.

The lights themselves were not unusual, but they had an odd quality: sometimes—though not always—they were visible to some persons but not to others who should have been able to observe them.

A *London Daily Mirror* reporter related a sighting he experienced in the company of the newspaper's photographer. The two had stationed themselves one evening in Egryn, where they hoped to see the lights. At 10 P.M., after a three-and-a-half hour vigil, a light resembling an "unusually brilliant carriage lamp" appeared at a distance of 400 yards. As the reporter approached it,

> it took the form of a bar of light quite four feet wide, within a few yards of the chapel [from which Mrs. Jones conducted her ministry]. For half a moment it lay across the road, and then extended itself up the wall on either side. It did not rise above the walls. As I stared, fascinated, a kind of quivering radiance flashed with lightning speed from one end of the bar to the other, and the whole thing disappeared. "Look! Look!" cried two women standing just behind me. "Look at the Light!" I found they had seen exactly what had appeared to me. Now comes a startling sequel. Within ten yards of where that band of vivid light had flashed across the road, stood a little group of fifteen or twenty persons. I went up to them, all agog to hear exactly what they thought of the manifestations—but not one of those I questioned had seen anything at all!

The witness does not say what, if anything, his photographer saw, or why the latter took no photographs. (No photographs of the lights are known to exist, and some contemporary accounts even assert that the lights could not be photographed.) A skeptic would argue, if not especially compellingly, that the climate of excitement and expectation caused the reporter to hallucinate; but the *Daily Telegraph* writer was not the only journalist to report such an experience. If anything, the incident recounted by Beriah G. Evans of the *Barmouth Advertiser* is even more puzzling.

Evans wrote that while walking with Mrs. Jones and three other persons early on the evening of January 31, 1905, he saw "three brilliant rays of light strike across the road from mountain to sea, throwing the stone wall twenty or thirty yards in front into bold relief, every stone plainly visible. There was not a living soul there, nor house, from which it could have come." Half a mile later, a "blood-red light" appeared in the middle of the village street, a foot above the ground, and immediately in front of them. It then vanished suddenly. Only the reporter and the evangelist saw these things.

"I may add," Evans wrote in a subsequent magazine article, "that a fortnight later a London journalist had an almost identical experience. He, and a woman standing near, crossing the road near the chapel, and climbing and resting upon the wall. A group of half a dozen other people present at the same time saw nothing. Others have had an almost precisely similar experience."

Still, other light manifestations claimed not only multiple but independent witnesses. Once, as Mrs. Jones was holding a revival meeting in a chapel in Bryncrug, a ball of fire casting rays downward illuminated the church. It was also observed by passers-by. On another occasion, Mrs. Jones and three companions were traveling in a carriage in broad daylight when a bright light with no apparent source suddenly shone on them. The occupants of two trailing carriages, including two skeptical journalists, witnessed the sight, as did Barmouth residents who were awaiting her arrival.

Some representative sightings:

December 22, 1904, 5:18 P.M.: Three observers saw a large light "about half way from the earth to the sky, on the south side of Cape Egryn, and in the middle of it something like [a] bottle or black person, also some little lights scattering around the large light in many colors."

January 2, 1905, 10:40 P.M.: "Hovering above a certain farmhouse … it appeared to me as three lamps about three yards apart … very brilliant and dazzling, moving and jumping like a sea-wave under the influence of the sun on a very hot day. The light continued so for ten minutes. All my family saw it at the same time."

Early January, between 10 and 10:30 P.M.: "I saw two very bright lights, about half a mile away, one a big white light, the other smaller and red in color. The latter flashed backwards and forwards, and finally seemed in the same place again, but a few minutes after[,] we saw another light which seemed to be a few yards above the ground. It now looked like one big flame, and all around it seemed like one big glare of light. It flamed up and went out alternately for about ten minutes."

On February 23 the *Advertiser* took note of a recent report by two men, one a prominent farmer, of a "gigantic human form rising over a hedgerow. Then a ball of fire appeared above and a long ray of light pierced the figure, which vanished."

In the midst of all this, Mrs. Jones and some of her flock were also encountering Jesus Christ and angels, who would manifest themselves in dreams and visions. One dark night, as she walked along a country road, Mrs. Jones said she encountered a shadowy figure that turned into a black dog and charged her, only to be dissuaded when she broke into a hymn. The attacker was, of course, Satan. These sorts of experiences are invariably personal and subjective and thus susceptible, to those so disposed, to secular psychological explanations. The lights, on the other hand, remain a mystery more than a century later.

The appearance of the lights in the context of an evangelical revival may or may not be coincidental. Certainly it is true, if we look at the broader historical view, that anomalous luminosities are usually observed in a purely secular context. Still, there are precedents. During a religious revival in Ireland in 1859, a

> One dark night, as she walked along a country road, Mrs. Jones said she encountered a shadowy figure that turned into a black dog and charged her....

"cloud of fire" was seen to descend from the sky and then hover over open-air assemblies of the faithful.

Lights attached to one place

In hundreds, possibly even thousands of places around the world, "strange lights haunt the earth," the late anomaly chronicler Vincent H. Gaddis wrote. "These types of UFOs are not flying saucers or balls of lightning. They are unusually small in size and appear close to the ground. Their outstanding characteristic is that they are localized to one area or place."

Such lights become the focus of legends, not infrequently of lantern-bearing ghosts searching for something they lost in life, such as (in not a few of the more morbid traditions) a head. Not many of these have ever been properly investigated, but on those rare occasions when scientists or other serious researchers have addressed themselves to the task, the results generally have been disappointing—at least to those who wish to have their mysteries remain forever enigmatic or who, on the other hand, have their own more exotic explanatory hobbyhorses to ride.

Many of the lights turn out, for example, to emanate from the headlights of cars on distant highways, or from stars and planets refracted through layers of air of varying temperatures. Sometimes the claim—that the lights were a part of folklore even before the invention of the automobile or the locomotive—proves itself to be folklore. Yet even ghost lights that are convincingly explainable in prosaic terms yield up occasionally puzzling reports, as if to confuse those who want to keep things simple.

Brown Mountain lights

Brown Mountain (alt. 2,600 feet), situated in the Blue Ridge Mountains of western North Carolina near Morganton, is celebrated in story and song—most famously the often-covered bluegrass ballad "Brown Mountain Light," composed in 1961 by Scotty Wiseman and inspired by legends passed on by his "Uncle Fate" Wiseman—as the place where luminous phenomena have baffled observers for many decades. Exactly how many, however, is a matter of dispute.

In 1925 Robert Sparks Walker had this to say of the Brown Mountain mystery:

The descriptions of the strange lights made by various observers do not agree. One person says that it is pale white, as is ordinarily observed through a ground-glass globe, with a faint, irregular halo encircling it. He claims that it is restricted to a prescribed circle, and appears from three to four times in rapid succession, then conceals itself for 20 minutes, when it reappears within the same circle. Another observer, who was standing about eight miles from Brown Mountain, says that suddenly after sunset there blazed into the sky above the mountain a steady glowing ball of light. To him, the light appeared yellowish, and it lasted about half a minute, when it disappeared rather abruptly. It appeared to him like a star from a bursting skyrocket, but much brighter.

To some people it appears stationary; to others, it moves sometimes upward, downward, or horizontally. A minister says that it appeared like a ball of incandescent light in which he could observe a seething motion.

In a letter to the editor of a North Carolina newspaper, *Gastonia Daily Gazette* (December 15, 1927), R. K. Babington of Atlanta quoted a letter he had received from J. Stokes Penland, a Linville Falls, North Carolina, man who "assisted the famous botanist Asa Gray in his explorations of the Blue Ridge and is a venerable patriarch of the mountains." Penland told him that he had seen the phenomena on Brown Mountain "40 years ago." Babington went on to remark, "The letter is dated 16th June, 1922, thus setting as 1882 the year when he first saw them"—well before electrical power had been installed and automobiles were rolling down area highways.

Many reports of mysterious lights have turned out to merely be the result of car headlights mistaken for something more paranormal.

So far as is known, the first printed reference to the lights appeared in the *Charlotte Daily Observer* for September 13, 1913. Citing the testimony of a band of fishermen, the newspaper reported that the "mysterious light is seen just above the horizon almost every night.... With punctual regularity it rises in the southeasterly direction just over the lower slope of Brown Mountain.... It looks much like a toy fire balloon, a distinct ball, with no atmosphere about it ... and very red." Not long afterwards, D. B. Sterrett of the U.S. Geological Survey investigated and concluded that locomotive headlights were responsible. But participants in a 1916 expedition swore that they had seen the lights just below the summit and, moreover, floating to the southeast in a horizontal direction and in and out of the ravines.

While the Brown Mountain light occupied the attention of local newspapers, in October 1918 a correspondent to the *Wilkesboro Patriot* wrote from Stony Point, about forty miles to the north-northeast of Morganton, to insist that other luminous mysteries were to be glimpsed:

> At Stony Point, in Alexander county, there is to be seen, any night, about 9 or 10 o'clock, two lights—a large one and a small one—standing over the wood east of the village, apparently some mile [sic] away. The small

light rises up out of the wood and moves up and down for a while slowly, gradually growing dimmer until, in the course of a couple of hours[,] it vanishes away.

The large light rises up out of the woods until far above the treetops and stands still for some time. Then suddenly it either moves over to where the small light is, and then returns to its former place, or, as it has done on several occasions, moves slowly over to the edge of the village, lighting up to the end of the walk of some of the houses in the village, lighting up the rooms in the houses, through the windows, then suddenly it vanishes away. Many have gone there to see these lights and "explain" the reasons for [them], while many more have gone there to prove that there were no such lights in existence; but the former have always come away wholly unable to explain, and the latter have always come away equally convinced of their reality. The small light seems to be about the size of a large lamp light. The large one looks to be about the size of a gallon bucket. Any one who might be interested in these strange lights may go to Stony Point and see them; for they appear any night, rain or shine.

If these lights existed, their manifestation was short-lived. The luminosities of Brown Mountain, however, continued. In 1921, U.S. Weather Bureau physicist W. J. Humphreys pronounced the phenomenon a "brush discharge of lightning ... which takes place either from the earth to the clouds or from the clouds to the earth around Brown Mountain." Humphreys likened the discharges to St. Elmo's fire.

Apparently, the U.S. Geological Survey was unconvinced. It sent one of its scientists, George Rogers Mansfield, to the area in March and April 1922. He devoted seven evenings to personal observations and supplemented these with a survey of the mountains and with interviews of local residents. He attributed forty-four percent of the lights to automobiles, thirty-three percent to trains, ten percent to stationary lights, and ten percent to brush fires. Besides leaving three percent unaccounted for, Mansfield was acknowledging what by now seemed obvious: no single explanation covered all the phenomena. He did speculate that the 1916 witnesses had seen nothing more than fireflies, even though he conceded that a government entomologist whom he had consulted held that identification to be "improbable" for various reasons.

In the spring of the next year, a writer using the by-line "J. A." recounted his and his companions' recent answers-seeking expedition. He left still puzzled, noting that lights had been sighted on the mountain "before the time of automobiles, and during the near flood here in 1916, when there was not a train running between Salisbury and Asheville.... From Brown mountain we could see artificial lights plainly, but it was also easy to see that they were artificial lights." The actual light "has a reddish glow and seems to come from nowhere and go to the same place."

After reading the USGS report, an Elizabethton, Tennessee, engineer named Frank D. Ruggles pursued his own field inquiries. "I cannot reconcile my opinions and my observations to [Mansfield's] decisions," he wrote in the *Charlotte Observer* in September 1932. He went on:

He speaks of the Brown Mountain "Light." Why not "Lights," as there were actually hundreds of them, clearly and distinctly visible to the naked eye? Looking at these lights, we found that they did not vary in intentness [sic], though they did appear and disappear from time to time. At no time did all of them disappear though they each one seemed to come and go at irregular intervals. Seen through glasses they did girate [sic] at all times and not only that but appeared like strong city street lights supported on limber poles which appeared to sway (all in one direction), with a gust of wind. In fact, these lights appear to me far more like the result of fumes of some incandescent form than anything else that I can think of…. Another point: I found the lights to be located on the side of the [sic] Brown Mountain, not above it.

In the years since then, witnesses have reported phenomena that they state resemble "toy balloons," "misty spheres," "flood lights," and "sky rockets." In a few instances, they claim to have heard a sizzling noise. A 1977 experiment beamed a 500,000-candlepower arc from a town twenty-two miles away to a location west of the mountain where observers lay in wait. The blue-white beam looked like an "orange-red orb apparently hovering several degrees above Brown Mountain's crest." The investigators concluded that refractions of distant lights were largely responsible for the sightings.

Other theorists, such as Britain's Paul Devereux, hold that the lights are evidence of the presence of little-understood, so-far-unrecognized geophysical phenomena he calls "earthlights." Local folklore has it that people were seeing the light long before the age of trains and cars, but the evidence for that is uncertain at best. Still, if this claim is ever validated, it will demonstrate that the Brown Mountain light, or lights, have not yet surrendered all their secrets.

Yakima enigma

The thinly populated reservation in Washington state is 3,500 miles square, divided between rugged wilderness in the west and flat lands in the east. Beginning in the late 1960s (though sporadic sightings had occurred before then), forest rangers, fire-control personnel, and others began reporting the movement of bright white lights low in the sky over rough terrain on both the north and south sides of Toppenish Ridge, which cuts through the reservation's east-central section.

When these reports came to the attention of W. J. (Bill) Vogel, chief fire-control officer, by his own account he would greet them "with knowing smiles, an embarrassed shuffling of papers, and advisement to 'keep us informed.'" Then late one night, as he was on patrol south of Toppenish, he saw something above a hill. "It was easy to see then that the object most certainly was no aircraft," he recalled. "Also there was no discernible lateral movement. Even without binoculars the object's teardrop shape, with the small, pointed end above, was obvious. Brilliantly white in the center, the outer edges were fluorescent tan or light orange

J. Allen Hynek worked for the U.S. Air Force as a consultant. He persuaded American Indians in the Simcoe Mountains in Washington state to allow an observer onto their land, and in 1972 he witnessed strange lights over the hills.

with a surrounding halolike glow. Its most awe-inspiring feature was a mouselike tail or antenna protruding from the small end and pointing upward. The antenna, as long as the object itself, was segmented into colors of red, blue, green, and white which were constantly changing brilliancy and hue."

Over the next ninety minutes Vogel took a series of photographs of the object, which eventually vanished to the south over the Simcoe Mountains. It would be only the first of a number of sightings he would make. Soon Vogel was busy collecting and investigating sightings on the reservation. Most of the reports he gathered were from his own fire lookouts, all trained and reliable observers, but he also interviewed many local people who had seen the lights.

Later investigators included astronomer and former U.S. Air Force UFO consultant J. Allen Hynek. Hynek persuaded the Tribal Council to allow an observer to set up equipment on the reservation and to monitor the lights' activity. The observer, David Akers, of the Aerial Phenomena Research Organization (APRO), brought with him cameras and other devices. On August 19, 1972, his first night on the reservation, Akers, accompanied by Vogel, saw two round, glowing, reddish orange lights circling, changing places, and going on and off as they maneuvered beneath the tops of hills west of White Swan, a town in the reservation's north-central region. He took four photographs. Other sightings and other photographs followed until Akers left the reservation at the end of the month.

Unfortunately, technical problems with his equipment prevented him from getting the other kinds of hard data he was seeking, but Akers left convinced that "something very strange and unusual is taking place." He returned to the reservation over the next few days to interview witnesses, and to see and photograph more strange aerial phenomena.

In subsequent years Greg Long (who would write a book on his research) joined the investigation, working closely with Vogel (since deceased). Examining the detailed records of Vogel and Akers, Long found lights that appeared at ground level, above ground level, and at high altitudes.

Some of the strangest cases reported by fire lookouts involved apparent mental communications. Though most of their sightings were of distant lights, on occasion lookouts saw the phenomena at no more than several hundred yards, yet somehow were prevented from getting close. Lookouts reported "hearing" a voice inside their heads saying, "Stay back, or you'll get hurt," and feeling restrained. One lookout saw a shaft of bright, purple-colored light shining down around her cabin. When she tried to go outside to investigate, she felt as if "two magnets [were] repelling each other" and blocking her exit. Puzzled but determined, she even ran at the entrance several times but could not get through.

Observers often reported feeling as if they were seeing something they were not meant to see, and more often than not they removed themselves from the presences of the lights or objects they had come to investigate.

It must be noted that some reports were of craft-like structures and a few were of alien beings (described as skinny, long-haired, and long-nosed). Consequently, the Yakima phenomena may have more to do with UFOs than with the pure light manifestations with which we are concerned here. Still, as UFOs, those at Yakima are out of the ordinary in being bound to one place and in looking like—at least in most of their appearances—ghost lights. In any case, the sightings have subsided substantially since 1986.

Hessdalen

The Hessdalen lights subsided in frequency in 1984, but they remain a target of investigation conducted by ufologists, scientists, and locals. From a high of fifteen or twenty events a week, they now occur no more than ten or twenty times a year, tracked by automatic monitoring. The Hessdalen Valley, stretching across seven and a half miles of central Norway, near the border with Sweden, and holding no more than 150 residents, began to experience odd, recurring luminous phenomena in November 1981. (Such lights were first noted in the 1940s, but their appearances were sporadic and relatively rare.)

At times the lights appeared as often as four times a day, often below the horizon along mountain tops, near the ground, or on the roofs of houses. Usually white or yellow white, they typically were shaped like cigars, spheres, or an "upside down Christmas tree." In this last instance, according to miner Bjarne Lillevold, it was "bigger than the cottage beside it. It was about four meters [about 13 feet] above the hill and had a red blinking light on it; there seemed also to be a curious 'blanket' over the whole thing. The object moved up and down like a yo-yo for about 20 minutes. When it was close to the ground, the light faded, but at the height of the maneuver it was so bright that I could not look at it for long. When the light was near the ground, I could see through it as though it was made of glass."

Occasionally, according to other witnesses, a red light maintained a position in front. The lights hovered, sometimes for an hour, then shot off at extraordinary speed. Most of the time they traveled from north to south.

Researchers from UFO Norge brought valley residents together to discuss their sightings on March 26, 1982. Of the 130 who attended, thirty-five said they had seen the lights. Soon afterwards, two Norwegian Air Force officers interviewed natives and later told reporters that the "people of Hessdalen have been seeing luminous objects since 1944, but many years passed before they dared to talk about the sightings."

In the summer of 1983, Scandinavian ufologists formed Project Hessdalen and secured technical assistance, including the active participation of scientists from the universities of Oslo and Bergen. A variety of equipment was set up on three mountains. The results from the month-long winter vigil (January 21 to February 26, 1984) were interesting but inconclusive: some sightings, radar trackings, and photographs. When laser beams were aimed at passing lights, the lights seemed to respond. Once, on February 12, one such object "changed its flashing sequence from a regular flashing light to a regular double flashing light, i.e., flash-flash ... flash-flash ... flash-flash. After about ten seconds we stopped the laser and the light immediately changed back to its previous flashing sequence. After about another ten seconds we repeated the exercise and again the light responded by changing to a double-flash sequence. In all we repeated this exercise four times and every time we got the same reaction from the light."

> **When laser beams were aimed at passing lights, the lights seemed to respond.**

The investigators disagreed on what the phenomena could be, with some holding forth for a geophysical explanation and others suspecting some guiding intelligence. Scientist Erling Strand, one of Project Hessdalen's directors, thought it "strange that [the lights] existed for a five-year period" to be "recorded in Hessdalen and nowhere else." Another investigator, Leif Havik, wrote of the "coincidences" that enlivened the investigation:

On four separate occasions, it happened that we came to the top of Varuskjolen, stopped the car, went outside, and there "it" came immediately and passed by us. The same thing happened once on Aspaskjolen. All these instances happened at different times of the day and most of the time it was on impulse which made us taken an evening trip to Hessdalen by car.... On some occasions other observers had been looking for hours without success.... "Coincidences" also happened to the video equipment which recorded the radar screen. One evening the pen of the magnetograph failed to work. At the same time the video tape had come to an end, and the phenomenon appeared less than one minute later. The next evening we made certain that the pen had sufficient ink and turned on the video recorder ten minutes later than the night before. We thought that now everything was ready for the usual 10:47 "message." (One light appeared regularly at 10:47 P.M.) The video tape ran out at 10:57 P.M. and we thought tonight "it" had failed us. But at 10:58 the usual phenomenon appeared.

In terms of hard scientific data, the results were disappointing. Project investigators logged 188 sightings. Some, they determined, were of passing aircraft. Of four photographs taken through special lens gratings, only two showed light spectra of sufficient clarity to be analyzed. Project advisor Paul Devereux said of these, "One spectrum of one 'high strangeness' object was analyzed and showed a wavelength range from 560 nm [nanometers] to the maximum the film could respond to—630 nm.… The spectrum analyzer did not register anything unusual while lights were being seen, but odd readings were obtained at times.… These showed up as 'spikes' at approximately 80 mHz [megahertz]." In forty percent of the sightings, changes in the magnetic field registered on the instruments.

The lights have never been explained. In place of answers, theories ranging from plasma phenomena to unusual piezoelectrical effects have been proposed.

Other luminous anomalies

Writing of anomalous lights, sociologist of science James McClenon observes that the circumstances of a report frequently determine its interpretation. A ball lightning effect that occurred during an electrical storm would be termed "'ball lightning'.… Other cases with the exact same appearance but occurring in other circumstances would be called UFOs, psychic lights, or will-o'-the-wisps depending on the context and the observer's assumptions and interpretation." He then relates a story, which the informant "solemnly affirms to be true," of a ball of light witnessed during his youth. The ball, one foot in diameter, approached the boy's bedroom from outside, magically opened a window, sailed around the house, and left via the front door, which also opened. "The respondent has not previously reported this observation," according to McClenon, "because it seems to defy classification."

Ball lightning, whose existence few physicists and meteorologists dismiss these days, continues to defy explanation—at least in the sense that so far no one has been able to find a physical mechanism that accounts for all its features. We do know that ball lightning nearly always appears during thunderstorm activity, is seen just after and near a lightning strike, lasts a few seconds to (rarely) a minute or two, and often disappears in an explosion that leaves a sulphur-like odor. Clearly, whatever the surface similarity in shape and luminosity, true ghost lights are not examples of ball lightning.

Other hypotheses, notably Devereux's earthlights and Michael Persinger's "tectonic stress theory," propose geophysical explanations for such luminous phenomena, but neither explanation has won any significant scientific acceptance. Devereux's in particular seems a thin scientific veneer for a kind of British nature mysticism, and Persinger's has been criticized on a number of methodological grounds. Both hold that ghost lights are the product of subterranean processes that not only generate luminous energy on the surface but cause hallucinations in observers.

Probably, ghost lights are a number of different things, from the ridiculously mundane, to the exotically natural, and to the certifiably enigmatic.

Further Reading:

Bessor, John Philip. "Mystery of Brown Mountain." *Fate* 4,2 (March 1951): 13–15.

"Brown Mountain Light." On Country Gentlemen, *Can't You Hear Me Callin': Early Classics 1963–1969*. Rebel Records, 2003.

Clark, Jerome. "UFO Update." *Omni* 11,10 (July 1989): 73.

Devereux, Paul. *Earth Lights: Towards an Understanding of the UFO Enigma*. Wellingborough, Northamptonshire, England: Turnstone Press, 1982.

———. *Earth Lights Revelation: UFOs and Mystery Lightform Phenomena: The Earth's Secret Energy Force*. London: Blandford Press, 1989.

Evans, Beriah G. "Merionethshire Mysteries." *Occult Review* Pt. I 1,3 (March 1905): 113–20; Pt. II 1,4 (April 1905): 179–86; Pt. III 1,6 (June 1905): 287–95.

Evans, Hilary. "Seeing the Lights." *Fate* Pt. I 38,10 (October 1985): 82–87; Pt. II 1,6 (November 1985): 87–92.

———, ed. *Frontiers of Reality: Where Science Meets the Paranormal*. Wellingborough, Northamptonshire, England: Aquarian Press, 1989.

Gaddis, Vincent H. *Mysterious Fires and Lights*. New York: David McKay Company, 1967.

Havik, Leif. "Project Hessdalen." *MUFON UFO Journal* 237 (January 1988): 4–7.

Jones, T. Gwynn. *Welsh Folklore and Folk Custom*. Totowa, NJ: Rowan and Littlefield, 1979.

"Lights and Fireballs." *The News* 9 (April 1975): 9–11, 14, 20.

Long, Greg. *Examining the Earthlights Theory: The Yakima UFO Microcosm*. Chicago: J. Allen Hynek Center for UFO Studies, 1990.

McClenon, James. *Deviant Science: The Case of Parapsychology*. Philadelphia: University of Pennsylvania Press, 1984.

Maclagan, R. C. "Ghost Lights of the West Highlands." *Folk-Lore* 8 (1897): 203–56.

Rudkin, Ethel H. "Will o' the Wisp." *Folklore* 49,1 (March 1938): 46–48.

Strand, Erling. *Project Hessdalen 1984: Final Technical Report, Part One*. Duken, Norway: Project Hessdalen, 1985.

Walker, Robert Sparks. "The Queer Lights of Brown Mountain." *Literary Digest* 87 (November 7, 1925): 48–49.

Green Fireballs

A strange aerial phenomenon briefly appeared in the earth's lower atmosphere for a three-year period between late 1948 and 1951. For a time sightings, virtually all of which occurred in the southwestern United States, were taking place with such intensity that military and civilian government agencies feared enemy agents had penetrated some of America's most sensitive national security bases.

The epidemic of "green fireballs" first attracted official attention on the evening of December 5, 1948, when pilots flying over New Mexico reported two separate observations, twenty-two minutes apart, of a pale green light that was visible for no more than a few seconds. The witnesses insisted these were not meteors but flares of a decidedly peculiar kind. On the sixth, a similar "greenish flare" was sighted for three seconds at the supersecret atomic installation Sandia Base, part of the Kirtland Air Force Base complex in New Mexico.

That same day, the Seventh District Air Force Office of Special Investigations (AFOSI), at Kirtland, commenced a probe. On the evening of the eighth, the two investigators, both pilots, saw one of the objects from their T–7 aircraft. They described it this way:

> At an estimated altitude of 2000 feet higher than the airplane ... the object was similar in appearance to a burning green flare of common use in the Air Forces. However, the light was much more intense and the object appeared to be considerably larger than a normal flare. No estimate can be made of the distance or the size of the object since no other object was visible upon which to base a comparison. The object was definitely larger and more brilliant than a shooting star, meteor, or flare. The trajectory of the object was almost flat and parallel to the earth. The phenomenon lasted approximately two seconds at the end of which the object seemed to burn out. The trajectory then dropped off rapidly and a trail of glowing fragments reddish orange in color was observed falling toward the ground. The fragments were visible less than second before disappearing. The phenomenon was of such intensity as to be visible from the very moment it ignited and was observed a split second later.

The next day one of the officers, Capt. Melvin E. Neef, conferred with Lincoln La Paz, director of the University of New Mexico's Institute of Meteoritics and an Air Force consultant with Top Secret clearance. La Paz said these were un-

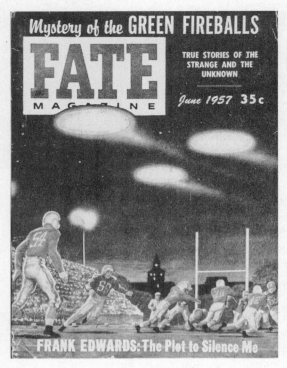

The June 1957 cover of *Fate* magazine depicts unexplained green fireballs.

like any meteors he had ever heard of. Within days La Paz had seen one of the objects himself. Two inspectors from the Atomic Energy Security Service (AESS) independently witnessed it; from their observation and his own, La Paz was able to establish that it had flown too slowly and too silently to be a meteor. He wrote in a confidential letter to the Seventh District AFOSI commanding officer that "none of the green fireballs has a train of sparks or a dust cloud…. This contrasts sharply with the behavior noted in cases of meteoritic fireballs—particularly those that penetrate to the very low levels where the green fireball of December 12 was observed."

Acting on La Paz's suggestion, the AESS organized patrols to try to photograph the fireballs. As the sightings continued, scientists and engineers at New Mexico's Los Alamos Scientific Laboratory set up an informal group to evaluate the reports, and the Army and the Air Force grew increasingly concerned. By late January 1949, La Paz, who had interviewed witnesses to some of the sightings, was convinced that the objects were artificial.

On February 16, a "Conference on Aerial Phenomena" brought military officers and scientists to Los Alamos, where they were told that whatever the nature of the objects, they were not the product of a "classified training exercise." La Paz challenged conference participants to "find anywhere among meteorites examples of conventional meteorites that move over long horizontal paths reserving nearly constant angular velocities and therefore, on the average, constant linear velocities, at elevations of the order of eight to 10 miles."

Late in April Maj. Charles Cabell, director of Air Force Intelligence in the Pentagon, and Theodore von Karman, chairman of the Air Force Scientific Advisory Board, dispatched physicist Joseph Kaplan to Kirtland. Kaplan, La Paz, and others discussed plans to establish an observational and instrumental network around several New Mexico installations. Meanwhile, since early March tiny white lights or "flares" had appeared regularly near Killeen Base, a nuclear-weapons storage site inside Camp Hood in central Texas, leading both to high-level alarm and to efforts to set up observation posts. Col. Reid Lumsden, commander of AFOSI at Kelly AFB, San Antonio, declared that the "unknown phenomena in the Camp Hood area could not be attributed to natural causes."

The testimonies of virtually all local experts and witnesses notwithstanding, the word came down from Washington: the fireballs and lights were natural, even if they had features that were, as Kaplan acknowledged, "difficult to explain." Yet the sightings continued, and in the summer, analyses of samples of the New Mexico atmosphere revealed an unusually large and unexplained quantity of copper particles, apparently associated with the fireball sightings. "I know of no case in which even the tiniest particle of copper has been reported in a dust collection supposedly of meteoritic origin," La Paz wrote to Lt. Col. Doyle Rees.

After meeting with high-ranking Air Force intelligence and scientific personnel, Kaplan urged the creation of a photographic and spectrographic patrol whose purpose would be to obtain quantitative data on the fireballs and lights. A Los Alamos conference discussed the situation and backed the plan, to be run by Air Materiel Command's Cambridge Research Laboratories. Project Twinkle was established, and it set up shop with an operations post manned by two observers at Holloman AFB in New Mexico. One of its critics was La Paz, who thought the matter was of sufficient gravity to deserve a far more "intensive, systematic investigation."

Despite some interesting sightings, Twinkle shut down in December 1951, owing to the incompetence of its personnel, poor funding, bureaucratic infighting, and inadequate instrumentation. It was a tragically missed opportunity to obtain solid information on at least one kind of unidentified flying object. Many of the scientists who participated in the investigation remained convinced that the fireballs were artificially created. In 1953, when Capt. Edward J. Ruppelt, head of the Air Force's Project Blue Book, talked with Los Alamos scientists, they expressed the conviction that the objects were projectiles fired from extraterrestrial spacecraft.

Further Reading:

Clark, Jerome. *The UFO Encyclopedia: The Phenomenon from the Beginning.* Second edition. Detroit, MI: Omnigraphics, 1998.

Gross, Loren E. *UFOs: A History, Vol. 1—July 1947–December 1948.* Fremont, CA: The Author, 1982.

———. *UFOs: A History, Vol. 2—1949.* Fremont, CA: The Author, 1982.

———. *UFOs: A History—1950: January–March.* Fremont, CA: The Author, 1983.

Moore, William L., ed. *The Mystery of the Green Fireballs.* Prescott, AZ: William L. Moore Publications and Research, 1983.

Ruppelt, Edward J. *The Report on Unidentified Flying Objects.* Garden City, NY: Doubleday and Company, 1956.

Hairy Bipeds

One night in January 1992, two men driving on a dark country road were startled to see two figures illuminated in their headlights. The larger figure stood seven to eight feet tall and appeared to weigh more than 500 pounds; the shorter was five feet and 300 pounds. The creatures were advancing in the car's direction. Frightened, the driver backed up the vehicle, all the while keeping the figures in the lights, until he found a place to turn around. Looking over their shoulders on the way out, the witnesses saw that the larger creature was still heading in their direction.

This story sounds as if it came out of the Pacific Northwest, reputed home of Sasquatch, otherwise known as Bigfoot, the controversial giant hominid that some researchers think represents an ape-like human or human-like ape. If to skeptics Sasquatch's existence seems deeply improbable, only the most determined hardcore critics deem it flatly impossible; the wilderness area that comprises northern California, Oregon, Washington, and British Columbia is vast, and it is at least dimly imaginable that a small population of such creatures, especially if they possess a degree of intelligence, could survive, and still be glimpsed only rarely.

The above report, however, comes from Tuscola County in eastern Michigan. It was, local investigator Wayne King said, the county's thirty-eighth hairy-biped report since 1977. In fact, similar sightings have been chronicled in virtually every state and province in the United States and Canada. It is hard to argue seriously that great numbers, or for that matter small numbers, of unknown ape-like animals could exist, at least in any biological sense, in the Midwest, East, or South—or even southern California, site of a number of extraordinary reports.

Despite a number of surface details, the Sasquatch reports and (as we shall call them here) hairy-biped (HB) stories harbor some fundamental differences. Whatever their cause, Sasquatch sightings and attendant evidence (footprints, samples of hair and scat) do not challenge the most hallowed precepts of consensus reality. To all indications, the phenomena act as if they were answerable to zoological laws, and indeed a growing number of physical anthropologists and other biological scientists accept the possibility, or even likelihood, of the animals' existence. They may well have, in other words, a place in the natural order. But where HBs are concerned, just about anything goes, as we shall see. As we

At the Granby Zoo in Quebec, Canada, this puppet of Bigfoot was on display, representing how people think the large, hairy biped might look.

leave Sasquatch's northwestern region and head east and south, we enter the Goblin Universe.

Hairy men of the woods

In its issue of January 4, 1785, the *Times* of London carried this short item (spelling modernized):

> There is lately arrived in France, from America, a wild man, who was caught in the woods, 200 miles back from the Lake of the Woods [in present-day Minnesota], by a party of Indians; they had seen him several times, but he was so swift of foot, that they could by no means get up with him; till one day, having the good fortune to find him asleep, they seized and bound him. He is near seven feet high, covered with hair, has but little appearance of understanding, and is remarkably sullen and untractable: when he was taken, half a bear was found lying by him, which he had just killed.

There was no follow-up. Nor was there follow-up to a story a number of newspapers published in December 1839, alleging that a "wild child" had been seen near Fish Lake, Indiana. "It is reported to be about four feet high," a story datelined December 4 from Michigan City alleged, "and covered with a light coat of chestnut-colored hair." A fast runner, it made hideous shrieks and whines and "seems to make efforts at speaking." The following spring, newspapers cited Florida sightings of something that "is said by those who saw it to resemble somewhat the baboon." In early 1850, the *Houston Telegraph* related that a figure, five feet tall and thought to be female, "resembling a human being, but covered with hair of reddish brown color," and running with the "speed of a deer" was seen on the banks of the Navidad River near Lake Texana. In Greene County, Arkansas, according to the *Memphis Sentinel,* in the spring of 1851, "an animal bearing the unmistakable likeness of humanity" and "of gigantic stature" ran with astonishing speed and left footprints thirteen inches long. It had been seen for at least seventeen years in Greene, St. Francis, and Poinsett Counties.

Many hundreds of comparable stories appeared in the nineteenth-century press, well before the monikers "Sasquatch" and "Bigfoot" (the latter coined in the mid–1950s) were in the common vocabulary. The meaning of these yarns is, as often as not, far from straightforward —even if we assume, as nobody literate in the freewheeling ways of the early American press is likely to do without serious reservation, that these certainly describe real events.

For purposes of comparison, we can separate stories of HBs into three categories: ape-like entities (ones most reminiscent of Sasquatch), wild men (usually partially clothed, carrying weapons or implements, presumed to be feral humans, but often having non-human features such as hairy bodies and great heights), and two-legged monsters of outlandish appearance ("nondescripts," in the language of the time, "unclassifiables" in current terminology).

Ape-like entities

Near Lancaster, Pennsylvania, December 1858: "A thing like a man, but hairy as a bear, has been seen by the people. It was very wild and strong. It was once seen in a pen, sucking the cows, and when discovered it started as if to fight, and then turned and fled, bounding like a deer. It walks upright and is supposed to be a wild man" (*Grand Traverse Herald,* Michigan, December 17).

Near Crawfordsville, Indiana, circa January 1869: While coon hunting one night, a Mr. Hardee encountered a creature that "appeared like a gigantic ape, sitting in the path in front of him.... He hesitated about approaching it. His dog, meanwhile, crouched down at his feet, and refused to stir.... Mr. H. waved his torch until it flamed brilliantly, and made a few steps towards the monster, when it uttered a yell so terrific and appalling, that it well nigh froze the blood in his veins. At the same time it seemed to beat upon its breast with long, uncouth arms. Mr. Hardee ... beat a hasty retreat" (*Fort Wayne Daily Democrat,* January 25, citing *Crawfordsville Review*).

Near Lafayette, Indiana, summer 1883: "Mrs. [Frank] Coffman was passing through the timber, when she suddenly saw on her right, a hideous creature, formed like a woman, with long black hair floating in the wind, and the whole body covered with short grey hair. The creature was breaking twigs from the sassafras bush and eating the bark.... Frozen with horror, the farmer's wife stood and gazed on the remarkable creature before her. Suddenly the wild woman turned, and, facing her civilized sister, glared at her with a baleful light of hate. Raising her long, hairy arms, she gave an unearthly shriek, and darted away into the forest. Almost paralyzed with fear, Mrs. Coffman gazed after the wild creature for a moment, then with agonized screams she fled homeward.... Soon half a hundred men and boys, accompanied by dogs, were on the trail of the wild woman. She was hotly pursued, and several times came near being caught, but eluded her pursuers, with wonderful skill and cunning. For fully half a mile of the chase, she was never out of sight. Her feet touched the ground but seldom. She would grab the underbrush with her long, bony hands, and swing from bush to bush and limb to limb with wonderful ease.... Coming to a swamp, she disappeared as suddenly and effectively as an extinguished light, and no searching served to ascertain her whereabouts" (*Victoria Daily Colonist*, British Columbia, August 2).

Near Calcutta, Ohio, December 1883: "One day last week Messrs. A. Rauch and Robt. Bradley left town for a hunt in the woods north of this place.... While Rauch and Bradley were walking along the top of a bluff in the thick of these woods they were startled by a peculiar cry. They could at first see nothing, but soon a creature of formidable aspect rushed out from a cleft in the rocks. It was about the average size of a man and somewhat resembled a gorilla. It stood perfectly erect and was covered from head to foot with hair. After staring a few moments at the hunters the creature gave another cry and jumped away into the woods.... One of the hunters raised his gun and fired, wounding the animal in the arm. It turned with a horrible scream of rage and pursued the hunters, who threw away their guns and ran at the top of their speed. The creature gained on them until they reached a clearing and a fence, over which they jumped. The animal then ran back into the woods" (*Lynchburg Virginian*, December 18).

Rockaway Beach, New York, December 1, 1885: "Rockaway Beach is still excited over the mysterious wild man of the sea and last night a company of New York men went down to the beach to see the strange creature. They saw the figure and declare that his body is covered with auburn hair as long as a horse's mane. John B. Ennis declared this morning that at eight o'clock last night he met the wild man near the Atlantic Park. Ennis came upon the dweller in the sea suddenly. He was dancing like one deranged, until, catching sight of Ennis, he gave a peculiar screech and darted into the sea" (*Brooklyn Daily Eagle*, December 2).

Near Mehalfley, Pennsylvania, July 1888: "Some persons ... report that they met a wild man.... They report him as being ten feet high, and covered with hair[,] and his tracks in the sand measure 16 inches. That Nicktown whiskey must be terrible stuff" (*Indiana Weekly Messenger*, Pennsylvania, August 1).

Near Vernon, Indiana, circa early spring 1891: "Recently Alexander Shepard and a friend from Vernon, while strolling through the hills in that vicinity, dis-

(Continued on page 82)

UNEXPLAINED! Strange Sightings, Incredible Occurrences, and Puzzling Physical Phenomena

In the Mongolian language Almas means "wildman." These strange creatures, half human, half ape, are reputed to dwell in the Altai mountains in western Mongolia and in the Tien Shan mountains of neighboring Sinkiang in the People's Republic of China.

The earliest known printed reference to Almases is in a journal written by Bavarian nobleman Hans Schiltberger. In the 1420s he traveled through the Tien Shan range as a prisoner of the Mongols. "In the mountains themselves live wild people, who have nothing in common with other human beings," he recorded. "A pelt covers the entire body of these creatures. Only the hands and face are free of hair. They run around in the hills like animals and eat foliage and grass and whatever else they can find." Schiltberger saw two of them himself, a man and a woman whom a local warlord had captured and given as presents to the Bavarian's captors.

A late eighteenth-century Mongolian manuscript on natural history contains a drawing of a wildman. The caption (in the Tibetan, Chinese, and Mongolian languages) identifies the figure as a "man-animal." All of the other illustrations in the book are of indisputably real animals, indicating that the Almas was not viewed as a supernatural being. In fact, Almases are not an element of the otherworldly folklore of the Mongolian people; they are considered ordinary creatures of flesh and blood.

A yeti is depicted in this April 13, 1952, issue of *Radar* magazine.

Prof. Tsyben Zhamtsarano conducted the first systematic scientific study of Almases, collecting reports mostly from nomads and others in the remote regions where the creatures—adults and children—were said to live. He plotted the sightings on maps and brought an artist with him on his field trips to interview witnesses. Unfortunately, while living in Leningrad in the 1930s, Zhamtsarano fell victim to the Stalinist terror (he was deemed a "bourgeois nationalist" for his interest in Mongolian folklore) and died in the gulag around 1940. The records of his Almas research have been lost.

Nonetheless, one of his associates, Dordji Meiren, has testified that their information indicates Almas sightings decreased significantly in number during the later decades of the nineteenth century. The Almases apparently largely disappeared from southern Outer Mongolia and Inner Mongolia (south of Outer Mongolia), perhaps suggesting that they were migrating westward to escape from encroaching civilization. Another early researcher, anatomist V. A. Khakhlov, submitted findings from his Almas studies to the Russian Imperial Academy of Sciences in 1913. These, too, seem to have been lost.

In 1936 M. K. Rosenfeld's *The Ravine of the Almases* incorporated the creatures into the plot of an otherwise routine adventure novel. Rosenfeld had heard of the creatures during a trip across Mongolia in the 1920s. By this time another Mongolian scholar, Y. Rinchen, was conducting his own research, and in the 1950s, in the wake of renewed interest in the Himalayas' yeti ("abominable snowman"), the Soviet Academy of Sciences established a Commission for the Study of the Snowman Question. The commission's principal figure, Boris Porschnev (who later wrote a book dealing in part with the Almas), encouraged Rinchen to publish some of his material. Rinchen concluded, as had his predecessors, that the Almas population was shrinking and retreating. Since then, other Russian and Mongolian scholars have published Almas

accounts gleaned from eyewitness testimony and literary sources. Zhamtsarano's associate Meiren claimed to have seen an Almas skin being used as a ritual carpet in a Buddhist monastery in the southern Gobi region of Mongolia. The creature had been skinned by a straight cut down the spine, so its features were preserved. The body had red, curly hair, and there was long hair on the head, but the face was hairless except for eyebrows. The nails at the ends of the toes and fingers were essentially human in appearance.

Adult Almases have been described as five feet or slightly taller, hairy, and shy, with prominent eyebrow ridges, a receding chin, and a jaw that juts out. They subsist on small mammals and wild plants and use simple tools, but have no language. According to British anthropologist Myra Shackley, their "very simple lifestyle and the nature of their appearance suggests strongly that Almas[es] might represent the survival of a prehistoric way of life, and perhaps even of an earlier form of man. The best candidate is undoubtedly Neanderthal man."

Another British anthropologist, Chris Stringer, while open-minded on the question of the Almases' possible existence, disputes this conclusion. He cites reports that "include mentions of bent knees, an unusual gait, turned in feet (with six toes in one case), long arms, forearms, hands and fingers, small flat noses, 'Mongolian' cheekbones, and a lack of language, cul-

(Continued from previous page)

ture, meat-eating and fire. None of these readily matches accepted ideas about the Neanderthals."

Itinerant British cryptozoologist Adam Davies found Almas traditions very much alive in Mongolia in the twentieth century. A hunter recounted his sighting in the 1990s, near a river, of a figure that stood erect but scampered away on all fours in the fashion of a chimpanzee. The Almas is considered a real animal, specifically an unusual ape. Davies found no evidence to support the belief that Almases are a form of early human.

Further Reading:

Bord, Janet, and Colin Bord. *The Evidence for Big-foot and Other Man-Beasts*. Wellingborough, Northamptonshire, England: Aquarian Press, 1984.

Davies, Adam. *Extreme Expeditions: Travel Adventures Stalking the World's Mystery Animals*. San Antonio and New York: Anomalist Books, 2008.

Heaney, Michael. "The Mongolian Almas: A Historical Reevaluation of the Sighting by Baradiin." *Cryptozoology* 2 (1983): 40–52.

Sanderson, Ivan T. *Abominable Snowmen: Legend Come to Life*. Philadelphia: Chilton Book Company, 1961.

Shackley, Myra. *Still Living? Yeti, Sasquatch and the Neanderthal Enigma*. New York: Thames and Hudson, 1983.

Stringer, Chris. "Wanted: One Wildman, Dead or Alive." *New Scientist* (August 11, 1983): 422.

(Continued from page 79)

covered the opening of a cave, and providing themselves with a lantern, they explored the interior until they found themselves confronted with a form resembling that of a gorilla or a wild man, covered with a rough coat of brown hair. The strange creature looked at them for a second and then ambled off, and the gentlemen were too much alarmed to follow. While retracing their steps the explorers found a storeroom partly filled with potatoes, corn and wheat, with bones of fowls, etc. Farmers in the vicinity have frequently complained of the loss of farm products, and it is believed a clue has been found to the thievery" (*Galveston Daily News*, Texas, April 10).

Near Womelsdorf, Pennsylvania, July 1891: "The wild woman who roamed over South Mountain near this place years ago ... has made her appearance again. One of a party from this place while picking huckleberries says he saw her: 'While [we were] going through a ravine ... our attention was drawn to a peculiar noise on the incline above. We ventured near the spot, and saw to our amazement a woman with long hair growing over her face and body, and one arm and leg shorter than the others. She was hanging on a vine suspended from a large tree, swinging to and fro, and as if humming a lullaby. Upon seeing us, she leaped from tree to tree and was soon lost to sight, chattering to herself as she disappeared.' The affair has caused considerable talk here" (*New York Times*, August 2).

Gladwin County, Michigan, October 1891: "George W. Frost and W. W. Vivian, both reputable citizens, report having seen a wild man on the banks of the Tittabawassee river.... The man was nude, covered with hair, and was a giant in proportions. According to their story he must have been at least seven feet high, his arms reaching below his knees and with hands twice the usual size. Mr. Vivian set his bull dog on the crazy man and with one mighty stroke of his monstrous hand he felled the dog dead. His jumps were measured and found to be from twenty to twenty-three feet long" (*Daily Northwestern*, Oshkosh, Wisconsin, October 28).

Near Cole Harbor, Nova Scotia, early January 1892: "The residents ... are excited over a strange animal that has appeared in the woods. It is seven feet high, and looks like a gorilla" (*Manitoba Daily Free Press*, Winnipeg, January 9).

Johnson County, Kansas, June 1893: "The people living along Cedar Creek ... near Olathe ... are greatly excited over the antics of some strange animal that roams through the woods.... Robert Sanders ... said he had been chased over a mile by a hideous monster that appeared to be half man and half devil. The next morning a man employed on the farm of Edward Lane, living half a mile north of Olathe[,] reported having seen the man. Since then several others have described the animal as it appeared to them. All agree upon the description and say that it appears to be fully seven feet tall with a heavy covering of brown hair, and perfectly naked. It stands in a half stooping posture, with long arms crossed over its breast, but when startled or in pursuit, it gets over the ground rapidly with a swinging gate. Robert Wilson, who owns a dairy farm two and a half miles northwest of Olathe, reports that the monster had killed two cows and a calf belonging to him.... A heavily armed party of men are scouring the woods in search of the strange beast. Two of the party ... found that the carcasses are so torn and mangled that they must have been killed by a most powerful animal. It is thought by many to be an African gorilla that has escaped from some traveling menagerie" (*Sioux Valley News*, Correctionville, Iowa, June 22).

> **S**he was hanging on a vine suspended from a large tree, swinging to and fro, and as if humming a lullaby.

Near Rome, Ohio, mid-1897: "The wild man who created so much terror among the inhabitants ... several weeks ago by his strange actions has again been seen. Charles Lukins and Bob Forner, while cutting timber a few miles from Rome, claim they encountered a wild man and after a severe struggle they were able to drive the gorilla-like object into his supposed retreat among the cliffs. They describe the terror as being about six feet tall, and his only covering, apparently, a mat of long, curly hair. From their description ... he is undoubtedly the same seen a number of times several weeks ago" (*Lima Times-Democrat*, Ohio, reprinted from *Cleveland Plain Dealer*).

Wild people

Camas Prairie, Idaho, November 1, 1882: "Two cowboys ... relate an experience which will probably go a great way toward re-establishing the popular faith in the wild man's tradition.... Searching for cattle lost in the storm, [they] passed over some lava crags and ... [saw] before them the form so often described to them.... Mustering courage and drawing their revolvers they dismounted and gave chase, but the strange being skipped from crag to crag as nimbly as a mountain goat. After an hour's pursuit both young men were so completely worn out that they laid [sic] down, seeing which the wild man gradually approached them and stopped on the opposite side of the gorge of lava, from which point he regarded the cowboys intently. The wild man was considerably over six feet in height, with great muscular arms which reached to his knees.... His chest was as broad as that of a bear. Skins were twisted about his feet and ankles and a wolf skin about his waist. All parts of his body to be seen were covered by long, black hair, while from his head the hair flowed over his shoulders in coarse tangled rolls and mixed with a heavy beard. His face was dark and swarthy and his eyes shone brightly, while two tusks protruded from his mouth. His fingers were the shape of claws, with long, sharp nails, and he acted very much as a wild animal which is unaccustomed to seeing a man. The boys made all kinds of noises, at the sound of which he twisted his head from side to side and moaned.... The two boys fired their revolvers, whereupon the wild man turned a double summersault and jumped fifteen feet to a low bench and growling terribly as he went" (*Ford County Globe*, Dodge City, Kansas, November 28).

Near Kingston, Ontario, July 1883: "One of Mr. Peter McLaren's drivers ... has seen a strange sight. He was sitting in his tent, when suddenly, upon the foreground of the shadows produced by the departing fire, he distinctly saw the outlines of a man appear, whose height was about eight feet. His hair was long and shaggy, and hung about his face. He had a vest, but no sleeves to his coat, knickerbocker pants, with hairy legs and arms. He stood still at the threshold of the brightness, and was questioned whence he came. There was no response, whereupon the citizen picked up a large stone, and, hurling it with all his force, struck the strange object amidship, and it fell with a splash into the water. Hastening to the spot he saw the stranger arise and depart swiftly, and though he searched for many hours there came no reward" (*Toronto Daily Mail*, July 28).

Near Pembroke, Ontario, on Prettis Island, summer 1883: "The people are so terrified that no one has dared to venture on this island for several weeks. Two raftsmen named Toughey and Sallman, armed with weapons, plucked up sufficient courage to scour the wood in hope of seeing the monster. About 3 o'clock in the afternoon their curiosity was rewarded. He emerged from a thicket having in one hand a tomahawk made of stone and in the other a bludgeon. His appearance struck such terror to the hearts of the raftsmen that they made tracks for the boat which was moored by the beach. The giant followed them, uttering demoniacal yells and gesticulating wildly. They had barely time to get to the boat and pull a short distance out into the stream when he hurled the tomahawk after them, striking Toughey in the arm and fracturing it. Sallman fired two shots, but neither took effect, the giant retreating hurriedly at the first shot of firearms.... The townspeople will arrange an expedition to capture, if possible, what Toughey describes as a man who looks like a gorilla, wandering about in a perfectly nude condition, and, with the exception of the face, completely covered with a thick growth of black hair" (*Newark Daily Advocate*, Ohio, August 1).

Grover Crossing, Ohio, mid–1886: "The people ... are in a state of great excitement over the advent of a wild man.... He is described as being gigantic in size, and wearing no clothing except an old slouch hat and a pair of boots. His hair is long and matty, his body tanned until it is a mud color, and he is very ferocious, and has a frightful appearance. He is very bold in his adventures and can run like a racehorse. His eyes flash like fire, and his unintelligible utterances are thrilling and blood-curdling. The first seen of this strange monster was in the latter part of last May. Since that time he has been seen on many occasions and viewed at short range" (*Burlington Hawk-Eye*, Iowa, June 30).

Norwell, Massachusetts, September 4, 1891: "Mrs. Ensign Damon and another woman while engaged in picking blueberries ... were startled on seeing the form of a man suddenly arise almost as from the ground in front of them. The trunk of a large hemlock tree lay in front of them, and from a narrow opening in the side there dashed forth a queer-looking creature. It looked like a man, and it was almost naked.... Mrs. Damon ... said, 'He was a weird looking thing, and of course we were frightened and ran as hard as we could.... We know he was a man, and he certainly looked like one of the wild men whom we have read about. His body was covered with hair down to his feet, but he seemed to be awfully frightened'" (*Boston Daily Globe*, September 9).

> **H**e is described as being gigantic in size, and wearing no clothing except an old slouch hat and a pair of boots. His hair is long and matty....

Bonesteel, South Dakota, July 1899: This is not a wild-man story, but it touches on questions central to the period controversy about the line between man and beast. "Upon the question of whether his victim was brute or human depends Archie Brower's guilt or innocence of the crime of murder. Brower was one of the owners of a small tent show. Among the attractions was a creature of seemingly a higher form of animal life than a monkey and lower than a man. Brower and Thorndyke called the animal the 'missing link' and laid great stress on the alleged fact that no one was able to say whether it belonged to the human or brute creation. Brower now says that the freak was a monkey. In a scuffle with it the showman became angry and seizing a heavy club dealt his antagonist a hard blow over the ear, from the effects of which it died in a few hours. The local authorities immediately placed Brower under arrest on a charge of murder. At the preliminary hearing his lawyers set up the defense that their client did not take the life of a human being, but the magistrate bound him over to the Grand Jury" (*Bismarck Daily Tribune*, North Dakota, July 17).

Near Kissimmee, Florida, September 1900: "Great excitement exists about here over the fact that a wild-man is roaming through the woods.... One day last week Mrs. Arthur Shiver, who lives a mile from town, saw a strange creature skulking about near the house. It had the figure of a man about four feet high. It was without clothing and was covered with short, shaggy black hair. Its skin was red and the hair on its head was black and hung below its shoulders. It walked on its feet in a crouching attitude, and held between its leg a sort of stick, which it rode, as children do, dragging one end on the ground. Its arms were long and the fingers looked like claws. Mrs. Shiver called to neighbors who were at the house and tried to catch the creature, but it bounded into a ditch and disappeared. They tracked it up the ditch to a swamp, where it was seen crawling into a big bunch of palmettos. Search was made, but no further sign of it was seen.... [Its track] was about six inches long, with a deep imprint of the ball of the foot and a claw mark showing that the nail of the big toe was an inch long at least.... Before the monster took to the ditch Mrs. Shiver's daughter, while trying to cut it off at a fence[,] came within a few feet of it unexpectedly and had a good look at it, and she said it growled and shook the club" (*Davenport Daily Leader,* Iowa, September 28).

Chesterfield, Idaho, January 1902: "An eight-foot, hair-covered human monster ... was first seen on Jan. 14, when he appeared among a party of young people who were skating on the river. The creature showed fight, and flourishing a large club and uttering a series of yells, started to attack the skaters, who managed to reach their wagons and get away in safety. Measurements of the tracks showed the creature's feet to be twenty-two inches long and seven inches broad, with the imprint of only four toes. Stockmen report having seen the tracks along the range west of the river" (*Dubuque Telegraph-Herald,* Iowa, January 29).

Near Beaver Dam, Pennsylvania, April 1902: "The creature is described as resembling a man, although possesses features course and rough, and is said to be covered with hair. The inhabitants ... are half crazed with excitement.... It is firmly believed that the strange creature is an insane person who has been at large for some time. The being is attired in dress peculiar to one of the male sex, although scantily clad" (*Delphos Daily Herald,* Ohio, April 14).

Bizarre beings on two feet

Waldoboro, Maine, January 2, 1854: "Mr. Editor:—On the morning of Jan. 2d, while engaged in chopping wood ... I was startled by the most terrific scream that ever greeted my ears: it seemed to proceed from the woods near by. I immediately commenced searching round for the cause... but after a half hour's search I resumed my labors, but had scarcely struck a blow with my axe when the sharp shriek burst out upon the air. Looking up quickly, I discovered an object about ten rods from me, standing between two trees, which had the appearance of a miniature human being. I advanced towards it, but the little creature fled as I neared it. I gave chase, and after a short time succeeded in catching it. This little fellow turned a most imploring look upon me, and then uttered a sharp shrill shriek, resembling the whistle of an engine. I took him to my house and tried to induce him to eat some meat, but failed in the attempt; I then offered him some water, of which he drank a small quantity. I next gave him some dried beach nuts, which he cracked and ate readily. He is of the male species [sic], about eighteen inches in height, and his limbs are in perfect proportion. With the exception of his face, hands, and feet, he is covered with hair of a jet black hue" (*Hornellsville Tribune*, New York, January 25, reprinted from *Thomaston Journal*, Maine, whose editor subsequently expressed his skepticism in mocking words).

Warren County, Mississippi, 1868 and thereabouts: "About twenty five miles from this city ... is a small stream known as Clear Creek, which empties into the Big Black river. The margin of both these streams, in that vicinity for miles back, is an almost impenetrable swamp.... For some time past, strange stories have been told by the negroes of an extraordinary animal, seen near these swamps.... One peculiarity ... was that from his tracks he seemed to be going both ways at once. That is, one foot pointed to the front and the other to the rear.... This extraordinary creature had often suddenly presented himself ... in the early twilight.... He is described ... as being about eight feet high, each eye ... 'as large as a hen's egg,' with no nose and no upper lip, his two eye teeth as large as a man's thumb, extending down over his chin about eight inches; his right foot points directly to the front and the left to the rear, and the measurement of the track is just twenty-three inches in length, his finger nails are perfectly hard and solid, and are about six inches long; the hair on his head which is stiff and wiry—sweeps the ground as he walks, and is parted in the rear and brought down in front on each side of his singular chest, which is not round or flat, but is angular like that of a fowl. The hair on the body of this singular being is very stiff and grows to the rear, parting at the angle of the breast bone, growing back and uniting with a long stiff growth on his spine which extends back about one foot like the spinal fin of a fish.... The hair on his arms is parted and grows in the same way making a long thick brush on the back of the arms, extending from his shoulders to the point of his middle finger; the same peculiarity is observable on his legs.... Several attempts have been made to capture it, but up to the present time without success" (*Coshocton Democrat*, Ohio, March 31, reprinted from *Vicksburg Herald*, Mississippi).

Near Olney, Indiana, January 1885: "Some hunters a few days ago were startled by the appearance of an uncouth, horrible-looking animal, south of the O. and M. railroad bridge over the Fox River.... Their attention was attracted by a noise to the top of a fallen tree, and looking up they beheld a monster such as they had never seen before. They describe the beast as the ugliest looking animal they ever saw. Its head and face resembled that of a negro, with a very large mouth full of sharp, fang-like teeth. Its neck was two or three feet long and covered with short red colored hair; it body was five or six feet in length, and was covered with scales that looked bright like those of a sun-fish; its tail was two or three feet long and curved up over its back; its legs were short and the feet webbed, and the toes had long claws. One of the hunters, who got too near in trying to throw a rope over its head, was struck by the animal's tail, and he tumbled headlong twenty feet away. The animal then made for the creek and disappeared. The beast had been devouring a hog.... The parties who describe it are good men and perfectly reliable" (*St. Louis Globe-Democrat*, January 17).

Pike County, Pennsylvania, February 1890: "The Paupack Creek … is the dwelling place of a monster … if one can believe the stories told by people in the vicinity. They describe the beast as having a head like an ape and square shoulders like a human being. From the shoulders of the creature there extend legs [and] arms, which terminate in great claws. The body of the monster, which is full six feet in length, is of a reddish brown tint, very like that of a lizard, and terminates in a tail like that of a fish. The creature's body is bare of any covering, but about the head and neck is a mane of reddish color. It is needless to say that the county is excited over the strange animals" (*Chillicothe Constitution*, Missouri, February 21).

Before Bigfoot

The Bigfoot/Sasquatch of the Pacific Northwest stepped outside regional lore and into international consciousness in the late 1950s. As we have seen, stories of ape-like hairy bipeds were told in many places elsewhere in North America long before. The episodes cited above exist only in print and probably could be dismissed in their entirety as pranks and newspaper hoaxes if not for the persistence, and robustly so, of HB reports into our time.

That said, tales of the more outlandish two-footed monsters, sometimes suspiciously detailed, are not credible, and they are mentioned only to lay out something of the background to modern monster stories. If we put aside the question of whether such monsters exist in any conventional sense, we can at least open the possibility of encounters in a purely experiential context. Even on that level, the tales of "nondescripts" fail to persuade. In another category, wild men have long figured in world mythology and folklore, and the press accounts above may simply have exploited that tradition in the interest of entertaining readers. On the other hand, the frontier's wide-open spaces, as well as nineteenth-century America's abundant forests, may have provided abodes for hermits, anti-social individuals, or the mentally ill or challenged. Even so, skepticism here is hardly unwarranted. Wild men made for good copy, a probably irresistible subject for correspondents (their tongues firmly in cheek) in outlying districts. They become rare, albeit not quite nonexistent, after the first decade of the new century.

Curiously, it was the HB that survived, and even with the less freewheeling journalistic standards of the modern newspaper era, reports continued. As early as January 8, 1905, no less than the *Washington Post* reported on sightings of a shrieking "yaho"—named after the sound it made and described as "similar to a gorilla, only taller," near Unionville, Maryland. In woods near Dover, New Jersey, people claimed to have encountered a hairy "half monkey," which ran both on all fours and on two legs. In the spring of 1921, residents of Kingston, New York, reported that at night on several occasions, "an ape or an animal resembling an ape" had chased dogs. A "gorilla" reportedly prowled the streets of Gettysburg, Pennsylvania, in the warm months of the same year. A "wild man, half man, half beast" covered with hair haunted the western slope of the Colorado Rockies in 1922. According to the *Washington Post* of July 26, 1929, a "huge gorilla" had been seen wandering in woods near Elizabeth, Illinois, the day before. Residents of northwestern Ohio allegedly sighted a "hairy ape" in 1930. At midnight of July 1, it was observed in a front yard in Toledo. Other "ape" sightings, sparking the usual futile searches, were recorded in Ohio in 1920 and 1932. A number of sightings of a "gorilla," which left big footprints in the mud of the Missouri river bottoms, were reported in western Iowa in November 1930. A spate of 1938 reports in South Carolina (especially around Rock Hill) and Alabama of a "terrible smelling" gorilla-like creature, which ran both upright and four feet, was ascribed dismissively to "frightened Negro folk." A "furry thing resembling an ape" chased people in Erie County, Pennsylvania, in September of that year, according to local newspaper accounts.

The descriptions of wild men in North America often compare these creatures to gorillas, African animals that resemble human beings in many ways.

Such stories—those mentioned above are only a sampling—saw sufficient circulation that the occasional paper on the subject found its way to journals tracking popular culture. In 1946, *Hoosier Folklore* noted a 1941 report from Mount Vernon, Illinois, where the Rev. Lepton Harpole was hunting squirrels along a creek when a "large animal that looked something like a baboon" leaped out of a tree and approached him on two legs. The reverend struck it with his gun barrel, then fired a couple of shots into the air. The creature fled. Over the next months hunters and rural families heard terrifying shrieks and found mysterious footprints. There were other sightings, some of them as much as forty or fifty miles from the Mount Vernon area.

A letter published in the *Decatur Review* on August 2, 1972, suggests a long tradition of such creatures in south-central Illinois. A woman named Ruth Schroat wrote:

> I am 76 years old. My home used to be south of Effingham [50 miles due north of Mount Vernon]. My two brothers saw the creatures when they were children. My brothers have since passed away.

> They are hairy, stand on their hind legs, have large eyes and are about as large as an average person or shorter, and are harmless as they run away from the children. They walk, they do not jump.

> They were seen on a farm near a branch of water. The boys waded and fished in the creek every day and once in a while they would run to the

house scared and tell the story.... This occurred about 60 years ago or a little less.

In Ontario, in the early decades of the century, newspapers chronicled occasional sightings of "Yellow Top," an ape-like creature with a light-colored mane. Near Goose Bay, Labrador, between the winters of 1913 and 1914, according to Elliott Merrick's *True North* (1933):

> One of the little girls was playing [near the settlement of Traverspine] in an open grassy clearing one autumn afternoon when she saw come out of the wood a huge hairy thing with low-hanging arms. It was about seven feet tall when it stood erect, but sometimes it dropped to all fours. Across the top of its head was a white mane. She said it grinned at her and she could see its white teeth. When it beckoned to her she ran screaming to the house. Its tracks were everywhere in the mud and sand, and later in the snow. They measured the tracks and cut out paper patterns of them which they still keep. It is a strange-looking foot, about twelve inches long, narrow at the heel and forking at the front into two broad, round-ended toes. Sometimes its print was so deep it looked to weigh 500 pounds. At other times the beast's mark looked no deeper than a man's track. They set bear traps for it but it would never go near them. It ripped the bark off trees and rooted up huge rotten logs as though it were looking for grubs.... A dozen people have told me they saw its track with their own eyes and it was unlike anything ever seen or heard of. One afternoon one of the children saw it peeping in the window. She yelled and old Mrs. Michelin grabbed a gun and ran for the door. She just saw the top of its head disappearing into a clump of willows. She fired where she saw the bushes moving and thinks she wounded it. She says too that it had a ruff of white across the top of its head.

Later interviewed by Canadian biologist Bruce Wright, Mrs. Michelin said, "There was blood where it had stood." She was certain it was not a bear, adding, "I have killed 12 bears on my husband's trapline, and I know their tracks well. I saw enough of this thing to be sure of that." Wright noted that sightings and tracks were being recorded as late as 1940.

In a 1947 interview focused on their fifteen years of medical work in Labrador, Dr. and Mrs. C. Hogarth Forsythe referred to reports of "ape-men," occasioned by "many reports of giant barefoot tracks in the snow. Usually they are found by trappers whose living depends on their knowledge of tracks. Trappers have traced the tracks to 'nests' under trees in the open.... The trail usually runs out on glare ice or in running water. But such trails have been followed as much as fifteen miles over rough country. Whatever made them climbed easily over stumps and other obstructions where an ordinary man would have gone around. And whatever it was walked on two feet."

In the early 1970s, while teaching at Newfoundland's Memorial University, American folklorist David J. Hufford collected a story from Newfoundland, from an elderly man who claimed to have had a comparable experience early in the century. He and a party of men had gone to Trinity Bay on a fishing expedition. They set up camp, only to find it in disarray every time they returned. They ascribed the trouble to "Indians," even though no Indians had lived on the island for a century and, Hufford said, it is "very unlikely that any of the men had ever seen an Indian." Finally, they saw "two Indians" sitting on a log and—shockingly under the circumstances—opened fire on them, killing one.

"They described this dead 'Indian' as being seven feet tall, covered with short reddish brown fur and wearing no clothes," Hufford wrote. "There was no room to put the corpse in the boat so they towed it behind with a rope, taking it to their home community where they buried it after showing it to others in the community. As a result, the spot where the killing took place is now called Red Indian Point."

Later, during the Bigfoot era (commencing in the late 1950s), a number of persons came forward to testify to sightings earlier in the century. A woman wrote Ivan T. Sanderson, a biologist and the first writer to give the phenomena of Sasquatch and other HBs wide publicity, to relate a 1911 incident that occurred when she was living in far northern Minnesota. There, she said, two hunters saw a "human giant which had long arms and short, light hair" and which left strange prints. A man recalled that in 1942, while he was cutting spruce in a New Hampshire forest, a "gorilla-looking" creature followed him for some twenty minutes. In 1914, according to an account given in 1975, a boy saw a gorilla-like beast sitting on a log in his backyard in Churchville, Maryland.

The new age of HBs

From the 1950s to the present, HB reports have been catalogued in startling numbers. Some representative reports:

Monroe, Michigan, August 11, 1965: As they rounded a curve in a wooded area, Christine Van Acker, seventeen, and her mother gaped in astonishment as a hairy giant stepped out into the road. In her panic Christine hit the brakes instead of the accelerator. As she frantically tried to restart the car, the creature, seven feet tall and smelly, reached through the open window and grabbed the top of her head. The screams of the two women, not to mention the honking of the car horn, may have caused the HB to withdraw into the woods. Nearby workmen came on the scene moments later, finding the two women nearly incoherent with fear. Somehow in the course of the incident—it is not clear how—Christine contracted a black eye. The story attracted national publicity, with a photograph of Christine's bruised face appearing in hundreds of newspapers around the country.

Rising Sun, Indiana, May 19, 1969: At 7:30 P.M., as George Kaiser was crossing the farmyard on his way to the tractor, he spotted a strange figure standing twenty-five feet away. "I watched it for about two minutes before it saw me," he reported. "It stood in a fairly upright position, although it was bent over about in the middle of its back, with arms about the same length as a normal human

A frame from a film of Bigfoot taken by Roger Patterson on October 20, 1967, at Bluff Creek, California.

being's. I'd say it was about five-eight or so, and it had a very muscular structure. The head sat directly on the shoulders, and the face was black, with hair that stuck out of the back of its head. It had eyes set close together, and with a very short forehead. It was covered with hair except for the back of the hands and the face. The hands looked like normal hands, not claws." The creature made a grunting sound, turned around, leaped over a ditch, and dashed off at great speed down the road. Plaster casts of the tracks it left show three toes plus a big toe.

Putnam County, Indiana, August 1972: Randy and Lou Rogers, a young couple living outside tiny Roachdale (pop. 950), forty miles west of Indianapolis, became recipients of regular late-night visitations from a shadowy creature. Occasional brief glimpses revealed it to be a large, hairy "gorilla." Most of the time it was bipedal, but when it ran, it did so on all fours. Lou Rogers reported that "we could never find tracks, even when it ran over mud. It would run and jump, but it was like somehow it wasn't touching anything. When it ran through weeds, you couldn't hear anything. And sometimes when you looked at it, it seemed you could see *through* it." Nonetheless, an area farmer, Carter Burdine, allegedly lost all but thirty of his 200 chickens to the creature, which ripped them apart. Burdine, his father, and his uncle saw the HB in the chicken house and chased it into the barn. The uncle opened fire on it as it fled from there to a nearby field. "I shot four times with a pump shotgun," Bill ("Junior") Burdine said. "The thing was only about 100 feet away when I started shooting. I must have hit it. I've killed a lot of rabbits at that distance." Even so, the HB seemed unaffected. At least forty persons claimed to have seen the HB before sightings ceased late in the month.

Noxie, Oklahoma, September 1975: Farmer Kenneth Tosh and his neighbors reported seeing and hearing at least two HBs. First seen on the first of the month, twenty feet from Tosh's house, it stood six or seven feet tall and had dark brown hair all over its body, except around the eyes and nose. "The eyes glowed in the dark, reddish pink eyes," Tosh said. "They glow without a light being on them." On three occasions over the next days, Marion Parrett would fire on the creature with a .30 hunting rifle. He was convinced he hit it each time, but only once did it respond, by swatting its arm as if at a fly. The HB smelled "like rotten eggs or sulphur." It left a three-toed track (all primates have five toes). Toward the end of the episode, Tosh and his brother-in-law found themselves between two

HBs as they called to each other. "One of them had red eyes, and the other one had yellow," he said. "They was about 300 yards away from each other.... One of them, the one with red eyes, was more like a woman screaming. The other one sounded more like a baby bawling. The one with yellow eyes was more of a grayish color than the other one. And it was about half a foot shorter. They probably weighed between 300 and 500 pounds."

Vaughn, Montana, December 26, 1975: In the late afternoon two teenaged girls went to check on their horses, which seemed agitated. They observed, 200 yards from them and twenty-five yards from a thicket, a huge figure, seven and a half feet tall and twice as wide as a man. Intending to frighten it off, one of the girls fired a .22 rifle into the air. When nothing happened, she fired again, and this time the creature dropped to all fours, walked a short distance, then resumed its original bipedal stance. The girls took off running. One looked over her shoulder and saw three or four similar creatures with the first one, all heading toward the thicket. Law enforcement officers asked the girls to take a polygraph test, which they passed. Other sightings, hearings, and tracks of HBs were chronicled in Montana in the mid–1970s.

Southeastern Nebraska, August 1976: Near dusk a woman sitting on the back porch of a farmhouse south of Lincoln noticed a sudden eerie silence among the animals. Three hundred yards away, silhouetted against the sky, stood a huge, hairy figure. The figure moved rapidly through the pasture toward her, panicking the dogs, which knocked her down in their frantic effort to get inside the house. The HB broke down the wire fence and was only thirty feet from her when it vanished in front of her eyes. Nonetheless, this cryptozoological ghost somehow managed to leave hair samples on the fence. When the witness brought these into the state's Game and Parks Commission for analysis, however, it refused them.

Salisbury, New Hampshire, October 1987: Two or three days after a hunter had told him of seeing two strange beasts walking across a field next to Mill Brook, Walter Bowers Sr., hunting at the same location, sensed that he was being watched. Between two stands of trees he saw a "thing ... at least nine feet" tall, "maybe less, maybe more." He asserted, "The whole body was covered with hair ... kind of a grayish color." Because the sun was in his eyes, he could not make out the creature's face, but he noted that the "hands were like yours or mine, only three times bigger, with pads on the front paws, like a dog.... Long legs, long arms. It was just like ... a gorilla, but this here wasn't a gorilla." The HB ran into a swamp, and Bowers ran to his car and sped away. A reporter characterized him as a "man of sound mind and sober spirit."

Furry objects and flying objects

Late one evening, in August 1972, a luminous object hovered briefly over a corn field in rural Roachdale, Indiana, before seeming to "blow up," according to an observer. An hour and half later, the Roachdale HB (see above) allegedly made its presence known to a young woman, Lou Rogers, who lived on the other side of the field.

Taken in isolation, this incident tells us little if anything. The witness could, after all, have been mistaken about the object's proximity to the corn field. It could have been much higher in the atmosphere and only seemed to be close by—a common optical illusion in meteor sightings. Perhaps this was a bolide, an exploding meteor.

Or perhaps not. A handful of cases link HBs with UFOs in more straightforward fashion, and several investigators, notably Stan Gordon and Don Worley, have held that HBs are a variety of UFO occupant. Even by the generally thin nature of HB evidence, this is a slender thread indeed. Still, a few provocative incidents have been logged, including this one:

Uniontown, Pennsylvania, October 25, 1973: Having observed a red light hovering above a field just outside town, a twenty-two-year-old man and two ten-year-old boys rushed to the site in a pickup truck. The light, now revealed to be a dome-shaped UFO, had turned white and now rested on the ground "making a sound like a lawn mower." "Screaming sounds" could be heard nearby. Two large apelike creatures with glowing green eyes were walking along a fence. The taller, eight-foot HB was running its left hand along the fence, while the other nearly dragged the ground; behind it, a shorter, seven-foot creature tried to keep up with the first. A whining sound emanating from both seemed to be a means of communication between the two. The oldest witness, who was bearing a rifle, fired directly into the larger HB, which reacted by whining and reaching out to its companion. At that moment the UFO vanished. The two creatures disappeared into the trees. A state trooper summoned to the scene soon afterwards noticed a 150-foot luminous area where the UFO had sat. He also heard loud crashing sounds in the woods, apparently made by someone or something big and heavy. The twenty-two-year-old witness, who accompanied the officer, suffered an emotional breakdown at this juncture.

Investigator Stan Gordon's *Silent Invasion* (2010) relates dozens of extraordinary HB episodes reported in western Pennsylvania, some with paranormal or UFO connections, over a period from January 1973 through December 1974. Gordon writes, "Even with reports of shooting at the creatures with various types of firearms, there were neither bodies recovered nor any indisputable, solid, physical proof to support the existence of these unknown hairy beings. There seemed to be no doubt, however, that strange encounters were indeed going on." In some instances, when the creatures were shot at—in one case from a distance of six feet—the creatures vanished in a flash of light. Reports continue, though at a less intense rate. As we have seen, Pennsylvania has a long tradition of HB sightings.

For eight years a wealthy benefactor, Robert Bigelow, sponsored a scientific investigation, complete with electronic and other monitoring, and the services of scientists and engineers, of a ranch in northeastern Utah where many strange phenomena were being reported. On one occasion, in the early morning hours of

August 25, 1997, one of the investigators spotted a faint light at an elevation lower than the one on which they stood. One tried to photograph it, while another studied it through night-vision binoculars.

As they watched, the light got brighter and started to expand. Through binoculars it became apparent that the "light" was in fact some kind of tunnel suspended perhaps two feet off the ground. The investigator looking at it through the glasses was shocked to see something crawling by its elbows through the tunnel, a big, black bipedal creature which then dropped to the ground. The thing looked to be six feet tall, perhaps weighing as much as 400 pounds. It walked away silently into the darkness. The light then faded away.

Though badly shaken, the two rushed down to the site but found nothing. They did, however, smell a pungent, sulphuric odor of the sort they had encountered in previous strange encounters at the ranch. Beyond that, there was nothing unusual. Photographs that had been focused on the light/tunnel were "disappointing, showing only a single very faint blurry light in one [photograph]

This drawing, which appeared in *UFO Report* Vol. 2, depicts a Bigfoot leaving a UFO near a Missouri town.

and nothing on the rest of the roll of film," according to Colm A. Kelleher and George Knapp's book-length treatment of the larger research project.

High strangeness

On March 28, 1987, at 11:45 P.M., Dan Masias of Green Mountain Falls, Colorado, happened to look out his window to see "these creatures … running down the road in front of my house, which at one point is 30 feet from my front window. The whole road there was covered with about a quarter of an inch of fresh, cold snow that had fallen. They ran down the road in a manner with their arms hanging down, swinging in a pendulum motion. The first impression I got was that they were covered with hair. It was the most incredible thing I've ever seen."

After Masias's sighting was recounted in the newspapers, other residents of the area, near the Pike National Forest, came forward with their own reports, about which they had kept quiet for fear of ridicule. Sightings and hearings (of unearthly howls and growls) continued, and persons who followed HB tracks in snow swore they vanished in midstride.

As befits creatures whose mere presence in Colorado, Oklahoma, Indiana, New Hampshire, or elsewhere in populated America is a biological and ecological absurdity, HBs give every indication of *being* appropriately absurd. When they leave tracks, which (as we have seen) they do not always seem to do, these tracks may be two-, three-, four-, five-, or even six-toed. In a handful of accounts, we are told that HBs were shot or killed; more often, witnesses allege that bullets or shotgun pellets either did not affect the creatures at all or simply elicited mild expressions of discomfort from them. Creatures that are supposed to disappear instantaneously like ghosts (or hallucinations) also are said to shed strands of hair while crossing a fence.

Even worse, the phrase "hairy biped" is in some ways generic. It does not always denote a paranormal version of Sasquatch. In a small but persistent minority of reports, beings with fangs and vaguely wolf- or dog-like facial features are described. Such were among the five varieties of HBs reported in western Pennsylvania during the wave of reports mentioned above. In the spring of 1973, during a spate of sightings in the Enfield, Illinois, area, some witnesses reported seeing an ape-like creature; others claimed to have encountered, as did one farmer who said he saw it from a distance of no more than several feet, a three-legged creature with a "short body, two little short arms coming out from its breast area, and two pink eyes as big as flashlights." (He swore it was not a kangaroo. Hissing like a wildcat, it bounded away and covered seventy-five feet in three steps.)

Some witnesses, in locations as far apart as southern California and South Dakota, have even reported invisible HBs. During a spate of sightings at an Indian reservation in South Dakota in 1977, a creature was seen intermittently from the afternoon of November 3 into the evening, by which time locals and law enforcement officers had the area staked out. One of them, rancher Lyle Maxon, related this weird event: "We were out there walking in the dark, and I could hear very plainly something out of breath from running.... I put my flashlight right where I could plainly hear it, only where it should have been, there was nothing in sight. Now what I'm wondering is, can this thing make itself invisible when things get too close for comfort?" In their book on HB sightings in southern California, *Bigfoot* (1976), B. Ann Slate and Alan Berry tell of similar occurrences.

At least some reports are surely hoaxes—stories told by the less than sincere, in other words, or by those sincerely fooled by pranksters wearing masks. To all available evidence, however, such hoaxes are uncommon, at least in the modern era. Thus, unless one is prepared to reject the testimony (which by now is overwhelming) wholesale, rewrite the witnesses' descriptions, and then "explain" what one has invented, we can only be modest about what we do and do not know. The conundrum is a familiar one—credible persons report incredible things—and thus far no theory, mundane or extraordinary, convincingly answers any of the interesting questions.

Yet it is undeniably true that, from some perspectives, the evidence is modest enough to leave the question open, but too modest to inspire a scientific revolution. This, it should be added, has nothing to do with the question of whether three-toed, glowing-eyed Midwestern ape-like bipeds are seen or exist in some sense; it has to do instead with the kind of evidence science requires to take a question into consideration to start with—the kind of evidence that is sufficient, in other words, to make that question appear ultimately resolvable. Where HBs are concerned, the implications are staggering, but the evidence, such as it is, is simply not enough to go on, much less to use as a stick with which to beat conservative scientists into confessing that the early twenty-first-century map of reality has ignored some of the landscape's most fascinating features.

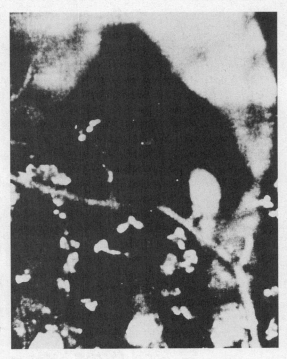

A rather indistinct photo of a hairy biped taken October 1966 in Labland, Ohio.

Still, scientists could do better. They *could* look at such evidence as has been collected more often than they do. It seems a shame that the Nebraska woman could not interest authorities in her samples of HB hair (see above). On the other hand, if an analysis of the hair produced genuinely anomalous results, where could the scientists go from there?

Perhaps what they can do—in fact, by ignoring the question for the most part, that is what they are doing in effect—is to refrain from making any pronouncements that are based on ignorance. The proper answer to the question of whether HBs are real, or what the observers' reports really mean, is not that all witnesses are liars, or that people are too stupid and hysterical to be able to tell the difference between a monstrous biped and a passing moose (a scientist's proposed explanation for the Salisbury, New Hampshire, episode above). Neither of these propositions is based on overwhelming evidence or logic.

At the same time, some advocates' endorsement of extraordinary hypotheses is unwise at this stage. To claim, as some do, that HBs are dropping out of another dimension or reality is to say nothing meaningful. Not, of course, that this *could not* be true (and perhaps that is just what the two Utah investigators witnessed); it is just that, given our present state of knowledge, we cannot prove it is true either. The proper answer to the HB question is on one level disappointing, on another intriguing and rife with the prospect of future discovery: We just don't know.

Further Reading:

Arment, Chad. *The Historical Bigfoot: Early Reports of Wild Men, Hairy Giants, and Wandering Gorillas in North America.* Landisville, PA: Coachwhip Publications, 2006.

"Bipedal Humanoids in Nebraska: A Chronology of Events." *Journal of the Fortean Research Center* 2,1 (April 1987): 4–6.

Bord, Janet, and Colin Bord. *Alien Animals*. Harrisburg, PA: Stackpole Books, 1981.

———. *The Bigfoot Casebook*. Harrisburg, PA: Stackpole Books, 1982.

———. *The Evidence for Bigfoot and Other Man-Beasts*. Wellingborough, Northamptonshire, England: Aquarian Press, 1984.

Chorvinsky, Mark, and Mark Opsasnick. "A Field Guide to the Monsters and Mystery Animals of Maryland." *Strange Magazine* 5 (1990): 41–46.

Dobbins, David L. "Colorado Bigfoot." *Fate* 41,11 (November 1988): 70–77.

Donovan, Roberta, and Keith Wolverton. *Mystery Stalks the Prairie*. Raynesford, MT: T.H.A.R. Institute, 1976.

French, Scot. "The Man Who Spied Bigfoot Comes Forward." *Concord Monitor*, New Hampshire (November 13, 1987).

Gordon, Stan. *Silent Invasion: The Pennsylvania UFO-Bigfoot Casebook*. Greensburg, PA: The Author, 2010.

Harris, Jesse W. "Myths and Legends from Southern Illinois." *Hoosier Folklore* 5 (March 1946): 14–20.

Hufford, David J. "Humanoids and Anomalous Lights: Taxonomic and Epistemological Problems." *Fabula* 18, 3/4 (1977): 234–41.

Keel, John A. *Strange Creatures from Time and Space*. Greenwich, CT: Fawcett Gold Medal, 1970.

Kelleher, Colm A., and George Knapp. *Hunt for the Skinwalker: Science Confronts the Unexplained at a Remote Ranch in Utah*. New York: Paraview Books, 2005.

Lake, Bonnie. "Bigfoot on the Buttes: The Invasion of Little Eagle." *UFO Report* 5,6 (June 1978): 28–31,67,69,71–72,74.

Opsasnick, Mark. *The Maryland Bigfoot Reference Guide*. Greenbelt, MD: The Author, 1987.

Roberts, Leonard. "Notes and Queries: Curious Legend of the Kentucky Mountains." *Western Folklore* 16,1 (January 1957): 48–51.

Sanderson, Ivan T. *"Things."* New York: Pyramid Books, 1967.

Schwarz, Berthold Eric. "Berserk: A UFO-Creature Encounter." *Flying Saucer Review* 20,1 (July 1974): 3–11.

Shoemaker, Michael T. "Searching for the Historical Bigfoot." *Strange Magazine* 5 (1990): 18–23,57–62.

Slate, B. Ann, and Alan Berry. *Bigfoot*. New York: Bantam Books, 1976.

Smith, Dwight, and Gary S. Mangiacopra. "Canada's 'Ape-Men' of Labrador." *North American BioFortean Review* 7,1 (2005): 18–21.

Worley, Don. "The UFO-Related Anthropoids: An Important New Opportunity for Investigator-Researchers with Courage." In Mimi Hynek, ed. *Proceedings of the 1976 CUFOS Conference*, 287–94. Evanston, IL: Center for UFO Studies, 1976.

Wright, Bruce. *Wildlife Sketches Near and Far*. Fredricton: University of New Brunswick Press, 1962.

Lake Monsters

On July 12, 1892, as two boys trolled for bass near the south shore of Lake Geneva, they were startled to see the head of an extraordinary serpent-like creature rise out of the water twenty to thirty yards away. It opened its huge mouth, revealing several rows of sharp, hooked teeth, and focused its fierce eyes on the terrified onlookers. It began swimming toward them, and the boys, literally paralyzed with fear, were unable to move.

Fortunately for them, the creature executed an abrupt turn when it got within a few feet of them. As it swam toward the middle of the lake, the boys could see that it was at least 100 feet long. "When last seen," the *Chicago Tribune* reported two days later, "the serpent was still carrying his head out of the water and slowly moving up the lake toward Keye's Park."

On February 22, 1968, at 7 P.M., farmer Stephen Coyne went to the dry bog near Lough Nahooin, one of a series of small lakes linked by streams that run through Connemara. With him were his eight-year-old son and the family dog. On reaching the bog, Coyne noticed a black object in the water and assumed that it was the dog. When he whistled for it, however, the dog came bounding up from elsewhere. The moment it saw the object in the water, it stopped and stared.

The object proved to be a strange animal with a narrow, pole-like head (without visible eyes) and a neck nearly a foot in diameter. It was swimming in various directions, occasionally thrusting its head and neck underwater. Whenever this happened, two humps from its back would emerge into view as would, sometimes, a flat tail. On one occasion this tail was observed near the head, indicating that the animal was both long and flexible. The skin was black, slick, and hairless. The creature appeared to be at least twelve feet long.

Once, apparently annoyed by the dog's barking, it swam toward the group, its mouth open. Coyne stepped forward to protect the dog, and the creature returned to resume its casual, directionless movement through the water. Soon father and son were joined by the other five members of the Coyne family. It remained clearly in view, sometimes from as little as five or six yards away. The beast was still there when darkness fell and the Coynes decided to go home.

These two stories, the first from Wisconsin, the second from Ireland, span the spectrum of lake-monster reports, from the predictably bogus to the unexpectedly credible. The Lake Geneva tale is, to all appearances, a nineteenth-century newspaper hoax; though the *Chicago Tribune* account refers to "thousands of people … flocking to the shore" of Lake Geneva in a state of intense excitement, not a single reference to the event appears in any other contemporary source. Readers of American newspapers of the nineteenth century were often regaled with comparably fantastic tales.

Whatever else it may be, the Coyne family's sighting is no newspaper hoax. Soon after the encounter, a team of experienced cryptozoological investigators, including University of Chicago biologist Roy P. Mackal, interviewed the adult and child witnesses and concluded that their sincerity was not open to question. A few months later, as they were engaged in an unsuccessful effort to snare the creature via a dragging operation through the tiny lake (measuring 100 yards by 80 yards), they met a local man, Thomas Connelly, who saw the same or a similar creature in September, as it plunged into the water from the banks. They also heard reports from other lakes in this remote area of western Ireland.

In cases like these, misperception or misidentification seems nearly as unlikely as the creature the Coynes claimed to have seen. Reports of lake monsters abound even in the modern world. If some are reducible to hoaxes and mistakes, some of the most detailed sightings are puzzling indeed, fitting comfortably into no explanatory scheme, not even the conventionally cryptozoological.

Monsters in the magical universe and consensus reality

Traditions of giant freshwater monsters are ancient, ubiquitous, and generally unhelpful to any modern, scientifically minded inquirer who seeks to extract zoological signals from the deafening noise of mythology and folklore. Our ancestors inhabited a magical universe in which the most fantastic and grotesque creatures were possible and even, in some sense, experienced. Lake monsters of the Middle Ages and earlier go by various names—great serpents, dragons, water horses, and innumerable others—and they share water and land with a bewildering array of supernatural entities.

The pre-modern freshwater monster is usually a great serpent, not entirely aquatic in its habits, and often dangerous. In 1636, for example, according to a Norwegian cleric named Nicolas Gramius, "In the last flood, a great serpent from the waters came to the sea; he had lived up to that point in the Mjos and Branz rivers. From the shores of the latter river, he crossed the fields. People saw him moving like a long ship's mast, overturning all that he met on his path, even trees and huts."

Norwegians believed that monsters grew in the lakes until they were too big to live there any longer; then they migrated to the sea. It is not entirely impossible that these creatures were large eels, which have been known to migrate as much as twenty miles overland.

Aside from accounts (nearly all of them sketchy) that describe more or less biologically plausible, and even more or less recognizable, lake monsters, most of

"Battle of Two Sea Monsters" by Andrea Mantegna, circa 1475. Sea monsters filled the imaginations and fears of sailors throughout the world for most of human history. Might some of the stories be true?

the early stories seem purely fabulous, and no more believable than tales (of which there were more than a few) of dragons in the sky. The freshwater dragon of legend surfaced as late as October 18, 1946, in the Clearwater River near Rocky Mountain House, Alberta. Farmer Robert Forbes claimed to have seen a huge, scaly-skinned monster with fiery eyes, long, flashing teeth, and a horn dart its head out of the water long enough to swallow whole a calf that happened to be eating on the banks.

Cryptozoologists sometimes link modern reports, especially those from the monster-haunted lochs and loughs of Scotland and Ireland, with earlier traditions of "water horses." As the argument goes, these supernatural beliefs, nonsensical if read literally, cloak the existence of real, if unusual, aquatic animals. But such a link is hardly certain.

Lake-monster reports and water-horse traditions intersect, with rare exception (see the Loch Duvat story below), at only two points: both are associated with fresh water, and the former creatures are frequently said to have heads reminiscent of horses'. Beyond these, the water horse (known as the "kelpie" in the

Scottish Highlands) is another order of entity entirely: a dangerous shape-changer that can appear either as a shaggy man, who would leap out of the dark onto the back of a solitary traveler and frighten or—if in an especially foul humor—crush him to death, or as a young horse that after tricking an unwary soul onto its back would plunge to the bottom of the nearest lake, with predictably fatal consequences for the rider.

Though water horses are widely remarked on in folklore texts, sighting reports—as opposed to traditions, beliefs, and rumors—are rarer. One, however, is attributed to Mary Falconer of Achlyness, West Sutherland, Scotland. On an afternoon in the summer of 1938, while walking with a companion near Loch Garget Beag, she noticed a herd of thirteen ponies grazing near the water. Mrs. Falconer, who was carrying a sack full of venison, thought one of the horses, a white one, looked like a neighbor's. She decided to borrow it to carry her burden for the rest of the trip to Rhiconich.

But as she approached the animal, she found that it was too big to be her friend's horse. When she saw that it had water weeds entangled in its mane, she knew immediately that it was a water horse. At that moment it and its dozen companions bolted for the lake and disappeared below the surface. "Her companion corroborated her story in every particular," according to folklorist R. Macdonald Robertson. Robertson wrote that Mrs. Falconer had a local reputation as a "seer."

Were beliefs in water horses based on experiences like this one? Since, as this book attests, people see all kinds of unlikely things, the question is not a trivial one: the relationship of modern, more "scientific" (as opposed to "superstitious") images of lake monsters to current sightings. In this regard, the folklorist/debunker Michel Meurger writes of the cultural evolution of lake monsters, "The original mythical monster has been progressively covered over with an ideological crust of pretended facticity. This hardened layer will resist any critical investigation, because the new monsters are adapted to the European mind."

The scientific investigation of anomalies such as lake monsters has a short history (though sporadic efforts were mounted in the eighteenth and nineteenth centuries) and even now, as a not quite respectable enterprise, is plagued by the habitual anomalists' problem of inadequate resources.

Few scientists are willing to risk reputation and career associating themselves with "monster hunts," and the funding sources on which scientific research depends are typically unavailable to scientific heretics, however well credentialed. Thus, little about lake monsters is certain and the information that might provide certain answers is unavailable to us because the question itself is deemed illegitimate.

As a consequence, virtually all we know about early popular beliefs concerning such creatures comes from antiquarians and folklorists, who had no obligation to document reports by collecting evidence and assessing their credibility. Folklorists recorded the stories, even the first-person testimonies, simply *as* stories and, that accomplished, snapped their notebooks shut. Many also implicitly rejected supernatural, or even merely extraordinary, testimony. As David J. Hufford, a scholarly critic of such "traditions of disbelief," has written, since it is supposed that "supernatural beliefs arise from and are supported by various kinds of error … the research design begins with the question 'Why and how do some people manage to believe things which are so patently false?'… Such a perspective has its usefulness but … it is ethnocentric in the most fundamental sense. It takes a body of knowledge and considers it to be simply 'the way things are' rather than a product of culture. It says over and over again: 'What *I* know I *know*; what you know you only *believe*.'"

One would like to know more about a story collected on June 5, 1897, by Father Allan McDonald, from a Highlander. McDonald wrote:

Ewen MacMillan, Bunavullin, Eriskay, of Skye descent, aged about 50 tells me that four years ago at the end of May or beginning of June he had gone to look after a mare and foal that he had at about nine or ten o'clock P.M. He went up to Loch Duvat (Eriskay) to see them. There was a foggy haze. He passed at the west end a horse belonging to John Campbell, Bunavullin, and a horse belonging to Duncan Beag MacInnes. He saw an animal in front of him on the North side of the lake which he took to be his own mare and was making up to it. He got to within twenty yards of it but he could not distinguish the color on account of the haze, but in size it appeared to be no larger than a common Eriskay pony. When he came to within twenty yards of it the creature gave a hideous or unearthly scream … that terrified not only MacMillan but the horses that were grazing at the West end of the lake, which immediately took to flight. MacMillan ran the whole way home and the horses did not stop till they reached home. These horses were not in the habit of coming home though they might come home of their own accord occasionally.

The tantalizing ambiguity of an unsettling image of a strange creature, whatever it may or may not have been, glimpsed darkly through nocturnal haze resonates richly in the imagination. It bears noting, however, that reports of unidentified large animals, as opposed to supernatural apparitions, were noted, taken seriously, and discussed in the nineteenth century, as we shall examine in more detail presently. In March 1856 the *Times* of London reprinted this piece from the *Inverness Courier* (the city of Inverness lies just west of Loch Ness):

The Sea Serpent in the Highlands.—The village of Leurbost, parish of Lochs, Lewis [an island northwest of Scotland in the Outer Hebrides], is at present the scene of an unusual occurrence. This is no less than the appearance in one of the inland fresh water lakes of an animal which from its great size and dimensions has not a little puzzled our island naturalists. Some supposed him to be a description of the hitherto mythical water-kelpie; while others refer it to the minute descriptions of the "sea serpent," which are revived from time to time in newspaper columns. It has been repeatedly seen within the last fortnight by crowds of people, many of whom have come from the remotest parts of the parish to witness the uncommon spectacle. The animal is described by some as being in appearance and size like a "huge peat stack," while others affirm that a "six-oared boat" could pass between the huge fins [humps?], which are occasionally visible. All, however, agree, in describing its form as that of an eel; and we have heard one, whose evidence we can reply upon, state that in length he supposed it to be about 40 feet. It is probable that it is no more than a conger eel after all, animals of this description having been caught in Highland lakes which have attained a huge size. He is currently reported to have swallowed a blanket inadvertently left on the bank of the lake by a girl herding cattle. A sportsman ensconced himself with a rifle in the vicinity of the loch during a whole day, hoping to get a shot, but did no execution.

Monsters in the nineteenth-century press

North American newspapers of the 1800s carried lake monster stories even more frequently than they ran other kinds of "snake stories" (as they were called then, the phrase being roughly translated as "preposterous yarns") involving gigantic land serpents and reptiles in stomachs. Stomach reptiles were certainly fiction—the phenomenon described is flatly impossible for biological reasons no rational person would dispute—and anecdotes of enormous snakes were viewed with amused skepticism even then; tellingly, neither they nor their gastrointestinal cousins are heard of anymore. That lake monster sightings continue—if more rarely—makes it more difficult to dismiss the reports out of hand. (It should be noted, by the way, that "lake monster" is a relatively recent phrase; large, unidentified creatures even in freshwater bodies were often referred to by the generic term "sea serpents" in nineteenth-century accounts.) Some representative examples of accounts that at least *sound* more plausible than others:

Lake Ontario, June 10, 1867: "About 8 o'clock, a party of four ladies and four gentlemen of this city went out … for a ride in a four-oared row-boat. They went up the lake about two miles.… The evening was pleasant, with almost no wind, and the moon … made objects plainly discernable.… At about 10 o'clock, the occupants … heard a peculiar noise which attracted their attention. About two hundred feet ahead of them and within one hundred from the shore, they saw what they at first thought to be a log floating in the water. The peculiar noise was repeated, and this time it was apparent that it came from the vicinity of the 'log'.… The party all saw a most horrible sight. The form of a huge snake was raised fully fifteen feet into the air, and brought down into the water three or four times in quick succession. A noise similar in nature to that heard previously, but greatly increased in power, was heard; the reptile settled into the water, and with its horrid head elevated two feet above the surface, began to move off toward the center of the lake, repeating the noise, which sounded like the bellow of a bull, and lashing the water into foam for a distance of at least forty feet behind the head.… They were not near enough to see the shape of the head, but unite in saying that the body of the animal was at least two feet thick at the neck, and gradually increased in size down to the water. The belly seemed of a light color, and the back black" (*Oswego Palladium*, New York, June 11).

Lake Simcoe, Ontario, summer 1881: "The latest 'sea serpent' story … is told by Mr. Allan G. Canava, Dominion Land Surveyor, in a letter to his uncle, Mr. Charles Gibbs.… Mr. Canava has been employed lately in examining the waters of Lake Simcoe and Couchiching and the marshes adjoining.… He was engaged with an assistant examining the swamps bordering on Lake Simcoe.… They were in a boat and moving slowly along when their attention was attracted by a peculiar puffing sound.… A few seconds later they saw emerging from the rushes an extraordinary creature, having a head as large as that of an adult human being and a body resembling a serpent, and increasing in thickness downwards. It seemed frightened and made a peculiar puffing sound like a small engine. After going out into deep water it stopped for a short time, and with the cessation of locomotion there was an end to the puffing noise.… Mr. Canava and his companion propelled their boat forward a short distance to have a better view of the creature, upon which the puffing recommenced more vigorously than before; and it moved off at the rate of fifteen miles an hour. It carried its head out of the water as it went" (*Fort Wayne Daily Gazette*, Indiana, August 12).

A "ribbon fish" sea monster is depicted in this 1921 illustration that appeared in the *London News*.

Goose Lake, Florida, October 1881: "Fishing parties … tell of a monster unlike anything ever seen or heard of before. J. Z. Scott first saw it, and says that it has a body between fifteen and twenty feet in length, and as large around as a common horse. It has a head like a dog and tail like a catfish. No fins or feet have ever been observed, though it seems to move with the motion of a fish, rather than that of a snake. All those portions of the body which have been exposed are covered with long hair of a dark color. It swims with astonishing rapidity, and will follow a lighted boat at night. Messrs. Aaron Terry and N. G. Osborne were out in a boat gig fishing, when the monster approached within striking distance, and they drove the gig deeply into it. The animal freed itself with a violent effort, twisting the prongs of the gig like so many straws" (*Chester Daily Times*, Pennsylvania, October 25).

Walled Lake, Michigan, spring 1884: "This monster was first seen by Jas. Monroe, who lives near the lake. He says, and his family entertain no doubt as to the truthfulness of his assertion, that this snake measures, according to his calculations, no less than 30 feet in length, and is seemingly about 10 inches in diameter. Hundreds of curious people are daily seen on the shores surrounding the lake watching for the frequent appearance of the huge reptile" (*Grand Traverse Herald*, Traverse City, June 19).

Lake Cowichan, British Columbia, circa November 1885: "As Mr. Charles Morrow, accompanied by an Indian man and woman, was paddling in a canoe … he was suddenly transfixed with astonishment and terror at the appearance of an extraordinary object which quickly lifted its head out of the water, and continued to raise it until it was about 20 feet above the surface. The head was eel-like in shape and the part of the body that appeared above the water resembled that of a gigantic snake, being of a reddish brown hue on the back and a dull white star on the belly. The monster, Mr. Morrow says, was 'as big around as Amelia's smokestack.' After surveying the party in the canoe for a few moments the serpent (for such it appeared to be) took a 'header' and disappeared, leaving the water as agitated as were the occupants of the canoe. In conversation with some old Indians afterwards Mr. Morrow was told that there was a tribal tradition that many years ago several huge water snakes were often seen in the lake and that the forefathers of the Indians now living were in the habit of shooting arrows into them" (*Victoria Daily Colonist*, November 17).

Cayuga Lake, New York, summer 1886: "A Mr. Tailby and his wife … had first seen the monster while walking near their home on the shore [at Little Point]. The snake when seen was lying around a rock and only a portion of his body was exposed to view. As near as could be judged it was about twenty feet long and six or eight inches in diameter. It was brown in color, with white spots. On seeing the reptile Mr. Tailby at once thought of his gun, but his wife … feared to be left alone with the serpent and volunteered to go for the weapon while he remained on guard. In her haste … she forgot to procure ammunition upon her first trip home and before this commodity so necessary to the effectiveness of a gun could be obtained, the cause of all the excitement suddenly disappeared. Several children were afterward very much frightened by a sight of the snake basking in the sun on the shore near the place where he had first been seen. A Mr. Watson also viewed the monster in the lake with its head, which he compared in size to a cigar box, a foot or eighteen inches above the water" (*Syracuse Herald*, July 18, quoting *Ithaca Democrat*).

Narrow Lake, Michigan, summer 1886: "A genuine sea monster abounds in the waters … 10 miles south of this city [Charlotte]. The monster, it is claimed by the habitués of that vicinity, raises itself out of the water on moonlight nights to a height of 10 feet and then disappears. Its body is said to be about the size of a stove pipe and its head to resemble that of a serpent" (*New York Times*, September 3).

Skiff Lake, New Brunswick, August 1887: "The famous land-locked sea-serpent which has long been said to inhabit the depths … was seen last week by at least three reputable eye-witnesses disporting itself on the bosom of the lake. According to one of the witnesses the serpent appeared to be about thirty feet in length. At times he lay on the surface, and then again he would slough through the water at a frightful rate of speed, lashing the water into foam with his head and tail. His course lay off McMullen's landing toward Northcote Island, a distance of three miles, during which he was plainly visible to the men on the hill overlooking the lake ... until an intervening island cut him out of their sight. This is at least the third appearance of this singular reptile" (*Adirondack News*, August 27, reprinted from *Woodstock Press*, New Brunswick).

Thunder Bay, Ontario, June 1888: "The residents for a long distance along Thunder Bay are terrified over the appearance of a monster lake serpent. A farmer named Isaacson recently found a trail about a foot wide through a plowed field. It led down to the bay, where there were indications of its presence. Mr. Isaacson's boy, Grant, was planting potatoes in a field near the house, and was frightened to see a huge snake moving toward him. The boy had with him a double-barreled shot-gun, and fired twice at the monster, when it went over the ground as lively as a horse and glided into the bay. The boy's father, attracted by the gun reports, followed the snake's track to the water. The boy described the snake as about twenty five feet long and over a foot thick. The body is black, with yellow spots and a yellow tail. The head was covered with long black hair" (*Dunkirk Observer-Journal*, New York, June 19).

La Crosse, Wisconsin, July 31, 1889: "A monster serpent [was] seen in the river bottoms near that place.... The snake had a head as big as a man's, its body was eight inches through, and it was thirty feet long" (*Winona Daily Republican*, Minnesota, August 2, citing *La Crosse Chronicle*).

Lake Erie, July 13, 1892: "Early [that] morning, while the schooner Madeline Dowing, on its way from Buffalo to this city [Toledo, Ohio], was passing the Dunning, about 150 miles east of here, in Lake Erie, Captain Patrick Woods saw, about half a mile ahead, the waters of the lake lashed into foam. Drawing near, to the surprise of the captain and all on board, a huge serpent, wrestling about in the waters as if fighting with an unseen enemy, was seen. It soon quieted down and lay at full length on the surface of the water.... The serpent was about 50 feet in length and not less than four feet in circumference of body. Its head projected from the water about four feet ... a terrible looking object. It has viciously sparkling eyes and a large head. Fins were plainly seen, seemingly sufficiently large to assist the snake in propelling itself through the water.... The body was dark brown in color, which was uniform all along" (*Fort Covington Sun*, New York, August 4).

Lake Michigan, April 1893: "The first sea serpent of the year ... was seen ... off Fort Sheridan [north of Chicago], and Captain Brinkerhoff and Lieutenant Blauvelt of the Fifteen United States Infantry are his vouchers. Captain Brinkerhoff said of it: 'The creature poked its head up, and we saw it, plainly with our naked eyes and through our glasses. The head was very large, dark above and light colored underneath. We could not see the features distinctly, but it looked like an alligator's head. It appeared to be disabled in some way and began to struggle. The effort seemed to revive it. It disappeared, but quickly came to the surface again at the identical spot where we had first got a good view of it. It looked toward us for an instant and then turning around made its way directly out into the lake. It described almost a letter S with its body in turning, and we got an excellent view of

A *Lophius americanus,* or fishing frog, is depicted in oversize proportions as a sea monster in this 1856 illustration.

it. The serpent or whatever it was I estimated to be 30 feet long. I could not describe it, except that it looked like a huge alligator deprived of its legs.... The creature went swiftly through the water for several hundred feet due east. Then it turned suddenly, its body again describing the letter S, and headed for the shore, aiming evidently at a point a quarter of a mile north of us. It changed its intention, however, and turning about passed out of our sight toward Waukegan [to the north]'" (*Marion Daily Star,* Ohio, April 22).

Lake Monona, Wisconsin, June 11, 1897: "The Monona sea-serpent has made its appearance about two months earlier than usual this season, according to several people in the vicinity of East Madison, who aver that they saw the monster last evening. They say it was at least 20 feet long, and traveled east on the surface of the lake until Eugene Heath ... fired two shots into it, when it turned and came back; at this juncture either the snake or the spectators appear to have disappeared. It is probably the same animal which is credited with having swallowed a dog ... swimming in the lake a few days ago. Mr. Schott and others who saw the 'thing,' whatever it may be, insist that it is a reality.... Its appearance is not that of a serpent. Mr. Schott says, however, that he saw it plainly in the bright moonlight, and its shape was like the bottom of a boat, but it was about twice as long. Mr. Schott's two sons saw it" (*Wisconsin State Journal,* Madison, June 12).

Gull Lake, Michigan, August 19, 1900: "Summer visitors at Allendale, Gull lake, are seriously wrought up over the unexpected appearance there of a marine [sic] monster, the like of which was never before known in Michigan waters....

The strange reptile first made its appearance in the little bay at the southeast end of the lake on Sunday morning, and was discovered by Harry Kemper and Miss Carrie Wirthlin, of Cincinnati, who were fishing…. They first lost a half dozen spoon hooks and lines, then their minnow pail, which was astern, trailing in the water. Noticing the water strangely agitated near by, Kemper started to row to shore. Something grabbed one of his oars and it came up with a piece torn out. Then a hideous head appeared above the water that swayed from side to side and emitted a hissing sound. Some twenty or twenty-five feet distant the tip of the reptile's tail could be seen lashing the water. Kemper rowed for his life toward shore … the monster pursuing them and endeavoring to seize the boat. When about twenty rods from shore Kemper beat the monster off with his oar, and in doing so capsized the boat. They were rescued from drowning by a passing launch. Kemper describes the serpent as having short, thick forelegs and a head as large as a [calf's], with bulging eyes, a large mouth, and vicious-looking teeth. On its forehead was a thick growth of hair, and its body was covered with scales that emitted a phosphorescent glow in the twilight. Kemper says the monster had a face almost human in its expression…. In 1894 a strange water nondescript of a similar character killed hundreds of sheep and fowls along the shores of the lake. It was unsuccessfully hunted for weeks at that time" (*Fort Wayne Sentinel*, Indiana, August 21).

Whatever inspired these sightings—sincere sightings, mistakes, or fictions of one kind or another—the salient fact must be that no bodies of such creatures were ever recovered.

Twentieth century and beyond

In the twentieth century, press accounts of North American lake monsters grew much rarer than previously, no doubt reflecting more professionalized journalism. Still, contrary to what one might have expected, reports did not cease. Continuing, puzzling sightings came most prominently from Lake Champlain (of the monster known as "Champ"; see below) and British Columbia's Lake Okanagan ("Ogopogo"). Some zoological authorities, notably Roy P. Mackal, have remarked on the Ogopogo animals' resemblance to zeuglodons, snakelike prehistoric whales. The occasional scientific inquiries directed toward monster reports at specific lakes tend to conclude with positive assessments of the eyewitness testimony. If the evidence is soft, it is not always easy to dismiss. Of course, mirages, oversized fish, big turtles, sea lions, logs, and tall tales provide plausible explanations for other sightings.

The popular modern image of the lake monster as a long-necked, plesiosaur-like animal seems just that. The handful of nineteenth-century reports of such creatures exist only in the retrospective testimony, typically decades later, of aging witnesses. Interestingly, in the nineteenth century some participants in the great debate about sea serpents championed plesiosaurs as the animals most likely responsible for the sightings. The late Bernard Heuvelmans, the leading modern historian of the subject, points, however, to significant discrepancies: the plesiosaur's neck is shorter and its tail longer than those associated with the animals described in sea-serpent reports. It is, on the other hand, imaginable that after tens of millions of years of subsequent evolution, the physical characteristics of plesiosaurs could have been altered.

If worldwide in scope, lake-monster reports are only spottily documented. A list of the planet's allegedly creature-haunted lakes—approximately 300—appeared in the Spring 1979 issue of *Pursuit*. Possibly, the real number is larger, bolstered by aquatic monster stories that are only locally known. (An example of a monster tradition known only to its local community will be cited shortly.)

Nessie: case history of a Scottish lake monster

The story of the world's best-known lake monsters begins, according to those who hold that such animals exist, more than 10,000 years ago. During the last Ice Age, glaciers carved out the largest freshwater lake (at least twenty miles long, one and a half miles wide, and in places 1,000 feet deep) in what one day would be called Scotland. When the thaw began, the sea moved to fill up the fjord the glaciers had created. As the ice disappeared, the land rose slowly, and eventually the fjord became Loch Ness. Over time fresh water replaced the salt water. The descendants of the animals that had swum into the loch when it was attached to the sea lived on in their new, altered environment.

In 565 C.E. a man swimming in the River Ness (which empties toward the sea from the north end of Loch Ness) died under bizarre circumstances. St. Columba, who came on the scene soon afterwards, encountered men carrying the body. A monster had killed the man, they said. Columba sent a companion into the river, attracting the attention of the creature, which rose up from the bottom and moved menacingly toward the swimmer. As the others looked up in terror, the saint formed a sign of the cross and commanded the monster to depart in the name of God. According to a Latin text compiled by St. Adamnan a century later, the "beast, on hearing this voice of the saint, was terrified and fled backwards more rapidly than he came."

This account did not describe what the "beast" looked like and ascribed to it aggressive behavior of a sort not associated with the modern Loch Ness monster. Still, most chroniclers of the mystery consider this the first known report of what the press would call "Nessie."

Ambiguous references to large animals in the loch appeared in other documents over the centuries. After the monster became a worldwide sensation in the 1930s, residents of the Loch area and other persons came forward with their own reports from earlier in the century and even before. For example, in 1934 D. Mackenzie wrote Rupert T. Gould, author of the first book on the Ness phenomenon, to recount a sighting in 1871 or 1872. At noon on a sunny October day, he recalled, he saw what looked "rather like an overturned boat ... wriggling and

Descriptions of lake monsters are sometimes reminiscent of plesiousaurs, aquatic reptiles that lived in the Triassic Period over two hundred million years ago.

churning up the water." On October 20, 1933, *The Scotsman* published a letter from the Duke of Portland, who remembered that "when I became, in 1895, the tenant of the salmon angling in Loch Oich and the River Garry, the forester, the hotelkeeper and the fishing ghillies used often to talk about a horrible great beastie as they called it, which appeared in Loch Ness." In 1879 and 1880 two groups of witnesses sighted, if their retrospective testimony is to be credited, a large elephant-gray animal with a small head at the end of a long neck as it "waddled" from land into the water.

Such words as upturned boat, elephant-gray color, small head, long neck, and even horrible would be applied to Nessie in numerous later reports. Ness chroniclers estimate the number of sightings to be in the thousands. Writing in the mid-1970s, biologist Roy P. Mackal asserted, "Over the years there have been at least 10,000 known *reported* sightings at Loch Ness but [fewer] than a third of these *recorded*."

The August 27, 1930, edition of the *Northern Chronicle,* published in Inverness near the loch, reported that a month earlier three local men, while fishing from a boat, saw, as one put it, "a commotion about 600 yards up the loch. I saw a spray being thrown up into the air at a considerable height.... It continued until it was about 300 yards away and then whatever was causing it turned southwards in a large half circle and moved away from us. It must have been traveling at fifteen knots. My estimation of the part of it we saw would be about twenty feet, and it was standing about three feet or so out of the water. The wash it created caused our boat to rock violently." Though he did not describe what the cause of the commotion looked like, he said it was "without doubt a living creature" and not "anything normal." Though the account brought letters (published in the September 3 issue) from other readers attesting to their own or other people's encounters with unidentified animals in the loch, the matter attracted no wider attention.

All that would change with an incident that occurred on the afternoon of April 14, 1933, near Abriachan, a village on the northwest side of Ness. A couple in a passing car watched an "enormous animal rolling and plunging" out on the loch. On May 2 the *Inverness Courier* carried the story, written by Alex Campbell, who would go on to become a controversial promoter of the monster and, allegedly, a witness himself. The *Courier*'s editor, Evan Barron, dubbed the animal a "monster," and the report attracted a fair amount of attention in the Scottish press. Other sightings followed, and the larger world took notice. By October, with more than twenty reports noted since the April 14 incident, the "Loch Ness monster" was born.

Over the years a composite picture of the "monster" has emerged. The classic Nessie has a long, vertical neck, with a head of comparable circumference. On the neck, near the end, some witnesses have said they have seen what looked like a mane of hair. The head may have a horse-like appearance. The long, tapering body may have one, two, or three humps. Persons who claim to have seen Nessie on land usually report fin-like appendages that allow for clumsy forward movement outside the water and (evidently) rapid movement within it. Its color is variously said to be dark gray, dark brown, or black, though occasionally witnesses speak of a lighter color. It surfaces and descends quickly and vertically. It almost always appears when the lake is calm.

If the loch indeed harbors something unusual, common sense and biology require that more than one specimen of it exists. Early writers such as Gould naïvely assumed that the loch harbored a single creature, but Ness proponents long ago abandoned that view and now hold that a breeding population resides in the loch. Indeed, reports of multiple Nessies, if infrequent, are made from time to time. The *Scottish Daily Press* of July 14, 1937, for example, told of eight persons who observed "three Monsters about 300 yards out in the loch. In the center were two black shiny humps, 5 ft. long and protruding 2 ft. out of the water and on either side was a smaller Monster." (In late 1997 a reporter for the *London Financial Times* claimed, apparently seriously, to have seen five "plesiosaur-type monsters," one an evident juvenile, from a distance of some fifteen yards.)

If taken at something approximating face value, the varying size estimates alone indicate that not every sighting is of the same animal. Estimates of length range from as little as three feet (in rare reports of "baby monsters") to as much as sixty-five feet. Some Nessie investigators reject these latter kinds of estimates as exaggerated, though others speculate that such reports may be of an older "bull." Most estimates are between fifteen and thirty feet.

The case for the Ness phenomenon begins with a large body of eyewitness testimony from individuals whose honesty and mental health do not appear to be open to question. Beyond that, the evidence for Ness includes photographs, films, and sonar traces. (In the last instance, there were approximately twenty anomalous detections between 1954 and 1982.) Such evidence seems to attest to the presence of unknown animate objects at or below the loch surface. Chemistry professor and Ness chronicler Henry H. Bauer notes examples of the sonar evidence:

> Sonar echoes stronger than from fish and often from moving objects have been obtained in Loch Ness on many occasions since the 1950s. In 1968 engineers from Birmingham University testing a new digital sonar detected large objects rising apparently from the bottom, coming swiftly up hundreds of feet and then returning to the bottom.... In 1969 a big object moved parallel to the sonar-equipped boat at several miles per hour, then turned back and moved away.... During the summer of 1980, several dozen large echoes were obtained over deep water by the Loch Ness & Morar Project.... During Operation DeepScan in 1987, three substantial contacts were fleetingly made in deep water.....

This 1954 illustration depicts the Loch Ness monster—looking rather like a dinosaur—frightening a local waitress.

Echoes from apparently large and moving objects have been obtained from a great variety of types of sonar instruments: fixed as well as moving, side-scanning as well as fish-finding, scanning-and-tracking mounted on boats. It seems unlikely that all of those modes would record artifacts that similarly mimic large, moving objects.

Such sightings, pictures, and trackings continue to the present, notwithstanding periodic pronouncements that the Ness monster—or, in the skeptics' version, the Ness myth—is dead.

Champ: case history of an American lake monster

According to standard accounts, Champ is Lake Champlain's version of the Loch Ness monster: a large, long-necked animal bearing a general resemblance to the long-extinct plesiosaur. In fact, witnesses' reports, of which there are hundreds, offer up a more complex picture than that.

Formed approximately 10,000 years ago out of melting glaciers, Lake Champlain is a deep, cold, 109-mile-long body of water. It stretches north from Whitehall, New York, along the New York–Vermont border and ends about six miles into Quebec. There, at Sorel, it drains into the St. Lawrence River; the St. Lawrence flows into the North Atlantic Ocean of which Champlain's parent,

Champlain Sea, was once an estuary. The largest North American water body outside the Great Lakes, it harbors some eighty different species of fish—more than enough to feed a family of monster-sized predators, if such exist.

In popular lore—some trace it to an article by the late Marjorie L. Porter in the Summer 1970 issue of *Vermont Life*; but in fact, it was mentioned in print at least as early as 1929—the first white man to see the monster was Samuel de Champlain, after whom the lake is named. Champlain is supposed to have mentioned the creature in a 1609 account of his explorations of the St. Lawrence and associated rivers, but that source, which few writers on the subject seem to have consulted directly, indicates only that he saw a large fish, identifiable from his description as a gar, whose undisputed presence in Champlain continues to this day.

If Champ is a real animal, it is—obviously—part of a breeding population. In other words, the generic name covers all members of the species. Indeed, a handful of reports speak of two or more such entities. Others refer to a "baby Champ."

The Champ saga really begins, more or less, in 1873. The qualification has to do with a curious fact that many proponents of the monster would later obscure: namely, the early monster and its modern equivalent do not appear to be the same animal. The former, invariably described as a gigantic serpent, is no plesiosaur.

The earlier known story about a monster in Lake Champlain was published in an upstate New York newspaper, *Whitehall Times*, for July 9, 1873. (In its July 5, 1946, issue, reporting a recent sighting, the *Essex County Republican* of Keeseville, New York, states, "Newspaper files of this area reveal that the Lake Champlain sea serpent was first seen in 1819 in the vicinity of Bulwaggy Bay, near Port Henry." These articles have yet to surface, and the author's extensive survey of relevant newspapers found no mention of a Champlain serpent or serpents prior to 1873.) The *Times* recounts the adventure of a railroad work crew which, while laying track on the lake shore near Dresden, New York, "saw a head of an enormous serpent sticking out of the water and approaching them from the opposite shore." So terrified that at first they could not move, crew members stood in shock for some moments before scattering. The monster then turned toward the open water and departed. The *Times* reported:

> As he rapidly swam away, portions of his body, which seemed to be covered with bright silver-like scales, glistened in the sun like burnished metal. From his nostrils he would occasionally spurt a stream of water above his head to an altitude of about 20 feet. The appearance of his head was round and flat, with a hood spreading out from the lower part of it like a rubber cap often worn by swimmers with a cape to keep the rain from running down the neck. His eyes were small and piercing, his mouth broad and provided with two rows of teeth, which he displayed to his beholders. As he moved off at a rate of 10 miles an hour, portions of his body appeared above the surface of the water, while his tail, which resembled that of a fish, was thrown out of the water quite often. Its head was said to be

20 inches in diameter. A quarter-mile into the lake, the creature sank suddenly out of sight.

Except for this last detail about the sinking (as opposed to diving), little of this story resembles reports from the twentieth and twenty-first centuries. There is nothing mentioned here, for example, about the hump or humps on which many later witnesses would remark, and the "scales" are a discordant detail that would, however, show up in subsequent early reports. Seen in February 1880 by a group of Vermont men, it was said to be "covered with scales which glistened like the precious metals in the sun," according to a Vermont newspaper, *Newport Express and Standard*, February 24.

> **I**n caves along the waterside, locals claimed, "bright and hideous looking eyes" could sometimes be seen in the darkness.

Within a few days of the Dresden sighting, farmers were complaining of missing livestock. Tracks and other marks in the ground indicated that something had dragged the animals into the lake. In caves along the waterside, locals claimed, "bright and hideous looking eyes" could sometimes be seen in the darkness. A few days later a young farmer saw the serpent in a lakeside marsh, with something that looked like a turtle in its mouth. He fired on it, and the creature disappeared into the water.

Other sightings and livestock kills followed, and search parties prowled the shoreline and surrounding farms. In early August a small steamship, *W. B. Eddy*, struck the serpent and nearly overturned. The head and neck of the creature surfaced 100 feet away. On August 9 the crew of the *Molyneaux* believed it had the monster trapped in the thick weeds of Axehelve Bay. Though no one could actually see it, the decision was made to fire into the thickets and await the result. According to the *Whitehall Times* (August 13):

> At a signal, the first three shots were sent. The smoke curled up from the muzzles of the guns as the contents went crackling in among the bushes. As three more muskets sent an echoing noise among the crags and peaks of Dresden, a terrible crackling and whistling noise greeted our ears. The noise was similar to that made by a great engine when it is discharging steam as its piston enters the steam chest. First, it was a low, suppressed bass whistle; then it gradually rose in strength and tone until our ears were greeted by a most unearthly noise.... The order was given (by Captain Belden) to steam away as the head of the mammoth snake appeared through the tangled vines and brushwood. The grayish hood upon his head flopped backwards and forwards like the immense ears of an elephant when being punished by his keeper. Great ridges of silver appeared above the surface of the water, undulating and scintillating in the bright sun like the highly polished surface of a warrior's silver helmet. The fan-like tail of the horrid monster was waved in the air about six feet above the water's surface. His eyes resembled two burning coals, fairly snapping fire, as its rage increased, while the rows of long and formidable teeth, pearly white and wicked looking, sent an indescribable thrill through us, which we shall

never forget. The body seemed to be about 18 to 20 inches thick in the middle, and 36 to 40 feet long while it gradually tapered off to both extremes.... Our vessel began moving downstream. Shots were discharged at the great moving, waving mass of silver. Two streams of water arose high above the monster's head, the wind blowing the spray over us all on the boat.... Shots were sent toward the monster by members of the party, and as he lashed the water with his fishlike tail and gave great spasmodic, powerful lurches with his broad flat head, we were confident that the shots were telling.... Only about 25 feet was between us and the infuriated serpent. Hon. Charles Hughes and General Barrett discharged each a shot at it, when the head was seen to turn, the immense body began to curve.... Streams of red blood spurted from its head.... At last the excited party observed the serpent give on spasmodic twist of its immense length, forming a circle by bringing its head toward its tail; then the great serpent, which had caused so much excitement in this vicinity, disappeared beneath the red sea of blood, never to rise more by its own exertions.

Attempts to raise the body proved unsuccessful. Searchers hoped to collect a $50,000 reward from P. T. Barnum, who wired the Whitehall newspaper to express his interest in the "hide of the great Champlain serpent to add to my mammoth World's Fair Show." These supposed events, whose authenticity is not automatically to be assumed, took place in the Dresden area at the southwestern edge of the lake. When the monster returned a few years later, it had moved north to the shore near Plattsburgh, along Champlain's northwest side.

On July 31, 1883, the *Plattsburgh Morning Telegram* reported Clinton County Sheriff Nathan H. Mooney's sighting of an "enormous snake or water serpent ... 25 to 35 feet in length." Beginning in the summer of 1886, sightings were registered almost daily from just about every part of the lake. One man fishing near Plattsburgh claimed to have hooked what he first thought was an enormous fish, but when its head reared out of the water, he and three other witnesses saw it was a "horrible creature." The line snapped, and the unwanted catch disappeared underwater.

Around this time a St. Albans, Vermont, man hunting ducks along the Mississquoi River, which flows out of the lake, said he came upon an "enormous serpent coiled up on the swampy shore and asleep ... as large around as a man's thigh." When he reached back to retrieve his gun, the slight noise he made was enough to awaken the creature, which shot toward the underbrush, "making as much noise ... as a large hound would."

Sightings continued into the next year. At two o'clock one morning in May 1887, for example, a farm boy heard strange sounds and went out to the shore. A mile out in the water a big serpent was "making noises like a steamboat." In several cases witnesses claimed that the creature had acted aggressively, swimming menacingly toward them, and causing them to beat a hasty retreat. Most spectacularly, it reportedly appeared in the view of a party of Charlotte, Vermont, picnickers who were on an early July outing near the lake. Seventy-five feet long and as big around as a barrel, it bore down on the group until several members cried out and the creature turned around and swam off.

Shortly afterwards this report was published in the *Plattsburgh Morning Telegram*:

> The sea serpent ... has left the lake and is making his way overland in the direction of Lake George [near Champlain's southernmost tip]. He was seen last night about five o'clock by a farmer driving to his barn with a load of hay. Chancing to look behind him ... he saw ... not five rods behind him, gliding along like a snake with its head raised about four feet above the ground ... an immense monster anywhere from 25 to 75 feet in length, with gray and black streaks, running lengthwise of its body which was covered with scales.

In September 1889 a party of fishermen on the lake chased the creature. Fifteen feet of it was visible, and they made out an unserpent-like detail: it had, they said, "many large fins" (*Essex County Republican*, September 26). In the summer of 1899, a witness, described only as a "wealthy New Yorker," reported seeing a serpent, thirty-five feet long, with an arched back, a head "like an inverted platter" (whatever that means), and a broad flat tail raised a few feet out of the water (*Plattsburgh Republican*, August 5). This last detail indicates the animal—assuming for the moment that this report is not a hoax—was a mammal, not a reptile.

The monster's return was noted in a late-June 1946 issue of the weekly *North Countryman*, published in the village of Rouses Point, on Champlain's western shore. (It was reprinted in Keeseville's *Essex County Republican* on July 5.) Boating on the lake on the evening of June 25, Mrs. Henry G. Augins glimpsed the "serpent's" head as the beast was churning the water 200 yards from shore. The newspaper account reports, "It disappeared suddenly but was judged to be from 18 to 20 feet in length, judging by the bulge it made and the wake in the water, caused by the rate at which it was traveling."

> Thomas E. Morse reported "what appeared to be a monstrous eel with white teeth that raked rearward in the mouth."

The plesiosaur-like Champ apparently did not become a feature in reporting until the 1970s. So far as we know, not a single sighting recorded at the time of its occurrence refers to a long, thin neck attached to a bulky reptilian body. The few early reports of this sort of animal are from testimony collected years afterwards, as in an account related at least four decades later by an elderly woman. She stated that sometime in the 1920s or 1930s she and her brother had witnessed the sudden surfacing of a creature with three camel-like humps and a head like a boa constrictor's. In an instance like this, involving distant memory and nothing else, it is impossible to prove anything one way or another.

In fact, many pre–1970s reports are so devoid of essential detail that it is difficult to understand just what the witnesses thought they were seeing. In those in which something like an adequate description is offered, the animal is often said to look like a huge snake, as in the nineteenth-century accounts. Some sightings apparently are of large fish, presumably sturgeons, and in a few instances the appearances are likened to (nonprehistoric) whales and eels.

In one of the very rare twentieth-century land sightings, this one made from a passing car in the spring of 1961, Thomas E. Morse reported "what appeared to be a monstrous eel with white teeth that raked rearward in the mouth." It was resting on the shore of Champlain's North West Bay in Westport, New York.

A sighting from the summer of 1970 is of particular interest for two reasons. One, it involves not only multiple, but independent, witnesses, and two, it tells us something of how a serpent-like entity is transformed into a Nessie-style plesiosaur in the imaginations of those who think of them as similar animals. In the August 9, 1978, issue of the *Plattsburgh Valley News,* two accounts appear, written by Champ witnesses who had not spoken in the eight years since their mutual sighting. One of them, Richard Spear, tells of seeing the creature with his thirteen-year-old daughter Susanne, as the two of them sat atop a ferry heading toward the Essex, New York, shore midway down the lake.

Spear writes that the creature, ninety yards or so from shore and "dark brownish-olive" in color, was "the size and shape of a barrel in cross-section. When first seen two 'bumps' were in evidence, each rising to about three feet above the surface and four feet in length, separated by about the same distance." As he helped his daughter with binoculars, she saw its head, which she said looked like a horse's. By the time Spear turned his head back, the creature was disappearing below the surface.

A theorist with such an inclination would have no trouble equating "bumps" with "humps" and noting, correctly, that many witnesses at Ness have said the animal's head looked like a horse's. But another ferry witness, Happy Marsh, who gave her separate testimony in the same issue of the newspaper (and who said that she had seen an identical creature in 1965 or 1966), said that "it was a large snake-like creature, swimming with her head above water, held as snakes do, with coils behind. I am no judge of size, but I should say she was between 18 and 20 feet long. It was black, and swimming slowly. Her head was about three feet long, wrinkled like a raisin, with a small ridge down the back, a snake body[,] and was blackish brown."

This more detailed description hardly resolves the issue. The animal Marsh evokes has the features generally of a giant snake, eel, and zeuglodon (a prehistoric, serpent-like eel proposed as one candidate for lake monsters) without being any one of them in particular. In any case, it is not a plesiosaur, or anything like one.

Reviewing Joseph W. Zarzynski's *Champ—Beyond the Legend* (1984), Henry H. Bauer, a leading academic authority on the Ness phenomenon, complained that the author's effort to link the two has "little specific justification. The listed sightings include a goodly number of descriptions as 'snake-like,' which has never been said of Nessie; smooth skin is reported whereas Nessie's is rough, warty; eyes are featured several times, and fins and manes, which are almost totally lacking in reports from Loch Ness."

This artist's image of Nessie gives it a snakelike appearance, unlike what witnesses report.

Still, some clear and specific reports of a Ness-like animal do exist. For example, Orville Wells's sketch of the "prehistoric monster" he claims to have seen in Champlain's Treadwell Bay in 1976 could easily have been drawn from a Loch Ness experience. Several witnesses have said specifically that what they saw looked like a "dinosaur." Perhaps such cases could be explained or rationalized away if it were not for the fact of the Mansi photograph.

In early July 1977, a Connecticut couple, Anthony and Sandra Mansi (then engaged, later married), were visiting Sandra's relatives in Vermont. Just past St. Albans Bay and somewhere near the Canadian border (they would never be able to recall the exact site), they stopped so that Sandra's two small children from a previous marriage could play in Champlain's water.

After parking their car, they walked 100 to 200 feet across a field, then descended a six-foot bank to the waterline. As the children waded near the shore, Anthony went back to the car to retrieve his sunglasses and a camera.

Some moments later Sandra noticed "some sort of turbulence in the water" about 150 feet away. In short order a huge animal with a small head, long neck, and humped back rose to the surface. As it moved its head—some eight feet above the water—from right to left, Sandra thought it resembled a creature from a prehistoric age.

By this time Anthony had returned, and he, too, witnessed the thing with mounting alarm. He and Sandra called the children (who, unaware of what was happening in the water behind them, never saw the creature). "He helped me back up the bank," Sandra recalled. "At that point I went down to my knees, turned around, and saw that the creature was getting all fidgety.... I picked up the camera and took one photograph."

At that point the animal sank—it did not dive—under the water, apparently frightened by the powerboat that came into view moments later. The sighting had lasted, Sandra would estimate, between six and seven minutes.

Fearing ridicule, the Mansis did not publicize their experience. Instead they placed the photograph, which had turned out remarkably well, into a family album. In time they lost the negative. Eventually, Sandra showed the photo to friends at her place of work, and by 1980 someone who had seen it informed Zarzynski, a Wilton, New York, social studies teacher and Champ researcher. Zarzynksi approached the couple and commenced an investigation.

He showed the photograph to a number of experts, including George Zug, of the Department of Vertebrate Zoology at the Smithsonian Institution's National Museum of Natural History. Zug said it bore no resemblance to any known animal in the lake or anywhere else. Roy Mackal, biologist and vice president of the International Society of Cryptozoology (ISC), also examined it. Soon afterwards, B. Roy Frieden, of the University of Arizona's Optical Sciences Center, conducted an extensive analysis.

Frieden determined that the photograph was not a montage. In other words, it had not been doctored by someone's posting the image of Champ over a photograph of the lake. The wave pattern around the object purporting to be Champ suggested vertical rather than horizontal disturbance, indicating that the object had come up from under the surface instead of moving along the surface, as would be the case if it were an artificial device being pulled by a rope.

Frieden could not determine its size because the photograph provided no clear points of reference. It did not, for example, show precisely where the shoreline began, which would have helped investigators determine the dimensions of the object and its distance from the observers. But University of British Columbia oceanographer Paul LeBlond found another method of estimating at least an approximate size: by measuring the length of the waves around the object. Using a formula that relates the speed of the wind and the distance of the open water over which the wind blows to wave properties, LeBlond estimated the waves to be between sixteen and thirty-nine feet in length. When he compared the "unknown object" with the waves in its vicinity, he found that it occupied one and a half to two wavelengths. Therefore, he concluded, the part of the object that was above water could not be less than twenty-four feet or more than seventy-eight feet. In short, the object was enormous.

If this was a hoax, it is truly an extraordinary one, and also an enormously expensive one. But if that were the case, why did Sandra Mansi wait for more than three years before allowing it to become public? Even more to the point, why did she take only *one* photograph?

In the intervening decades no evidence of a hoax has emerged. Which is not say, of course, that none could ever emerge; it's just that this does not seem, on the evidence available currently, to be the most compelling explanation. The other modestly plausible prosaic solution holds that the "creature" is a rotting log or tree, which the object in the photograph in no way resembles.

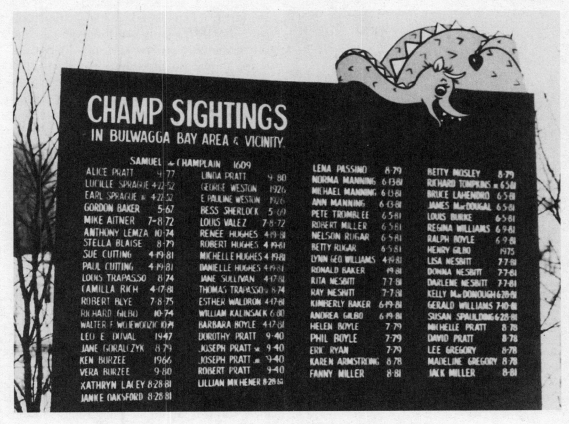

This sign at Port Henry, New York, records Champ sightings around Bulwagga Bay.

The Champ mystery continues, albeit with intriguing new evidence. In June 2003 a crew from Fauna Communications Research, under the direction of the well-regarded bioacoustic specialist Elizabeth von Muggenthaler, with financing by the Discovery Channel, conducted sonar investigations at the lake's Button Bay. Sonar detected the presence of an animal whose soundings were ten times stronger than anything that a known creature in the lake could have emitted; in fact, they were like those associated with a beluga whale or a dolphin, neither of which is a Champlain resident. The readings registered on three instruments over three days. Some lasted as long as ten minutes, and on one occasion the target seemed only thirty feet from the boat.

Phantoms in Scandinavian lakes

Outside North America and the British Isles, most of the investigation has occurred at Scandinavian lakes. One of particular fascination is Storsjön, a deep mountain lake in central Sweden.

When it comes to monster hunts, even royalty gets in on the game, at times. King Oscar II of Norway contributed his efforts in 1894 to verify reports of a strange lake creature in Storsjön.

In 1898, Peter Olsson, a high school zoology teacher with a particular interest in marine biology, launched an investigation of reports of strange animals in Storsjön. He collected accounts dating back as early as 1820, but a particularly impressive one was much more recent. One morning in October 1893 two young women, eighteen and twenty-one years old and regarded as truthful, had gone to the shore to wash clothes when they saw an object moving rapidly toward them from out in the lake. They watched it over the next hour and a half as it rose and fell in the water.

They said the creature had shiny gray skin and black spots. Its fins were smaller near the shoulders than at its rear. Its head—large, round, three feet long and three feet wide—housed big eyes and what looked like short, clipped ears. Its mouth was wide and open, with a tongue that flicked out at regular intervals. Its neck was eight or nine feet long, the body to which it was attached something like fourteen feet long.

In 1894 a wealthy woman provided money to fund a company to capture the creature. Even King Oscar II is said to have contributed to the effort, which came to naught. A Norwegian whaler spent a year on the lake without detecting anything, and soon the company went bankrupt.

Local people, however, sighted the creature on occasion; the year 1898 was particularly rich in reports. Olsson eventually concluded that the animal was a giant, long-neck seal, an explanation for sea serpents favored by the pioneering Dutch zoologist/cryptozoologist A. C. Oudemans, in an influential 1892 book on the subject.

That was not the last of Lake Storsjön's curious inhabitants. It or its relatives still pass before astonished viewers every once in a while. While some sightings appear genuinely mysterious, others—of an animal, unlike most lake monsters, with large ears—may be generated by a swimming moose; the area hosts an abundant local moose population, according to cryptozoologist Lars Thomas.

In recent decades most attention has been focused on a Norwegian lake, Seljörd, where "sea horses" have been written about since at least 1750. In that year a man named Gunleik Verpe had his boat attacked as he was rowing across the water. Verpe survived to tell others of his frightening encounter with what he called a "huge sea-serpent." Of the creature, local chronicler Hans Jacob Wille wrote in 1786, "It is very peculiar and the most poisonous of all. It moves on the surface like an eel, and some years ago it bit a man in the big toe." As she washed laundry on the shore one day in 1880, Gunhild Bjorge was shocked to see a repulsive-looking serpent crawl out of the water toward her. She struck it with a stick and drove it way. The creature is usually described as around thirty feet long with a head variously characterized as resembling a horse's or a crocodile's.

Globe-hopping British cryptozoologist Adam Davies remarks:

There are, in my opinion, three massive arguments against it. First, although the lake is not exactly crowded, there has been a sustainable population of towns around Lake Seljörd for centuries. I find it difficult to believe that there could have been no tangible proof of its existence in all that time, no matter how elusive the creature. Second, how could a lake of this size and depth—it is roughly fifteen kilometers [9.3 miles] long and nearly two kilometers [1.25 mile] with a maximum depth of 150 meters [490 feet]—contain such a creature? The water had always been considered to have a low nutritional value. Small-scale fishing does take place on the lake, but how could the lake possibly support a population of large beasts? Third, and *most* pertinently, there was never a lake at all until about ten thousand years ago, when the land was completely covered with ice.

But this would not be the end of the story, for either the lake monsters (sometimes collectively nicknamed "Selma") or Davies himself. While on expedition at Seljörd in August 1999, Davies saw the creature with his own eyes. It rose out of the water fifteen yards from the boat carrying him and fellow researchers, then proceeded toward the lake's deepest area. "It was black," Davies would write, "and I could clearly see three humps as it moved in an undulating manner." He never saw its head.

All the while a video camera held by another investigator, Andrew Sanderson, was capturing the sight. (Unfortunately, Sanderson was holding the camera while standing up in an unsteady boat; nonetheless, stills of the shaky video images show three mysterious, widely separated moving humps in the water.) Sound recordings were also made. According to Davies, Auld von Soldal of Bergen's Marine Research Institute, working with colleagues, analyzed the sound tapes, concluding, "It astounds me to say that this is a unique species."

Much of the history of cryptozoology, alas, is a function of Davies's paradox: logical to irrefutable *a priori* reason to dismiss a cryptid's existence, countered by compellingly puzzling sighting reports and a nagging quantity of instrumented evidence sufficient to keep the question open.

Other lakes where lake monsters are said to appear include Börringe, Kranke, Vomb, Sövde, and Vättern.

Continuing tradition, persistent mystery

Though the number of native monster-haunted lakes is much smaller than it used to be, traditions and sightings persist. Some—such as the giant serpent seen for decades at Pickerel Lake in northeastern South Dakota—have received no publicity at all (witnesses include, among others, persons to whom the author is related by family and a former marriage). They remain known only to those who live near, or have occasion to boat on, a body of water and to encounter its unexpected inhabitant.

It is hard to believe that all eyewitnesses are mistaken, especially since those who make the reports are usually manifestly sincere and some sightings occur at close range and in good viewing conditions, and that all of their testimony arises from ulterior motives. It will not do, as one prominent debunker notoriously does, to lay all reports to misperceptions of logs and otters. Nor will it do to rush to the opposite sorts of conclusions, especially in the telling absence of bodies. In rare instances photographic evidence and sonar data apparently back up the anecdotes, but without resolving the conflicts and the confusion.

If at least a few lakes harbor real, large, and so far uncatalogued animals—mammal, reptile, amphibian, or fish—one presumes they will be found, eventually. Perhaps they would have been found before now were it not for the ridicule that surrounds the subject and discourages most qualified inquirers. In other words, the fact that no lake monster has yet been caught may not necessarily tell us that no lake monster exists to be caught. It may mean only that the proper resources have not been brought to bear, including funding for the sophisticated, expensive equipment needed to document or even capture such creatures.

Or it may not. It may be that some fantastic things are neither wholly real nor wholly imaginary. They're here, sometimes, to be experienced or to hint at an existence which remains forever, frustratingly elusive—residing in some liminal zone where the vividly experienced never transcends perception, memory, and testimony.

Further Reading:

Bauer, Henry H. *The Enigma of Loch Ness: Making Sense of a Mystery*. Urbana: University of Illinois Press, 1986.

———. Review of Binns's *The Loch Ness Mystery Solved*. Blacksburg, VA: The Author, n.d.

———. "The Case for the Loch Ness 'Monster': The Scientific Evidence." *Journal of Scientific Exploration* 16,2 (2002): 225–246.

———. "Common Knowledge about the Loch Ness Monster: Television, Videos, and Films." *Journal of Scientific Exploration* 16,3 (2002): 455–477.

Binns, Ronald. *The Loch Ness Mystery Solved*. Buffalo, NY: Prometheus Books, 1984.

Bord, Janet, and Colin Bord. *Alien Animals*. Harrisburg, PA: Stackpole Books, 1981.

Brown, Charles E. *Sea Serpents: Wisconsin Occurrences of These Weird Water Monsters in the Four Lakes, Rock, Red Cedar, Koshkonong, Geneva, Elkhart, Michigan and Other Lakes*. Madison: Wisconsin Folklore Society, 1942.

Campbell, John L., and Trevor H. Hall. *Strange Things: The Story of Fr Allan McDonald, Ada Goodrich Freer, and the Society for Psychical Research's Enquiry into Highland Second Sight*. London: Routledge and Kegan Paul, 1968.

Coleman, Loren, and Patrick Huyghe. *The Field Guide to Lake Monsters, Sea Serpents, and Other Mystery Denizens of the Deep*. New York: Jeremy P. Tarcher/Penguin, 2003.

Costello, Peter. *In Search of Lake Monsters*. New York: Coward, McCann and Geoghegan, 1974.

Dash, Mike. "Status Report: Lake Monsters." *Fortean Times* 102 (1997): 28–31.

Davies, Adam. *Extreme Expeditions: Travel Adventures Stalking the World's Mystery Animals*. San Antonio and New York: Anomalist Books, 2008.

Dinsdale, Tim. *Loch Ness Monster*. Boston: Routledge and Kegan Paul, 1961. Fourth edition, 1982.

Gould, Rupert T. *The Loch Ness Monster and Others*. London: Geoffrey Bles, 1934.

Haas, Joseph S., Jr. "Lake Monsters." *Pursuit* 12,2 (Spring 1979): 56–57.

Heuvelmans, Bernard. *In the Wake of the Sea-Serpents*. New York: Hill and Wang, 1968.

Holiday, F. W. *The Dragon and the Disc: An Investigation into the Totally Fantastic*. New York: W. W. Norton and Company, 1973.

———. "Water Monsters: The Land Sighting Paradox." *INFO Journal* 4,4 (March 1976): 2–4.

Hufford, David J. "Traditions of Disbelief." *New York Folklore Quarterly* 8,3–4 (Winter 1982): 47–55.

Mackal, Roy P. *The Monsters of Loch Ness*. Chicago: Swallow Press, 1976.

———. *Searching for Hidden Animals*. Garden City, NY: Doubleday and Company, 1980.

Magin, Ulrich. *Investigating the Impossible: Sea-Serpents in the Air, Volcanoes that Aren't, and Other Out-of-Place Mysteries*. San Antonio and New York: Anomalist Books, 2011.

———. "A Brief Survey of Lake Monsters of Continental Europe." *Fortean Times* 46 (1986): 52–59.

Mangiacopra, Gary S. "Water Monsters of the Midwestern Lakes." *Pursuit* 12,2 (spring 1979): 50–56.

Robertson, R. Macdonald. Jeremy Bruce-Watt, ed. *Selected Highland Folk Tales*. North Pomfret, VT: David and Charles, 1977.

Shuker, Karl. *Alien Zoo*. Bideford, North Devonshire, England: CFZ Press, 2010.

Thomas, Lars. *Weird Waters: The Lake and Sea Monsters of Scandinavia and the Baltic States*. Bideford, North Devonshire, England: CFZ Press, 2011.

Witchell, Nicholas. *The Loch Ness Story*. Baltimore: Penguin Books, 1975.

Zarzynski, Joseph. *Champ—Beyond the Legend*. Port Henry: Bannister Publications, 1984.

Lake Worth Monster

Though little known, the monster scare that rocked Lake Worth, on the northwest edge of Fort Worth, Texas, in the summer of 1969 is among the most intriguingly attested to in the tangled history of hairy-biped reports.

Early on the morning of July 10, John Reichart, his wife, and two other couples showed up at a Fort Worth police station. They were so manifestly terrified that, as improbable as their story sounded, the officers had no trouble believing the six had seen something truly out of the ordinary. As the witnesses' story went, they had been parked along Lake Worth around midnight when a huge creature leaped out of a tree and landed on the Reicharts's car. It was, they said, covered with both scales and fur and looked like a cross between a man and a goat.

Four police units rushed to the scene but found nothing. They were impressed, however, by the eighteen-inch scratch running along the side of the witnesses' car. Swearing that it had not been there before, the Reicharts were sure it was a mark from the monster's claws.

In the previous two months other reports of a monster had come to police attention but were attributed to pranks. The officers assumed that the Reicharts and their friends had been similarly victimized, but the frightening, aggressive nature of this latest incident made them take the matter more seriously than heretofore.

Almost exactly twenty-four hours after this encounter, Jack Harris, driving on the only road going into the Lake Worth Nature Center, allegedly spotted the creature crossing in front of him. It ran up and down a bluff and soon was noticed by thirty to forty people who had come to the area hoping to see it, after the *Fort Worth Star Telegram* headlined a story titled "Fish Man-goat Terrifies Couple Parked at Lake Worth." Within a short time officers from the sheriff's department were on the scene as well, observing the incredible sight. But when it appeared that some of the onlookers were going to approach it, the creature fired a spare tire, complete with rim, and the witnesses retreated to their cars. It then escaped into the underbrush.

The witnesses testified that it was seven feet tall, with an estimated weight of 300 pounds. It walked on two feet and had whitish gray hair. The creature had a "pitiful cry—like something was hurting him," Harris told reporter Jim Marrs. "But it sure didn't sound human."

In the weeks ahead parties of searchers, many carrying guns, made nighttime forays into the woods and fields along the lake. Most thought it resembled a "big white ape." It left tracks, unfortunately not preserved, that reportedly were sixteen inches long and eight inches wide at the toes. On one occasion searchers fired on it and followed a trail of blood and tracks to the edge of the water. Three men claimed that one night the creature leaped on their car and got off only after the vehicle collided with a tree. Another three individuals spent a week tracking it without ever seeing it, though they heard its cry and smelled the foul odor associated with it. They also came upon dead sheep with broken necks—victims, they believed, of the creature. Allen Plaster, owner of a dress shop, took a fuzzy black and white photograph said to show the creature at close range. Anomalists and cryptozoologists view it with considerable suspicion.

"**I** remember being confused and shaken, but I immediately pushed Gary to get his attention so that he could see the strange, hairy creature as well."

Sporadic sightings would be logged for years afterwards, but the last report of the 1969 scare is attributed to Charles Buchanan. Buchanan said he had been dozing inside his sleeping bag in the back of his pickup when suddenly something lifted him up. It was the monster. Buchanan grabbed a bag with chicken in it; the creature stuffed it into its mouth, then plunged into the lake and swam to Greer Island. This event allegedly occurred on November 7.

Helmuth Naumer, a spokesman for the Fort Worth Museum of Science and Industry, and Park Ranger Harroll Rogers theorized that the creature was a bobcat—a preposterous explanation by any standard. Less silly though not without its own problems was a rumor, never confirmed, that police caught pranksters with a costume. If one or more pranksters were indeed responsible they must have been, considering how many searchers were armed and trigger-happy, either remarkably brave or incredibly stupid.

✳

Lake Worth monster, or something like it

Unpublished till now, the following reports come from two brothers known to the author. Fred and Gary Davis are natives of Dallas, Fort Worth's sister city, and still live in the area. Fred (who is a friend of the author) is a senior employee of a Dallas-based corporation, and Gary is a retired U.S. Army captain. Fred Davis wrote the first account, recounting an incident from their pre-teen years in early 1966, with his brother's approval of the text:

The Southeast side of Dallas (Piedmont area) to this day has the thickest forest and vegetation in and around Dallas County. We lived on Modesto Drive which took a dead end into the entrance to the forest. We would often have to cut our way through the brush and weeds to make our way.

On one particularly cold late afternoon … we noticed a stench in the air, which resembled [that of] a dead animal. We stopped and looked around and did not see anything of particular interest up until I looked up into a huge sycamore tree about 20 feet away and then saw what can only be described as a large beast with all four limbs to the tree about 15 feet up.

I remember being confused and shaken, but I immediately pushed Gary to get his attention so that he could see the strange, hairy creature as well. We then looked up in the tree simultaneously, and when we did so, the "monster" moved its head toward us so that it could get a better view of us. Once this thing confirmed to us that it was actually a live, breathing creature, we took off running as fast as we possibly could.

The creature, as we both recall, looked to be about 7–8 feet tall based on how much of the tree trunk he was covering. It had long (3–4-inch) strands of thick, light brown to dirty blond hair covering its entire body. Its hands and feet were huge. Its eyes (I will never forget) were piercing and seemed hypnotic. The facial features were prominent and not covered entirely with hair, almost humanlike, and its expression seemed inquisitive....

We *never* said a word of this event to *anyone* ever until we were both sitting on my back patio one evening in 1998 having a beer or two. For whatever reason, we began talking about this event. Our stories were identical.

Gary Davis had a second sighting while in Fred's company, though Fred saw nothing:

I was hiking in the same woods in Southeast Dallas with two of my friends and Fred during the summer of 1966. [We were] walking along a narrow path in single file, [and] I was the last person in line. As we all passed a small, grassy clearing and entered the woods again, I turned to look behind me and saw the beast again on the edge of the forest [from which] we all had first entered the clearing. It was about 30 yards away. It looked at us and then the creature just went into the woods in the opposite direction that we were all traveling.

I tried to get everyone's attention, but by the time everyone stopped, nothing was there. It was gorilla-like except for the fact that it had long brown hair and it stood erect on two long legs like a man.

Further Reading:

Chorvinsky, Mark. "Our Strange World: The Lake Worth Monster." *Fate* 45,10 (October 1992): 31–35.

Clarke, Sallie Ann. *The Lake Worth Monster of Greer Island, Ft. Worth, Texas.* Fort Worth, TX: The Author, 1969.

Coleman, Loren, and Patrick Huyghe. *The Field Guide to Bigfoot, Yeti, and Other Mystery Primates Worldwide.* New York: Avon Books, 1999.

Davis, Fred, and Gary Davis. Communications to author, September 2011.

Green, John. *Sasquatch: The Apes among Us.* Seattle, WA: Hancock House, 1978.

Lindorms

In the mid-eighteenth century, Erik Pontopiddan, the bishop of Bergen, Norway, and author of a major work on north-country natural history, remarked on a belief held by residents of the Nordic coast. Sea serpents, he wrote, "are not generated in the sea, but *on land*, and when they are grown so big that they cannot move about on the rocks, they then go into the sea and afterwards attain their full growth." Many farmers, he went on, had seen land snakes of "several fathoms length." They called these "the Lindormen, or great snake." Similar creatures also lived in the freshwater lakes of Scandinavia, according to popular lore.

Such creatures, or at any rate beliefs in such creatures, persisted into the nineteenth century and beyond. They coexisted with traditions of the dragon, a staple of Scandinavian (and other) folklore, ordinarily thought to be a supernatural creature in the fashion of ghosts and trolls. Sweden's lindorms, on the other hand, appeared to belong to this world, as real as other fauna, whatever scientists and academics, who denied their existence, argued to the contrary. Consequently, lindorms figured not only in legends but also in a body of firsthand reports.

By 1885 the pioneering Swedish folklorist Gunnar Olof Hyltén-Cavallius (1818–1889), encouraged by several prominent countrymen who had come to a similar conclusion, was persuaded from his field work that the lindorm was an actual, if so far uncatalogued, animal. That year—a second, expanded edition followed in 1886—he published a book titled (in English translation) *On the Dragon, Also Called the Lindorm,* which carried forty-eight verbatim accounts, half of them involving multiple witnesses. Hyltén-Cavallius offered this summary:

> In Värend [in Småland in the south]—and probably in other parts of Sweden as well—a species of giant snakes, called dragons or lindorms, continues to exist. Usually the lindorm is about 10 feet long but specimens of 18 or 20 feet have been observed. His body is as thick as a man's thigh; his color is black with a yellow-flamed belly. Old specimens wear on their necks an integument of long hair or scales, frequently likened to a horse's mane. He has a flat, round or squared head, a divided tongue, and a mouth full of white, shining teeth. His eyes are large and saucer-shaped with a frightfully wild and sparkling stare. His tail is short and stubby and the general shape of the creature is heavy and unwieldy.

This runestone from eleventh-century Sweden depicts a lindorm.

Hyltén-Cavallius's reports indicated that the lindorm (sometimes spelled lindwurm) was powerful and ill-tempered. "When alarmed," he wrote, "he gives off a loud hissing sound and contracts his body until it lies in billows; then he raises himself on his tail four or six feet up and pounces upon his prey." It was most likely to be encountered in wild, unpopulated areas such as marshes, swamps, caves, and lakes. Such encounters usually traumatized witnesses, often rendering them physically ill or afflicting them with nightmares for years afterwards. Lindorms, which could be slain only with great difficulty, gave off an appalling stench in death.

Convinced that these were reports of real animals—the witnesses included a member of the Swedish parliament and other presumably reliable individuals—Hyltén-Cavallius distributed a poster offering a reward for a lindorm's remains. From his perspective this was a perfectly reasonable approach with a decent chance of success; after all, a dozen of his reports concerned the killings of such creatures. But no takers stepped forward. For his efforts, however, the previously respectable scholar, whose contributions to the study of his country's folk traditions are honored even today, found himself the object of ridicule from scientists. Beneath the sarcastic rhetoric was an undeniable truth: no specimens had ever been produced—notwithstanding claims by a few witnesses that they had killed lindorms in the course of violent confrontations—nor were there any photographs.

Still, in the reports lindorms acted more like reptiles—large snakes specifically—than like supernatural creatures. Lindorms were also known as "lime tree serpents" because they were said to lay their eggs under lime-tree bark. As modern chronicler Richard Svensson remarks:

A typical lindorm tale is similar to an account of encountering a large snake in the jungle. Someone is out walking, stumbles on the big reptile and flees. Sometimes there is a violent confrontation and the monster is overcome. That's it. There's no moral to the story, no allegory or witty twist. It would appear that what you're reading (or hearing) is a retelling of an actual event. The lindorm cannot fly or breathe fire and doesn't have any magical powers. It's simply a very big, nasty reptile.

Lindorms—references to which have been traced to the ninth century—did have the unusual habit of vomiting a vile venom. The creatures were often observed near lakes and ponds in the spruce-tree forests of southern Sweden. Their eyes were striking. "The eyes were shiny, like those of the asp, about the size of hazelnuts," witness Johan Sedig recalled of his sighting of a twelve-foot lindorm on an island on Lake Läen. "Its stare was sharp and terrible."

If lindorms by that name have passed into folk history, it is not quite accurate to refer to sightings of them in the past tense. In the 1980s, folklorist Jan-öjvind Svahn collected testimony from more than twenty people who claimed they had seen comparable creatures. They did not refer to them as lindorms, however, even though the description was largely the same. In each case the creature, observed swimming in a body of water, was referred to in more modern terminology as a lake monster.

To Michel Meurger, a scholar with a fiercely skeptical reading of the lake-monster tradition, the nineteenth-century lindorm reports were part of the "process of the naturalization of dragons," blending "archaic and modern elements. The traditional attributes of the monster are preserved, but the creature is now conceived more as a snake than as supernatural creature." This would be a more plausible interpretation if not for the firsthand accounts, which are specific and unambiguous; why not condemn the reporters as liars and be done with it? Meurger is reduced to unpersuasively broad speculation: Witnesses have been "projecting traditional fabulous creatures onto local animals [such as grass snakes] perceived as monsters under specific conditions."

If such is the case—which frankly seems something of a stretch—we can only conclude that Swedes harbored prodigiously gifted imaginations. At the same time Hyltén-Cavillius was certainly wrong in believing the lindorms to have been animals in the zoological sense. As with other claims in which fabulous, folkloric elements converge confusingly into vivid experience, no explanation that convincingly addresses all aspects exists, or even seems possible.

Further Reading:

Meurger, Michel. "In Jormungandra's Coils: A Culture Anthropology of the Norse Sea-Serpent." *Fortean Times* 51 (Winter 1988/1989): 63–68.

Meurger, Michel, with Claude Gagnon. *Lake Monster Traditions: A Cross-Cultural Analysis*. London: Fortean Tomes, 1988.

Rosén, Sven. "The Dragons of Sweden." *Fate* 35,4 (April 1982): 36–45.

Svensson, Richard. "The Serpents of Sweden." *Fortean Times* 264 (2010): 32–37.

Living Dinosaurs

Do dinosaurs still exist? The question sounds absurd. After all, conventional wisdom—not to mention the fossil evidence—holds that these giant reptiles lapsed into extinction some sixty-five million years ago. Still, occasional reports from remote regions of the earth have kept the issue alive, if only to readers of tabloid newspapers and to the handful of scientists, adventurers, nature writers, anomalists, and young-earth creationists who have tried to make sense of the accounts and, where possible, to investigate them.

Much of the investigation has centered on a legendary creature generally referred to as mokele-mbembe and described as a sauropod-like reptile, with a long neck, small head, bulky body, and tail. The first printed mention of the huge, plate-shaped tracks associated with the beast appears in a 1776 history of French missionaries in west-central Africa. In 1910 newspapers around the world mentioned "native stories of a huge monster, half elephant, half dragon, dwelling in the depths of the great swamps … some kind of dinosaur seemingly akin to the brontosaurs." Over many decades, missionaries, colonial authorities, hunters, explorers, and natives provided strikingly consistent descriptions of such animals and their spoor. A 1920 issue of *Literary Digest* quotes big-game hunter Walter Winans:

> The late [animal collector] Carl Hagenbeck told me before the war that two of his travelers, on different expeditions and in different years, had seen the brontosaurus in swarms in central Africa. I do not think it is impossible that some of the prehistoric animals have survived, and when several explorers have seen glimpses of what they think must be such animals they are most probably right.... These men are always on the lookout for new species and know all the animals by sight.

Sighting reports in recent decades have been confined largely to the swampy, remote Likouala region of the Republic of the Congo.

In 1980 and 1981 University of Chicago biologist Roy P. Mackal led two expeditions to the area, the first in the company of herpetologist James H. Powell, Jr., who had heard mokele-mbembe stories while doing crocodile research in west-central Africa. Neither expedition produced a sighting, though Mackal and his companions interviewed a number of native witnesses. Greatly feared, the creatures were said to live in the swamps and rivers. A band of pygmies supposedly killed one at Lake Tele around 1959.

Though the Mackal expeditions were unable to reach the nearly inaccessible Tele, a rival group, headed by the late American engineer Herman Regusters, successfully made the journey in late 1981. Over a period of two to three weeks, he and his wife, Kia Van Dusen, would claim, large, long-necked animals came into view on several occasions, both in the water and in the swampy areas around the lake. (According to one allegation, some of the native guides who had accompanied the expedition later denied to Dutch biologist and mokele-mbembe seeker Ronald Botterweg that they had witnessed anything out of the ordinary.) Congolese biologist Marcellin Agagna, who had participated in Mackal's second expedition, arrived there in the spring of 1982 (or 1983; sources vary) and reported a single sighting. Both Regusters and Agagna alleged that camera problems frustrated their attempts to obtain photographic evidence of these fantastic sights. Other expeditions consisting of a variety of personnel from several nations have been mounted, with inconclusive results, into the current century.

Walter Winans (1852–1920), an American big-game hunter, artist, and horse-breeder, reported in *Literary Digest* that some of his friends had encountered dinosaur-like creatures in Africa. Winans did not discount the possibility that their tales could be true.

If—that's a big if, needless to say—there is such a thing as a living dinosaur, mokele-mbembe is surely it. Other proposed candidates cannot marshal a comparably interesting case. Nonetheless, it is significant that no fossils of dinosaurs that may have survived extinction and lived on for tens of millions of more years have ever been uncovered. The reality of changing environmental and geological conditions (even in central Africa) undercuts the sometimes-argued notion that dinosaurs could have survived in a climate and ecology not so stable as alleged. The African rainforests in which mokele-mbembe and possibly other relic creatures are reported to dwell are no more than a few thousand years old. Moreover, absent flesh, skin, or bones, mokele-mbembe's existence remains unproven—an intriguing long-shot possibility at best, an absurdly inflated legend at worst. As is so often the case with extraordinary claims, however, seemingly puzzling testimony exists alongside a curious vacuum of physical evidence.

Enigma of the *sirrush*

Around 600 B.C.E., during the reign of King Nebuchadnezzar, a Babylonian artist fashioned bas reliefs on bricks used in the enormous archway of the Ishtar

Gate and the high walls of the approach road. The bas reliefs consist of three animals, and each row of bricks displays numerous images of one of them. The rows alternate, some showing lions, others *rimis* (as the Babylonians called them), and still others *sirrushes* (dragons).

Though extinct in Mesopotamia, the *rimi* was a real animal which was either remembered or known through the specimens brought over from Eurasia, where these wild oxen (called *urus* or *aurochs*) lived on until 1627. The dragon, of course, was a purely imaginary beast. Or was it?

Science writer Willy Ley described the *sirrush*, which he considered a "zoological puzzle of fantastic dimensions," as having, "a slender body covered with scales, a long slender scaly tail, and a long slim scaly neck bearing a serpent's head. Although the mouth is closed, a long forked tongue protrudes. There are flaps of skin attached to the back of the head, which is adorned (and armed) with a straight horn."

The *Apocrypha*'s Book of Bel and the Dragon relates a curious story: that in the temple of Bel, Lord of the World, Nebuchadnezzar's favored god, the priests kept a "great dragon or serpent, which they of Babylonia worshipped." The king challenged the Hebrew prophet Daniel, who had been sneering about nonliving gods of brass, to dispute this god, who "liveth, and eateth and drinketh; you canst not say that he is no living god; therefore worship him." To remove himself from this quandary, Daniel poisoned the animal.

The fortieth chapter of Job in the Old Testament, composed somewhere between the seventh and second centuries B.C.E., may refer to the *sirrush* by another name:

> Behold now Behemoth … he eateth grass as an ox. Lo now his strength is in his loins, and his force is in the navel of his belly. He moveth his tail like a cedar: the sinews of his stones are wrapped together. His bones are as strong pieces of brass, his limbs are like bars of iron.… He lieth under the shady trees, in the cover of the reed, and fens. The shady trees cover him with their shadow; the willows of the brook encompass him about.… His nose pierceth through snares.

The behemoth's identity has long puzzled biblical scholars, who have not doubted that Job was writing of a real animal, even if no satisfactory candidate among known animals seems to exist. Mackal offers this interpretation: "The behemoth's tail is compared to a cedar, which suggests a sauropod. This identification is reinforced by other factors. Not only the behemoth's physical nature, but also its habits and food preferences are compatible with a sauropod's. Both live in swampy areas with trees, reeds and fins (a jungle swamp)."

The discoverer of the Ishtar Gate, German archaeologist Robert Koldeway, gave serious thought to the possibility that the *sirrush* may have been an actual animal. Unlike other fantastic beasts in Babylonian art, he noted, images of the *sirrush* remained unchanged over centuries. What struck him about these depictions was the "uniformity of [the *sirrush*'s] physiological conceptions."

The ancient Mesopotamians left behind works of art depicting exotic creatures such as the *rimi* and this tile dragon from the Ishtar Gate in Babylon.

The *sirrush*, he said, was more like a saurian than any other animal. Such creatures did not coexist with human beings, he wrote, and the Babylonians, who were not paleontologists, could not have reconstructed a saurian from fossil remains; yet the Old Testament states explicitly that the *sirrush* was real. All this considered, he was reduced to speculating that the Babylonian priests kept "some reptile" in a dark temple and led the unsuspecting to believe it was a living *sirrush*.

The Babylonians are known to have penetrated equatorial Africa, home of the mokele-mbembe, and Ley, Bernard Heuvelmans, and Mackal have all suggested that in the course of their travels they heard of such creatures, perhaps sighted them, or even brought a specimen home with them. This is not an unreasonable hypothesis, at least if we assume that mokele-mbembe exists.

On the other hand, some modern scholars, for example Adrienne Mayor, dispute the assumption that the ancients did not know of, or had no interest in, prehistoric animals. Mayor observes, "Reliable ancient sources relate that, when fossils were discovered in antiquity, they were transported with great care, identified, preserved, and sometimes traded. Reconstructed models or the remains of 'unknown' species were displayed in Greece and Rome." She adds that ancient writings seem to indicate that "some representations and descriptions of crypto-

"Momo" comes from a fusion of Missouri—Mo.—and the first two letters of monster. For a few days in the summer of 1972, it was the major story of the "silly season," the subject of tongue-in-cheek coverage in newspapers all over America.

The Momo scare was played out in and around Louisiana, a small town (pop. 4,600) in northeastern Missouri. In July 1971, two picnickers in a wooded area north of town reportedly spotted a "half-ape and half-man" with a hideous stench. Stepping out of a thicket, it walked toward them, making a "little gurgling sound," and they locked themselves inside their car. The creature ate an abandoned peanut butter sandwich and ambled back into the woods. The women reported the incident to the Missouri State Patrol but did not come forward publicly until a year later, and then only after numerous others had reported a similar sight.

The monster got its name after a series of sightings that began on the afternoon of July 11, 1972, when three children saw a creature, "six or seven feet tall, black and hairy," standing next to a tree. It was flecked with blood, apparently from the dead dog it carried under its arm. That same afternoon a neighbor heard strange growling sounds, and a farmer found that a newly acquired dog had disappeared.

Three evenings later, as the children's father, Edgar Harrison, stood talking with some friends outside the Harrison home, they saw a "fireball" come over near Marzolf Hill and apparently alight behind an abandoned schoolhouse across the street.

animals in antiquity were based on reconstructions from skeletons of living or extinct animals." If such was the case with the *sirrush*, however, the fossilized remains would have had to be brought in from elsewhere. Dinosaur fossils did not exist in Mesopotamia.

Other African dinosaurs

While at Lake Tele, Herman Regusters would report, he and his associates heard a peculiar story. Some months earlier, in February 1981, according to local people, the bodies of three adult male elephants had been found floating in the water. The cause of death seemed to be two large puncture marks in the abdomen of each. These were not bullet holes, and the elephants still had their tusks, indicating that poachers had not killed them. The natives attributed the deaths to a mysterious horned creature that lived in the nearby forests.

Five minutes later another followed suit. Not long afterwards, a loud growl emanated from the hilltop and seemed to come down and toward the listeners, though its source was not visible to them. The police investigated but found nothing.

An hour or two later, as they poked around the hilltop in the darkness, Harrison and others found an old building suffused with a pungent, unpleasant odor of the kind that was associated with Momo's appearances. On several occasions witnesses claimed to have seen a small glowing light that exploded and left the stench in its wake.

The scare continued for two more weeks, during which others reported seeing a hairy biped with both ape and human features. Some claimed to have heard disembodied voices. One said, "You boys stay out of these woods," and another asked for a cup of coffee. Footprints allegedly made by the creature were found on several occasions, but the only one to undergo scientific analysis was dismissed as a hoax by Lawrence Curtis, director of the Oklahoma City Zoo. A number of Louisiana residents reported fireballs and other unusual aerial objects. One, described as a UFO with lighted windows, allegedly landed for five hours on a hilltop. One family claimed to have seen a "perfect gold cross on the moon.... The road was lit up as bright as day from the cross."

Further Reading:

Coleman, Loren. *Mysterious America: The Revised Edition*. New York: ParaView Press, 2001.

Crowe, Richard. "Missouri Monster." *Fate* 25,12 (December 1972): 58–66.

This creature is called *emela ntouka* ("killer of elephants"). Reports consistently describe it as the size of an elephant, or larger, with heavy legs that support the body from beneath (as opposed to the side, as in crocodiles) and a long, thick tail. Its face is said to be generally rhinoceros-like, with a single horn that protrudes from the front of the head. It is semi-aquatic in habit, eats foliage, and kills elephants and buffaloes with its great horn. Possibly, it is what a friend of Col. H. F. Fenn allegedly saw in Lake Edward, on the border between what is now the Democratic Republic of Congo and Uganda, the *irizima* ("the thing that may not be spoken of"), described in a 1927 article in *Chambers's Journal* as "like a gigantic hippopotamus with the horns of a rhinoceros upon its head."

In *A Living Dinosaur?* (1987), Mackal suggests that such animals, if they exist, are likely to be a kind of prehistoric rhinoceros or a horned dinosaur of the triceratops variety. If the former, it is a mammal.

A creature sighted in the area of what is now Uganda and the Democratic Republic of Congo resembled a huge hippopotamus with rhinoceros-like horns. Could it have been a survivor of the Eocene called Uintatherium?

Mackal also has collected a handful of vague reports of *mbielu mbielu mbielu*, "the animal with planks growing out of its back," said to resemble a stegosaur. More compelling were sightings of *nguma monene*, an enormous serpent-like reptile with a serrated ridge along its back and four legs situated along its sides. Among the witnesses was American missionary Joseph Ellis, who said he saw such a creature emerge from the Mataba River and disappear into the tall grass one day in November 1971. Ellis did not get a good look at its entire body, though he was only 200 feet away and had the creature under observation for two minutes. He never saw its head and neck, but from the portions of the body above water, he determined that it had to be more than thirty feet long.

As one well familiar with the Congo's fauna, he was positive that the animal could not have been a crocodile. Native reports, which do include descriptions of a head and extended tail, suggest to Mackal that "we may be dealing with a living link between lizards and snakes," perhaps a "lizard type ... derived from a primitive, semi-aquatic group known as dolichosaurs, rather than more advanced monitors."

In 1932, biologist Ivan T. Sanderson and animal collector W. M. (Gerald) Russell had a bizarre and frightening experience in the Mamfe Pool, part of the

Mainyu River in western Cameroon. The two men, with native guides, were in separate boats and passing cliff-like river banks dotted with deep caves when suddenly they heard ear-shattering roars, as if huge animals were fighting in one of the caves.

Swirling currents sucked both boats near the cave's mouth. At that point, Sanderson would recall, there "came another gargantuan gurgling roar and something enormous rose out of the water, turned it to sherry-colored foam and then, again roaring, plunged below. This 'thing' was shiny black and was the head of something shaped like a seal but flattened from above to below. It was about the size of a full-grown hippopotamus—this head, I mean."

Sanderson and Russell chose not to stick around to see anything more. Upstream they found big tracks that could not have been placed there by a hippopotamus because hippos do not live in the area. This was because the creatures had killed them all, the natives said. The creatures were not carnivorous, however; their diet consisted of the liana fruits that grew along the rivers. The natives called these creatures, in Sanderson's phonetic rendering, "m'kuoo m'bemboo."

Nonetheless, if the part of the animal the party saw really was its head, the animal was not the sauropod-like mokele-mbembe. Sauropods by definition have small heads. Mackal found during his own expeditions, fifty years later, that some local people used "mokele mbembe" as something of a generic description of any large, dangerous animal—including those described above—living in rivers, lakes, or swamps.

Dinosaurs in the lost world

In his 1912 novel, *The Lost World*, "perhaps his finest work in fiction" according to one biographer, Sir Arthur Conan Doyle imagined the discovery, by a band of hardy English explorers, of a plateau on the Amazon basin where prehistoric monsters thrived many millions of years past their time. Conan Doyle took his inspiration from periodic claims of relic dinosaurs in South America.

One such account was published in the January 11, 1911, issue of the *New York Herald*. Its author, a German named Franz Herrmann Schmidt, of whom little if anything is known, claimed that in October 1907 he and a companion, Capt. Rudolph Pfleng, along with Indian guides, entered a valley composed of swamps and lakes in a remote region of the Peruvian interior. There they discovered some strange, huge tracks, and crushed trees and vegetation indicating the presence of more than one unknown animal in the waters. They also noticed the curious absence of alligators, iguanas, and water snakes.

In spite of the guides' visible fear, the party camped in the valley that night. The next morning expedition members got back into their boat and resumed their search for the animals. Just before noon they found fresh tracks along the shore. Pfleng declared that he was going to follow them inland, however perilous the quest. Just then they heard the screams of a troop of monkeys that had been gathering berries nearby. According to Schmidt's account:

A large dark something half hidden among the branches shot up among [the monkeys] and there was a great commotion.

One of the excited Indians began to paddle the boat away from the shore, and before we could stop him we were 100 feet from the waterline. Now we could see nothing and the Indians absolutely refused to put in again, while neither Pfleng nor myself [sic] cared to lay down our rifles to paddle. There was a great moving of plants and a sound like heavy slaps of a great paddle, mingled with the cries of some of the monkeys moving rapidly away from the lake…. For a full 10 minutes there was silence, then the green growth began to stir again, and coming back to the lake we beheld the frightful monster that I shall now describe.

The head appeared over bushes 10 feet tall. It was about the size of a beer keg and was shaped like that of a tapir, as if the snout was used for pulling things or taking hold of them. The eyes were small and dull and set in like those of an alligator. Despite the half dried mud we could see that the neck, which was very snakelike, only thicker in proportion, was rough knotted like an alligator's side rather than his back.

Evidently the animal saw nothing odd in us, if he noticed us, and advanced till he was no more than 150 feet away. We could see part of the body, which I should judge to have been eight or nine feet thick at the shoulders, if that word may be used, since there were no fore legs, only some great heavy clawed flippers. The surface was like that of the neck.

As far as I was concerned, I would have waited a little longer, but Pfleng threw up his rifle and let drive at the head. I am sure that he struck between the eyes and that the bullet must have struck something bony, horny or very tough, for it cut twigs from a tree higher up and further on after it glanced. I shot as Pfleng shot again and aimed for the base of the neck.

The animal had remained perfectly still till now. It dropped its nose to the spot at which I had aimed and seemed to bite at it, but there was not blood or any sign of real hurt. As quickly as we could fire we pumped seven shots into it, and I believe all struck. They seemed to annoy the creature but not to work any injury. Suddenly it plunged forward in a silly clumsy fashion. The Indians nearly upset the dugout getting away, and both Pfleng and I missed the sight as it entered the water. I was very anxious to see its hind legs, if it had any. I looked again only in time to see the last of it leave the land—a heavy blunt tail with rough horny humps. The head was visible still, though the body was hidden by the splash. From the instant's opportunity I should say that the creature was 35 feet long, with at least 12 of this devoted to head and neck.

In three seconds there was nothing to be seen except the waves of the muddy water, the movements of waterside growth and a monkey with its hind parts useless hauling himself up a tree top. As the Indians paddled frantically away I put a bullet through the poor thing to let it out of its misery. We had not gone a hundred yards before Pfleng called to me and pointed to the right. Above the water an eighth of a mile away appeared

An illustration from the 1912 novel *The Lost World* by Sir Arthur Conan Doyle.

the head and neck of the monster. It must have dived and gone right under us. After a few seconds' gaze it began to swim toward us, and as our bullets seemed to have no effect we took flight in earnest. Losing sight of it behind an island, we did not pick it up again and were just as well pleased.

This story appears in the course of an otherwise generally credible-sounding narrative about an expedition along the Solimes River. Schmidt writes that a few months later, on March 4, 1908, his companion Pfleng died of fever. Thus the story cannot be independently verified. Mackal remarks, "The details ... seem to ring true and probably reflect the experiences of an actual expedition. It does not necessarily follow that the encounter with the alleged creature also occurred." When they searched through records, cryptozoologists Dwight Smith and Gary Mangiacopra could find no evidence that an explorer named Franz Schmidt ever existed.

Whatever its factual basis (or, more likely, absence of same), Schmidt's is not the only reference to a huge swamp-dwelling beast in the South American backwaters. In the early twentieth century Lt. Col. Percy H. Fawcett surveyed jungles for Britain's National Geographic Society. A careful, accurate reporter, Fawcett wrote that native informants had told him of "tracks of some gigantic animal" seen in the swamps along the Acre River, near where the borders of Peru, Bolivia, and Brazil intersect (and 500 to 600 miles from the site of Schmidt and Pfleng's alleged encounter). The natives said they had never actually seen the creature responsible for the tracks.

Farther south, according to Fawcett, along the Peru-Bolivian border "some mysterious and enormous beast has frequently been disturbed in the swamps—possibly a primeval monster like those reported in other parts of the continent. Certainly tracks have been found belonging to no known animals—huge tracks, far greater than could have been made by any species we know."

On March 31, 1922, the *New York Times* carried an interview with John Barrett, who had served as President Theodore Roosevelt's ambassador to Argentina and later been director of the Pan American Union. Barrett had read reports by Martin Sheffield, "an American of whom I have personal knowledge," who claimed to have seen a plesiosaur-like creature in a lake in the southern Andes. He went on to say that "nearly 20 years ago, in November 1903, when I was Minister to Argentina, a clear-headed typical American prospector and explorer, whose name I have forgotten, came to the legation. In a convincing way, he proceeded to relate to me a story almost identical with that now reported by Sheffield, to the effect that he had seen swimming in a lake a huge lizard-like monster with a curved neck."

The individual, who stated he had fought alongside Roosevelt during the Spanish-American War, pleaded with Barrett to inform the President of what he had seen. After Barrett had done so, Roosevelt replied with an enthusiastic letter saying he remembered the man well and urging him to write him personally with a full account. According to the former ambassador:

> The man meanwhile sent word that he was off again on a mineral and timber prospecting tour in Southern Argentina and Chile, but giving no address and no names of those he might represent.
>
> In April, five months later, just before I went to Panama as first American Minister, I received a letter from the prospector written from … Patagonia. He was almost enthusiastic in his story of how he had again found a fresh trail of a strange animal leading to the waters of a lake, although he had not actually again seen the beast as in his first experience.…
>
> When I returned to the United States the first salutation President Roosevelt gave me as I entered his office in the White House was: "Well, Old Pan-American, where is your Argentine amphibian and what has happened to ———" calling the man's name.… The President for half an hour discussed, as an enthusiastic naturalist and scientist, the possibility of there being some huge surviving amphibian [sic] descended from the ancient plesiosaurians, and actually took stock … in the story of the American prospector, whom he said he well remembered.

In the 1920s at least two expeditions, one organized by Buenos Aires Zoo curator Clementi Onelli (a friend of Sheffield's), the other by Australian adventurer Gayne Dexter, sought evidence, preferably in the form of a body, of an animal described as a "dinosaur" and said to live in an Andean lake. In the latter instance, Dexter remarked in a newspaper dispatch on the presence of unexplained tracks and the testimony of more than a dozen witnesses. Of Sheffield, Onelli stated, "I have not the least doubt that he has seen a large and strange animal with a swan-like neck swimming in the lake as he asserts." Over the years Onelli had also heard other reports of a plesiosaur-like creature in the region. Neither expedition, however, turned up much.

In two articles published in *Pursuit* between 1977 and 1979, Silvano Lorenzoni suggested that the flat-topped, steep mountains of the Guayana Massif may harbor surviving dinosaurs. For his intriguing idea, however, Lorenzoni had only thin supporting evidence: a trader's report of three "plesiosaur like things" in a lake on one such plateau, Auyantepuy, in southeastern Venezuela where Angel Falls originates. He also noted reports of exceptionally large, lizard-like reptiles in mountain valleys near the Venezuelan coast.

North American dinosaurs

If living dinosaurs in Africa and South America seem at least marginally conceivable, the presence of such creatures in North America is—it hardly need be stated—pretty much impossible, at least this side of the twilight zone. Probably unsurprisingly, this consideration has not prevented the occurrence of sighting reports represented as factual.

Some of the stories were featured in the freewheeling American press of the nineteenth century. In 1886 a number of newspapers, including the *Omaha Bee* for August 15, carried this account:

> A stage driver and two tourists, while near Yellowstone lake, claim to have seen an enormous reptile which, while running through the grass, carried its head ten to fifteen feet above the ground. They think it must have been at least thirty feet long. A party was organized to pursue the reptile. Col. [David W.] Wear, superintendent of the park, and his assistant, Captain [Jack] Barronette, while near the cave of an extinct geyser in the vicinity of the lake, heard a hissing and saw the head of the reptile thrust out some fifteen feet and immediately withdraw. Parties are searching for another sight of the monster.

With sketchy details it is not clear what the witnesses are supposed to have seen. Newspapers of the period delighted in what were called "snake stories"—a euphemism for outlandish tall tales, usually involving encounters with giant serpents. On the other hand, the following tales seem clear enough in their references:

Sometime in the 1880s, so the *Atlanta Constitution* (January 2, 1888) had it, a mine owner, identified only as Mr. Alexander, traveling via burro in the San Andres Mountains (in what is now the state of New Mexico) observed an enormous reptile heading toward a crater a quarter mile to the east:

> He says it appeared to be about 60 feet in length; but what surprised him most [were] the queer proportions of the creature. The fore parts were of

Plesiosaur-like animals have also been rumored to swim in an isolated lake in the Andes in South America, as well as in Guayana.

enormous size, its head being fully as large as a barrel. A few feet behind the creature's head two large scales were visible, which glittered in the sun like polished shields; further back were two huge claws on either side, about two feet apart, which were all the monster had in the shape of feet. The rest of the body was comparatively small and tapering to the end of the tail; it traveled at a rapid gait, sometimes rearing its whole body from the ground, and walked on its four claws.

Alexander chose not to follow the beast when it disappeared over a hill. The article further alleged that the monster was well known to locals, who believed it lived inside the crater. It was also ferocious, and thought to have killed several persons.

Decades later, a Carlsbad, New Mexico, man chronicled his own supposed encounter with a dangerous dinosaur, though he did not characterize it specifically as such. Readers had been reporting their own strange experiences in a series of letters published in the city's *Daily Current-Argus*, inspiring Fowler Merritt to contribute this account in the July 6, 1948, issue:

I do not want to alarm anyone or to cause undue apprehension, but I honestly think there is a real menace in the hills west of Carlsbad. About ten years ago I was out in the flats at the base of the hills west of Happy Valley. I had my little son and a dog with me. I had a .12 gauge shotgun, pump, and a .45 Colt automatic.

Just before dark a horrible thing rushed out of a deep canyon toward the boy and the dog who had strayed off to one side as boys do. I was almost paralyzed but the boy streaked toward me. The dog stood his ground but his terror was pitiful. This apparition, or whatever, had the body of a good-sized horse and the head of a snake on a long neck. The head was stretched out toward my boy and the drumming of the animal's feet and the screams of the boy and the frantic barking of the dog kept me frozen.

I did manage to pump several loads of bird shot into the thing at rather long range and it slowed down. My boy got to me and behind me and then the thing seemed to notice the dog. Its long neck stretched out with this nasty head on the end of it and the jaws grabbed the dog. As it wheeled and started back into the canyon I grabbed the .45 and emptied it at the thing's head. I know some of the shots took effect but some missed. Our heroic dog was carried away before our eyes and we were afraid to follow. I was thankful that the boy escaped, but he was sick with brain fever for weeks. Even now, a grown man with the battles of the Pacific behind him, he won't talk of this and he refuses to go past Happy Valley.

You may laugh … [but] it is no joke to me, I assure you.

"Snake stories" were a nineteenth-century euphemism for tall tales, usually involving huge serpents, published in the period press—which was not always known for accuracy or even truthfulness. Dinosaur reports may be a variety of snake story, and oversized snakes and big dinosaurs may overlap as fantastic-creature categories. Still, it can be said that the creature of Death Valley, California, chronicled in newspapers in 1892 (for example, *Chicago Journal*, June 10), was no snake, if it was anything beyond a figment of some editor's imagination. One supposed witness, identified as Los Angeles-based geological surveyor Oscar W. Clark, is said to have provided this account to a reporter as well as another to the Smithsonian Institution:

> Happening to glance to the southwest, through the gaze peculiar to the desert, I saw a strange body moving along about one mile away. I went toward it and was soon both elated and horrified by seeing an animal fully 30 feet long that differed from any of the known forms of the present epoch. It was an immense monster, walking part of the time on its hind feet and at times dragging itself through the sands and leaving tracks of a configuration in the sand whenever it changed its form of locomotion and dragged itself. The forelimbs of the animal were extremely short and it occasionally grasped the nearest shrub and devoured it. The thumb of the three-pronged forefoot was evidently a strong conical spine that would be a dangerous weapon of attack. Whenever the animal stood upright it was fully 14 feet high. The head was as large as that of an elephant, with a long tail extending from the hindquarters something like that of an alligator.
>
> When I saw it the strange animal was on the edge of a great sink hole of alkaline water—a sink hole, by the way, that my guides told me was a bottomless pit, and evidently a remnant of the days when Death Valley was an inland sea. I approached within 300 yards of the monster, crawling cautiously over the sand, and watched it for fully half an hour. Suddenly the beast began to bellow, and the sound was of a most terrifying and blood-curdling character. Its immense eyes, fully as large as saucers, projected from the head, and gleamed with a wild and furious fire, while from the enormous mouth of the monster streams of steam-like vapor were exhaled, and as they drifted toward one the effluvia was something awful. The animal was liver color, with bronze-like spots.

Two other men, E. W. Spear and Henry Brown, both of nearby Daggett, allegedly saw the creature on separate occasions.

A frankly unbelievable story of an immense reptile living on an island in the south part of Salt Lake in Utah made the rounds in early September 1903. Other persons, unnamed, are said to have seen the monster, but a press-wire account (published in *Quincy Daily Journal*, Massachusetts, September 7, and elsewhere) cites in particular the testimony, real or imagined, of hunters Martin Gilbert and

John Barry, who from direct observation and study of tracks estimated the thing to be between fifty and sixty-five feet tall. The account describes the creature thus:

> The head is like that of an alligator, the eyes fiercely glowing, the jaws capable of opening a distance of 10 feet from the top of the upper to the lower, are provided with a fearful array of sharp saw-edged teeth; the body, so far as observation goes, is incased with heavy, horny scales. As to this Gilbert and Barry are not positive, as the constant diving of the beast, if such it may be called, into the strong brine of the lake has incrusted it with a thick coating of salt, which, save near the wings, completely hides the body.

A dinosaur-like something was killed in the woods near Richmond, Indiana, in the fall of 1910, if we are to credit a short report in the *Star and Sentinel* (November 16) of Gettysburg, Pennsylvania. The shooter was identified as Fremont Webster:

> The creature resembles several kinds of reptiles. It has a tail about one and one-half feet long and similar to that of a snake. It has four legs, resembling those of an alligator, except the toes, the ends of which are hooked like claws. Its body is like that of a lizard, only much larger than those seen in that section and covered with a tough skin. On its back is a furlike ridge. The head is very large, resembling a fish, while under the head and attached to the throat is a large pouch. The animal measures five feet in length and weighs about eighteen pounds. It has been presented to the Earlham College Museum.

An inquiry to that institution produces the unsurprising reply that it knows of no such specimen.

Less obviously fanciful are reports from the Canadian prairie province Saskatchewan, in some (albeit not all) ways reminiscent of Scandinavian lindorm traditions. In early September 1927 the *Regina Leader* took note of strange sightings in the vicinity of Killaley, quoting a letter a local man, Charles Whall, wrote to the province's deputy minister of education, A. H. Ball:

> It was first sighted about four miles from Killaley. Since then a gang of men has hunted the creature with no success as we cannot get its exact location until it has had sufficient time to move a considerable distance.

> We would very much like to know what this creature might be and whether or not it is dangerous. The creature travels like a snake and when it is molested it rears up its head and makes a noise similar to a cow roaring but coarser. When stones that were thrown at it struck the creature it roared loudly and jumped about four feet towards the man who threw the stone.

> It is eight feet long and has traveled more than a mile in 27 hours from the time it was first seen, August 26. It was seen again the next day by a farmer's son who was cutting wheat. The horses he was driving were terribly afraid of the creature. They snorted and jumped when they were within 50 yards of it.

> The creature had a forked tongue. Its mouth is extremely red and is big enough to hold a ball of twine comfortably. At the thickest part of its

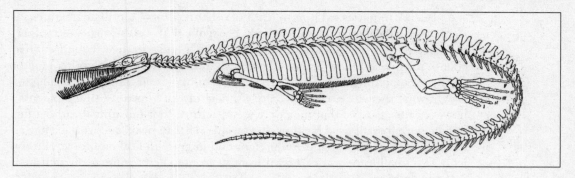

A sketch of the skeleton of a *Mesosaurus brazilianus* from a 1914 publication. This animal lived over 250 million years ago during the Permian period, but it is highly reminiscent of animals encountered in Indiana.

body it is about one foot in diameter and it is estimated to weigh between 100 and 150 pounds. Down the back of its head and neck it has thin hair about an inch long. It has four small legs close up to its body. The back of the creature is of a brown color.

Mr. Ball, the recipient of the letter, recalled that in 1904, while serving as a school inspector and living with a local farm family, he had heard of a comparably described creature. On one occasion, after the hired man heard its unsettling roar, the two of them searched for it along the banks of a lake but did not see it.

In a letter published in the August 22, 1982, issue of *Empire Magazine*, the *Denver Post* Sunday supplement, Myrtle Snow of Pagosa Springs, Colorado, wrote that in May 1935, when she was three years old, she saw "five baby dinosaurs" near her home town. A few years later a local farmer shot one after it took some of his sheep. "My grandfather took us to see it the next morning," she said. "It was about seven feet tall, was gray, had a head like a snake, short front legs with claws that resembled chicken feet, large stout back legs and a long tail."

But these were not her only sightings. There were two more: (1) "I saw another one in a cave in 1937, but it was dark green." (2) "On October 23, 1978, as I was returning from Chama, New Mexico, about 7:30 P.M., in a driving rain, I saw another one going through the field towards the place where I had seen the one in 1937."

Interviewed in 2001, by anthropologist and cryptozoologist Nick Sucik, Snow repeated the stories, giving every appearance of being sincere about them. "What is perplexing," he would write, "is that she cites actual people who supposedly were involved in the incidents she describes," though most had died or moved away. "I was able to speak with surviving kin, but no one I contacted ever recalled hearing their deceased relatives mention anything about a dinosaur or giant lizard or monster of any sort."

Subsequently, he found a man who as a child in the early 1950s recalled a sighting of something like a giant lizard, perhaps five feet long, a few miles south of Pagosa Springs.

Sucik's inquiries led him to learn of other reports of reptilian creatures in southwestern Colorado and elsewhere. He spoke with two women—a mother and daughter—who one hot evening in July 2001 had a strange encounter on a county road near Yellow Jacket. (There was a third witness, the mother/grandmother.) Something darted across the road in front of their car, whose headlights caught what the witnesses immediately thought to be a fawn. Within moments, however, they grasped that they were seeing a three-foot-tall animal without fur or hair, with a small head bending downward on a thin neck, and with a lengthy tail perhaps two feet long. It ran upright and in graceful fashion on two skinny legs. Two small forelimbs extended from its front. The creature soon vanished into the darkness.

Through the owner of the Reptile Reserve in Cortez, Sucik was put in touch with a woman, identified only as Bea, who had had a remarkably similar sighting in daylight—around 11 A.M.—in 1996. She had never heard of the Yellow Jacket sighting (which the witnesses had not confided even to other family members). Bea's reaction, Sucik writes, "was emotional, giving sighs of immense relief." Such a response, he adds, "was common to other witnesses about whom I later would learn. The overwhelming majority found their experience to be isolating."

Some of the other reports Sucik received from a short classified ad in a local newspaper were, he was certain, of collard lizards (their size exaggerated), which are semi-bipedal lizards native to the area. But in one instance, from early July 2002, the creature was observed immediately in front of the car, making a height estimation—at least three feet, which is too tall for a lizard—a more certain proposition.

The most dramatic account came about through a casual conversation with a newspaper reporter who happened to be visiting the Navajo reservation, where Sucik was engaged in anthropological investigation. The woman mentioned a close friend's "dinosaur" sighting near Snowflake, Arizona. When he spoke with the witness, Eugene Atcitty, at the time of the incident a member of the Navajo Nation Emergency Management staff, Sucik learned that the encounter took place in the middle of the afternoon of February 17, 1993:

> He was the lead driver in a convoy of five vehicles heading for Phoenix for a Department Retreat. Within a mile of approaching a junction between Snowflake and Heber, Arizona, the highway took a sudden dip before climbing back to ground level. His vehicle had just climbed out of the dip, while the second vehicle entered it. It was after the climb out that he saw a large upright creature quickly cross the highway into the large brush area. The height of the animal he placed at 10–12 feet. It had small arms that made him think of a T-Rex and its tail carried above ground as it ran. In moments the creature was gone from view. [Because he was] traveling at approximately 55 to 60 mph, and being the lead vehicle, stopping was impossible. At the fuel stop in Payson, Arizona, a co-worker who was driving the third vehicle came up to him and quietly asked if he'd seen "that thing." It turns out that as the second vehicle was in the dip in the highway the third driver had caught sight of it as well. Both agreed to keep

quiet about it for fear of ridicule and concern that the creature, whatever it was, would end up being hunted and killed if learned of.

If the near-defining characteristic of anomalous claims is an ordinary person's experience of the extraordinary, it is just as often true that "extraordinary" is a stand-in for "impossible." No sane and reasonable reader will read any of the above as evidence that dinosaurs survive in the wilds of Western states. That doesn't make the stories, paradoxically, any less puzzling.

Further Reading:

Arment, Chad. "Dinos in the U.S.A.: A Summary of Northern American Bipedal 'Lizard' Reports." *North American BioFortean Review* II,2 (2000). http://www.strangeark.com/nabr.html.

Doyle, Sir Arthur Conan. *The Lost World*. London: Hodder and Stoughton, 1912.

Fuhlan [pseud. of William Hichens]. "On the Trail of the Brontosaurus: Encounters with Africa's Mystery Animals." *Chambers's Journal* 7,17 (1927): 692–95.

Greenwell, J. Richard. "Interview: The Father of Cryptozoology Gives His Views on Many Matters." *ISC Newsletter* 3,3 (autumn 1984): 1–6.

Hall, Mark A. "More Living Dinosaurs." *Wonders* 10,2 (June 2006): 51–64.

Heuvelmans, Bernard. *On the Track of Unknown Animals*. New York: Hill and Wang, 1958.

———. *In the Wake of the Sea Serpents*. New York: Hill and Wang, 1968.

———. "The Birth and Early History of Cryptozoology." *Cryptozoology* 3 (1984): 1–30.

———. "How I Conquered the Great Sea Serpent Some Twenty-Five Years Ago." *Strange Magazine* 3 (1988): 10–13,56–57.

Higham, Charles. *The Adventures of Conan Doyle: The Life of the Creator of Sherlock Holmes*. New York: W. W. Norton and Company, 1976.

Keel, John A. *Strange Creatures from Time and Space*. Greenwich, CT: Fawcett Gold Medal, 1970.

Ley, Willy. *Exotic Zoology*. New York: Viking Press, 1959.

Lorenzoni, Silvano. "Extant Dinosaurs: A Distinct Possibility." *Pursuit* 10,2 (Spring 1977): 60–61.

———. "More on Extant Dinosaurs." *Pursuit* 12,2 (summer 1979): 105–09.

Mackal, Roy P. *Searching for Hidden Animals*. Garden City, NY: Doubleday and Company, 1980.

———. *A Living Dinosaur? In Search of Mokele-Mbembe*. New York: E. J. Brill, 1987.

Mayor, Adrienne. "Paleocryptozoology: A Call for Collaboration Between Classicists and Cryptozoologists." *Cryptozoology* 8 (1989): 12–26.

Powell, James. "Some Field Notes on African Neodinosaurs." *Pursuit* 9,1 (January 1976): 8.

"Queer Reptile with Roar Like Car [sic] Causes Excitement in Saskatchewan Town." *Lethbridge Herald*, Alberta, September 12, 1927, quoting *Regina Leader*, Saskatchewan.

Rickard, Bob. "A Reprise for 'Living Wonders.'" *Fortean Times* 40 (1983): 4–15.

Sanderson, Ivan T. *More "Things."* New York: Pyramid Books, 1969.

———. "There Could Be Dinosaurs." *Saturday Evening Post* 220 (January 3, 1948): 53–56.

Smith, Dwight G., and Gary S. Mangiacopra. "An [sic] 1900s Prehistoric Amazon Monster—An Explorer's Account, Crypto Fiction, or a Combination of Both?" *North American BioFortean Review* 6,1 (2004). http://www.strangeark.com/nabr/NABR14.pdf.

Sucik, Nick. *Dinosaur Sightings in the United States*. Flagstaff, AZ: The Author, n.d.

"To Bring Home a Dinosaur Dead or Alive." *Literary Digest* 64,9 (February 28, 1920): 76–77, 80.

"Unidentifieds on Land." *The News* 15 (April 1976): 9–11.

Morag

Loch Morar lies seventy miles to the southwest of the infinitely more famous Loch Ness. Eleven miles long and a mile and half across at its widest point, it is separated from the sea by a quarter mile, sits thirty feet above sea level, and averages 200 feet in depth. At its center, however, it descends to more than 1,000 feet, surpassing any other lake in the British Isles. According to reports that date back many years—but now are exceedingly rare, perhaps nonexistent—it hosts a monster much like that reported at Ness and other Scottish and Irish lakes.

On April 3, 1971, Ewen Gillies, a lifelong resident of a house overlooking Loch Morar and a member of a family with centuries-old roots in the region, saw the creature for the first time. Alerted by his twelve-year-old son, John, who had noticed it a few minutes earlier while walking down a road near the shore, Gillies stepped outside and looked out on the water. It was a clear, sunny morning, around 11 o'clock. Not quite half a mile away a huge animal lay in the water, its three- or four-foot neck pointed straight up and curving slightly at the top. The head was barely distinguishable from the neck itself. Two or three humps, moving up and down slightly, ran along its back. The skin was black and shiny. The creature was approximately thirty feet long.

Gillies went into the house to retrieve a Brownie camera. He took two pictures from an upstairs window just before the creature lowered its head, straightened its body, and sank below the waterline. The pictures did not turn out, but no one accused Gillies, a respected member of the community, of making up the story.

Early history

He and his son had seen Morag. The name comes from the Gaelic *Mhorag*, traditionally believed to be the spirit of the loch and conceived of as a shape-changing mermaid, whose appearance was an omen of death if glimpsed by a member of the Gillies clan. With the passage of time and the thinning of population in this wild, remote region, the older folklore faded from memory and *Mhorag* (pronounced "Vorack") became Morag, a strange but not supernatural beast, seen by some but seldom spoken of.

Loch Morar in Scotland is where Ewen Gillies and his son John reported seeing a huge creature in 1971.

Possibly because Morag the animal is lost to view, or seen only in distorted form through the folkloric fog that hangs over the loch's history, researchers have had a hard time tracing reports beyond the late nineteenth century. As early as 1907 a local writer named James MacDonald, author of the privately published *Tales from the Highlands*, asked, "Who has not heard of the Mhorag?" An older song from the Highlands mentions *Morag ... giant swimmer in deep-green Morar/ The loch that has no bottom/There it is that Morag the monster lives*. In the early 1970s investigator Elizabeth Montgomery Campbell interviewed elderly residents who recalled sightings in their youth. Campbell also learned of a "persistent tradition of hideous hairy eel-like creatures that were pulled up by fishermen long ago and thrown back into the loch because they were so repulsive."

Folklorist R. Macdonald Robertson collected this story, describing an un-dated experience from early in the last century, from Alexander Macdonnell:

> Some years ago, we were proceeding one morning down the loch in the estate motor launch from Meoble to Morar pier with some schoolchild-ren and other persons on board. As we were passing Bracarina Point, on the north side, some of the children excitedly shouted out: "Oh look! What is that big thing on the bank over there?" The beast would be about the size of a full-grown Indian elephant, and it plunged off the rocks into the water with a terrific splash.

Robertson noted that "Loch Morar's monster is said to have been seen by a number of persons of unquestionable veracity." A typical sighting is expressed in the words of one witness: "a huge, shapeless, dark mass rising out of the water like a small island."

Some who saw the shape thought it was, as they told travel writer Seton Gordon in the 1930s, a "boat without sails towing one or two smaller boats after it." Those were ghost ships, they presumed. Later witnesses at Morar, Ness, and elsewhere often say the creature's back looks like an "overturned boat."

In an unpublished memoir written in the early 1940s, Lady Brinckman, who had lived on an estate near the loch five decades earlier, recalled this incident from the summer of 1895:

> One evening, it was getting towards dinner time and I was sitting looking back, when suddenly, I saw a great shape rise up out of the loch, a good way off. I called the attention of Theodore [her husband] and McLaren [an employee] to it and asked if it was the launch and that it did not seem to be coming the right way. McLaren pointed a long way to the left as being where the launch would come from, and then, while we were watching, it disappeared. McLaren said, "It'll just be the monster," and he said it was a well known thing that one was seen from time to time.

In September 1931, young Sir John Hope, who as Lord Glendevon would go on to become a privy councilor and undersecretary of state for Scotland, had a curious experience which, while it involved no direct sighting, clearly suggested the presence of some huge unknown animal in the loch.

He, his brother, a friend, and a local guide had gone out on a boat to fish in a deep part of Morar. Hope, who was holding a long trout rod, felt something grab his line, dragging it "directly downwards at such a pace that it would have been madness to try and stop it with my fingers. In a very few seconds the whole line including the backing had gone and the end of the rod broke." Whatever had taken the bait, it was "something … heavier than I have experienced before or since."

It could not have been a salmon. Even if there had been one that size in the loch, it would have traveled parallel to the surface rather than making a steep vertical descent. Such descents, however, are described in any number of lake monster reports. The only other conceivable candidate is a seal, but no seals are known to exist at Loch Morar. Glendevon recalled that when they asked their guide what the animal could have been, "he mumbled something and said he thought we had better go home." Glendevon suspected that he knew more than he was telling.

After 1933, the year the Loch Ness monster emerged into world consciousness, note was taken of Morag, and a few witnesses came forward to describe observations either of large, fast-moving humps in the water or of long-necked creatures, usually said to be thirty feet long. But as a cryptozoological mystery Morag is far less richly documented than Nessie, the focus of a nearly unending investigation spanning decades. Photographs, sonar trackings, and a large body of eyewitness testimony have afforded Ness' monstrous denizen a credibility Morag cannot begin to claim.

In February 1970, several members of the Loch Ness Investigation Bureau formed the Loch Morar Survey to pursue the biological, operational, and historical aspects. Over the next few years they conducted sporadic investigations as limited time and funds permitted. These included a number of underwater probes in a submersible vehicle, with disappointing results.

But on July 14, 1970, one member, marine biologist Neil Bass, spotted a "hump-shaped black object" in the water at the north end of the loch. He called to his associates, but the hump had vanished by the time they started to look for it. "Following this, within half a minute," Bass reported, "a disturbance was witnessed by all of us ... followed by radiating water rings which traveled to form a circle, at maximum 50 yards in diameter." Bass said the apparent motion was inconsistent with an eel's; in any case it would have to be a "very, very big eel! My personal opinion is that it was an animate object of a species with which I am not familiar in this kind of habitat."

This infamous photograph of the Loch Ness monster was taken by London surgeon Robert K. Wilson, April 19, 1934. In 1994 this photo was labeled a hoax, an assertion now generally accepted.

The most dramatic Morag encounter took place on August 16, 1969. It is also among the very few sightings to be reported in newspapers all over the world shortly after its occurrence. It happened as two local men, Duncan McDonell and William Simpson, were on their way back from a fishing trip at the north end of the loch. It was just after 9 P.M. The sun had gone down, but there was still plenty of light.

Hearing a splash behind them, McDonell, who was at the wheel, turned to determine its cause. To his astonishment, it turned out to be a creature coming directly toward them, at a speed later estimated to be between twenty and thirty m.p.h. Within seconds it struck the side of the boat, then stopped or slowed down. Though McDonell had the impression that the collision had been accidental, that did not allay his fear that the creature, simply by virtue of its bulk, could cause the boat to capsize. He grabbed an oar and tried to push it away. Meanwhile, Simpson had rushed into the cabin to turn off the gas. He returned with a rifle and fired a single shot at the beast, to no apparent effect. It slowly moved away and sank out of sight. These events took five minutes to run their course.

When interviewed by representatives from the Loch Ness Investigation Bureau, the two agreed that the creature had been some twenty-five to thirty feet long, with rough, dirty brown skin. Three humps or undulations, about eighteen

A number of other lakes in Scotland have traditions of aquatic monster sightings, including Loch Assynt, shown here.

inches high, stood out of the water, and at one point McDonell spotted the animal's snake-like head just above the surface. It was, he thought, about one foot across the top.

Theories

Morar lies in a glacially deepened valley on Inverness-shire's west coast. Twelve thousand years ago, as the ice retreated, sea water is believed to have invaded the loch, bringing with it an abundance of marine life. Even after the sea water retreated, for a few thousand years the sea animals now in the loch may have had fairly ready access to their oceanic home, because the loch level and the low-tide level were only one-third then what they are today. The sea level at high tide would have been within a few feet of loch level.

There is no doubt that Loch Morar at least once possessed an adequate food supply—fish, plankton, and detritus—to support a population of large animals. In recent decades pollution has decimated the salmon population. It is also one of nine Highland lochs with monster traditions and reports. (Besides Ness and Morar, the others are Oich, Canisp, Assynt, Arkaig, Shiel, Lochy, and Quoich.) Most sightings at Morar and elsewhere describe creatures bearing an undeniable resemblance to the supposedly long-extinct plesiosaur. If such animals survive, however (and there is no confirmation of this in the fossil record), they would have had to adapt to far colder water temperatures than their ancestors could handle. Roy P. Mackal, a biologist with a keen interest in lake monsters, has argued that Morag, Nessie, and their relatives are zeuglodons, primitive, snake-like whales generally believed to have ceased their existence over twenty million years ago.

If the idea of relic prehistoric reptiles and mammals seems too fantastic to be considered, plesiosaurs and zeuglodons at least *look like* what people usually report when they recount their observations of the monsters of the Highland lochs. "Conventional" explanations pointing to sharks, seals, eels, or even mats of vegetation typically begin with the outright rejection of the witnesses' testimony and the implicit assumption that these individuals could not have seen what they said they saw; thus, they saw something else, which the explainer is always happy to supply, even when it defies nearly every word of the viewers's testimony. Such an approach may have its uses on occasion, but more often than not, it takes us only so far. Often it is easier to believe that the witnesses are lying outright than that they suffered from such massive breakdowns of their perceptual apparatus.

In any event, reports of large, unknown animals in Morar, whatever their cause, are unheard of today. Visits to the area (which is hard to get to) by outside inquirers are rare, and those who do make it find the locals reluctant to discuss the monster, or perhaps simply too little interested to do so. Unlike the communities along Ness, Mallaig—a small but vibrant port village two and a half miles north of Morar—does not promote Morag among its tourist attractions. Nor does the tinier town of Morar on the loch's west side, though shielded from sight of the water by hills and wooded islands. Whatever it is or isn't, was or wasn't, Morag seems well on its way to becoming more a distant legend than a living mystery.

Further Reading:

Bauer, Henry H. *The Enigma of Loch Ness: Making Sense of a Mystery*. Urbana: University of Illinois Press, 1986.

Campbell, Elizabeth Montgomery, and David Solomon. *The Search for Morag*. New York: Walker and Company, 1973.

Costello, Peter. *In Search of Lake Monsters*. New York: Coward, McCann & Geoghegan, 1974.

Gordon, Seton. *Afoot in Wild Places*. London: Cassell, 1937.

Holiday, F. W. *The Great Orm of Loch Ness: A Practical Inquiry into the Nature and Habits of Water Monsters*. New York: W. W. Norton and Company, 1969.

———. *The Dragon and the Disc: An Investigation into the Totally Fantastic*. New York: W. W. Norton and Company, 1973.

———. *The Goblin Universe*. St. Paul, MN: Llewellyn Publications, 1986.

Mackal, Roy P. *The Monsters of Loch Ness*. Chicago: Swallow Press, 1976.

Robertson, R. Macdonald. Jeremy Bruce-Watt, ed. *Selected Highland Folktales*. North Pomfret, VT: David and Charles, 1977.

Whyte, Constance. *More Than a Legend*. London: Hamish Hamilton, 1957.

Wignall, Sydney. "Morag of Morar." *Pursuit* 15,2 (Second Quarter 1982): 50–51, 56, 63.

Pterosaur Sightings

The flying reptiles known as pterosaurs, including pterodactyls and their cousins the pteranodons, lived from the lower Jurassic to nearly the end of the Cretaceous period—in other words, from approximately 160 to 60 million years ago.

About sixty million years later, on January 11, 1976, two ranch hands near Poteet, just south of San Antonio, Texas, sighted a five-foot-tall birdlike creature standing in the water of a stock tank. "He started flying," Jesse Garcia reported, "but I never saw him flap his wings. He made no noise at all."

Around the same time, two sisters, Libby and Deany Ford, observed a "big black bird" near a pond northeast of Brownsville, which lies along the Texas-Mexico border. "It was as big as me," Libby said, "and it had a face like a bat." Later, as the two girls looked through a book in an effort to identify the creature, they found out what it was.

Driving to work on an isolated rural road southwest of San Antonio a few weeks later, on the morning of February 24, three elementary school teachers saw a shadow cast over the entire road. The object responsible for it, passing low overhead, looked like an enormous bird with a fifteen- to twenty-foot wingspan. "I could see the skeleton of this bird through the skin or feathers or whatever, and it stood out black against the background of the gray feathers," one of the witnesses, Patricia Bryant, said. According to David Rendon, "It just glided. It didn't fly. It was no higher than the telephone line. It had a huge breast. It had different legs, and it had huge wings, but the wings were very peculiar like. It had a bony structure, you know, like when you hold a bat by the wing tips, like it has bones at the top and in between."

Never having seen anything remotely like it, the three witnesses went to the encyclopedia as soon as they got to school. After some searching they found what they were looking for. They learned that the animal they had observed was not unknown after all.

At 3:55 A.M. on September 14, 1982, James Thompson, an ambulance technician, was driving along Highway 100 four miles east of Los Fresnos, Texas, midway between Harlingen and Brownsville, on his way back from an inspection on South Padre Island. He suddenly spotted a "large birdlike object" pass low over the highway 150 feet in front of him. Its strange-looking tail almost literally stopped

An artist's concept of pteranodons in flight. Pteranadons and pterodactyls were two types of flying animals from the Cretaceous Period. Even in modern times some witnesses claim to have seen them.

him in his tracks. He hit the brakes, pulled the vehicle to the side of the road, and stared intently at the peculiar object, which at first he had a hard time believing was a living creature.

"I expected him to land like a model airplane," Thompson said. Then "he flapped his wings enough to get above the grass.... It had a black, or grayish, rough texture. It wasn't feathers. I'm quite sure it had a hide-type covering." Its thin body, which ended with a "fin," stretched more than eight feet; its wingspan was five to six feet. The wings had "indentations" on their tops and possibly their bottoms as well. At the back of the head it had a hump like a Brahma bull's. There was "almost no neck at all."

Later he consulted books in an effort to identify the "bird." Like the Ford sisters and the San Antonio teachers more than six years earlier, he had no particular trouble finding out what he had seen. The trouble was, however, that the books told him he had seen a pterosaur.

Out of Africa

In the early twentieth century, a traveler and writer named Frank H. Melland worked for the British colonial service in Northern Rhodesia (now Zambia).

While there, he learned of a flying creature that lived along certain rivers. Called *kongamato* ("breaker of boats"), it was considered extremely dangerous. Native informants described it as "like a lizard with membranous wings like a bat." Melland wrote in his 1923 book, *In Witch-Bound Africa*:

> Further enquiries disclosed the "facts" that the wing-spread was from 4 to 7 feet across, that the general color was red. It was believed to have no feathers but only skin on its body, and was believed to have teeth in its beak: these last two points no one could be sure of, as no one ever saw a *kongamato* close and lived to tell the tale. I sent for two books which I had at my house, containing pictures of pterodactyls, and every native present immediately and unhesitantly picked it out and identified it as a *kongamato*. Among the natives who did so was a headman (Kanyinga) from the Jiundu country where the *kongamato* is supposed to be active.

> The natives assert that this flying reptile still exists, and whether this be so or not it seems to me that there is presumptive evidence that it has existed within the memory of man, within comparatively recent days. Whether it is scientifically possible that a reptile that existed in the mesozoic age could exist in the climate conditions of to-day I have not the necessary knowledge to decide.... The evidence for the pterodactyl is that the natives can describe it so accurately, unprompted, and that they all agree about it. There is negative evidence also in the fact that they said they could not identify any other of the prehistoric monsters which I showed them.

In 1942 Col. Charles R. S. Pitman recalled his African days in a memoir, *A Game Warden Takes Stock*:

> When in Northern Rhodesia I heard of a mythical beast, alleged to have a similar death-dealing attribute, which intrigued me considerably. It was said to haunt formerly, and perhaps still to haunt, a dense, swampy forest region in the neighborhood of the Angola and Congo borders. To look upon it too is death. But the most amazing feature of this mystery beast is its suggested identity with a creature bat- and birdlike in form on a gigantic scale strangely reminiscent of the prehistoric pterodactyl. Where the devil does the primitive African derive such a fanciful idea?

> The kongamato is said to have a taste for decaying human flesh.

A 1947 book, Frederick Kaigh's *Witchcraft and Magic in Africa*, refers to a spot on the "Rhodesian-Congo border near the north-eastern border of the Jiundu Swamp, a foetid, eerie place in which the pterodactyl is locally supposed to survive with spiritual powers of great evil."

On April 2, 1957, the *Rhodesia Herald* reported the 1956 experience of an engineer named J.P.F. Brown. On his way home to Salisbury (now Harare, Zimbabwe), Brown stopped at Fort Rosebery to refill his canteen. The time was around 6 P.M. He noticed two strange-looking creatures flying directly and silently above him. Large, with wingspans of approximately three and a half feet, their tails strikingly long, they looked "prehistoric," he thought. When one opened its mouth,

Brown observed pointed teeth. In 1957, it is alleged, a patient came into a Fort Rosebery hospital with a severe chest wound, claiming to have been attacked by a giant bird in the nearby Bangweulu Swamp. When the physician asked him to draw what the bird looked like, the victim allegedly sketched what appeared to be a pterosaur. In 2010 a creationist group, Genesis Park, as part of an effort to prove that *Homo sapiens* and dinosaurs have coexisted both historically and currently, dispatched an expedition to the region, but the researchers reported finding "no definitive evidence" for the kongamato.

Cryptozoologist Karl Shuker holds a model of the Congolese mokele-mbembe.

Ropens

In recent years much of the focus of investigation and speculation about living pterosaurs has been on *ropens* (*duahs* in the language of another island tribe, roughly translated as "demon flyers"), said to be leather-skinned flying creatures inhabiting the mountain area of Papua New Guinea as well as east-coast islands Rambutyo and Umboi. Both native people and missionaries have observed them. British cryptozoologist Karl Shuker describes them as having "a wingspan of 3–4 ft., a long tail terminating in a diamond-shaped flange, and a long beak brimming with sharp teeth ... startlingly reminiscent of an early prehistoric pterosaur known as *Rhamphorhynchus*." They live in caves and ordinarily hunt at night. Like the kongamato, they have a taste for rotting human flesh, even digging up graves seeking it. Fishermen say they attack boats for fish either aboard or in the process of being brought aboard from the water.

An especially curious aspect is the widespread belief that these creatures are bioluminescent. In other words, they glow in the dark, the light coming from patches under their wings. At night or in early-morning hours witnesses see mysterious glowing lights moving from mountaintop to mountaintop. (Shuker speculates that "highly reflective scales or adhering phosphorescent fungi may be responsible.") Analysis of videos of the phenomenon, taken for example by investigator Paul Nation in 2006, seems to eliminate conventional natural causes or hoaxes. The first Western witness to these nocturnal lights, British entomologist Evelyn Cheesman, described them in her 1935 book, *The Two Roads of Papua*. Though she did not liken them to living pterosaurs, she could not explain them either.

Investigations in Papua New Guinea, the Solomon Islands, and other regions of the Southwest Pacific where such creatures allegedly appear are continuing. The prominent involvement of creationists, Christian fundamentalists engaged in a rearguard struggle against evolutionary science (in this case to establish that "prehistoric" reptiles and *Homo sapiens* have coexisted), has placed an additional layer of controversy on an already contested and heretical claim. Jonathan Whitcomb's *Searching for Ropens* (2007), for example, is as much evangelical polemic as cryptozoological text.

Flying snakes and other terrors

In a dispatch out of Columbia, South Carolina, on May 30, 1888, the *New York Times* reported that three evenings earlier, at dusk, Ida Davis and her two younger sisters while on a stroll through the woods of Darlington County

> were suddenly startled by the appearance of a huge serpent moving through the air above them. The serpent was distant only two or three rods when they first beheld it, and was sailing through the air with a speed equal to that of a hawk or buzzard but without any visible means of propulsion. Its movements in its flight resembled those of a snake, and it looked a formidable object as it wound its way along, being apparently about 15 feet in length.... The flying serpent was also seen by a number of people in other parts of the country early in the afternoon of the same day, and by those it is represented as emitting a hissing noise which could be distinctly heard.

Area papers asserted that the sky serpent was seen that day over the town of Grassland, ten miles to the southeast. According to the account, the creature circled the Methodist church steeple, adorned by a metal dove, which it mistook for a real dove. When it did so, "with a fierce swash of its tail, [it] knocked the weathercock from its fastenings and sent it to the ground below in a hundred pieces. Some of the fragments picked up are stained with blood." The church's pastor, the Rev. Richard Medway, and his wife (who fainted at the sight) supposedly witnessed the incident.

Reports of similar phenomena continued in the Carolinas until at least 1904, if press accounts are to be credited. Stories of sky serpents, often indistinguishable from the dragons of tradition, are ubiquitous in the often freewheeling American press of the nineteenth-century. The most extravagant are plainly hoaxes and jokes; others, especially those printed in small-town newspapers identifying local individuals by name and lacking obvious humor markers, seem genuinely puzzling. Their relationship to pterosaur reports, if any, is less than certain. (For a full discussion of the sky-serpent phenomenon, see pp. 229–253 of my *Hidden Realms, Lost Civilizations, and Beings from Other Worlds*.)

In the twentieth century sightings of extraordinary flying reptiles have been logged in various parts of the world. For example, Izzet Göksu of Bursa, Turkey, related his mother's encounter one day in 1947, when she was twelve years old and living in Bulgaria:

I used to go and fetch fresh water from the spring 200 meters [600+ feet] from our house. One lovely summer evening, I picked up two buckets and started to walk towards the spring. After about 40 meters [130 feet], I noticed what looked like branches on the path, but as I got closer I saw them moving. They were black, gray and white, thin and one or two meters [three to six feet] long. I stopped, thinking they might be snakes, but they were moving in a straight line, not like snakes at all.

As I got closer, something alarmed them or they noticed me. They gave the weirdest cry I have ever heard before taking off and flying two or three meters above the ground straight as arrows. They flew all the way to the spring about 150 meters [450+ feet] away and disappeared behind the trees. I don't remember seeing any wings on them. Whenever I remember that cry, it makes the hair on my arms stand on end.

"As she told me this story," Göksu wrote, "I clearly saw the hairs rising on her arms."

Among the best documented (if still unproven) reports of flying reptiles come out of Africa.

In the late 1930s J.L.B. Smith, a South African chemist with a keen interest in ichthyology (the study of fish), and an associate, Marjorie Courtenay-Latimer, entered zoological history as the co-discoverers of the coelacanth, a large fish heretofore known only from the fossil record and assumed to have been extinct for some sixty million years.

Smith was also fascinated with other reports of animals generally believed no longer to exist, and at one point he had correspondence (since lost, but referred to in his memoir of the coelacanth episode, *Old Fourlegs* [1956]), with members of a German missionary family. They told him that while living near Mount Kilimanjaro (in northeast Tanzania near the Kenya border), one member had had a close sighting of a "flying dragon." This flying dragon was known prior to the incident through numerous reports native witnesses had given them.

For her part Courtenay-Latimer once investigated reports of similar creatures in southern Namibia (then South-West Africa). In one instance, native shepherds had walked off their job after complaining that their employer, the white owner of a large ranch, did not take seriously their insistence that a large flying snake lived in the mountains nearby. With no one else to watch the livestock, the farmer dispatched his sixteen-year-old son to the site. When he failed to return that evening, a search party set out to the mountains to look for him. He was found unconscious.

Even after regaining consciousness, for three days the young man could not speak—owing, his attending physician said, to shock. Finally the son related that he had been relaxing beneath a tree when a sudden roaring noise, like a powerful wind current, startled him. As he looked up, he saw a huge "snake" flying down from a ridge. The closer it got, the louder was the roaring sound. All around, the sheep were scattering. The creature landed in a cloud of dust. The boy noticed a strong odor reminiscent of burned brass. At this point he passed out.

Courtenay-Latimer, who arrived on the scene soon afterwards, interviewed witnesses, including other farmers and local police officers, and examined marks on the ground reportedly left by the creature. She was told that a police party had seen the creature disappear into a crevice in the mountain. Sticks of dynamite were heaved into the opening, from which a low moaning sound subsequently emanated, followed by silence. The creature was seen no more.

Cryptozoologist Roy P. Mackal corresponded years later with Courtenay-Latimer about the episode. Reflecting on it, he wrote, "A snake, even a very large one, hurtling or falling over a ledge or mountain precipice hardly would disturb the air as described. In fact, it is hard to attribute such a disturbance even to a large gliding creature, suggesting instead that some kind of wing action must have been involved." Mackal asks, "Could some species of pterodactyl with elongated body and tail still survive?"

According to Carl Pleijel, of the Swedish Museum of Natural History, a sighting of such a pterosaur-like creature occurred in Kenya in 1974. The witnesses were members of a British expedition, Pleijel told (sometimes controversial) cryptozoological journalist Jan-Ove Sundberg, citing as his source an unnamed person he deemed credible. Sundberg allegedly interviewed a "museum superintendent here in Sweden … whose name I don't want to mention" and from him heard of an American expedition's sighting over a swamp in Namibia in late 1975. No further details have been forthcoming.

If the rumors out of Sweden are vague and inadequately documented, continuing reports from Namibia seem more substantial. In the summer of 1988, Mackal traveled to that nation with a small group of associates. From an isolated private desert area owned by Namibians of German descent, he said, come continuing reports of "flying snakes." Witnesses with whom Mackal spoke said the animals indeed had wings—of thirty feet, no less—but no feathers. The creatures apparently live in caves and crevices in the many kopjes (small veld hills) that dot the landscape.

Expedition members found ostrich bones in almost inaccessible spots atop kopjes, possibly evidence that the kills had been carried there by flying creatures. One expedition member who stayed on after Mackal had left to return to the United States reported seeing one from a thousand feet away. It was, he said, black with white markings and had enormous wings that it used to glide through the air.

In 1995 a South African television documentary, *In Search of the Giant Flying Snake of Namibia*, featured the testimony of witnesses who estimated the creature's length to be nine to fifteen feet long.

Further Reading:

Cheesman, L. Evelyn. *The Two Roads of Papau*. London: Jarrolds Ltd., 1935.

Clark, Jerome. *Hidden Realms, Lost Continents, and Beings from Other Worlds*. Detroit: Visible Ink Press, 2010.

Coleman, Loren. *Curious Encounters, Phantom Trains, Spooky Spots, and Other Mysterious Wonders*. Boston: Faber and Faber, 1985.

Göksu, Izzet. "Letters: Flying Snakes of Bulgaria." *Fortean Times* 78 (1994/1995): 57.

Heuvelmans, Bernard. *On the Track of Unknown Animals*. New York: Hill and Wang, 1958.

———. "Of Lingering Pterodactyls." *Strange Magazine* 6 (1990): 8–11, 58–60.

———. "Lingering Pterodactyls, Part 2." *Strange Magazine* 17 (1996): 18–21, 56–57.

"Is This a Pterodactyl?" *Fortean Times* 134 (2000): 21.

Jeffreys, M.D.W. "African Pterodactyls." *Journal of the Royal African Society* 43, 171 (April 1944): 72–74.

Mackal, Roy P. *Searching for Hidden Animals*. Garden City, NY: Doubleday and Company, 1980.

Pittman, Charles R.S. *A Game Warden Takes Stock*. London: J. Nisbet and Company, 1945.

Shuker, Karl. *Alien Zoo*. Bideford, North Devonshire, England: CFZ Press, 2010.

———. "Flying Graverobbers." *Fortean Times* 154 (2002): 48–49.

Smith, J.L.B. *Old Fourlegs: The Story of the Coelacanth*. London: Longmans, Green and Company, 1956.

Sundberg, Jan-Ove. "The Monster of Sraheens Lough." *INFO Journal* 5,6 (March 1977): 2–9.

Sutherly, Curt. "Pterodactyls and T-Birds." *Pursuit* 9,2 (April 1976): 35–36.

Sea Serpents

The American ship *Silas Richards* was sailing off St. George's Bank south of Nova Scotia at 6:30 P.M. on June 16, 1826, when its captain, Henry Holdredge, and a passenger, Englishman William Warburton, saw a most peculiar sight: an enormous, many-humped, snake-like creature slowly approaching the vessel. Warburton raced to inform the other passengers, who were below deck, but only a handful responded. Warburton recalled, "The remainder refused to come up, saying there had been too many hoaxes of that kind already."

Even in the early years of the nineteenth century, the sea serpent had a reputation as, in Bernard Heuvelmans's words, the "very symbol of a hoax." That reputation would withstand a battering in the later years of the century, with the publication of a number of reports that could not reasonably be ascribed to mistakes, delusions, or lies, and emerge intact in our time to figure in inane clichés about the "silly season."

That the sea serpent has such a reputation says more about the capacity of human beings for blind incredulity than it does about the quality of the testimonial evidence for the creature once called the "great unknown." Some might argue that the sea serpent is due for a revival. With the initiation of systematic deep-sea research in recent decades, marine biologists have discovered a bewildering variety of life forms, some never suspected, others thought extinct for millions of years. An article in the June 2, 1992, issue of the *New York Times* remarks, "Scientists concede that other creatures, perhaps even larger and stranger than the monstrous *Architeuthis* [giant squid], may continue to defy discovery in their vast water refuges." Twenty years later, however, the sea serpent remains more elusive than ever.

Early history

Though sea serpents are ubiquitous in myths and legends, the first attempt to describe them as figures in natural history appears in a 1555 work by Olaus Magnus, the exiled Catholic archbishop of Uppsala, Sweden. The archbishop wrote that sailors off the coast of Norway had often seen a "Serpent ... of vast magnitude, namely 200 feet long, and moreover 20 feet thick." A dangerous beast, it lived in caves along the shore and devoured both land and ocean creatures, in-

The kraken was a gigantic squid said to have terrorized sailors in past centuries, pulling their ships down beneath the waves.

cluding the occasional seaman. "This Snake disquiets the shippers," Olaus Magnus wrote, "and he puts up his head on high like a pillar."

Except for this last detail, Magnus's is an exaggerated and unbelievable account, but we know from chroniclers who came after him that "serpents" were reported regularly in the North Sea, though not everyone regarded them as dangerous. In 1666, Adam Olschlager wrote of a sighting of a "large serpent, which seen from afar, had the likeness of a wine barrel, and 25 windings. These serpents are said to appear on the surface of the water only in calm weather and at certain times."

In 1734 a Protestant priest, Hans Egede, saw a "monster," estimated to be 200 feet long, rise from the water off the coast of Greenland. He recorded the experience in a book published in 1741, and ignited a still-ongoing controversy about what the creature may or may not have been. A few years later, the most influential of the early treatments appeared: *The Natural History of Norway* (1752–53), by Bishop Erik Pontoppidan.

In one chapter, destined to be cited frequently in the controversies of the following centuries, the bishop addressed the question of merfolk, the kraken (known to us as the giant squid and, though once deemed mythical, recognized by science since the late 1800s), and the sea serpent, all of which he believed, on the testimonies of individuals of good reputation, to exist. The reports indicated, Pontopiddan wrote, that more than one kind of animal was involved. Egede's monster, for instance, was distinctly different from those seen off the Scandinavian coasts. For example: "The head in all the kinds has a high and broad forehead, but in some [as in Egede's] a pointed snout, though in others that is flat, like that of a cow or horse, with large nostrils, and several stiff hairs standing out on each side like whiskers."

In the New World

In *An Account of Two Voyages to New England*, published in 1674, John Josselyn recalled a 1639 conversation with residents of the Massachusetts colony: "They told me of a *sea-serpent* or snake, that lay coiled upon a rock at Cape Ann." This is the first known printed reference to an American sea serpent. In the next century and a half, thousands of residents of New England and Canada's maritime provinces would observe comparable creatures.

One of the better of these early reports comes from Capt. George Little of the frigate *Boston*:

In May, 1780, I was lying in Round Pond, in Broad Bay [off the Maine coast], in a public armed ship. At sunrise, I discovered a huge Serpent, or monster, coming down the Bay, on the surface of the water. The cutter was manned and armed. I went myself in the boat, and proceeded after the Serpent. When within a hundred feet, the mariners were ordered to fire on him, but before they could make ready, the Serpent dove. He was not less than from 45 to 50 feet in length; the largest diameter of his body, I should judge, 15 inches; his head nearly the size of that of a man, which he carried four or five feet above the water. He wore every appearance of a common black snake.

A year earlier the crew of the American gunship *Protector* had an extraordinary encounter in Penobscot Bay. One of the witnesses was an eighteen-year-old ensign, Edward Preble, who would go on to become a commodore and a notable figure in the history of the Navy. In his biography of Preble, James Fenimore Cooper recounts this event:

The day was clear and calm, when a large serpent was discovered outside the ship. The animal was lying on the water quite motionless. After inspecting with the glasses for some time, Capt. [John Foster] Williams ordered Preble to man and arm a large boat, and endeavor to destroy the creature; or at least to go as near to it as he could.... The boat thus employed pulled twelve oars, and carried a swivel in its bows, besides having its crew armed as boarders. Preble shoved off, and pulled directly towards the monster. As the boat neared it, the serpent raised its head about ten feet above the surface of the water, looking about it. It then began to move slowly away from the boat. Preble pushed on, his men pulling with all their force, and the animal being at no great distance, the swivel was discharged loaded with bullets. The discharge produced no other effect than to quicken the speed of the monster, which soon ran the boat out of sight.

There were sporadic sightings in the following decades, but the New England sea serpent did not become an international cause célébre until the second decade of the nineteenth century. Over a period of several years, from Boston up to Cape Ann at the northeastern tip of Massachusetts, numerous witnesses on both ship and shore saw the animal. Some representative reports:

Hawkins Wheeler, June 6, 1819: "I had a fair and distinct view of the creature, and from his appearance am satisfied that it was of the serpent kind. The creature was entirely black; the head, which perfectly resembled a snake's, was elevated from four to seven feet above the surface of the water, and his back appeared to be composed of bunches or humps, apparently about as large as, or a little larger than, a half barrel; I think I saw as many as ten or twelve.... I considered them to be caused by the undulatory motion of the animal—the tail was not visible, but from the head to the last hump that could be seen, was, I should judge, 50 feet."

Solomon Allen III, August 12, 13, and 14, 1817: "I have seen a strange marine animal, that I believe to be a serpent, in the harbor in ... Gloucester. I should judge him to be between eighty and ninety feet in length, and about the size of a half barrel.... I was about 150 yards from him.... His head formed something like the head of a rattlesnake, but nearly as large as the head of a horse. When he moved on the surface of the water, his motion was slow, at times playing about in circles, and sometimes moving nearly straight forward. When he disappeared, he sunk [sic] apparently down."

Samuel Cabot, August 14, 1819: "My attention was suddenly arrested by an object emerging from the water at the distance of about one hundred or one hundred and fifty yards, which gave to my mind at the first glance the idea of a horse's head.... I perceived at a short distance eight or ten regular bunches or protuberances, and at a short interval three or four more .... The Head ... was serpent shaped[;] it was elevated about two feet from the water.... He could not have been less than eighty feet long."

On August 19, 1817, the Linnean Society of New England met in Boston and selected three men—a judge, a physician, and a naturalist—to conduct inquiries. They were to interview witnesses and secure affidavits from them. The sightings went on almost daily through the end of the month. From all this testimony, and from that of other witnesses in 1818 and 1819, a composite description of the sea serpent emerged: a huge snake-like creature, dark on top, lighter on its underside, moving with vertical undulations.

Whatever else it may have been, the animal was not a serpent. Reptiles move laterally, not vertically. Nonetheless, the Society investigators concluded that the animal, an enormous reptile, was appearing close to shore because it had laid its eggs there. No such eggs were found, in spite of repeated searches, but

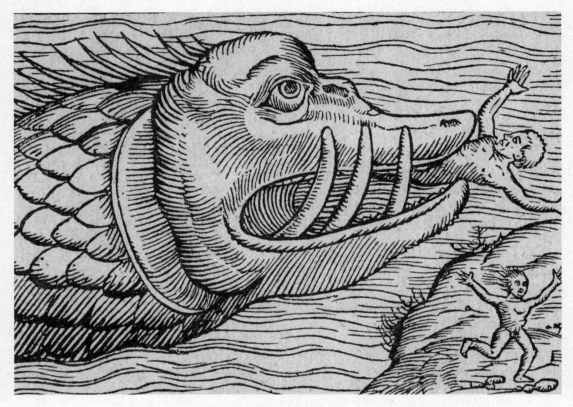

A 1550 illustration of a hungry sea monster swallowing ill-fated sailors.

when a farmer killed a three-foot black snake in a field just off Cape Ann, he noticed it had a series of bumps along its back—just as the sea serpent was reported to have.

The Society foolishly endorsed the farmer's suggestion that this was a recently hatched baby sea serpent. Subsequently, another scientist, Alexandre Lesuerur, showed that the specimen was no more than a deformed version of the common black snake. Though Lesuerur did not intend to discredit the sightings of the much larger New England sea serpents, his analysis was seized upon by skeptics and their journalistic allies, and the entire affair ended in derision.

The "great unknown"

No amount of laughter, however, could stop the sightings, which kept coming in from all over the world, though it could discourage some people from reporting them. When the great American statesman Daniel Webster saw a sea serpent, while on a fishing trip off the Massachusetts coast, he pleaded with his companion, according to Henry David Thoreau, "For God's sake never say a word about this to anyone, for if it should be known that I have seen the sea serpent, I should never hear the last of it."

For all the attempts to explain them conventionally—one scoffer averred that every sighting arose from "defective observation connected with an extravagant degree of fear"—the sea serpent did not lose all its supporters in the ranks of the rational and the learned. Sightings saw print mostly in newspapers but also occasionally in scientific periodicals. In 1835 the *American Journal of Science*, after reporting one clear observation, remarked, "We must therefore consider this case as settling the question of the real existence of a Sea Serpent. The absence of paddles or arms forbids us from supposing that this was a swimming saurian."

Of course this did not settle the matter at all, and in 1837 a German zoologist, Hermann Schlegel, "proved" that sea-serpent sightings were caused by observations of rows of porpoises. The sea serpent was fortunate enough, however, to attract the attention of *Zoologist* editor Edward Newman, who in 1847 opened the pages of his journal to open-minded discussion of the subject. He was well aware, naturally, that he was defying convention. In an editorial he noted, "It has been the fashion for ... many years to deride all records of this very celebrated monster." He proceeded to chide critics for *a priori* approaches that ignored "fact and observation" on the grounds that the sea serpent "ought not to be." "Fact-naturalists," on the other hand, "take a different road to knowledge, they enquire whether such things *are*, and whether such things *are not*."

The following year the most famous sea-serpent report of all time took place. It occurred on the later afternoon of August 6, 1848, and the witnesses were the captain and crew of the frigate *Daedalus*, on their way back to England from the Cape of Good Hope. Soon after its arrival at Plymouth on October 4, several newspapers took note of rumors of a spectacular twenty-minute sea-serpent sighting, and the Admiralty asked Peter M'Quhae, the captain, to supply a report either denying or detailing the incident. On the eleventh M'Quhae wrote Adm. Sir W. H. Gage a letter that the *Times* of London reprinted two days later. It reads, in part:

> The object ... was discovered to be an enormous serpent, with head and shoulders kept about four feet constantly above the surface of the sea, and as nearly as we could approximate by comparing it with the length of what our main-topsail yard would show in the water, there was at the very least 60 feet of the animal [above water], no portion of which was, to our perception, used in propelling it through the water, either by vertical or horizontal undulation. It passed rapidly, but so close under our lee quarter, that had it been a man of my acquaintance, I should easily have recognized his features with the naked eye; and it did not, either in approaching the ship or after it passed our wake, deviate in the slightest degree from its course to the S.W., which it held on at the pace of from 12 to 15 miles per hour, apparently on some determined purpose.
>
> The diameter of the serpent was about 15 or 16 inches behind the head, which was, without any doubt, that of a snake, and it was never during the 20 minutes that it continued in sight of our glasses, once below the sur-

face of the water; its color a dark brown, with yellowish white about the throat. It had no fins, but something like the mane of a horse, or rather a bunch of seaweed, washed about its back. It was seen by the quartermaster, the boatswain's mate, and the man at the wheel, in addition to myself and officers above mentioned.

The *Zoologist* soon afterwards published the private notes of another witness, Lt. Edgar Drummond, who confirmed M'Quhae's account in all particulars but one. What M'Quhae had called a mane Drummond deemed a dorsal fin. Then years later another officer recalled the incident in a letter to the *Times*: "My impression," he wrote, "was that it was rather of a lizard than a serpentine character, as its movement was steady and uniform, as if propelled by fins, not by any undulatory power."

> The world was now too well explored for it to harbor unknown beasts of great size, the reasoning went.

These accounts sparked an uproar. Those who could not credit the sea serpent, even when reported by sane, sober, and experienced British officers, scrambled to concoct alternative explanations. One held that M'Quhae and the others had seen a patch of seaweed. Slightly less preposterous was a notion advanced by Sir Richard Owen, the great anatomist best remembered for his role, a few years in the future, as one of the most implacable foes of Charles Darwin's theory of evolution. Owen declared that the animal M'Quhae saw could not have been a reptile—here he was certainly correct—and so it must be a giant seal, with the witnesses' excitement and overwrought imagination supplying the unseal-like details.

Writing in the November 28 issue of the *Times*, M'Quhae boldly took on the esteemed professor, who happened to be the Admiralty's consultant on sea serpents, whose existence he had pronounced less likely than that of ghosts. The captain flatly rejected Owen's speculations, citing the quotations out of context and false conclusions that the scientist had employed to buttress his argument. "Finally, I deny the existence of excitement, or the possibility of optical illusion," he stated. "I adhere to the statement, as to form, color, and dimensions, contained in my official report to the Admiralty, and I leave them as data whereupon the learned and scientific may exercise the 'pleasures of imagination' until some more fortunate opportunity shall occur of making a closer acquaintance with the 'great unknown'—in the present instance assuredly no ghost."

Science writer Richard Ellis, generally skeptical of cryptozoological claims but less dogmatic about it than Owen, theorizes that the *Daedalus* crew saw an animal then unrecognized, but since embraced, by science. The creature's head, in this reading, is in reality "the tail section of an enormous cephalopod," according to Ellis. "No vertebrate can move through the water without some visible means of propulsion, but a squid, which uses water ejected from the funnel or the mantle to move, could easily be conformed to M'Quhae's description."

Though their contemporaries thought M'Quhae got the better of the argument and the sea serpent still had a few prominent champions (such as the famous naturalist Philip Gosse), the weight of scientific opinion continued its slide into negativism. Despite a multitude of reports by men and women of responsible position and impeccable reputation, despite sightings by whole ship crews, and notwithstanding statements under oath, the creature was more and more viewed as an impossibility. The world was now too well explored for it to harbor unknown beasts of great size, the reasoning went. Moreover, if they existed, why did such creatures never get stranded on beaches, leaving carcasses that would settle the question for once and always? Of course the latter was something of a self-fulfilling prophecy, because prejudice against sea serpents had become so entrenched that when unusual carcasses were found, often scientists refused to examine them. On the other hand, when examinations were accomplished, the carcasses typically proved to be from known sea animals, notably the basking shark.

Final solutions to the sea-serpent mystery were regularly declared. One caustic observer of these attempts to bury the monster, Richard A. Proctor, wrote in 1885:

> Because one captain has mistaken a lot of floating sea-wreck half a mile away for a sea monster, therefore the story of a sea creature seen swiftly advancing against wind and sea, at a distance of less than 200 yards, meant nothing more than misunderstood sea-weed. Another mistakes a flight of birds in the distance, or a shoal of porpoises, and even a range of hills beyond the horizon, for some sea-serpentine monster, and forthwith other accounts, however manifestly inconsistent with such explanations, are regarded as explained away. Then, worst of all, some idiot invents a sea-serpent to beguile his time and find occupation for his shallow pate, and so soon as the story is shown to be only a story, men of sense and standing, as incapable of the idiocy of inventing sea-monsters as I am of inventing a planet, are supposed to have amused their leisure by sending grave reports of non-existent sea-monsters to men under whom they (the seamen, not the monsters) held office, or by taking oath before the magistrates that they had seen sea creatures which they had invented, and by parallel absurdities.

In 1892 A. C. Oudemans revived the question in a classic work, *The Great Sea Serpent*, which as a summary and analysis of the evidence would be unmatched until the publication, in 1968, of Bernard Heuvelmans's *In the Wake of the Sea-Serpents*. In 591 pages Oudemans, a respected Dutch zoologist, reviewed 187 cases and from them concluded that all sea-serpent sightings were of a single species of animal, a gigantic long-necked seal.

The twentieth-century serpent

In 1933 reports of strange animals in a Scottish lake caused a sensation, and the legend of the Loch Ness monster entered international popular culture. Though within fairly short order Ness' alleged inhabitants would acquire a reputation, at least among those who had not bothered to pay attention to the evidence (inconclusive but certainly intriguing), as creatures in an absurd tall tale, for a period of time the Ness story reminded scientists and others of the still-unsolved mystery of the sea serpent. Oudemans, for instance, assumed that one of the Ness animals would soon be caught or killed and the identity of the sea serpent would be known with certainty.

In the 1920s and 1930s a rash of reports described a sea serpent off the coast of British Columbia. Occasional sightings had occurred in the past, going back to at least 1897, but the Loch Ness uproar gave water monsters generally a new cachet. Soon the Canadian animal was given the name Cadborosaurus, which combined Cadboro Bay, on Victoria Island's southeast coast, and saurus. Cadborosaurus soon was shortened to "Caddy."

The first widely publicized sighting took place on October 8, 1933, and involved a witness of high repute: Maj. W. H. Langley, a barrister and clerk of the British Columbia legislature. Sailing his sloop past Chatham Island early in the afternoon, he spotted a greenish brown serpent with serrated body, "every bit as big as a whale but entirely different from a whale in many respects." He estimated its length at eighty feet.

Two scientists, University of British Columbia oceanographer Paul LeBlond and marine biologist Edward Bousfield, of the Royal Ontario Museum, have spent years investigating reports like these. By 1992 they were willing to endorse the reality of the animals in a formal lecture to the American Society of Zoologists. They went on to write a book on the subject, though their identification of the creatures as plesiosaurs has met with criticism and skepticism, even from colleagues sympathetic to the notion that Caddy exists as an unknown animal.

According to the British Columbia Scientific Cryptozoology Club, which has pioneered much of the investigation:

> Cadborosaurus (known by the some of the coastal First Nations peoples of B.C. as Hiyitlik, also known locally as Tzarta-saurus, Sisiutl, Penda, Amy, Saya-Ustih, Sarah the Sea Hag, Kaegyhil-Depgu'esk, Say Noth-kai and Klematosaurus) is not limited to the waters of British Columbia alone and is to be found from Alaska (where it is known as Pal-Rai-Yuk) to the Gulf Of Monterey in California.... A number of similar aquatic cryptids [have been] seen off the Oregon and Washington coast known variously as Colossal Claude and the Yachats serpent.

> Although it is thought that this creature has tended to remain in the deeper oceanic waters off the coast of British Columbia[,] it has been seen in and around Vancouver at Siwash Point, Stanley Park, Burrard Inlet, Indian Arm off North Vancouver; False Creek; Kitsilano Beach: at the mouth of the Fraser River off UBC and in the river at the foot of Main Street. Sightings around Victoria have taken place at the Inner Harbour; Cadboro Bay: Oak Bay; Cordova Bay; off Dallas Road; Race Rocks Chatham Island; Witty's Lagoon; Willow Beach; Sooke and Ross Point.

Occasional video footage of a large unidentified animal with a turtle- or camel-shaped head has not settled the issue, but it, along with continuing sightings by reputable individuals, has kept it alive.

Another sea serpent, prominent a few decades ago but since faded from public attention, is Chessie, the Chesapeake Bay monster. Though sightings were reported in the late 1960s, a particularly spectacular one occurred in 1978, when a retired CIA employee and his neighbor observed four such creatures seventy-five feet out in the water. In 1980, twenty-five people aboard four charter boats sighted a creature they described as twenty-five to forty feet long and a bit less than one foot across. Its head was oval and dark, and it was serpent-like in contour, but no fins or limbs were visible.

On May 2, 1982, at 7 P.M., while entertaining guests outside their home overlooking the bay at Love Point on the northern tip of Kent Island, at the mouth of the Chester River, Robert and Karen Frew saw a strange animal 200 feet from shore in calm water only five feet deep. Frew watched it through binoculars for a few minutes before securing his video camera and focusing on the object, which submerged and reap

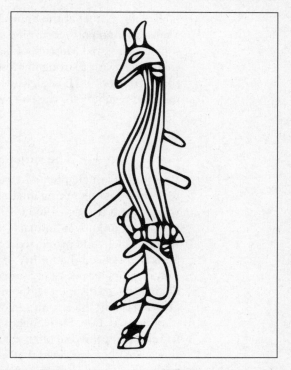

This drawing is based on a pteroglyph discovered near Sproat Lake on Vancouver Island, Canada. It appears to be an ancient drawing of a plesiosaur-like animal.

peared several times during the sighting. The closest the creature came was within 100 feet of shore and within fifty feet of some boys who were playing on a pile of submerged rocks. Though the Frews and their friends shouted to alert the boys (their cries and all other comments made during the event are recorded on the videotape), the boys never heard them and so apparently never saw the animal.

The witnesses estimated the animal to be thirty to thirty-five feet long but slightly less than a foot in diameter. Much of it remained under water, but as it surfaced repeatedly, more and more of it became visible. Frew said, "The first time up, we saw its head and about four feet [of back]. The next time about 12 feet, the next time about 20." The visible part of the back seemed to have humps. Its head was shaped like a football, only "a little more round." Observers could not discern eyes, ears, or mouth. It was the odd shape of the head more than anything else that led Frew to reject the idea that the animal was some kind of snake. Familiar with a wide variety of sea life, the Frews rejected theories that they had misperceived a conventional seal.

On August 20, seven scientists from the Smithsonian Institution, along with representatives of the National Aquarium and Maryland's Department of Natu ral Resources, met at the Smithsonian to view and discuss the Frew videotape. In a subsequent report recounting the group's conclusions, George Zug of the Smithsonian's National Museum of Natural History wrote: "All the viewers of the tape came away with a strong impression of an animate object.... We could not identify the object.... These sightings are not isolated phenomena, for they have been reported regularly for the past several years."

The varieties of sea-serpent experience

In the last chapter of *In the Wake of the Sea-Serpents*, at the end of a detailed recitation and searching analysis of every sea-serpent report, credible or otherwise, known through 1966 (587 in all, of which he judged 358 authentic observations of unknown animals [some of which have been disputed; see below]), Bernard Heuvelmans parted company with nearly all of his predecessors. He bluntly conceded the futility of trying to force-fit from these sightings a description of a single species of animal. Virtually every other commentator, including Oudemans and Rupert T. Gould (author of the important *The Case for the Sea Serpent* [1930]), had dismissed or rationalized away all discordant detail as due to error or invention. Heuvelmans found, however, that these supposedly anomalous features reappeared so often that they had to be taken into consideration. And if they were, they suggested that "sea serpent" is a generic term covering several unrecognized marine animals. Among them:

Long-necked (forty-eight sightings). Description: A long neck, angled toward the head; hump or humps on the back; no tail; two horns, sometimes de-

He bluntly conceded the futility of trying to force-fit from these sightings a description of a single species of animal.

scribed as ears. Sample report: In the summer of 1950, John Handley, bathing in the surf on the Kent coast, saw a long-necked creature rise out of the water less than 500 yards away. It had ears and a horselike head more than two feet across. A woman also observed the creature. Classification: Almost certainly a pinniped (seal). Range: Cosmopolitan.

Merhorse (thirty-seven sightings): Description: Floating mane, medium to long neck, big eyes, hair or whiskers on the face. Sample report: In November 1947, Vancouver Island fisherman George W. Saggers encountered a strange serpent-like animal in Ucluelet Harbor, at a distance of 150 feet. Its head and neck were four feet above the water; it had "two jet black eyes just three inches across and protruding from the head.... It appeared to have some sort of mane.... The color of the mane was dark brown," he wrote. Classification: Probably a pinniped. Range: Cosmopolitan.

Many-humped (thirty-three sightings). Description: String of dorsal humps, slender neck of medium length, small but prominent eyes, striped dark on top of the body, white on underside, white stripes on neck. Sample report: On June 20, 1815, Capt. Elkanah Finney focused a telescope on a sea serpent in Cape Cod

Bay: "I then had a good view of him through my glass, at the distance of a quarter of a mile. His appearance in this situation was like a string of buoys. I saw perhaps thirty or forty of these protuberances or bunches, which were about the size of a barrel. The head (front part visible above water) appeared to be about six or eight feet long, and where it was connected with the body was a little larger than the body. His head tapered off to the size of a horse's head.... What I supposed to be his under jaw had a white stripe extending the whole length of the head, just above the water. While he lay in this situation, he appeared to be about a hundred or a hundred and twenty feet long." Classification: Cetacean (whale, porpoise, or dolphin). Range: North Atlantic.

Many-finned (twenty sightings). Description: Triangular fins looking up like a huge crest; short, slender neck. Sample report: In December 1878, an Englishwoman named Mrs. Turner was aboard the liner *Poonah* anchored off Suez or Aden, she could not remember which, when she related her experience to Robert P. Greg, who subsequently wrote a letter to Oudemans. She observed an extraordinary animal motionless on the surface 150 feet away. Greg wrote, "She saw both the head and 7 or 8 fins of the back, all at the same time in a line. She cannot remember exactly how many dorsal fins there were, but they were large, slightly curved back and not all the same size.... The head looked 4–6 feet diameter, like a large tree trunk.... The color was nearly black like a whale. The whole length appeared considerable, perhaps as long as an ordinary tree, or moderate sized ship!" Classification: Cetacean. Range: Tropical waters.

Super-Otter (thirteen sightings). Description: Slender, medium-length neck; long, tapering tail; several vertical bends in the body. Sample report: Hans Egede, a Protestant missionary known as the Apostle of Greenland, record this 1734 manifestation, witnessed while he was on his second voyage to Greenland: "This Monster was of so huge a Size, that coming out of the Water, its Head reached as high as the Mast-Head; its Body was bulky as the Ship, and three or four times as long. It had a long pointed Snout, and spouted like a Whale-Fish; great broad Paws, and the Body seemed covered with shell-work, its skin very rugged and uneven. The under Part of its Body was shaped like an enormous huge Serpent, and when it dived again under Water, it plunged backwards into the Sea, and so raised its Tail aloft, which seemed a whole Ship's Length distant from the bulkiest part of its Body." Classification: Uncertain, but possibly a surviving form of primitive cetacean. Range: North Atlantic (possibly extinct; last known sighting in 1848). See below for a critique of Heuvelmans's treatment of this incident.

Super-Eel (twelve sightings). Description: Serpentine body; long, tapering tail. Sample report: Two British naturalists aboard the yacht *Valhalla,* on a scientific cruise fifteen miles off the mouth of the Parahiba in Brazil, spotted a strange animal in the water at mid-morning on December 7, 1905. E.G.B. Meade-Waldo wrote: "I ... saw a large fin or frill sticking out of the water, dark seaweed-brown in color, somewhat crinkled at the edge. It was apparently about 6 feet in length, and projected from 18 inches to 2 feet from the water." After securing field glasses, he watched a "great head and neck [rise] out of the water in front of the frill; the neck did not touch the grill in the water, but came out of the water *in front* of it, at a distance of certainly not less than 18 inches, and from 7 to 8 feet was out of the water; head and neck were all about the same thickness. The head had a very turtle-like appearance, as had also the eye…. It moved its head and side in a peculiar manner; the color of the head and neck was dark brown above, and whitish below—almost white, I think." Classification: Fish. Range: Cosmopolitan.

Heuvelmans acknowledged, "I cannot claim to have entirely solved the problem of the great sea-serpent, but I have cleared up a good deal of it. To solve the whole complex problem, without being able to examine the remains of the animals in question, we need many more detailed and exact reports." He noted that hoaxes and misidentifications of known marine animals have added no small measure of confusion. Aside from reports that had to be eliminated from the analysis because of lack of detail, Heuvelmans counted forty-nine hoaxes and fifty-two mistakes among the reports he collected.

(Some of the most outlandish hoaxes would be perpetrated in the decade after *In the Wake* saw print. They included widely published photographs, allegedly taken by an untraceable "Mary F.," allegedly of the Cornish sea serpent Morgawr off Falmouth Bay. An account in *Strange Magazine*, the results of an extensive investigation conducted by Mark Chorvinsky, identifies the hoaxer as professional prankster Tony "Doc" Shiels, though Shiels [who like Chorvinsky has since died] admitted nothing then or later. There is, in any event, no doubt that the photographs are bogus. Shiels also took dubious-looking pictures of what he maintained was the Loch Ness monster.)

In common with every other twentieth-century commentator, Heuvelmans rejected the idea that sea serpents are serpents as such. All but one of the proposed candidates above are mammals. But he did leave the door open slightly for the possibility that an unknown reptile may have been observed on rare occasion. His collection included a scant four reports of what he called a "marine saurian," a huge lizard or crocodile-shaped creature encountered in tropical waters. If it exists, it may be, in Heuvelmans's view, "a surviving thalattosuchian, in other words a true crocodile of an ancient group, a specifically and exclusively oceanic one, which flourished from the Jurassic to the Cretaceous periods. But it could also be a surviving mosasaur, a sea cousin of the monitors of today. It would not be surprising if it had survived for so long in the sea, since it is well designed to dive deep and remain unseen."

Curiously enough, though Heuvelmans did not mention the fact, some witnesses claim to have sighted giant "crocodiles," "alligators," or "salamanders" in Loch Ness, though writers and investigators—focused on the notion of the classic long-necked, plesiosaur-like Nessie—have tended to ignore or downplay such sightings.

To the most frequently stated objection to sea serpents—the absence of stranded carcasses—Heuvelmans wrote that the kinds of beasts responsible for such sightings "all belong by nature to the category of animals least likely to be stranded, and quite capable of getting off the shore again, if by misfortune they are." Apparently, he thought, they die far out at sea.

Heuvelmans disputed

As one would expect given the controversial nature of his subject matter, Heuvelmans has his critics. The most vociferous of them is the German debunker Ulrich Magin, who is not given to understatement; to him, cryptozoology itself is no less than a "pseudoscience" and Heuvelmans, its founder, a purveyor of absurd myths.

In a wide-ranging attack in the journal *Fortean Studies*, Magin condemns Heuvelmans for sometimes sloppy research, leading him to include in his classification system instances of clear misidentifications of conventional animals or of outright hoaxes. He also charges that the system does not exist outside Heuvelmans's imagination. Magin writes:

Cryptozoologist Bernard Heuvelmans speculated that sea serpents are able to move onto land like crocodiles or sea lions.

> Sightings are based on real animals like whales, seals, large turtles and sharks, and natural effects like standing waves and seaweed in the tide, which are interpreted as sea monsters. I notice that every May and June, when basking sharks migrate along the British shores, we get the first reports of sea serpents from fishermen. When basking sharks leave the area, the reports stop. But the witness, surprised by the gigantic creature, sees the phenomenon in terms from mythology or newspaper reports. This can explain the strange hybrid arising when witnesses mix characteristics they know from previous reading or storytelling to be typical of the monster with the forms they have actually seen.

In those last two sentences Magin appears oddly oblivious to the consideration that the same might be said of his comparably all-knowing skeptic's rejection of uncongenial reports. To a strikingly similar degree, the critic and the criticized are engaged in mind-reading (and worse) of persons whom they have never met and are unlikely ever to meet. While he scores some points in his dissection of Heuvelmans's treatment of individual reports, Magin—in the fashion of would-be debunkers who preceded him—cannot resist overstating his case. Even Richard Ellis, for example, acknowledges the 1817 to 1819 Gloucester, Massachusetts, sightings to be "one of the great unsolved mysteries of sea-serpent lore." Just as it is wise to be cautious about these matters, it seems futile to pretend that all of the interesting questions have been answered or that all of the eyewitness testimony merits nothing more than sneering dismissal.

A more restrained critic than Magin, Lars Thomas looks at Heuvelmans's evidence for Hans Egede's "super-otter" and finds it wanting. Heuvelmans, it turns out, relied on a faulty translation. When Thomas located the actual text, in a book by Paul Egede, Hans's son, he learned that his father had not been a witness—he had not even been on the ship at the time of the sighting—and had learned of it secondhand from the witnesses. A more accurate translation of the description, according to Thomas, reveals an animal that could not possibly have been an otter, even one of enormous proportions. Its features are reminiscent of a zeuglodon's, in Thomas's judgment.

Heuvelmans revised

In 2003, cryptozoologist Loren Coleman and science journalist Patrick Huyghe reexamined and revised Heuvelmans's classification system. In their assessment Heuvelmans had sometimes failed to consider "various behaviors, individual characteristics, and regional and temporal variations" before proposing separate species. For his Super-Otters, Super-Eels, and some Many-humped, they suggest a single category, "Classic Sea Serpent." These are marine creatures described as resembling giant snakes, even if "the animal may turn out to be a mammal." And they brought Merhorses and Long-necks into a single category.

They expanded categories of sea-going cryptids into new areas, such as Mystery Cetacean, Giant Shark, and Mystery Manta, and others for a total of fourteen categories. Some of these ostensibly uncatalogued animals are less controversial than others.

Sea serpents in our future

Most marine zoologists who have reflected on the question agree that as many as several dozen large marine creatures remain to be discovered. Of course, it will take an actual specimen to silence the skeptics.

Nonetheless, as the dimensions of our ignorance about the fauna and flora of the ocean depths become ever more apparent, *a priori* objections to the existence of gigantic unknown sea animals have fallen by the wayside. Perhaps the sea serpent's time is just around the temporal horizon.

Further Reading:

Aldrich, Hal B. "Was It a Plesiosaur?" *INFO Journal* 6,3 (September/October 1977): 13–14.

Bandini, Ralph. "I Saw a Sea Monster." *Esquire* (June 1934): 90,92.

Bayanov, Dmitri. "Black Sea Serpents." *Fortean Times* 51 (1988/1989): 59.

Bradford, Gershom. "Sea Serpents? No or Maybe." *The American Neptune* 13,4 (October 1953): 268–76.

Burr, Malcolm. "Sea Serpents and Monsters." *The Nineteenth Century and After* 115 (February 1934): 220–30.

Chorvinsky, Mark. "The 'Mary F.' Morgawr Photographs Investigation." *Strange Magazine* 8 (Fall 1991): 8–9,11,46–48.

Chorvinsky, Mark, and Mark Opsasnick. "A Field Guide to the Monsters and Mystery Animals of Maryland." *Strange Magazine* 5 (1990): 41–46.

Coleman, Loren, and Patrick Huyghe. *The Field Guide to Lake Monsters, Sea Serpents, and Other Mystery Denizens of the Deep.* New York: Jeremy P. Tarcher/Penguin, 2003.

Colombo, John Robert. *Mysterious Canada: Strange Sights, Extraordinary Events, and Peculiar Places.* Toronto: Doubleday Canada, 1988.

Corliss, William R., ed. *Strange Life: A Sourcebook on the Mysteries of Organic Nature, Volume B–1.* Glen Arm, MD: Sourcebook Project, 1976.

Ellis, Richard. *Monsters of the Sea.* New York: Alfred A. Knopf, 1994.

Geller, L. D. "Notes on Sea Serpents of Coastal New England." *New York Folklore Quarterly* 26,2 (June 1970): 153–60.

Gould, Rupert T. *The Sea Serpent.* London: Huggins and Company, 1923.

———. *The Case for the Sea Serpent.* London: Philip Allan, 1930.

———. *The Loch Ness Monster and Others.* London: Geoffrey Bles, 1934.

Heuvelmans, Bernard. *In the Wake of the Sea-Serpents.* New York: Hill and Wang, 1968.

———. "How I Conquered the Sea-Serpent Some Twenty-Five Years Ago." *Strange Magazine* 3 (1988): 10–13,56–57.

LeBlond, Paul H. "A Previously Unreported 'Sea Serpent' Sighting in the South Atlantic." *Cryptozoology* 2 (1983): 82–84.

Lester, Paul. *The Great Sea Serpent Controversy: A Cultural Study.* Birmingham, England: Protean Publications, 1984.

Ley, Willy. *Exotic Zoology.* New York: Viking Press, 1959.

McLellan, Wendy. "A Serpent Lurking in the Deep?" *Vancouver Province,* British Columbia (August 2, 1992).

Magin, Ulrich. "Irish Sea Serpent Wave of 1850." *Strange Magazine* 14 (1994): 30–31, 56.

———. "St. George Without a Dragon." In Steve Moore, ed. *Fortean Studies, Volume 3,* 223–34. London: John Brown Publishing, 1996.

Mangiacopra, Gary S. "The Great Unknowns of the 19th Century." *Of Sea and Shore* (Winter 1976–77): 201–05, 228.

Mawnan-Peller, A. *Morgawr: The Monster of Falmouth Bay: A Short History.* Falmouth, Cornwall, England: Morgawr Productions, 1976.

Meurger, Michel. "In Jormungandra's Coils: A Cultural Archaeology of the Norse Sea-Serpent." *Fortean Times* 51 (1988/1989): 63–68.

Moore, Gary. "The Gloucester Moncester." *Boston Herald American Beacon* (January 9, 1977): 20–22, 26–27.

Oudemans, A. C. *The Great Sea Serpent.* Leiden, Netherlands: E. J. Brill, 1892.

Proctor, Richard A. "Monster Sea-Serpents." *Knowledge* 7 (1885): 273–74.

Saggers, George W. "Sea Serpent off Vancouver." *Fate* 1,2 (Summer 1948): 124–25.

Sansom, John H. "Fabulous Lunkers." *Fate* 41,3 (March 1988): 62–69.

"Sea Serpent." *American Journal of Science* 1,11 (1826): 196.

Thomas, Lars. "Appendix: No Super-Otter After All?" In Steve Moore, ed. *Fortean Studies, Volume 3,* 234–36. London: John Brown Publishing, 1996.

"On the History of the Great Sea Serpent." *Blackwood's Edinburgh Magazine* 13,3 (April 1818): 32–42.

Westrum, Ronald. "A Note on Monsters." *Journal of Popular Culture*. 8,4 (Spring 1975): 862–70.

———. "Sea-Serpent Reporting Dynamics." *Pursuit* 8,4 (October 1975): 86–88.

———. "Knowledge about Sea Serpents." In Roy Wallis, ed. *The Sociological Review Monograph No. 27: On the Margins of Science: The Social Construction of Rejected Knowledge*, 293–314. Great Britain: University of Keele, March 1979.

Wood, J. G. "The Trail of the Sea-Serpent." *The Atlantic Monthly* 53,320 (June 1884): 799–814.

Yoon, Carol Kaesuk. "In Dark Seas, Biologists Sight a Riot of Life." *New York Times* (June 2, 1992).

Tatzelwurm

Though zoologists discount claims to its existence, relegating reports to mistakes and hoaxes, and the name is fading into obscurity, the lizard-like creature sometimes called the tatzelwurm (German for "worm with claws") was reported for more than two centuries, and likely longer. Mostly—albeit not quite entirely; some French and Italian reports exist—it was said to inhabit the Swiss and Austrian Alps. A close examination of the reports, however, raises questions about whether "tatzelwurm" had any other than a broadly generic meaning.

Aside from vague folk traditions of a mountain-dwelling dragon with a cat-like head and spiked ridges along its back, the documented sighting history begins in the eighteenth century. In Italy in 1750, for example, witnesses told of encountering a hairless animal, something like a fast-moving lizard, with two front paws and dragging hindquarters. It was once seen killing a rabbit.

A later, more famous report is associated with a certain Hans Fuchs, who in 1779 spotted two tatzelwurms as they appeared unexpectedly in front of him. Unable to shake off the terror he had experienced, not long afterward he suffered a stress-related fatal heart attack. Before he died, he detailed what he had seen to his family. In a painting, which an unidentified individual prepared in the wake of the supposed event, two large, lizard-like creatures are featured. German cryptozoologist Ulrich Magin remarks, "This depiction of the two monsters is still the best we have of the creature." Or maybe not; the creatures here have four legs. A 1934 picture taken by a Swiss man, while represented as a photographic image of a tatzelwurm and answering to the unusual shape tradition attests, is generally judged dubious; the so-called tatzelwurm is probably a ceramic figure.

In the later nineteenth century, asserted sightings grew more frequent, with witnesses often relating their glimpses of a thick, light-colored cylindrical body, along with two long legs in front with three toes on each foot. A wide mouth held sharp teeth in a feline-looking head. The back legs were said to be tiny, vestigial, or nonexistent. The creature had either a short neck or no neck at all, and at times it was heard emitting a whistling sound; other observers spoke of snorting, spitting, or hissing. Length estimates were anywhere from one to six feet. Most observers thought it had smooth skin, but a significant plurality believed they had

(Continued on page 184)

Dover Demon

The scare began at 10:30 on the evening of April 21, 1977, as three seventeen-year-old boys were driving north through Dover, Massachusetts, Boston's most affluent suburb. One of them, Bill Bartlett, thought he spotted something creeping along a low wall of loose stones on the left side of the road.

As the figure turned its head and stared into the headlights of the car, Bartlett said, he saw two large, round, glassy, lidless eyes shining brightly "like orange marbles." Its head, resting atop a thin neck, was big and watermelon-shaped and fully as large as the rest of the body. Except for its oversized head, the creature was thin, with long spindly arms and legs, and large hands and feet. The skin was hairless and peach-colored and appeared to have a rough, sandpaper-like texture. No more than four feet tall, it had been making its way uncertainly along the wall, its long fingers curled around the rocks, when the car lights surprised it.

Neither of Bartlett's companions, whose attention was elsewhere, noticed the creature, which was visible for only a few seconds. They testified later, however, that their friend had seemed genuinely upset. When Bartlett arrived at his home, his father noticed his distraught state and heard the story from his son, who drew a sketch of what he had seen.

Around 12:30 A.M. fifteen-year-old John Baxter, walking home from his girlfriend's house, reportedly saw a short fig-ure approaching him. Thinking it was a small-statured friend, he called out his name but got no response. When the figure got closer it stopped, causing Baxter to do the same. Trying to get a better look, Baxter took one step forward, and the figure scurried off to the left, running down a shallow, wooded gully and up to the opposite bank.

Baxter followed it down the slope, then stopped and stared across the gully. The creature—which looked like nothing he had ever seen or heard of—stood in silhouette about thirty feet away, its feet "molded" around the top of a rock a few feet from a tree. It was leaning toward the tree with the long fingers of both hands entwined around the trunk. Though he would claim not to have heard of Bartlett's report at that point, his description of it would be exactly the same. Baxter backed carefully up the slope and walked quickly away from the scene.

The next night Bartlett told his close friend Will Taintor, eighteen, about his experience. That night, while Taintor was driving fifteen-year-old Abby Brabham home, Brabham said she spotted something in the car's headlights. On the left side of the road a hairless creature crouched on all fours, facing the car. Its body was thin and monkey-like, its head large, oblong, and devoid of nose, ears, and mouth. The facial area around the eyes was lighter, and the eyes glowed green. Brabham insisted on this last detail even after investigators in-

formed her that Bartlett had said the eyes were orange. Taintor said he caught only a brief glimpse.

The well-known anomalist Loren Coleman, then living in the area, learned of Bartlett's report through an acquaintance who knew the teenager. Subsequently he, along with ufologists Walter N. Webb and Ed Fogg, interviewed Bartlett and the other witnesses along with their parents, school officials and teachers, and police officers. They uncovered no evidence of a hoax; to the contrary, those who knew the teenagers described them as credible (though one teacher expressed some reservations about Bartlett). Coleman gave the creature the nickname "Dover Demon," and the moniker has stuck both locally and in the literature of anomalous entities.

Debunker Martin S. Kottmeyer later proposed that the witnesses saw no more than a yearling moose, blaming the confusion on darkness and the briefness of all sightings except Baxter's. "Bartlett's placing of the eyes matches the placement of eyes just above the hip of the muzzle on a moose's head," he wrote. "The lack of a discernable nose and mouth is easily laid to the fact that nostrils and mouth are very far down on the muzzle. A drawing of a young moose presents the ears swept back along the line of the head and would not discernably stick out, thus accounting for the absence of visible ears."

Notwithstanding a vague superficial plausibility, Kottmeyer's theory is almost certainly baseless. Coleman, who had the advantage of having investigated first-

(Continued from page 181)

seen small scales. It was given various colors. Nearly all agreed, on the other hand, that it had a short, blunt, unlizard-like tail.

There was wide agreement about the tatzelwurm's behavior. If it did not flee as soon as it noticed it was being seen, it turned on the witness, sometimes taking huge leaps (accounting for one of its alternate names, springwurm, or "jumping worm") and exhaling a snorting or whistling sound while in flight. If the witness did not run fast enough, the creature would bite him or her, on occasion with fatal consequences; in the less extreme cases, the victim suffered paralysis, usually temporary, of the affected limb. An Austrian case, from the summer of 1921, has a tatzelwurm—with a cat's head and a length of about three feet—leaping ten feet through the air toward two onlookers. Witnesses often spoke, too, of its terrifying fixed, nearly hypnotic stare and scary, menacing eyes.

The tatzelwurm reportedly hibernated during the winter, resting in crevices on mountainsides (thus yet another name, stollenwurm, German for "worm that lives in holes"). Occasionally, however, farmers found the creatures sleeping in hand, observes, "A skinny, four-foot-tall, upright (coming down on all fours sometimes), sandpaper-skinned, five-huge-fingered, bright orange-eyed 'baby moose' would be more of a wonder than the Dover Demon itself, I'm afraid." Additionally, the moose would have had to be a very young one without antlers, and even a young one, at 600 pounds, is too large to be a plausible candidate for the small, thin creature. Moreover, moose are rare in Massachusetts—only two interactions between officials and the animals are recorded between 1976 and 1977—and are to be found, if at all, in the central and western parts of the state, far from the Boston/Dover area. No evidence of a moose's presence there in the time period exists. This explanation seems literally a product of a debunker's imagination.

In 2006 the *Boston Sunday Globe* interviewed Bartlett, now an artist and family man living in a nearby community. Bartlett stated, "I have no idea what it was. I definitely know I saw something.... It was definitely weird. I didn't make it up. Sometimes I wish I had."

Nothing like the Dover Demon has been reported since.

Further Reading:

Coleman, Loren. *Mysterious America: The Revised Edition*. New York: ParaView Press, 2001.

"The Dover Demon." *Real Paper* (Cambridge, Massachusetts), May 21, 1977.

Kottmeyer, Martin S. "Demon Moose." *The Anomalist* 6 (1998): 104–10.

Sullivan, Mark. "Decades Later, the Dover Demon Still Haunts." *Boston Sunday Globe* (October 29, 2006).

the hay. One farmer claimed he killed a hibernating tatzelwurm, from whose mouth a green liquid then drained. In 1924 two men, who thought it resembled a lizard's, found a five-foot-long skeleton. A veterinary student who examined it concluded it was the remains of a roe.

In a significant minority of cases, "tatzelwurm"—notwithstanding its employment in the narrative—seems an inaccurate characterization. Some observers report two pairs of feet. In some rare instances, multiple pairs of feet are mentioned. In a 1927 Italian incident, one Josef Reiterer, walking in the twilight just after sundown, noticed a "worm" resting on a stone in his pathway. The thing abruptly rose to stare threateningly at him as it supported itself on its tail. The startled Reiterer noticed large front legs, followed by progressively smaller pairs the closer they got to the tail. The "worm" was approximately sixteen inches long, and a pointed tongue darted from its mouth, set in a "strange, square head." Its body was gray and hairless, its texture snail-like. A Catholic priest named Father Trafojer interviewed the witness on three occasions be-

An 1836 wood engraving from Germany of a tatzelwurm.

tween 1937 and 1947. It bears noting that an 1881 Austrian report alleges "two or three pairs of hind legs."

An 1893 story, set near Salzburg, Austria, links the tatzelwurm to what Americans of the period called a "glass snake"—a reptile that if struck would shatter into pieces. Such creatures once were a tall-tale staple, though also, once in a while, the subject of a supposed personal encounter. In this instance the tale is secondhand, from an individual identified only as Count Platz. As he approached a narrow footbridge over the Enns River, a professional hunter in the count's employ noticed a weasel on the other bank moving in his direction. It stopped abruptly to stare at something, and when the hunter followed its line of vision, he spotted a tatzelwurm coiled on the bridge. The weasel dashed into the woods and returned with a root in its mouth. It tossed the object at the tatzelwurm, which then disintegrated. Told of the incident, the count expressed disbelief, but the hunter swore that he was telling the truth.

As the twentieth century wore on, published reports grew less frequent. Those who thought the tatzelwurm might be real wondered if it had become extinct. Eventually, the tatzelwurm was relegated to the status of minor popular superstition (perhaps a dim echo of the once-ubiquitous dragon legend), from the skeptic's point of view, or to cryptozoological footnote, from the point of view of those who think the stories may be of a genuine unknown animal. In the first decade of the twenty-first century, uncatalogued reptiles, albeit not classic tatzelwurms, possessing extraordinary characteristics returned in some dramatic reports.

An undated incident, apparently occurring before 2005, allegedly took place in Tresivio, an Italian region in the Valtelina Valley along the Swiss border, when a young agricultural student encountered a creature right out of *Jurassic Park*. At the time nobody believed her, but subsequent developments—namely sightings by others of the same or a similar beast in the area in subsequent years, culminating in press accounts in 2009—led to a reassessment of the matter. Reinterviewed then, the woman, now a research assistant, swore, "I was not dreaming! I saw it clearly with my own eyes. It approached me, walking on its hind legs. The anterior legs were very small. It resembled a prehistoric velociraptor, and generally it was like a monitor lizard. Yet while monitors move on four legs, this one went upright. Its back was nearly 80cm [two feet eight inches] above the ground, with the head nearly a meter. I guess it was one and a half or two meters long [five to six feet six inches]."

Further Reading:

Coleman, Loren, and Jerome Clark. "Tatzelwurm." In *Cryptozoology A to Z: The Encyclopedia of Loch Monsters, Sasquatch, Chupacabras, and Other Authentic Mysteries of Nature*, pp. 231–32. New York: Fireside/Simon & Schuster, 1999.

Eberhart, George M. "Tatzelwurm." In *Mysterious Creatures: A Guide to Cryptozoology*, pp. 537–39. Santa Barbara, CA: ABC-CLIO, 2002.

Heuvelmans, Bernard. *On the Track of Unknown Animals*. New York: Hill and Wang, 1958.

Magin, Ulrich. "European Dragons: The Tatzelwurm." *Pursuit* 19,1 (First Quarter 1986): 16–22.

———. "The Tatzelwurm Lives!" *Fortean Times* 272 (2011): 55.

Meurger, Michel, with Claude Gagnon. *Lake Monster Traditions: A Cross-Cultural Analysis*. London: Fortean Tomes, 1988.

Thunderbirds

A belief once widespread among North American Indian tribes held that giant supernatural flying creatures, known as thunderbirds, cause thunder and lightning. They accomplish the former by flapping their wings, the latter by closing their eyes. Thunderbirds also war with other supernatural entities and sometimes grant favors to human beings. They are frequently depicted on totem poles.

The link between these mythological beasts and the "real" giant birds of modern reports is problematic. But there is no doubt that, if it means nothing else for anomalists, the tradition has provided a name for what people long have claimed to see (the first recorded sightings were in the 1840s) in the heavily forested Alleghany Plateau of north-central Pennsylvania.

"Thunderbirds are not a thing of the past," Pennsylvania writer Robert R. Lyman declared in 1973. "They are with us today, but few will believe it except those who see them. Their present home is in the southern edge of the Black Forest of the Susquehanna River, between Pine Creek at the east and Kettle Creek at the west. All reports for the past twenty years have come from that area."

Lyman himself claimed to have seen one of the birds in the early 1940s. When first observed, it was sitting on a road north of Coudersport. It then rose a few feet into the air, spreading wings that measured at least twenty feet, then flew into—not above—the dense woods lining the highway. It negotiated the dense second-growth timber with "no trouble," according to Lyman. In common with many—in other words, those who don't describe it as an immense eagle—who report seeing a thunderbird, Lyman thought it looked like a "very large vulture," brown, with short neck and eyes, and with "very narrow" wings. He also inferred it was a young representative of the species.

In 1969, the wife of Clinton County sheriff John Boyle, while sitting in front of the couple's cabin in remote Little Pine Creek, saw an enormous gray-colored bird land in the middle of the creek. A few moments later it rose to fly away, and "its wingspread," she said, "appeared to be as wide as the streambed, which I would say was about 75 feet"—making the creature truly otherworldly. That same summer three men allegedly saw a thunderbird snatch up a fifteen-pound fawn near Kettle Creek. In late September 1992, driving near a wildlife refuge in rural Lycoming County, Kim Foley and her young son reportedly observed "a very big bird

This nineteenth-century drawing from the North American Haida tribe is of a doubled thunderbird.

eating a dead deer. It was huge," she stated, "dark brown, almost black, an ugly beak. [It] looked right at us in the car, it was that tall."

Over in the Jersey Shore, Pennsylvania, area, just east of Clinton County, numerous reports of thunderbirds have been logged over the years. On October 28, 1970, several people driving west of town sighted what one of them, Judith Dingler, described as a "gigantic winged creature soaring towards Jersey Shore. It was dark colored, and its wingspread was almost like [that of] of an airplane." In the summer of 1992, Allison Stearn, who was hiking near Shingletown, spotted a huge, eagle-like bird, "dark brown or black," the size of an airplane.

Attack of the giant vultures

In July 1925, two visitors to Consolation Valley in the Canadian Rockies of Alberta spotted what they thought was an eagle at some considerable altitude. As it approached the Tower of Babel, a 7,500-foot-high peak within the range, they noticed that it was huge and brown and, even more startlingly, carried a large animal in its talons. Shouts from the observers caused it to drop its prey, which turned out to be a fifteen-pound mule deer fawn.

All conventional ornithological knowledge tells us that such reports describe the impossible. The largest predatory birds such as the eagle attack only "small mammals, reptiles, fish, and, perhaps, some other birds," according to the late wildlife authority Roger A. Caras. The largest American birds, the rare and endangered California condors, have a wingspan of slightly more than ten feet, though one captured specimen early in the twentieth century was measured at eleven feet, four inches. Even so, their weak feet do not permit them to carry their prey; instead they feed on carrion.

Here are some representative sightings of the vulture variety of thunderbird:

Kentucky, 1870: A "monster bird, something like the condor of Sinbad the Sailor," landed on a barn owned by James Pepples in rural Stanford. Pepples fired on the creature, wounding it, and took it into captivity. A contemporary press accounts says, "On measurement, the bird proved to be seven feet from tip to tip. It was of a black color, and both similar and dissimilar in many ways, to an eagle." Nothing is known of its fate.

Illinois, 1948: A number of persons told of seeing an immense bird said to be the size of a Piper Cub airplane and to look like a condor.

Puerto Rico, 1975: During a spate of unexplained nocturnal killings of farm and domestic animals, owners sometimes reported being awakened by a "loud screech" and hearing the flapping of enormous wings. Several witnesses claimed daylight sightings of what one called a "whitish-colored gigantic condor or vulture."

Northern California, 1975: Residents of a Walnut Creek neighborhood saw an immense bird, over five feet tall with a "head like a vulture" and gray wings, dwarfing a nearby eucalyptus tree. Five minutes later it flew away, revealing a fifteen-foot wingspan. Around the same time, in nearby East Bay, a number of persons observed the same or a similar bird sitting on a rooftop.

A remarkable series of events that took place in 1977 attracted wide publicity. They began on the evening of July 25 in Lawndale in central Illinois's Logan County. Three boys, one of them ten-year-old Marlon Lowe, were playing in the backyard when they saw two large birds come out of the south. They swooped out of the sky toward Travis Goodwin, who jumped into a swimming pool to escape. They then turned their attention to Marlon, who was grabbed by the straps of his sleeveless shirt and lifted two feet above the ground. As Marlon screamed, his parents Jake and Ruth Lowe and two friends, Jim and Betty Daniels, heard him and witnessed the bizarre sight of the boy held in the talons of a flying bird. Marlon was beating at it with his fists until finally, after carrying him about forty feet into the front yard, it dropped him. By this time Mrs. Lowe, who had headed off in pursuit, was so close to the birds that she had to back up. Then, she said, "the birds just cleared the top of the camper, went beneath some telephone wires and flapped their wings—very gracefully—one more time." They flew off toward the north and in the direction of the tall trees along Kickapoo Creek.

According to the witnesses, the birds, about four feet long, were black with white rings on their long necks and at the tips of their wings. Their beaks were curved. They looked, the Lowes decided after consulting books in a library, like condors.

The authorities wasted no time in declaring that all concerned were liars. Logan County Conservation officer A. A. Mervar stated bluntly, "I don't think the child was picked up." Illinois Department of Conservation biologist Vern Wright hastened to echo the sentiment. The Lowes found themselves at the receiving end of harassing phone calls and public ridicule. Marlon himself suffered from nightmares for weeks afterwards, though there were no physical injuries.

The Lowes and their friends were not the only people who reported seeing strange birds in the area. On July 28 a woman driving near Armington, not far from Lawndale, at 5:30 P.M. briefly glimpsed a huge bird flying at rooftop level and larger than the hood of her car. She noticed that it had a ring of white around its neck. Two and a half hours later, at the Stanley Thompson farm near Covell in McLean County (to the north of Logan County), six persons flying model airplanes suddenly noticed an enormous bird about to land atop the barn. Their shouts apparently caused it to change its mind, but it circled them and stayed in sight for some minutes before heading north in the direction of Bloomington. Its wingspan was estimated to be ten feet, its body six feet long. The wings had white tips at the ends, and the body was brown.

At 5:30 the following morning, between Armington and Delavan, mail carrier James Majors stopped to watch two large birds in the sky. As one remained behind, another descended until it was just above a cornfield. Extending its claws two feet, it closed in on a nearby pig farm. It snatched what Majors thought was a forty- or fifty-pound baby pig, passed across the road in front of him within thirty or forty feet, and joined up with its companion. At this point Majors could hear the flapping of their wings, which made a noise like that of a "jet taking off." These were, in other words, thunderbirds in an almost literal sense. Majors thought they looked like condors, only larger. He estimated their wingspans at eight feet.

Other sightings followed. One of the more interesting ones was also among the last. It occurred on August 11, on a farm south of Odin, Illinois. At 7 A.M. a large, gray-black bird flew out of the northeast and in a circle about 300 feet away, as if looking for a tree big enough to hold it. Finally it landed on one near a small pond close to the house. John and Wanda Chappell were able to watch it closely for five minutes—making theirs the most detailed report of all.

"It looked like a prehistoric bird," Mrs. Chappell said. "It was really fantastic. The head didn't have any feathers, and it had a long neck, crooked, kind of 'S' shaped. The body was covered with feathers.... We couldn't tell much about the feet, but it had long legs." Her husband judged its wingspan at ten to twelve feet, she at fourteen. They agreed, however, that it was four feet high; the distance from the tip of the beak to the back of the neck was eight inches.

After a few minutes the bird left in a southwest direction.

The official explanation for the reports, which required authorities to ignore actual witness descriptions, was "turkey buzzard." Or, as psychiatrist Donald P. Spence once observed, "It would appear that we cannot tolerate the absence of explanation."

Monster eagles

A century or more ago, it was not uncommon to read newspaper reports like these:

St. John's Island (now Prince Edward Island), Canada, August 1881: "A bald-headed eagle ... suddenly swooped down and attempted to carry off a two-year-old child of Mr. Clancy's ... playing in the field alone. The light clothing gave way with every tug of the voracious bird and torn into ribbons. Some men working near by came up in time to save the child from injury, but the eagle refused to go away until shot at" (*Reno Evening Gazette*, August 26, reprinted from *Toronto Globe*).

Franklin County, Pennsylvania, August 1886: "An eagle attacked a nine year old son of I. Martin of Hamilton township ... and attempted to carry him off. The glorious bird did not succeed in this but the boy was badly injured" (*Wellsboro Agitator*, August 31).

Truckee, California, September 1887. "A few days ago a child of a Mrs. Smith living on West River street was playing in the back-yard when a monstrous eagle swooped down, and fixing its talons in the child's clothing attempted to fly away. The screams of the child attracted the mother, who rushed out of doors at which the big bird flew away. It is thought that the eagle measured ten feet from tip to tip, and had it not been for the timely arrival of the mother[,] the child would certainly have been carried off" (*Weekly Nevada State Journal* [Reno], reprinted from *Truckee Republican*).

Eagle Valley, New York, late summer 1897: "A resident ... says that a big eagle swooped down into his yard a few days ago and tried to carry off his child. Its mother saw the little one's peril and drove the hungry bird away with a club" (*Middletown Daily Argus*, September 6).

Pinedale, New York, September 1899: "A bald eagle, measuring more than six feet between its wing tips, flew into the yard of William H. Berry ... and attacked his 2-year-old son. Mrs. Berry ran screaming into the yard and the eagle rose, being joined by its mate, and both circled over the house" (*Hornellsville Weekly Tribune*, September 8).

Near Pitcairn, New York, February 2, 1900: For days an immense eagle had been eating food that farmer Josiah Olmtree had put out for his sheep. His efforts to shoot the creature came to nothing. Then, as his five-year-old daughter played about the barnyard, the eagle flew by and snatched her. Alerted by her cries, Olmtree rushed out of the barn and began shouting. Evidently startled by the sounds, the eagle dropped her on the roof of a nearby building. Her father fired at the fleeing bird, but aside from losing a few feathers, it escaped (*Washington Post*, February 4).

Near Waterville, Pennsylvania, November 1900: Mrs. Isaac Holden heard screaming from outside, where her two-year-old son Clayton was playing. When she ran outside, she saw a huge eagle trying to carry off the little boy. With the broom in her hands, she struck the bird, which then turned on her and tried to peck her eyes. Eventually, it tired of the struggle and flew away (*Indiana Weekly Messenger*, November 28).

Denver, Colorado, December 1900. "Two wires which are strung across the lawn at the courthouse yesterday saved a 4-year-old boy from feeling the talons of [an] eagle in his tender flesh. That it was the intention of the bird when it swooped down to carry off the child there can be little doubt, but that it could have done so is doubtful.... The bird is an unusually large black eagle. A number of them have been seen about the city lately and it is assumed that the recent snows in the mountains have driven them to the plains" (*Anaconda Standard*, Montana, reprinted from the *Denver Republican*).

Marie Delex is carried off by a giant eagle in the French Alps in 1838.

Near Coweta, Oklahoma, January 1907: "The five-year-old son of [farmer] Nero Charles ... was attacked by a large gray eagle a few days ago, and narrowly escaped with his life after being carried 50 yards by the fierce bird. So far as known, this is the first time in the history of Indian Territory that a child has actually been picked up and carried by an eagle.... The child weighs 50 pounds, and at no time did the eagle succeed in getting more than eight to ten feet above the ground with him. The child was not injured save for bruises and scratches when his parents found him" (*Ada Evening News*, February 2).

Of such claims, Roger Caras wrote, "The stories about eagles carrying off human babies and even small children are ... pure myth, yet the stories persist."

Scientists who have investigated such reports have not always been so confident of their unreality, though it is certainly true that the capacity of any conventionally sized eagle (which never weighs much over seven pounds) to carry anything but the smallest animals has never been demonstrated. Yet at least one such abduction, however unlikely, seems well documented. Certainly, no one has been able to propose a plausible counter-explanation, notwithstanding a number of attempts. The principal in the story, Svanhild Hansen (married name Hartvigsen), swore to its truth all her life, which ended on November 12, 2010.

The incident took place in early June 1932. At the time Svanhild was three and a half years old, small for her age, perhaps weighing as little as 19 pounds. She and her family lived on a tiny island in the Hortavær complex off Norway's central coast. They had gone to a nearby, larger island, Leka, home to the village of Kvalø, where a church stood (there were none in remote Hortavær) and a baby brother could be christened. They stayed with relatives on their farm outside town.

The service took place on Sunday, June 5. The family then returned to the farm for dinner. Afterwards, the adults stayed inside while the children went out to play. Around three o'clock the boys wandered off to the seashore, leaving little Svanhild alone in the yard. At 3:30, when family members checked, the girl was nowhere to be seen. As many as 200 persons, many of them individuals who had come to town to attend church, joined in the search.

As anxious hours passed, that search expanded inland more than a mile to the middle of the island, all the way to the Haga Mountains, where a shoe identified as the girl's was found. One of the party remarked that earlier that morning, he had seen unusual activity by the sea eagles that lived in an eyrie on the mountain. Apparently this was said in the context of speculation that an eagle may have abducted Svanhild. Three young men decided to climb up the peaks to see what they could find. One of them, Karl Haug, related many years later in a filmed interview, "We were not prepared at all. We still had church clothes on and had no food, but we were determined to get up to the nest. It seemed unlikely that the eagle should have taken the child, but we saw no other solution." As they climbed, they came upon the girl's handkerchief.

> As they crept up below the nest, an eagle, claws extended, shot dangerously close to them.

As they crept up below the nest, an eagle, claws extended, shot dangerously close to them. Undeterred, they looked up at a tiny ledge with an overhang situated below the eyrie. Though all they could see was its underside, they wondered if the object of their quest might be lying on it. To check, searcher Jentoft Svensson positioned himself on the others' shoulders for a better view, which allowed him to see that yes, indeed, the girl was there. When Svensson crawled to the crevice, he observed her lying motionless. One shoe was missing, her clothes were torn, and her hands were stained with blood. He shouted down to the others that she was dead. And then the startled, sleeping child screamed. It took her a moment or two to realize that she had been rescued.

As she would tell the story in her adult life, "I was ... playing with some stones when suddenly I saw the eagle coming towards me. The next thing I remember is that I'm lying on a ledge, and then I see the eagle dive towards me. I remember how she came at me with those big claws. It was horrible." She crawled under the overhang for protection, meanwhile throwing stones at the eagle whenever it threatened her. "I was only three years old," she added, "but I had an instinct to fight, to survive.... It would probably have torn me to pieces and carried me up to the nest to feed its kids." Eventually, she fell asleep from sheer exhaustion.

Because no one witnessed the actual abduction, the story has remained controversial, at least in Scandinavia, where it is still remembered and was revived on the occasion of Svanhild Hartvigsen's death. No one could question her sincerity, though, and no one could satisfactorily explain how a tiny child managed to climb so far up nearly inaccessible peaks. As a grown woman she expressed resentment of critics who doubted that such a thing could have happened. "I know myself what I experienced," she said. For the rest of her life, she had difficulty being in open country or within viewing distance of eagles. She revisited the mountain in 1971 and suffered deep anxiety, though she returned four years later for a filmed recreation of the story. The filmmakers also interviewed surviving rescuers Karl Haug and Leif Andersen.

Other cases, though less documented, are interesting in their own ways. All of them do not have happy endings. A nineteenth-century nature encyclopedia (Felix A. Pouchet's *The Universe* [1871]) tells this sad story from the French Alps, in 1838:

A little girl, five years old, called Marie Delex, was playing with one of her companions on a mossy slope of the mountain, when all at once an eagle swooped down upon her and carried her away in spite of the cries and presence of her young friend. Some peasants, hearing her screams, hastened to the spot but sought in vain for the child, for they found nothing but one of her shoes on the edge of a precipice. The child was not carried to the eagle's nest, where only the two eagles were seen surrounded by heaps of goat and sheep bones. It was not until two months later that a shepherd discovered the corpse of Marie Delex, frightfully mutilated, and lying upon a rock half a league from where she had been borne off.

A Tippah County, Mississippi, school teacher recorded the following in the fall of 1868:

A sad casualty occurred at my school a few days ago. The eagles have been very troublesome in the neighborhood for some time past, carrying off pigs, lambs, etc. No one thought that they would attempt to prey upon children; but on Thursday, at recess, the little boys were out some distance from the house, playing marbles, when their sport was interrupted by a large eagle sweeping down and picking up little Jemmie Kenney, a boy of eight years, and when I got out of the house, the eagle was so high that I could just hear the child screaming. The eagle was induced to drop his victim; but his talons had been buried in him so deeply, and the fall was so great, that he was killed—either would have been fatal.

As late as 1929, a Wisconsin newspaper, *Sheboygan Press*, reported that three-year-old Edith Dorschell, who vanished at a picnic near Sturgeon Bay, may have been carried away by two "giant eagles which have attacked sheep flocks in this vicinity for two weeks..... The child wandered away from the group and disappeared in a wild wooded area nearby. Picnickers recalled that the eagles had hovered over the picnic grounds shortly before the child had disappeared."

Blue herons such as this one, as well as eagles, cranes, and other large birds, have been mistaken for thunderbirds.

A tale with a less tragic conclusion goes back to July 12, 1763, and the mountains of Germany, where a peasant couple left their three-year-old daughter lying asleep by a stream as they cut grass a short distance away. When they went to check on her, they were horrified to find her missing. A frantic search proved fruitless until a man passing by on the other side of the hill heard a child crying. As he went to investigate, he was startled at the sight of a huge eagle flying up before him. At the spot from which it had ascended, he found the little girl, her arm torn and bruised. When the child was reunited with her parents, they and her rescuer estimated that the bird had carried her well over 1,400 feet.

Twentieth-century zoologist C. H. Keeling characterizes this as the only eagle-abduction story he finds "even remotely convincing"—notwithstanding the "simple and unalterable fact ... that no eagle on earth can carry off more than its own weight."

The problem of explanation

No trained ornithologists have ever concerned themselves with the thunderbird phenomenon in its entirety, and few have ever had any participation even in specific reports, beyond the rejection of them out of hand. The skepticism is not difficult to understand.

Illinois State University ornithologist Angelo P. Capparella, who harbors a sympathetic interest in cryptozoology, remarks, "The lack of interest of most ornithologists is probably due to two factors. First, there is the lack of sightings from the legions of competent amateur birdwatchers.... The number of good birdwatchers scanning the skies of the U.S. and Canada is impressive. Every year, surprising observations of birds far from their normal range are documented, often photographed. How have Thunderbirds escaped their roving eyes?" A second reason, Capparella writes, is that such creatures lack an adequate food source in the areas where they have been reported.

In some instances—if not the ones cited above—witnesses have mistaken cranes, blue herons, and turkey buzzards for more extraordinary and mysterious birds. In other cases—the ones here, for example—it is easier to believe (even in the absence of evidence to the effect) in pure invention than in honest misidentification. And indeed hoax is about the only option left to those who believe that if something seems impossible, it cannot happen. Those who believe otherwise are those who accept—or acknowledge—fantastic possibilities beyond the scope of current knowledge.

Further Reading:

Bord, Janet, and Colin Bord. *Alien Animals*. Harrisburg, PA: Stackpole Books, 1981.

Capparella, Angelo P. Review of Mark A. Hall's *Thunderbirds! The Living Legend of Giant Birds*. *Cryptozoology* 9 (1990): 94–96.

Caras, Roger A. *Dangerous to Man: The Definitive Story of Wildlife's Reputed Dangers*. Revised edition. South Hackensack, NJ: Stoeger Publishing Company, 1977.

Coleman, Loren. *Curious Encounters: Phantom Trains, Spooky Spots, and Other Mysterious Wonders*. Boston: Faber and Faber, 1985.

Hall, Mark A. *Thunderbirds! The Living Legend of Giant Birds*. Bloomington, MN: Mark A. Hall Publications and Research, 1988.

———. "Birds That Carry Off People." *Wonders* 7,3 (September 2002): 67–84.

———. "Benoit Crevier Pursues the 'Monster Eagle' of Quebec (1892)." *Wonders* 10,1 (March 2006): 18–22.

Maruna, Scott. "Aviation Abductions: Lawndale Was Last." *Biofort* (November 24, 2007).

Michell, John, and Robert J. M. Rickard. *Living Wonders: Mysteries and Curiosities of the Animal World*. New York: Thames and Hudson, 1982.

Pouchet, Felix. *The Universe: Or the Infinitely Great and the Infinitely Little*. New York: Scribner's, 1871.

Rickard, Bob. "Necrolog: Svanhild Hartvigsen." *Fortean Times* 272 (2011): 24–25.

Robiou Lamarche, Sebastian. "UFOs and the Mysterious Deaths of Animals." *Flying Saucer Review* 22,5 (1976): 15–18.

Spence, Donald P. "The Mythic Properties of Popular Explanations." In Joseph de Rivera and Theodore R. Sarbin, eds. *Believed-in Imaginings: The Narrative Construction of Reality*, 217–28. Washington, DC: American Psychological Association, 1998.

Stein, Gordon. "Unidentified Flapping Objects." *Fate* 41,5 (May 1988): 66–71.

Thylacines

One of the liveliest ongoing cryptozoological controversies concerns an Australian animal that, though officially judged extinct, may yet be alive. What makes the matter particularly fascinating is that it is a mystery on two levels, the first intriguing, the other possibly even more so.

History and prehistory

The thylacine, a carnivorous marsupial, came into existence on the Australian mainland late in the age of mammals. Though it looked something like a cross between a fox, a wolf, a tiger, and a hyena, it was in fact related to the opossum, with which zoologists believe it shared a common ancestor.

The male thylacine, which measured more than six feet long from head to tail, was the size of a large dog, weighing between sixty-five and seventy-five pounds. Its head looked much like a fox's or a dog's, if larger in proportion to its body, and its jaws were huge; they could open as much as 80° to 90°. Beginning mid-back and extending all the way to the tail, the thylacine had tiger-like stripes (thus its popular nickname "Tasmanian tiger"). Its bunched and extended rear, reminiscent of a hyena's, ended in a stiff, unwagging tail. Its fur was coarse and sandy brown. Females were slightly smaller, but with twice the number of stripes, and these started just behind the neck. Females also had a pouch, as all marsupials do, but it faced the rear, presumably to protect its young as it moved through undergrowth.

Twelve thousand years ago, the land bridge linking Tasmania to the continent sank under water as sea levels rose. Approximately 3,000 years ago (or, as some authorities estimate, some hundreds of years later), thylacines disappeared from the mainland, probably because of competition from more effective predators, the dingoes, who were brought over by Indonesian mariners. It is surmised that the surviving animals were those isolated on Tasmania, now an island off Australia's southeast coast. The first published mention of a thylacine is in a 1905 Tasmanian newspaper, where the animal is called "destructive." The thylacines' days were numbered.

Convinced that they were responsible for the mass slaughter of sheep, which had been brought to Australia in 1803, authorities commenced a campaign to

This Australian stamp shows a thylacine, a marsupial carnivore that supposedly became extinct in the 1930s, though continuing sighting reports have put that claim into question.

wipe out the "tigers." (In fact, according to modern experts, feral dogs and "duffers" [rustlers] were a far greater threat to livestock than the hated thylacines ever were.) Both private companies (in the 1830s) and government agencies (as of 1888) offered rewards for thylacine scalps, and the killing began. By the early twentieth century thylacines had become a rare sight. Bounty hunters were not their only enemy, however; a distemper epidemic decimated much of the population, and settlers were claiming ever more of their habitat. But it was the relentless hostility of armed human beings that ensured the thylacines' extinction. "Farmers continued to see the creature as a menace," two historians of the thylacine write, "long after it was capable of reproducing itself in any numbers."

According to the standard histories, the last specimen for which a bounty was paid was shot in 1909. The final one shot was gunned down in 1930. Captured in 1933, the last known one on Earth died on September 7, 1936, in Tasmania's Hobart Domain Zoo, just two months after Tasmania passed a law declaring the thylacine a protected species. "Benjamin," as the one remaining thylacine was named, "was tame and could be patted," its keeper, Frank Darby, recalled, but "it was frequently morose and showed no affection." Considering what humans had done to its species, one can hardly blame it.

The first mystery

Only after it was gone for good did most Tasmanians—who, along with the zoo staff and visitors, had mostly ignored Benjamin—begin to regret what they had done. In time, the Tasmanian coat of arms would depict two thylacines, and Australians would informally adopt it as their most beloved lost animal, its disappearance nothing less than a national tragedy.

Yet as little as a year after Benjamin's death and the thylacine's official passing from the domain of living species, Australia's Animals and Birds Protection Board sent two investigators into the mountains of northwestern Tasmania to look into the possibility that a few thylacines might have survived. They returned with a handful of intriguing sighting reports collected from residents of the area. Though hardly conclusive, they encouraged the board to sponsor further searches. A 1938 expedition found the first physical evidence: footprints with the thylacine's distinctive five-toed front legs and four-toed hind legs.

World War II got in the way of further investigation, but in late 1945 a private expedition viewed a set of tracks and heard some sighting reports, though none of its members saw anything themselves. After that, Australian wildlife specialists essentially abandoned the question for a number of years. Then, in 1957, zoologist Eric R. Guiler, chairman of the Animals and Birds Protection Board, went to Broadmarsh, where a mysterious marauder had killed some sheep. The tracks were, Guiler thought, unmistakably those of a thylacine. Converted to belief in living thylacines, Guiler mounted nine expeditions between 1957 and 1966, during which he garnered a mass of evidence but, again, produced no body; nor did he have a personal sighting.

In 1968 other researchers established a Tiger Center, to which witnesses could report sightings. Search parties continued to prowl the bush. A late–1970s project sponsored by the World Wildlife Fund (Australia) set up a number of automatic-camera units at locations where witnesses said they had seen thylacines. Bait was placed to lure the animals across an infra-red beam that would trigger a camera. The camera caught nine different species, most prominently the Tasmanian devil (which on occasion has been mistaken for the thylacine), and in his official report in 1980, project leader Steven J. Smith of the National Parks and Wildlife Service (NPWS) expressed the view that thylacines are, indeed, extinct.

In 1982, however, in a published survey of 104 sightings reported to the NPWS between 1970 and 1980, he moderated his conclusions. Writing with D. E. Rounsevell, he observed, "If thylacines still exist in Tasmania, they are few, and the difficult task of rediscovering them may be facilitated by careful analysis of the growing collection of reported sightings"—the majority clustered in the northern regions of the state, where in earlier decades most of the bounties had been collected.

Guiler also conducted a hidden-camera operation, with similarly disappointing results, but remained convinced that the animals still existed because of sightings and tracks he thought otherwise inexplicable.

Events in the affair took a new turn one rainy night in March 1982. A park ranger for the NPWS working in a forested area of northwestern Tasmania woke from a nap in the back seat of his car. He turned on his spotlight and shined it on an animal only twenty feet away. It was, he quickly deduced, a thylacine, "an adult male in excellent condition, with 12 black stripes on a sandy coat." Unfortunately, the rain wiped out any tracks it may have left.

The NPWS held up an announcement of the encounter until January 1984, in an effort to discourage curiosity-seekers who might threaten the animal and whatever companions might live in the same area. Yet the NPWS statement did not amount to an official certification of the thylacine's return from the dead. There was still, after all, no body. But more important than scientific concerns were the potential economic and political problems. What financial hardship or other inconvenience would befall a mining or timber company on whose property thylacines were found to be living? The animals, after all, were endangered and in need of protection; would mineral or timber rights—along, of course, with the tax revenues associated with them—have to be surrendered? And who would pay the compensation?

Since then other expeditions have been launched, but Tasmania's thylacine remains elusive. Skeptics, of whom there remain many, dismiss the reports as the consequence of wishful thinking or misperceptions of other animals, in particular feral dogs (which in the past undeniably have been mistaken for thylacines). In any case, sightings continue. In 1991 as many as thirteen reports were logged, and the Tasmanian Parks Wildlife and Heritage Authority deemed three of them "very good." Zoologist Bob Green remarked of thylacines, "They are extremely cunning animals. For every one that's seen, I believe they see a thousand humans. I have received samples of dung and footprints sent in by experienced bushmen who know what they have seen. I believe that the thylacine not only exists but is coming back strongly."

Continuing sightings of apparent thylacines seem to support that optimistic analysis. The Australian press reported as many as a dozen appearances in East Gippsland between October 1996 and February 1997. One woman, who saw the animal "for a good 30 seconds," said, "It was about the size of a cattle dog, dark gray with tan and dark brown stripes and a greyhound-like face." Even so, in May 2001 the State Government of Tasmania pronounced the species "presumed extinct." Since then others have told of encounters. A photograph, interesting but inconclusive, surfaced in 2006, and a video of a blurry, but suggestive, moving quadruped with apparent thylacine features sparked discussion in 2009. Expeditions continue to be mounted from time to time. A March 2005 offer of a $983,000 reward, offered by the Australian magazine *The Bulletin*, for proof of the creature's continued existence has gone unclaimed. The controversy drags on, awaiting resolution, if resolution is to be had on the other side of a twilight zone of continuous ambiguity.

At the same time, thylacines—thought gone from New Guinea for something like 2000 years—figure in reports in the province of Irian Jaya in the western part of the country. Though skeptical of surviving thylacines, senior London Zoo curator Simon Tonge remarks that if the creature "is going to turn up anywhere, it would be there." In March 1997 the *Melbourne Herald-Sun* reported that villages in the province had seen a creature answering to a thylacine's description attacking livestock. Its appearance was so fierce that it intimidated witnesses from trying to kill it, though a report a few weeks later alleged that three had been slain. Unfortunately, their bodies were not preserved or otherwise presented to scientists.

The second mystery

In 1981, following a number of sightings of an unusual animal in an area of southwestern Western Australia, the state's Agricultural Protection Board hired Kevin Cameron, a tracker of aboriginal descent, to investigate. In due course, Cameron would claim to have seen the animal himself and to have identified it as a thylacine.

Even those inclined to take seriously the notion of surviving thylacines in Tasmania blanch at reports like these. Not only is there no fossil evidence of a mainland thylacine in the past 12,000 years, but there is no indication that the animal was known either to Australian aborigines or to the Europeans who settled the country in the nineteenth century.

In 1951 a man from Dwellingup came to the Western Australian Museum in Perth, where he showed photographs and casts of tracks of what he insisted was a thylacine—which he said he had seen with his own eyes. But the staff zoologist with whom he spoke rejected the report and the supporting evidence out of hand. Some years later, other reports of a strange sheep-killing animal led that same zoologist, Athol M. Douglas, into the bush, where he tracked and killed the culprit: a feral Afghan hound with long, matted hair. The experience only reinforced his skepticism about thylacine reports. Even so, over the years he occasionally examined carcasses of kangaroos and sheep and noted, uneasily, that the animals had been slain exactly the way thylacines—and not dogs or dingoes—slay their prey.

In February 1985 Douglas's doubts took a serious hit when Cameron handed him five color photographs. They showed the profile of an animal burrowing at the base of a tree. Though its face was hidden in the brush, its striped back and long, stiff tail belonged to no creature but the thylacine. Cameron would not tell Douglas where he had taken the pictures, but he did produce casts of its prints. Douglas thought Cameron's account of its behavior rang true to reports in the scientific literature—all the more impressive evidence of the witness' credibility, in his view, since Cameron was barely literate.

A nineteenth-century drawing of a thylacine.

Still, Cameron's odd, secretive behavior warned Douglas that something was amiss. Cameron gave, retracted, then granted permission to Douglas to use the photographs in an article to appear in *New Scientist*, a British popular-science weekly. Just before the manuscript was submitted to the magazine, Douglas would later recall in *Cryptozoology*:

> Cameron accompanied me to the photographic laboratory to have the enlargements made. This was the first time I saw the negatives with full-frame, good-quality enlargements. When I saw the negatives, I realized Cameron's account with regard to the photographs was inaccurate. The film had been cut, frames were missing, and the photos were taken from different angles— making it impossible for the series to have been taken in 20 or 30 seconds, as Cameron had stated. There were no photographs of the animal bounding away. Furthermore, in one negative, there was the shadow of another person pointing what could be an over-under .12 shotgun. Cameron had told me he had been alone. It would have been practically impossible for an animal as alert as a thylacine to remain stationary for so long while human activity was going on in its vicinity. In addition, it is significant that the animal's head does not appear in any of the photographs.

Some *New Scientist* readers noticed a couple of glaring discrepancies: one, the animal did not seem to move at all at all from photograph to photograph, and two, markedly varying shadow patterns suggested that a difference of at least an hour, possibly more, separated some pictures from the rest. To the critics this could only mean that Cameron had photographed, in fairly leisurely fashion, a stuffed model of a thylacine.

On the other hand, Douglas thought it more likely that one of the pictures, evidently the first, showed a living thylacine. "The full frame of this negative is the one which shows the shadow of the man with a rigid gun-like object pointing in the direction of the thylacine at the base of the tree," he wrote. "This shadow was deliberately excluded in the photo published in *New Scientist*. If I am correct in this supposition, the thylacine was alive when the first photo was taken, but had been dead [and frozen in *rigor mortis*] for several hours by the time the second photograph was taken."

Douglas hoped that someone would find the carcass, "presumably shot by persons unknown," but none ever surfaced. If the photo depicts an authentic thylacine, one may infer that this is because Australian law decrees that anyone convicted of killing the (paradoxically officially extinct) thylacine is subject to a $5,000 fine.

In 1966, a Western Australian Museum team recovered a thylacine carcass in a cave near Mundrabilla Station. Carbon dating placed its age at 4,500 years. In fact, according to Douglas, the carcass may be more recent—much more recent—than that. The condition of the body indicated it died no more than a year before, and probably less. "During my 1986 visit to the cave," he recalled, "I found a dingo carcass; it was hairless, dry and odorless, and its skin was like parchment. The thylacine carcass had been—and is—in a far superior state of preservation than this dingo carcass, yet the dingo carcass would not have been in the cave for more than 20 years." The "inaccurate dating would have resulted from contamination from the groundwater which saturated the carcass," he suggested.

This may be the second item of physical evidence for a Western Australian thylacine. In a 1974 issue of the *Journal of the Royal Society of Western Australia*, University of New South Wales sociologist Michael Archer wrote that bones found in a cave in the Kimberleys (a plateau region in the northern part of the state), in 1970, had been carbon-dated to less than eighty years old. The bones were of small animals, and they were in a cave too small for human occupation. Another item, though too tiny and fragile to be carbon-dated without destroying it, was from a thylacine shoulder bone. The implication—which could not be proved, of course—was that it was contemporary with the other bones, perhaps of animals on which it had preyed.

Western Australia (which covers one-third of Australia's continental land mass) is not the only mainland state to claim thylacine sightings. According to cryptozoological investigator Rex Gilroy, author of *Mysterious Australia* (1995), a book full of fascinating but often hard-to-believe stories, numerous "reports of large striped dog-like animals, possibly thylacines," have been made from "a wide area of the rugged eastern Australian mountain ranges, from far north Queensland through New South Wales to eastern Victoria." Moreover, "plaster casts have been made of tracks found on the mainland"; these "compare with others from Tasmania, leaving little doubt as to the animal's identity."

Gilroy claims he once saw the animal himself. As he and a friend drove toward the Blue Mountains west of Sydney (in New South Wales), something dashed out of the scrub along the highway and ran in front of them. It was "almost the size of a full-grown Alsatian dog, with fawn-colored fur and a row of blackish stripes. For a few seconds it stood there in the glare of the headlights before running off into the scrub, towards the Grosse Valley nearby. I have no doubt that it was a thylacine; its appearance matched that of stuffed specimens in Government museums."

Among those who say they have seen thylacines in the mountainous wilderness of the Namadgi-Kosciusco National Park along the New South Wales-Victoria border is ranger Peter Simon, who saw one for several seconds in broad daylight in 1982, from a distance of 100 feet. In 1990, after writing an article about the thylacine mystery in *The Age*, Melbourne's leading newspaper, Graeme O'Neill received cards and letters from Victoria residents who reported their own sightings. "The way they told their stories, and the internal consistency of each account, left me in no doubt," he remarked, "that each had seen something unusual [and] … broadly consistent with the appearance of a thylacine."

In their comprehensive *Out of the Shadows* (1994), a survey of Australia's cryptozoological mysteries, Tony Healy and Paul Cropper write that concentrations of mainland reports come mostly (though not exclusively) from "the relatively well-watered, forested areas in the east and southeast of the continent, within a couple of hundred kilometers [124 miles] of the sea." Reports have been sufficiently frequent that some of the animals have acquired local nicknames, sometimes ending in "monster." In 2001, speaking at a cryptozoological conference, researcher Peter Chapple declared that he and his organization, the Victoria-based Australian Rare Fauna Research Association, had "collected and analyzed some 4,300 sightings [allegedly] of thylacines from the mainland of Australia, around 1,400 of which we believe are highly credible." All but 200 of these were from Victoria, probably representing little more than inevitable selection bias.

The southern tip of Victoria has the "Wonthaggi monster," an appellation coined after farmers reported unusual livestock kills and glimpses of a mysterious animal. Over the years some witnesses got a better look at the creature. Among them were Mr. and Mrs. Charlie Thorpe, who on the afternoon of November 6, 1975, saw one pass in front of their car as they were driving in the Promontory's National Park. At one point it hesitated briefly before resuming its trek across the road. According to Mr. Thorpe:

> We … were not moving fast, probably about 40 km/h [25 mph]…. It was taller than my Labrador but was lower in the hindquarters. It moved with a peculiar hopping gait. The tail was very thick at the base and longer than a dog's, tapering to a point. It appeared to be a dark to light gray in color and had distinct darker bands around its hindquarters. The stripes did not appear to be black but were a darker gray than the rest of the body.

In the border area of southwestern Victoria and southeastern South Australia, residents speak of the "Tantanoola tiger" and the "Ozenkadnook tiger." The latter got its name, in 1962, from press reports of a marauding animal in the vicinity of the small town of Ozenkadnook in Victoria's Wimmera district. Vague stories have the creature's presence noted as early as the mid-nineteenth century.

A bus full of school children spotted a strange animal just yards away from their vehicle one day in July 1967. It loped alongside the bus for about a mile, so the children and the driver got a very good look at it. The encounter took place near Lucindale, South Australia, and one of the witnesses was thirteen-year-old Rosalie Anderson. Her mother, Dawn, who had a keen interest in wildlife, had her draw a picture, which depicted something that looked very much like a thylacine. Soon joined by Kath Alcock, who lived in a nearby community, Dawn Anderson began collecting casts of footprints and investigating reports, such as this one from a man who described an encounter in January 1968:

> The animal was sighted about 4:30 to 5 P.M. I was only about 30 to 40 yards away from it as it trotted across the road.... The animal was very much larger than a fox. It seemed to have a long face, but I could not see it properly as the animal looked neither to right nor left. (This was unusual, as a dog or fox will nearly always turn its head.)

> It just kept going and took its time as it crossed the road. It was in sight for several seconds, and I was able to get a reasonable look at it. It was a kind of gray-blue with light off-white stripes down the back and tail. The tail was long and thin and hung rigid, the back was high and thin, and in front the animal was thickset.

That same month Anderson and her eleven-year-old son, Peter, driving through a scrubby area near their property, saw a thylacine in the ditch beside the road. The two were able to observe it in plain sight for fifteen minutes. She would have two other encounters, though these were much briefer. Anderson did not subscribe to any fantastic notion about how all this could have come about; she believed that these creatures had not in fact survived extinction on the mainland and lived in secrecy ever after, but that they were the spawn of specimens brought up from Tasmania in the early part of the century and released into the wild. There, they established breeding populations and over the years evolved into a subspecies, with distinctive features such as paler stripes or, on occasion, no stripes at all.

An intriguing but controversial photograph was snapped near Goroke in western Victoria in 1964 by Rilla Martin, a Melbourne woman visiting relatives. Taken in daylight, it shows a large, striped animal with generally thylacine-like features (though with a larger, more feline head), walking amid foliage and shadows. No conclusive evidence of a hoax has ever emerged, but the picture met with such a frosty reception from zoologists that the witness soon ceased speaking about it. Even so, similar creatures are still reported in the region.

This is a photo of the last living thylacine, or Tasmanian tiger, to have been in captivity. It was taken in the 1930s at the Hobart Zoo in Tasmania.

And beyond

To Australian writer Tony Healy there is something downright weird about mainland thylacines. He notes that the night before Ranger Simon's sighting, his dogs, participants in the slayings of more than 300 wild pigs, refused to get out of the truck after they and their masters heard harsh, thylacine-like panting sounds in the bush. In 1982 a Western Australian farm couple, who claimed to have lost livestock to thylacines, told a Perth newspaper that a "prickly feeling" at the backs of their necks was invariably their first warning of the animals' presence.

If these are tiny threads on which to frame a fantastic hypothesis—that there is a paranormal aspect to the experience of mainland thylacines—or if even flesh-and-blood thylacines strain credulity, consider this 1974 report.

On April 7, at 3:30 A.M., Joan Gilbert spotted a "strange striped creature half cat and half dog" as it passed in front of her car's headlights. "It was," she recalled, "the most peculiar animal I have ever seen. It had stripes, a long thin tail, and seemed to be all gray, though it might have had some yellow on it. Its ears were set back like a member of the cat family, and it was as big as a medium-sized dog. It was thin, and it definitely was not a fox."

It was, she learned when she looked through reference books at the library, an animal she had never heard of: a thylacine. The sighting did not take place in Tasmania. It did not take place in Western Australia or Victoria or New South Wales. It happened on the outskirts of Bournemouth. In England.

Further Reading:

Beresford, Quentin, and Garry Bailey. *Search for the Tasmanian Tiger*. Sandy Bay, Tasmania, Australia: Blubber Head Press, 1981.

Critchley, Cheryl, and Jack Taylor. "Tiger Sightings on the Increase." *Melbourne Herald Sun* (February 20, 1997).

Dash, Mike, and Rex Gilroy. "The Lost Australians." *Fortean Times* 62 (1992): 54–56.

Douglas, Athol M. "Tigers in Western Australia?" *New Scientist* 110,1505 (April 24, 1986): 44–47.

———. "The Thylacine: A Case for Current Existence on Mainland Australia." *Cryptozoology* 9 (1990): 13–25.

Earley, George W. "Tasmanian Tiger Update." *INFO Journal* 64 (October 1991): 13–14.

Eberhart, George M. "Thylacine." In *Mysterious Creatures: Volume Two*, 547–50. Santa Barbara, CA: ABC-CLIO, 2002.

Gilroy, Rex. *Mysterious Australia*. Mapleton, Queensland, Australia: Nexus Publishing, 1995.

———. "On the Trail of a Tiger." *Fortean Times* 49 (1987): 46–47.

Goss, Michael. "Tracking Tasmania's Mystery Beast." *Fate* 36,7 (July 1983): 34–43.

Guilder, Eric R. *Thylacine: The Tragedy of the Tasmanian Tiger*. Oxford, England: Oxford University Press, 1985.

Healy, Tony. "The Riddles of Oz." *Fortean Times* 49 (1987): 42–45.

Healy, Tony, and Paul Cropper. *Out of the Shadows: Mystery Animals of Australia*. Chippendale, Australia: Ironbark, 1994.

Neale, Greg. "New Sightings Raise Hope Tasmanian 'Tiger' Lives." *Vancouver Sun*, British Columbia (April 2, 1997).

"Out of Place." *The News* 9 (1985): 15–20.

Parker, Heather. "Is It the Tasmanian Tiger?" *Australian Women's Weekly* (February 25, 1970): 35, 56, 61.

Rickard, Bob. "The Return of the Tiger?" *Fortean Times* 49 (1987): 5–7.

Shuker, Karl. *Alien Zoo*. Bideford, North Devonshire, England: CFZ Press, 2010.

"Thylacine Reports Persist After 50 Years." *ISC Newsletter* 4,4 (winter 1985): 1–5.

Wilford, John Noble. "Automatic Cameras Stalk Tasmania's Rare Tiger." *New York Times* (May 27, 1980).

Unidentified Submarine Objects

While sailing in the equatorial Atlantic Ocean in the early morning hours of October 28, 1902, the *Fort Salisbury* came upon an incredible sight. As second officer A. H. Raymer noted in the ship's log

Dark object, with long, luminous trailing wake, thrown in relief by a phosphorescent sea, seen ahead, a little on starboard bow. Look-out reported two masthead lights ahead. These two lights, almost as bright as a steamer's lights, appeared to shine from two points in line on the upper surface of the dark mass.

Concluded dark mass was a whale and lights phosphorescent. On drawing nearer dark mass and lights sank below the surface. Prepared to examine the wake in passing with binoculars.

Passed about forty to fifty yards on port side of wake, and discovered it was the scaled back of some huge monster slowly disappearing below the surface. Darkness of the night prevented determining its exact nature, but scales of apparent 1 ft. diameter and dotted in places with barnacle growth were plainly discernible. The breadth of the body showing above water tapered from about 30 ft. close aft where the dark mass had appeared to be about 5 ft. at the extreme and visible. Length roughly about 500 ft. to 600 ft.

Concluded that the dark mass first seen must have been the creature's head. The swirl caused by the monster's progress could be distinctly heard, and a strong odor like that of a low-tide beach on a summer's day pervaded the air. Twice along its length the disturbance of the water and a broadening of the surrounding belt of phosphorus indicated the presence of huge fins in motion below the surface.

The wet, shiny back of the monster was dotted with twinkling phosphorescent lights, and was encircled with a band of white phosphorescent sea.

Such are the bare facts of the passing of the sea serpent in latitude 5 deg. 31 min. S., longitude 4 deg. 42 min. W., as seen by myself being officer of the watch, and by the helmsman and look-out man.

The account's laconic tone notwithstanding, this incredible but supposedly true story challenges the reader's boggle threshold. To the late Bernard Heuvelmans, the father of cryptozoology and in his life the greatest authority on sea-serpent reports, it can only be "all nonsense." As Charles Fort wryly observed, "So doubly damned is this datum that the attempt to explain it was in terms of the accursed Sea Serpent."

But *are* we to believe the story? It was reported as true in the *London Daily Mail* (November 19, 1902), and when interviewed the ship's captain, not himself a witness, remarked of his second officer, "I can only say that he is very earnest on the subject and has, together with the lookout and the helmsman, seen something in the water, of a huge nature, as specified."

An even more fantastic story, if that is possible, was published in a Washington newspaper, the *Tacoma Daily Ledger,* on July 3, 1893. The witnesses, most of them named, were identified as members of a fishing party that left Tacoma on the afternoon of the first and camped that evening on Henderson Island, not far from a large band of surveyors. The narrative that follows is attributed to one of the fishermen:

It was, I guess, about midnight before I fell asleep, but exactly how long I slept I cannot say, for when I woke it was with such startling suddenness that it never entered my mind to look at my watch, and when after a while I did look at my watch, as well as every watch belonging to the party, it was stopped.

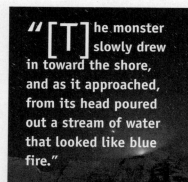

"[T]he monster slowly drew in toward the shore, and as it approached, from its head poured out a stream of water that looked like blue fire."

I am afraid that you will fail to comprehend how suddenly that camp was awake.

Since the creation of the world I doubt if sounds and sights more horrible were ever seen or heard by mortal man. I was in the midst of a pleasant dream, when in an instant a most horrible noise rang out in the clear morning air, and instantly the whole air was filled with a strong current of electricity that caused every nerve in the body to sting with pain, and a light as bright as that created by the concentration of many arc lights kept constantly flashing. At first I thought it was a thunderstorm, but as no rain accompanied it, and as both light and sound came from off the bay, I turned my head in that direction, and if it is possible for fright to turn one's hair white, then mine ought to be snow white, for right before my eyes was a most horrible-looking monster.

By this time every man in our camp, as well as the men from the camp of the surveyors, was gathered on the bank of the stream; and as soon as we could gather our wits together we began to question if what we were looking at was not the creation of the mind. But we were soon disburdened of this idea, for the monster slowly drew in toward the shore, and as it approached, from its head poured out a stream of water that looked like blue fire. All the while the air seemed to be filled with electricity, and the sensation experienced was as if each man had on a suit of clothes formed of the fine points of needles.

Mr. [W. L.] McDonald ... was struck with some of the water that the monster was throwing and fell senseless to the earth. By this time every man in both parties was panic-stricken, and we rushed to the woods for a place of safety, leaving the fallen men lying on the beach.

One of the men from the surveyors' camp incautiously took a few steps in the direction of the water that reached the man, and he instantly fell to the ground and lay as though dead.

As we reached the woods the "demon of the deep" sent out flashes of light that illuminated the surrounding country for miles, and his roar—which sounded like the roar of thunder—became terrific. When we reached the woods we looked around and saw the monster making off in the direction of the sound, and in an instant it disappeared off in the direction of the sound, and in an instant it disappeared beneath the waters of the bay, but for some time we were able to trace its course by a bright luminous light that was on the surface of the water. As the fish disappeared, total darkness surrounded us, and it took us some time to find our way back to the beach where our comrades lay. We were unable to tell the time, as the powerful electric force had stopped our watches. We eventually found McDonald and the other man and were greatly relieved to find that they were alive, though unconscious. So we sat down to wait the coming of daylight. It came, I should judge, in about half an hour, and by this time, by constant work on the two, both were able to stand.

This monster fish, or whatever you may call it, was fully 150 feet long, and at its thickest part I should judge about 30 feet in circumference. Its shape was somewhat out of the ordinary insofar that the body was neither round nor flat but oval, and from what we could see the upper part of the body was covered with a very coarse hair. The head was shaped very much like the head of a walrus, though, of course, very much larger. Its eyes, of which it apparently had six, were as large around as a dinner plate and were exceedingly dull, and it was about the only spot on the monster that at one time or another was not illuminated. At intervals of about every eight feet from its head to its tail a substance that had the appearance of a copper band encircled its body, and it was from these many bands that the powerful electric current appeared to come. The bands nearest the head seemed to have the strongest electric force, and it was from these first six bands the most brilliant lights were emitted. Near the center of its head were two large hornlike substances, though they could not have been horns for it was through them that the electrically charged water was thrown.

Its tail from what I could see of it was shaped like a propeller and seemed to revolve, and it may be possible that the strange monster pushes himself through the water by means of this propellerlike tail. At will this strange monstrosity seemed to be able to emit strong waves of electric current, giving off electro-motive forces, which causes any person coming within the radius of this force to receive an electric shock.

Amusingly, like Raymer, the narrator of the above tale, a tall one by any standard, insists on characterizing the "monstrosity" as a sea serpent rather than

(*Continued on page 214*)

Water Hounds

In a book published in 1684, *A Description of West or H-Lar Connaught*, Roderick O'Flaherty tells a frightening story of something that he says happened at Lough Mask, a lake in the west of Ireland:

There is one rarity more, which we may term the Irish crocodile, whereof [someone], as yet living, about ten years ago had sad experience.

The man was passing the shore just by the waterside, and spyed far off the head of a beast swimming, which he took to be an otter, and took no more notice of it, but the beast it seems lifted up his head, to discern whereabouts the man was; then diving swam under the water till he struck ground; whereupon he ran out of the water suddenly and took the man by the elbow whereby the man stooped down, and the beast fastened his teeth in his pate [head], and dragged him into the water; where[upon] the man took hold of a stone by chance in his way, and calling to mind he had a knife in his pocket, took it out and gave a thrust of it to the beast, which thereupon got away from him into the lake.

The water about them was all bloody, whether from the beast's blood, or his own, or from both he knows not. It was the pitch of an ordinary greyhound, of a black slimey skin, without hair as he imagines.

Old men acquainted with the lake do tell there is such a beast in it, and that a stout fellow with a wolf dog along with him met the like there once, which after a long struggling went away in spite of the man and his dog, and was a long time after found rotten in a rocky cave of the lake where the waters decreased. The like they say is seen in other lakes in Ireland; they call it Doyarchu, i.e., water-dog, or anchu which is the same.

More often called *Dobharchœ* (water-hound; also spelled *Dobharchú*), this creature appears both in folklore and in a handful of intriguing and puzzling first-person narratives from earlier centuries. Though no longer reported or even believed in, the "water hound" was once considered a real and dangerous inhabitant of the Irish landscape.

Stark testimony to that effect can be found in a gravesite in the County Leitrim town of Glenade, on the north side of Ben Bulben mountain, where a woman named Grainne Ni Conalai (Grace Connelly in English) is buried. The tombstone places her death on September 24, 1722, and carries a carving of an otterlike creature being stabbed by a dagger. According to local lore, she was a victim of a water hound.

She and her husband, Traolach Mac Lochlainn, lived in a village on the northwest corner of Glenade Lake. On the day in question, she took clothes down to the shore to wash them. When she did not return, her husband went out to look for her. He was horrified to come upon her bloody

(Continued from previous page)

body and even more shocked to see a water hound sleeping atop her corpse.

The man quietly returned to the house and retrieved a knife, which he then plunged into the creature's heart. Just before it died, however, it gave out a whistling sound which alerted a fellow water hound.

The distraught husband and his brother fled on horseback, the water hound in hot pursuit. At one point the husband's horse lost a shoe, forcing an emergency stop at a blacksmith's shop. When the monster appeared, the blacksmith urged the brothers to place their horses in front of the entrance; then when the water hound's head poked out from beneath the animals, they should take a sword and cut its head off. In that way the hound met its end.

As often occurred in the wake of unusual events, a ballad soon came into being, and it was sung in the streets of local towns for a time. The anonymous composer set the bloody scene:

She, having gone to bathe, it seems, within the water clear,

And not having returned when she might, her husband, fraught with fear,

Hasting to where he her might find, when oh, to his surprise,

Her mangled form, still bleeding warm, lay stretched before his eyes.

Upon her bosom, snow white once, but now besmirched with gore,

The Dobharchú reposing was, his surfeiting being o'er.

Her bowels and entrails all around tinged with a reddish hue:

"Oh, God," he cried, "'tis hard to bear but what am I to do?"

It is impossible to know what to make of these accounts, assuming they are not purely legendary. They provide us with little information about the creature's appearance, except that it bore at least a passing resemblance to an otter. Its behavior, however, is utterly unotterlike; otters are shy of humans and entirely unaggressive in their dealings with them. Nor does the creature sound much like the lake monsters that supposedly populate fresh-water bodies throughout the British Isles.

The only other entity the *Dobharchœ* brings to mind is one that is alleged to have crossed a road in Magalia, a small town in northern California, on the morning of May 24, 1996. Sheila Charles was driving her son Shane to school when it darted out in front of her. Swerving to avoid it, she lost control of the car and suffered an accident, which fortunately resulted in no serious injuries.

The thing's appearance no doubt had something to do with her reaction. It was, she said, four to five feet long, generally doglike, but with a sleek serpentine head set on a slender thirty-inch neck. Its eyes were "reptilian," and it was covered with shaggy black fur or hair. Its hind limbs

(Continued from previous page)

were long, its front limbs notably shorter, and it had no tail. The driver of the car behind Charles's also saw the creature.

Further Reading:

Shuker, Karl. "Alien Zoo." *Fortean Times* 98 (1997): 17.

———. "Alien Zoo." *Fortean Times* 100 (1997): 17.

Tohall, Patrick. "The Dobhar-Chœ Tombstone of Glenade, Co. Leitrim." *Journal of the Royal Society of Antiquaries of Ireland* 78 (1948): 127–29.

Walsh, Dave. "Lethal Lutra." *Nua Blather,* August 21, 1998.

(Continued from page 211)

an extraordinary technological device. Though we probably will never know for sure, one strongly suspects—more to the point, presumes—that this is just one of the many outrageous, less than strictly factual yarns with which nineteenth-century American newspapers regaled their readers, perhaps inspired by the classic proto-science fiction novel *Twenty Thousand Leagues under the Sea* (1869). There surely is more Jules Verne than veracity here.

Other USOs

If reports like the two above occasion a sense of disbelief more than of credibility, they do not necessarily relegate reports of unidentified submarine objects (USOs) to the realm of popular fantasy. Even in the nineteenth century some intriguing reports of such phenomena were recorded. Among the more impressive was one that occurred on June 18, 1845, in the eastern Mediterranean Sea. The crew of the brig *Victoria* saw three bright, luminous objects emerge from the sea and shoot into the sky, where they were visible for ten minutes.

Prof. Baden-Powell collected reports from these and other witnesses and published their testimony in an 1861 issue of *Report of the British Association.* One man who observed the sight independently from land said the objects were five times the size of the moon, with "sail-like or streamerlike" appendages. He and other witnesses, who had the objects in view for between twenty minutes and an hour, said they appeared to be joined together.

On November 12, 1887, near Cape Race, a "large ball of fire"—one account describes it as "enormous"—rose from the sea, ascended fifty feet, then approached a nearby ship, the British steamer *Siberian,* moving against the wind as it did so. It then retreated and flew away. The incident was reported and discussed in *Nature,* *L'Astronomie,* and *Meteorological Journal.*

Modern UFO literature records a number of supposed USO incidents. Most are sketchily documented and unimpressive. At least some seem explainable as sightings of terrestrial submarines in unexpected places, presumably pursuing espionage or other secret missions. From the 1960s into the 1990s, for example, Scandinavia was plagued with what its military believed to be submarines trespassing ominously in its territorial waters. They were thought to be of Russian origin, though Moscow repeatedly denied it knew anything about them; indeed, no evidence has yet emerged to contradict these denials. In the early 1990s some of the "submarines" were identified as small water mammals (notably minks) that had set off underwater detection devices. Many of the incidents, however, remain unaccounted for.

Here's a sampling of reports:

Hudson River, New York, July 1, 1924: Pilot D. P. Lott and photographer R. A. Smith, flying a small aircraft 5500 feet over the Hudson River at a location near the city of Ossining, observed two immense objects of curious appearance. An estimated 250 feet in length, the objects were moving upstream from under the water, pursuing a parallel course approximately 600 feet apart. Through a telephoto lens Smith snapped a picture, which depicts two pointed cylindrical structures with an arrow-shaped wake behind each. The Navy denied it had any submarines in the area. Though speculation about rum runners figured in press accounts, no evidence exists to substantiate the theory that traffickers in illegal alcohol—the incident took place in the midst of the Prohibition era (1920–1933)—ever plied their trade with submarines. In any event, the size alone, even if only generally accurate, is too great for any known underwater boats of the period.

Off the Alaska coast, summer 1945: Around sunset a large, round object, something like 200 feet in diameter, emerged from the sea about a mile from the U.S. Army transport *Delarof*. After ascending a short distance, it turned toward the ship, approached it, and circled it silently two or three times before it flew off and disappeared in the southwest.

South Pacific, between South America and Polynesian islands, mid-1947: "We saw the shine of phosphorescent eyes drifting on the surface on dark nights," the Norwegian anthropologist/explorer Thor Heyerdahl wrote in *Kon-Tiki* (1950), "and on one single occasion, we saw the sea boil and bubble while something like a big wheel came up and rotated in the air, while some of our dolphins tried to escape by hurling themselves desperately through space."

North Atlantic, late summer 1954: The crew of the *Groote Beer,* a ship owned by the Dutch government, observed a flat, moon-shaped object rise out of the ocean. Watching it through binoculars, Capt. Jan P. Boshoff noted its gray color and bright lights around the edges. It flew off at a 60° angle, covering thirty-two minutes of arc in one and a half minutes' time. It or another object was also seen by the Honduran freighter *Aliki P.*, sailing in the same general area. It radioed the Long Island Coast Guard: "Observed ball of fire moving in and out of water without being extinguished. Trailing white smoke. Moving in erratic course, finally disappeared."

Westchester County, New York, September 17, 1955: Around 1:30 A.M. a couple named Bordes, fishing enthusiasts, were rowing out onto a lake on Titicus Reservoir when they saw an object come out of the water a few feet from their boat

Thor Heyerdahl, the famous sea adventurer, wrote in his *Kon-Tiki* of an encounter with an apparent USO.

and toward the shore. Rose-colored and luminous, it was the size and shape of a basketball. After rising a foot into the air, it fell back into the water with a loud splash and disappeared. Unnerved, the Bordeses headed for shore. On their way they saw, 200 yards to the southeast and at the center of the lake, two parallel lights, wavy in shape but rigid, thirty feet in length, along or just under the surface. "Above these 'serpents' was a round light of lesser brilliance, more yellowish white in hue," an investigator reported. "Considerably smaller than full moon, and dimmer than a car headlight, it appeared the size of a basketball ... at a distance of a few hundred feet. It was not hovering in midair, but was apparently fixed to a solid body, which was only intermittently visible as a dim gray shape against the blackness." It appeared to be a rotating spotlight. The couple watched the object for a time and even tried to approach it. When they left, considerably shaken, it was still there. The couple emphatically rejected any suggestion that they had seen another boat.

Shag Harbor, Nova Scotia, October 4, 1967: What would be one of the best documented underwater-UFO cases began just before midnight when two men driving in a car saw a row of bright reddish orange lights. They "came off and on one at a time," according to a local newspaper, the *Yarmouth Light Herald* (October 12). "The lights were at an angle of 45°, dipping to the right, and the lights came on in order from bottom to top." Five other persons in a car stopped and watched the lights fly off the water half a mile from shore, where they changed into a single bright white light that bobbed on the waves. Numerous other people, including a Royal Canadian Mounted Police constable, also saw it, and a number of boats set out to find it. "Within an hour," the paper related, "the boats had arrived in the area where the object had disappeared, and reported finding a very large patch of bubbling water and foam. One fishermen described the froth as 80 feet wide and yellowish in color and said that he had never seen anything like it before in the area." This incident precipitated a series of strange events that played out over the next days but are beyond the scope of this treatment.

Underwater civilization?

Combining reports such as these with Bermuda Triangle lore, Ivan T. Sanderson wrote a book, *Invisible Residents* (1970), which treated the accounts as evidence that underwater OINTS (Other Intelligences) evolved on the earth and developed a sophisticated technological civilization. "If a superior technological type of intelligent civilization(s) developed on this planet under water," he wrote, "they would very likely have gotten much farther ahead than we have, having had several millions and possibly up to a billion years' headstart on us as we know it having started in the sea."

Nothing like actual evidence sustains these sweeping speculations. It is likely that Sanderson himself, given to casual thought exercises which often saw their way into print, did not mean for them to be taken especially seriously. The late Mac Tonnies revived a variant conjecture, in which "cryptoterrestrials"—his term—evolved as an advanced race alongside protohumans, eventually colonizing the oceans in order to keep themselves hidden. Others have suggested, on occasion, that extraterrestrial UFOs maintain bases in oceans and lakes, or that such craft are exploring the water regions along with the earth's land areas. Sometimes, usually under hypnosis (which adds another level of uncertainty to the testimony), abductees have related episodes in which aliens flew them to undersea bases.

Further Reading:

Coleman, Loren. *Mysterious America: The Revised Edition*. New York: ParaView Press, 2001.

Corliss, William R., ed. *Strange Phenomena: A Sourcebook of Unusual Natural Phenomena*, Volume G–1. Glen Arm, MD: The Author, 1974.

Dash, Mike. "Swedish Mystery Subs Mystery." *Fortean Times* 51 (1988/1989): 26–30.

Feindt, Carl W. *UFOs and Water: Physical Effects of UFOs on Water through Accounts by Eyewitnesses*. Privately published, 2010.

Fort, Charles. *The Books of Charles Fort*. New York: Henry Holt and Company, 1941.

Hall, Richard. "Aerial Anomalies at Sea." *INFO Journal* 4,3 (May 1975): 6–9.

Heuvelmans, Bernard. *In the Wake of the Sea Serpents*. New York: Hill and Wang, 1968.

Ledger, Don, and Chris Styles. *Dark Object: The World's Only Government-Documented UFO Crash*. New York: Dell, 2001.

Lingeman, Richard. "The Swedes and the Soviet Subs." *The Nation* (April 3, 1995): 452–54.

"More Lake Monsters." *INFO Journal* 6,3 (September/October 1977): 5.

Ribera, Antonio. "UFOs and the Sea." *Flying Saucer Review* 10,6 (November/December 1964): 8–10.

Sanderson, Ivan T. *Invisible Residents: A Disquistion upon Certain Matters Maritime, and the Possibility of Intelligent Life under the Waters of This Earth*. New York: World Publishing, 1970.

Tonnies, Mac. *The Cryptoterrestrials: A Meditation on Indigenous Humanoids and the Aliens among Us*. San Antonio and New York: Anomalist Books, 2010.

"USO Update." *INFO Journal* 4,1 (May 1974): 30–33.

Yowie

Driving in a wagon toward Minlaton, South Australia, one day in April 1880, a man identified only as Mr. O'Dea noticed that his horses were acting spooked about something. Looking down the road, he saw a strange-looking object less than twenty yards ahead. It had the general outline of a human being except that it appeared, on closer inspection, to be some kind of ape, fully seven feet tall and fully bipedal.

Because no wild primates were (and are) known to exist in Australia, O'Dea sensibly deduced that he needed a closer look in order to be sure he was seeing what he thought he was seeing. Yet however fast he forced his horses to gallop in the creature's direction, the farther away it got from him. Finally, after a 200-yard chase, it emitted a loud bellow, leaped over a fence, and vanished into the scrub.

The newspaper that related the encounter, *Western Australian* (April 23), seemed oblivious to a long history of this sort of crossing of paths of human and quasi-human. In fact (or at least in tradition) such creatures, if never recognized by science, have wandered the Australian landscape since before Australia as a nation existed. In South Australia, Aborigines call it *noocconah*. Elsewhere, names such as *quinkin* (north Queensland), *jurrawarra*, *myngawin*, and *puttikan* (various parts of New South Wales), *gubba*, *doolagarl*, and *gulaga* (Western Australia), and other identifications elsewhere. The words have a common meaning. Translated, it's Hairy Man.

The Hairy Man was a big, reclusive, apelike beast that native groups throughout the continent assigned a set of common characteristics: hirsute (obviously), tall, often foul-odored, fast-moving, and sometimes aggressive and dangerous in its behavior. It left huge footprints, significantly larger than a man's. It uttered guttural cries, and its diet consisted, in part, of kangaroo meat. It climbed trees, and it could walk on four legs or two. On occasion it thumped trees or the ground with its foot to announce its presence. Some traditions gave the creatures extraordinary talents, such as the ability to fly or hypnotize witnesses into drowsiness. Its feet, moreover, were pointed backwards so as to confuse those who might be tracking it.

By the middle decades of the nineteenth century, British settlers—the first British immigrants arrived in Australia in 1788—produced the first written records of native testimony concerning the creature. In 1842, *The Australian and New Zealand Monthly Magazine* addressed native "superstitions," such as their belief in what "they call Yahoo, or … *Devil-Devil*," and wondered if they were embellished descriptions of a genuine, but so far uncatalogued, antipodean primate:

> This being they describe as resembling man, of nearly the same height, but more slender, with long white straight hair hanging down from the head over the features, so as almost entirely to conceal them; the arms as extraordinarily long, furnished at the extremities with great talons, and the feet turned backwards, so that, on flying from man, the imprint of the foot appears as if the being had travelled in the opposite direction. Altogether, they described it as a hideous monster, of an unearthly character and ape-like appearance.… A contested point has long existed among Australian naturalists whether or not it does, and that from its scarceness, slyness, and solitary habits, man has not succeeded in obtaining a specimen, and that it is likely one of the monkey tribe.

Writing in *Notes and Sketches of New South Wales during a Residence in the Colony from 1839 to 1844* (1844), Mrs. Charles Meredith noted that the aborigines

> have an evil spirit, which causes them great terror whom they call "Yahoo," or "Devil-Devil": he lives in the tops of the steepest and rockiest mountains, which are totally inaccessible to all human beings.… The name Devil-Devil is of course borrowed from our vocabulary, and the doubling of the phrase denotes how terrible or intense a devil he is; that of a Yahoo, being used to express a bad spirit, or "Bugaboo," was common also with the aborigines of Van Diemen's land [Tasmania], and is as likely to be a coincidence with, as a loan from Dean Swift.

In Jonathan Swift's celebrated satire *Gulliver's Travels* (1726), yahoos were wild men, partially covered in thick brown hair, who lived on an island off the south coast of Australia. With "strong extended claws before and behind," they were given to loud, menacing roars and threatening expressions, and they smelled bad. Since "yahoo" is a simple, two-syllable word not unlike others aborigines used to describe the Hairy Man, it need not have derived from settlers' use of Swift's invention. On the other hand, it may well have. Yet again, some reports have *yahoo* associated with the creature's vocalizations. All we know from this distance, in any event, is that "yahoo" as a name for the Hairy Man was an expression in both native and colonial vocabularies in the nineteenth century.

The *Sydney Morning Herald* for January 21, 1847, mentioned reports by natives in the Hunter River country of New South Wales of the Yahoo, "having much resemblance in the form of the Human figure, but with frightful features." In 1849, as related in two contemporary newspaper accounts, a party of white men fired upon a large creature encountered at Phillip Island, Victoria. It was "in appearance half man, half baboon." In the 1850s, at Port Hacking—now a southern suburb of Sydney, then an isolated outpost occupied by one colonial family— William Collin and a friend, who were collecting seashells on the shore for resale

Gulliver confronts a Yahoo in Jonahan Swift's classic 1726 novel, *Gulliver's Travels*.

as lime, were told that the clan patriarch, one Charles Gogerly, had seen a "Yahoo, or wild man of the woods … about 12 feet high … and carrying a staff 20 feet long." In his memoir *Life and Adventures (of an Essexman)* (1914) Collin, who appears unfamiliar with the Hairy Man/Yahoo tradition (at least he makes no further reference to it), assumed that Gogerly had simply concocted the story for the purpose of scaring them off.

A particularly interesting account from a few years later is chronicled in Ernest Favenc's *The History of Australian Exploration From 1788–1888* (1888), related to a tragically failed 1848 transcontinental expedition launched by Ludwig Leichhardt. He and his men vanished in the interior and were never heard from again, their fate unlearned, though subject to both abundant speculation and follow-up searches.

In 1851 two would-be squatters, named Oakden and Hulkes, set out west of Lake Torrens, South Australia, hoping to locate good grazing land. They found lush, lake-filled territory and more of the same to their northwest from aborigines, who also regaled them with accounts of the wildlife that could be found there. They also offered, Favenc noted, "descriptions of strange animals," including the "*jimbra*, or apes, of Western Australia, which ruthless animals, according to blackfellows' legend, devoured the survivors of Leichhardt's party, as they straggled into the confines of that colony."

A decade later, members of another expedition passing through the region also heard of the *jimbra*, said to resemble a monkey but to be so fierce that it would kill a man if it caught one alone. "Thinking there might be a confusion of name," Favenc wrote, "the explorers asked if the *jimbra* or *jingra* was the same as the *ginka*—the native name for devil. This, however, was not so, as the natives asserted that the devil ... was never seen, but the *jimbra* was both seen and felt." A few weeks later, speaking with other aborigines in an eastern part of the region, they heard about the dead white men. The native informants assumed they had been from Leichhardt's group; the victims had died along a large salt lake either from *jimbra* attack or from thirst. In either case, the account had it, the creatures had eaten their bodies. Favenc remarked, "It must seem strange that the natives should in the *jimbra* have described an animal (the ape) they could not possibly have ever seen."

As more British and other Europeans occupied the continent, growing numbers of references to comparable creatures—sometimes retrospective, sometimes current—found their way into print. In one of the former, told in 1903, a respected tribal elder recalled witnessing the killing, by a large band of aborigines, of a Hairy Man west of Yass, in eastern New South Wales, in 1847, when he was ten years old. He said it was black-skinned and covered with gray hair. In the second category, this story appeared in the *Maitland Mercury & Hunter River General Advertiser* (New South Wales), April 2, 1868:

> The following narration we present to our readers for what it is worth, merely promising that our informant gave us the intelligence in all good faith, and appeared to believe most entirely in the truth of his statement. Patrick Hogan, a tree selector [tree farmer] on the other side of the Sugarloaf Mountain, towards Lake Macquarie, was falling trees in the bush at about three o'clock last Thursday afternoon [March 26], when from the surrounding forest, which is thereabouts very dense, there came a creature in all appearances like a man, but painted with various devices in brilliant colors upon a red ground from head to heel. The creature was most beautifully formed, and in all respects resembled one of the human species. It stood about five feet eight inches high, had long tangled hair, and some ornament or bracelet round each knee, also some appearance of clothes about the waist. It had in each hand a stick which it brandished as it walked along.... Hogan had a couple of dogs with him, one an old fashioned watch dog, which he thought would face anything, the other a young kangaroo pup. The old dog, upon being set upon the apparition, slunk away in fear, but the kangaroo, more bold, barked loudly, but produced no effect upon the wild man.... Seeing this, Hogan advanced and menaced the creature with his axe, having previously called to it to stand,

an order which it treated with as much disdain as the barkings of the pup, but when it was in likelihood of being "axed" to stand, it quickened its pace, and in two or three leaps disappeared. Hogan turned back to his hut to get a gun which he had there loaded, but on his return could find no traces of the creature, though it appeared that the kangaroo pup had followed it, as its yelpings were heard in the depths of the bush.... The hero of the adventure is not without an opinion as to the genus of his mysterious visitor; he says it is a gorilla.

According to the August 24, 1886, issue of the *Queanbeyan Age* (New South Wales):

Whilst a young man named Flynn was looking after stock at the back of the Bredbo station one afternoon last week, he was surprised to observe a hairy human form, about seven feet in height, walking in the bush. The wild man walked with an unsteady, swinging, and fast step, his arms being bent forward and nearly reaching the ground, whilst the colour was described as "bay," being between a red and chestnut. Flynn did not take a second look at the uncanny creature, but rode as fast as he could to the homestead of Mr. Crimmings, nearly two miles away, to whom he reported the strange, mysterious affair. Since then, Mr. Crimmings himself has [encountered] the monster, and his account tallies exactly with that given by Mr. Flynn. But Mr. Crimmings heard the animal make a cry that sounded very like "Yahoo." We hear that Mr. Joseph Hart, of Jingera, also saw the "Yahoo" as he was returning home one afternoon. The strange being is, no doubt, the "Wild man" that has been so often talked of about Jingera for so many years past.

> "The old dog, upon being set upon the apparition, slunk away in fear, but the kangaroo, more bold, barked loudly...."

The previous reports in the region included an account in the *Monaro Mercury* (published in Cooma, New South Wales) for December 9, 1871, chronicling separate sightings, one by a girl identified only as the "granddaughter of Mr. Joseph Ward, senior, of Mittagong" and the other by "Mr. Kelly, of the Jingeras, who says that he himself has seen the 'Wild Man'.... There is a tradition among the settlers of this place that the mysterious monster, the 'Yahoo,' is a denizen of the mountainous country where the 'wild man' has been discovered, and that it is only observable in stormy weather, or on the approach of bad seasons." Sightings of the same or similar creature were reported in May 1881. A local newspaper noted the return of the "Jingera hairy man.... It was seen on Saturday last by Mr. Peter Thurbon and one or two others. This was its first appearance for some considerable time. The animal, if such it be, has the appearance of a huge monkey or baboon, and is somewhat larger than man."

In his *Travel and Adventure in Northern Queensland* (1895), Arthur C. Bicknell tells a strange story, set sometime in the latter 1880s, of something he experienced near the Einasleigh River in Queensland. His account is peculiar in more than one sense: its content, surely, but just as much his curiously blinkered view of its significance. He wrote that he was alerted to the presence of an unusual animal by an old settler, who spoke of a "wood devil." He described it as a bipedal creature around six feet tall, possessed of big hands and long arms and given to moaning. The settler thought it had killed some of his dogs, which had disappeared mysteriously.

Determined to observe the creature and, in the trigger-happy custom of the time, to kill it, Bicknell hid himself in the branches of a tree and waited.

> I had not been long in the tree when I heard the peculiar moaning noise … and also the crashing and breaking of the brushwood…. It was nearly dark and the moon only just rising. I could see nothing. The noise had an unearthly ring about it. I am not easily frightened, but … slipping down from my perch … I waited a moment to fire two or three shots … in the direction the sounds came from, and then turned and bolted for the house. If the devil himself was after me I could not have made better time.

> When the old man appeared [the next morning] we got him to go with us to the place. There sure enough, he lay, as dead as any stone, shot through the heart…. He was nothing but a big monkey, one of the largest I have ever seen, with long arms and big hands, as the old man had described. These huge monkeys or apes are common in Nicaragua, but this one was certainly the largest I ever came across.

The sheer obtuseness of these remarks boggles comprehension. The distance between Nicaragua and Australia is vast, and the two countries do not have an overlapping primate population. Specifically, as already noted, there are no native apes and monkeys down under. Nor do the spider monkeys of Central America grow more than three and a half feet tall; they don't bother dogs, and they walk on four feet. One can only marvel at Bicknell's lack of comprehension. "Nothing but a big monkey," indeed.

On October 3, 1894, while riding in the New South Wales bush in the middle of the afternoon, Johnnie McWilliams said he spotted a "wild man or gorilla" that stepped out from behind a tree, gazed at him briefly, and dashed for a wooded hillside a mile away. Around the turn of the century Joseph and William Webb, camped in the range in New South Wales, reportedly fired on a "formidable-looking" ape-like creature that left "footprints, long, like a man's, but with longer, spreading toes; there were its strides, also much longer than those of a man." They found "no blood or other evidence of their shot['s] having taken effect," according to John Gale, in *An Alpine Excursion* (1903).

From yahoo to yowie

Writing in *The Yowie* (2006), the one book-length survey to provide a comprehensive overview of both the legendary background and the sighting testimony, Tony Healy and Paul Cropper remark, "Our records suggest that a large minority, possibly even the majority, of non-urban white Australians, were at least vaguely aware of the Hairy Man/yahoo/yowie phenomenon [during the colonial era]. It seems strange, therefore, that by the middle decades of the 20th century awareness of the yowie among non-Aborigenes was virtually zero." They suggest that the rapid urbanization of the nation starting in the very early years of the new century, coupled with the abandonment of many small rural towns and the attendant disappearance of a number of provincial newspapers, was partially responsible. Another reason, they argue, is the near-decimation of aboriginal culture, with its long traditions of the Hairy Man (and of course a great deal more), in the first half of the 1900s.

If infrequently chronicled—in their sighting catalog Healy and Cropper managed to recover a total of ten reports from contemporary sources from 1900 through 1974; the rest come from retrospective testimony, some of it going back decades—sightings were continuing, however scant the attention accorded them, up till 1975. In that year the Hairy Man/yahoo became the yowie and assumed its place in Australian popular culture, as sighting claims, now with places and persons (including a handful of active field investigators) to direct them, accelerated.

Perhaps the most interesting of the pre-yowie tales was related by a prominent Australian literary figure in the October 23, 1912, edition of the *Sydney Morning Herald*. The correspondent, cattle farmer and lyric poet Sidney Wheeler Jephcott, prefaced his account with the observation that he had lived in the bush for half a century without "the faintest scintilla of first-hand evidence ... that any animal of importance remained unknown in our country." Then just ten days before he set pen to paper, as he rode through a jungle area near Creewah, New South Wales, he noticed unusual scratches on the trunk of a white gum tree. The effect looked like something that three fingers and a thumb of a large, powerful right hand with big nails might produce. Starting at three and a half feet, the marks ascended to about seven feet. Though Jephcott deduced that "some animal unknown to science was at large," he conducted no search for it.

Not long afterwards, on October 12, he learned that a neighbor, George Summerell, had seen some animal of more than ordinary size, its back to him, drinking at a creek. Startled and confused, Summerell at first could only imagine that it was an "immense kangaroo." Then it stood up and turned around, revealing its height to be no less than seven feet. After staring quietly at Summerell for a few moments, "it walked steadily away up a slope ... and disappeared among the rocks and timber 150 yards away.... The face [was] like that of an ape or man, minus forehead and chin, with a great trunk all one size from shoulders to hips, and with arms that nearly reached to its ankles."

The next morning Jephcott rode to the site, where he noticed some twenty prints, noting that "the handprints where the animal had stooped at the edge of the water being especially plain. These handprints differed from a large human hand chiefly in having the little fingers set much like the thumbs (a formation explaining the series of scratches on the white gum tree)." Of the footprints Jephcott wrote that they were "enormously long," human-like, and "ugly," but with only four toes, each five inches in length. "Even in the prints which had sunk deepest into the mud," he added, "there was no trace of the 'thumb' of the characteristic ape's 'foot.'" Older tracks indicated that the creature had passed in the same direction about two weeks earlier.

Jephcott returned two days later to take plaster of Paris casts of two footprints and a handprint. "These I have now forwarded to Professor Davis, at the university, where, no doubt, they can be seen by those interested," he asserted. What "Professor Davis" did with them, if anything, is unknown, unfortunately. According to Healy and Cropper, sightings of a similar animal in the general area were reported as late as 1977 and 1997.

A rare mention of the mysterious beasts appears in a 1937 issue of the anthropological journal *Mankind*. Along the southeast coast of New South Wales, it states, native people spoke of a "creature called the Yaruma. According to them it was a creature closely resembling man, but of greater stature, and having hair all over the body." One native informant declared that "big hairy men" could be found on New South Wales' North Coast. "A Crown Lands Surveyor, S., informed me that he lived as a boy in the Mudgee district," W. J. Enright adds, "where a scrubby place was reputed to be the abode of a 'Yahu,' and a resident in the Maitland district told me a 'Yahu' was reputed to live in a thick scrub there. Each said he was a big hairy man." Knowing nothing more of the matter, oblivious to the many other reports by both aborigines and settlers, Enright could only wonder if the stories arose from vague memories of some dangerous, cannibalistic tribe.

> **[H]e noticed unusual scratches on the trunk of a white gum tree. The effect looked like something that three fingers and a thumb of a large, powerful right hand with big nails might produce.**

In 1971, when several Royal Australian Air Force surveyors landed in a helicopter on top of inaccessible Sentinel Mountain, they were astonished to find huge man-like tracks (though too big for a man) in the mud left over from a recent rain. They had no idea what to make of them.

It would take a controversial and flamboyant man, Rex Gilroy, to revive the Hairy Man question in the mid-1970s. A resident of the Blue Mountains region west of Sydney, Gilroy allegedly saw a gorilla-like biped pass a few yards in front of him at a location below the Ruined Castle Rock formation near Katoomba, New South Wales, on April 7, 1970. Five years later, he founded the Australian Yowie Research Center, making sure that all major media knew about it by flooding them with press releases and articles. Soon, the tabloid press, if not its more respectable counterpart, ran features, and he became a fixture on radio and television. Gilroy's stories did not always add up, and they were often sketchily documented, if that. His advocacy of a range of extreme notions did not help his credibility. Still, others without his baggage would pick up the Hairy Man mystery, and Gilroy's popularization of the name "yowie"—a term of nebulous origins, apparently a corruption of the native word *yourie*—would stick.

In August 1977, Canberra archivist Graham Joyner released a monograph titled *The Hairy Man of South Eastern Australia,* a collection of reports published between 1842 and 1935. Other early sightings would come to light as research efforts expanded. Other, more scientifically sophisticated investigators, including Healy, Cropper, Malcolm Smith, Gary Opit, Geoff Nelson, and others, began investigating reports in the states of New South Wales, Queensland, Victoria, and Western Australia.

Reports grew in number. On April 13, 1976, in Crose Valley near Katoomba, New South Wales, five backpackers allegedly encountered a foul-smelling, five-foot-tall yowie—a female judging from its pendulous breasts. On March 5, 1978, a man cutting timber near Springbrook on the Gold Coast reportedly heard what sounded like a grunting pig and went into the forest looking for it. "Then something made me look up," he related, "and there about 12 ft. in front of me was this big black hairy man-thing. It looked more like a gorilla than anything. It had huge hands, and one of them was wrapped around a sapling…. It had a flat black shiny face, with two big yellow eyes and a hole for a mouth. It just stared at me, and I stared back, I was so numb I couldn't even raise the axe I had in my hand."

In one celebrated instance twenty students from Southport School, at the edge of Lamington National Park in southeastern Queensland, experienced repeated daylight sightings on October 22 and 23, 1977. One of them, Bill O'Chee, grew up to be an award-winning athlete and, later, a well-regarded Australian senator. Interviewed years later, O'Chee verified the essential correctness of the original press account (*Gold Coast Bulletin,* November 17, 1977) and provided further details.

O'Chee said the creature was at least eight feet tall. "It was not really like a gorilla," he recalled. "In fact, it was more like Chewbacca out of *Star Wars*—except that its hair was not so long and its body was much broader; it was very heavy around the shoulders. It looked rather slumped or hunched over. Its arms hung down past its knees, and it took a couple of steps here and there with a sort of swaying, sideways movement. It seemed to be just looking around." This "swaying, sideways movement" is a consistent feature of yowie reports.

Healy also interviewed Craig Jackson, now tutor at the school, who had also seen the creature and who confirmed O'Chee's account. Jackson, however, thought his companion's estimate of its height was perhaps too conservative. Both recalled following the creature's prints into the woods and through a trail of pulverized underbrush. "A whole lot of saplings had been freshly twisted, shredded and broken off above the head height," Jackson said. "I started to think it might have become enraged." The two boys found an impression in the ground where they suspected the beast had lain.

Sightings have continued, if anything accelerated, through the first decade of the new century. Meanwhile, most Australian scientists remain resolutely skeptical. As one puts it, "The first and only primates to have lived in Australia were human beings." Australian National University anthropologist Colin P. Groves dismisses all the reports without exception as "of little value as evidence," asserting that people see what they want to see. Graham Joyner, historian of the yahoo (see above), holds to another, more nuanced, if rather bizarre, form of skepticism. "The Yahoo was an undiscovered marsupial of roughly bear-like conformation," he has written, "which was referred to intermittently throughout most of the 19th and early 20th centuries.... The Yowie, on the other hand, is a recent fiction which came into being in 1975.... It, of course, has no history, although one has been invented for it." Of course.

There can be no doubt, "of course," that zoologically speaking the yowie is a most unlikely beast. Even so, witness descriptions are strikingly alike, enough so that Healy and Cropper have reconstructed a composite yowie:

In 1977, Queensland resident Bill O'Chee encountered a hairy apelike creature that he compared to Chewbacca from the George Lucas science fiction film *Star Wars*.

> A full-grown adult is seven and a half to eight feet tall … and very heavily built; covered from head to foot in dark hair; its dome-shaped head may seem small in comparison to its very wide, but rounded, shoulders; skin is brown to black; eyes large and deep-set; ears small, set close to side of the head; nose flat; mouth wide, lips thin; teeth large and fearsome; upper canines sometimes protrude over the lower lip; neck extremely short and thick; arms very long and muscular; hands roughly human-like with very strong nails or claws; legs as long, proportionately, as those of a human.

Yet no bodies have ever been produced, notwithstanding legends and occasional anecdotal accounts of killings. Aside from tracks which do not seem to have been faked and to have been made by *some* kind of unknown animal (yet oddly, vexingly inconsistent in shape and toe number), Healy and Cropper remark, "people have reported car windows smashed, doors scratched, trees bitten and broken, strong bushes uprooted, heavy logs moved, heavy water tanks pushed over, horses injured, steers, goats, wallabies and possums killed and eaten."

Witnesses have also examined what they took to be "yowie nests." In one representative case, prominent bushman and television personality Maj. Les Hiddens came upon one while escorting scientists to a remote, leech-infested area in the western Australia jungle. He related the incident to a reporter for the *Townsville Bulletin* for December 8, 2004:

> In that country it takes a good hour to move 1 kilometer [slightly more than half a mile] through the scrub, so it's fairly slow going.... The forward

scout came upon this very strange construction … that left us quite baf-fled.… Someone or something had constructed a rectangular sleeping mat on the ground made from fronds. It was perhaps a little over a meter [slightly more than a yard] long and a meter wide. This mat had been slept on that very night, and the vegetation that made up the mat was ex-tremely fresh. We all stood around … this strange discovery.… None of us could come up with any sort of logical answer. We examined the ends of the fronds to see if they had been cut … but … they had been chewed off the main vine, not cut. Dr. John Campbell, our expedition archaeol-ogist, said that "If I were anywhere but here in Australia, I would have to say that was a primate nest."

American primatologist Henner Farhenbach studied four hair samples col-lected at other alleged yowie nests. Three, he concluded, were primate hair—cu-riously, very much like alleged Sasquatch samples this experienced professional had examined.

So stands the yowie controversy. It is a creature whom many eyewitnesses have seen at such close range that the comforting hypothesis of misidentification seems a very long shot indeed. At the same time the yowie, like the hairy bipeds of the American inland, is a most unlikely beast. Like so many other shadowy monsters, yowies dwell at the fringes of cryptozoology, itself a largely fringe pur-suit. They are neither quite here nor quite there. In their wake, in the fashion of phenomena that are less unexplained than inexplicable, they generate startled witnesses and extraordinary testimony, and beyond that, little more than puzzling and never definitive physical evidence. One would be surprised if that pattern changes in the future.

Further Reading:

Bayanov, Dmitri. "The Case for the Australian Hominoids." In Vladimir Markotic, ed. Grover Krantz, associate ed. *The Sasquatch and Other Unknown Hominoids,* 101–26. Calgary, Al-berta: Western Publishers, 1984.

———. Graham C. Joyner, and Colin P. Groves. "Comments and Responses." *Cryptozoology* 6 (1987): 124–29.

Bord, Janet, and Colin Bord. *Alien Animals.* Harrisburg, PA: Stackpole Books, 1981.

———. *The Evidence for Bigfoot and Other Man-Beasts.* Wellingborough, Northamptonshire, England: Aquarian Press, 1984.

Dash, Mike. "Just What Is a Bunyip Anyway?" *Fortean Times* 76 (1994): 38–41.

Enright, W. J. "The Yerri-Wahoo." *Mankind* 2,4 (1937): 91.

Favenc, Ernest. *The History of Australian Exploration from 1788 to 1888.* Sydney: Turner and Henderson, 1888.

Gilroy, Rex. *Mysterious Australia.* Mapleton, Queensland, Australia: Nexus Publishing, 1995.

Groves, Colin P. "The Yahoo, the Yowie, and Reports of Australian Hairy Bipeds." *Cryptozool-ogy* 5 (1986): 47–54.

Healy, Tony. "The Riddles of Oz." *Fortean Times* 49 (1987): 42–45.

———. and Paul Cropper. *Out of the Shadows: Mystery Animals of Australia.* Chippendale, New South Wales: Ironbark/Pan Macmillian Australia, 1994.

————. *The Yowie: In Search of Australia's Bigfoot.* San Antonio and New York: Anomalist Books, 2006.

Joyner, Graham. *The Hairy Man of South Eastern Australia.* Canberra, Australia: Union House, 1977.

————. "The Orang-utan in England: An Explanation for the Use of *Yahoo* as a Name for the Australian Hairy Man." *Cryptozoology* 3 (1984): 55–57.

————. "Scientific Discovery and the Place of the Yahoo in Australian Zoological History." *Cryptozoology* 9 (1990): 41–51.

Joyner, Graham C., and Colin P. Groves. "Comments and Responses: The Yahoo—An Improbable Hypothesis." *Cryptozoology* 8 (1989): 116–19.

Raynal, Michel, John Becker, Dmitri Bayanov, and Graham C. Joyner. "Comments and Responses." *Cryptozoology* 4 (1985): 106–12.

Smith, Malcolm. "Analysis of the Australian 'Hairy Man' (Yahoo) Data." *Cryptozoology* 8 (1989): 27–36.

Williams, Michael, and Ruby Lang. "Yowieland." *Fortean Times* 208 (2006): 40–44.

CURIOSITIES

Belled Buzzard

"While walking about the farm this afternoon," Pennsylvanian William P. Kinsey wrote his local newspaper on August 8, 1885, "I was surprised at hearing the sound of a sleigh bell in the air." The sound emanated from a nearby wooded area. As he headed that way to determine its source, Kinsey observed a buzzard on a limb. On his approach the bird rose into the air, and the farmer noticed a small bell—about the size of a walnut, he estimated—tied to its left leg. As it flew off toward the south, he noticed that when it flapped its wings, the bell tinkled.

This is just one of many curious stories published over the decades—roughly from the late 1860s into the mid–1940s—about a belled buzzard. More specifically, about *the* belled buzzard, usually treated, however wide its range (seemingly everywhere from Florida to the Dakotas) and however many its years of roaming, as a single entity.

The stories told of its origins were also many. In some versions the story begins in Paulding County, Georgia, in 1882, on the farm of a man named Freeman. It is said that one of his children caught a buzzard—technically, a turkey vulture (*Cathartes aura*)—and for some reason, presumably a poorly considered prank, tied a sheep bell to the bird's leg. Startled by the tinkling, it abruptly flew away. Or maybe it started in 1869 in Tennessee. Or maybe 1870 on Stony Creek in Giles County, Virginia, when James Bradley belled a buzzard and released it. Or perhaps it was Alabama in 1863 or Genoa, Italy, in 1874. Or somewhere in Indiana in 1882. Or rather in Shelbyville, Indiana, in 1879 or 1880 on the Tindall farm. Or was it the Carter farm east of Livonia in 1882? Or Westmoreland County, Maryland, in 1847? Or did it happen on the Sanford property in Belton, Texas, in the mid 1890s?

And what was the fate of the belled buzzard? Did it live on for years or even decades, only to be captured or killed or de-belled, then released? Did the bird end its career in Georgia in 1900? West Virginia or Maryland in 1910? Tennessee in 1911? Ohio in 1913? Georgia in 1926? Ohio in 1928? Maryland in 1930? Indiana in 1931? Ohio in 1934?

One of the earliest accounts appears in the *Memphis Appeal* in the early summer of 1869, a story reprinted in newspapers around the country. The phrase "belled buzzard" appears nowhere in the narration. It is simply related that on two separate farms south of Burnsville, Tennessee, persons sighted a buzzard with a small bell around its neck. The buzzard "appeared more than usually wild."

By the early 1880s the phrase "belled buzzard" was being used to characterize such sightings. Some selected reports:

Near Springport, Mississippi, circa late February 1883: "A young man named Petrie heard a bell ringing in his cornfield … and found that a 'belled buzzard' was the cause of the alarm. When the buzzard flapped his wings the bell rang, but it did not when he sailed smoothly" (*Palo Alto Reporter*, Emmetsburg, Iowa, March 3, quoting *Sardis Star*, Mississippi).

Pilot Point, Texas, April 25, 1893: "The belled buzzard was seen … by Mrs. Keys and family on their farm near town and as usual it was not accompanied by any of its kind" (*Dallas Morning News*, April 30).

Erath County, Texas, March 18, 1894: "Col. J. L. Hansel … always doubted [newspaper] reports concerning the famous 'belled buzzard.' He did not believe until yesterday afternoon that such a buzzard existed. He was out in his yard when above him he heard a bell ringing. Looking up he saw a buzzard with a bell hanging on its neck" (*Dallas Morning News*, March 20).

> "He saw it several times and distinctly heard the bell which he described as having a tin sound."

Longview, Texas, late June 1894: "A buzzard wearing a sheep bell was seen by several citizens yesterday morning [June 27]. This belled buzzard has been seen at numerous places in this state… Mr. O. H. Methvin and his son, over whose corn field he circled several times, thought it was a belled sheep or calf in their corn and tried some time to find it" (*Dallas Morning News*, June 29).

Mount Airy, North Carolina, early September 1894: "The belled buzzard has been seen in this neighborhood by several persons. One young lady heard the bell and thought a pet lamb of hers was coming home, but soon discovered that the bell was on the neck of a buzzard which was flying near by. The bell could be distinctly seen" (*Charlotte Observer*, September 9, quoting *Mount Airy News*).

South McAlester, Indian Territory (present-day Oklahoma), March 9, 1898: "A buzzard with a small bell fastened around its neck was seen near here this morning. It was feeding on some carrion near the Choctaw railway track. As the train passed the bird became scared and flew away towards the north" (*Dallas Morning News*, March 10).

Near Woodbury, Texas, October 29, 1900: "J. C. Goldfrey … informed The News correspondent that the celebrated belled buzzard spent the day on his farm yesterday. He saw it several times and distinctly heard the bell which he described as having a tin sound" (*Dallas Morning News*, October 31).

Boone County, Missouri, circa late August 1901: "The 'belled buzzard' has returned once more…. Such has been the rumor for several days, and today it was positively verified by C. S. Ballew of Hargo, Mo., six miles east of Columbia, who saw the great bird at close view.... This may be the last visit of the famous bird, for it is very old. Mr. Ballew said that the buzzard had turned gray. It seemed weary and sluggish, and apparently indifferent when he approached, and did not fly until he had a good view of the bell, the origin of which is unknown" (*Oshkosh Daily Northwestern,* Wisconsin, September 2, from press wire).

Near Laurel, Mississippi, March 21, 1909: "W. P. Bush reported to have seen a belled buzzard ... Sunday afternoon. The bell seemed to be very small, but was clearly heard when the carrier raised his great wings to pitch from his perch in the dead tree for a northern course" (*Laurel Ledger,* March 25).

Tifton County, Georgia, mid-January 1914: "Another Tifton county farmer, Henry Sutton, of the Brighton section, saw the belled buzzard this week. The buzzard flew within fifty yards of Mr. Sutton and he was first attracted by the noise of the bell. Mr. Sutton says the bell is suspended about six inches from the buzzard's neck and that it only rings when the bird flaps its wings" (*Atlanta Constitution,* January 16).

Shenandoah Valley, Virginia, July 1922: "The belled buzzard ... is reported back in his old haunts. Several farmers of this section report having heard the tinkling of a bell high over head during the last week, and in each case to have seen an unusually large buzzard winging his somber way down the valley" (*New Castle News,* Pennsylvania, July 14).

Hardy County, West Virginia, circa late September 1922: "The 'belled buzzard' has been seen again and is very much alive, skeptics to the contrary notwithstanding, according to two eye-witnesses—Edward S. Brown and his daughter, Mrs. Ruth Hott.... Mr. Brown and daughter said Saturday [September 30] they saw the buzzard recently in the neighborhood known as Bean's settlement. They were first attracted by the tinkling of a bell and, looking up, saw the buzzard flying over and circling as if making ready to descend. Mr. Brown said there had been a belled buzzard in Hardy county for many years" (*Cumberland Evening Times,* Maryland, October 2).

Sparta, Georgia, mid-October 1928: "The famous 'belled buzzard' or at least one of the species ... was seen by several workmen on the roof of Drummers' Home hotel here recently. The workmen said the buzzard flew over the roof, before seeing them, and they could plainly see the small bell attached to the buzzard's neck by a small leather collar and could hear the tinkle of the bell" (*Le Grand Reporter,* Iowa, October 26).

Brown County, Indiana, late April 1929: "[Neal] Ackerman and his companion were cutting out crossties ... near Maumee. Suddenly their attention was attracted by the faint tinkling of a bell which seemed to come from overhead. Looking up they saw a buzzard flying not much higher than the tree-tops and they were able plainly to discern a small bell about two or three inches in diameter attached to the bird's neck" (*Indiana Evening Gazette,* Pennsylvania, April 30).

The origin of the belled buzzard legend has vague roots dating back to the 1860s, when, according to legend, a child or children put a bell around a turkey vulture. Sightings of that mysterious vulture were reported for decades after that, much longer than the lifespan of the species would have allowed.

Falfurrias, Texas, early February 1931: "A belled buzzard may be seen daily in the Flowella section.... Mrs. J. F. Dawson and her son, Jimmie, were working in the yard ... when suddenly they heard the tinkle of a small bell, seemingly out of the blue sky. After straining their eyes in every direction for a short time they discovered his buzzardship lazily floating along, while with each flap of his wings the little bell tinkled" (*San Antonio Express*, February 15).

Woodpoint, Maryland, late February 1931: "That the belled buzzard, like the proverbial cat, comes back to its former haunts, was demonstrated a few days ago when Lesher Kreps, Williamsport, and two friends ... were driving along when they saw the buzzard flying low and distinctly heard the bell" (*Hagerstown Daily Mail*, Maryland, March 4).

Near Royal Center, Indiana, mid-October 1931: "John Cline and Mr. Ramer sighted the bird when it appeared at the Cline farm two and one half miles north of here. They say it wore a sheep bell about its neck" (*Logansport Pharos-Tribune*, Indiana, October 20).

Near Camden, Indiana, early May 1932: "[Frank] Albaugh was hunting mushrooms along Deer Creek ... when he heard the bell.... Through the trees he saw a large buzzard. The bird soared low enough for Mr. Albaugh to see the bell about its neck, and it stayed near the creek for several minutes" (*Logansport Press*, Indiana, May 10).

Harford County, Maryland, January 1935: "The belled buzzard of legendary fame has arrived ... and, residents complain, it has brought a flock of its friends. The countians had no objection to the arrival of the giant belled leader, apparently to take up quarters for the winter, but when some 500 others of its tribe appeared they were not so well pleased. Means are being sought to 'shoo' the flock from the county" (*Frederick News*, Maryland, January 5).

Near Gosport, Indiana, late March 1938: "John B. McKendall, who saw the belled buzzard as far back as 18 or 20 years ago, reported that he was building a fence on his farm when he heard a sheep bell tolling overhead and looked up squarely into the face of the bird" (*Hammond Times*, Indiana, March 27).

Coshocton, Ohio, June 12, 1938: "Paul A. Rice ...and a party of friends were on the Lake Hills golf course. Hearing the tinkling of a bell overhead, they saw the buzzard and someone recalled the old legend of the belled bird" (*Coshocton Tribune*, June 13).

Near Woodruff, South Carolina, mid-July 1941: "W. H. Phillips kept hearing the tinkling of a bell as he worked in a field. Finally looking up, he saw a large buzzard with a metal bell attached to its neck. The buzzard swooped low over a grazing cow which sought cover in the woods—ringing her own bell so loudly that the buzzard was frightened away" (*Hutchinson News*, Kansas, July 25).

A rare post-World War II account of a belled-buzzard encounter appears in a West Virginia newspaper, the *Beckley Post-Herald*, in Shirley Donnelly's column on December 7, 1961. Donnelly quotes a letter from reader E. C. Hitchcock recalling an experience in 1946. He, his son, his friend Carl Short, and others were hunting eight miles from Union when the son, separated from the others in the woods, fired a shot. He subsequently related that he had fired at a big buzzard with a bell around its neck. "Never having heard of buzzards with bells on," Hitchcock wrote, "I asked him if he was feeling all right." When a member of the party said that the boy had seen the notorious belled buzzard, the father thought both were crazy, until Short joined them to confirm that, at least according to widespread allegation, such a creature existed.

In the July 5, 2010, edition of Georgia's *Dublin Courier Herald*, columnist R. Scott Thompson surveyed reports in that state from 1877 to 1933 (when "newspaper stories ended"). On the day of the article's publication, Thompson related, "I received a call from Charles Taylor who way back about 60 years ago heard the tinkling of the belled buzzard as he was walking from his school in downtown Gillisville, Georgia." If "about 60 years ago" is correct, that would place such a sighting—surely among the very last—as late as circa 1950.

The lore of the belled buzzard

Newspaper stories document the rich folklore that surrounded the belled buzzard, including wildly conflicting—and unconfirmed—accounts of its origin, as noted above. Perhaps two stories deserve more detailed treatment, though it is wise to keep in mind that they are calling up memories of decades earlier and should be read with appropriate caution.

Interviewed by an International News Service reporter in March 1930, Shelbyville, Indiana, physician C. A. Tindall referred to a recent sighting in the area, remarking that it "calls to my mind an incident that occurred about 1879 or '80 on the old home farm, four miles of Shelbyville. My two brothers … and myself [sic] discovered a buzzard's nest in an old strawstack among some trees. We could slip up to the nest unobserved by the hen buzzard. This we did and caught her. We put a sheep bell with a leather strap around the body of the buzzard, in front of one wing and behind the other. As the buzzard soared away the bell tinkled. We saw her a time or two during the next few days, later read articles in some of the newspapers about a buzzard with bell on her in Eastern Indiana and Ohio."

In September 1968 (accompanied by her daughter) eighty-year-old Irma Sanford Eddleman returned for a visit to her native Belton, Texas, from her current home elsewhere in the state. The *Belton Journal* devoted an article to her in its September 26 issue. At her daughter's insistence Mrs. Eddleman reluctantly related a story from her early childhood. "I'm not at all proud of that," she said. "It was the unthinking act of a child, and not a kind one."

She grew up in town on a block-long lot, at the back of which the Sanfords maintained a barn, a stable, and chicken houses. When an old hen expired, a family employee tossed its remains on an ash pile, soon attracting the attention of buzzards looking for a meal. "My little brother and I decided to catch one," she remembered. "I did. It jerked me almost two feet off the ground, trying to get away, and how it stank. But I held on, and sent my brother into the barn to get a length of wire that had a bell on it. We wrapped the wire around that bird's neck, and let it go. My father worried for days about a bell ringing up in the air; he could hear it in the early morning up in the sky. My brother and I didn't dare say a word."

Besides the origin stories, press accounts abounded with yarns of the bird's death or capture. Some examples:

Peacher's Mills, Tennessee, circa early June 1888: "Recently while Alexander Johnson … was on a hunting expedition, and was walking through a dense woods, he came upon what he at first supposed to be a huge eagle, flapping and fluttering about on the ground. He raised his gun to his shoulder and fired, and the monster bird fell.… Johnson rushed up to it … and saw, to his great astonishment, that a bell hung to it, suspended by a small wire chain, of which some of the links had been worn almost to the thinness of paper. The bell attached—from which the clapper was missing—was round, and about three inches in diameter, bearing this inscription, evidently cut with a knife, or some sharp instrument: C. W. MOORE, ALABAMA, 1863" (*Quincy Daily Journal*, Massachusetts, June 14, quoting *Memphis Avalanche*).

Near Gist, Michigan, late July/early August 1891: "A buzzard with a bell about its neck was found dead in the cornfield of Cornelius H. Sibley.… A small bell was attached to its neck by a wire. On the tongue or clapper of the bell was the Roman numeral I and the letter D" (*Jackson Citizen-Patriot*, Michigan, 1891).

Near Nunn, Texas, early June 1894: "M. K. Ownsly and Will James caught a belled buzzard.… The bell was branded 'J' and was attached to the buzzard's neck by a leather collar" (*Dallas Morning News*, June 15).

Rankin County, Mississippi, January 1895: "While L. J. Dear … was out hunting, his attention was attracted by the tingling of a small bell, the sound of which seemed to come from nowhere in particular and everywhere in general. For some time he searched for the source of the ringing and was finally rewarded by discovering a buzzard flying over him with a bell suspended from its neck. He shot the bird and found the bell fasted on with a small leather strap, upon which was cut the name 'Parks,' presumably the name of the individual who fastened it on the bird" (*New Orleans Daily Picayune*, January 16, quoting the *Terry Headlight*, Mississippi).

Near Chatfield, Texas, April 3, 1898: "'The belled buzzard' has been captured. It was caught … last Sunday. The bell consisted of an oyster can securely tied about the bird's neck with a ten-penny nail as a bell clapper. It was trapped on the farm of Mr. T. B. Roberts, liberated from the burden, which had cut into the flesh, and the bird turned loose. The can is on exhibition at Shook's drug store" (*Dallas Morning News*, April 10, quoting the *Corsicana Chronicle*, Texas).

Near Mount Pleasant, North Carolina, mid-July 1900: "Almost every year some one sees a buzzard in some part of the county with a bell attached to it. The one this year was found last week at the McAllister place … by Mr. D. M. Blackwelder. Mr. Blackwelder says that the bird was on the ground and seemed unable to fly. Around its neck was attached a small brass bell with the following inscription on it: 'H. B., Havana, Cuba, Jan. 6, 1878'" (*Charlotte Daily Observer*, North Carolina, July 26, quoting the *Concord Standard*, North Carolina).

> "A small bell was attached to its neck by a wire. On the tongue or clapper of the bell was the Roman numeral I and the letter D."

Larkin, Kentucky, mid-June 1903: "Jack Martin … has captured a belled buzzard. The bell was made from a small tin can, in which a rude clapper had been fastened, the bell being strapped tightly around the bird's neck. Where it came from is a mystery" (*Earlington Bee*, Kentucky, June 18).

East Nottingham Township, Pennsylvania, late July or early August 1908: "Samuel Winchester, who captured the bird a few days ago, has decided to set it free" (*Suburbanite Economist*, Chicago, August 7, citing *Philadelphia Record*).

Near Union, West Virginia, December 31, 1909: "The belled buzzard … was captured a mile south of Union … by Ocie Raines, aged 18.… The big bird had descended to the ground and showed little fear when Ocie approached.… The buzzard seemed weak and mighty indifferent to his fate. He was evidently half starved, for when Ocie had placed him in a big chicken-coop and brought him a liberal allowance of hog livers he ate ravenously. Since then he has thriven [sic] powerfully on his generous prison fare and shows a strong disposition to fight his captor. The bell, which attracted the attention of so many, has been taken from the buzzard around which it had been hung by means of a copper-riveted leather strap. The bell is an ordinary sleighbell and on the outside is scratched the date '1872.' This is probably the buzzard belled on Stony Creek, Giles Co., Va., by Mr. James Bradley between 35 and 40 years ago, according to our Waiteville correspondent" (*Raleigh Herald*, West Virginia, January 13, 1910, quoting the *Monroe Watchman*, West Virginia).

Bridgeport, Alabama, mid-October 1911: "Marshall Glover … shot a belled buzzard.… Around its neck was fastened a bell with the inscription: 'Genoa, Italy, 1874.' It was a sleigh bell fastened by three copper wires, one of which was worn in two" (*Indiana Evening Gazette*, Pennsylvania, October 23).

Union County, Ohio, early June 1913: "The buzzard was caught in a trap by Milton and Ellsworth Loughrey of York township, who removed the bell from the big bird's neck before releasing it" (*Indiana Evening Gazette*, Pennsylvania, June 9).

Near Comer, Georgia, mid-April 1926: "This weird bird ... was killed the other day ... by W. C. Birchmore, a farmer who was out hunting for geese and brought down the buzzard by mistake. He stripped the bell from around the buzzard's neck and the chipped and scarred piece of brass is now on display in a jewelry store window at Athens. Scratched on the surface of the bell is the date 1882, indicating the amazing fact that the buzzard has lived for 44 years with this brass cowbell slung around its neck.... The carving on the surface of the bell was done with a blunt knife, and in addition to the date, the name 'Joel Mine, Lanville,' is easily discernible" (Consolidated Press Association, April 15).

> "Scratched on the surface of the bell is the date 1882, indicating the amazing fact that the buzzard has lived for 44 years with this brass cowbell slung around its neck...."

Near Richwood, Ohio, early July 1928: "No doubt the belled buzzard that had frequented this community for several years was the one found dead on the Elmer Parish farm.... Mr. Parish says he was evidently taking his last meal on a dead chicken. There was no sign of a struggle in the oatfield. The bell and strap shows long wear. It is evidently a small sized cow bell" (*Richwood Gazette*, July 19).

Hagerstown, Maryland, April 23, 1930: "Returning home from the quarry ... after 5 o'clock [in the afternoon], Mr. [Roy] Colbert happened to approach a large black bird standing moodily on the towpath of the canal.... Slowly then Mr. Colbert began to cover the rest of the distance to the bird ... and to his surprise he was able to walk right up and lay his hands on his prize.... He made from home with the buzzard as fast as he could travel under the huge weight and established him in his headquarters in the barrel.... The head of the bird was bald from the rubbing of a tightly fastened wire, which was badly rusted from many rains. To this wire hung an ancient type of sleigh bell. It was made entirely of iron, was solid at the bottom, and had a number of curves in the top. No bells like it have been used during the past 25 years, which is proof of the age of the bird and the basis for Mr. Colbert's claim that he is the original belled buzzard" (*Hagerstown Morning Herald*, April 24).

Spencer, Indiana, early April 1931: "The belled buzzard of fact, fiction and superstition is dead—the victim of an auto. Rufus Turner, local man, ended the tintinnabulations of the bird whose fame has spread through Indiana and half a dozen states to the South, when he drove into a flock of buzzards. The cowbell attached to the neck of the belled buzzard apparently impeded its rise from the ground, and it struck the windshield of Mr. Turner's machine" (*Valparaiso Vidette-Messenger*, Indiana, April 8).

Perry County, Ohio, mid-July 1934: "The famed 'Belled Buzzard of Perry County' is dead. Delbert Farmer, finding the huge bird on the edge of a cliff three miles west of Bremen, O., removed the strap and bell which had made it famous in this section for years" (United Press dispatch datelined Junction City, Ohio).

What is this?

In the popular imagination the belled buzzard took on a strangely mythical quality. Even to many skeptical people, it was no ordinary bird; to the contrary, it was judged so outlandish that it could only be the product of foolish people's imaginations. Consequently, those who claimed to have sighted it were sometimes subjected to ridicule and the usual questions about their sanity or sobriety. In 1897, when mystery airships (a late nineteenth-century equivalent to modern UFOs) were reported in various parts of the country, witnesses received the same treatment. In fact, mystery airships and belled buzzards were sometimes mentioned in the same humorous or unflattering sentences.

Mostly, to those of a superstitious disposition—contemporary newspapers identified them as unlettered rural folk—the belled buzzard was a harbinger of death and disaster. An article in an 1884 issue of the *St. Louis Globe-Democrat* recounts a recent sighting in Georgia in near-Gothic prose. When a resident of a cabin heard a ringing sound on his roof, he stepped outside to "ascertain the cause … and immediately the buzzard rose from its perch and flew away. The night was clear and cold, and as the inmates rushed out and beheld the great black object, and heard the tinkling of the bell hundreds of feet up in the air, great fear seized them, and they all took to their knees under the impression that the end of the world was approaching."

In 1908 the *Philadelphia Record* claimed that in Pennsylvania's East Nottingham Township, the buzzard's "hovering over a farmhouse has been regarded as an infallible sign that there was to be an addition to the family. Mothers instead of telling their children of the stork's visit informed them that the belled buzzard was the bearer of the little one."

In some newspaper stories from the latter nineteenth and early twentieth centuries, belled-buzzard stories are said to have begun in the 1810s or at least the middle part of the century. As noted, the research for this book uncovered nothing published before 1869, but of course earlier reports are possible. It does seem certain, though, that the creature did not gain great notoriety until the late 1870s or the 1880s. In its time a fiddle tune and a folk song sharing the title "The Belled Buzzard" were in circulation. By the middle years of the twentieth century, the tradition had passed out of collective memory, even of folklorists'.

There is no evidence that the belling of buzzards was once a common or accepted activity. If so, the notion that they existed and could be seen and heard would not have been so widely dismissed. It is perhaps arguable that the legends and sightings inspired a few scattered individuals to attempt it. Most published accounts of bellings, however, depend upon rumors or decades-old memories and are less than conclusively based in actual events.

All that can be stated confidently is that a belled-buzzard tradition was once ubiquitous in a good part of rural America, as were alleged sightings and claims of death or capture. Superstitious beliefs, often seeing the creatures as evil omens, surrounded the phenomenon. In their time belled buzzards were as controversial, if on a smaller scale, as ghosts and sea serpents. And like other extraordinary phenomena, they were more than just a folk belief. There was no shortage of those who swore they had personally experienced them.

Cosmic Jokers
and Saucer Critters

When we think of encounters with the otherworldly, certain words tend to attach themselves automatically to our responses: fear, astonishment, incredulity. But sometimes another word, one that ordinarily does not come to mind, best describes what the witnesses experience (or claim to have experienced): comic.

By "comic" we do not mean the preposterous yarns of the shameless hoaxer, such as the contactee who sells moon potatoes to the uniquely gullible, or the schlock magazine publisher who peddles tales of Midwestern towns leveled by marauding flying saucers. Sometimes persons, who from all available evidence have their sanity intact and their sincerity manifest, recount experiences that make it sound as if they were the unwitting victims of jokers from the cosmos.

Take for instance the tale of a couple we will call Frank and Kathy, whose bizarre experience Marc Hunker, a sober investigator for the Mutual UFO Network, examined not long after it allegedly occurred. It happened on a Saturday night in early April 1974 in rural Hancock County, Ohio.

Driving along a country road early in the evening, the couple observed a light low on the northern horizon. At first they thought it was from a fire, and they decided to head toward it to see if they could help. Then the "fire" shot up into the air and grew in size. "That ain't no barn fire," Frank, stating the obvious, remarked to Kathy. He later told Hunker that it "looked like the whole northeast section of the sky was on fire from it. It was pulsating and shooting off light. It was down on the ground level, treetop height and below, just nosing around along the ground there." It appeared to be about five miles from them.

"I got on channel 18 [of his citizens' band radio] and broke four other guys," Frank said, "and I told them, 'Fellows, this is the Longrifle Man out here on the Cromer Road and I got a saucer critter.... It's reddish orange and maybe two or three hundred yards acrost, and it's movin' around.'" He went on:

> While we were talkin' on the radio, that thing seemed to open up and eject, on the end of a rope or somethin', a large square box-kite contraption. It stuck 'em out, and they'd go whirly-whirly-whirly in the air for a while, and then it'd stick 'em back in and close the door. Appeared to me that it was takin' samples of some kind.

It turned towards us and approached. That's when I first said, "Kathy, let's get out of here. We don't want to get scooped up in that contraption." But when it started chasin' us, it quit pullin' 'em out.

When it turned slaunch ways—that's edgeways—it would look like a long cee-gar. But when it would straighten out, it'd look like a saucer. And when it came towards us—it came well within a half a mile—I could hear some kind of runnin' sound very faintly to it…. Anyway, we turned around and hauled tail out of there….

It must have got aggravated at me for tellin' the world where it was at and what it was doin' because it commenced to follerin' us…. It followed us for 47 miles according to my speedometer.

We finally caused it to leave when we turned out the lights. Seems like it was following us by watchin' the headlights. So I turned out the lights, and with a black car in a black night, it—I guess—finally gave up and left.

Frank and Kathy then turned their attention to more earthly concerns, namely their hunger, and they decided to seek out a nearby roadside restaurant, the Wigwam. It was now 2:15 A.M.

No sooner had they stepped inside than a short, bald, fat man approached them with a question: "What did you see in the sky?"

When Frank asked if he was one of the people he had spoken with over the CB, the stranger looked at him blankly and said no. And then, as Kathy remembered it, "he kept a-talkin' real dumb" in a slow, choppy voice that sounded like nothing so much as a record being played at too slow a speed. "What … did … you … see … in … the … sky?"

He ignored Frank's question about how he could possibly have known about their sighting. When he continued to press the couple for details, Frank snapped, "I don't think that it's any of your business." Still, he couldn't resist asking one more time about the source of the stranger's information concerning them.

> The man's nose seemed extraordinarily long, as were his fingers—the latter, in Frank and Kathy's estimation, twice the length of normal ones.

At this final question the man, Frank recalled, "got the stupidest look on his face, and then he said the weirdest thing I ever heard." The man opened his unusually large mouth "five inches at least" and declared, "I … live … by … visions!" As if this were not unsettling enough, "he bugged his eyes out of his head a good three inches." "Sometimes further," Kathy added.

There were other unusual features. The man's nose seemed extraordinarily long, as were his fingers—the latter, in Frank and Kathy's estimation, twice the length of normal ones.

Not unnaturally it occurred to Kathy that "I was seeing things. But … I knew we weren't seeing things." Yet whatever they were seeing, it didn't look as if anyone else were. To the couple's bafflement, nobody else in the crowded restaurant seemed to be paying any attention.

In any event, Frank was growing ever angrier. "I looked daggers at him," he recalled. "He was startin' to make me disgusted, saucer critter notwithstanding. He goes making eyes at my lady.... He turned away and went to the other end of the bar."

Shortly thereafter, as Frank and Kathy got up to leave, the stranger demanded to know, "Where do you think you're going? You get back here! I want to talk to you!" Frank turned to Kathy and said, "We don't want to talk to that poor white trash. Let's go!"

"Everything was all right for a couple miles," as Frank remembered. "And then there was two bright eyes that appeared like headlights, only they were real close-set together—closer-set than a jeep would be.... They appeared to vary from three inches in diameter and very intense to about 12 inches ... and they'd go back up and raise up."

The lights, which Frank feared were from a vehicle at the mercy of a drunk driver, were three miles away and closing fast. "I was rollin' along at 50," he said, "and he was closin' in like 90. So we turned. I didn't want no part of him."

Thinking of what he had done earlier, Frank turned off his lights. "All of a sudden, zoop! zoop! zoop!" he exclaimed. "Right down he went! He overrun the road, stopped in his tracks, backed up, turned down the road, and then took off.... I presumed that he left.... I turned on the lights again, and about two minutes later, blink! There he was, right behind us again."

This time the lights were five to six feet in the air. In other words, this was no car, at least not one of terrestrial manufacture. "We lost him again by turning out the lights again," Frank said. "I was, I must admit, becoming a little unnerved."

"Just about then," Kathy related, "it felt like a force came up behind me—behind my head—and made me turn around and look back. We were sitting there where the road ended and the other road comes through. And when I turned around, I seen this big orange ball coming up behind the car. And it acted like it was gonna suck us up.... I went to say, 'Frank, the orange ball!' But all I could say was a bunch of mumbles."

The car seemed to be in the grip of the "force." The lights—the ones the two had seen first—then reappeared on the other side of the orange ball. Meanwhile, in front of them, according to Frank,

> a little man on a little black object ... kept a-goin' back and forth. It was just like a little black man. Like a devil or something. It looked like it had an odd-sized top on it. It was all funny-shaped. I can distinctly remember the triangle on the end of the tail. I was sittin' still, tryin' to make up my mind whether to cross 12 and go south or go in on 12....

> But I made up my mind that we better go straight across. And then all this transpired, and instinct took over, and I pulled him into low gear, and away we went across. I let in the clutch and did give it gas, and nothing happened. "Come on, come on, let's go! We ain't gonna wait around for this thing!" And I realized that the rear tires had broken traction....

(Continued on page 249)

Nazca Lines

At some time before 1000 B.C.E. the Nazca Valley, a desert region on Peru's southern coast, was occupied by a people whose sophisticated agricultural technology enabled them to build an irrigation system, improve their crops, and expand the area of cultivatable land. Over the next 1,500 years they also made advances in weaving, pottery, and architecture. The most celebrated of their cultural achievements, however, was the creation of a remarkable ground art whose precise function remains a mystery.

The so-called Nazca lines, of which there are thousands, consist of five kinds of markings. William H. Isbell writes:

> Most common are the long straight lines. Thousands of these crisscross the desert in every direction.... Sometimes the lines turn back on themselves to form elaborate geometric complexes with zigzags or long parallel sets of oscillating lines. Second are the large geometric figures—elongated trapezoids or triangles—which were first noticed from the air.... Third are representational drawings of animal and plant forms accomplished with curving lines.... Frequently these three types of markings are combined in a single layout.... A fourth class of ground markings incorporates several kinds of rock piles.... The fifth class of ground art consists of figures on steep hillsides.

The lines may be as narrow as six inches or as wide as several hundred yards. Some run for several miles. The Nazca people created them by removing the dark surface stones and placing them in the desired pattern. "Walking or sweeping the resulting figure disturbs a thin brown surface coating of material called desert varnish, which accumulates over time," William E. Shawcross writes. "This action exposes the creamy pink soil underneath." These light areas comprise the Nazca lines which, owing to the dry, stable climatic conditions of the area, have remained essentially unchanged over many centuries.

What has made these lines a curiosity that otherwise would interest only South American archaeologists is the fact that some (though not all) of the forms are visible only from the air. Within conventional archaeological circles this aspect has given rise to different interpretations; one, that the figures, which probably had some religious significance (they were not "roads," as some popular opinion had it), were not meant to be seen in their entirety, at least by human eyes, and two, that the Nazca people built balloons that enabled them to fly over the sites. This latter interpretation, though not flatly impossible, seems devoid of supporting evidence.

Beacons of the gods?

The Nazca lines entered popular culture not long after the commencement of the UFO age, with its suggestions of extraterrestrial visitations. In the 1950s, as

(Continued from previous page)

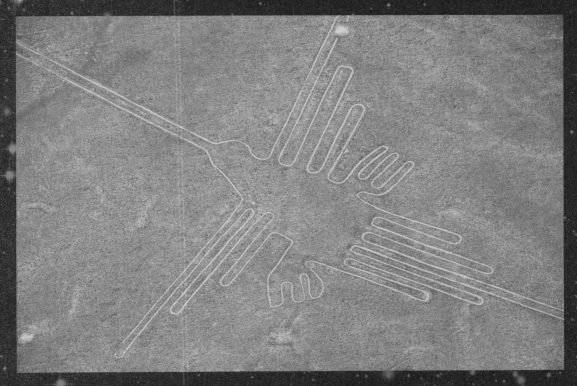

An example of the mysterious Nazca lines, this one depicting what looks like a humming-bird.

books and magazine articles about UFOs proliferated, some writers looked back to ancient history and mythology for evidence of early space contacts. In an article in the October 1955 issue of *Fate,* amateur archaeologist and UFO buff James W. Moseley suggested that since the markings were largely invisible from the ground, the Nazca people must have "constructed their huge markings as signals to interplanetary visitors or to some advanced earth race [presumably Atlanteans] that occasionally visited them."

Picking up on the theme, fringe archaeologist and flying-saucer contactee George Hunt Williamson devoted an entire chapter, "Beacons for the Gods," of his *Road in the Sky* (1959) to the lines. He wrote:

There were "sky gods" who came to Earth in the dim past. But why did they come and what was the necessity of immense astronomically perfect [sic] lines?.... These "gods" or heavenly messengers must have been in communication with some highly

Another example of Nazca lines looks like a monkey.

advanced civilizations on Earth; perhaps these people assisted the "gods" in the building of the lines and surfaces, or perhaps the "gods" were only the master architects and the Earth races did the actual building.

The "highly advanced civilizations" to which Williamson referred were from the lost continents of Lemuria and Atlantis, and of course the "gods" were space people. Williamson thought that archaeologically interesting sites, including the lines,

had been built at "magnetic centers" at which spaceships could refuel.

In the early 1960s, a French bestseller (published in England as *The Dawn of Magic,* and in America as *The Morning of the Magicians,* in 1963) by Louis Pauwels and Jacques Bergier offered a hodgepodge of speculations about what soon would be called "ancient astronauts" and mentioned the Nazca lines. Such speculations got their widest circulation in Erich von Däniken's *Chariots of the Gods?,* first published in West Germany in 1968, and subsequently reprinted in translated editions around the world. To Von Däniken the lines represented an "air field" on which spacecraft landed and from which they took off.

In fact, nothing in the nature of these lines sustains this interpretation. A Von Däniken critic remarked indignantly, "It hardly seems reasonable that advanced extraterrestrial spacecraft would require *landing strips*"; besides, he wrote, Nazca's "soft, sandy soil ... is hardly the kind of surface that would be required for an airport." Still, the notion was touted in a hugely successful documentary film based on Von Däniken's book, and comparable speculations were endlessly recycled during the ancient-astronauts boom of the 1970s and wowed the ignorant and impressionable. Even now, occasional "true mystery" shows on cable television revive the concept.

Further Reading:

"Guardian Spirit of Nazca Lines." *New Zealand Herald,* Auckland (November 4, 1991).

Isbell, William H. "Solving the Mystery of Nazca." *Fate* 33,10 (October 1980): 36–48.

Kozok, Paul, and Maria Reiche. "Ancient Drawings on the Desert of Peru." *Archaeology* 2 (1949): 206–15.

Moseley, James W. "Peruvian Desert Map for Saucers?" *Fate* 8,10 (October 1955): 28–33.

Pauwels, Louis, and Jacques Bergier. *The Dawn of Magic.* London: Anthony Gibbs and Phillips, 1963.

Shawcross, William E. "Mystery on the Desert—The Nazca Lines." *Sky & Telescope* 68,3 (September 1984): 198–201.

Story, Ronald. *The Space-Gods Revealed: A Close Look at the Theories of Erich Von Däniken.* New York: Harper and Row, 1976.

Von Däniken, Erich. *Chariots of the Gods? Unsolved Mysteries of the Past.* New York: G. P. Putnam's Sons, 1970.

Williamson, George Hunt. *Road in the Sky.* London: Neville Spearman, 1959.

(Continued from page 245)

I stopped, put it in reverse, and backed up, and I definitely felt it wham something solid. Yanked it into low and floored it, and it broke loose three times and then pulled itself across Route 12. And then the critter started followin' us again.

"We saw two white lights, and they were just like glued to the window," according to Kathy. "We kept seein' this thing—the little man—goin' back and forth, back and forth."

The object remained until the couple got within a quarter of a mile of Frank's house in Findlay, where it stopped and hovered. Half an hour to forty-five minutes later, when they next looked, the UFO was gone.

Marc Hunker was able to interview the couple several days later. He also spoke with the Wigwam waitress, who confirmed that Frank and Kathy had indeed been at the restaurant at the stated time. She could not, however, confirm the weird story they had told. Nonetheless, she recalled seeing a strange man sitting alone at the bar and wondering who he was and why he was there by himself at such a late hour. Hunker located two CB operators who said they had heard the "Longrifle Man's" UFO report. One claimed to have seen the object himself.

For their part Frank and Kathy insisted they wanted no publicity. They refused Hunker's request for a second interview, though he heard later from a source that Frank and a friend had gone back to the sighting area and there observed "hundreds of white lights moving about the roads and fields."

For all its outlandish and humorous qualities, Frank and Kathy's story is not unique. The men in black of saucerdom's dark-side folklore sometimes are said to utter nonsensical declarations and to speak in strangely slowed speech. In a close encounter case from November 1966, a Gallipolis, Ohio, farm woman reported witnessing a landing and speaking briefly with the occupants, who talked like a "phonograph record playing at the wrong speed."

> [A] Gallipolis, Ohio, farm woman reported witnessing a landing and speaking briefly with the occupants, who talked like a "phonograph record playing at the wrong speed."

Even the assertion that no one else seemed to witness the weird goings-on at the Wigwam is echoed in the curious phenomenon sometimes reported by witnesses and called by English ufologist Jenny Randles the "Oz factor," which she defines as the "sensation of being isolated, or transported from the real world into a different environmental framework … where reality is slightly different."

The men from Oz

Another man-who-was-sort-of-there story is told by Peter M. Rojcewicz, very much unlike Frank and Kathy in background and education. Rojcewicz is currently Vice President of Academic Affairs and Dean of Faculty at Antioch University in Seattle. In November 1980, however, he was a graduate student at the University of Pennsylvania, doing research for a dissertation on UFO folklore.

On a late afternoon at the library, he would write, "I sat alone in a wing facing a large window to the south. I had the table closest to the window, facing the window. Without any sound to indicate that someone was approaching me from behind, I noticed from the corner of my right eye what I supposed was a man's black pant leg. He was wearing rather worn black leather shoes."

Walking around the table, the stranger, tall, thin, clad in a rumpled, oversized suit, glanced out the window, his back to Rojcewicz. Then he turned around and sat down. Rojcewicz saw a man with a dark complexion and sunken eyes. As he spoke in what sounded like a "European" accent, he inquired about what the student was up to. Rojcewicz, who had no interest in an extended conversation, spoke briefly about his UFO-related project, then returned to his study materials. The stranger persisted, wanting to know if Rojcewicz had himself seen a UFO.

Rojcewicz replied that at the moment he was more interested in stories of flying saucers than in the question of whether they exist as physical spacecraft.

As if offended the stranger suddenly exclaimed, "Flying saucers are the most important fact of the century, and you're not interested!" Startled, wondering if he were dealing with a lunatic, Rojcewicz sought to calm him, and the man appeared to relax. A few moments later, he stood up "as if he were mechanically lifted." Placing his hand on the young man's shoulder, he said (to the best of Rojcewicz's recollection), "Go well in your purpose," and walked away. Shortly thereafter, the student was struck by the strangeness of the episode and thought he should see where the stranger had gone:

> I got up, walked two steps in the direction he had left in, turned around, and returned again to my seat. Got up again. I was highly excited and finally walked around the stacks to the reference desk and nobody was behind the desk. In fact, I could see no one at all in the library. I've gone to graduate school, and I've never been in a library where there wasn't *somebody* there! No one was even at the information desk across the room. I was close to panicking and went quickly back to my desk. I sat down and tried to calm myself. In about an hour I rose to leave the library. There were two librarians behind each of the two desks!

In October 1981 Grant Breiland, a young man from Victoria, British Columbia, experienced a UFO sighting. Three days later he was in the city's business district waiting to meet a friend, who did not show up. Seeking to find out why, he called from a pay phone situated between two glass doors leading to and from a popular department store. After putting down the phone, he turned to see two dark-suited men staring at him expressionlessly. They were strange-looking: "sun-tanned" and unblinking. Worst of all, when they addressed him, their lips did not move.

Breiland did not respond when one asked his name, likewise when the other inquired as to where he lived. The second man then asked an even stranger question: "What is your number?" Breiland remained silent, and a few seconds later the strangers walked in a curiously mechanical fashion through one of the doors and out onto the rainy street. Puzzled and curious, the young man followed them. The men ignored him as they crossed the road and entered a muddy, plowed field about eighty feet across. Three quarters of the way through it, they vanished from sight. They left no footprints.

This all happened, Breiland told investigator P.M.H. Edwards, on a busy Friday mid-afternoon. All during the time the strangers were in sight, he saw not a single soul. Cars sat parked, but no vehicles passed down the street. Cars and people returned only after the strange men were gone.

Further Reading:

Edwards, P.M.H. "M.I.B. Activity Reported from Victoria, B.C." *Flying Saucer Review* 27,4 (January 1982): 7–12.

Hunker, Marc. Letters to Ron Westrum (July 30 and August 19, 1975).

Keel, John A. *The Mothman Prophecies*. New York: Saturday Review Press/E. P. Dutton and Company, 1975.

Randles, Jenny. *UFO Reality: A Critical Look at the Physical Evidence*. London: Robert Hale, 1983.

Rojcewicz, Peter M. *The Boundaries of Orthodoxy: A Folkloric Look at the UFO Phenomenon*. Ph.D. dissertation, University of Pennsylvania, Philadelphia, 1984.

———. "The 'Men in Black' Experience and Tradition: Analogues with the Traditional Devil Hypothesis." *Journal of American Folklore* 100 (1987): 48–60.

Schwarz, Berthold E. "The Man-in-Black Syndrome." *Flying Saucer Review* Pt. I. 23,4 (January 1978): 9–15; Pt. II. 23,5 (February 1978): 22–25; Pt. III. 23,6 (April 1978): 26–29.

Swords, Michael D. *Grassroots UFOs: Case Reports from the Center for UFO Studies*. San Antonio and New York: Anomalist Books, 2011.

Entombed Animals

"Many well-authenticated stories of the finding of live toads and frogs in solid rock are on record," declared a writer for *Scientific American* in 1890. Twenty years later a *Nature* editor snarled, "It matters little to tell the reporters of such occurrences that the thing is absolutely impossible, and that our believing it would involve the conclusion that the whole science of geology (not to speak of biology also) is a mass of nonsense."

Both are right. The thing is absolutely impossible, and there are many well authenticated stories of it. As the Polish writer Stanislaw Lem once observed, "No matter how unlikely a thing is, if it happens, it happens." William R. Corliss, probably the world's leading authority on anomalies of nature, remarks, "If miracles do happen, then toads can be found in solid rocks. It may be that nature operates this way, violating the 'logical' laws we try to impose with some low frequency, after the fashion of the 'forbidden transitions' in quantum physics."

Because of its outrageousness the phenomenon of entombed toads, frogs, and other animals is seldom discussed in the scientific literature of our time, but it made frequent appearances in learned journals of the nineteenth and earlier centuries. An early example is this account, related by a sixteenth-century figure, Ambroise Paré, chief surgeon to Henry III of France, and reprinted in the 1761 edition of the *Annual Register*:

> Being at my seat near the village of Meudon, and overlooking a quarryman whom I had set to break some very large and hard stones, in the middle of one we found a huge toad, full of life and without any visible aperture by which it could get there.... The laborer told me it was not the first time he had met with a toad and like creatures within huge blocks of stone.

In September 1770, when a live toad was found encased in plaster in a castle wall that had stood for some forty years, scientist Jean Guéttard investigated the incident personally. The following February he presented his findings to the French Academy of Sciences and also provided an extended overview of other cases preserved in academic and popular literature. Guéttard's work inspired other scientists and educated lay inquirers, some of whom conducted tests whose purpose was to determine whether toads could survive for long entombed. The results—negative—provided fuel for skeptics, then and now. Even so, the reports continued.

One of the most famous, most often cited cases, however, may not be all it appears to be. At Hartlepool, England, on April 7, 1865, laborers doing excavation work found a block of magnesium limestone, twenty-five feet below the surface.. As they were breaking it up, they related, it split open to expose a cavity in which, to their astonishment, they saw a living toad. "The cavity was no larger than its body, and presented the appearances of being a cast of it," the *Hartlepool Free Press* reported on April 15. "The toad's eyes even shone with unusual brilliance, and it was full of vivacity on its liberation."

It seemed at first to be experiencing difficulty breathing, probably because its mouth was sealed shut. At first a "barking" sound came out of its nostrils, possibly related to inhalation and exhalation problems. Soon this ceased, though it would emit a startled bark whenever it was touched. When discovered, the toad was of a pale color indistinguishable from that of the stone in which it had been embedded, but in short order it grew darker until it became olive brown. "The claws of its forefeet are turned inwards," the newspaper noted, "and its hind ones are of extraordinary length and unlike the present English toad."

S. Horner, president of the Natural History Society, took possession of it. The *Zoologist* reported that it had also been examined by a local clergyman and geologist, the Rev. Robert Taylor, who confirmed the strange circumstances of its recovery. Then a group from the Manchester Geological Society studied the rock. One of them reported feeling chisel marks inside the cavity and grew suspicious enough to accuse the collier who allegedly found it of fraud. After denying it, the workman lapsed into silence. The Reverend Taylor withdrew his endorsement. Though nothing was proved one way or another, under the circumstances, skepticism of the story seems the only appropriate response.

The *Free Press* appended this commentary to its original article:

The world now had another story of a toad in a hole ... illustrations of which the toad's perilous passion for holes abound in our literature and, if we turn over the leaves of our local chronicles, numerous examples present themselves.

We read of the discovery within the last hundred years of live toads in all sorts of possible and impossible situations; in the solid slate of a quarry in Barnard Castle, in a block of freestone at Blyth, in a limestock block at Saeham and at Ryhope, and in a seam of coal down a deep pit at Sunderland.

Another of his race, profiting by repairs, emerged from the battlements of Flambard's Bridge in 1828, and gave rise to unavailing speculation as to his antiquity. A beech tree at Shawdon and an American oak at Blyth fell into the hands of sawyers, when a "living toad" started out of each of them, and exchanged a life of solitude for the publicity of a paragraph in Sykes or Latimer.

As these words indicate, embeddings have been reported not only in rocks but in trees. In 1719 the *Memoires* of the French Academy of Sciences related, "In the foot of an elm, of the bigness of a pretty corpulent man, three or four feet

An illustration depicting a May 8, 1733, incident in which a living toad was discovered at a quarry in Gotland, Sweden. The toad had been encased in solid stone.

above the root and exactly in the center, has been found a live toad, middle-sized but lean and filling up the whole vacant space." In the fall of 1876, according to the South African newspaper *Uitenhaage Times* of December 10, sawyers cutting a sixteen-foot trunk into lumber had just removed the bark and the first plank when a hole the size of a wine glass was uncovered. Inside this space were sixty-eight small toads, each the size of the upper joint of a human little finger. "They were … of a light brown, almost yellow color, and perfectly healthy, hopping about and away as if nothing had happened. All about them was solid yellow wood, with nothing to indicate how they could have got there, how long they had been there, or how they could have lived without food, drink or air."

Next to toads, frogs are the most popular stars of entombed-animal stories. One example was made known to the eminent twentieth-century biologist-philosopher Sir Julian Huxley, in a letter from gas fitter Eric B. Mackley of Barnstaple, Devonshire. Mackley wrote:

It became desirable to widen the Barnstaple-Ilftacombe road some years ago, taking in part of the long gardens in front of a row of bungalows which had gas meters housed just inside the front gates; these of course had to be moved back to the new front wall line. The meter-houses were brick-walled but rather massively concrete-floored, and the concrete had to be broken up to allow me to get at the pipes for extension. My mate was at work with a sledge hammer when he dropped it suddenly and said, "That looks like a frog's leg." We both bent down and there was the frog.... The sledge was set asided and I cut the rest of the block carefully. We released 23 perfectly formed but minute frogs which all hopped away to the flower garden.

Tilloch's Philosophical Magazine related this lizard-in-stone story in 1821:

A short time since, as David Virtue, mason, at Auchertool, a village four miles from Kirkaldy, in Scotland, was dressing a barley millstone from a large block, after cutting a part, he found a lizard embedded in the stone. It was about an inch and a quarter long, of a brownish yellow color, and had a round head, with bright sparkling projecting eyes. It was apparently dead, but after being about five minutes exposed to the air it showed signs of life. One of the workmen, very cruelly, put snuff in its eyes, which seemed to cause it much pain. It soon after ran bout with much celerity; and after half an hour was brushed off the stone and killed. When found, it was coiled up in a round cavity of its own form, being an exact impression of the animal. This stone was naturally a little damp; and about half an inch all round the lizard was a soft sand, the same color as the animal. There were [sic] about 14 feet of earth above the rock, and the block in which the lizard was found was seven or eight feet deep in the rock; so that the whole depth of the animal from the surface was 21 or 22 feet. The stone had no fissure, was quite hard, and one of the best to be got from the quarry of Cullaloe—perhaps the best in Scotland.

The *Los Angeles Herald* printed this brief account in its April 26, 1909, issue:

BISBEE, Ariz., April 25.—Miners working in the shaft of the Denn mine discovered a toad buried in the limestone and still alive. The animal was found at a depth of 1265 feet and the men on shift at the time felt all sorts of chilly shivers chasing each other over their backs when the antediluvian creature hopped from the little cavity where it had rested for thousands of years. This is not the first instance of such a discovery, but it probably is the first time in the history of the Warren district.

In December 1914, a crew doing repairs on a science hall at Yankton College in South Dakota found a toad entombed in a basement air shaft, apparently there since 1892 when the building was constructed. "The toad had resided in its brick tomb so long it was 'brick red' on the underside," a local correspondent informed the *New York World*. Though large in size, it lacked claws, which it apparently wore off trying to escape its confinement. "How it had lived is a mystery," the writer observed. "Not a drop of moisture could have reached the toad in all the years it had been a prisoner."

One account, from a World War II British soldier, has two animals entombed together:

In Algeria in the early part of 1943, I was working with a team whose job was to quarry stone that was then used for making roads and filling bomb craters. The method was used to set small charges of explosives into the rock face and crack open the rock, which we then pried away and broke down before it was used. One morning, we had set off the charges as usual and I started to pry away the rock from the quarry face when I saw in a pocket in the rock a large toad, and beside it a lizard at least nine inches long. Both these animals were alive, and the amazing thing was that the cavity they were in was at least 20 feet from the top of the quarry face. Try as we might, we couldn't find how it was possible for the two creatures to be where they were—there were no inlets, cracks or fissures leading to the cavity. In fact, it was quite a topic of conversation among us all for some days.

The last known entombment case occurred in New Zealand in November 1982, when a crew working on a road extension on the North Island supposedly found a frog inside a recently broken rock. Another was found later in the day under similar circumstances, according to Auckland's *New Zealand Herald* of December 9.

Attempts to explain

To human beings mysteries may be appealing, but they are also abhorrent. Thus, inevitably, in common with other mysteries, entombed-animal reports have faced as much disbelief and ridicule as wonder and excitement. Unable to mock such things out of existence, critics have concocted "solutions" so patently inadequate as to make outright hoax charges a more plausible alternative.

"The true interpretation of these alleged occurrences," wrote the same *Nature* writer who had relegated entombment tales to the realm of the absolutely impossible, "appears to be simply this—a frog or toad is hopping about while a stone is being broken, and the non-scientific observer immediately rushes to the conclusion that he has seen the creature dropping out of the stone itself."

There is no way to square such an attempted explanation with most of the reports (try applying it, for instance, to Mackley's experience). Aside from its complacent, implicit assumption that reporters of the phenomenon go through the world trying to function with what amounts to a chimpanzee's level of intelligence, it fails to consider a consistent feature of the phenomenon: the presence of a "smooth" or "polished" cavity, only slightly larger than the creature's body, inside the rock, concrete, or tree; as often as not, the animal is seen within that cavity before liberating itself or being liberated from it. There is also the fact that, in many cases, the toad or frog is decidedly unusual, its general appearance suggesting that it has indeed been confined somewhere for a period of time.

It is not hard to imagine how animals might get embedded in concrete. An indulged imagination conceives of ways they could meet such a fate within trees. Rocks, however, are quite another matter. The animals' survival, too, seems in-

This toad, entombed in stone, was found in a pile of flints in Sussex, England, in 1901. The stones were given to Booth Museum by Charles Dawson, a known hoaxer.

explicable. How could they have breathed, and what could they have eaten? Amphibians, the most common embedding victims, have, at the outer extreme and under the best of circumstances, a lifespan of three decades. But how old are these embedded animals?

In rare cases we have an answer. In August 1975, as they broke up concrete that had been laid over a year earlier, Fort Worth, Texas, construction workers were startled to find a living green turtle within it, and the smooth, body-shaped cavity in which it had resided during its imprisonment clearly visible. The animal's rescue, alas, proved its undoing. It died within ninety-six hours of its liberation.

Where rocks are concerned, we seem indeed to be dealing with an event not significantly short of miraculous, as Corliss says. Occasionally conventionalists have speculated that these animals were able to sustain themselves by drinking water that seeped through cracks. Even if we discard testimony that specifically denies the presence of such openings, we still leave unanswered the monumental question of how the animal got there in the first place. The implication, it need hardly be stressed, is that it was there a *long* time.

Nothing about this phenomenon makes any kind of sense. It seems to defy not only natural but even any conceivable outlandish explanation. Of the phenomenon all we can do is to acknowledge that while it is entirely impossible, it apparently happens anyway.

Further Reading:

Corliss, William R., ed. *The Unexplained: A Sourcebook of Strange Phenomena*. New York: Bantam Books, 1976.

————, ed. *Unknown Earth: A Handbook of Geological Phenomena*. Glen Arm, MD: Sourcebook Project, 1980.

Daniels, C. "Toads in a Tree." *Zoologist* 2,11 (1876): 4805.

"Embedded Frogs." *Fortean Times* 40 (1983): 7.

"Embeddings." *Fortean Times* 36 (1982): 17–19.

Hricenak, David. "The Mystery of Entombed Animals." *INFO Journal* 8,1 (May/June 1979): 5–6.

Michell, John, and Robert J. M. Rickard. *Phenomena: A Book of Wonders*. New York: Pantheon Books, 1977.

————. *Living Wonders: Mysteries and Curiosities of the Animal World*. New York: Thames and Hudson, 1982.

Sanderson, Sabina W. "Entombed Toads." *Pursuit* 6,3 (July 1973): 60–64.

Screeton, Paul. "The Enigma of Entombed Toads." *Fortean Times* 39 (1983): 36–39.

Skinner, Bob, ed. *Toad in the Hole: Source Material on the Entombed Toad Phenomenon*. London: Fortean Times, 1986.

Splitter, Henry Winfred. "The Impossible Fossils." *Fate* 7,1 (January 1954): 65–72.

Thorn, Marjorie. "Fossils That Came Alive." *Fate* 19,3 (March 1966): 71–72.

"Toads and Frogs in Stones." *Nature* 83 (1910): 406–07.

"Toads in Rocks." *Scientific American* 63 (1890): 180.

Green Children

The tale of the green children dates from the middle of the twelfth century, in the realm of either King Stephen or his successor, King Henry II. In Suffolk, England, according to medieval chroniclers, two green children, weeping inconsolably, were found wandering in a field. Seized by reapers, they were taken to the nearest village, Woolpit, and held in captivity at the home of Sir Richard de Calne, where local people came to gape at them.

According to William of Newburgh (c. 1136–1198), the children were clad in "garments of strange color and unknown materials." They could speak no English and refused all food offered them. A few days later, on the brink of starvation, they were brought "beans cut off or torn from stalks," wrote Abbot Ralph of Coggeshall (d. c. 1226), who allegedly had the story from Calne himself and who is responsible for the claim that the boy and girl traveled a "long journey by passages under the ground." The children "broke open the beanstalks, *not* the pod or shell of the beans, evidently supposing that the beans were contained in the hollows of the stalks. But not finding beans within the stalks they again began to weep, which, when the bystanders noticed, they opened the shells and showed them the beans themselves. Whereupon, with great joyfulness, they ate beans for a long time, entirely, and would touch no other food." In British tradition, as some folklorists examining the tale have noted, beans are the food of the dead. Still, the boy and girl were obviously not dead.

Soon the children were baptized, and not long afterwards the boy weakened and died. The girl learned to eat other foods and was restored both to health and to normal skin color. She learned to speak English and took employment in service to a knight and his family. She "was rather loose and wanton in her conduct," Ralph of Coggeshall wrote.

Asked about her native country, "she asserted that the inhabitants, and all that they had in that country, were of a green color; and that they saw no sun, but enjoyed a degree of light like what is after sunset." She said that, as they followed their flock of sheep, she and her brother entered a cavern. On the other side of it, they entered a land of light and higher temperature than they were used to. "Struck senseless," in Ralph's phrase, they lay down for a long time. Eventually, they heard the sounds of an approaching group of people and were frightened; but when they tried to return to the cavern, they could not find it and were soon captured.

In William of Newburgh's account, the children stated that their country was called St. Martin's Land. Its people were Christians. There was no sun there, but across a broad river a bright, shining land could be seen. Eventually, it is alleged, the woman married, bore thirteen children, and lived for years at Lenna in Suffolk.

Newburgh remarked, "Although the thing is asserted by many, yet I have long been in doubt about the matter, deeming it ridiculous to credit a thing supported by no rational foundation, or at least one of a mysterious character; yet, in the end, I was so overwhelmed by the weight of so many competent witnesses that I have been compelled to believe and wonder over a matter I was unable to comprehend and unravel by the powers of my intellect." A modern writer, the late British folklorist Katharine Briggs, observed, "This is one of those curiously convincing and realistic fairy anecdotes which are occasionally to be found in the medieval chronicles." Another authority, science fiction historian John Clark, acknowledges, "The story seems strangely convincing."

Sign in Woolpit, Suffolk, England, depicting the Green Children.

Another recent chronicler, Paul Harris, speculates that the children were not aliens from another realm but simply lost, undernourished children—a green cast of skin is associated with food deficiency—who had wandered into flint mines in the vicinity of Thetford Forest, near the village of Fordham St. Martin. "Perhaps from the twilight of the thick woodlands the children could see a less forested and therefore sunnier land across the river Lark," he writes. They may have spoken an English dialect "unintelligible to the insular 12th Century farmworkers of Woolpit."

Critics, however, counter that geographical and other considerations render that reconstruction unlikely to be accurate. The theory calls for starving children to have walked more miles than they could have managed. Furthermore, no underground passages link Thetford Forest to Woolpit.

As early as 1621, Robert Burton, author of *Anatomy of Melancholy,* suggested that "the rest of the Planets are inhabited, as well as the Moone.... It may bee those two greene children, which [William of Newburgh] speakes of in his time, that fell from Heaven, came from thence." Newburgh said no such thing, of course; he remarked that according to general belief, they had come up from the earth. In the late twentieth century, nonetheless, Scottish astronomer/science fiction writer Duncan Lunan revived the extraterrestrial theory of their origin, even specifying the characteristics of their home planet. Harold T. Wilkins, a mid-century English writer of books on UFOs and other unexplained phenomena, thought the children had wandered here from another dimension. He thought, "There is, so to speak, 'a hole in the wall,' or, to vary the metaphor, the occurrence of a vortex in matter-energy through which certain people ... may pass, and from which there may or may *not* be a return to the world from which they were 'teleported.'" The green children's "fourth dimensional world existed side by side with ours.... It may also—who can say?—imply that they had been teleported from some world in space, beyond the earth, where men live underground."

In any case, that the children were ordinary human beings, as opposed to fairyfolk, extraterrestrials, or visitors from a parallel reality, seems effectively undeniable. Unfortunately, the particulars that would tell us all we would like to know about them are lost to history.

Further Reading:

Briggs, Katharine. *An Encyclopedia of Fairies: Hobgoblins, Bogies, and Other Supernatural Creatures*. New York: Pantheon Books, 1976.

———. *British Folktales*. New York: Dorset Press, 1977.

Clark, John. "'Small, Vulnerable ETs': The Green Children of Woolpit." *Science Fiction Studies* 33 (2006): 209–229.

Harris, Paul. "The Green Children of Woolpit." *Fortean Times* 57 (1991): 39,41.

———. "The Green Children of Woolpit: A 12th Century Mystery and Its Possible Solution." *Fortean Studies* 4 (1998): 81–95.

Keightley, Thomas. *The Fairy Mythology*. London: G. Bell, 1878.

Lunan, Duncan. "Children from the Sky." *Analog* (September 1996): 39–53.

Wilkins, Harold T. *Strange Mysteries of Time and Space*. New York: Citadel Press, 1958.

Hoop Snakes and Joint Snakes

"The hoop snake is supposed to be an acrobatic serpent that takes his tail in his mouth and rolls merrily along hoop-fashion when he wants to go places," herpetologist Percy A. Morris once wrote. Jutting vertically from the tip of the tail is a horn which this dangerously venomous snake holds in its mouth as it propels itself. "Although stories about this creature are not uncommon," Morris chirpily intoned, "it is always someone's uncle's brother's cousin that sees it."

Not quite. Up till a few decades ago, newspapers covered alleged hoop-snake sightings, citing names and locations, even if in sometimes tongue-in-cheek fashion. Occasionally, newspaper editors' dismissal of hoop snakes (and joint snakes, to be discussed presently, as well) generated responses from readers who insisted that they had seen such creatures themselves. Any scientist who publicly dismissed them was certain to receive letters from lay witnesses arguing from what they insisted were personal experiences.

In 1912, after a Pennsylvania zoologist offered a reward for a specimen of a hoop snake, which he deemed nonexistent, he was besieged with letters (albeit not specimens). According to an article in the *Reading Eagle* (August 9):

> One woman in Chelsea, Mich., writes … that when she was a small girl, while berrying, she saw two old hoop snakes with five young ones, and when they were disturbed they took their tails in their mouths and rolled out of danger. A man in Redlands, Cal., says he and his brother saw a hoop snake which was captured and is now in the State Normal School in Illinois. From McCleansburg, Ill., and Long Island, N.Y., come letters from people who say that they have seen hoop snakes that took the horny protuberances on their tails in their mouths and forming a perfect hoop rolled away.

The same article makes the point, with clearly skeptical intention, that such alleged experiences reportedly occurred years or decades ago. Some newspaper stories, however, claimed reported incidents from as little as a day before, such as one attributed to Howard Shaffer of Pleasantville, Pennsylvania, in July 1905. Shaffer, it was said, encountered a snake, fully seven feet long, in a meadow near town. When he chased it, it "rolled up like a hoop" until he caught it and killed it. As is usually the case, unfortunately, there is no word of what happened to the slain specimen.

"There are many people who refuse to believe that there is such a thing as a hoop snake," Pennsylvania's *New Castle News* remarked in its June 24, 1903, edition, "but the fact remains that every once in a while some one bobs up who claims at some time or another to have seen one." The paper had just related that lately, Capt. George W. Crede Jr., a shooter at a local range, killed a three-foot-long snake "with a horn-like tip to his tail about an inch and a half long." No one had seen the creature propelling itself in a rolling hoop with the tip in its mouth, but the horned tail is one defining characteristic of the hoop snake.

Reports of reptiles with one or more hoop-snake characteristics go back to colonial America. A 1688 letter John Clayton wrote to the Royal Society mentions the "Horn snake, so called from a sharp horn it carries in its tail, with which it assaults anything that offends it," so forcefully that it could penetrate the butt of a musket "from whence it is not able to disengage itself."

Writing in *A New Voyage to Carolina* in 1709, John Lawson recorded:

Reports of reptiles with one or more hoop-snake characteristics go back to colonial America.

Of the horn snakes, I never saw but two that I remember. They are exactly like the rattlesnake in color, but rather lighter. They hiss exactly like a goose when anything approaches them. They strike at their enemies with their tail (and kill whatsoever they wound with it), which is armed at the end of a horny substance, like a cock's spur. This is their weapon.

I have heard it credibly reported, by those who said they were eye-witnesses, that a small locust tree, about the thickness of a man's arm, being struck by one of the snakes at ten o'clock in the morning, then verdant and flourishing, at four in the afternoon was dead, and the leaves red and withered.

In 1722, discussing the fauna to be found in the Virginia Colony, Robert Beverly noted the "Horn snake, so called from a sharp horn it carries in its tail, with which it assaults anything that offends it." In a 1779 work, Alexander Hewatt notes the presence of the "horn snake … which takes its name from a horn in its tail, with which he defends himself, and strikes it with great force into every aggressor. This reptile is deemed very venomous."

Five years later, in *Tour in the U.S.A.*, J.F.D. Smyth, writing of a stay in western North Carolina, provided what may be the first printed reference to hoop snakes by that name:

While I was at Sawra [sic; Saura] Town, one day a little lad of Mr. Bayley's came to acquaint us that he had killed a horn-snake, which being a curiosity that I was extremely desirous of observing and examining with particular attention, I accompanied him to the place where he said he had left it; but when we arrived there, to my great disappointment, it was not to be found. He assured me that it must not have been quite dead, and had recovered so much as to be able to crawl from the spot on which he had left it, and had secreted itself somewhere among the leaves.

However, everyone, and all the inhabitants, with the great confidence asserted, and avowed their having seen such snakes, though very seldom.

They represented them to me as the most formidable and direful foes in existence to the human race, and to all animation; poisonous and fatal to a degree almost beyond credibility.

He is described as something resembling a black snake, but thicker, shorter, and of a color more inclining to dark brown. He never bites his adversary, but has a weapon in his tail, called his sting, of a hard horny substance, in shape and appearance very much like to a cock's spur: with this he strikes his antagonist, or whatever object he aims at, when he least expects it, and if it penetrates the skin it is inevitable and sudden death.

So very virulent in his poison that it is reported, if he should miss the object he pointed at, and should strike his horn through the bark of a young sapling tree, if it penetrates into the sap or vital parts, the bark or rind will, within a few hours, swell, burst, and peel off, and the tree itself will perish.

As other serpents crawl upon their bellies, so can this; but he has another method of moving peculiar to his own species, which he always adopts when he is in eager pursuit of his prey; he throws himself into a circle, running rapidly around, advancing like a hoop, with his tail arising and pointed forward in the circle, by which he is always in the ready position of striking.

It is observed that they only make use of this method in attacking; for when they fly from their enemy they go upon their bellies, like other serpents.

From the above circumstance, peculiar to themselves, they have also derived the appellation of hoop snakes.

Two early books on South Carolina, John Drayton's in 1802 and Robert Mills's in 1826, mention hoop snakes by name. J. H. Hinton's *History and Topography of the United States* (1832) remarks, "The accounts of the deadly venom of the Horn-snake ... are considered to be unfounded," though without quite making clear whether it is horn snakes themselves, or just their poisonous stings, that are mythical.

Newspapers from the nineteenth and early twentieth centuries not infrequently related recent alleged sightings of hoop snakes, even though skepticism of their existence was even then widespread, perhaps more among zoologists than among lay people. A few defenses of the hoop snake stirred editorial writers, such as one in an 1886 issue of the *St. Louis Globe-Democrat*, arguing while the creature is surely rare, "that it exists is a settled fact."

Some representative reports from the press of the period:

Saline Fork, Arkansas, summer 1879: "Dr. Alvord, County Clerk Masterson, and Mr. Leahy have just returned from a hunt.... The party had stationed themselves in the tree platforms about Yokum Blue Lick.... The lick is at the bottom of a steep hill. Dr. Alvord suddenly noticed something like a hoop come rolling down the hill and across the wet lick. It was followed by three others, which rolled to where it had stopped.… The snakes played around for a few minutes, and then resuming their former position, standing on edge with their tails in their mouths, deliberately began to roll up the hill" (*St. John Daily Sun*, New Brunswick, September 1, quoting *Zellville Sabre*, Arkansas).

Marietta, Georgia, August 5, 1883: "While waiting in her garden, a lady of this place saw a veritable hoop snake. It had its tail in its mouth and was rolling when it was seen" (*Atlanta Constitution*, August 10). The same day, a witness "discovered on the Western and Atlantic railroad track, just above the railroad bridge, a large snake about three feet long, black in color with yellow spots on its sides. Apparently it had its tail in its mouth, and was rolling over like a hoop. It disappeared among some bushes on the side of the railroad embankment, and an hour's search for it proved fruitless. It was doubtless of that species known as the hoop snake" (*Atlanta Constitution*, August 12, quoting *Marietta Journal*).

> **M**r. Nolan … noticed that when he touched the body with a stick the tail at once struck the stick with considerable force.

Peru, Indiana, May 1886: "James Nolan … discovered the reptile in a ravine, and when it saw him it rolled up in the shape of a hoop, but he struck it with a club and disabled it. Mr. Nolan had never seen a hoop snake, but had heard of it and noticed that when he touched the body with a stick the tail at once struck the stick with considerable force. He experimented some time until thoroughly convinced that he had found a genuine hoop snake. After it was entirely dead, Mr. Nolan cut off the needle in the end of the snake's tail, and now has it in a bottle where all can see it who are disposed to make the trip to his residence. The needle or sting is 7/10ths of an inch long, looks like a thorn from a locust tree, and is of black color. The snake is 5 feet and 6 inches long, of a black color, showing a golden color as it moved. The under surface of the monster was a dirty yellow. The remains are still where the snake was killed" (*Logansport Pharos*, June 7, citing *Peru Sentinel*).

Near Syracuse, Ohio, August 1886: "Phillip Mumaw killed a genuine hoop snake on the Bartels farm.… This snake had a horn on the end of its tail two inches long. The horn-like tail was fiery red" (*Athens Messenger*, September 2).

Near Floris, Iowa, June 1888: "A genuine hoop snake has been captured by George Milton, a farmer, and is now on exhibition at this place. It is about 15 inches in length, is streaked with black and white with a spiked tail, and is of a bronzed color on top of its head. Between the eyes is a small socket in which the end of the spike tail fits when coiled up like a hoop. Mr. Milton was in the field plowing when he saw an object like a hoop roll down and strike his plow beam with its tail. He saw that it was a snake, and when it attempted to roll away he struck it on the head with a club and killed the reptile. Mr. Ramsey, a druggist, has preserved it in alcohol. It is a reptile rarely seen in this country" (*New York Times*, June 11).

Near Port Byron, New York, August 28, 1902: "Two young men were driving along a country road … when their horse became frightened from a cause not at first apparent to them. The horse suddenly bolted and ran down the road and they did not discern the cause until they glanced down and saw a large hoop snake rolling along beside the horse.... When they quieted the horse they got out and killed the snake, which measured four feet" (*Ogdensburg Daily Journal,* September 1).

Pleasantville, Pennsylvania, July 1905: "If any one doubts the existence of 'hoop snakes' a talk with Howard Shaffer ... will change his mind. Mr. Shaffer was out on the meadows yesterday, when he encountered a huge snake, which, when pursued, 'rolled up like a hoop,' according to his story. He killed it and found that it measured nearly seven feet in length" (*New York Sun,* July 30, citing *Philadelphia Record*).

Near Cross Hill, North Carolina, September 1917: "Deputy Sheriff Jones, while out hunting in the mountains, saw what he believed to be a hoop rolling down upon him. He dodged and the hoop followed. Realizing it was a hoop snake, he ran behind a tree and the snake struck the tree with such force the small end of its tail penetrated the bark. Jones killed the snake at his leisure and brought it home as a souvenir" (*Des Moines Daily News,* Iowa, September 13).

Hickory, North Carolina, August 3, 1918: "Messrs. Oscar and Mack Hefner ... killed a hoop snake.... As the young men were working in the field Saturday afternoon three dogs struck a rabbit's trail and were running it. Across the cornfield they ran and into the hoop or horn snake. The reptile coiled into a roll, with its two-inch horn projecting from its head, and struck out after the dogs. It hit a small dog in the chest and the wounded animal ran about 25 steps before falling dead. The snake struck two other dogs but the poison was emitted with the first stroke. The horn is located in the tail and as the snake runs it winds itself into a ball, with the horn protruding, and strikes with much velocity. Mr. [Oscar] Hefner said he went to view the dead snake Sunday afternoon and there saw [a] blacksnake swallowing it. He killed the black reptile. Horn snakes are not supposed to be in this part of the country, but have been seen many times in the mountains" (*Statesville Landmark,* August 9, citing *Hickory Record*).

Near Middle Grove, Missouri, July 16, 1929: "Miss Ruth Blaker ... was picking blackberries ... near the home and on returning from the berry patch to the path that led to the house she heard something at the side, and, looking around, noticed a large blacksnake stretched out on some bushes, the reptile being about six feet long.... She [also] heard something on the ground close to her feet, and there saw another snake of a different kind. She succeeded in finding a piece of rail close by, and captured the snake. Miss Blaker carried it to the house and inquiry was made as to what kind of snake it was. Examination showed it to have a needle on the end of its tail, and, when bothered or pressed on its back, would thrust out the needle quite a bit further. The snake was about three feet six inches long, and was brownish-black in color, covered with small yellow spots. Many people have viewed the snake, and some of them, more than seventy years old, say it is the first hoop snake they ever saw. The hoop snake is very poisonous, killing whatever it strikes with the tail needle" (*Monitor-Index and Democrat,* Moberly, July 23).

(*Continued page 269*)

Monstrous Serpent

The story that follows exists only as an anecdote told to folklorists decades ago, but it was told as a true story, and it is by any standard as strange as any tale ever related about a fabulous beast. Even harder to believe than many of the accounts related in these pages, it is repeated here not because it is convincingly documented—it isn't—but because of its eerie, even mind-boggling, nature.

It allegedly occurred sometime in the late nineteenth century in Somerset County, Pennsylvania, at a country schoolhouse. The new school had been built near the crossroads in Jenner Township to replace an older, more remote one, far from any road. William Johnson, then sixteen, and other students and parents often attended nighttime functions in the building. These functions, however, were anything but routine because to enter the door one had to step over the long, scaly body of ... something.

The something had the body of an immense snake, though neither its head nor its tail was ever visible. It was assumed that these were under the schoolhouse. Its body was a foot in diameter, and it had sharp scales on which it was unwise to step. Anyone who did so was instantly hurled to the ground.

The snake appeared only at that time of the month when there was no moon in the sky. Not everyone could see it, according to Johnson, but even those who didn't would be thrown if they stepped on it unknowingly.

The original owner of the land became so frightened that he sold the property and left. The man who purchased it raised a large family there, apparently having made his peace with the monster. Sometimes other men, often under the influence of alcohol, would attack it with sharp stakes and other weapons, to no avail. When Johnson moved away from the area at age thirty, the snake was still making appearances.

Johnson's testimony has led Fortean writer Michael Winkle to wonder what such a creature could be —assuming for one giddy moment the truth of this literally monstrous yarn. "A multi-dimensional reptile, perhaps?" he speculates. "Such a creature might project part of its body into our universe while other parts—its head and tail, say—would remain in a higher spatial dimension."

Further Reading:

Whitney, Annie Weston, and Caroline Canfield Bullock. "Folk-Lore from Maryland." *Memoirs of the American Folk-Lore Society* 18 (1925): 193.

Winkle, Michael. "Fabulous Beasts: The Worm Ouroboros." *INFO Journal* 76 (Autumn 1996): 30–31.

(Continued from page 267)

Hoop-snake sightings did not end in the early decades of the twentieth century, but like other kinds of outré experiential claims, persons who believed they had encountered such reptiles did not rush to publicize it.

In a December 1, 2000, article *Houston Chronicle* writer Leon Hale recalled a recent lunch at the upscale Riverdale Country Club. There, a woman told him of a strange experience which commenced when she heard her husband's voice shouting from the distance, "Open the door! Open the door!" When she opened the back door, she saw him running at high speed. Close behind was a large snake, its tail in its mouth, rolling like a wheel after him. The husband rushed into the house and slammed the door. The hoop snake disappeared under the house. "I have heard dozens of hoop snake stories over the past 40 years," Hale remarked without elaborating.

Software engineer Robert Benjamin, who grew up in rural Pennsylvania, has written of his and his father's sighting, sometime in the late 1960s, of a whistling hoop snake. The two were alerted to its presence when they heard the whistling. "Soon," Benjamin asserts, "we could see a snake come rolling down the field in our direction. Dad started up the tractor and waited a bit as the snake got closer. As it neared us, Dad moved the tractor forward just as the snake passed by and flung itself in our direction." The barb in its tail penetrated a tractor wheel, causing it to deflate and angering the father, who promptly killed the snake, still stuck in the tire. He cut off its spike and showed it to young Robert, who recalls that it "resembled a spine I had seen before in bullheads and catfish."

As everybody from folklorists to herpetologists has assured the rest of us for at least two centuries, no such snake exists in nature. After all this time, there is no reason to dispute that assessment. Apparently, however, hoop snakes exist in people's experiences of them. They are usually "explained" as known but harmless snakes, radically misperceived by persons too frightened or unschooled to know any better. As is so often the case when explainers confront discordant testimony, that testimony is reinvented in order to make it behave.

Which brings us to their cousins, the joint snakes.

Snakes like glass

We are told that one day in the spring of 1883, a North Carolina tenant farmer named Jake Barringer, plowing a field, turned up a snake three feet long. Fearing it might be venomous, he grabbed a stick and hit it. This is how the *Charlotte Observer* reported what happened next:

> At the first blow, the snake fell all to pieces, the head part going one way and the tail part another, and the two body pieces jumped off in different directions. The amazed [Barringer] resumed his ploughing [sic], went to the end of the furrow, and on his return was surprised to see the snake all together again except the tail piece, and watching a few minutes, saw the tail coming up to join the body, taking sharp, quick little jerks. It came

nearer and nearer until within a few inches of the three-fourth snake, when it gave a sudden jump and hitched on its proper place with a fuss resembling the popping of a camp. [Barringer] knocked it to pieces several times, and each time it came together again.

In 1885, according to a story in the *Chicago Times*, citing the *Proceedings of Academy of Sciences* (without, alas, specific citation, though the reference is to the Chicago Academy of Sciences, founded in 1857), a speaker identified only as Dr. Bartlett—no first name; possibly prominent Chicago physician John Bartlett—"presented letters and affidavits he had received in reference to a species of snake which is said to infest the Illinois prairies." The testimony was from three residents of tiny Rockport, near the Missouri border. The claimants were identified as Mrs. Triall, Mrs. Buell, and Rev. T. J. Keller. (Inquiry establishes that the last of these did indeed exist; Keller headed the Disciples of Christ Church in Rockport and died in 1914.) Each swore to an experience—in one instance multiple experiences—with a joint snake.

The two women said that they had been together when they saw the creature in their flower beds. As they approached it, it stood on its tail. Mrs. Triall struck it with a stick, knocking it into four separate pieces. The head wriggled around for a few moments, then collected the other parts and speedily joined into the single reptile it had been. An affidavit from Mrs. Buell backed up the testimony.

The Reverend Keller stated that he had observed the same phenomenon on a number of occasions. Once, he said, the snake had broken into four pieces. The head slithered away about ten feet for a short period, during which the reverend handled the other parts, which felt hard and dry. Then the head returned, and all the pieces were rejoined "as if by magic." Keller was surprised to learn that such things were little known and ordinarily disputed.

The academy report concludes:

Dr. [Edmund] Andrews [surgeon and president of the Chicago Academy of Sciences] said he had taken some pains to inquire into the story, and had found the affiants earnest, reputable people, and he had no reason to doubt their entire sincerity, nor yet that they actually believed that they had seen what they narrated. He could not, however, dispel a few doubts he had on the entire subject. In the first place he regarded it as improbable for a snake to stand erect upon its tail; then again, he could not convince himself of the possibility of the bowels, arteries and spinal cord of the snake, or anything else, being suddenly separated, except at the cost of life, much less of the possibility of their being united, as had been claimed. Other members share in the same opinions ... but nothing short of the presence of one of the most remarkable snakes will satisfy the academy.

All true enough, but what did the Rockport people see?

In its April 18, 1886, issue the *Fort Wayne Sunday Gazette* declared that, based on the evidence, "we are inclined to think that the 'joint snake' is a real-

Anniella pulchris, or the California legless lizard, is an example of a reptile species that can detach its tail. The purpose of this adaptation is to distract predators, allowing the lizard—or most of it—to escape with its life.

ity, and by far the most wonderful and curious reptile in all the world." It went on to print a letter from Oregon resident S. P. Lowell, who related that in the spring of 1860, while traveling from Minneapolis, Minnesota, to Lafayette, Wisconsin, to visit a brother, he spotted a "green glassy-looking snake about a foot long." After realizing that it was a glass or joint snake, he encouraged S. P. to strike it, but not hard enough to kill it. The letter continued:

> I did so and its tail-half fell in several pieces. I then stuck a stick by them and we proceeded to the depot and stayed there about fifteen minutes, until the train passed, then returned to look after my snake, and to my surprise no snake or piece of snake could be found. My brother said that several had experimented with them and were convinced of the fact of their disjointing and reuniting at will. I make this statement for what it is worth as a matter of fact and not as a "snake story."

The paper carried two other stories, one from Illinois "about forty years ago," the other a more recent one, set along the banks of Florida's Suwannee River in the fall of 1884.

According to period press reports, George D. Pemberton of Spotsylvania, Virginia, was walking on his farm one spring day in 1899 when

I came across a copper-colored snake about 2 ½ feet long. I struck the reptile a blow on the head with a stick, and to my surprise the snake fell apart in four pieces. Near by was a hole, and into this the head went, and, although I worked for half an hour trying to get it, I failed. I then examined the body, which was as hard as if it had been frozen, and, as far as I could discover, it was entirely lifeless. Thinking it was a jointed snake, I left the pieces of the body on the ground and went to the house. Shortly afterward I returned, but the portion of the body that I had left disappeared, and no trace of it could be found.

The less than automatically reliable press of the nineteenth century occasionally printed stories in which pieces of joint snakes were allegedly preserved. In May 1893, for example, Georgia's *Americus Recorder* carried the story of an Oak Hall man, Si Hawkins, who on a recent Sunday afternoon ride in his wagon encountered a snake in the road. When Hawkins struck it with a whip, it fell into a dozen pieces, each three inches long. The head, attached to a foot's worth of the body, fled into the bushes and did not reappear, though Hawkins waited for a period of time. He brought the remaining pieces to town as curiosities, and that is the last we hear of the matter.

The joint snake was sometimes conflated with the hoop snake, one principal characteristic of which has always been a horn in its tail. In the summer of 1889, a correspondent to the *Atlanta Constitution* reported that Linton Richardson of Hartwell had killed a joint snake. "It was about two feet long," the writer claimed, "and had a horn on its tail." The tail of a joint snake supposedly encountered in Dublin, Georgia, in late 1882 had a "horn, evidently a weapon of defense, about as long as a needle, and quite as sharp," according to a letter published in the *Dublin Gazette*.

While any printed dismissal of joint snakes (as with hoop snakes) was sure to generate angry letters from readers who insisted they had seen the creatures themselves, skepticism was widespread among educated elites, including those that determined how the subject was treated in the press. "The so-called glass snake does not break to pieces at the sight of an enemy, as is commonly supposed," Michigan's *Ironwood Times* sniffed in an 1896 editorial, "but, like some lizards, throws off its tail in an effort to escape." The remark apparently grants that the reptile in question is indeed a snake, but even then, the snakelike glass lizard (without legs) was widely thought to be the culprit—a lizard known in some Southern states for a tail that breaks off and regrows. As the other details—that it is not the tail that breaks but the entire body, and into many pieces—explainers were and are reduced to dismissing them as exaggerations.

The nonexistence of a joint snake as a part of the natural world—as opposed, say, to the experiential realm—is a settled question. As the saying goes, there ain't no such animal. Still, the testimony, some parts of it puzzling, persists. Even a hundred and more years ago, scientists were too skeptical to be inclined to investigate, but on the highly infrequent occasion (as in the Rockport, Illinois, episode from the mid–1880s) they found seemingly honest people who were more likely to be lying than to be mistaken.

Joint snakes and hoop snakes have an existence, if a shady one, *somewhere*, in that ambiguous realm where cultural imagination and individual experience briefly occupy the same space.

Further Reading:

Dorson, Richard M. *Man and Beast in American Comic Legend*. Bloomington: Indiana University Press, 1982.

Hewatt, Alexander. *An Historical Account of the Rise and Progress of the Colonies of South Carolina and Georgia*. Volume I. London, 1779.

Sass, Herbert Ravenel. "The Great Horned Serpent." *The Atlantic Monthly* (May 1935): 619–28.

Ice Falls

Dominick Bacigalupo stood up from a kitchen chair and took a step or two just before his roof caved in. When he managed to recover his senses and get back on his feet, he was able to reconstruct what had happened, and it still did not make much sense. A seventy-pound chunk of ice had crashed through both the top of his house and the attic and had fallen in three big pieces in the cooking area.

It was not storming in Madison Township, New Jersey, on the evening of September 2, 1958. Bacigalupo's fourteen-year-old son, Richard, said he had seen two airliners flying by just before the bizarre fall, but airport officials denied that the craft were carrying ice. The Rutgers University meteorology department said atmospheric conditions could not have created ice of such size and weight. So where did it come from?

Falls of ice comprise one of meteorology's great mysteries, though meteorologists have only reluctantly addressed the question, and usually only when asked. Most often the falls are "explained" as resulting from the accumulation of ice on aircraft. This explanation, however, is a nonstarter for several reasons. One is that electrical heating systems on most modern aircraft prevent ice build-ups on wings or other surfaces. Moreover, even on older planes without such heating systems, speed and construction ensure, according to the Federal Aviation Agency, that "the possibility of accumulating" significant amounts of ice—here the FAA was referring specifically to a fall of a ten-pound block—"is extremely rare." Finally, some of the fallen ice is of such enormous proportions that were a plane carrying it even for a short time, it would be in serious danger of an imminent crash.

On the other hand, anomalist Peter Hassall notes the inevitable exceptions. On occasion, ice *does* fall from aircraft holding tanks. "Blue chunks that smell of chemicals, or greenish-yellow pieces that smell of urine (not to mention rarer cases of brown pieces smelling of something even worse) certainly originate in this way," he writes. Clearly, these are neither mysterious nor relevant to the present subject.

Large blocks of ice were raining out of the sky long before the invention of the airplane. Late in the eighteenth century, for example, a block "as big as an elephant" reportedly fell on Seringapatam, India, and took three days to melt. Though poorly documented, it is not inherently incredible, inasmuch as later accounts of similarly oversized ice blocks are not exactly rare. In 1849 the *Edinburgh New Philosophical Journal* took note of the following event, in August of the same year, in Scotland:

> A curious phenomenon occurred at the farm of Balvullich, on the estate of Ord, occupied by Mr. Moffat, on the evening of Monday last. Immediately after one of the largest peals of thunder heard there, a large and irregularly shaped mass of ice, reckoned to be nearly 20 feet in circumference, and of a proportionate thickness, fell near the farmhouse. It had a beautiful crystalline appearance, being nearly all quite transparent. If we except a small portion of it which consisted of hailstones of uncommon size, fixed together, it was principally composed of small squares, diamond-shaped, of from 1 to 3 inches in size, all firmly congealed together. The weight of this large piece of ice could not be ascertained, but it is a most fortunate circumstance, that it did not fall on Mr. Moffat's house, or it would have crushed it, and undoubtedly have caused the death of some of the inmates. No appearance whatever of either hail or snow was discernible in the surrounding district.

On December 16, 1950, another Scottish man, driving near Dumbarton, watched a mass of ice rain out of the sky, nearly hitting him, and crashed on the road. When the police got there and weighed the pieces, they came to 112 pounds. This was only one of a number of ice falls that occurred in Great Britain over a two-month period between November 1950 and January 1951. In Kempton, West Germany, in 1951 a block of ice six feet long and six inches around fell on a carpenter working on a roof and killed him. In February 1965, a fifty-pound mass of ice smashed through the Phillips Petroleum Plant's roof in Woods Cross, Utah.

The largest recognized hailstones are slightly more than five inches in diameter and weigh a little more than two pounds. They fall, of course, during storms, held aloft prior to their descent by vertical winds or updrafts. Ice falls, on the other hand, as often as not, come out of a clear sky on a calm day.

Scientists investigate

Among the best documented cases is one witnessed by British meteorologist R. F. Griffiths. While waiting at a street junction in Manchester on April 2, 1973, he saw a large object strike the ground ten feet to his left and shatter on impact. He picked up the largest chunk, weighing three and a half pounds, and rushed home to store it in the freezing compartment of his refrigerator. He later wrote, "The ice sample displays a puzzling collection of features. Whilst it is clearly composed of cloud water, there is no conclusive evidence enabling one to decide precisely how it grew.... In some respects it is very much like a hailstone, in others it is not." A review of flight records determined that no aircraft were passing overhead at the time.

The fall took place nine minutes after another meteorological oddity, with which it may or may not have been linked. While walking down the street, Grif-

Golfball-sized hailstones are not uncommon on the American plains and in the Midwest, especially, but falling ice stories involve strange precipitation when no clouds are to be seen.

fiths saw a "single flash of lightning. This was noted by many people," he remarked, both "because of its severity, and because there were no further flashes."

There were, Griffiths found, "unusual meteorological conditions" in England that day, including gales and heavy rains. Snow had fallen on Manchester that morning but had cleared up by early afternoon, when the ice came down. Not long after the ice fell, sleet arrived, accompanied by a breeze too slight for its direction to be determined. He concluded (in an article in *Meteorological Magazine*, 1975), "The lightning was triggered off an aeroplane which flew into the storm [in progress to the east, over Liverpool]. No definite conclusion as to the origin of the sample has been arrived at, except that it was composed of cloud water."

A less well known, but in many ways even stranger, occurrence was investigated by Pennsylvania meteorologists in 1957. Early on the evening of July 30, farmer Edward Groff of Bernville, hearing a "whooshing noise," looked up and saw a large white, round object sailing out of the southern sky. After it crashed and shattered a few yards from him, another similar object struck a flower bed near him and his wife. The first of these was a fifty-pound ice cake; the second was half the size and weight of the first.

The witnesses immediately notified Matthew Peacock, a meteorologist who lived in nearby Reading. Peacock had a colleague, Malcolm J. Reider, examine it in detail. It was cloudy and white, as if it had been frozen rapidly, and permeated with "sediment"—dust, fibers, algae—and was put together like a "popcorn ball." In other words, it was made up of numerous one-inch hailstones frozen together in a single mass. Yet the chemical contaminants were not those associated with conventional ice or hailstones. According to one account, "Iron and nitrate were entirely absent, which is never true of ordinary 'ground water' or ice made by rapidly freezing such water; in contrast, salt and other dissolved minerals were present in an amount that would be excessive in drinking water, and the ice was *alkaline*."

Reider was perplexed, and another scientist who examined the material, Paul Sutton, chief of the U.S. Weather Bureau station at Harrisburg, declared that the ice "was not formed by any natural process known to meteorology."

Theories

From a wide range of scientific journals, Charles Fort first brought together the many reports of extraordinary ice falls. He as much as anyone showed that these were not isolated events but manifestations of a larger, continuing, and not infrequent phenomenon. Typically, Fort could not resist the temptation to indulge in extravagant, if tongue-in-cheek, speculation about the cause: "I shall have to accept that, floating in the sky of this earth, there are fields of ice as extensive as those on the Arctic Ocean." During violent thunderstorms some of this ice would get dislodged and plummet to earth.

The UFO age brought the sorts of "explanations" to the mystery that ufologist M. K. Jessup posited:

> It seems most natural that a space contrivance, if made of metal, and coming from cold space, would soon become coated with ice. That the ice should fall off, or be pushed off by de-icing mechanisms, or even melt off when the space ships are heated by friction with the air, or become stationary in the sunshine, seems equally natural. If these contrivances are drawing power from surrounding media via an endothermic process, the space structure will become colder and colder the more power it draws, and, in the atmosphere, ice would tend to form on it, just like the frosting of the coils in a refrigerator.

In fact, few ice falls are associated with UFO sightings. Fort noted one rare, though arguable, exception, recorded in an 1887 issue of *Monthly Weather Review*. On March 19 of that year, at 5 P.M., the Dutch bark *J.P.A.* found itself in the middle of a severe storm in the North Atlantic. Capt. C. D. Swart noticed

> a meteor in the shape of two balls, one of them very black and the other illuminated. The illuminated ball was oblong, and appeared as if ready to drop on deck amidships. In a moment it became dark as night above, but below, on board and surrounding the vessel, everything appeared like a sea

of fire. The ball fell into the water very close alongside the vessel with a roar, and caused the sea to make tremendous breakers which swept over the vessel. A suffocating atmosphere prevailed, and the perspiration ran down every person's face on board and caused everyone to gasp for fresh air. Immediately after this solid lumps of ice fell on deck, and everything on deck and in the rigging became iced, notwithstanding that the thermometer registered 19 degrees Centigrade. The barometer during this time oscillated so as to make it impossible to obtain a correct reading. Upon an examination of the vessel and rigging no damage was noticed, but on that side of the vessel where the meteor fell into the water the ship's side appeared black and the copper plating was found to be blistered. After this phenomenon the wind increased to hurricane force.

If the captain's description is even broadly accurate, the object could not have been a "meteor." It may have been a particularly extraordinary manifestation of ball lightning. It may also have been a genuine unidentified flying object. Whatever it was, no incident like it has been reported since, and consequently, it tells us almost nothing at all about the cause or nature of ice falls.

Ice falls are almost certainly some strange variety of natural phenomenon. William R. Corliss suggests that "some unappreciated mechanism in hailstorms permits the sudden aggregation of many hailstones." At least as likely perhaps, as some theorists—once ridiculed, now being taken more seriously (though still skeptically)—have proposed, the ice chunks are true meteorites. Unfortunately, as the late critic Ronald J. Willis observed, "there is little indication of high speed entry into the atmosphere that we would expect from any meteorite, whatever its origin." Also, the sample studied by Griffiths was composed of "cloud water," suggesting an atmospheric origin.

It is always possible that the falls are of diverse origin. There is enough variety in the reports to sustain this interpretation, if not to prove it. Meanwhile the falls continue—and continue to confound the would-be-explainers.

Further Reading:

Corliss, William R., ed. *Handbook of Unusual Natural Phenomena*. Glen Arm, MD: Sourcebook Project, 1977.

———, ed. *Tornados, Dark Days, Anomalous Precipitation, and Related Weather Phenomena: A Catalog of Geophysical Anomalies*. Glen Arm, MD: Sourcebook Project, 1983.

Dennis, Jerry. *It's Raining Frogs and Fishes: Four Seasons of Natural Phenomena and Oddities of the Sky*. New York: HarperCollins, 1992.

"Falls." *The News* 3 (March 1974): 8–10.

"Falls." *The News* 13 (December 1975): 7–11.

"Farmer Puzzled Over Fall of Ice and Fire." *Tyrone Daily Herald*, Pennsylvania (August 3, 1957).

Foght, Paul. "Ice-Falls Continueth." *Fate* 13,2 (February 1960): 27–31.

Fort, Charles. *The Books of Charles Fort*. New York: Henry Holt and Company, 1941.

Hassall, Peter. "Look Out Below!" *Fortean Times* 263 (2010): 46–49.

Hitching, Francis. *The Mysterious World: An Atlas of the Unexplained*. New York: Holt, Rinehart and Winston, 1978.

"Ice Falls." *Fortean Times* 43 (1985): 20–21.

"Ice Falls." *Fortean Times* 45 (1985): 16.

Jessup, M. K. *The Case for the UFO*. New York: Citadel Press, 1955.

Laprade, Armand, ed. *Shapes in the Sky*. Marshall, AR: Would-You-Believe Publications, 1985.

Lorenzen, Coral E. *The Shadow of the Unknown*. New York: Signet, 1970.

Martin, M. W. "Are There Icebergs in the Sky?" *Fate* 23,9 (September 1970): 54–58.

Michell, John, and Robert J. M. Rickard. *Phenomena: A Book of Wonders*. New York: Pantheon Books, 1977.

Rickard, Bob. "Falls." *Fortean Times* 27 (1978): 3–5.

———. "Falls." *Fortean Times* 36 (1982): 26–27,41.

———. "Falls." *Fortean Times* 39 (1983): 22–23.

———. "Falls." *Fortean Times* 40 (1983): 31–33.

Wilkins, Harold T. "Mystery of the Falling Ice." *Fate* 4,4 (May/June 1951): 22–27.

Willis, Ronald J. "Ice Falls." *INFO Journal* 1,3 (Spring 1968): 12–23.

Jersey Devil

The origins of the Garden State's favorite monster are as much a matter of dispute as its subsequent history. One popular version of the Jersey devil's genesis is set in Estellville, New Jersey, and pegs the year of the monster's birth as 1735. It came into the world, it is said, when a practicing witch, one Jane Leeds, learning she was pregnant for the thirteenth time, declared disgustedly that she'd as soon have a devil as another child. In the fashion of good legends everywhere, that's just what it turned out to be.

A grotesque creature possessing bat's wings, horse's head, cloven hoofs, and tail, it flew off into the remote pine barrens of South Jersey, where it has lived ever since, as evidenced by mysterious livestock deaths, enigmatic footprints, eerie cries in the night, and—on occasion—sightings. First known as the Leeds devil, by the nineteenth century the beast was also being referred to as the Jersey devil.

Stories of the Jersey devil often read more like folk humor than anything meant to be believed for longer than the duration of a joke, though this may be a misleading impression an outsider gets from the invariably—one might add, frustratingly—tongue-in-cheek reporting of the legend by journalists. Still, the Jersey devil is inherently even harder to swallow than other strange creatures chronicled here. There is also a muddled quality to the whole business, as if the Jersey devil is a stand-in for a range of weird reports and rumors of varying credibility.

The Jersey devil's "finest hour," as two folklorists once put it, fell in the early twentieth century. If press accounts are to be credited—not something one ought to do reflexively—approximately 100 persons in thirty different towns saw the thing as it rampaged through eastern Pennsylvania and southern New Jersey.

The first known sightings took place at 2 A.M. Sunday, January 17, 1909. In Bristol, Pennsylvania, postmaster E. W. Minster saw a glowing monster flying over the Delaware River. It had, he said, a ramlike head with curled horns and kept itself aloft with long, thin wings. It had short legs, the rear ones longer than the front ones, and it emitted cries that sounded like a combined squawk and whistle. At the same time, another Bristol man, John McOwen, heard strange sounds emanating from his backyard "like the scratching of a phonograph before the music begins" with "something of a whistle to it." While on patrol, police officer James Sackville, alerted by a chorus of barking dogs in the neighborhood, turned to observe a hopping, winged creature letting out a terrifying scream. As he charged toward it, it retreated on foot before rising into the air. Sackville fired at it with his revolver but missed.

It was seen at six o'clock the following morning in Burlington, where it prowled through an alley. The witness, Mrs. Michael Ryan, said it had long, bird-like legs, a horse's head, and short wings. A day or two later, at 4 P.M., Mrs. Davis A. White encountered it in her backyard in Philadelphia. This time it had alligator skin and breathed fire from its mouth. Her screams alerted her husband, who dashed outside and chased the devil to Sixteenth Street, where shortly thereafter a trolley car nearly hit it. That evening, at Salem, New Jersey, a police officer spotted a "devil bird" with one foot like a horse's, the other like a mule's. It had a horn on its head and an ostrich's tail, and it was eleven feet long.

On the evening of the nineteenth a Moorestown fisherman allegedly encountered it. Now it was three feet high and, except for its dog's face and devil's split hooves, monkeylike. At Camden, a witness thought it was "something like a possum, the size of a dog, with a shrill bark, flapping its wings and taking off into the air."

On the twenty-first, at 2 A.M., Nelson Evans of Gloucester City heard something on the roof of his shed in his backyard. On investigating he found (according to the *Philadelphia Public Ledger* of January 22) the following:

> It was about three feet and a half high, with a head like a collie dog and a face like a horse. It had a long neck, wings about two feet long, and its back legs were like those of a crane, and it had horse's hoofs. It walked on its back legs and held up two short front legs with paws on them. It didn't use the front legs at all while we were watching. My wife and I were scared, I tell you, but I managed to open the window and say, "Shoo!" It turned around, barked at me, and flew away.

Several hours later Daniel Flynn of Leiperville, Pennsylvania, observed the devil as it ran at a brisk pace along the Chester Pike toward Chester. It stood six feet high, he said, and had skin like an alligator's. The next morning Mary Sorbinsky of Camden, New Jersey, raced outside after she heard her dog screaming. A huge creature rose up from the ground and took flight. It had taken a chunk out of her pet, Mrs. Sorbinsky reported.

Or so the story goes. At least this much is undeniably true:

In the course of this brief panic, newspapers and zoos offered rewards for the devil's capture, though presumably with no expectation that they would have to pay up. Less certainly true, albeit perhaps possible, is an allegation many years later, made by the prominent anomalist and cryptozoologist Ivan T. Sanderson (d. 1973), a longtime New Jersey resident, in a letter to Loren Coleman. Sanderson claimed that the 1909 episode grew out of a real-estate hoax. "Crafty trickster-purchasers wanted to buy up rural property" before they became more valuable once a planned development was announced. Owners terrified by a monster's appearance would presumably sell their land at a modest price. Paraphrasing Sander-

This sketch of the Jersey Devil is based on a description by Mr. and Mrs. Nelson Evans of Gloucester City, New Jersey.

son, Coleman writes that he "even found in an old barn the fake feet to make the footprints in the snow." Unfortunately, we have only Sanderson's word for this, and he was sometimes inclined to exaggeration.

Even so, whatever the Jersey devil is or was about, hoaxing is likely a good part of it. Whatever the rest—the part that is not pure invention—the bulk of it survives in old newspaper accounts. Some examples:

Staunton, Virginia, early February 1910: "David Meeze has just seen what some declare is the famous Jersey Devil.... Meeze says that the strange bird or beast was flying directly over him and had a head like a horse and feet and legs like a mule. It soars along on great red wings. It is said that the animal was seen in West Virginia some months ago" (*Hagerstown Mail*, Maryland, February 4).

York, Pennsylvania, circa early September 1910: "William Smuck first saw the animal in a woodland near his farm, and describes it as being about the size of a large dog, but with legs shaped like those of a kangaroo. Others who saw it claim that it has quills like a porcupine" (*Williamsport Gazette and Bulletin*, September 10).

Margate City, Absecon Island, New Jersey, March 2, 1924: "It was a black, black night ... when Chief of Police [William] Devereaux stepped out of the city hall.... What he saw waiting for him he refuses to identify, but those who say they saw next day prints of cloven hoof and spiked tail in the sand lot adjoining agree only one thing could have left them there. The Jersey devil is back again" (*Sioux City Journal*, Iowa, March 6).

Swedesboro, New Jersey, early August 1927: "Slightly behind its usual schedule comes the perennial 'Jersey Devil.' Huckleberry pickers hereabouts report the appearance—at a distance—of a feathered quadruped about the size of a fox, with a cry 'half bark, half hoot'" (Associated Press, August 4).

Woodbury Heights, New Jersey, late December 1929: "The town ... is much exercised, the police being called out to search the surrounding woods[,] and an armed posse of twenty men combed the country side. All of this is the result of the death by violence of three hogs and the frightening tale of two school children. The children Robert Eberhart, thirteen, and Phyllis Pisecco, 15, were chased by a shaggy black monster with a pig's snout and four-footed, four-toed tracks were found. Uncanny cries have been heard and the community is terror stricken. Periodically for the past fourteen years this monster is said to have made its appearance and it has been termed the 'Jersey Devil'" (*Orange County Independent*, Middletown, New York, December 26).

Downington, Pennsylvania, July 27, 1937: "The strange monster was reported shortly after 9 P.M. by Cydney Ladley, who lives near Milford Mills, just north of here. Rushing into town ... Ladley, his wife and Mrs. Chester Smith, a neighbor, told of seeing the creature on a back road near their home just as dusk was settling.... 'It leaped across the road in front of my car,' Ladley said. 'It was about the size of a kangaroo, was covered with hair four inches long, and it hopped like a kangaroo. And eyes! What eyes!' 'And how it jumped,' chimed in Mrs. Ladley" (*Philadelphia Evening Bulletin*, July 28).

Gibbstown and Paulstown, New Jersey, November 1951: "The Jersey devil ... [has] caused ... upset among [Gibbstown] residents, particularly school children.... Paul May, 10, first reported seeing the half-human 'monster' through the window of a youth club. A club attendant said the boy became hysterical. On Sunday [November 18], Ronald Jones ... said he heard 'eerie screams' in nearby Cedar Swamp and a neighbor investigated" (*Chester Times*, Pennsylvania, November 22).

A website called The Devil Hunters: The Official Researchers of the Devil collects anecdotes from readers who report encounters with a range of odd creatures, all presumed to be the Jersey devil. The alleged witnesses are anonymous, and their stories are brief and devoid of detail. For instance:

> I was driving down a dirt road very early in the morning, around 3, when I saw a large figure on the side of the road. It was about 7 feet tall. It had big red eyes, bat-like wings, and a big head. It stared at me as I drove by. I was terrified. I know it was the Jersey Devil.

As to the question of what the Jersey devil is, if anything, the answer seems to be: many things, or nothing in particular.

Further Reading:

Beck, Henry Charlton. "The Jersey Devil and Other Legends of the Jersey Shore." *New York Folklore Quarterly* 3,1 (spring 1947): 202–06.

Bord, Janet, and Colin Bord. *Alien Animals*. Harrisburg, PA: Stackpole Books, 1981.

Coleman, Loren, and Bruce G. Hallenbeck. *Monsters of New Jersey: Mysterious Creatures in the Garden State*. Mechanicsburg, PA: Stackpole Books, 2010.

Devil Hunters. http://njdevilhunters.com/post.html.

MacDougall, Curtis D. *Hoaxes*. New York: Dover Publications, 1958.

Martin, Douglas. "Is Jersey Devil Still a Spirited Affair, a Wild Ghost Chase?" *Wall Street Journal* (October 31, 1979).

Sullivan, Jeremiah J., with James F. McCloy. "The Jersey Devil's Finest Hour." *New York Folklore* 30,3 (September 1974): 233–39.

Kangaroos in America

A strange, yet comic, event occurred on Chicago's northwest side at 3:30 in the morning of October 18, 1974. Two police officers, responding skeptically to a bizarre report from a man who claimed to have seen a kangaroo on his porch, were duly astonished to encounter the creature at the end of a dark alley. Not sure what else to do, Officer Michael Byrne attempted to handcuff the animal, at which point, he would relate, it "started to scream and get vicious." An altercation then ensued, during which the five-foot-tall kangaroo landed some good swift kicks on the shins of Officer Leonard Ciagi. The policemen retreated and summoned help, which was arriving as the animal departed down the street at an estimated speed of twenty mph.

Over the next two or three weeks kangaroo sightings were logged not only in Chicago but in Plano, Illinois, fifty miles to the west. On the evening of November 2, two separate groups of witnesses in both of these places reported seeing a kangaroo at almost the same time. Things got no less crazy over the next couple of weeks, when sightings came out of Lansing, Illinois, and Rensselaer and Carmel, Indiana. Just after 8 A.M. on November 15, a kangaroo was seen back in Chicago, standing in a vacant lot. The witness said it was five feet tall and "black all over, except for the stomach and face, which were brown." The last known sighting took place on November 25, when Sheridan, Indiana, farmer Donald Johnson spotted a kangaroo on a deserted rural road. It was "running on all four feet down the middle of the road." When it noticed Johnson, it bounded over a barbed-wire fence and disappeared into a field.

The kangaroo, or kangaroos, were never killed, captured, or explained. Strange as this episode was, however, it was neither the first nor the last of its kind. Errant kangaroos have been a part of the American landscape for nearly a century.

Out of place

"A strange animal is roaming around Carter county, Mo.," a newspaper noted in November 1889, "which, from the description, is supposed to be a kangaroo that has escaped from some circus."

In the middle of a major storm on June 12, 1899, a New Richmond, Wisconsin, woman saw a kangaroo run through her neighbor's yard. At the time a circus happened to be in town, so some assumed the kangaroo was an escapee. In fact, the circus owned no kangaroo.

The following year, near Mays Landing, New Jersey, in the middle of Jersey devil country, a farm family heard a scream emanating from near the barn. Its source was, according to one witness, "this thing that looked like a kangaroo. It wasn't such a great big animal—it was about the size of a small calf and weighed about 150 pounds. But the noise is what scared us. It sounded like a woman screaming in an awful lot of agony."

Subsequently, the family often saw the animal's tracks, eight to ten feet apart, leading to a large cedar swamp at the rear of the property.

The following story appeared in newspapers around the United States in early November 1907:

This controversial picture allegedly depicts a kangaroo photographed in Waukesha, Wisconsin, on April 24, 1978.

Pennsburg, Pa.—Tales of a kangaroo that is said to be roaming the wooded hills in the vicinity of Pleasant Run, a few miles west of here, have occasioned intense excitement. Several persons, among them Erwin Styer and Martin Stengel, have seen the strange animal within the past week, and while it is so fleet that no one has been able to obtain a good view of it, the descriptions substantiate the theory that it is a kangaroo. It is described as being of gray color, with a head shaped like that of a sheep and a body of large proportions. Upon the approach of a human being it darts away at tremendous speed.

Dogs have attacked it, but were always worsted. They were not bitten but apparently the animal flung them off with terrific force in the manner that a kangaroo defends itself with its hind legs and tail.

People living in the neighborhood are afraid to venture away from home after nightfall and there is little disposition to linger at the village store or tavern in the evening. Young men say that the customary outdoor rural amusements are no longer safe. "It ain't that I'm afraid of any wild beast that ever roamed the jungles of Montgomery county," said one young swain, "but I certainly do object to the disgrace of being knocked out by the hind legs or the tail of a kangaroo. So I guess we fellows won't do much sitting up with the girls for some time to come."

(Continued on page 288)

Alligators in the Sewers

A popular American contemporary legend has it that alligators dwell in the New York sewer systems. They got there, it is said, when baby alligators purchased as pets grew too big for their owners' comfort and were dispatched down toilets. The animals reportedly survived under the city and became so large as to threaten the well-being of sewer workers. New York City officials deny, however, that any such creatures currently exist, and no evidence has surfaced to contradict the official stance.

Though the rumor was circulated most widely in the 1960s, its origins are in an oft forgotten series of events in the 1930s. The first incident took place on June 28, 1932, when "swarms" of alligators were seen in the Bronx River and a three-foot-long specimen was found dead along its banks. Then, in March 1935 and June 1937, both live and dead alligators were recovered.

The most remarkable of these incidents was chronicled in the February 10, 1935, issue of the *New York Times*. Several teenage boys were shoveling snow into an open manhole near the Harlem River when they spotted something moving in the icy water about ten feet down. It turned out to be an alligator trying to free itself. The boys retrieved a rope, fashioned it into a lasso, and pulled the animal to the surface; but when one of them tried to take the rope off its neck, the alligator snapped at him. In response the young men beat it to death with their shovels.

The boys dragged the body to a nearby repair shop, where it was determined that the animal weighed 125 pounds and was seven and a half feet long. Later the police were notified, and a city department of sanitation employee drove the remains off to be incinerated.

Around that time, Teddy May, New York City's superintendent of sewers, was receiving complaints about alligators. At first, he claimed, he thought they were the result of alcohol consumption, and he even hired investigators to check on the drinking habits of his employees. When the investigators came up empty-handed, May himself descended into the sewers with a flashlight, which soon enough uncovered the presence of alligators. A shaken May subsequently had the animals killed by poison and gunshot. Or maybe not. It is said that May himself was a colorful and not automatically credible yarn-spinner.

In any event, alligators and crocodiles have a way of showing up in the most unexplained places. Between 1843 and 1983, according to anomalist Loren Coleman, no fewer than eighty-four such animals were seen or recovered, dead or alive, all across the United States and Canada. Coleman writes, "Pet escapee explanations cannot deal adequately with these accounts of alligators in northern waters—when it is caimans (Central or South American crocodilians similar to alligators but often superficially resembling crocodiles) that are being sold as pets."

(Continued from previous page)

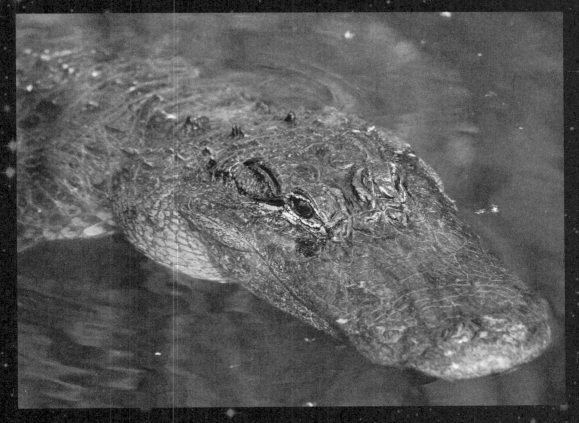

A popular American legend concerns people flushing baby alligators down toilets. They end up in the sewer, where they grow to become enormous, dangerous predators.

Further Reading:

"Alligator Found in Uptown Sewer." *New York Times* (February 10, 1935).

Brunvand, Jan Harold. *The Vanishing Hitchhiker: American Urban Legends and Their Meanings.* New York: W. W. Norton, 1989.

Coleman, Loren. "Erratic Crocodilians and Other Things." *INFO Journal* 3,4 (February 1974): 12–18.

———. "Alligators in the Sewers: A Journalistic Origin." *Journal of American Folklore* 92,365 (July/September 1979): 335–38.

Corliss, William R., ed. *Strange Life: A Sourcebook on the Mysteries of Organic Nature, Volume B–1.* Glen Arm, MD: Sourcebook Project, 1976.

Michell, John, and Robert J. M. Rickard. *Living Wonders: Mysteries and Curiosities of the Natural World.* New York: Thames and Hudson, 1982.

(Continued from page 285)

It is not clear whether the creature that supposedly terrified rural Tennessee in January 1934 belongs in a history of anomalous kangaroos. All we know is that those who reported they had seen it said, in the words of one, "It was as fast as lightning and looked like a giant kangaroo running and leaping across the field." But the alleged witnesses also claimed that it attacked or killed dogs, geese, and ducks. Conventional kangaroos—though not their prehistoric ancestors—are generally unaggressive and vegetarian.

These stories, which were reported in newspapers all over the country, sparked massive ridicule and charges of journalistic hoaxing. It is true that no other "killer kangaroo" has ever been reported, a consideration that surely suggests we ought to judge the Tennessee stories with proper caution.

One night, in January 1949, the headlights of a Greyhound bus picked up a strange form crossing a highway near Grove City, Ohio. "It's about five and a half feet high, hairy, and brownish in color," said driver Louis Staub. "It has a long pointed head. It leaped a barbed-wire fence and disappeared. It resembled a kangaroo, but it appeared to jump on all fours. I'm certain it wasn't a deer."

From 1957 through 1967 residents of Coon Rapids, a Minneapolis suburb, repeatedly sighted kangaroos, on occasion two of them, which apparently lived in a wooded area near the Anoka County Fairgrounds. In 1958 kangaroos were reported in the vicinity of Nebraska towns as far as 100 miles from each other. One witness, brewery owner Charles G. Wetzel, who saw one while stepping out of his cabin along the Platte River, even gave one of his brands the name "Wetzel Kangaroo Beer."

In the 1970s and 1980s kangaroos appeared in Illinois, Wisconsin, Colorado, Delaware, California, Utah, Oklahoma, and North Carolina and in the Canadian provinces of Ontario and New Brunswick. In 1999 a spate of sightings broke out in rural Iowa. As late as 2005 sightings were reported near Poole, Kentucky, Charleston, West Virginia, and Latah, Idaho. A red, 130-pound kangaroo was captured in a snowstorm in Iowa County, Wisconsin, in early January of that year. After two months' of failed efforts to locate the presumed owner, authorities gave the animal to a zoo in Madison.

Considering the quality and the obvious sincerity of the witnesses—a not-insignificant number of them being police officers—it seems beyond dispute that kangaroos *are* being seen from time to time far away from their native Australian home. How they got here is, of course, one more question with no immediate answer.

Further Reading:

Coleman, Loren. *Mysterious America: The Revised Edition.* New York: Paraview Press, 2001.
Quinn, Ron. "Cryptoletters." *ISC Newsletter* 1,1 (spring 1982): 10.
Shoemaker, Michael T. "Killer Kangaroo." *Fate* 38,9 (September 1985): 60–61.

Mad Gassers

In the late summer of 1944, lasting notoriety came to Mattoon, a small city in east-central Illinois (pop. 15,827 in the 1940 census), in the person of an elusive attacker whose reign of terror lasted two long weeks. By the time events had run their course, the attacker would be pronounced nonexistent. The "mad gasser of Mattoon" survives in cultural memory as a classic example of social panic. Still, the controversy has not been entirely laid to rest. Some writers continue to argue that the episode amounts to a bizarre unsolved crime with spooky overtones, and a few have even treated it as at least quasi-paranormal.

Mattoon's phantom attacker first made his presence known on August 31, when Urban Raef awoke feeling ill and struggled to the bathroom, where he threw up. On returning to the bedroom, he asked his wife if she had left the gas on. She said she hadn't, but when she attempted to get up to be sure, she found she could not move. A visiting couple sleeping in another room experienced nothing out of the ordinary. Elsewhere in town, however, a young mother who heard her daughter coughing in another room also tried to leave her room, with similar lack of success.

At around 11 P.M. on September 1, Aline Kearney and her daughter Dorothy retired for the night. The two had just crawled into bed when a "sickening sweet odor in the bedroom" seemed to enter the room. As it grew stronger, Mrs. Kearney grew alarmed, less certain that it came, as first thought, from the flowers outside the window. Her throat got dry, and she "began to feel a paralysis of my legs and lower body," she reported. "I got frightened and screamed." Her visiting sister Martha Reedy rushed to her assistance. Noticing the odor, she ran next door to seek the next-door neighbor, Earl Robertson, who called the police. They investigated but, finding nothing, shrugged off the matter. An hour and a half later Aline's husband, Bert, a late-night taxi driver who hurried home after learning about the apparent attack on his family, observed a strange man standing at the bedroom window. Kearney, who would describe him as "tall, dressed in dark clothing and wearing a tight-fitting cap," gave chase, but the prowler escaped.

These events took place before anyone had heard of a "mad gasser" or "phantom anesthetist," and whatever inspired the stories, mass hysteria is not the explanation that immediately pops to mind. Unfortunately, at this stage the *Mattoon Daily Journal-Gazette* picked up the story, calling Mrs. Kearney the "first victim," which not only was untrue but also implied that more "victims" would join her. (The headline of the article was an unsettling "Anesthetic Prowler on the Loose.") As it happened, other alleged attacks did in fact—or anyway in allegation—follow, reported by the town newspaper in sometimes overwrought prose that frightened more than informed.

Several other residents complained to police that the sudden infusion of a "sickly sweet odor"—soon dubbed "gardenia gas"—had paralyzed them for as long as ninety minutes. No one else had seen the gasser, but late on the evening of September 5, after she and her husband, Carl, had returned home through the rear entrance, Beulah Cordes noticed a white cloth positioned on the front screen door. Curious as to how it got there, she stepped out for a closer look. She noticed that its middle was soaked in some kind of liquid. On sniffing it, "I had a sensation similar to coming in contact with an electric current," she related. "The feeling raced down my body to my feet and seemed to settle in my knees. It was a feeling of paralysis." She required her husband's assistance in getting back inside.

> **S**everal other residents complained to police that the sudden infusion of a "sickly sweet odor"—soon dubbed "gardenia gas"—had paralyzed them for as long as ninety minutes.

In short order her lips swelled and cracked, and her mouth and throat burned. She started spitting blood. A doctor was summoned. After he left and her strength was restored, Mrs. Cordes found a worn skeleton key and a largely empty lipstick tube near the porch. The Cordeses called the police, who took the evidence—if that's what it was—and sent it, along with the cloth, to the Illinois State Police Laboratory the next morning. (The results proved inconclusive, possibly because any chemical that may have existed had dissipated in the interim.) Meantime, the police picked up a young man seen wandering the neighborhood, releasing him after he persuaded them that he was merely lost.

Near midnight a woman called police to report that a man had tried to force his way through her door. Her screams frightened him off. According to press accounts, the man resembled the gasser's general description, whatever that meant. Probably the incident had nothing to do with the "phantom anesthetist," as he was coming to be called, but it was the kind of story that served to ratchet up the paranoia.

At 10 o'clock the following evening, Laura Junkin, who kept an apartment in the back of the restaurant she managed, stepped into her bedroom, and detected something like a "cheap perfume" which, when inhaled, caused her legs to buckle. Others were reporting comparable odors and effects. One couple called the police about a suspicious prowler near their house, and an hour later their eleven-year-old daughter, Glenda Henderschott, was awakened from sleep feeling nauseous. The parents linked the two events.

Other supposed attacks continued into the early-morning hours. The most dramatic occurred at about 1 A.M. when sixty-year-old Fred Goble awoke violently ill and spent the next two hours vomiting. Robert Daniels, Goble's neighbor, would assert that he had seen a "tall, thin man" running from Goble's house and across his yard.

In a September 8 summary, the *Herald* (published in nearby Decatur) noted, "Victims report that the first symptom is an electric shock which passes completely through the body. Later nausea develops, followed by partial paralysis. They also suffered burned mouths and throats and their faces become swollen."

As the days passed, the mad gasser generated United Press stories and became a national sensation. As the perceived assaults went on, the community was outraged that the local police—comprising two officers and eight patrolmen whose cars lacked radio communication—had not been able to catch the perpetrator. (In the course of the scare, however, state police and officers from nearby communities assisted the overwhelmed Mattoon authorities. Two FBI agents quietly entered town to see if they could determine what kind of gas was being used.) Illinois officials managed to dissuade local leaders who had planned a mass protest rally for the ninth.

Meanwhile, gun-toting locals roamed the streets at night, in defiance of Police Commissioner Thomas V. Wright's plea for them to get a grip on themselves. He said that a "gas maniac exists" but "many of the attacks are nothing more than hysteria. Fear of the gas man is entirely out of proportion to the menace of the relatively harmless gas he is spraying." Rumors were flying: the gasser was a lunatic, an "eccentric inventor" (the commissioner's pet theory, soon to be abandoned), or even (as proposed by a local psychic, who said she had seen him wielding a spray can) a Neanderthal-like "ape man."

The scare climaxed on September 10, a Sunday night, with two attacks that felled a total of five persons. In one of them, said to have occurred in the early morning hours of the eleventh, a widow named Bertha Bence claimed that strange noises outside her front bedroom window woke her up. Then a sweet gas filled the room, inflicting nausea and light-headedness. Hearing her expressions of alarm, her sons bolted from bed in time to see a short, fat, dark-clad man fleeing down a back alley. As we have seen, other reports alleged that the gasser was tall and thin, though the description of the clothing is the same.

Examining the window through which the spraying had occurred—Scott Maruna, a chronicler of the episode, writes that the window was "cut and ruined," though without citing a source for this important-if-true allegation—the two spotted what they believed to be footprints from a woman's high-heeled shoes in the soft soil of the flowerbed just outside the window.

By the next morning police were talking more skeptically, pointing to the absence of solid evidence and stipulating that all further complainants undergo examination at Mattoon Memorial Institution. Within hours police treated gas-attack calls as false alarms. Practically nobody doubted that some citizens of Mattoon had become seriously unhinged. Press treatment in the area and throughout the state (the Chicago papers had given the story particularly prominent play) turned abruptly—almost literally overnight—toward dismissal and ridicule.

At a press conference on the morning of the twelfth, Chief of Police C. E. Cole told reporters, "Local police, in cooperation with state authorities, have checked and rechecked all reported cases, and we find absolutely no evidence to support stories that have been told. Hysteria must be blamed for such seemingly accurate accounts of supposed victims." On the thirteenth the *Journal-Gazette* noted that calls about gas attacks had declined to a "vanishing point."

A week later, responding to a ribbing of Mattoon by a Decatur newspaper, the *Journal-Gazette*'s editors wrote that it was an "undisputable fact" that a mad gasser existed, remarking, "There are two principal reasons why he was not caught. One is that our police failed to take the case seriously enough at first. The other is that, when the police finally decided there was 'something to it,' mass hysteria and outside interference combined to make their efforts unsuccessful."

The perpetrator named?

"For some reason, women are more susceptible to mass suggestion than men," Donald A. Laird, "Ph.D., Sci.D., Internationally Known Psychologist and Lecturer," wrote in the December 3, 1944, issue of the newspaper supplement magazine *American Weekly*. Laird's was the first more or less formal statement by a mental health professional to codify the hysteria explanation for all of, not just the later, depredations of the supposed gasser. Laird, who had conducted no personal investigation, relied on armchair speculation about the witnesses and on the undeniable fact that no attacker had been caught.

The most influential—one might say defining—study would be Donald M. Johnson's paper published in an early 1945 issue of the *Journal of Abnormal and Social Psychology*. At the time Johnson, who would go on to a distinguished academic career in psychology, was a lowly University of Illinois at Champaign-Urbana first-year undergraduate student whose formal professional education probably consisted of a mere introductory psychology course. Even so, Johnson apparently conducted a conscientious inquiry, given that he entered the investigation on the presumption that the Mattoon gasser was a psychological creation. He interviewed many of the victims, pored over newspaper accounts, and examined police records. He declared, "The case of the 'phantom anesthetist' was entirely psychogenic.... The hypothesis of a marauder cannot be supported by any verifiable evidence. The hypothesis of hysteria, on the other hand, accounts for all the facts."

When the *Abnormal and Social Psychology* issue saw print, the *Journal-Gazette* of March 8 merely summarized Johnson's conclusions (dramatically elevating his academic status to "Professor" Johnson in the process) without comment. The newspaper did not seek out the alleged victims for their opinions, nor did it interview Johnson for elaboration. One has the sense that where official Mattoon was concerned, the mad gasser had more than worn out his welcome.

Only a few have challenged this interpretation in the decades since, even as the true cause of these curious occurrences can remain only conjectural. Even in their time they made little sense. If nothing else, the hysteria explanation filled the vacuum created by the absence of any more compelling interpretation. It can also be said that hysteria, valid or invalid, amounted to a blame-the-victim strategy.

The late Willy Smith, a physicist, rejected the social-panic hypothesis, arguing in the 1980s:

> The best-documented cases of [mass hysteria] have occurred in enclosed spaces, such as workplaces or schools. The contagious behavior usually stems from a single case, or *trigger* event, and is characterized by a specific item, such as a bug bite or an odor.... For the Mattoon case there was no event that could have triggered a mass hysteria. The three initial incidents—August 31 and September 1—were real, but had no immediate influence, as they were not publicized until September 2. Even then, and in spite of the sensationalist headlines and the extensive newspaper coverage, they failed to generate new cases until September 5.

Drawing of the Mad Gasser of Mattoon.

In a more recent effort to devise a plausible counter-interpretation, Scott Maruna, a Jacksonville, Illinois, high-school chemistry teacher who grew up near Mattoon, produced a short, self-published book which flatly identifies the perpetrator by name: "Farley Llewellyn was the Mad Gasser of Mattoon."

In his thirties, Llewellyn, a member of a Mattoon family that had seen better days (though Farley's father was well liked for his kindness and charity), lived as an eccentric—some thought deranged—recluse in a trailer house, where he had installed a small laboratory. He had also been a chemistry major at the University of Illinois. According to Maruna, Llewellyn held a grudge against the town and set about playing a prank, using a nitromethane gas he had managed to synthesize, to frighten residents. He had some degree of assistance, Maruna infers, from one or both of his sisters, thus the heavy-set, apparently feminine, high-heeled attacker described in the Bences' story.

The attacks stopped when Farley Llewellyn was taken into custody and placed in a mental institution (where he spent the next twelve years) around September 10. His sisters Florence and Katherine continued the attacks for another three days to deflect suspicion from their brother.

According to Maruna, all of these individuals are long dead; consequently, no confession will ever be forthcoming. On a visit to Mattoon in the summer of

2004, British writer Jonathan Downes found that where longtime Mattoon residents were concerned, Farley Llewellyn's responsibility was certain:

> I visited several shops and spoke to a number of the older members of the community I found there. Everybody knew of the Mad Gasser; everybody knew that it was Farley; and everybody told me that, because Farley's father had been such a well-loved and popular member of the community, nobody had been prepared to pillory the family in public just because his son was insane. In order to protect the reputation of Farley's family, the whole town had put up with 50 [sic] years of visiting UFO freaks, conspiracy theorists, and assorted nutcases.... Now [that] there were no longer any living relatives, people were prepared to talk, and several told me they were happy to do so because—at long last—the myth of Mattoon's Mad Gasser could be laid to rest.

All that is known with reasonable certainty is that at one point the police had considered Farley Llewellyn a suspect. At least, from their point of view, he had the look—tall and thin—and the requisite chemical knowledge to make for a plausible phantom anesthetist. Nothing more than this kind of broadly circumstantial evidence, however, links him to the crimes.

The Botetourt gasser

Whatever its meaning and significance, the Mattoon scare was preceded by another, this one in Botetourt (BOT-a-TOT) County, Virginia, a little more than a decade earlier. It received little attention outside the affected area.

The first alleged attack took place on the Cal Huffman farm near Fincastle on the evening of December 22, 1933, when three separate infusions (the last in an early-morning hour of the next day) of gas sickened eight members of a family and a visitor. Some of the victims thought they saw a man fleeing in the darkness. The gas caused nausea, headaches, facial swelling, and constriction of mouth and throat muscles. One victim, twenty-year-old Alice Huffman, suffered convulsions for weeks afterwards. A police officer who arrived between the second and third attacks—after staying an hour, he left, and soon gas wafted through both floors of the house—found only one clue: the print of a woman's heel under the window the gas was believed to have passed through (presaging the already discussed detail in a Mattoon case).

Over the next two weeks other persons reported similar nocturnal attacks. In one case, witnesses saw a 1933 Chevrolet, with a man and woman inside, passing back and forth in front of a house around the time its occupants experienced the mysterious gas. In another instance, a young mother attending to her baby said she heard a rattling window shade and mumbling voices outside. Suddenly the room filled with gas, and her body felt numb. While on his way to summon police after a gassing at his farm, F. B. Duval saw a man run toward a car parked on a rural road and drive away quickly. Duval and an officer examined the site soon afterwards and found prints of a woman's shoe.

Amid growing panic, residents of the county armed themselves and prowled back roads in search of suspicious strangers. On one occasion a searcher fired on a fleeing figure. On another, moments after a gas attack, one of the victims dashed outside in time to glimpse four men running in the direction of the nearby Blue Ridge Mountains. By the time the witness returned with a gun, he could no longer see them, but he could hear their voices. Despite skepticism in some quarters concerning the gasser's (or gassers') existence, physicians who had called on victims were certain he was (or they were) real. County Sheriff C. E. Williamson was likewise convinced.

Another gas attack was reported near Lithia in nearby Roanoke County. In its wake the victim found discolored snow with a sweet-smelling, oily substance in it. When analyzed, it turned out to consist of sulfur, arsenic, and mineral oil—something like the components, authorities thought, of insecticides. A trail of footprints led from the house to the barn, but none away from the barn. They were, according to press accounts, a "woman's tracks."

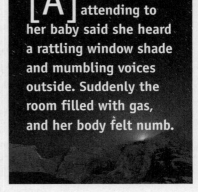

[A] young mother attending to her baby said she heard a rattling window shade and mumbling voices outside. Suddenly the room filled with gas, and her body felt numb.

In February 1934 the attacks were focused in Roanoke County. The first week of the month saw steadily escalating reports of gassings and the presence of suspicious cars, but police came to believe that the source was panic. None of them smelled anything out of the ordinary, and in several cases they thought they were able to track the gases to conventional sources such as automobile exhaust. The *Roanoke Times* declared, "Roanoke Has No Gasser," and the matter faded away.

Writer Michael T. Shoemaker noted the scare's many similarities to the later one at Mattoon. "In both Mattoon and Botetourt," he noted, "the principal physical effects were the same: a sickeningly sweet odor, nausea, paralysis, facial swelling and unconsciousness." Robert E. Bartholomew, an academic psychologist and authority on social panics, attributes both incidents to public fear of gas warfare, a favorite subject in the press of the period. People were "preoccupied with the threat of chemical weapons" and so "began to define various mundane events and circumstances as gasser-related."

A footnote

In 2011, an article from a Tavares, Florida, newspaper, *Lake County Citizen*, came to light. Dated November 8, 1935, it relates a story largely similar to other mad-gasser attacks, but with its own distinctive details:

> It seems there's a man wandering loose in Lake county who has training and put it to criminal use.

The bold bad bandit who for the past five months has been driving the police authorities of Lake county gradually daffy, is using a spray gun—not loaded with mosquito dope—filled with a very potent fluid which lulls his victims into even sounder sleep.

Officers in Eustis this week disclosed, following a break-in at the home of Frank Smith, that some drug was being used to prevent victims waking. Authorities had been mystified for some time as to how the thief could enter a home[,] ransack the house, dumping bureau drawers about, without being detected.

The bandit has been at work in Eustis, Mt. Dora, Leesburg and Umatilla. He has stolen approximately $300 since he began his activities last May. He has entered homes while the entire family was in bed asleep, ransacked desks, bookcases, clothing and bureaus and walked off unmolested.

Further Reading:

Coleman, Loren. *Mysterious America*. Revised edition. New York: ParaView Press, 2001.

Downes, Jonathan. "In Search of the Mad Gasser." *Fortean Times* 216 (2006): 36–39.

Evans, Hilary, and Robert E. Bartholomew. *Outbreak! The Encyclopedia of Extraordinary Social Behavior*. San Antonio and New York: Anomalist Books, 2009.

Johnson, Donald M. "The 'Phantom Anesthetist' of Mattoon: A Field Study of Mass Hysteria." *Journal of Abnormal and Social Psychology* 40 (1945): 175–86.

Laird, Donald A. "Manhunt for 'Mr. Nobody.'" *The American Weekly* (December 3, 1944).

Maruna, Scott. *The Mad Gasser of Mattoon: Dispelling the Hysteria*. Jacksonville, IL: Swamp Gas Book Company, 2003.

Shoemaker, Michael T. "The Mad Gasser of Botetourt." *Fate* 38,6 (June 1985): 62–68.

———. "Resurrections." *Fortean Times* 49 (1987): 53.

Smith, Willy. "The Mattoon Gasser: A Modern Myth." *International UFO Reporter* 9,6 (November/December 1984): 7–9,14.

———. "The Mattoon Phantom Gasser." *Skeptic* 3,1 (1994): 33–39.

Merbeings

In the coastal town of Kiryat Yam, Israel, for a few days in August 2009, dozens of persons, together or independently, reported something unthinkable: a mermaid cavorting in the sea not far from shore. Local authorities took the claims seriously, according to the Israeli press and the *New York Daily News*. The incidents occurred at twilight, and the "half girl, half fish," as it was described, was seen either in the sand or in the water.

One alleged witness, Shlomo Cohen, told a reporter, "I was with friends when suddenly we saw a woman [lying] on the sand in a weird way. At first I thought she was just another sunbather, but when we approached, she jumped into the water and disappeared. We were all in shock because we saw she had a tail. At least five of us saw it, and we all couldn't believe it."

Merbeings—so we shall call them; mermen figure prominently in the lore as well—are usually assumed to be purely mythological, extant only in folklore and fantasy, not in any actual human being's supposed experience. The reality, however, is that experience drove the tradition. "Medieval belief in the mermaid," a folklorist writes, "was widespread and substantiated." This supposed substantiation consisted of claimed sightings, at least some of which were associated with individuals generally viewed as sane and sensible. As the Israeli stories—and countless others over time—indicate, the "sightings" did not end in the Middle Ages.

Still, the notion of a human/fish hybrid is undeniably a zoological absurdity. Furthermore, no physical evidence—in other words, no body—supports centuries of testimony by sailors and land-dwellers. There is no reason to believe that such creatures are even possible. The Irish historian and folklorist Douglas Hyde demanded of his colleague W. Y. Evans-Wentz, then writing a book destined to be well known even now, *The Fairy-Faith in Celtic Countries* (1911): "Are we to believe that all those [supernatural] beings equally exist, and, on the principle that there can be no smoke without a fire, are we to hold that there would be no popular conception of the banshee, the leprechaun, or the *Maighdean-mhara* (sea-maiden, mermaid), and consequently no tales told about them, if such beings did not exist, and from time to time allow themselves to be seen like the wood-martin and the kingfisher?" To Evans-Wentz, who held the heretical opinion (based on testimony he had collected from informants he judged credible) that fairies may be real entities of some kind, Hyde countered that such thinking could only lead to madness—even to acceptance of merbeings.

Even so, most authorities who have paid attention have accepted the need to explain the sightings, and they have offered a variety of theories about what the witnesses "really" saw. As is not infrequently the case with anomalous claims, efforts to reduce wild tales to tame orthodoxy may betray evidence of strain, sometimes to the breaking point. So what to make of this? First, let's consider what we are dealing with.

The mythic background

Merbeing legends, or their equivalents, have an ancient lineage. The earliest story known concerns the Babylonian god Oannes, human to the waist and fish-shaped from there on, who rose from the Erythrean Sea to impart knowledge and culture to the human race. (In modern times Oannes would reemerge into prominence as a prime candidate for an early extraterrestrial visitor, nominated by no less than the late celebrity astronomer Carl Sagan.) Merbeing-like gods and goddesses were worshipped in Syria, India, China, Greece, and Rome.

> **[A] human/fish hybrid is undeniably a zoological absurdity. Furthermore, no physical evidence ... supports centuries of testimony by sailors and land-dwellers.**

In later centuries they would figure in a nearly universal folklore. We know them as merbeings, merfolk, mermaids, or mermen because of the Old English word for sea: *mere*. Such creatures, by various names, were known all over Western Europe and just about everywhere else.

Among the first known chroniclers of the phenomenon was Pliny the Elder, a first-century naturalist who accepted their existence, remarking—as if to acknowledge even then the objections of skeptics—"it is no fabulous tale that goeth of them." He went on, "Only their body is rough and scaled all over, even in those parts wherein they resemble a woman." He referred to a sighting by coastal residents who clearly saw one such creature, apparently more than once. Later they heard it dying, making a "piteous moan, crying and chattering very heavily." Bodies were found: "Many of these Nereides or Mermaids were seen cast upon the sands and lying dead."

Over the centuries, explicitly supernatural elements entered the lore of what had been heretofore thought of mostly as a rare and exotic sea animal. A variant of merbeing legends concerned the North European seal-folk or selkie, described succinctly in the dark Orkney folk ballad "The Grey Selkie of Sule Skerry": *I am a man upon the land/I am a selkie in the sea*. When repairing to land to pass themselves off as people, selkies simply removed their seal skin. In many folktales merbeings do the same, enabling them to marry landbound mortals and even produce children by these unions, until at last the inevitable homesickness for the sea overtakes them and they are gone in a splash.

Sailors usually regarded the sighting of a mermaid as a dire omen of imminent death, usually in the storm that follows such an encounter. In "The Mermaid," a well-known and still-sung traditional ballad thought to have originated in the mid-eighteenth century, a ship's crew spots such a creature sitting on a rock with a comb and a glass in its hand. The captain speaks up:

> *This fishy mermaid has warned me of our doom*
> *And we shall sink to the bottom of the sea…*
> *And three times around spun our gallant ship…*
> *And she went to the bottom of the sea.*

Merbeings sighted

To settle a furious and persistent national controversy—even then, skepticism of such things was widespread, especially among the educated—the Danish government set up an official inquiry into the authenticity of merbeings. The Danish Royal Commission declared that if merbeings were determined to be a mere fantasy, those who continued to speak of them would find themselves in trouble with the law. Freedom of expression on such matters was preserved, however, when members of the commission themselves spotted a merman near the Faroe Islands. On the approach of their ship, it sank into the water but surfaced shortly afterwards to stare intently at them with its deep-set eyes. A few minutes of this scrutiny proved so unsettling that the ship effected a retreat. As it was doing so, the merman puffed out his cheeks and emitted a "deep roar" before diving out of sight.

Three decades later, writing in his *Natural History of Norway* (1752–53), Bishop Erik Pontoppidan had this to say about merbeing sightings: "Here, in the diocese of Bergen, as well as in the manor of Nordland, there are several hundreds of persons to credit and reputation who affirm, with the strongest assurance, that they have seen this kind of creature."

According to Canada's National History Society, a prominent fur-trader and merchant made this deposition at the Court of King's Bench in Montreal on November 13, 1812:

> That in the year 1782, on the 3d of May, when on his return to Michilimackinac [present-day Mackinac Island, Michigan, on Lake Huron] from the Grand Portage, he arrived at the south end of Lake Pate [Pie Island, near present-day Thunder Bay, Ontario, on Lake Superior], where he formed his encampment to stop for the night. That a little before sunset, the evening being clear and serene, deponent was returning from setting his nets, and reached his encampment a short time after the sun went down. That on disembarking, the deponent happened to turn towards the lake, when he observed, about an acre or three quarters of an acre distant from the bank where he stood, an animal in the water, which appeared to him to have the upper part of its body, above the waist, formed exactly like that of a human being. It had the half of its body out of the water, and the

In the 2005 movie *Harry Potter and the Goblet of Fire* the title hero encounters frightening merpeople while trying to rescue a friend. Depictions of mermaids and mermen in film and literature have ranged from the frightening to, as in *The Little Mermaid,* the benign.

novelty of so extraordinary a spectacle excited his attention, and led him to examine it carefully. That the body of the animal seemed to him about the size of that of a child of seven or eight years of age, with one of its arms extended and elevated in the air. The hand appeared to be composed of fingers exactly similar to those of a man: and the right arm was kept in an elevated position, while the left seemed to rest upon the hip, but the deponent did not see the latter, it being kept under the water. The deponent distinctly saw the features of the countenance, which bore an exact resemblance to those of the human face. The eyes were extremely brilliant; the nose small but handsomely shaped; the mouth proportionate to the rest of the face; the complexion of a brownish hue, somewhat similar to that of a young negro; the ears well formed, and corresponding to the other parts of the figure. He did not discover that the animal had any hair, but in the place of it he observed that wooly substance about an inch long, on top of the head, somewhat similar to that which grows on the heads of negroes. The animal looked the deponent in the face, with an aspect indicating uneasiness, but at the same time with a mixture of curiosity. And the deponent, along with three other men who were with him at the time, and an old Indian woman to whom he had given a passage in his canoe, attentively examined the animal for the space of three or four minutes.

The deponent formed the design of getting possession of the animal if possible, and for this purpose endeavored to get hold of his gun, which was loaded at the time, with the intention of shooting it; but the Indian woman, who was near at the time, ran up to the deponent, and seizing him by his clothes, by her violent struggles, prevented his taking aim. During the time which he was occupied in this, the animal sunk under water without changing its attitude, and disappearing, was seen no more. The woman appeared highly indignant at the audacity of the deponent in offering to fire upon what she termed the God of the Water and Lakes; and vented her anger in bitter reproaches, saying they would all infallibly perish, for the God of the Waters would raise such a tempest as would dash them to pieces upon the rocks…. The deponent … remained quietly where he had fixed his encampment. That at about ten or eleven at night, they heard the dashing of the waves, accompanied with such a violent gale of wind, so as to render it necessary to drag their canoe higher up on the beach; and the deponent … was obliged to seek shelter from the violent storm, which continued for three days, unabated.

That it is in the knowledge of the deponent, that there exists a general belief diffused among the Indians who inhabit the country around this island, that it is the residence of the God of the Waters and of the Lakes, whom in their language they call Manitou Niba Nabais, and that he had often heard that this belief was peculiar to the Sauteux [Chippewa] Indians. He further learned from another voyageur, that an animal exactly similar to that which deponent described, had been seen by him on another occasion when passing from Pâté to Tonnerre, and the deponent thinks the frequent appearance of this extraordinary animal in this spot has given rise to the superstitious belief among the Indians, that the God of the Waters had fixed upon this for his residence.

That the deponent, in speaking of the storm which followed the threats of the Indian woman, merely remarked it as a strange circumstance, which coincided with the time, without attributing it to any other cause than what naturally produces such an effect, and which is a well known occurrence to voyageurs; that fish in general appear most numerous near the surface, and are most apt to show themselves above water on the approach of a storm.

And further the deponent saith not.

Signed VENANT ST. GERMAIN
Sworn before us, 13th November, 1812
Signed, P. L. Panet, J.K.B.
I. OGDEN, J.K.B.

The reader may have noticed with wry amusement that while St. Germain confessed to having seen a mercreature, he wanted it plainly understood that he had no time for superstitious beliefs. Possibly more to the point, note his reference to it as an "animal" as opposed to a sentient humanoid. We will encounter such characterization repeatedly in other testimony.

In the September 30, 1819, issue of *The New Times* (London), a correspondent signing himself—presumably pseudonymously—as "A. Salamé" contributed a letter recalling a curious sighting:

In the month of August, 1805, I was on board of a brig, on my voyage through the Red Sea, in latitude between 14 and 15 degrees, North, quite becalmed, in the centre of the gulf. On a morning, about 11 o'clock, I saw a whale at a little distance from us; and a short time after, I saw something about the size and shape of a coffin jumping just by our side, out of the water as high as nearly to the main-top, when on its dropping down, I observed the lower part was like a dolphin, and the upper part, to my astonishment, was exactly of the form of a female's bust, composed of a head with long hair, dropping backwards, a fine and correct profile, and an elegantly prominent bosom; but I do not remember that I saw any arms or hands. My anxiety and curiosity were, of course, warmly excited, till to my full satisfaction I saw her jumping again four or five times, on which opportunities I had the gratification to make ample observations. I considered her jumping out of the water to be occasioned by her being pursued by the whale I saw before.

Now, Mr. Editor, I am very glad to find that this animal has been found in this quarter of the globe [a reference to an article recently reprinted from the *Galway Advertiser*], the existence of which was doubted, because when I related my story several times, my hearers were rather doubtful of the fact.

A subsequent letter to the editor expressed skepticism in part because Salamé had mentioned Red Sea whales, as if the alleged witness had made a tell-tale error. In his response Salamé insisted, correctly, that the Red Sea houses such marine mammals. Still, a letter composed by an untraceable individual doesn't amount to much as evidence. Other accounts, however, are tied to named witnesses and, sometimes, official inquiries and thus, if still difficult to swallow, are not so easily set aside.

"A phenomenon almost incredible to naturalists"

Writing in *A Tour to Milford Haven in the Year 1791*, compiled from a series of letters the author wrote during her stay on that Welsh inlet, Mary Morgan recounted a statement made to George Phillips, M.D., of Haverfordwest, in late December 1782 (spelling modernized):

Henry Reynolds, of Pennyhold, in the parish of Castlemartin in the county of Pembroke, a simple farmer, and esteemed by all who knew him to be a truth-telling man, declares the following most extraordinary story to be an absolute fact, and is willing, to satisfy such as will not take his bare word for it, to swear to the truth of the same. He says he went one morning to the cliffs that bound his own lands, and form a bay near Linny Stack. From the eastern end of the same he saw, as he thought, a person bathing very near the western end, but appearing, from almost the middle up, above water. He, knowing the water to be deep in that place, was much surprised at it, and went along the cliffs, quite to the western end, to see what it was. As he got towards it, it appeared to him like a person sitting in a tub. At last he got within ten or twelve yards of it, and found it then to be a creature much resembling a youth of sixteen or eighteen years age, with a very white skin, sitting in an erect posture, having, from somewhat about the middle, its body quite above the water; and directly under the water there was a large brown substance, on which it seemed to float. The wind being perfectly calm, and the water quite clear, he could see distinctly, when the creature moved, that this substance was part of it. From the bottom there went down a tail much resembling that of a large Conger Eel. Its tail in deep water was straight downwards, but in shallow water it would turn it on one side. The tail was continually moving in a circular manner. The form of its body and arms was entirely human, but its arms and hands seemed rather thick and short in proportion to its body. The form of the head, and all the features of the face, were human also; but the nose rose high between its eyes, was pretty long, and seemed to terminate very sharp. Its head was white like its body, without hair; but from its forehead there grew a brownish substance, of three or four fingers' breadth, which turned up over its head, and went down over its back, and reached quite into the water. This substance did not at all resemble hair, but was

An illustration of mermaids by the famous artist Arthur Rackham for Nathaniel Hawthorne's story "The Three Golden Apples."

thin, compact, and flat, not much unlike a ribbon. It did not adhere to the back part of its head, or neck, or back; for the creature lifted it up from its neck, and washed under it. It washed frequently under its arms and about its body; it swam about the bay, and particularly around a little rock which Reynolds was within ten or twelve yards of. He stayed about an hour looking at it. It was so near him, that he could perceive its motion through the water was very rapid; and that, when it turned, it put one hand into the water, and moved itself round very quickly. It never dipped under the water all the time he was looking at it. It looked attentively at him and the cliffs, and seemed to take great notice of the birds flying over its head. Its looks were wild and fierce; but it made no noise, nor did it grin, or in any way distort its face. When he left it, it was about a hundred yards from him; and when he returned with some others, it was gone.

Apparently such creatures were active off the coast of Scotland during this period. London's *Monthly Magazine* carried a letter signed by Elizabeth Mackay and her cousin C. Mackenzie, though composed by the former. The header notes that the letter, dated May 25, 1809, was addressed to "Miss Innes Dowager, of Sandside, Reay Manse," and identified Miss Mackay as the "daughter of the Rev. David Mackay, Minister of Reay":

While she and I were walking by the seashore, on the 12th of January, about noon, our attention was attracted by seeing three people who were on a rock at some distance, shewing signs of terror and astonishment at something they saw in the water; on approaching them, we distinguished that the object of their wonder was a face resembling the human countenance, which appeared floating on the waves; at that time nothing but the face was visible; it may not be improper to observe, before I proceed further, that the face, throat, and arms, are all I can attempt to describe; all our endeavours to discover the appearance and position of the body being unavailing. The sea at that time ran very high, and as the wave advanced, the Mermaid gently sunk under them, and afterwards re-appeared. The face seemed plump and round, the eye and nose were small, the former were of a light grey colour, and the mouth was large, and, from the shape of the jawbone, which seemed straight, the face looked short; as to the inside of the mouth I can say nothing not having attended to it, though sometimes open. The forehead, nose, and chin, were white; the whole side face of a bright pink colour. The head was exceedingly round, the hair thick and long, of a green oily cast, and appeared troublesome to it, the waves generally throwing it down over the face; it seemed to see the annoyance, and, as the waves retreated[,]with both its hands frequently threw back the hair and rubbed its throat, as if to remove any soiling it might have received from it. The throat was slender, smooth, and white; we did not think of observing whether it had elbows; but from the manner in which it used its arms, I must conclude that it had. The arms were very long and slender, as were the hands and fingers; the latter were not webbed. The arms, one of them at least, was frequently extended, over its head, as if to frighten a bird that hovered over it, and seemed to distress it much; when that had no effect, it sometimes turned quite round several times successively. At a little distance we observed a seal. It sometimes laid its right hand under its cheek, and in this position floated for some time. We saw nothing like hair or scales on any part of it; indeed the smoothness of the skin particularly caught our attention. The time it was discernible to us was about an hour. The sun was shining clearly at that time; it was distant from us a few yards only. These are the few observations made by us during the appearance of this strange phenomenon....

I have stated nothing but what I clearly recollect; as my cousin and I had frequently, previous to this period, combated an assertion which is very common among the lower class here, that Mermaids had been frequently seen on this coast, our evidence cannot be thought biased by any former prejudice in favour of the existence of this wonderful creature.

"It is interesting to note," twentieth-century Scottish folklorist R. Macdonald Robertson would write, "that whereas in all the traditional mermaid stories the maid of the sea has golden hair, in eye-witness accounts it ranges in color from green to black."

After one of the witnesses published her account—which, understandably, sparked a sensation—William Munro wrote this time to the *London Courier*, which published the following in its September 7 edition:

About 12 years ago, when I was Parochial Schoolmaster at Reay, in the course of my walking on the shore of Sandside Bay, being a fine warm day in summer, I was induced to extend my walk toward Sandside Head, when my attention was arrested by the appearance of a figure resembling an un-clothed human female, sitting upon a rock extending into the sea, and apparently in the action of combing its hair, which flowed around its shoulders, and was of a light brown color.

The forehead was round, the face plump, the cheeks ruddy, the eyes blue, the mouth and lips of a natural form, resembling those of a man; the teeth I could not discover, as the mouth was shut; the breasts and the abdomen, the arms and fingers of the size of a full-grown body of the human species; the fingers, from the action in which the hands were employed, did not appear to be webbed, but as to this I am not positive.

It remained on the rock three or four minutes after I observed it, and was exercised during that period in combing its hair, which was long and thick, and of which it appeared proud; and then dropped into the sea, from whence it did not reappear to me.

I had a distinct view of its features, being at no great distance on an emi-nence above the rock on which it was sitting, and the sun brightly shining.

Immediately before its getting into its natural element it seemed to have observed me as the eyes were directed towards the eminence on which I stood.... Previous to the period I beheld this object, I had heard it fre-quently reported by several persons, and some of them persons whose ve-racity I never heard disputed, that they had seen such a phenomenon as I have described, though then, like many others, I was not disposed to credit their testimony on this subject. I can say of a truth, that it was only by seeing the phenomenon I was perfectly convinced of its existence.

If the above narrative can in any degree be subservient towards estab-lishing the existence of a phenomenon, hitherto almost incredible to nat-uralists, or to remove the skepticism of others, who are ready to dispute every thing which they cannot fully comprehend, you are welcome to it.

Another mermaid sighting at the same general location is said to have taken place in mid-April. Observed by four or five individuals over the period of an hour and a half, it was said to have perfectly formed breasts, long arms, green hair, and pink skin. It displayed no signs of alarm, and the witnesses, according to the *Edinburgh Journal*, were of "unquestionable integrity."

Reports of Scottish merbeings continued. In its November 29, 1811, edi-tion *The Times* of London related that a young man named John McIsaac of Cor-phine, Kintyre, had sworn before Kintyre's Sheriff-Substitute that he had seen a similar creature sitting on a black rock along the sea coast on the afternoon of October 13. He provided a detailed description, paraphrased in the *Times* article:

A drawing of a real "mermaid" that was exhibited in London, England, around 1875.

He states that the upper half of it was white, and of the shape of a human body; the other half, towards the tail, of a brindled or reddish grey colour, apparently covered with scales; but the extremity of the tail itself was of a greenish red shining colour; that the head was covered with long hair; at times it would put back the hair on both sides of its head, it would also spread its tail like a fan; and while so extended, the tail continued in tremulous motion, and when drawn together again, it remained motionless, and appeared to the deponent to be about twelve or fourteen inches broad; that the hair was long and light brown; that the animal was between four and five feet long: that it had a head, hair, arms, and body, down to the middle, like a human being; that the arms were short in proportion to the body, which appeared to be about the thickness of that of a young lad, and tapering gradually to the point of the tail; that when stroking its head, as above-mentioned, the fingers were kept close together, so that he cannot say whether they were webbed or not; that he saw it for nearly two hours, the rock on which it lay being dry; that after the sea had so far retired, as to leave the rock dry to the height of five feet above the water, it tumbled clumsily into the sea; a minute after[,] he observed the animal above water, and then he saw every feature of its face, having all the appearance of a human being, with very hollow eyes. The cheeks were of the same colour with the rest of the face; the neck seemed short; and it was constantly, with both hands, stroking and washing its breast, which was half immersed in the water. He therefore cannot say whether its bosom was formed like a woman's or not. He saw no other fins or feet upon it but as described. It continued above water for a few minutes, and then disappeared. He was informed that some boys in a neighbouring farm saw a similar creature in the sea, close to the sea, on the same day. The Minister of Campbeltown, and the Chamberlain of Mull, attest his examination, and declare they know no reason why his veracity should be questioned.

Three prominent citizens, the Rev. Dr. George Robertson, Campbeltown minister Norman MacLeod, and lawyer James Maxwell, who were there when McIsaac delivered his testimony, remarked, "From the manner in which he delivered his evidence we are satisfied that he was impressed with a perfect belief."

Five days later, on November 2, another eyewitness made sworn testimony to Kintyre's Sheriff-Substitute Duncan Campbell. Katherine Loynachan stated that on the afternoon of October 13, as she was herding cattle near the sea shore, she saw a creature sliding off one of the rocks and dropping into the water, then resurfacing six yards out. It had long, dark hair, white skin on its upper part, and dark brown skin on its lower part, which was fishlike. In Campbell's account of her testimony, it

> turned about with the fact of it towards the shore, where the declarant was standing, and having laid one hand, which was like a boy's hand, upon another rock that was near the first rock it came nearer to the shore than it was; that at this time the declarant saw the face of it distinctly which had all the appearance of the face of a child and as white, and at this time the animal was constantly rubbing or washing its breast with one hand, the fingers being close together.... After this animal continued to look towards the declarant for about half a minute, it swam about and disappeared, but in a very short time thereafter she saw the head and fact of this animal appearing above water again, and swimming away south toward the farm of Corphine, but soon after disappeared, and the declarant saw it no more.

> The girl was so reluctant to credit the testimony of her own senses that at first she told herself this was a boy who had fallen out of a boat and was seeking rescue. Campbell interviewed, and secured sworn testimony from, the witness' father, who recalled his daughter's running home to tell him about a strange boy who was swimming along the shore. The father, mother, and daughter all went to look but saw nothing.

A series of sightings took place off Scotland's west coast in the summer of 1814. When a frightened boy reported seeing a creature half human and half fish, he got nothing but ridicule for his efforts. A month later a group of children saw what they thought was a drowning woman, whom closer examination revealed to be something else entirely. According to a letter from a local informant in the *York Chronicle* of September 1:

> The upper part was exactly like a woman, the skin appeared very white, and a good deal of colour in the cheeks, and very long darkish looking hair; the arms were very well proportioned above, but tapered very much towards the hands, which were no larger than a child's of eight or ten years old, the tail was like an immense cuddy fish ... in color and shape.

Some of the children had gone off to alert nearby farmers. By the time they arrived, the creature had swum close enough to shore so that one man, who bore a rifle, expressed his intention to shoot it, but the others dissuaded him from acting on such pointless blood lust. He contented himself with whistling at the creature. The whistle caused it to turn around and glance at him. It "remained in sight for two hours, at times making a hissing noise like a goose." It was seen on two subsequent occasions, "always early in the morning and when the sea was calm."

At Port Gordon, on August 15 of that same year, fishermen Thomas Johnstone and William Gordon were a quarter mile from shore when they spotted, not far from them, a merman. The local schoolmaster, George McKenzie, interviewed them shortly afterwards and the next day sent an account to the editor of the *Caledonian Mercury*. The merman, he reported, was of "swarthy" countenance, with small eyes, flat nose, large mouth, and remarkably long arms. After fifteen seconds it dived under water, resurfacing farther away from the boat, now accompanied by "another, whom the men assumed to be female, as they could perceive she had breasts, and her hair was not curled, but reached to a little below the shoulders; the skin of this last one, too, was fairer than the other's." Terrified, Johnstone and Gordon raced for the shore. The two creatures continued to gaze at them even after they made land.

Ireland had its sightings as well. One that gained international prominence in a widely reprinted piece from the *Galway Advertiser* comes from the summer of 1819, from coastal Derrygimia in Connemara, a region comprising the western part of County Galway. The press story refers to the creature as an "animal half female and half fish," first glimpsed by a "female of the lower order," presumably because she was pregnant and apparently unmarried. Suddenly the creature emitted a shrieking sound, then plunged toward the retreating water as the tide went out. When it was able to return to the sea, it seemed in no hurry to swim out farther. It was visible, the article claimed, to no fewer than 300 witnesses, including "Thomas Evans, Esq., of Cleggan, a gentleman well known to many of our readers." Evans provided this account:

> It was about the size of a well grown child of ten years of age; a bosom prominent as a girl of sixteen, a profusion of long dark brown hair; full dark eyes, hands and arms formed like the human species, with a slight web connecting the upper part of the fingers, which were employed in throwing back her flowing locks, and running them through her hair; her movements in the water seemed principally directed by the finny extremity; for near an hour she remained in apparent tranquility ... until a musket was leveled at her, which having flashed in the pan, she immediately dived, & was not afterwards seen. Mr. Evans declares she did not appear to him to possess the power of speech, for her looks appeared vacant, & there was an evident want of intelligence.

The "female of the lower order" was so traumatized by the experience that she suffered a miscarriage and was confined to bed for some time afterwards. It was this sighting, incidentally, that led "A. Salamé" to recall his own alleged encounter in the Red Sea in 1805 (see above).

The *Drogheda Journal* printed a statement by three residents, one the parish clerk, of Termonfechin, in the Irish county of Louth, attesting to a sighting on August 18, 1824. Standing on the sea shore in mid-afternoon, George Hoey (the clerk), Owen Maguire, and Patrick Taaffe looked out to see what they recognized as a mermaid from having heard about such in books. They and others saw it at sufficiently close range as to make them certain they could not be mistaken about what it was, a creature of human size swimming toward the River Boyne. "Its body was remarkably white, with long arms," the statement read, "which it frequently used to drive away the sea-gulls which were hovering over it." It had dark hair, as was its tail, "which it frequently showed when plunging … shaped like the tail of a fish." They watched it for about fifteen minutes, and it was still visible when, rather incredibly, they walked away.

The newspaper noted, "We questioned the above-named persons on Saturday [August 21], relative to the extraordinary appearance on our coast, and received such satisfactory answers as to leave no doubt on our minds of its identity."

According to an 1828 article in *Welsh Magazine*, a farmer whose house was located 300 yards from Wales' west-central coast, near Aberystwyth, rose early, leaving other family members still in their beds, and decided to take in a view of the rising sun's light on the ocean. Gazing out into the water, he was startled to see what he first thought was a woman bathing. Though she was within a stone's-throw distance, the sea was deep enough at the location—six feet, he thought—that he couldn't understand how she could be upright. Embarrassed at viewing what he took to be a naked woman, he retreated. Overcome by curiosity (or something), however, he soon sneaked back and watched from behind a rock for the next half hour.

This statue of the Little Mermaid watches over the ocean by Copenhagen. It honors the famous tale by Hans Christian Andersen.

Convinced that he was seeing something truly out of the ordinary, he returned to the house. Several of his children had just risen, and they went to the site with their father. The wife and youngest child followed soon thereafter. By now the supposed bather was closer to the shore, and the wife boldly walked toward her. The article relates:

> But as soon as the Mermaid saw her, she sank into the water and swam away, till she was about the same distance from the land as she was first seen at; and the whole family ran along the shore for more than half a mile, and for nearly the whole time, saw her in the sea, and sometimes her entire head and shoulders were quite above the water.

> There was in the sea a great stone, more than a yard high, on which she would stand when she was first seen. [This is a confusing statement. Perhaps what is meant is "*against which* she would stand."] And the whole family testify that she was exactly such [a] one, in repose, of shape and size, as a young woman would be of about eighteen years of age. Her hair was pretty short, and of colour dark; her face extremely handsome, her necks and arms were as usual, her breasts [illegible], and her skin whiter than that of any person they had seen before. Her face was towards the

land. She often [illegible] she was taking up water, and then she put her hand before her face for about half a minute.

When she so bent herself, something black was seen, as if it had been a short tail, turning up behind her. She often made a sort of sound like sneezing, which made the rock resound. The farmer, who had an opportunity of beholding her for so long a time, said that he saw but very few women so fair to look upon as this Mermaid. The whole family, the youngest of whom is eleven years of age, is now living. And we had this account, word for word as it is here given, from themselves within the last month.

In 1857, *Shipping Gazette* took note of a recent report by Scottish sailors, who claimed to have observed a creature "in the shape of a woman with full breast, dark complexion, comely face." Early the same year, the *Portland Guardian*, published in the Australian state of Victoria, stated, "We have heard a strange story of a person having very lately seen in Portland swamp what he himself declares to be a mermaid. The observer to whom we refer positively declares that in a part of the swamp near the foot of Mr. Trangmar's paddock, and down among the reeds[,] he saw a living object, in shape half-woman, half-fish, with long flowing hair, which (as we understand) said mermaid was engaged in smoothing, apparently as if combing her tresses."

Sightings in the Orkney Islands (off Scotland's north coast) attracted international attention in the late part of the century. In the spring of 1890, a farm woman from Birsay observed a strange creature in water near the rocks just off shore. Unable to recognize it and feeling alarmed, she went to get her husband. When the two returned, they observed it, or at least the four feet of it above sea, and tried to capture it. But the creature evaded them and dived beneath the water. The wife said it appeared to be "a good-looking person"; the husband characterized it as "a woman covered over with brown hair." A widely distributed newspaper account concludes, "An animal of similar description was seen by several people at Sheerness [Orkney] two years ago."

Reports continued over the next few years. In the summer of 1895 dozens of persons reportedly witnessed the creature, or one very much like it. In the spring of 1896, an Orkneys correspondent of the *London Telegraph* filed this story:

What is said to be a mermaid has been seen for some weeks at stated times at South Side Deerness. It is about six feet in length, according to the evidence, and is of the shape of a well-proportioned woman. The head, which is rather small, is of a dark brown or black color. The neck, breast, arms, and, in fact, the entire body, is [sic] of snowy whiteness. In swimming, it appears exactly like a human being in a similar act, making as regular strokes with its arms as any woman or man would make. At times it comes very close to the shore, and appears to bask on the surface or to be seated upon a sunken rock. While so reposing it often appears to wave its hands at the sightseers on the shore. A waving motion is kept up at any rate, whether the creature knows what it is doing or not. It has never been seen entirely out of the water, but the portions which have been exposed are surprisingly humanlike in their outlines.

Merbeings caught

In 1762, a French newspaper reported that "two girls on the island of Noirmontier," while searching for shells in rock crevices, encountered "an animal of a human form, leaning on its hands." One girl promptly stabbed it with a knife. It moaned and died. Afterwards a physician went to the site and examined the body, finding it "as big as the largest man" with the white skin of a drowned person's and "the breast of a full-chested woman; a flat nose; a large mouth; the chin adorned with a kind of beard, formed of fine shells; and over the whole body, tufts of similar white shells. It had the tail of a fish, and at the extremity of it a kind of feet."

A highly unusual account from the Calf of Man, a tiny island off the southwest coast of the Isle of Man (between Ireland and Great Britain), is set in late 1810. A correspondent there wrote that, hearing sounds like a kitten's cries, "three respectable tradesmen" found two strange creatures. One was dead, its body apparently ravaged in the violent storm the night before. The other, still alive, was taken to Douglas, the isle's capital city, and described thus:

> It is one foot eleven and three quarter inches in length, from the crown of its head to the extremity of its tail; five inches across the shoulders; its skin is pale brown, and the scales on its tail are tinged with violet; the hair on its head is light green; it is attached to the crown of the head only, hanging loose about the face, about four inches in length, very gelatinous to the touch, and resembling the green sea weed, growing on rocks; its mouth is small and has no appearance of teeth. It delights much in swimming in a tub of sea water, and feeds chiefly on muscles and other shell fish, which it devours with great avidity; it also now and then swallows small portions of milk and water, when given to it in a quill.

As is usually the case, the sequel, if any, to this episode (if it occurred at all) is unrecorded. Usually, not always, as the following story attests.

Around 1830, people at work along the shore of Benbecula, one of the islands in the Hebrides chain (off Scotland's northwest coast), spotted a small creature, half woman and half fish, in the water a few feet away. It was turning somersaults in the water as it play. When some men tried to capture it, it evaded them. Finally a little boy hit it on the back with some stones, and it disappeared. A few days later the body washed up on shore two miles away.

According to Duncan Shaw, the district sheriff, who conducted an examination of the body, "The upper part of the creature was about the size of a well-fed child of three or four years of age, with an abnormally developed breast. The hair was long, dark and glossy, while the skin was white, soft and tender. The lower part of the body was like a salmon, but without scales." It was "interred in the presence of a large assemblage of the Hebridean people in the burial-ground at Nunton, where the grave is pointed out to this day," R. Macdonald Robertson stated in 1961. "I have seen it myself." Unfortunately, "it" is the grave, not the creature's remains.

An affidavit records the alleged capture of a mermaid—or something like it—in the Shetland Islands north of Scotland:

In the presence of Arthur Nicholson of Lochend, J.P.—William Manson, Daniel Manson, John Henderson, residing in Cullivoe in the parish of North Yell, who being sworn deposit—That, in the beginning of July last [1833], they at the deep-sea from 30 to 60 miles from land, and about midnight took up a creature attached by the back of the neck to a hook, which was about 3 feet long, and about 30 inches in circumference at the broadest part, which was across the shoulders. From the navel upwards, it resembled a human being—had breasts as large as those of a woman.

Attached to the side were arms about 9 inches long, with wrists and hands like those of a human being, except that there were webs between the fingers about half their length. The fingers were in number and shape, like those of a man. The little arms were close on the outside of the breasts and on the corner of each shoulder was placed a fin of a round form which, when extended, covered both the breasts and the arms.

The animal had a short neck, on which rested a head, about the length of a man's but not nearly as round, and somewhat pointed at the top. It had eyebrows without hair, and eyelids covering two small blue eyes, somewhat like those of a human being—not like those of a fish. It had no nose, but two orifices for blowing through. It had a mouth so large that when opened wide it would admit a man's fist. It had lips rather thicker than a man's of a pure white colour. There was no chin, but they think the lower jaw projected a little further than the upper one. There were no ears.

The whole front of the animal was covered with skin, white as linen, the back with skin of a light-grey colour, like a fish. From the breasts the shape sloped towards the tail, close to which was only about 4 inches in circumference. The tail was flat, and consisted of two lobes which, when extended, might be 6 inches together in breadth, and were set at right angles with the face of the creature; it resembled the face of a halibut.

The animal was very nearly round at the shoulders. It appeared to have shoulder bones and a hollow space between them. The diminution of size increased most rapidly from the navel, which might be 9 inches below the breasts. There was between the nostrils a thing that appeared to be a piece of gristle one on each side of the head, but not so long, which the animal had the power of moving backwards and forwards, and could make them meet on top of the skull.

When the men spoke the animal answered, and moved these bristles, which led them to suppose that the creature heard by means of them. They did not observe what sort of teeth the creature had, nor the parts of generation. There was no hair upon any part of the body which was soft and slimy.

There is an old opinion among fishermen that it is unlucky to kill a mermaid and therefore, after having kept it in the boat for some time, they slipped it [back into the water].

All of which is the truth, so help me God.

A man who interviewed the boat's skipper as well as the crewmen forwarded an account to Edinburgh University's Natural History Department:

> Not one of the six men dreamed of a doubt of its being a mermaid.... The usual resource of skepticism that the seals and other sea animals appearing under certain circumstances operating upon an excited imagination and so producing an ocular illusion cannot avail here. It is quite impossible that six Shetland fishermen could commit such a mistake.

In late 1838 the *Derry Sentinel* and other northern Irish newspapers straight-facedly announced the capture of a mermaid, caught in a salmon net near Fahan, County Donegal:

> It weighs about seventy pounds, and is altogether *human* [italics in original] in its *outward* organization from the head to the navel ... and the remainder is formed very like the

Fishermen accidentally net a mermaid in this 1919 illustration published in the periodical *Chatterbox*.

extremity of a large dolphin. The skin of the face and the breast is a whitish brown.... It looks to be twelve or fourteen years old, and regards people, occasionally, as if it had an *inclination* to speak.

Needless to observe, everything about this suggests an audacious hoax, journalistic or other.

Reports of merbeings in the seas off Scotland continued through the rest of the nineteenth century and even into the twentieth. In August 1949, fishermen off Craig More claimed to have had several sightings.

New World merbeings

Of all purported sighters of merbeings (or sighters of purported merbeings), Christopher Columbus is easily the most famous. On his voyage of discovery into the West Indies, he saw three of them "leaping a good distance out of the sea" and found them "not so fair as they are painted." In fact, this vague description—if we can draw any conclusion from it at all—is consistent with the behavior of dugongs.

A more detailed story comes from a seventeenth-century explorer of America, John Smith. Sailing through the West Indies in 1614, Smith noticed what he first took to be a young woman in the water. In Smith's appreciative, but not uncritical, appraisal she had "large eyes, rather too round, finely shaped nose (a little too short), well-formed ears, rather too long, and her long green hair imparted to her an original character by no means unattractive." Just as Smith began to "feel the first pangs of love," she moved in such a way as to reveal that "from below the waist the woman gave way to the fish."

"One may be inclined to question the veracity of the susceptible Captain Smith," Sir Arthur Waugh, a scholarly authority on merbeing lore, observes, then adds, "It is much more difficult to doubt the detailed reports of ... sober and responsible people," among whom he numbers a Capt. Whitbourne. In 1610, while sailing a small boat into harbor at St. John's, Newfoundland, Whitbourne spotted a strange creature swimming in his direction and "looking cheerfully as [if] it had been a woman, by the Face, Eyes, Nose, Ears, Neck and Forehead." It did not get a cheerful reception. Deeply alarmed, Whitbourne backed hastily away. The creature then turned around and attempted to board a companion boat belonging to William Hawkridge, who banged it on the head. It disappeared under the water. Hawkridge later offered this laconic comment: "Whether it was a mermaid or no ... I leave it for others to judge."

The mermaid should have considered itself lucky that it did not suffer the fate of a merman who that same century tried to climb into a boat in Casco Bay, off the coast of southern Maine. The boat's occupant, a Mr. Mitter, is said to have slashed off one of its arms. It sank, "dyeing the waters purple with its blood," in the words of a contemporary chronicler.

A second sighting, not long after that in the waters off Nova Scotia, occurred to the crew of three French vessels. This time they chased and attempted to capture a merman with ropes, but to no avail. "He brushed his mossy hair out of his eyes which seemed to cover his body as well—as much as seen above water, in some places more, in other less," the captain of one of the ships recorded. The merman dived, never to be seen again, "to the great dejection of the fishermen."

Another of Waugh's "sober and responsible people," the celebrated New World explorer Henry Hudson, noted the following in his journal on June 15, 1610:

> This evening one of our company, looking overboard, saw a mermaid, and, calling up some of the company to see her, one more of the crew came up, and by that time she was come close to the ship's side, looking earnestly on the men. A little after[,] a sea came and overturned her.

> From the navel upward, her back and breasts were like a woman's, as they say that saw her; her body as big as one of us, her skin very white, and long hair hanging down behind, of color black. In her going down they saw her tail, which was like the tail of a porpoise, speckled like a mackerel. Their names that saw her were Thomas Hilles and Robert Rayner.

Of this incident the eminent Victorian naturalist Philip Gosse remarked, "Seals and walruses must have been as familiar to those polar mariners as cows to a milkmaid. Unless the whole story was a concocted lie between the two men, reasonless and objectless, and the worthy old navigator doubtless knew the character of his men, they must have seen some form of being as yet unrecognized."

In 1797 a Dr. Chisholm visited the tiny island of Berbice in the Caribbean. He spent time with Gov. Van Battenburgh and others who told him of repeated sightings, in the island's rivers, of strange creatures known to the Indians as *mene mamma* (mother of waters). In his 1801 book, *Malignant Fever in the West Indies*, Chisholm wrote:

> The upper portion resembles the human figure, the head is smaller in proportion, sometimes bare, but oftener covered with a copious quantity of long black hair. The shoulders are broad, and the breasts large and well formed. The lower portion resembles the tail portion of a fish, is of immense dimension, the tail forked, not unlike that of the dolphin.… The color of the skin is either black or tawny.… They have been generally observed in a sitting posture in the water, none of the lower extremity being discovered until they are disturbed; when by plunging, the tail appears, and agitates the water to a considerable distance round. They have been always seen employed in smoothing their hair, or stroking their faces and breasts with their hands, or something resembling hands. In this posture, and thus employed, they have been frequently taken for Indian women bathing.

At Branford, Connecticut, in 1710, a party of fishermen attested to a sighting of a half-woman/half-fish creature sitting on off-shore rocks. A Connecticut historian, Judge Sherman W. Adams, could not resist expressing his firm command of the obvious: "This very much resembled the description of the mermaid."

And there is this from an 1820 issue of the *American Journal of Science*:

> Extract from the log book of the ship Leonidas, sailing for New York towards Havre [France]. Asa Swift master; May 1817, Lat. 44 degrees, 6 degrees north. First part of the day light variable winds and cloudy; at two P.M. on the larboard quarter, at the distance of about half the ship's length, saw a strange fish. Its lower parts were like a fish; its belly was all white; the top of the back brown, and there was the appearance of short hair as far as the top of its head. From the breast upwards, it had a near resemblance to a human being and looked upon the observers very earnestly; as it was but a short distance from the ship, all the afternoon, we had a good opportunity to observe its motions and shape. No one on board ever saw the like fish, before; all believe it to be a Mermaid.

> The second mate Mr. Stevens, an intelligent young man, told me the face was nearly white, and exactly like that of a human person; that its arms were about half as long as his, with hands resembling his own; that it stood erect out of the water about two feet, looking at the ship and sails with great earnestness. It would remain in this attitude, close along side, ten or fifteen minutes at a time, and then dive and appear on the other side. It remained about them six hours. Mr. Stevens also stated that its hair was black on the head and exactly resembled a man's; that below the arms, it

was a perfect fish in form, and that the whole length from the head to the tail [was] about five feet.

In the nineteenth century, North American newspapers occasionally related stories—some apparently serious, some clearly tongue in cheek, others ambiguous—of merbeing encounters. In 1894, the *Brooklyn Eagle* quoted the testimony of a local man, Frederick Carruthers, who as a seaman "many years ago" had, he said, an extraordinary sighting while standing on the dock of a bark at anchor in Demerara, in present-day Guyana. He observed a dark-skinned mermaid on a rock just thirty feet away:

> The face was quite round, a perfect human face of small size, and the hair hung far down the back.… The neck was human, and the shoulders somewhat resembled the shoulders of a woman, but the body rapidly became fish, with big fins and a regular fish tail.

He called to the ship boy, but the sound of his voice startled the creature, and it slipped away. By the time this potential second witness arrived, the creature was no longer visible.

One story—published in the *Port Jervis Evening Gazette*, New York, for August 10, 1869, and probably other papers—related this story, set in Atlantic water just off Toms River, New Jersey:

> Two fishermen, while pursuing their vocation a few days ago in the Inlet, effected the capture [of an unknown marine creature] after a violent struggle. At seeing the animal its captors became hugely frightened and took to their heels. After a while they mustered up sufficient courage to return and look at their prize. In appearance it more resembled a human being than a fish, having a face frightfully like that of a man or woman, with body and breasts exactly resembling the latter. The lower part terminated in a fish tail. The fishermen, after looking at the monster, became so superstitious, that they threw it back into the sea. It's a pity they did not preserve it.

Its lower parts were like a fish; its belly was all white; the top of the back brown, and there was the appearance of short hair as far as the top of its head.

At a beach in Brewster, Massachusetts, on Cape Cod, a group of children and one adult, a woman identified simply as Mrs. Young, spotted something strange on the beach on July 16, 1873, according to the *Provincetown Advocate*. "The head of this object," the paper related, "resembled exactly that of a child, while the rest was of fish form." Because the creature lay motionless, it could not be determined if it was alive or dead. As their adult supervisor uneasily kept her distance, the children approached and threw sand into the creature's face. In response it "uttered cries like that of a child," then proceeded to roll over and over until it reached water. As it swam out to sea, it kept its head above water and disappeared into the distance.

The *Cape Breton Herald* ran this story (subsequently widely reprinted in the Canadian press) of something said to have happened in the water off Gabarus, Nova Scotia, in July 1886:

While Mr. Bagnell, accompanied by several fishermen, was out in a boat, they observed floating on the surface of the water a few yards from the boat what they supposed to be a corpse. Approaching it for the purpose of taking it ashore for burial, they observed it to move, when, to their great surprise, it turned around in a sitting position and looked at them and disappeared. A few minutes after[,] it appeared to the surface and again looked toward them, after which it disappeared altogether. The face, head, shoulders, and arms resembled those of a human being, but the lower extremities had the appearance of a fish. The back of its head was covered with long dark hair resembling a horse's mane. The arms were shaped exactly like a human being's, except that the fingers on the hands were very long. There is no doubt that the mysterious stranger is what is known as a mermaid and the first seen in Cape Breton waters.

In the twentieth century

While it is tempting to dismiss these reports as long ago, far away, and therefore easily dismissible, claimed merbeing sightings were logged throughout the deeply skeptical twentieth century. Most of the stories, unfortunately, lack detail, owing less to the witnesses than to the newspaper reporters who judged the incidents too absurd to merit comprehensive treatment.

In December 1911 two fishermen, William Rivers and Ernest Williams of Greenwich, Connecticut, were half a mile from shore in Cos Cob Harbor (on Long Island Sound) when they noticed what they first took to be a woman on a sandy beach. She seemed to be gesturing to them, or at least her arms were extended. Wondering if she needed help, the two rowed toward her. When they got close enough for a good look, they were dumbfounded to see that she was half fish. Badly frightened, they fled the scene as fast as they could depart it. They did not report the incident to the authorities, but police eventually learned of it via rumors circulating through the area. They dismissed the figure as "some woman who was taking an unseasonable sea bath."

Three years later, if one is to credit an odd account in Iowa's *Waterloo Evening Courier and Reporter* (June 30, 1914), something with at least broad merman characteristics haunted a summer resort on Clear Lake. Vacationers and fishermen in boats on the lake's north side saw a man swimming "with the speed of a fish." As the boatmen approached, the man dived beneath the water and was not seen again. The paper said witnesses—several sightings were reported—described him as resembling a fifty-year-old man "whose body seems to be covered with scales like a fish.... Others claim it is impossible for the creature to be a man because of the long time it stays under water." Over the period of a few days others encountered the figure, and some complained of the mysterious disappearance of food left on the pier. There was a mental hospital nearby, but investigators found

(Continued on page 320)

Ringing Rocks

Southeastern Pennsylvania is dotted with sites where rocks ring when struck by a hammer. These include the Stony Garden (Haycock, Bucks County), the Devil's Race Course (Franklin County), and others in the South Mountain region and at Pottstown. By far the most famous site, and the most studied, is in Upper Black Eddy in Bucks County. It is located a mile west of the Delaware River near the New Jersey state line.

Set in a forested area, the Ringing Rocks appear in a field that has no vegetation except lichens. Ten feet thick and seven acres around, the rocks are composed of diabase, in other words part of the earth's basic crustal structure. There is nothing unusual about them except that when struck hard, they ring. In June 1890, backed by a brass band, Dr. J. J. Ott played a few selections on the rocks for an appreciative Buckwampum Historical Society gathering. Ott, in short, had learned what other investigators have since confirmed: that the rocks don't have to be in their natural location to ring. They do not even have to be intact.

Curiously, though made up of the same materials, not all of the Ringing Rocks ring—only about thirty percent of them, according to those who have experimented with them.

While this is undoubtedly a natural phenomenon, it is an odd one for which no fully satisfactory explanation has ever been proposed. In 1965, geologist Richard Faas, of Lafayette College, Easton, Pennsylvania, conducted laboratory experiments using sensitive equipment. He learned that when he struck a ringing rock, a series of sub-audible frequencies were produced, and these added up to a tone that could be heard by the human ear. He could not, however, determine a specific physical cause.

Some writers have made remarkable—almost occult—claims for the ringing rocks, asserting that something about the rock field spooks animals, even insects, which make a point of keeping their distance. There is nothing especially mysterious about this, according to investigator Michael A. Frizzell, since the area is barren, open, and hotter than the surrounding forest during the summer, thus generally inhospitable to living creatures.

More interesting is a claim made by the late anomalist Ivan T. Sanderson, though since then there has been no published replication. "There are some larger rocks which, when hit appropriately, give rise to a whole scale: ... two different ringers when knocked together while suspended on wires produced (invariably, it seems) but one tone, however many different combinations are used."

In April 1899 press accounts detailed a related anomaly:

> People who have recently visited the large surface deposit of dark stones known as "Ringing Rocks" near Pottstown, Penn., tell a story of a

(Continued from previous page)

Anomalist Ivan T. Sanderson investigates Ringing Rocks in Pennsylvania.

most unusual sight there.... During the first spring thunder storm recently the night was quite dark. Persons passing the rocks were startled to see a light bluish flame rise from the ground and spread over a space of ten or twelve yards square. This flame rose and fell after the manner of the Northern Lights, sometimes entirely disappearing and then flaming up again, lighting up the darkness around it. They stood and watched this mysterious light from a distance and then went close to it to see what cause there was for it. Some old residents in the neighborhood said they had seen the strange lights on nights during violent storms.

Ringing rocks have been noted all over the world. Surprisingly, the kinds of rock possessing such talents vary. The absence of clear patterns in the creation of such odd geological phenomena continues to frustrate theorists.

Further Reading:

Corliss, William R., ed. *Strange Planet: A Sourcebook of Unusual Geological Facts, Volume E–1*. Glen Arm, MD: Sourcebook Project, 1975.

———, ed. *Unknown Earth: A Handbook of Geological Enigmas*. Glen Arm, MD: Sourcebook Project, 1980.

Frizzell, Michael A. "The Riddle of the Ringing Rocks." *Fate* 36,10 (October 1983): 70–76.

Gibbons, John, and Steven Schlossman. "Rock Music." *Natural History* 79 (December 1970): 36–41.

"Rocks That Glow in Storms." *Delphos Daily Herald,* Ohio (April 26, 1899).

Sanderson, Ivan T. *"Things."* New York: Pyramid Books, 1967.

"Why Do Rocks Ring?" *Pursuit* 4 (April 1971): 38–41.

(Continued from page 317)

that nobody was missing from it. If there was any sequel to this curious episode, it has gone unrecorded.

An alleged sighting from 1922 is of a more traditional mermaid, though it included a novel detail. In November, according to a brief account in the *Los Angeles Times*, sailors two miles off the coast of Redondo Beach, California, observed a sad-eyed mermaid just feet from their vessel. It had a child of the species at its bosom.

In the summer of the next year, along the coast of Brittany in France, more than 100 residents of the village of St. Giles Croix DeVie saw what they took to be a mermaid. The first was fisherman Jules Cuesac, who spotted it when it rose up from under the sea fifty yards from his boat, two miles offshore. He described it as having a kind of phosphorescence around its body, giving it a glow. Witnesses said it had blue eyes and green hair, though it was never seen more than halfway out of the water; consequently no one saw its tail, if one existed.

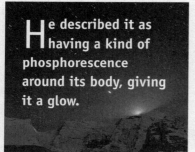

He described it as having a kind of phosphorescence around its body, giving it a glow.

In 1930, *Havana American* reporter Marie Cappick, who had been pursuing the rumor for three years, located and interviewed a retired sea captain who may have had a mermaid encounter in the Bahamas in his youth. Sam Lowe, who lived in Key West, Florida, told Cappick, "I don't know if it was a mermaid I saw or not," but his story was certainly a peculiar one.

"I went one day to a place known in Bahama waters as Conch Rocks," he recalled. His friend Edwin Saunders accompanied him. "The day was clear and cloudless," he went on. "We could see for miles around us, and there was not a living thing in sight until we reached Conch Rocks, and there we sighted a woman." The sight was so unlikely and so unexpected that Lowe and Saunders could only deduce that she was a survivor from a ship wreck. Yet there was no wreckage in sight.

Lowe said, "We continued to sail nearer and nearer to the object until about 20 feet from where the woman sat. We called and signaled her, thinking to rescue her from her position, for it was a dangerous place...." A part of Conch Rocks extends over what is known as Ocean Hole, a place that is so deep that no one has ever ascertained its exact depth.

"This woman, or whatever it was, sat there running her arms upward through her hair. If she had hands and fingers we could not tell, because her hair was coarse and black and grew close to her face. She paid no attention to us, if she saw us, and never as much as looked in our direction. Her gaze was fixed oceanward and not on the two young men in the boat near enough to shout at her and make her hear.... Just then it struck me that there was something about this creature that put a queer feeling over me. Just what it was I cannot describe, but there we two boys stood looking at her pop-eyed and open-mouthed. Finally Saunders gave the boat a shove that sent it away from the rock. It was plain that he was frightened."

If both witnesses felt misgivings about leaving the woman alone, at the same time they had the clear impression that she had no interest in being rescued or even in acknowledging their presence. That evening, when Lowe told her about the uncanny experience, his mother suggested that the woman was a mermaid, something Lowe had never heard of till that moment. He told Cappick, "When I was a man and commanded my own vessel I frequently sailed to Conch Rocks to see if the woman was there, but I never saw her again."

Cappick concluded her article by remarking, "Captain Lowe is well known in Key West and his word is unquestioned by those who know him."

In early September 1937, Michael Warde and Thomas O'Toole, Irish fishermen on the Connemara coast, noticed something following their boat—a merman with shaggy, strawlike hair, a beard, bushy eyebrows, and red lips. One of them tossed the creature a mackerel, which it caught before diving under the water. It reappeared, without the mackerel, soon afterwards. The terse Associated Press account told no more.

Merbeings apparently never abandoned the waters around the Isle of Man. In 1961 AP devoted an article to reports along the isle's west coast. Royal Air Force Wing Cmdr. Roy MacDonald, fishing five miles out to sea, sighted two red-haired mermaids "moving at about 12 knots. No human being could swim at such speed.... Before I could get the anchor up, they vanished." The mayor of the village of Peel told of seeing a red-haired mermaid on rocks off Peel Castle.

Groping for explanations

In the summer of 1978, Filipino fisherman Jacinto Fetalvero let slip the secret of his recent fishing success. One moonlit night he had met a mermaid with "amiable bluish eyes, reddish cheeks, and green scales on her tail." She helped him "secure a bountiful catch." A torrent of ridicule ensued, and Fetalvero thereafter refused to discuss the subject.

Though merbeings are still experienced, few witnesses are so naïve as Fetalvero about the certain reception to testimony to that effect. It is also true that belief in them has given rise to numerous hoaxes. In the mid–1820s, in a famous instance, the eccentric Robert S. Hawker "used to disguise himself as a mermaid," folklorist Horace Beck writes, "sit on a rock and sing in the moonlight—much to the awe of the villagers about." In the mid-nineteenth century Japanese fishermen supplemented their incomes by manufacturing mermaid corpses by attaching the top halves of dead monkeys to the bottom halves of fishes. P. T. Barnum and any number of sideshow hustlers since him have separated fools from their money by offering views of dead and living mermaids.

Probably few people today are even aware that their ancestors, or some of them anyway, believed they had actually *observed* merbeings. As we have seen, however, published accounts in respected newspapers, magazines, and journals insisted on the credibility of witnesses, who sometimes gave sworn testimony. In the words of folklorists Gwen Benwell and Arthur Waugh, respected authorities on the tradition:

> The witnesses in these stories made no attempt to reconcile the sea-creatures they had seen with the merman and mermaid of legend. Except on rare occasions the half-human, half-fish creatures they describe neither sing nor speak; they neither foretell the future nor bring about disaster. They seldom conform to the beautiful mermaid of legend. Indeed some descriptions are unpleasing.... All these accounts look to be sincere, straightforward narratives of what eye-witnesses saw, or believed they saw. The temptation to embroider—to bring the creature into line with the mermaid of legend—is resisted.

Other modern analysts of this testimony—scientists and folklorists mostly; anomalists and paranormalists tend to shy away from it for obvious reasons—take it seriously and agree that it poses questions that merit better than a brush-off. Among the proposed solutions have been sea cows, manatees, and dugongs, which as scientist Richard Carrington once put it "became 'transformed' into a mermaid by the expectant attention of the superstitious mariners who saw it." Science journalist Richard Ellis, who pays no heed to witnesses' contrary descriptions, deems the explanation so self-evidently true as to merit the linking of the words with a slash mark: "manatee/mermaid."

Such identifications suffer from two immediate problems:

(1) According to a sighting survey by Benwell and Waugh, nearly three-quarters reportedly occurred far from areas where sea cows, dugongs, and manatees are known to exist. (2) Moreover, though plausible in cases of long-distance sightings where perceptual errors may be expected to occur, these animals (the latter two, incidentally, found only in tropical climes) in hardly any way resemble the creatures described in the most interesting sightings, which characteristically claim not only a close view, but an extended one. As Benwell and Waugh remark, "It is asking a lot of a maritime race to believe that sailors, with the trained powers of observation which their own safety, and that of their ship, so often depend, could commit such a blunder" of monumental misperception.

That, however, is not quite reason to abandon such explanations in all cases. Consider this, in a 1927 *Illustrated London News* article, naturalist W. P. Pycraft remarked on a recent mermaid sighting:

> A journalist brought me a letter for my comment, written by a lady who, in passing quite recently down the Red Sea, had seen a "veritable mermaid." Hitherto, she averred, she had regarded such creatures as mere figments of the imagination, but now she no longer doubted, for had she not just seen one with her own eyes? It was some nine feet long, very much like a woman, but emphatically ugly. Its face was hideous; its hands looked as though they had been thrust into some fingerless glove; but it had no legs. The body terminated in a great round, flat tail, and its skin, which was bare, was dark-grey in color. But there it was, indubitable "mermaid"! The letter was written in all seriousness.

According to one popular speculation, witnesses to ostensible merbeings are really seeing manatees.

Pycraft rightly deduced that the woman had seen a dugong. From that he concluded, less convincingly, that it was now established that dugongs are the cause of mermaid sightings. Unfortunately, he failed to give any thought to this not-irrelevant consideration: that while the woman's identification of the animal was absurdly mistaken, her description of it was accurate, and she had not described a mermaid.

On the other hand, the people of New Ireland, an island province of Papua New Guinea, *did* describe merbeings. Called ri (and pronounced *ree*), these creatures were said to look like human beings down to their genitals; the legless lower trunk ended in a pair of lateral fins. Or so native informants told a visiting American anthropologist, Roy Wagner, in the late 1970s. The native witnesses claimed that the creatures reminded them of the mermaids on tuna-fish cans, though they did not regard them as intelligent beings. On one occasion Wagner himself saw a "long, dark body swimming at the surface horizontally." His companions identified it as a ri.

Though Wagner was positive these creatures were not dugongs, in fact, people who lived farther north on the island considered ri just another name for dugong. A February 1985 expedition by American cryptozoologists produced underwater photographs of a ri—an unambiguous dugong—and solved at least part of the puzzle. Expedition member Thomas R. Williams pondered the remaining mystery, for which he had no answer, of "how myths of merfolk can arise and persist in the face of the obvious reality of the dugong."

We have no way of knowing how widely the lessons from this episode can be applied, for the simple reason that in our time no one else has ever mounted a scientific investigation of merbeing sightings as they were occurring. Nearly all commentary on the matter focuses on reports from the distant past to the nineteenth century, and therefore theories can only be speculative.

Perhaps the most ingenious is that proposed by two *Nature* contributors who tied Norse merman reports to optical effects produced by a "moderate [atmospheric] inversion," showing how the resulting distortions on the ocean surface could make killer whales, walruses, and jutting rocks look much like what the sailors reported they saw. The authors respected the witnesses' testimony, including their assertion that storms followed merbeing appearances. As behavioral scientist David J. Hufford remarks of this study, "an improved understanding of naturally occurring atmospheric optical anomalies did result from a serious consideration of an apparently fabulous medieval belief"; furthermore, the scientists "were able to document with a high degree of confidence the role of accurate observations in the development of a medieval tradition, and the accurate correlation of these observations with impending storms, apparently achieved by properly performed inductive reasoning and empirical generalization."

This sort of explanation will not necessarily enable us to unravel the enigma of the European and New World sightings recounted earlier. If anything, cloudy matters only get mistier. If we assume that these sightings are not outright hoaxes—and few scholars of the subject believe that is all they are—we must also assume that the observers were wildly mistaken, that what they thought they saw was only vaguely related to what they really saw. Remember, some of these sightings are supposed to have been from a distance of no more than a few feet.

If misperception under these circumstances seems inconceivable, remember the ri. But don't remember *only* the ri; remember, too, the Norse mermen that, if they did not exist as the sailors thought they did, were described precisely enough for scholars centuries later to discern their cause.

In short, to the vital question of whether we ought to trust the reports, no answer leaps up to satisfy us with any certainty. Some observations are precise and credible. Others are startlingly at variance with demonstrable reality. Beyond this, the paucity of modern investigations frustrates further understanding. It forces those who take up the question to dump a mountain's worth of theory on a mole hill's worth of solid information.

Merbeings as unknowns

Michel Meurger, a French folklorist and student of the lore of fabulous water beasts, derides biological explanations of merbeing sightings as naïve and reductionist. He considers them "visionary experiences," by which he means vivid hallucinations that take their shape from images out of popular superstition. He has a point, but probably not the one intended. While merbeing "sightings" are almost certainly not of real biological creatures, the notion of hallucination as ordinarily understood looks labored when placed against the testimonies of multiple witnesses. If merbeings don't "exist," which is surely true, neither can encounters with them be contained with current knowledge.

Another problem is that the merbeing of experience and the merbeing of popular superstition are manifestly different entities. The latter, intelligent entities with supernatural powers, can speak like normal human beings and even shed their fishy bottoms to live on land and romance or wed dwellers on the land. As noted already, the merbeings of sightings neither speak nor communicate anything but animal-like sounds, if that. For that matter, they give no particular indication of possessing more than an animal's level of intelligence. Witness nearly always attach the pronoun "it" to the entity they believe they have observed.

So could they be animals of some unknown type? Addressing the issue only reluctantly, after dismissing it virtually out of hand in his earlier writings, the late Bernard Heuvelmans, the father of cryptozoology, stated in a 1986 paper, "Only a still-unrecorded species of recent Sirenia [dugongs, manatees, sea cows], or possibly—though much less likely—an unknown form of primate adapted to sea-life, could explain the abundance and persistence of merfolk reports in certain seas up to modern times." Benwell and Waugh come to essentially the same conclusion.

Even if not supernatural, such an animal would be extraordinary indeed. It is hard to believe any such thing exists, not only because *a priori* it seems beyond zoological reason, but also because no bodies have washed ashore and found their way into scientists' hands. (Reports of bodies are just that: reports.) These would not be, it should be stressed, creatures living in remote depths, from which remains would not surface, but animals that cavorted frequently in shallow offshore waters. If merbeings were real, flesh-and-blood citizens of the oceanic regions of consensus reality, we would have more than sightings to document them.

Which does not explain everything, of course. One could argue that merbeing reports have as much claim to our attention as those of other exotic, uncatalogued creatures haunting water and land even now, according to worldwide testimony. The latter do not make much sense, either. But someone else could retort that at least with these, there are living persons to interview, and sometimes a tantalizing fragment of what may be physical evidence—a footprint, a strand of hair, a blurry photograph—to take into account, not to mention to take to a laboratory.

Yet it is in the nature of such things that huge claims are nearly always married to small evidence. The evidence for merbeings, consisting (with the occasional exception) of the words of long-dead men and women, is minuscule, and it shrinks with each passing year. In the end it does not permit us—if, at any rate, we demand scrupulous intellectual honesty of ourselves, even in the face of the unthinkable—to laugh into oblivion the questions that remain. Neither, however, does it compel us to reinvent the world so that merbeings may comfortably occupy a place in it.

Further Reading:

"An Account of the Mermaid." *South-Carolina State Gazette and Columbia Advertiser* (November 8, 1828). Reprinted from *Welsh Magazine*.

Beck, Horace. *Folklore and the Sea*. Middletown, CT: Marine Historical Association/Wesleyan University Press, 1973.

Benwell, Gwen, and Arthur Waugh. *Sea Enchantress: The Tale of the Mermaid and Her Kin*. New York: Citadel Press, 1965.

Berman, Ruth. "Mermaids." In Malcolm South, ed. *Mythical and Fabulous Creatures: A Source Book and Research Guide*, 133–45. New York: Greenwood Press, 1987.

Blyth, Harry. "A Mermaid." *Notes and Queries* 5,3 (February 27, 1875): 168.

Bondeson, Jan. *The Feejee Mermaid and Other Essays in Natural and Unnatural History*. Ithaca, NY: Cornell University Press, 1999.

Cappick, Marie. "Three-Year Search for Man Who Saw Mermaids Ends on Porch of Key West Dwelling." *Key West Citizen*, Florida (July 24, 1930). Reprinted from the *Havana American*.

Carrington, Richard. *Mermaids and Mastodons: A Book of Natural and Unnatural History*. New York: Rinehart and Company, 1957.

Carthy, Martin, and Dave Swarbrick. "Mermaid." *Straws in the Wind*. Topic Records, 2006.

Chambers, Paul. "Fishy Tales: An Unnatural History of the British Mermaid." *Fortean Times* 254 (2009): 32–34, 36.

Christie, Peter. "Fortean Extracts from the *Gentleman's Magazine*." In Steve Moore, ed. *Fortean Studies, Volume 2*, 246–71. London: John Brown Publishing, 1995.

"Connecticut's Wild Animals." *McKean County Miner*, Pennsylvania (February 28, 1896).

Costello, Peter. *The Magic Zoo: The Natural History of Fabulous Animals*. New York: St. Martin's Press, 1979.

"A Dead Mermaid Found Near Lewes." *Chester Daily Times*, Pennsylvania (January 9, 1880).

"Did the Mermaid Exist?" *Shetland Times* (July 21, 1961).

"Douglas, Isle of Man." *British Press* (December 5, 1810).

Eberhart, George M. "Mermaid." In *Mysterious Creatures: A Guide to Cryptozoology*. Volume One: A-M, 329–33. Santa Barbara, CA: ABC-CLIO, 2002.

Ellis, Richard. *Monsters of the Sea*. New York: Alfred A. Knopf, 1994.

"English Isle Will Sponsor Mermaid Hunt." Associated Press dispatch. *Florence Morning News*, South Carolina (March 6, 1961).

Farish, Lucius, ed. *Omega*. Worcester, MA: Controversial Phenomena Bulletin, 1965.

"The First Seen in These Waters." *Canadian Statesman* (July 30, 1886).

Hall, Mark A. "A Primer on Mermaids." *Wonders* 6,2 (June 2000): 35–59.

"He Saw a Mermaid." *Hornellsville Weekly Tribune*, New York (November 16, 1894).

Heuvelmans, Bernard. "Annotated Checklist of Apparently Unknown Animals with Which Cryptozoology Is Concerned." *Cryptozoology* 5 (1986): 1–26.

Hufford, David J. *The Terror that Comes in the Night: An Experience-Centered Study of Supernatural Assault Traditions*. Philadelphia: University of Pennsylvania Press, 1982.

"'Human Fish' at Clear Lake Excites Natives and Visitors." *Waterloo Evening Courier and Reporter*, Iowa (June 30, 1914).

"An Irish Mermaid." *London Times* (September 1, 1824).

Lapowsky, Issie. "Mermaid Fever Sweeps Israel Beach Town of Krivat Yam As Many Report Sightings of Fabled Creature." *New York Daily News* (August 12, 2009).

Lehn, W. H., and I. Schroeder. "The Norse Merman as an Optical Phenomenon." *Nature* 289 (1981): 362–66.

"A Live Mermaid, and No Mistake." *Daily National Intelligencer* (November 9, 1838). Reprinted from the *New York American*.

McEwen, Graham J. *Sea Serpents, Sailors and Skeptics*. Boston: Routledge and Kegan Paul, 1978.

"May Have Been Mermaid." *Coshocton Morning Tribune*, Ohio (December 27, 1911).

"Mermaid Evidently Domestic." *Frederick News*, Maryland (November 16, 1922). Reprinted from the *Los Angeles Times*.

"A Mermaid on View." *Marion Daily Star*, Ohio (May 28, 1892).

"The Mermaid, Seen on the Coast of Caithness." *London Courier* (September 7, 1809).

Meurger, Michel, with Claude Gagnon. *Lake Monster Traditions: A Cross-Cultural Analysis*. London: Fortean Tomes, 1988.

"Now It's Merman!" *Lethbridge Herald*, Alberta (September 7, 1937).

Phillips, John Pavin. "A Story of a Mermaid." *Notes and Queries* 2,9 (May 12, 1860): 360–61.

Pycraft, W. P. "The World of Science: Mermaids." *Illustrated London News* (February 19, 1927): 294.

Rickard, R.J.M. "Strange Tales: Mermaids." *Fortean Times* 27 (Autumn 1978): 38–39.

Robertson, R. Macdonald. Jeremy Bruce-Watt, ed. *Selected Highland Folktales*. North Pomfret, VT: David and Charles, 1977.

Swift, Asa. "Mermaid." *American Journal of Science* 1,2 (1820): 178–79.

T.G.S. "Minor Notes: Mermaids in Scotland, 1688." *Notes and Queries* 2,149 (November 6, 1858): 371.

Wagner, Roy. "The *Ri*: Unidentified Aquatic Animals of New Ireland, Papua New Guinea." *Cryptozoology* 1 (1982): 33–39.

Waugh, Sir Arthur. "The Folklore of the Merfolk." *Folklore* 71 (June 1960): 73–84.

Williams, Thomas R. "Identification of the *Ri* through Further Fieldwork in New Ireland, Papua New Guinea." *Cryptozoology* 4 (1985): 61–68.

Woon, Basil. "French Coast Stirred over Mermaid Tale." *Indianapolis Star* (August 19, 1923).

Wright, A. R. "Correspondence: Mer-folk in 1814." *Folklore* 40,1 (March 1929): 87–90.

Wyman, Walker D. *Mythical Creatures of the U.S.A. and Canada*. River Falls: University of Wisconsin River Falls Press, 1978.

Moving Coffins

Barbados, an island located at the easternmost edge of the West Indies, is the site of a curious story that some writers have treated as one of the great mysteries of the nineteenth century. The enigmatic events in question, said to have taken place inside the Chase vault between 1812 and 1819 or 1820, involved the apparently inexplicable movement of coffins.

According to the first published account, Sir J. E. Alexander's *Transatlanic Sketches* (1833):

> Each time that the vault was opened the coffins were replaced in their proper situations, that is, three on the ground side by side, and the others laid on them. The vault was then regularly closed; the door (a massive stone which required six or seven men to move) was cemented by masons; and though the floor was of sand, there were no marks or footsteps or water.

> The last time the vault was opened was in 1819, Lord Combermere [governor of the colony] was then present, and the coffins were found confusedly thrown about the vault, some with their heads down and others up. What could have occasioned this phenomenon? In no other vault in the island has this ever occurred.

In its September 14, 1858, issue, the *New York Times*, citing the *Charleston Courier*, identified the individuals whose coffins had been affected:

> In 1807, the first coffin that was deposited in it was that of a Mr. GODDARD; in 1818, a Miss A. M. CHASE was placed in it; and in 1812, Miss D. CHASE. In the end of 1812, the vault was opened for the body of the Hon. T. CHASE; but the three first coffins were found in a confused state, having been apparently tossed from their places. Again was the vault opened to receive the body of an infant, and the four coffins, all of lead, and very heavy, were found much disturbed. In 1816 a Mr. BREWSTER'S body was placed in the vault, and again great disorder was apparent among the coffins. In 1819 Mr. CLARKE was placed in the vault, and, as before, the coffins were in confusion.

Over time, various versions of the story saw print. Even one of the alleged witnesses, the Rev. Thomas H. Orderson, the rector of Christ Church, gave conflicting accounts to inquirers. Other accounts were published in 1844 (Sir Robert Schomburgk's *History of Barbados*) and 1860 (Mrs. D. H. Cussons's *Death's Deeds*). In the December 1907 issue of *Folk-Lore,* the noted English folklorist Andrew Lang reviewed the affair, drawing not only on printed sources but on his brother-in-law Forster M. Alleyne's investigation in Barbados. Alleyne had examined vault records but found nothing to substantiate the story, and the island's newspapers of the period had nothing to say on the subject. He did, however, come upon an unpublished description by Nathan Lucas, who witnessed the final interment of the vault in April 1820. Alleyne's father, who was on the island in 1820, alluded to the coffin disturbances in correspondence that survives from that year.

Lang's interest in the affair was fueled by another intellectual fascination of his, psychical research. He noted a report of similar events in a Lutheran cemetery at Ahrensburg on the Isle of Oesel, in the Baltic Sea, said to have taken place in 1844. The evidence for its occurrence, he conceded, consisted in its entirety on an anecdote passed on to American diplomat Robert Dale Owen (who reported it in *Footfalls on the Boundary of Another World* [1872]); no written records were known to exist, and none have surfaced since.

A securely locked door protected the vault from unauthorized disturbance. In the first indication of something out of the ordinary, visitors heard strange underground sounds.

Owen's account credits as its primary—and sole—source "Mademoiselle de Guldenstubbé … who was residing in her father's house at the time and was cognizant of each minute particular…. They were confirmed to me, also, on the same occasion, by her brother, the present baron." It alleges that the events occurred in a vault located in a basement beneath a family chapel. A securely locked door protected the vault from unauthorized disturbance. In the first indication of something out of the ordinary, visitors heard strange underground sounds. Horses hitched in front of the chapel fell victim to unexplained terrors. One day in July the sounds grew so loud that passersby were alarmed and horses badly frightened. Once alerted, the owners rushed to the scene but could find no cause.

Soon afterwards, a member of the family (Buxhoewden) died and was prepared for burial. At the funeral, held in the chapel, mysterious rumblings and (some thought) groans emanated from the vault below. When the service was over, three or four bold men entered the vault where they found, "to their infinite surprise, that, of the numerous coffins which had been deposited, there in due order side by side, almost all had been displaced and lay in a confused pile," Owen wrote. "They sought in vain for any cause that might account for this. The doors were always kept carefully fastened, and the locks showed no signs of having been tampered with. The coffins were replaced in due order."

Subsequently, people reported seeing dark apparitional shapes hovering nearby. An official inquiry commenced, led by the Baron de Guldenstubbé (father of Owen's informant), who with two Buxhoewden family members visited the vault and found the coffins again in disorder. Later, the investigating committee, consisting of the baron, the local bishop, and other prominent citizens, reentered the vault, to find the coffins again inexplicably scattered. Only three remained in place, two holding children, the third a grandmother known for her saintly conduct in life. Eventually, there being no other evidence of entry, the theory emerged that perhaps vandals or individuals seeking vengeance against the family had dug a tunnel under the vault. When workmen were hired to dig, they uncovered nothing suspicious. Commission members opened coffins to determine whether valuables had been stolen from the corpses; none had.

Finally, the doors were doubly sealed and wood dust scattered about the chapel, stairs, and vault so as to catch footprints of potential intruders. For three days guards from the local garrison watched the chapel to be sure no one unauthorized entered it. At the end of that period, commission members descended on the scene. Until they unlocked the vault, nothing seemed out of the ordinary. Then:

> Not only was every coffin, with the same three exceptions as before, displaced, and the whole scattered in confusion over the place, but many of them, weighty as they were, had been set on end, so that the head of the corpse was downward. Nor was even this all. The lid of one coffin had been partially forced open, and there projected the shriveled right arm of the corpse it contained, showing beyond the elbow; the lower arm being turned up toward the ceiling of the vault!…. They approached … the coffin from one side of which the arm projected; and … they recognized it as that in which had been placed the remains of a member of the Buxhoewden family who had committed suicide.

Or so goes the story. Lang thought it was at least possible that Owen's informants "plagiarized" the Barbados tale, adding a few flourishes of their own.

Another moving-coffins story, however, could not have been based on the Barbados incident because it saw print before the supposed West Indian events became known. *European Magazine*, for September 1815, related the case of "The Curious Vault at Stanton in Suffolk," in which coffins were "displaced" several times under mysterious circumstances. Nathan Lucas, one of the alleged witnesses to the final (1820) interment at the Chase Vault, mentions this English case, even quoting the article, in his privately written 1824 account.

A final tale is told by F. A. Paley in *Notes and Queries*, November 9, 1867, of an "instance which occurred within my own knowledge and recollection (some twenty years ago) in the parish of Gretford, near Stamford, a small village, of which my father was the rector. Twice, if not thrice, the coffins in a vault were found on reopening it to have been disarranged." He quotes a letter written by an unnamed woman and dated the previous October 15. The woman attributed the effect to flooding, a hypothesis with which Paley apparently concurred.

A hoax charge and a conspiracy theory

These spottily documented nineteenth-century incidents have no known twentieth-century equivalents, but they have attracted the attentions of such

Tales of coffins that have moved during the night, apparently of their own volition, were told in the nineteenth century but have not been related since then.

thoughtful latter-day writers as Lang, Rupert T. Gould, and Joe Nickell, who are responsible for the most thorough modern examinations.

Of these writers, only Nickell comes to a firm conclusion, one that is at once skeptical and conspiratorial. He focuses on the Barbados episode, the only one for which much (ostensible) information is available, arguing it is loaded with symbols and phrases that Freemasons would recognize. Nickell, a lifelong debunker of unorthodox claims such as those with which this book concerns itself, had earlier investigated a Masonic hoax involving a tale of buried treasure. He contends that the Barbados story was fashioned around the Masonic allegory of a "secret vault" that, according to a Masonic text, was:

> … in the ancient mysteries, symbolic of death, where alone Divine Truth is to be found…. We significantly speak of the place of initiation as "the secret vault, where reign silence, secrecy and darkness." It is in this sense of an entrance through the grave into eternal life, that the Select Master is to view the recondite but beautiful symbolism of the secret vault. Like every other myth and allegory of Masonry, the historical relation may be true or it may be false; it may be founded on fact or the invention of imagination; the lesson is still there, and the symbolism teaches it exclusive of the history.

Along with other suggestive evidence, Nickell quotes these words from Lucas: "I examined the walls, the arch and every part of the vault and found every part old and similar; and a mason in my presence struck every part of the bottom with his hammer and all was solid." Nickell remarks:

> In the Royal Arch degree of Masonry—to which the "arch" above may have been in cryptic reference (just as the "vault" suggests the "secret vault" which, in Masonry, is said to have been "curiously arched")—there is a reference to the "sound of a hammer." According to Macoy's *Illustrated History and Cyclopedia of Freemasonry*, "The blow of the Master's hammer commands industry, silence, or the close of labour, and every brother respects or honors its sound."

Nickell goes on to quote from the Royal Arch degree ("We have examined the secret vault") and notes that the striking of stone—to determine its soundness—"is the means by which the secret vault is sought for and finally located!" Of course, Nickell adds, Lucas's use of the word "mason" is also interesting.

Through his investigation Nickell (conducted with associate John F. Fischer) learned that the men who supposedly participated in the events were Freemasons—as was Robert Dale Owen, chronicler of the alleged episode at Oesel. He also speculates that prominent French Freemasons knew of the hoax. Another Freemason who may have participated in the fabrication, Nickell proposes, was Sir Arthur Conan Doyle. While discussing the Barbados coffins in a December 1919 article in *The Strand*, Doyle used a word ("effluvia") whose significance only Masons would recognize. The word is "well known to Masons since it appears in the Master Mason degree," according to Nickell; "not only that, but it does so specifically in reference to the grave!" That seems a stretch. Though credulous and often prey to fraudulent spiritualist mediums, Doyle himself has no reputation as a hoaxer.

Still, though based entirely on circumstantial evidence (aided and abetted by exclamation points), Nickell's speculations are certainly ingenious, if unsettlingly akin to something like a conspiracy theory, with all the baggage conspiracy theories bring to any discussion. His ideas are also unprovable, and they beg the question of what the point of perpetrating such arcane hoaxes would have been. In any case, because concrete evidence for the claims is thin to nonexistent, skeptical inferences are inescapable.

Moving coffins of another kind

A very strange story of floating coffins (a phrase more often used, at least in the past, to denote disease-ridden ships) was published in a small-town Texas newspaper, the *Batesville Advocate*, and was reprinted in other papers, including New York's *Dunkirk Evening Observer* on March 22, 1884:

> Last week Mrs. Reneau, who with her husband and family lived on Coryell Creek, some five miles from Turnersville, died rather suddenly. At the time of her death several neighbors were present, together with the attending physicians, Dr. J. D. Calaway, of Turnersville, and Dr. Toland, of Jones-

boro. When the spirit had parted from the body and wended its way to the home above, a sight was seen which, to the faithful ones who were watching by the couch, was as startling as it was real. The spectacle presented itself just above the house and was frightful in the extreme. Six coffins of different sizes were seen to come and hover immediately above the house. The night was dark, and ordinary objects at any distance were invisible, but the coffins were as plainly seen as they would have been in broad daylight. When the gaunt and ghastly coffins had been visible for some time they disappeared, and as they seemed to glide gently upward[,] sounds of the sweetest and most melodious music seemed to accompany the dark omens in the journey toward the skies. We did not see any of the parties who saw the strange phenomenon, but no doubt can be entertained of their veracity, or the facts regarding the strange sight as herein stated. The phenomenon was indeed a curious one and we do not remember to have ever chronicled such a rare occurrence before.

Floating coffins appear occasionally, albeit infrequently, in folk belief and testimony. In a private communication the folklorist Thomas E. Bullard draws attention to an account from rural Kentucky, from the early decades of the twentieth century. William Lynwood Montell's *Ghosts along the Cumberland* (1987) quotes the words of a woman who told of seeing a floating coffin which came to rest on her front porch, then rose into the air, circled nearby houses, and passed over a field. A few days later, her husband died.

Further Reading:

Gould, Rupert T. *Oddities: A Book of Unexplained Facts*. New Hyde Park, NY: University Books, 1965.

Lang, Andrew. "'Death's Deeds': A Bi-Location Story." *Folk-Lore* 18,4 (December 1907): 376–90.

Macoy, Robert. *Illustrated History and Cyclopedia of Freemasonry*. New York: Macoy Publishing, 1908.

Montell, William Lynwood. *Ghosts along the Cumberland: Deathlore in the Kentucky Foothills*. Knoxville: University of Tennessee Press, 1987.

Nickell, Joe, with John F. Fischer. *Secrets of the Supernatural: Investigating the World's Occult Mysteries*. Buffalo, NY: Prometheus Books, 1988.

Ouitanon, Frederick J. "The Ahrensburg Mystery." *Fate* 4,4 (August 1950): 33–36.

Owen, Robert Dale. *Footfalls on the Boundary of another World*. Philadelphia, PA: J. B. Lippincott & Co., 1872.

Paley, F. A. "Disturbance of Coffins in Vaults." *Notes and Queries* 3rd Series 12 (November 9, 1867): 371.

Onza

The onza was Mexico's most famous mystery feline, reported for centuries in the remote Sierra Madre Occidental Mountain range in the northwestern part of the country.

To the Aztecs the onza (or, as they called it, *cuitlamiztli*) was an animal distinct from the other two large cats, the puma and the jaguar, with which they shared an environment. After the Spanish conquerors arrived, they called on the emperor Montezuma, who showed them his great zoo. In it, Bernal Diaz del Castillo observed, were "tigers [jaguars] and lions [pumas] of two kinds, one of which resembled the wolf."

The later Spanish settlers of northwestern Mexico noted the presence in the wild of a wolflike cat—with long ears, a long, narrow body, and long, thin legs—and gave it the name *onza*, from the Latin *uncial*, referring to the cheetah of Asia and Africa. They also remarked on its ferocity. "It is not as timid as the [puma]," Father Ignaz Pfefferkorn, a Jesuit missionary stationed in Sonora, wrote in 1757, "and he who ventures to attack it must be well on his guard." According to Father Johann Jakob Baegert, who worked with the Guaricura Indians in Baja California in the mid-eighteenth century, "One onza dared to invade my neighbor's mission while I was visiting, and attacked a 14-year-old boy in broad daylight and practically in full view of all the people; and a few years ago another killed the strongest and most respected soldier" in the area.

Yet outside its range the onza was virtually unknown. The occasional published references to it made no impression, and zoologists continued to assume that only pumas and jaguars lived there. No serious scientific field expeditions into the rugged terrain, inaccessible in many places even to horses, were ever mounted to investigate the question.

Then, in the 1930s, two experienced mountain hunting guides, Dale and Clell Lee, were working in the mountains of Sonora when they heard for the first time of the onza. In time they moved their operation 500 miles to the south, to Sinaloa, where they took Indiana banker Joseph H. Shirk to hunt jaguars on the wildlife-rich La Silla Mountain. There they treed and killed a strange cat which they immediately concluded was something other than a puma. In fact, it looked exactly like the onzas that locals said lived in the region. After measuring and photographing it, they butchered the animal. Shirk kept the skull and skin. Their present whereabouts are unknown.

Certain they had found something of importance, the Lees described the animals to American zoologists. They were stunned when both the scientists and the newspapers scoffed at their story. Conservative and cautious by nature, unused to having their word questioned, the brothers withdrew and ceased discussing the experience—until the 1950s, when an Arizona man, Robert Marshall, befriended Dale Lee and sympathetically recorded his testimony. Marshall even went down to Mexico to conduct further investigations, the results of which he recounted in a 1961 book, *The Onza*, which, aside from a single (unfavorable) review in a scientific journal, attracted no attention whatsoever.

The onza in the age of cryptozoology

In 1982, at a meeting at the Smithsonian Institution in Washington, D.C., the International Society of Cryptozoology (ISC) came into being (only to cease operation in 1996), and for the first time biological scientists interested in unknown, unrecognized, or obscure animals had a formal structure through which research could be conducted. Cryptozoologists were among the few nonresidents of northwestern Mexico to have heard of the onza.

The ISC Secretary, J. Richard Greenwell, lived in Tucson where, so he would learn, Robert Marshall also resided. So, as it happened, did Dale Lee. Marshall possessed an onza skull, and he gave Greenwell a cast of its upper tooth row. Greenwell subsequently showed it to a German mammalogist, Helmut Hemmer, who had proposed that onzas were relics of a prehistoric species of North American cheetah (*Acinonyx trumani*). Eventually, comparison of skulls eliminated that identification from further consideration, but the very fact that the discussion had happened at all indicated that the onza was finally about to get its due.

While engaged in unsuccessful pursuit of the long-missing Shirk skull, Greenwell and Marshall coordinated their efforts with two interested mammalogists, Troy Best and E. Lendell Cockrum, respectively of the Universities of New Mexico and Arizona. Through Cockrum they met Sinaloa rancher Ricardo Urquijo, Jr., who had the intact skull of an onza killed by another rancher, Jesus Vega, in the same area as the onzas associated with the other two skulls. Meanwhile, Best, an authority on puma skulls, located another onza skull in the Academy of Natural Sciences in Philadelphia.

At 10:30 on the evening of January 1, 1986, two deer hunters in the San Ignacio District of Sinaloa shot and killed a large cat. It clearly was not a jaguar, and they had no idea what it was. Recalling that a few months earlier a couple of gringos (Greenwell and Marshall) had talked with a rancher friend about their interest in an unusual animal, they alerted Manuel Vega, who recognized the creature as an onza as soon as he saw it. Vega's father, in fact, had once shot an onza.

To the Spanish colonizers of the Americas, the onza was a large, elusive native cat.

Through the help of the wealthy Urquijo family (one of whose members had supplied Cockrum with the Vega skull), the body was placed in a freezer at a commercial fishery company in Mazatlan, and Greenwell was notified. In due course, Greenwell and Best photographed and dissected the creature in that city, at the Regional Diagnostic Laboratory of Animal Pathology, an agency of Mexico's Ministry of Agriculture. Greenwell wrote:

> Upon inspection, the cat, a female, appeared to be as described by the native people. It had a remarkable gracile body, with long, slender legs and a long tail. The ears also seemed very long for a puma (about 100 mm.) and small horizontal stripes were found on the inside of its forelimbs, which, as far as has been determined to date, are not found in pumas. Well-developed mammae were observed, and its age was determined to be at least 4 years. It weighed about 27 kg. (in life, prior to freezing, it probably weighed a little more), compared to a range of from 36 to 60 kg. in adult female pumas. Its total length, at 186 cm., fell within the normal range of female pumas of from 150 to 233 cm. The tail, however, was 73 cm. in length, very long for a female puma of comparable size; the range in female pumas is from 53 cm. to 81 cm.

Tissue samples and organs were taken to the United States for further analysis. Unfortunately, in the intervening years Greenwell and Best would not pursue the matter with any great vigor, pleading lack of time and commitment to other projects. A preliminary comparison of tissue samples of pumas and the onza, conducted at Texas Tech University, indicated great similarities and no significant differences, but the analysts prepared no technical report. In any case, no conclusions could be drawn from a single test of this sort, since animals of different species are often quite close genetically.

In 1998, after further analysis, the long-awaited test results were released, solving the onza mystery. The tests revealed no "significant difference between the 1986 specimen and a typical *Felis concolor*." In other words, the onza, while real enough, is simply a local variant of the puma.

Further Reading:

Carmony, Neil. *Onza! The Hunt for a Legendary Cat*. Silver City, NM: High-Lonesome Books, 1995.

Dratch, Peter A., et al. "Molecular Genetic Identification of a Mexican Onza Specimen as a Puma (*Puma Concolor*)." *Cryptozoology* 12 (1996): 42–49.

"ICSEB III Cryptozoology Symposium." *The ISC Newsletter* 4,3 (autumn 1985): 7–8.

Marshall, Robert E. *The Onza: The Story of the Search for the Mysterious Cat of the Mexican Highlands*. New York: Exposition Press, 1961.

"Onza Identity Still Unresolved." *The ISC Newsletter* 7,4 (winter 1988): 5–6.

"Onza Specimen Obtained—Identity Being Studied." *The ISC Newsletter* 5,1 (spring 1986): 1–6.

"Two New Onza Skulls Found." *The ISC Newsletter* 4,4 (winter 1984): 6–7.

Pwdre Ser

For centuries the phenomenon of *pwdre ser* (a Welsh phrase meaning "star rot")—also known as star jelly—was known to everyone, from peasants in the field to scientists in the universities, and it figured in everything from folklore to academic discourse. Today, after long neglect, it is receiving a degree of attention from naturalists and meteorite specialists, more willing than their counterparts of earlier generations to acknowledge that *pwdre ser* comprises a genuine puzzle.

In 1541 the poet Sir John Suckling wrote:

As he whose quick eye doth trace
A false star shot to a mark't place
Do's run apace
And, thinking it to catch,
A jelly up do snatch.

Or in John Dryden's words in 1679:

When I had taken up what I supposed a fallen star
I found I had been cozened with a jelly.

What Sucking and Dryden had in mind were the sorts of stories that follow.

On October 21, 1638, during a fierce thunderstorm, lightning hit and destroyed a church in Dartmoor, England. A foul odor emanated from the destroyed tower. When he went to investigate its source, a man found, according to a contemporary account, "a round patch as broad as a bushel, which looked thick, slimy, and black, to which he put his hand, and found it soft, and bringing some from the wall, came down and showed that strange compound. It was like a slimy powder, tempered with water ... odious beyond expression."

From a paper on meteors published in the *American Journal of Science* (1829):

A Mr. John Treat, a respectable farmer, and a man of veracity, stated to us, that he was with the army of Gen. Washington, in the campaign against Gen. Howe, after his landing at the Head of Elk. On the night [September 10, 1777] previous to the battle of Brandywine, as he was standing centinel [sentinel], a shooting star fell within a few yards of him. He instantly went to the spot, and found a gelatinous mass, which, if we recollect right, was still sparkling, and he had kept his eye on it from its fall. A very respectable lady mentioned, that as she was walking in the evening with one or two others, a similar meteor fell near them, and she pointed out the very place where it struck.

At 4 P.M. on May 16, 1808, on a warm, cloudless day, the sun dimmed for an unknown reason, and as soon as that happened, a correspondent wrote in *Transactions of the Swedish Academy of Sciences* (1808), "There appeared on the western horizon, from where the wind blew, to arise gradually, and in quick succession, a great number of balls, or spherical bodies, to the naked eye of a size of the crown of a hat, and of a dark brown color." As these curious objects approached the sun, they grew darker until they became "entirely black." For a brief period they ceased their flight and hovered in the air. When they resumed their motion, they picked up speed, traveling in a nearly straight line until they disappeared in the eastern horizon. The correspondent recorded:

> During this course, some disappeared, others fell down.... The phenomenon lasted uninterruptedly, upwards of two hours, during which time millions of similar bodies continually rose in the west, one after the other irregularly, and continued their career in exactly the same manner. No report, noise, nor any whistling or buzzing in the air was perceived. As these balls slackened their course on passing by the Sun, several were linked together, three, six, or eight of them in a line, joined like a chain shot by a thin and straight bar; but on continuing again a more rapid course, they separated, and each having a tail after it, apparently of three of three or four fathoms length, wider at its base where it adhered to the ball, and gradually decreasing, till it terminated in a fine point. During the course, these tails, which had been the same black color as the balls, disappeared by degrees.

This photograph of alleged pwdr ser shows the slimy, jelly-like substance next to a coin. Several theories have been put forward as to what it is, ranging from a type of slime mold to jelly from a deposit of frog eggs to an alien life form brought to Earth from meteors. (Source: geograph.org.uk).

Some of the balls fell to earth not far from an observer, who happened to be an official of the Swedish Academy, K. G. Wettermark. Wettermark noticed that as the objects came downward, they lost their dark color, then vanished from view briefly, only to become visible again but now with changing colors, "in this particular exactly resembling those air-bubbles which children use to produce from soapsuds by means of a reed. When the spot, where such a ball had fallen, was immediately after examined, nothing was to be seen, but a scarcely perceptible film or pellicle, as thin and fine as a cobweb, which was still changing colors, but soon entirely dried up and vanished."

(Continued on page 342)

White River Monster

From about 1815 through the early 1970s, residents of Newport in northeastern Arkansas occasionally reported seeing a "monster" in the White River, which flows through the town. Sightings were not continuous but tended to occur in spates. In July 1937, for example, at least half a dozen local people either saw the strange disturbances in the water or caught a glimpse of the cause.

One witness was Bramblett Bateman, a plantation owner, who in an affidavit swore he had seen "something appear on the surface of the water" on or around July 1. "From the best I could tell, from the distance [375 feet], it would be 12 feet long and four or five feet wide. I did not see either head nor [sic] tail, but it slowly rose to the surface and stayed in this position for some five minutes. It did not move up or down the river at this particular time, but afterward on different occasions I have seen it move up and down the river, but I have never, at any time, been able to determine the full length or size of said monster."

Jackson County Deputy Sheriff Z. B. Reid was with Bateman when the creature appeared later that July. They saw, Reid testified, "a lot of foam and bubbles coming up in a circle about 30 feet in diameter some 300 feet from where we were standing. It did not come up there but appeared about 300 feet upstream. It looked like a large sturgeon or cat fish. It went down in about two minutes."

Within a couple of weeks a plan had been laid to capture the creature at its lair, believed to be in the mile-long, sixty-foot eddy of the river, six miles south of Newport. Organized by state toll-bridge inspector W. E. Penix, the plan was to employ small boats to help drop a large net into the water. Penix acknowledged that the scheme could take days to fulfill, and the creature—estimated to be anywhere from 600 to 1,500 pounds—could be a struggle to subdue. Nothing came of any of this, however.

The next known sightings occurred in June and July 1971. One witness reported seeing a "creature the size of a boxcar thrashing ... the length of three or four pickup trucks" and two yards across. "It looked as if the thing was peeling all over, but it was a smooth type of skin or flesh," he said. Other sighters, one of whom took a blurry photograph of a large surfacing form on June 28, described (as had witnesses in previous decades) a roar associated with the creature's appearance, a combination of a cow's moo and a horse's neigh. On those rare occasions its face was seen, if only briefly, it was said to have a protruding "bone" on its forehead.

In the most frightening encounter, Ollie Ritcherson and Joey Dupree were cruising near Towhead Island looking for the monster when their boat collided with something. The boat rose into the air on the back of some huge animal that they were not able to see clearly. The two had

Cryptozoologist Roy P. Mackal speculated that the large creature observed in Arkansas in 1973 was actually some type of elephant seal. If true, how did this large sea mammal find its way so far from its native territory on the Pacific shoreline?

come to the site because two weeks earlier huge tracks leading to and from the river had been found on the island. Each of the three-toed tracks was fourteen inches long and eight inches wide, with a large pad and another toe with a spur extending at an angle. There was evidence, in the form of bent trees and crushed vegetation, that a large animal had walked on the island and even lain down at one point.

In February 16, 1973, in a tongue-in-cheek exercise the Arkansas senate passed

a resolution, sponsored by Sen. Robert Harvey, honoring the River near Newport as the "White River Monster Sanctuary and Refuge." It went on to render it "unlawful to molest, kill, trample or harm the White River Monster while in its native retreat."

The "monster," sightings of which seem to have ceased, was likely a conventional beast in an out-of-place location. According to biologist and cryptozoologist Roy P. Mackal, "The White River case is a clear-cut instance of a known aquatic ani-

(Continued from previous page)

mal outside its habitat or range and therefore unidentified by the observers unfamiliar with the type. The animal in question clearly was a large male elephant seal, either *Mirounga leonia* (southern species) or *Mirounga angustirostris* (northern species)." Mackal suggests that the creature wandered up through the mouth of the Mississippi River to the White River, which branches off from the Mississippi in east-central Arkansas.

A more startling hypothesis was suggested by another maverick biologist,

Ivan T. Sanderson, who labeled it "a truly gigantic penguin."

Further Reading:

"Arkansas Has a Problem." *Pursuit* 4 (October 1971): 89–95.

Mackal, Roy P. *Searching for Hidden Animals: An Inquiry into Zoological Mysteries.* Garden City, NY: Doubleday and Company, 1980.

"The Monster Has a Home." *Northwestern Arkansas Times* [Fayetteville] (February 16, 1973).

"Rope Net Devised to Catch Monster." *Hope* [Arkansas] *Star* (July 3, 1937).

(Continued from page 339)

In 1819 the *American Journal of Science* reported an extraordinary incident that had taken place on August 13 of that year. According to Prof. Rufus Graves, between 8 and 9 P.M. a fireball "of a brilliant white light resembling burnished silver" descended slowly from the sky and onto the front yard of an Amherst, Massachusetts, man, Erastus Dewey. Two women had seen its light reflected on the wall just before it settled on the ground. In the morning, twenty feet from his front door, Dewey found, according to Graves, who soon examined the material, a

> circular form, resembling a sauce or salad dish bottom upwards, about eight inches in diameter and one in thickness, of a bright buff color, with a fine nap upon it similar to that on milled cloth.... On removing the villous coat, a buff color pulpy substance of the consistence of good soft soap, of an offensive, suffocating smell, appeared; and on a near approach to it, or when immediately over it, the smell became almost insupportable, producing nausea and dizziness. A few minutes exposure to the atmosphere changed the buff into a livid color resembling venous blood. It was observed to attract moisture very rapidly from the air. A half-pint tumbler was nearly half filled with the substance. It soon began to liquefy and form a mucilaginous substance of the consistence, color, and feeling of starch when prepared for domestic use.

Within two or three days the substance had vanished from the tumbler. All that remained was a dark-colored residue on the sides and bottom of the glass. When this material was rubbed between the fingers, it became a fine, odorless ash. (In 1712, when the Rev. John Morton of Emmanuel College burned some *pwdre ser,* he noted that "there was left a film like isinglass, and something like the skins and vessels of animal bodies.")

During the famous mass meteor shower of August 13, 1833, residents of Rahway, New Jersey, found lumps of jelly on the ground. At Loweville, New York, on November 11, 1846, an alleged meteor which "appeared larger than the sun" and remained "in sight nearly five minutes" fell into a field near the village." According to a contemporary issue of *Scientific American,* "a large company of the citizens immediately repaired to the spot and found a body of fetid jelly, four feet in diameter."

> **W**here the presumed meteorite had come down, however, there was now a gray, gelatinous mass, which shook when they poked it with a stick.

Late on the evening of October 8, 1844, two men walking in a plowed field near Coblentz, Germany, were startled to observe the fall of a luminous object that crashed to earth not twenty yards from them. Because it was too dark to investigate, they marked the spot and returned early the next morning. Where the presumed meteorite had come down, however, there was now a gray, gelatinous mass, which shook when they poked it with a stick. They did not try to preserve it, according to the *Reports of the British Association.*

This report appeared in the *Milwaukee Daily Sentinel* (October 13, 1864) and other newspapers around the country:

> Another meteor has fallen at Hubbardstown, Mass. It was first discovered on the 9th [of September] and on examination proved to be a mass as large as a hogshead, of a gelatinous, light colored, semi-transparent substance. A specimen was presented to the Natural History Society of Worcester, Monday evening [October 10], and although tightly corked in a bottle, it had diminished considerably in bulk, and was partially dissolved. It was of a light straw color and had a strong odor of sulphuretted hydrogen, with sulphurous taste.

The rise of skepticism

By the late decades of the nineteenth century, most scientists discounted such reports, in part because new understanding of the nature of meteors and meteorites seemed to eliminate any possibility that they could contain, or be, organic matter. Moreover, some botanists were certain that the material was nostoc, a blue-green algae, or—if not that—perhaps bird vomit. Edward Hitchcock, an Amherst College chemistry professor, was convinced, for example, that he recognized the Amherst material as a "species of gelatinous fungus, which I had sometimes met with on rotten wood in damp places, during dog days." He declared that it was an "entire mistake" that had caused observers to connect it with the falling object, though his colleague Prof. Graves adamantly insisted that there could be "no reasonable doubt that the substance found was the residuum of the meteoritic body."

One can hardly blame scientists for being reluctant to embrace so incredible a phenomenon as *pwdre ser*, which makes no sense in terms of anything we know about meteoritics—unless, of course, this phenomenon is wholly separate from meteorites and should not be classed with them at all. The Swedish case above may indicate as much.

Modern cases

Reports of falls of star jelly are recorded from time to time. One much-publicized case took place in August 1979 in Frisco, Texas, a Dallas suburb. On the night of August 10, a bright light was seen to descend in the neighborhood where Martin and Sybil Christian lived. The next morning Mrs. Christian found three purple blood blobs in her front lawn. One of the blobs dissolved; the other two were frozen and sent for analysis. The result was an "identification" as industrial material from a nearby battery-processing plant. In fact, the factory denied any responsibility. Furthermore, chemical analysis showed significant differences between the two substances, and they did not even look alike to the naked eye.

Because even eyewitnesses can't always tell precisely where a meteorite has fallen, it is not easy to establish a link between a fireball observed in the evening and jelly discovered the next morning. In a case from Kempton, Tasmania, on the morning of November 3, 1996, Marlene Smith awoke to find "queer stuff, white/clear jelly oodles of it," on the concrete in front of her house. "I've lived here for 56 years," she said, "and I've never seen anything like it. We could have got a bucket of it." The previous night, significantly or otherwise, had seen a rainstorm preceded by the fall of a yellowish fireball that Barry Smith, Marlene's husband, observed. A quick analysis in a laboratory revealed that the material contained unspecific "micro-organisms," though it was not clear (as noted in a later case) if the organisms had attached themselves to the jelly in the wake of the latter's appearance.

After a 2009 incident in Scotland, experts at Edinburgh's Royal Botanic Gardens examined samples without being able to explain what it was. Neither plant nor animal, it was devoid of DNA, thus eliminating such long-favored "explanations" as frog spawn, avian stomach disorder, stag semen, and algae. Television journalist Euan McIlwraith, responsible for bringing the substance to several laboratories at the behest of the National Geographic Society, remarked, "It's a case of Nature 1, Science 0 at the moment."

Further Reading:

Brandes, Counsellor Dr. "Examination of a Substance Called Shooting Star, Which Was Found in a Wet Meadow." *American Journal of Science* 16 (1829): 20–27.

Burke, John G. *Cosmic Debris: Meteorites in History.* Berkeley: University of California Press, 1986.

Corliss, William R., ed. *Handbook of Unusual Natural Phenomena.* Glen Arm, MD: Sourcebook Project, 1977.

————, ed. *Tornados, Dark Days, Anomalous Precipitation, and Related Weather Phenomena*. Glen Arm, MD: Sourcebook Project, 1983.

"Queer Jelly Found after UFO Sightings." *Fortean Times* 95 (1997): 19.

Reid, Melanie. "Nature 1, Science 0 as Finest Minds Fail to Explain Star Jelly." *Times of London* (September 18, 2009).

Schultz, Ted. "Blobs from Space?" *Fate* 34,12 (December 1981): 85–90, 92.

Stuart's Monsters

There may be no stranger book in the literature of flying saucers than John Stuart's *UFO Warning*—strange not only because it is implausible, even ridiculous, but because its author appeared to believe every unbelievable word of it.

It was published in 1963 as a small, amateurishly produced, large-sized paperback under the Saucerian Books imprint. Saucerian, which specialized in fringe literature (such as *From Outer Space to You* [1959], in which New Jersey sign-painter Howard Menger reported his many meetings with Venusians), was a one-man operation run by a colorful promoter named Gray Barker, of Clarksburg, West Virginia. Interested in UFOs since the early 1950s, Barker had been chief investigator for the International Flying Saucer Bureau before its director, Albert K. Bender, closed the organization in the fall of 1953. Bender's claim that mysterious agents had threatened him into silence gave rise to the legend of the men in black, and it was the subject of Barker's paranoia-drenched best-seller, *They Knew Too Much about Flying Saucers* (1956).

Part of one chapter of *They Knew* concerns two Hamilton, New Zealand, UFO enthusiasts, John Stuart and Doreen Wilkinson, who together comprised an "organization" called Flying Saucer Investigators. Barker quotes from letters in which Stuart relates a few personal experiences reminiscent of those traditionally associated with poltergeists. In the final chapter, Stuart tells Barker that subsequently someone had called on him and that, as a result of that visit, Stuart is leaving ufology. "I can't, at the moment, tell you any more," he says.

Stuart kept his silence until 1962, when he produced a manuscript titled *The Kiwi under UFO Attack*. Barker published an edited version as *UFO Warning* the following year. In his introduction Barker, ordinarily not at a loss for words, confessed, "I cannot completely understand this volume, and I doubt if many others can either."

The story begins on a peculiar note, albeit not a paranormal one. The married Stuart writes that every evening, often into the early hours of dawn, he and Doreen Wilkinson, described as young, single, and attractive, met to conduct "research" together. Stuart complains bitterly about what the "evil minds" of the neighborhood made of these, uh, investigations.

Beyond this the story gets progressively harder to swallow, starting with Stuart's assertion that his and Wilkinson's relationship was an innocent one. (In fact, as private correspondence that became available after Stuart's death makes clear, they were—as any adult reader of the book will have assumed all along—lovers.) Soon, however, weird things happen, most dramatically the appearance of a ghostly spaceman who beams a telepathic warning that Wilkinson will be in danger if the two do not stop their research.

Soon afterwards John sees a UFO from his front lawn, and the next evening he and Doreen hear whispering sounds and breathing, with no discernible source. A few nights later Doreen (whom Barker gave the pseudonym "Barbara Turner" in the book, though she had been correctly identified in *They Knew*) goes out to buy cigarettes. John grows anxious at her prolonged absence. Then, he writes,

House painter and flying-saucer contactee Howard Menger, with his wife, Marla.

> the front door flew open, and a figure rushed into my arms. [Doreen] said in a voice filled with fear, "There's something out there!"

> Quickly releasing her, I hurried outside, stopping on the top step as a terrible stench struck me. I almost fainted in terror. It was like burnt plastic and sulphur. I stood there for a moment, and then walked down to the front gate, neither seeing nor hearing anything. I searched the rear of the grounds, finding nothing, and had just started to return to the door when I heard distinct sounds behind me. I stopped and shone my torch [flashlight]. There was nothing there. I walked on. The sounds followed. I stopped and the sound stopped. I moved. It moved. Again I stopped, was amazed and startled when "it" kept on! The peculiar shuffling, scraping sound went past me, and I felt something solid brush against my shoulder! This was the first indication I'd had that "they" were as solid as I!

Walking around the house, John and Doreen are horrified to see a grotesque eight-foot-tall creature about thirty feet from them.

> The monster's head was large and bulbous. No neck. A huge and ungainly body supported on ridiculously short legs. It had webbed feet. The arms were thin and not unlike stalks of bamboo. It had no hands, the long fingers jutting from the arms like stalks. Its eyes were about four inches across, red in color. There was no nose, just two holes, and the mouth was simply a straight slash across its appallingly lecherous face. The whole was a green lime in color, and it was possible to see red veins running through its ungainly form. The monster was definitely male.

The creature moves toward them, its "filthy eyes" on Doreen, who ... well, it depends on which account you prefer to believe: the bowdlerized account in *Warning* or the lurid one in the original manuscript. The former has Doreen standing transfixed, the latter taking off her clothes. All the while the monster is beaming "very obscene" thoughts into her brain. Just as it reaches her, it suddenly floats backward and vanishes.

Events reach their climax in December 1954, when three invisible entities attack and violate Doreen in her apartment. She leaves town and abandons ufology forever. The demoralized Stuart, who tries to carry on, has one more encounter. Sitting at his desk at 1:30 A.M., he is shocked when the monster appears before him:

> The thing was about four or five feet from me. It was facing me in all its vile, base hideousness. Its body resembled, vaguely, that of a human. From the waist up it was a man, and from the waist down that of a woman. Its flesh, stinkingly putrid, seemed to hang in folds. It was a grayish color. Evil exuded from the entire thing. The slack mouth was dribbling, and the horrible lips began to move, but there was no sound....

> It told me [telepathically], "Your friend knew too much and had to be silenced. We sent one of us to her as a warning"....

> The thing told me in obscene words what [Doreen] had experienced, and each word was accompanied with what seemed to be laughter....

> The thing seemed to waver, and grow less distinct; then materialized again into solidity. I almost collapsed in horror as the male and female areas of its body had been changed.

> "You have been warned! Take heed! Should you fail there will be others to suffer!"

The creature dissolves and disappears.

Shattered, Stuart abandons ufology and returns to his native Auckland, where he spends the next two years with his mother. On his return to Hamilton, he resumes UFO research but later gives it up, explaining, "I knew my wife was too important to me to take any further risks," concluding piously, "She was more to me than solving the enigma of the 'flying saucers.'"

That's one version. The other, recounted in a tape Stuart made for Barker around 1962, tells a different story. In this one John suffers an "attack of amnesia" after Doreen's departure and wanders the streets in a dazed state, finally to be rescued by a woman named Gayleen (who is also mentioned in Stuart's private letters). He lives with her for a time before returning to Hamilton, where in September 1955 he receives a telegram from Doreen, who asks him to come see her at a private nursing home where she has given birth to an out-of-wedlock baby boy. The two have a tense exchange in which Doreen first ascribes the otherworldly attack to "nerves," then assails John for not protecting her from it. John storms out, and they do not see each other again. His correspondence, which has a distinctly misogynistic tone, depicts Doreen as foul-mouthed and sluttish.

Though the flavor of *Warning* cannot be conveyed in a single adjective, "steamy" is one that comes to mind. "Creepy" (on both levels of meaning) is another. "Believable," however, is not. Nonetheless, the reader puts down this short book harboring the irritating suspicion that the author is sincere. The reader, moreover, is dogged with thoughts such as these: Why would Stuart, if a hoaxer, have put himself at risk of legal retribution from an irate Wilkinson? Would she not have taken outraged exception to being inserted into a sex-drenched fantasy novel that, worse, pretended to be true? The reader mulls over these questions without ever quite abandoning the certainty that the events recounted could not have happened.

New Zealand UFO historian Murray Bott has recovered a considerable portion of Stuart's letters from the early 1950s into the early 1970s. Paradoxically, the correspondence both sheds light on the mystery and deepens it.

They make clear, for one thing, that Stuart genuinely believed that he and Doreen had undergone terrifying experiences. In fact, he lived much of the rest of his life in their shadow. As he struggled to find an explanation that made sense, he speculated briefly that Doreen had used her erotic allure to seduce him into a kind of hypnotic state. But in the end, he was always forced back to the distressing conclusion that no comfortingly conventional solution existed.

A 1953 issue of the *Saucerian,* published by Gray Barker, a promoter of fringe literature about UFOs and alien invaders.

Meantime, he contended with the skeptics—in this case fellow New Zealand ufologists who made little effort to conceal their disbelief. In correspondence with one, Stuart writes in exasperation, "I can whole-heartedly assure you that [the events] truly and honestly happened to us.... I DO NOT WANT TO EXPERIENCE ANYTHING LIKE IT AGAIN!"

It is hard to imagine what would have motivated Stuart to concoct a bogus tale. He can have made little—and probably no—money from *Warning,* marketed to the minuscule audience of hard-core saucerians who comprised Barker's mailing list. Unlike what's found in most contactee books, there is no cosmic uplift here, nothing with which to pursue further business—spiritual or financial. Just an absurd, disturbing, and (in many ways) revolting yarn constructed around the alleged experiences of one little man, apparently sane, but not heroic, and not even very appealing. One can ascribe it all to "psychological experience" without, perhaps, explaining much.

Who, in any case, would embrace the notion that lust-crazed space monsters drove two libidinous saucer fans out of UFO "research"? Nobody but the most credulous, surely. Whatever it was, the truth is unrecoverable. Stuart, who dropped out of sight in the mid–1960s, died in the late 1980s. No one interviewed him to find out what he might have said in later years. In this story, if not in her life (about which no more is known), Doreen survives only in Stuart's account of her and in a single photograph. It would have been interesting to hear her side. One suspects she was a victim, and not just of space monsters.

Further Reading:

Barker, Gray. *They Knew Too Much about Flying Saucers*. New York: University Books, 1956.

Stuart, John. *Concerning the "Strange Experiences"*. Hamilton, New Zealand: Flying Saucer Investigators, 1956.

————. *The Kiwi under UFO Attack*. Hamilton, New Zealand: The Author, 1962.

————. *UFO Warning*. Clarksburg, WV: Saucerian Books, 1963.

Teleportation

Teleportation—a word coined by Charles Fort to characterize the instantaneous transport of a person or object from one place to another—is best known to readers of science fiction. Less known is the fact, or at least allegation, that it takes place in real life. Though there is no shortage of stories attesting to these occurrences, convincing reports are rare. There are, moreover, a number of unambiguously fraudulent claims of teleportation.

The last of these appear not infrequently in accounts from nineteenth-century Spiritualist circles. There physical mediums of dubious reputation plied their trade to mostly unquestioning sitters and from time to time persuaded them that they had moved through space in some inexplicable manner. Because psychic claims are outside the scope of this book, these episodes will not be reviewed here. Our discussion will concentrate on those incidents said to have occurred spontaneously in a natural setting.

Into the fourth dimension

Of all teleportation tales, perhaps none has been so widely told as that of Tennessee farmer David Lang, who one afternoon in 1880, while crossing a field, vanished in full view of witnesses, including three members of his family. Most chroniclers have speculated that Lang, in common with other persons who have disappeared mysteriously, fell into the "fourth dimension." (Or, as Fort remarked in *Lo!* [1931], "Oh yes, I have heard of 'the fourth dimension,' but I am going to do myself some credit for not lugging in that particular way of showing that I don't know what I'm writing about.") In the 1970s an investigation by the late writer Robert Schadewald determined that neither David Lang nor any of the "witnesses" had ever existed and that the narrative bore a suspicious resemblance to the plot of Ambrose Bierce's late-nineteenth-century short story "The Difficulty of Crossing a Field." (See coverage of the David Lang disappearance elsewhere in this volume.)

A more credible-sounding story, this one about a presumed *near*-disappearance into another dimension, figures in several December 1873 articles in the *Bristol Daily Post* and the *London Times,* where it is treated more as an unusual court case than as a brush with the unknown. On December 8, Mr. and Mrs.

In the *Star Trek* television series, transportation is achieved with advanced technology, but some occultists believe it can be achieved through spiritual means.

Thomas B. Cumpston, two elderly, respectable residents of Leeds, arrived in Bristol, signed themselves into the Victoria Hotel, and some hours later found themselves under arrest for disorderly conduct. At the railway station where they were arrested, a terrified Cumpston told the night superintendent, "My wife and I have escaped from a den of thieves and rogues. We had to defend ourselves with a pistol." Cumpston had fired twice, once into the roof and later into the street. Suspecting them of insanity, the superintendent notified police.

In police court the couple said that early in the evening they had heard strange, loud sounds in or near their room. They complained to the landlady, who also heard them but shrugged them off. The sounds ceased, and the Cumpstons went to bed. At three or four o'clock in the morning the sounds resumed, this time accompanied by an alarming sensation that the floor was giving out. The couple's shouted words echoed weirdly or else were repeated by unseen presences. The floor "opened," and Mr. Cumpston felt as if he were being dragged into it. His wife pulled him out, and the two jumped out a window. In their panic and confusion they thought criminals had attempted to kidnap them and were following them as they ran to the station.

The landlady testified that she had indeed heard unusual sounds, though she proved unable to provide any meaningful description of them. The police said they had checked out the room and seen nothing out of the ordinary. The court concluded that the Cumpstons had suffered a "collective hallucination" and discharged them into the company of someone from Leeds.

Though the true nature of the couple's experience will never be known, the event, unlike the David Lang disappearance, undoubtedly happened. Those unsatisfied with the hallucination solution prefer another, more fantastic answer. Eighty years later Harold T. Wilkins would suggest:

> The strange noises and the hole in the floor described by the Cumpstons are impossible to explain unless one assumes that under certain conditions an unknown force operates which is able to create a vortex in solid matter.... Matter is "solid" only relative to human perceptions; on the atomic level it may be described as mostly empty space. A human being drawn into such a vortex, or whirlpool, in matter may be deposited in some spot dozens or even thousands of miles from his starting point. On occasion, in fact, it seems that a vortex could operate over astronomical distance so as to teleport a being from one planet to another.

Teleported people

Teleportations of human beings are not hard to find in folkloric and religious contexts. One early example of the former, recorded by the Rev. Robert Kirk in his classic work on seventeenth-century Scottish fairy traditions, *The Secret Common-Wealth* (1691), remarks on one unfortunate man's plight (spelling modernized):

> His neighbors often perceived this man to disappear at a certain place, and about one hour after to become visible, and discover himself near a bow-shot from the first place. It was in that place where he became invisible, said he, that the Subterraneans [fairies] did encounter and combat with him.

Another seventeenth-century story, known to us through an affidavit signed by Swedish clergyman Peter Rahm, recounts a troll's appearance at the Rahms' doorstep late one evening in 1660. After repeated entreaties Mrs. Rahm agreed to accompany the little man to his residence where his wife was giving birth. On her return Mrs. Rahm told her husband, according to his account, "it seemed to her as if she was carried along in the wind" on her way both to and from the fairy realm.

Mrs. Rahm's description of the physical sensation associated with teleportation is echoed in the Old Testament, wherein the prophet "Elijah went up by a whirlwind into heaven" (II Kings 2:1).

The great first-century pagan philosopher and physician Apollonius of Tyana, for example, was said to have transported himself instantaneously to Ephesus to treat

sufferers from a plague. Many Christian saints, according to legend, removed themselves, often carried by angels, from one location to another with similar swiftness. Early in his career, though for some reason no longer, Sathya Sai Baba (who died on April 24, 2011), a modern Indian religious teacher said to have miraculous supernatural powers, teleported himself in full view of others. "As we were approaching the river and passing a hill on our right-hand side," one witness told the late Icelandic psychologist Erlendur Haraldsson, Baba "would sometimes suddenly disappear. He would, for example, snap his fingers and ask those around him to do the same. And hardly had we snapped our fingers when he had vanished from amongst us and we could see him on the top of the hill waiting for us." Haraldsson devoted an entire chapter of his book-length investigative report on Baba, *Modern Miracles* (1987), to similar accounts.

Apollonius of Tyana (c. 15–100 C.E.), was said to have transported himself instantaneously to Ephesus to treat sufferers from a plague.

In 1901, shortly after the Pansini family moved into a large house in Ruvo, Italy, poltergeist phenomena of various kinds erupted. Seven-year-old Alfredo Pansini fell into trances, during which "angels" allegedly spoke through him and he experienced clairvoyant visions. He also took to vanishing suddenly from the house and reappearing in a dazed state elsewhere in town or in nearby towns. These alleged teleportations occurred frequently for three years, ending when he reached puberty in 1904. Just before then, however, Alfredo's younger brother Paolo began teleporting as well, and on one occasion both disappeared from their house and appeared aboard a fishing boat a few miles out at sea from the port of Baletta.

Joseph Lapponi, a medical adviser to Popes Leo XIII and Pius X, interviewed witnesses and wrote a book on the case. Once, according to Lapponi, Bishop Bernardi Pasquale locked the two boys in their room, sealing all doors and windows; yet within a few minutes the youths disappeared. Even so, one cannot help suspecting that a couple of clever boys were having fun at their elders' expense.

Teleported objects

The noted psychical researcher Hereward Carrington, who was interested in the common human experience of misplaced objects, thought that something other than absent-mindedness and inattention may underlie some such episodes. Carrington wrote of one incident:

Miss K., a nurse and a most methodical person, had the habit of invariably placing her bunch of keys on the dining room table the moment she entered her flat. One day she did this as usual (so she declared) and, a short time afterwards, looked for them as she was about to leave the apartment, on another "case." Her keys had disappeared. She looked for them everywhere; they were not to be found. She finally had to have other keys made for the front door, etc. Several days later, she wished to get a cork for a medicine bottle, having broken the old one. These corks were kept in a tin box, in the bottom portion of a trunk, standing in the hall. She does not (she says) have occasion to open this drawer on the day in question, nor subsequently until she looked for the cork. Nevertheless, her keys were there, peacefully reposing in the tin box.

The late Raymond Bayless, a Los Angeles artist with parapsychological interests, reported a 1957 experience that took place while he was holding a long-handled brush and speaking with a student. The room was empty except for two stools and an easel, and there was no rug or carpet on the floor. A large northern window brought in abundant sunlight. Suddenly the brush slipped from his hand. Both he and the student heard a clicking sound as it hit the floor. When Bayless reached down to retrieve it, he was astounded to find it nowhere. A thorough search of the stark room uncovered no sign of it. "It had just vanished into the air," Bayless concluded.

Where an instance like the first is concerned, one is free to speculate that the woman suffered a brief spasm of amnesia and herself placed her keys in the bottom of a trunk. Of course no evidence supporting such speculation exists, but such off-the-cuff explanations appeal to us for the simple reason that it is easier to believe in memory lapses than in teleportation. Nonetheless, Bayless's experience does not seem to lend itself to easy accounting.

Besides Carrington, D. Scott Rogo was the only serious anomalist to collect cases of "spontaneous dematerialization" in any systematic way. Rogo believed he had experienced it on a number of occasions in his own life. After he wrote about it and other people's possible paranormal thefts in *Fate*, he was inundated with mail from readers with their own stories.

The author of this book has his own puzzling experience to relate. I do my writing in an office in my home, surrounded by large numbers of books, magazines, and files. I also share space with most of my extensive CD collection and usually listen to music as I write. Several years ago, I decided I wanted to hear something from the Watersons, a venerable English family group whose repertoire consists of traditional British folk songs. Arranged alphabetically, my CDs are easily located. When I went to retrieve the desired disc, I was taken aback to discover that most of my Watersons albums were missing. My first thought was that, since they were at the end of the shelf, they must have fallen onto the floor. They hadn't. I then began to search through boxes on the floor near the shelf, removing all their contents and sorting through them. No luck. I was frustrated and be-

(Continued on page 357)

Skyquakes

On July 4, 1808, while exploring the Rocky Mountains, the Lewis and Clark expedition had an odd experience. It was recorded thus in the expedition journal:

Since our arrival at the Falls we have repeatedly heard a strange noise coming from the mountains in a direction a little to the north of west. It is heard at different periods of the day and night, sometimes when the air is perfectly still and without a cloud, and consists of one stroke only, or five or six discharges in quick succession. It is loud, and resembles precisely the sound of a six pound piece of ordnance at the distance of three miles.

Such phenomena, sometimes described as sounding like muffled thunder or cannon fire, have long been noted. They figure in American Indian and other legends, and in our time they have been incorporated into our own reigning folklore; some writers have linked them to UFOs and parallel universes. The best known of these "skyquakes" are the Barisal Guns of India and the Moodus Noises of Connecticut, but comparable sounds have been heard all over the world.

For example, members of an exploration party along the Darling River, near what is now Bourke, New South Wales, Australia, were startled by mysterious sounds that erupted one afternoon in February 1829. The leader's diary recorded the event:

About 3 P.M. on the 7th Mr. Hume and I were occupied tracing the chart upon the ground. The day had been remarkably fine, not a cloud was there in the heavens, nor a breath of air to be felt. On a sudden we heard what seemed to be the report of a gun fired at the distance of between five and six miles. It was not the hollow sound of an earthly explosion, or the sharp cracking noise of falling timber, but in every way resembled a discharge of a heavy piece of ordnance. On this all were agreed, but no one was certain where the sound proceeded. Both Mr. Hume and myself [sic] had been too attentive to our occupation to form a satisfactory opinion; but we both thought it came from the N.W. I sent one of the men immediately up a tree, but he could observe nothing unusual.

The confusion about the location of the source is typical. It explains why the sounds are known as skyquakes; to many who hear them, they seem to be coming out of the air. In truth, as a natural, if unusual, phenomenon linked to earthquakes and seismic activity, the sounds actually emanate from underground. Scientists do not know why earthquake activity (sometimes so slight as to be measurable only with instruments) generates these peculiar noises in some places and not in others. Since 1981, however, the Weston Observatory of Boston College has been monitoring earthquake activity in New England and has amassed considerable data on the Moodus phenomena.

Possibly answers to the physical mechanisms behind skyquakes will emerge from this research.

Further Reading:

Brooks, Harrison V. "Thunder of the Mackimoodus." *Fate* 28,10 (October 1975): 70–79.

Cleland, J. Burton. "Barisal Guns in Australia." *Nature* 81 (1909): 127.

Corliss, William R., ed. *Handbook of Unusual Natural Phenomena*. Glen Arm, MD: Sourcebook Project, 1977.

Fort, Charles. *The Books of Charles Fort*. New York: Henry Holt and Company, 1941.

Gould, Rupert T. *Enigmas: Another Book of Unexplained Facts*. London: Philip Allan, 1929.

Rierden, Andi. "A Steady Observer for Trembling Moodus." *New York Times* (August 6, 1989).

Robinson, Charles H. "Barisal Guns." *Nature* 53 (1896): 487.

(Continued from page 355)

wildered. Finally, some instinct told me that further effort was useless and hopeless, but that the CDs would eventually show up.

A few days later, as I opened a drawer elsewhere in the office while looking for something else, I was surprised to find a plastic bag neatly wrapped around unseen contents. I knew I had not placed such a package—or any package—inside that particular drawer, which was used for other purposes. On opening it, I found myself gaping at the missing albums. My wife denied knowing anything about it, and I believe her. Even now, the only "prosaic" explanation I can think of is that—though leaving no other evidence of his presence—someone broke into the house simply to pull a pointless prank on me, and that makes no sense.

As random events subject to other interpretations (valid or invalid), incidents like these do not constitute serious evidence for extraordinary conclusions about teleportation or other dimensions—though one cannot help being attracted to the implicit argument that such phenomena are part of the common experience of all of us.

Some theorists have suggested that teleportation is responsible for falls from the sky and for appearances of animals far away from their native habitats (see the entry about kangaroos in the Midwest). Ivan T. Sanderson, a trained zoologist and an imaginative anomalist, even wrote that it is "reasonable to suspect" that ants have "developed teleportation as a system of moving precious stuff around in an emergency."

Further Reading:

Carrington, Hereward. "Mysterious Disappearances." *Psychic Research* 24 (1930): 8–10.

Creighton, Gordon. "Teleportations." *Flying Saucer Review* 11,2 (March/April 1965): 14–16.

Fodor, Nandor. *Mind Over Space*. New York: Citadel Press, 1962.

Fort, Charles. *The Books of Charles Fort*. New York: Henry Holt and Company, 1941.

Haraldsson, Erlunder. *Modern Miracles: An Investigative Report on Psychic Phenomena Associated with Sathya Sai Baba*. New York: Fawcett Columbine, 1987.

Keightley, Thomas. *The Fairy Mythology*. London: G. Bell, 1878.

Knight, Damon. *Charles Fort: Prophet of the Unexplained*. Garden City, NY: Doubleday and Company, 1970.

Michell, John, and Robert J. M. Rickard. *Phenomena: A Book of Wonders*. New York: Pantheon Books, 1977.

Palmer, Stuart. "How Lost Was My Father?" *Fate* 6,7 (July 1953): 75–85.

Rogo, D. Scott. *The Haunted Universe: A Psychic Look at Miracles, UFOs and Mysteries of Nature*. New York: New American Library, 1977.

———. *Miracles: A Parascientific Inquiry into Wondrous Phenomena*. New York: Dial Press, 1982.

———. *Beyond Reality: The Role Unseen Dimensions Play in Our Lives*. Wellingborough, Northamptonshire, England: Aquarian Press, 1990.

Sanderson, Ivan T. *"Things."* New York: Pyramid Books, 1967.

Sanderson, Stewart, ed. *The Secret Common-Wealth and a Short Treatise of Charms and Spells by Robert Kirk*. Totowa, NJ: Rowman and Littlefield, 1976.

Schadewald, Robert. "David Lang Vanishes … Forever." *Fate* 30,12 (December 1977): 54–60.

Wilkins, Harold T. "They Fly through the Air." *Fate* 6,11 (November 1953): 88–92.

Wheels of Light

Passing between Oyster Reed and Pigeon Island in the Indian Ocean late on a calm, starlit January evening in 1880, Commander R. E. Harris and other crew members of the steamship *Shahihehan* saw an incredible sight. Harris's account was published in the *Calcutta Englishman* on January 21:

I ... observed a streak of white matter on the horizon bearing south-south-west. I then went to the bridge and drew the third officer's attention to it. In a few minutes it had assumed the shape of a segment of a circle measuring about 45 degrees in length and several degrees in altitude about its center. At this time it shone with a peculiar but beautifully milky whiteness, and resembled (only in a huge mass, and great luminous intensity) the nebulae sometimes seen in the heavens. We were streaming to the southward, and as the bank of light extended, one of its arms crossed our path. The whole thing appeared so foreign to anything I had ever seen, and so wonderful, that I stopped the ship just on its outskirts, so that I might try to form a true and just conception of what it really was. By that time all the officers and engineers had assembled on deck to witness the scene, and were all equally astonished and interested. Some little time before the first body of light reached the ship I was enabled, with my night glasses, to resolve in a measure what appeared, to the unassisted eye, a huge mass of nebulous matter. I distinctly saw spaces between what again appeared to be waves of light of great luster. These came rolling on with ever-increasing rapidity till they reached the ship, and in a short time the ship was completely surrounded with one great body of undulating light, which soon extended to the horizon on all sides. On looking into the water it was seen to be studded with patches of faint, luminous, inanimate matter, measuring about two feet in diameter. Although these emitted a certain amount of light, it was most insignificant when compared with the great waves of light that were floating on the surface of the water, and which were at this time converging upon the ship. The waves stood many degrees above the water, like a highly luminous mist, and obscured by their intensity the distant horizon; and as wave succeeded wave in rapid succession, one of the most grand and brilliant, yet solemn, spectacles that one could ever think of was here witnessed. In speaking of waves of light I do not wish to convey the idea that they were mere ripplings, which are sometimes caused by the fish passing through a phosphorescent sea, but waves of great length and breadth, or in other words, great bodies of light. If the sea could be converted into a huge mirror and thousands of powerful electric lights were made to throw their rays across it, it would convey no adequate idea of this strange yet grand phenomenon.

As the waves of light converged upon the ship from all sides they appeared higher than her hull, and looked as if they were about to envelop her, and as they impinged upon her, her sides seemed to collapse and expand.

Whilst this was going on[,] the ship was perfectly at rest, and the water was like a millpond.

After about half an hour had elapsed the brilliance of the light somewhat abated, and there was a great paucity of faint lustrous patches which I have before referred to, but still the body of light was gone, and, if emanating from these patches, was out of all proportion to their number.

This light I do not think could have been produced without the agency of electro-magnetic currents exercising their exciting influence upon some organic animal or vegetable substance; and one thing I wish to point out is, that whilst the ship was stopped and the light yet some distance away, nothing was discernible in the water, but so soon as the light reached the ship a number of luminous patches presented themselves, and as these were equally as motionless as the ship at the time, it is only natural to assume that they existed and were actually in our vicinity before the light reached us, only they were not made visible till they became the transmitting media for the electro-magnetic currents. This hypothesis is borne out by the fact that each wave of light in its passage was distinctly seen to pass over them in succession, they also became less distinct, and had actually disappeared so soon as the waves of light ceased to exist.

On May 15, 1879, on a clear night, the captain of the H.M.S. *Vulture* recorded a similarly extraordinary phenomenon, observed in the Persian Gulf:

I noticed luminous waves or pulsations in the water, moving at great speed and passing under the ship from the south-south-west. On looking towards the east, the appearance was that of a revolving wheel with center on that bearing, and whose spokes were illuminated, and looking towards the west a similar wheel appeared to be revolving, but in the opposite direction. I then went to the mizzen top (fifty feet above water) with the first lieutenant, and saw that the luminous waves or pulsations were really traveling parallel to each other, and that their apparently rotatory motion, as seen from the deck, was caused by their high speed and the greater angular motion of the nearer than the more remote part of the waves. The light of these waves looked homogenous, and lighter, but not so sparkling, as phosphorescent appearances at sea usually and extended from the surface well under water; they lit up the white bottoms of the quarter-boats in passing. I judged them to be twenty-five feet broad, with dark intervals of about seventy-five between each, or 100 from crest to crest, and

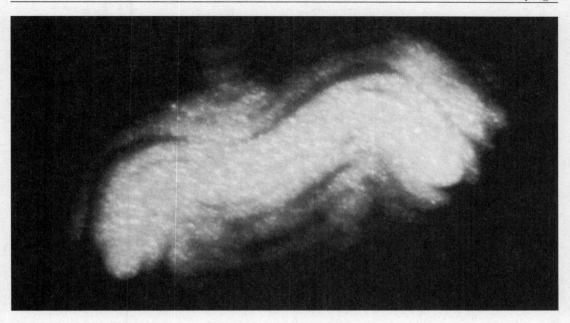

Strange lights that contort and change shape have frequently appeared over Hessdalen, Norway. One such light was captured in this 1983 photo.

their period was seventy-four to seventy-five per minute, giving a speed roughly of eighty-four English miles an hour.

From this height of fifty feet, looking with or against their direction, I could only distinguish six or seven waves, but, looking along them as they passed under the ship, the luminosity showed much further.

The phenomenon was beautiful and striking, commencing at about 6h. 3m. Greenwich mean time [9:40 P.M. local time], and lasting some thirty-five minutes. The direction from which the luminous waves traveled changed from south-south-west by degrees to south-east and to east. During the last five minutes concentric waves appeared to emanate from a spot about 200 yards east, and these meeting the parallel waves from south-east did not cross, but appeared to obliterate each other at the moving point of contact, and approached the ship, inclosing an angle about 90 degrees.

This incident appears in the 1910 yearbook of the Danish Meteorological Institute (translation by Thomas Brisson Jørgensen):

The night between June 18 and 19, 1909, at approximately three o'clock in the morning, Captain Gabe of the Danish-East Asian Company steamship *Bintang* was awakened by his second in charge because of a strange phenomenon he wanted him to see. The second-in-charge officer had first seen many "waves of light" in the water out in the distance, which started to take the shape of "arms" ... rotating from west to east around some kind of center. The arms accelerated faster and faster, but only the front of this "wheel" was visible, and the center was also too far in the distance to see. At this point the captain came up, describing it like the light of a fast-spinning lighthouse, without being able to see the actual lighthouse itself. After a while it started moving away, still spinning, but gradually losing intensity until at last completely gone. The sighting lasted about 15 minutes all in all.

The captain notes that the arms of light were all very similarly shaped, all having a kind of crooked bent to them, and all being about six feet in width where the beams hit the ship, and the distance in between the arms being about 12 feet. At its fastest, the arms of light hit the ship about every second or so. The captain concluded that it must have come from underwater, since no light hit any part of the ship that was above water. Some of the light extended to the back of the ship, but only very little.

Such strange phenomena continue to be seen to the present day, mostly (though not exclusively) in the Indian Ocean. Sometimes they appear in association with luminous parallel bars, as in this September 17, 1959, incident from the East Indian Archipelago. This account appeared in the journal *Marine Observer* in 1960:

The first indication of anything unusual was the appearance of white caps on the sea here and there, which made me think that the wind had freshened, but I could feel that this was not so. Then flashing beams appeared over the water, which made the Officer on watch think that the fishing boats were using powerful flashlights. These beams of light became more intense and appeared absolutely parallel, about 8 ft wide, and could be seen coming from right ahead at about ½ sec intervals. At this time, I thought I could hear a swish as they passed, but decided that this was imagination. They did not appear like rings or arcs of a circle, unless it was a circle so big as to make them appear as straight lines. It was like the pedestrian's angle of a huge zebra passing under him whilst he is standing still. While this part of the phenomenon was at its height it looked as if huge seas were dashing towards the vessel, and the sea surface appeared to be boiling, but it was more or less normal around a fishing vessel which we passed fairly close. The lights of various fishing vessels were visible through the beams of light, though dimmed by the brightness of the latter. The character of the flashes changed and took on the appearance of beams from a lighthouse situated about two miles on the starboard bow; or as if the center of a giant wheel was somewhere on the starboard bow with the beams as its spokes. As the beams from the vessel on the starboard bow weakened, the same pattern appeared on the port bow at the same distance and regularity. The wheel on the starboard bow revolved counterclockwise and the only one on the port bow revolved clockwise, i.e., both wheels were revolving towards the ship. The wheel on the starboard bow diminished as the one on the port bow increased; when the latter was at its peak the one on the starboard bow had disappeared. The next change was that the beams appeared to be traveling in the exact course of the ship, i.e., the beams now seen were a reversal of those seen at first.

More than a hundred well-attested sightings like these have been recorded in the last century and a half. To the extent that scientists have paid attention, they have been forced to acknowledge that these phenomena seem to defy explanation. Nearly all witnesses and commentators agree that the glow comes from bioluminescent organisms in the sea. The problem is explaining what triggers the luminescence and what causes the organisms to manifest in long-lasting, fast-moving, stable, complex geometric patterns.

Not surprisingly, these marine apparitions have inspired speculation about "vast wheel-like constructions," in the words of Charles Fort. Fort's disciple Ivan T. Sanderson theorized that "some source of energy starts broadcasting some invisible 'waves' on the electromagnetic (or other) spectrum which stimulate or activate the light-producing mechanisms of the *Noctiluca* [single-celled bioluminescent sea creatures].... This energy is broadcast in the form of a series of radiating bands whose source of origin is revolving; we would then have a progressive and, to our eyes, instantaneous turning on and off of the *Noctiluca* as the beams swept by them."

Such speculations would be more compelling if, for one thing, witnesses reported the kind of water displacement one would expect from the rapid passage, not far under the surface, of a vast structure. Instead, witnesses insist on the sea's placidity during the sighting.

We would also expect sightings of airborne structures of comparable description. Even Fort, who thought the wheels to be of extraterrestrial origin, found only one—a December 20, 1893, report of an "enormous wheel" over three Southeastern states—and its relevance is by no means certain. As Sanderson points out, the "'wheels of light' are not wheels at all but might better be called 'sunbursts,' like the old Japanese flag."

Nonetheless, one intriguing report leaves the question of a UFO/light-wheel link open at least a crack. It is said to have taken place in September 1961, near Leba, Poland, a resort on the Baltic Sea coast. Late one evening a vacationer, Czeslaw Kawecki, on a walk through the sand dunes that separate the sea from an inland lake, stopped to look out on the Baltic. After a short time he turned to go, only to hear a sound of rushing waters. He whirled around in time to see something rising out of the water 100 yards away. "It looked like a round hill—pushed up from beneath," he said. "Then splashes of water gushed from the top and [something] like fountain jets fell around the 'hole' in the waves. From this opening in the water emerged an object which at first I took to be an elongated triangle.... The object rose a few meters and hovered above the same spot, and there was now a whirlpool of water rushing inwards with a loud sucking and gurgling noise. The object itself was black and silent."

Leonard G. Cramp gives this account in his *Pieces for a Jig-Saw* (1966):

Suddenly there appeared a belt of steady white light segmented by a number of convex dark streaks. This light made glowing reflections on the lower rim of the object. It also lighted considerably the upper rim and all the rest. Now it became apparent that "the thing" had the shape of a huge funnel with two rims, separated by a belt of segmented light. About half way up the upper part was a thin strip of something whiter than the rest, of a rather dark body. The slim end of this "funnel" had a rounded top, from which protruded a stump, thinning upwards, and bent in the middle on one side.

The stillness of this object lasted about a minute.... Then, there appeared the glow of a second light under the object. Also a white one, but much stronger and sharper than that emitted by the augmented belt and almost immediately the "funnel" tilted slowly northwards revealing the bottom. After remaining in this position for about half a minute without changing, it glided about 50 meters eastwards, stopped but soon glided back and stopped again. All the time the bottom of the object was visible and consisted of a dark circular perimeter corresponding to the lower (and wider) rim of the "funnel." Towards the center was a wide ring of strong white light, with a number of dark, hook-shaped streaks upon it. Next was a dark ring with three evenly spaced triangular spokes, which protruded over half the width of the lit, streaky ring. Finally, there was a central disc which looked as if it was made of highly polished silver or crystal. It reflected the light with great brilliance.

"There was some rotating movement involved," Kawecki reported. "I could not make out whether the spikes were moving or the dark streaks gyrated under them. But I had no doubt that one or the other rotated. The light now became bluish and more intense. Then the object moved towards the north and upwards at a angle of about 45 degrees with a speed not exceeding that of a jet. It became just a diminishing spot of light until it finally disappeared. There was no sound. The entire observation lasted not more than four to five minutes."

The object was approximately eighteen feet wide and twenty feet high. After the UFO's departure he noticed several other persons who had also witnessed the bizarre sight.

On the whole, however, it must be said that wheels are probably not the marine equivalent of unidentified sky objects. What they are, on the other hand, is far from clear. We are unlikely to know more until scientists mount a real investigation of the phenomenon. At the very least, as authority Michael T. Shoemaker remarks, the solution is likely to "involve important biological or meteorological discoveries."

Further Reading:

Corliss, William R., ed. *Strange Phenomena: A Sourcebook of Unusual Natural Phenomena.* Glen Arm, MD: Sourcebook Project, 1974.

———, ed. *Handbook of Unusual Natural Phenomena.* Glen Arm, MD: Sourcebook Project, 1977.

————, ed. *Lightning, Auroras, Nocturnal Lights, and Related Luminous Phenomena: A Catalogue of Geophysical Anomalies*. Glen Arm, MD: Sourcebook Project, 1982.

Cramp, Leonard G. *Pieces for a Jig-Saw*. Cowes, Isle of Wight: Somerton Publishing Company, 1966.

Durant, Robert J. "Submarine Lightwheels." *Pursuit* 7,3 (July 1974): 58–59.

Fort, Charles. *The Books of Charles Fort*. New York: Henry Holt and Company, 1941.

Hall, Richard. "Aerial Anomalies at Sea." *INFO Journal* 4,3 (May 1975): 6–9.

Sanderson, Ivan T. *Invisible Residents: A Disquisition upon Certain Matters Maritime, and the Possibility of Intelligent Life under the Earth*. New York: World Publishing Company, 1970.

Shoemaker, Michael T. "The Lightwheel Wonder." In Steve Moore, ed. *Fortean Studies, Volume 2*, 8–63. London: John Brown Publishing, 1995.

FABLES

Cottingley Fairy Photographs

In 1917 two English girls, Frances Griffiths, ten, and her thirteen-year-old cousin, Elsie Wright, shared a house in Cottingley, near Bradford, Yorkshire. Frances and her mother had moved there from Cape Town, South Africa; Mr. Griffiths was serving as a British soldier in the Great War. One day Frances returned home soaking wet and offered the excuse that she had fallen into the brook while playing with the fairies they had befriended in a nearby glen. The parents were unmoved, and Frances was punished.

Feeling sorry for her cousin and best friend, Elsie hit upon an idea: they would borrow her father Arthur Wright's camera and photograph the fairies. After the parents believed them, the girls would announce that the picture was fake; they had lied about fairies just as their parents had lied to them about Father Christmas. Thus a kind of vengeance could be exacted for Frances's current misery.

Elsie approached her father and asked to borrow his camera, on the excuse that she wanted to take a picture of her cousin. He provided her with a single plate. An hour later the girls returned and said they now had proof of fairies. When the skeptical elder Wright developed the picture, he saw an image of Frances facing the camera as four miniature winged women dressed in filmy clothing danced in front of her.

The girls refused to admit that they had, as their elders were certain they had, photographed paper cutouts—or, as Elsie's father suspected specifically, "sandwich papers." Still, one month later Wright again reluctantly gave the girls access to a camera and a single plate, and they returned with a second picture, this one showing a sitting Elsie bidding a gnomish figure to jump up on her lap. Convinced that this was a joke that was getting out of hand, Wright forbade the girls further use of the camera.

The following year, when Frances's father returned from service, the Griffithses moved to Scarborough, Yorkshire. Just prior to the move, Frances wrote a South African friend and enclosed copies of the two fairy photographs. On the back of one, she noted, "Elsie and I are very freindly [sic] with the beck fairies. It is funny I did not see them in Africa. It must be to [sic] hot for them there." In the letter she referred to the fairies only briefly and in passing. When rediscovered and published (in the *Cape Town Argus*, November 22, 1922), Frances's words

The March 1921 issue of *Strand Magazine* published Sir Arthur Conan Doyle's article about the Cottingley Fairies.

would be cited as evidence of the girls' sincerity and of the photographs' authenticity.

The affair

What would prove to be one of the most bizarre controversies in the history of photography began in 1920, when Polly Wright, Elsie's mother, attended a lecture on folklore, including fairy beliefs. Afterwards Mrs. Wright mentioned the photographs, and the lecturer asked for prints, which subsequently she sent to Edward L. Gardner, a prominent London Theosophist. Gardner entered into correspondence with the Wrights. In time they loaned him the original plates, which he took to an acquaintance, H. Snelling, an authority on photography. Snelling's guardedly positive assessment of the pictures would be widely quoted for decades afterwards, though it would not be known until 1983 that he retouched the first photograph—badly overexposed—and transformed it into the very clear one with which all who knew of the Cottingley photographs would be familiar.

Gardner showed the pictures at a public lecture in May, and an audience member alerted Sir Arthur Conan Doyle, the prominent author, who was by then an ardent Spiritualist. Doyle urged Gardner to take the pictures to the Kodak laboratory in London. There, as Doyle would write later, "two experts were unable to find any flaw, but refused to testify to the genuineness of them, in view of some possible trap." (In fact, one of the consulted experts declared that "there is some evidence of faking.") Gardner finally met the Wrights that summer. He supplied Elsie with a modern camera, and subsequently she and Frances provided three more photographs of fairies.

In December, *The Strand* magazine published Doyle's article on the first two pictures, and the following March a follow-up included the later three. The story received worldwide publicity, much of it mocking and centering on the question of how the creator of Sherlock Holmes could have fallen for what most saw as an obvious hoax.

The aftermath

Yet attempts to debunk it were not notably successful. A claim by magician Harry Houdini and others that the fairy figures were patterned after those in a cer-

Frances Griffiths with the Cottingley fairies.

tain advertising poster proved groundless once the poster was produced. By this time Doyle had written an entire book on the case, *The Coming of the Fairies* (1922). The previous year Theosophist and clairvoyant Geoffrey Hodson had visited the beck in the girls' company and reportedly saw numerous fairies (the girls saw nothing), though efforts to photograph them subsequently proved unsuccessful.

There would be no more Cottingley fairy photographs, but the controversy would live on. In 1945 Gardner published a book-length account of the case, and the photographs were revived periodically in newspapers and magazines. Elsie and Frances seemed to stand by the pictures, or at least refused to admit their phoniness. When asked, they responded with the ambiguous assertion that the photographs were of "figments of our imaginations," which believers interpreted as meaning "thought forms" (paranormal entities formed out of the perceiver's psychic energy) and doubters as a virtual admission that the girls had made them up. In February 1972, however, Elsie sent the two cameras, along with other materi-

(Continued on page 373)

Oliver Lerch Disappearance

The story of a young man's tragic but mysterious fate at the hands of unearthly forces has been chronicled for decades, always as an authentic account.

In the most common version the incident occurs on Christmas Eve 1889, 1890, or 1900, on a farm outside South Bend, Indiana. Friends and family have gathered for a holiday party. At one point during the evening Oliver Lerch (or Larch), age twenty (eleven in some versions), sets out to the well to fetch water. It is a clear night, the clouds having passed earlier after dusting the ground with snow. Five minutes later horrible screams interrupt the Christmas celebration, and everyone dashes outside, where they see Oliver's tracks suddenly disappearing halfway to the well. A voice, apparently emanating from the sky, though its source is not visible, screams, "It's got me! Help! Help!" The pathetic pleas fade away after a few minutes, and Oliver Lerch is never seen or heard again.

"The facts of the case," one chronicler asserted, "are clearly written down for everyone to see in the police records."

An identical tale, differing only in the name of the victim and the location of the otherworldly abduction, is told of eleven-year-old Oliver Thomas of Rhayader, Wales. This version, apparently of relatively recent vintage, first appears in "true mystery" paperbacks in the 1960s. Subsequent archival investigations in Rhayader have established conclusively that Oliver Thomas never existed.

The Lerch/Larch story is decades older. The most influential version, in the sense that retellings of it brought the story between book covers for the first time (in, for example, M. K. Jessup's *The Case for the UFO* [1955] and Frank Edwards's *Strangest of All* [1956]), appeared in the September 1950 issue of *Fate*. Twenty-seven years later another *Fate* writer, Joe Nickell, persuaded the earlier contributor, Joseph Rosenberger, to confess, "There is not a single bit of truth to the 'Oliver Lerch' tale.... It was all fiction for a buck."

Though—presumably through faulty memory—Rosenberger claimed to have made it up himself, in fact the story was known well before 1932, when Rudolf H. Horst, managing editor of the *South Bend Tribune,* responded to an inquiry from British writer Harold T. Wilkins. Horst said the story "was purely imaginary. We frequently hear of this supposed incident regarding the Lerch family, but have never been able to locate such a family."

Inquiries by local newspaper reporters and librarians also found that the weather in the Decembers of 1889 and 1890 was unusually warm—in the 50s and 60s—meaning that there would have been no snow for any hypothetical Oliver Lerch to leave tracks in.

The yarn's plot comes from an early science-fiction story, "Charles Ashmore's Trail," published in an 1893 collection by Ambrose Bierce, *Can Such Things Be?* Set in Quincy, Illinois, in November 1878, it

(Continued from previous page)

tells of the title character's ill-fated trip to the well and of his family's horrified discovery of tracks that "abruptly ended, and all beyond was smooth, unbroken snow." Subsequently, family members hear his voice seeming to "come from a great distance, faintly, yet with entire direct-ness of articulation." No one has been able to determine how Charles Ashmore became Oliver Lerch, however, or how a tale never intended as anything but fan-tasy became a "true mystery."

Further Reading:

Begg, Paul. *Into Thin Air: People Who Disappear.* North Pomfret, VT: David and Charles, 1979.

Edwards, Frank. *Strangest of All.* Secaucus, NJ: Citadel Press, 1956.

Jessup, M. K. *The Case for the UFO.* New York: Citadel Press, 1955.

Nickell, Joe. "The Oliver Lerch Disappearance: A Postmortem." *Fate* 33,3 (March 1980): 61–65.

Rosenberger, Joseph. "What Happened to Oliver Lerch?" *Fate* 4,5 (September 1950): 28–31.

Steiger, Brad. *Strangers from the Skies.* New York: Award Books, 1966.

Wilkins, Harold T. *Mysterious Disappearances of Men and Women in the U.S.A., Britain and Europe.* Girard, KS: Haldeman-Julius Publications, 1948.

(Continued from page 371)

als related to the case, to Sotheby's for sale; with them went a letter confessing for the first time ever that the photographs were inauthentic. Sotheby's returned the letter, apparently failing to grasp what it had, on the grounds that it dealt only with antique documents.

Yet in 1975, when interviewed by a writer for *Woman* magazine, Elsie and Frances gave the impression (though without stating so explicitly) that the pho-tographs were real. The following year, on a Yorkshire Television program, Frances snapped, "Of course not," when asked if she and Elsie had fabricated the photos.

The first public acknowledgement to the contrary appeared in a 1982 issue of *The Unexplained.* At the same time, the *British Journal of Photography* was in the early installments of a major reappraisal of the case, based on an extensive inves-tigation by editor Geoffrey Crawley; it became a ten-part series between Decem-ber 1982 and April 1983. Frances and Elsie complained that the confessions cited by Joe Cooper in his *Unexplained* article were "unauthorized" (Cooper had been working with Frances on her [posthumously published] autobiography). Their first signed, formal confessions were given to Crawley in February 1983.

It was revealed that the two had agreed that the truth—that the pictures were a "practical joke" that "fell flat on its face"—be withheld until the deaths of the major advocates, Doyle, Gardner, and Gardner's son, Leslie. Elsie, a gifted young artist, had created the figures, using as her models fairies depicted in a pop-ular children's book of the period, *Princess Mary's Gift Book.*

According to Cooper, the first four photographs were all simple, single-exposure, open-air shots, but in Crawley's view the latter two were intentional double exposures. The fifth, showing a "fairy bower," was an unintentional double exposure. But even to the end the two women would not reveal the techniques they used, promising to reveal them in books they were writing. Both died, however, before finishing them, Frances in 1986, Elsie two years later.

Interestingly, professed fairy believer Frances, whose posthumously published *Reflections on the Cottingley Fairies* (edited by her daughter Christine Lynch, 2009) insists that the fifth picture was authentic, would always maintain—and reiterated as much in her communications with Crawley—that while the photographs were bogus, she *had* seen real fairies in the beck. Elsie, on the other hand, did not accept the existence of fairies, photographed or otherwise, thus implying her assessment of the fifth picture. (Winged fairies, it might be noted, are a creation of Victorian children's literature. "Real" fairies—the fairies of tradition—lack wings and otherwise do not much resemble their sentimental literary representatives.)

The story was revived in a well-received movie, *Fairy Tale: A True Story* (1997), with Peter O'Toole playing Doyle. The following year British bookseller Simon Finch bought Frances's collection of the photographs, with the intention of selling them to a higher bidder. Along with a first edition of Doyle's *Coming*, they were auctioned to a couple of unidentified Americans. Original copies are widely scattered and largely unrecoverable. Much of Gardner's collection of Cottingley-related materials went in 1972 to Leeds University, where most of it remains.

Further Reading:

Bord, Janet. "Cottingley Unmasked." *Fortean Times* 43 (1985): 48–53.

Clapham, Walter. "There *Were* Fairies at the Bottom of the Garden." *Woman* (October 1975): 42–43,45.

Cooper, Joe. "Cottingley: At Last the Truth." *The Unexplained* 117 (1982): 2338–340.

Crawley, Geoffrey. "That Astonishing Affair of the Cottingley Fairies." *British Journal of Photography* Pt. One (December 24, 1982): 1375–80; Pt. Two (December 31, 1982): 1406–11, 1413–14; Pt. Three (January 7, 1983): 9–15; Pt. Four (January 21, 1983): 66–71; Pt. Five (January 28, 1983): 91–96; Pt. Six (February 4, 1983): 117–21; Pt. Seven (February 11, 1983): 142–45, 153, 159; Pt. Eight (February 18, 1983): 170–71; Pt. Nine (April 1, 1983): 332–38; Pt. Ten (April 8, 1983): 362–66.

Doyle, Arthur Conan. *The Coming of the Fairies*. New York: George H. Doran Company, 1922.

———. "Fairies Photographed." *The Strand Magazine* (December 1920): 462–67.

Gardner, Edward L. *Fairies: The Cottingley Photographs and Their Sequel*. London: Theosophical Publishing House, 1945.

Hitchens, Christopher. "Fairy Tales Can Come True...." *Vanity Fair* 446 (October 1997): 204, 206, 208, 210.

Hodson, Geoffrey. *Fairies at Work and Play*. London: Theosophical Publishing House, 1925.

Sanderson, S. F. "The Cottingley Fairy Photographs: A Re-Appraisal of the Evidence." *Folklore* 84 (Summer 1973): 89–103.

Shepard, Leslie. "The Fairies Were Real." *Fortean Times* 44 (1985): 61–62.

Smith, Paul. "The Cottingley Fairies: The End of a Legend." In Peter Narváez, ed. *The Good People: New Fairylore Essays*, 371–405. Lexington: University Press of Kentucky, 1991.

Flight 19

Of the "mysterious disappearances" associated with the once-notorious Bermuda Triangle, none is more famous than Flight 19. As with many of the stories that comprise the legend, however, there are serious discrepancies between what can be verified and what Triangle chroniclers claimed.

At 2:10 on the afternoon of December 5, 1945, five Avenger torpedo bombers left the Naval Air Station (NAS) at Fort Lauderdale, Florida, and headed east. Flight 19 was made up of fourteen men, all students in the last stages of training, except for the commander, Lt. Charles Taylor. The five pilots had been transferred only recently from the Miami Naval Air Station. Taylor knew the Florida Keys well; but he did not know the Bahamas, in whose direction he and the others were heading.

The purpose of the exercise was to conduct a practice bombing at Hens and Chicken Shoals fifty-six miles away. Once that was accomplished, the Avengers were to continue eastward for another sixty-seven miles, then head north seventy-three miles. After that they would turn west-southwest and fly the remaining 120 miles straight home. In short, they were flying a triangular flight path through what would be called the Bermuda Triangle.

At 3:40 P.M. a pilot and flight instructor, Lt. Robert Cox, who was about to land at Fort Lauderdale, overheard a radio transmission addressed to someone named Powers. Powers replied, "I don't know where we are. We must have got lost after that last turn." Fort Lauderdale attempted to communicate with Powers (in fact Marine Capt. Edward Powers Jr.) but got no immediate response. A few minutes later Cox established contact with Taylor, the pilot who had spoken to Powers. Taylor told Cox that his compasses were not working, but "I'm sure I'm in the Keys, but ... I don't know how to get to Fort Lauderdale." Cox urged him to fly north toward Miami, "if you are in the Keys."

Taylor was not, however, in the Keys. He was in the Bahamas. By flying north he would only go farther out to sea. Efforts by Cox and others to establish the location of Flight 19 were hampered by poor communications. At one point, Taylor was urged to turn over control of the flight to one of the students, though apparently he did not do so; the occasional, overheard exchange between him and other Flight 19 pilots suggested some degree of dissension. Just after 4:30 P.M.

Donald E. Keyhoe's *Flying Saucer Conspiracy* suggested that a "giant mother ship" from space had snatched the Flight 19 planes.

Taylor radioed a question to Port Everglades Boat Facility, an Air Sea Rescue Unit near Fort Lauderdale: "Do you think, as my student does, that we should fly west?" Not knowing where he was, Port Everglades simply acknowledged receiving his transmission. If Flight 19 had flown west at this stage, it would have been saved.

At 4:45 P.M. Taylor indicated that the Avengers were going to go north-northeast for a short time, then head north "to make sure we are not over the Gulf of Mexico." By now the people on the ground were seriously concerned; it was clear that Taylor, far from being temporarily lost as happens to many pilots, had no idea where he was. As dusk approached, atmospheric interference with the radio signals increased. Through the static, two of the student pilots could be heard complaining that "if we would just fly west, we would get home." Nonetheless, they flew north, then veered off slightly to the east, for a few minutes. At 5:15 Taylor called in to Port Everglades, "We are now heading west." Taylor addressed his companions, telling them that they should join up; as soon as one of them ran out of fuel, they would all go down together.

The sun set at 5:29. With bad weather moving in from the north, the situation was growing ever more urgent, but no one on the ground knew where Flight 19 was. Around 6 P.M. reception improved for a short time. Taylor was urged to switch to 3,000 kilocycles, the emergency frequency, but refused to do so for fear his and the other planes would fall out of communication; unfortunately, interference from Cuban commercial stations, and the inability of other coastal stations to easily translate the Fort Lauderdale training signal, would effectively shut off Flight 19 from the rest of the world.

A few minutes earlier, at 5:50, the ComGulf Sea Frontier Evaluation Center thought it had pinpointed the flight's approximate position: east of New Smyrna Beach, Florida, and far to the north of the Bahamas. At 6:04 Taylor was heard ordering the others to "turn around and go east again." Two minutes later he repeated the order, explaining, "I think we would have a better chance of being picked up." Apparently he still believed the flight was over the Gulf.

So far no rescue aircraft had gone out because the position fix had not yet been passed on to all affected parties, not the least of them Taylor and his companions. But finally a Dumbo flying boat based at the Dinner Key seaplane base left Miami, heading northeast, at 6:30, on what amounted to a blind effort to reestablish contact. The Dumbo itself soon fell out of contact with shore, however, and for a while it was feared that it, too, was lost. The problem turned out to be icing on the antenna, and the Dumbo continued on what proved to be a futile search.

Within the hour other aircraft joined the search, including two Martin Mariners (Training 32 and Training 49), the second of which departed from the Banana River NAS at 7:27. This Mariner was to join up with the first, which had taken off twenty minutes earlier, east of New Smyrna Beach. Lt. Gerald Bammerlin, 32's pilot, later told naval investigators, "When we arrived in the area of Flight 19's 5:50 position fix, about 8:15, the overcast was at approximately 800 to 1,200 feet. There were occasional showers. The estimated wind was west-southwest 25 to 30 knots. The air was very turbulent and the sea very rough. We flew manually on instruments through the night, though whitecaps were visible below."

In the meantime 49 had failed to make its scheduled rendezvous, and it was not answering radio calls. At 7:50 the crew of the SS *Gaines Mill* observed an enormous sheet of fire caused by the explosion of an airplane. A few minutes later the ship passed through a big pool of oil and looked with no success for survivors or bodies. Though they saw some debris, crew members did not try to retrieve any of it because of the ocean turbulence. Weather conditions were deteriorating rapidly.

The Flight 19 aircraft now had exhausted their fuel and were assumed to be down. Taylor's last transmission was heard at 7:04. The search continued through the night, though at a diminished rate because of turbulence in the air and on the ocean. The next day hundreds of planes and ships looked in vain, on heavy seas, for the missing Avengers and Mariner. No trace of them turned up then, later, or ever.

On April 3, 1946, at the conclusion of an intensive investigation of this much-publicized air disaster, the Navy declared that the "flight leader's false assurance of identifying as the Florida Keys, islands he sighted, plagued his future decisions and confused his reasoning.... He was directing his flight to fly east ... even though he was undoubtedly east of Florida." When Taylor's mother and aunt refused to accept this verdict, the Navy set up a panel to review the report. In August this panel announced it could only agree with the original conclusion. Furious, the two women hired an attorney and secured a hearing the following October. On November 19 the Board for Correction of Naval Records retracted the original verdict and officially laid the disaster to "causes or reasons unknown."

The Mariner's fate seemed relatively clear. The Mariners were known as "flying gas bombs," which something so small as a lighted cigarette or an electrical spark could ignite. As for the Avengers, none of the investigating authorities doubted that the fifty-foot-high waves tearing across the ocean surface had chewed them up, and sent what remained to the bottom in no more than seconds.

Myth and mystification

What seems to have been the first suggestion that the disappearances might be something other than a conventional aviation tragedy was expressed in a letter to the science fiction magazine *Amazing Stories*. In the August 1946 issue, a Colorado man named Edward R. Walker wrote to say, "A couple of months ago I read another AP dispatch about SIX NAVY PLANES disappearing ALL AT ONE TIME off the coast of Florida…. This is one of the strangest happenings that I have ever heard of in my lifetime…. It wasn't even storming."

The magazine's colorful and controversial editor, Ray Palmer, who had been promoting a range of outlandish "true mysteries" in the magazine, replied, "Your editor would like to KNOW what happened, because it wasn't anything ordinary. As a matter of fact, this is only one of hundreds of mysteries of this type which have baffled the world in the past few years. But we hear nothing further about them because 'officialdom' and 'explainers of everything by means of book larnin' can't explain them."

In September 1950, Associated Press reporter E.V.W. Jones sent a story out on the wires. Its echoes would be heard for decades to come. In it he declared that a triangular area connecting Florida, Bermuda, and Puerto Rico comprised a "limbo of the lost" where planes and ships often "vanished in the thin air." An especially baffling mystery was the disappearance of Flight 19 and the Martin Mariner that had gone in search of it. An October 1952 article in *Fate,* a popular digest on "true mysteries" by then co-edited by the sensation-seeking Palmer, drew heavily on the AP piece, citing the Flight 19 story along with others that, by the 1960s, would evolve into the "Bermuda Triangle" concept.

In a 1955 book, *The Flying Saucer Conspiracy*, Donald E. Keyhoe, a retired Marine Corps major and leading proponent of UFOs as extraterrestrial visitors, suggested that a "giant mother ship" from space had snatched the planes. Like many other writers who would follow, Keyhoe claimed that the sea had been calm all during the episode. More influential, however, was an *American Legion Magazine* article by Allan W. Eckert, who contributed fictitious dialogue that other Triangle chroniclers later repeated endlessly. According to Eckert, Taylor had radioed Fort Lauderdale that "everything is wrong … strange … the ocean doesn't look as it should."

A later writer, Art Ford, reported he had interviewed a radio operator who heard Taylor say, "They look like they're from outer space—don't come after me." Nothing in the transcript of Taylor's exchanges with others during the flight substantiates this allegation. Though at one point, during his mid-afternoon conversation with Cox, Taylor had indeed said not to come after him, most believe he meant that he would be fine, not that spaceships were pursuing him.

In a February 1964 *Argosy* article, and the next year in a book, *Invisible Horizons*, Vincent Gaddis, coiner of the phrase "Bermuda Triangle," called Flight 19's fate the "most incredible mystery in the history of aviation." Other authors such as Charles Berlitz, Richard Winer, Alan and Sally Landsburg, and John Wallace Spencer told comparably fantastic and misleading versions of the episode. Having rejected all possible mundane explanations for the tragedy, these writers were free to speculate about marauding aliens, the fourth dimension, space-time warps, and extraordinary magnetic anomalies. At the conclusion of Steven Spielberg's 1977 science fiction film *Close Encounters of the Third Kind*, the Flight 19 crew returns to Earth via UFO.

In time, more cautious investigators revived, and sometimes expanded on, the Navy's original findings. Larry Kusche wrote an entire book, *The Disappearance of Flight 19* (1980), based on considerable original research. Kusche contended that the Navy's Correction Board ought not to have exonerated Taylor. Though the "decision was a kindness to Mrs. [Kathleen] Taylor [Charles's mother] … it was incorrect. The conclusion of the original Board of Investigation, that Charles Taylor was at fault, was correct."

Flight 19 was back in the headlines in the spring of 1991, when the crew of the salvage ship *Deep See*, hunting for sunken Spanish galleons, found the intact remains of five Avengers at 600 feet on the ocean bottom ten miles northeast of Fort Lauderdale. One plane bore the number 28, the same as Taylor's aircraft. But on June 4 Graham Hawkes, who had headed the search, conceded that further investigation had proved the craft were not from Flight 19. The numbers on the other planes were different from those on the fabled flight. Moreover, the craft were an older generation Avenger.

Ray Palmer was the controversial, colorful editor of *Amazing Stories*.

In 1985, reminiscing about the event, Willard Stoll, who had led Flight 18 half an hour in front of Taylor's flight, remarked, "What the hell happened to Charlie? Well, they didn't call those planes 'Iron Birds' for nothing. They weighed 14,000 pounds empty. So when they ditched, they went down pretty fast. But they found the *Titanic*, and maybe one day they'll find him and the others. Wherever they are, they're together."

Further Reading:

Begg, Paul. *Into Thin Air: People Who Disappear*. North Pomfret, VT: David and Charles, 1979.

Christensen, Dan. "After 40 Years, Story of Flight 19 Still Unknown." *West Palm Beach* [Florida] *Post* (December 8, 1985).

Clary, Mike. "Mystery of 'Lost Patrol' May Be Solved." *Los Angeles Times* (May 18, 1991).

Eckert, Allan W. "The Mystery of the Lost Patrol." *American Legion Magazine* (April 1962): 12–23, 39–41.

"Explorers Say Planes Aren't Lost Squadron." *Staunton* [Virginia] *Daily News Leader* (June 5, 1991).

Kusche, Larry. *The Bermuda Triangle Mystery—Solved*. Buffalo, NY: Prometheus Books, 1986.

———. *The Disappearance of Flight 19*. New York: Harper and Row, Publishers, 1980.

McDonell, Michael. "Lost Patrol." *Naval Aviation News* (June 1973): 8, 10–16.

Sand, George X. "Sea Mystery at Our Back Door." *Fate* 5,7 (October 1952): 11–17.

Hollow Earth

The idea that Earth possesses a hollow interior which houses an underground civilization is an old one—the widespread religious belief in hell is one variant of it—but the first American to try to prove it was the eccentric John Cleves Symmes (1779–1829). A War of 1812 hero and a self-taught naturalist, Symmes grew obsessed with the notion that the world consists of "solid concentric spheres, one within the other," which describes the earth's true geography. At the north and south poles are holes 4,000 miles wide.

On April 10, 1818, Symmes, then living in St. Louis, sent a document to a large number of institutions, politicians, governments, and scientists. Other copies went to major foreign universities. *Circular Number 1*—accompanied by a statement of Symmes's sanity, a strategic mistake and the occasion of much ridicule—declared the earth "hollow and habitable within.... I pledge my life in support of this truth, and am ready to explore the hollow, if the world will support and aid me in my undertaking." He asked for a party of 100 well-equipped explorers who in the fall would take off from Siberia, where he soon expected to find a "warm and rich land, stocked with thrifty vegetables and animals, if not men, on reaching one degree northward of latitude 82; we will return in the succeeding spring."

Few if any of the recipients doubted that Symmes was some species of madman, but undeterred, he mailed seven more circulars in 1818 alone. The next year, from his new home in Kentucky, he dispatched *Light between the Spheres,* which secured a wider audience after being reprinted in *National Intelligencer.* Unable, however, to persuade the nation's intellectual elites, he chose a path of less resistance: he decided to lay out his theories to more receptive listeners, namely those who lived in rural and small-town settings on the fringe of the then-Western frontier of Ohio and Kentucky. Though an uncharismatic man and a terrible speaker, he embarked on a lecture tour in 1820, delivering the message mostly to unlettered provincials and even to schoolchildren. He carried a wooden globe built with a series of concentric shells and a hole at each end to represent the two polar regions.

Even so, Symmes's hollow earth remained subject to occasional consideration in more influential quarters. In 1822, Sen. R. M. Johnson of Kentucky, citing Symmes, urged Congress to equip two ships and provide other aid for an expedition "to one or other of polar regions" to determine whether a race of human beings lives inside the earth. Johnson garnered some support from colleagues, but by the end of the day, his petition was permanently tabled. In 1824, sympathizer James McBride issued a thorough-going defense, *Symmes's Theory of Concentric Spheres*, which sought to counter all conceivable counter-arguments.

Before long, a young Ohio newspaperman named Jeremiah Reynolds chided Symmes for wasting his time in the outlying districts; he needed to take his theories to big-city audiences. When the nervous Symmes expressed reluctance, Reynolds promised to accompany him. In time, the smoother, more sophisticated companion effectively took control of the operation from the retiring—and now ailing—Symmes. Reynolds did most of the speaking. On noting what the audiences responded to most enthusiastically, he changed the focus to arctic exploration in general; hollow earth speculations faded into the background. Whatever they thought about a hollow earth, most people were curious about the then-unexplored poles.

In fact, Reynolds succeeded in securing funds from a wealthy benefactor, a Dr. Watson, for a South Pole expedition, which departed New York harbor in October 1829 in the SS *Annawan*, but proved unable to break through the surrounding icepack. On the return voyage, a mutiny by the crew—which then took up piracy—deposed Reynolds and Watson. Reynolds was stranded in Chile until 1831, when he found employment as a secretary on the frigate *Potomac*, which traveled around the world. On his return to America in 1834, he wrote a popular book on his experiences, then resumed lecturing on polar exploration and the hollow earth. A lecture in Baltimore so impressed one audience member, Henry Allan, that he later told his adopted half-brother all about it. Thus, Edgar Allan Poe went on to write the hollow earth's one great contribution to American literature, the 1838 proto-science fiction novella, *The Narrative of Arthur Gordon Pym*.

After two years at the home of a New Jersey friend, a gravely ill Symmes retired to his farm near Hamilton in southwestern Ohio. Not long afterwards, in May 1829, he succumbed to his various ailments. A monument in Hamilton (2010 pop. 62,447) still honors his resting place with a monument, though it is doubtful that more than a handful of its residents have any idea who he was.

Still hollow after all these years

John Symmes's son Americus picked up where his father had left off. He spent the rest of his life as a hollow earth advocate. He kept in touch with a network of like-minded theorists, and in 1878 he published an anthology of his father's lectures. By this time even the spirit world was echoing the theme. In 1871 medium M. L. Sherman brought out *The Hollow Globe*, based on supposed communications from the dead. Helena Petrova Blavatsky, founder of an influential school of occultism called Theosophy, wrote of the hollow earth in two classic works, *Isis Unveiled* (1877) and *The Secret Doctrine* (1888). Frederick Culmer weighed in with *The Inner World* in 1886, and exactly twenty years later William

Reed released his book *The Phantom of the Poles*. The fiction of fantastic voyages also brought forth Jules Verne's famous, still-read and occasionally filmed, *Journey to the Center of the Earth* (1864).

In a 1931 book, *Lemuria: Lost Continent of the Pacific*, H. Spencer Lewis added a new ingredient to the mix when he averred that remnants of a super race, survivors of the long-ago sinking of the great Pacific continent Lemuria, dwell within Mount Shasta in northern California. (In reality, the idea of "Lemuria" was invented in the nineteenth century, first by biologist Ernst Haekel as a hypothetical home for the original *Homo sapiens*, then elaborated by Blavatsky in her alternative history of the human race. There is no geological or biological evidence that such a place ever existed.) Lewis, founder of the Ancient Mystical Order Rosae Crucis (better known as the Rosicrucians), led his followers on expeditions to the mountain in search of the secret Lemurian colony. Lemurians would not have been hard to spot. They were, according to Lewis, seven feet tall with large foreheads, in the middle of which was a growth—a "third eye" for perception, both extraordinary and extrasensory. According to Lewis:

> Many years ago it was quite common to hear stories whispered in Northern California about the occasional strange looking persons seen to emerge from the forests and dense growth of trees in that region, and who would run back into hiding when discovered or seen by anyone. Occasionally one of these oddly dressed individuals would come to one of the smaller towns and trade nuggets or gold dust for some modern commodities. These odd-looking persons were not only peculiar in their dress and different in attire from any customer ever seen on the American Indian, and especially the California Indian, but distinctive in features and complexion; tall, graceful and agile, having the appearance of being what one would term foreigners, but with larger heads, much larger foreheads, headdresses that had a special decoration that came over the center of the forehead to the bridge of the nose, and thus hid or covered a part of the forehead that many have attempted to see and study.

These sorts of legends would persist well into the UFO age. In a 1993 publication, "Commander X" (pseud. of the late Jim Keith), allegedly a retired military officer privy to the deepest secrets of the UFO cover-up, declared that Mount Shasta "has a highly charged aura which prevents the forces of darkness from penetrating anywhere nearby. Teams of Lemurians, Space Brothers and elementals[,] working jointly, meditate daily underground here to heal the planet and to keep this sacred spot from either physical or mental attack."

Ufologist Bill Hamilton reports meeting "a young, very pretty blonde … with almond-shaped eyes and small perfect teeth," who was born in 1951, "in a city called Telos that was built inside an artificial dome-shaped cavern in the Earth a mile or so beneath Mt. Shasta, California." Identified only as "Bonnie," the woman told Hamilton that she, her friend, and fellow Telosians travel via tube shuttle to visit other subterranean cities populated by survivors of Lemuria and Atlantis. "One tube connects with one of their cities in the Mato Grosse [sic] jungle of

Brazil," Hamilton states. "The Lemurians have developed space travel and some flying saucers come from their subterranean bases." The Lemurians are members of a cosmic federation that links them to extraterrestrial intelligences.

Late in the nineteenth century a religion based on hollow earth doctrines came into being under the leadership of Cyrus Teed (1839–1908). Teed claimed to have been contacted by no less than the Mother of the Universe, who imparted some exciting news: he was to be the savior of the world. Teed founded a utopian community, based in Fort Myers, Florida, and dedicated it to "Koreshanity," according to which the "universe is a cell, a hollow globe, the physical body of which is the Earth; the sun is at the center. We live on the inside of the cell; and the sun, moon, planets and stars are all within the globe." In other words, the universe is inside out.

Less radical, relatively speaking, was a 1913 book, *A Journey to the Earth's Interior*, by Marshall B. Gardner, who returned to the Symmes model of the hollow earth (though

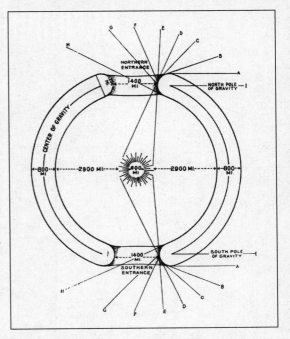

A diagram illustrating Earth as a hollow sphere, from Marshall B. Gardner's *Journey to the Earth's Interior.*

speaking ill of his mentor at every turn). Gardner thought there was an interior sun, though it was not *the* sun. This sun, 600 miles in diameter, gave the underworld a pleasant climate, allowing its inhabitants to live in tropical splendor.

By this time the hollow-earth concept, though disparaged by scientists as preposterous and physically impossible, had taken a firm hold in the imaginations of some occultists. The next major occult figure to pick it up was Guy Warren Ballard (1878–1939), whose *Unveiled Mysteries*, written under the pseudonym Godfré Ray King, told of an extraordinary experience the author had undergone four years earlier. Ballard wrote that while on an outing at Mount Shasta, he met a stranger who produced a creamy liquid and urged him to drink it. After consuming it, Ballard saw the man as he "truly" was: Count Saint Germaine, an eighteenth-century figure, thought by historians to have been a self-promoting charlatan but by Blavatsky to have lived on as an immortal Tibetan Master.

In his account Ballard met the count many times after that, and in his company he took numerous out-of-body tours under the earth, where he explored a beautiful world of scientific and spiritual marvels. In time he even started meeting space people under the earth. Under Wyoming's Grand Teton Mountains he attended a conference with a dozen Venusian masters. He related comparable tales in a follow-up book, *The Magic Presence* (1935), and until his death he, his wife,

(Continued on page 386)

Bermuda Triangle

The genesis of the Bermuda Triangle legend is an Associated Press dispatch of September 6, 1950, in which reporter E.V.W. Jones took note of what he characterized as unexplained vanishings of ships and planes between the Florida coast and Bermuda. Two years later, in an article in *Fate* magazine, George X. Sand recounted a "series of strange marine disappearances, each leaving no trace whatever, that have taken place in the past few years" in a "watery triangle bounded by Florida, Bermuda and Puerto Rico."

M. K. Jessup picked up on some of the same stories in his 1955 book *The Case for the UFO,* which suggested that alien intelligences were responsible, a view echoed by Donald E. Keyhoe (*The Flying Saucer Conspiracy* [1955]) and Frank Edwards (*Stranger Than Science* [1959]). It took Vincent H. Gaddis to coin the catch-all phrase that would enter popular culture; his article in the February 1964 issue of *Argosy* (the following year incorporated into his book *Invisible Horizons*) was titled "The Deadly Bermuda Triangle Mystery." Soon nearly every popular book on "true mysteries" included sections on the Bermuda Triangle, or as some called it, the "Devil's triangle" or the "hoodoo sea." Ivan T. Sanderson, author of *Invisible Residents* (1970), cited it as evidence of an intelligent, technologically advanced underwater civilization that is responsible for UFOs, among other mysterious phenomena.

A June 1930 issue of *Amazing Stories* includes a story about the Bermuda Triangle by Hyatt Verrill.

The first book specifically on the subject was a self-published work by John Wallace Spencer, *Limbo of the Lost* (1969), which as a 1973 Bantam paperback found a huge readership. In 1970 a feature-film documentary, *The Devil's Triangle,* brought the subject a new, larger audience. Bermuda Triangle fever peaked in 1974 with the publication of *The Bermuda Triangle,* a major bestseller (with five million sales worldwide) written by Charles Berlitz with J. Manson Valentine. That year two paperbacks, Richard Winer's *The Devil's Tri-*

(Continued from previous page)

angle and John Wallace Spencer's *No Earthly Explanation*, racked up impressive sales.

The articles and books on the subject betrayed little evidence of original research. Attentive readers could not help noticing that mostly the Triangle's chroniclers rewrote each other's work. In 1975 Larry Kusche, a librarian at Arizona State University, published a devastating debunking of what he called the "manufactured mystery." In the book, titled *The Bermuda Triangle Mystery—Solved,* he did the archival digging that other writers had neglected. Weather records, the reports of official investigating agencies, newspaper accounts, and other documents indicated that the Triangle literature had played fast and loose with the evidence. For example, calm seas in the literature turned into raging storms in reality; mysterious disappearances became conventionally caused sinkings and crashes; the remains of ships "never heard from again" turned out to have been found long since.

In an April 4, 1975, letter to Mary Margaret Fuller, editor of *Fate,* a spokesman for Lloyd's of London wrote, "According to Lloyd's Records, 428 vessels have been reported missing throughout the world since 1955, and it may interest you to know that our intelligence service can find no evidence to support the claim that the 'Bermuda Triangle' has more losses than elsewhere. This finding is upheld by the United States Coastguard [sic] whose computer-based records of casualties in the Atlantic go back to 1958."

If the Triangle's proponents had been able to mount any credible defense, the Triangle might have retained some claim to being an authentic anomaly. Instead there was virtual silence. An exchange in *Pursuit* between Berlitz and another Triangle critic, British writer Paul Begg, inspired little confidence in would-be believers. Berlitz's response to a long list of factual errors was to note that Kusche and Begg had not actually visited the Triangle and that Kusche had once asked him "whether *The New Yorker* was a New York newspaper."

Occasional reappearances in supermarket tabloids notwithstanding, the once-famous Bermuda Triangle survives only as a footnote in the history of fads and passing sensations.

Further Reading:

"Another 'Bermuda Triangle' Mystery Vanishes." *Pursuit* 9,1 (January 1976): 15–16.

Begg, Paul. *Into Thin Air: People Who Disappear.* North Pomfret, VT: David and Charles, 1979.

———. "Symposium: False Facts." *Pursuit* 9,2 (April 1976): 42–43.

———. "Mr. Berlitz—Again!" *Pursuit* 11,2 (spring 1978): 73–75.

Berlitz, Charles. *Without a Trace.* Garden City, NY: Doubleday and Company, 1977.

———, with J. Manson Valentine. *The Bermuda Triangle.* Garden City, NY: Doubleday and Company, 1974.

———. "An Observation on Critics Whose Appraisal of Phenomena Is Undisturbed by Personal

(Continued from previous page)

Knowledge or Experience." *Pursuit* 11.2 (Spring 1978): 75–76.

Chorvinsky, Mark. "The Invisible Horizons of Vincent H. Gaddis." *Strange Magazine* (April 1991): 14–18,54–55.

Eckert, Allan W. "The Mystery of the Lost Patrol." *American Legion Magazine* (April 1962): 12–13, 39–41.

Gaddis, Vincent H. "The Deadly Bermuda Triangle Mystery." *Argosy* (February 1964): 28–29, 116–18.

———. *Invisible Horizons: True Mysteries of the Sea*. Philadelphia, PA: Chilton Books, 1965.

Kusche, Larry. *The Bermuda Triangle Mystery—Solved*. New York: Harper and Row, Publishers, 1975.

———. "The Bermuda Triangle and Other Hoaxes." *Fate* 28,10 (October 1975): 48–56.

Sand, George X. "Sea Mystery at Our Back Door." *Fate* 5,7 (October 1952): 11–17.

Sanderson, Ivan T. *Invisible Residents: A Disquisition upon Certain Matters Maritime, and the Possibility of Intelligent Life under the Waters of This Earth*. New York: World Publishing Company, 1970.

(Continued from page 383)

Edna, and son Donald crisscrossed the United States and spoke to large audiences of seekers who would join the Ballards's occult group, The "I AM" Activity.

Shaver's mystery

Until Richard Sharpe Shaver came along, nearly all hollow earth proponents had spoken of the inner world's inhabitants as members of an advanced, benevolent race whom it would be desirable for human beings to meet and befriend. Shaver, however, had another story to tell. Shaver technologized hell. In doing so, it should be noted, he insisted he was not doing so from a hollow earth perspective. The evil of which he warned a disbelieving world was located deep inside caverns, not in the world's actual interior. Still, his was recognizably a variant of the tradition that Symmes had been the first to popularize in America.

Shaver announced himself with a letter sent to the Chicago office of the science fiction pulp magazine *Amazing Stories*. If the letter had not fallen into the hands of editor Ray Palmer, who had an instinct for outlandish promotions, it would have ended up in a waste basket and vanished. But Palmer thought he saw something in Shaver's claim that he had recovered an ancient Lemurian alphabet. The two struck up a correspondence, during which Shaver's story grew ever more fantastic.

He told Palmer he had encountered evil creatures known as "deros," short for "detrimental robots" (or something like that; the definition kept shifting). Deros were not robots as ordinarily understood; "robots" was simply a name given to races produced by genetic engineering that the "Titans," the giant people of

Lemuria (the ancient Earth, not the lost continent), performed. Along with another Elder race of extraterrestrial origin, the Atlans, the Titans—some of whom were as tall as 300 feet—lived on the earth's surface until 12,000 years ago, when they were forced to escape to distant planets. Most of the "robots" fled into great caverns under the earth to avoid deadly radiation from the sun. (Some genetic products of the Titans, however, stayed on the surface, adjusted, and became the present human race.) Deros—demons in all but name, and close enough to it even there—were degenerate, sadistic idiots who had access to the advanced Atlan/Titan technology, which they used to heighten sexual pleasure during the orgies to which they were addicted. They also used the machines in marathon torture sessions on kidnapped surface people and also on the "teros" (integrative robots, who were not robots but good subterraneans who, though vastly outnumbered, were fighting the deros). They also employed the machines to cause accidents, madness, and other miseries in the world above the caves.

How did the deros get that way? Shaver was never entirely coherent on the subject. Here is the answer he gave in the June 1947 issue of *Amazing*:

> A dero is a cavern wight whose ancestors had the habit of bringing in the sunlight over the penetrays. Their evil nature is due to a constant "hearing" (telepathic) of sun vibrants because these same penetrays they use to bring in the sunlight and warmth were designed to handle thought-waves, to detect and augment waves of those frequencies heard by the brain. Their brains got dis (infections) on the lipoid films of the brain cells, where thought is generated. This went on for centuries, for an age, and the hereditary result was a dero, the ancient "Devil" of mythology, and his people—humans whose minds handle only disintegrant pattern thought.

In any event, between 1945 and 1948, *Amazing* and its companion pulp *Fantastic Adventures* were filled with thrilling and terrifying tales of the underworld. Most of these stories bore Shaver's byline, but Palmer was at least a large editorial presence in them. The first, "I Remember Lemuria!," all 31,000 words of it, appeared in *Amazing*'s March 1945 issue, and in the introduction Shaver told readers of his vivid memories of life as "Mutan Mion, who lived many thousands of years ago in Sub Atlan, one of the great cities of ancient Lemuria!"

A flood of letters crossed Palmer's desk, some from individuals who claimed they, too, had met with the deros, or something like them anyway. Not all readers were pleased, however. Some were furious. Convinced that some sort of swindle was afoot (and given Palmer's reputation, this was not an unfounded suspicion), they feared that the so-called Shaver mystery would make all science fiction fans, hungry for respectability, look like fools—or worse. By 1948 their protests led Ziff-Davis, *Amazing*'s parent company, to order the series stopped. Voluntarily or otherwise (it has never been clear), Palmer left soon thereafter.

After co-founding *Fate*, with *Flying* editor Curtis Fuller, in 1948, and editing it under the house pseudonym Robert N. Webster (shared with Fuller) for its first years, Palmer moved to tiny Amherst, Wisconsin, to produce his own alternative-reality magazines, which carried occasional Shaver material. In 1961 Palmer introduced *The Hidden World*, a series of magazines in trade-paperback format, and over the next three years reprinted Shaver's original articles and ran new contributions from a diminishing band of enthusiasts.

Biographical research determined that between the 1930s and early 1940s Shaver had spent significant time in mental hospitals.

In later years a significant faction of Shaver's fan base consisted of persons whose interest was in Shaver as a colorful, if obscure, cultural figure. Few, if any, actually believed Shaver's stories to be true in any literal sense, but they found them interesting for a variety of reasons. Biographical research determined that between the 1930s and early 1940s Shaver had spent significant time in mental hospitals. In other words, during much of the period in which he claimed to have been living in the caves with tero allies, he was institutionalized. Shaver's tales arose not from non-pathological visionary experiences, apparently, but from schizophrenic hallucinations. Still, not many observers doubted his sincerity, and Shaver, who died in Arkansas in November 1975, swore to the inner world's reality to the end of his life.

In Rainbow City

Another *Amazing* reader who claimed to have met the deros was Maurice Doreal (born Claude Doggins). Like Ballard, he said he was friends with the Masters who live inside Mount Shasta, though unlike Guy Warren Ballard, he said they hail from Atlantis, not Lemuria. According to him, the Atlanteans and the Lemurians live in great caverns under the earth and regularly visit, and receive visits from, other star systems. His own occult group, the Brotherhood of the White Temple, headquartered in the Pleiades, engaged in complex interstellar diplomacy and warfare, which Doreal detailed at length in his various writings.

In 1946, W. C. Hefferlin published some items in *Amazing* about Rainbow City, a metropolis in a dumbbell-shaped valley surrounded by Antarctic ice and once occupied by a race of extraterrestrial giants who arrived on earth long ago while fleeing their enemies, a powerful alien race known as the Serpent People. "From the Temples and Libraries of a great city, one of seven built of plastics, here even now on this earth as it was 2 million years ago," Hefferlin intoned, "does our information come. Six of these great cities are encased in eternal ice, and the seventh only is in open ground and protected and warmed by hot springs. Yet it is isolated as to ordinary approachable means by ice walls ten thousand feet high." The hot springs keep Rainbow City at a pleasant 75° at all times, rendering it a veritable Shangri La.

Hefferlin's account of the space people's secrets, however, met a chilly reception from those readers who knew something about science. Typical of the responses was one from a reader who scoffed, "I honestly cannot see how anyone with a high school education could read Mr. Hefferlin's article without laughing."

Hefferlin dropped out of sight for a year, to reappear for a time with his wife, Gladys, under the sponsorship of Borderland Sciences Research Associates (BSRA), an occult-oriented group headquartered in Vista, California, with editorial standards even less demanding than *Amazing*'s.

As the Hefferlins told it, the source of their esoteric knowledge was a mysterious "Emery," whom they had met in 1927 in San Francisco. For a time they and Emery fell out of contact, but they reconnected in 1935, when they learned he was working "in radio circles" in New York. They began thought communication with him. The messages would come through Gladys, who was, like Emery, a gifted telepath.

Emery meantime would go off on unexplained trips to different parts of the world. Eventually, just as World War II was breaking out in 1939, Emery confided that for the past few years a group of Masters—the Ancient Three, who lived in an underground retreat under the Tibetan surface—had guided his efforts in fulfillment of a cosmic plan, which included the repopulation of Rainbow City. Rainbow City first had to be rediscovered, however. After a number of flights over Antarctica, Emery succeeded in locating it in 1942. He and his associates managed to enter it, where they found that six levels lay beneath. Though no one had lived there for a very long time, the technology continued to run, and vast gardens grew, tended to by immense butterflies. Tunnels from an enormous subway system stretch under much of the planet. The Hefferlins found one end of it on a mountainside near Sheridan, Wyoming. Flying saucers, the Hefferlins reported, are ships flown by agents of the Ancient Three in their quest to uncover remains of additional lost cities.

Rainbow City was revived in 1951, in Robert Ernst Dickhoff's self-published *Agharta: The Subterranean World*, and again in 1960, in *Rainbow City and the Inner Earth People*, by Michael Barton. Writing as Michael X, Barton also revived the Shaver mystery (which the Hefferlins had specifically disavowed), adding the detail that Venusians and Masters were then allied in a struggle to wipe out the deros. He further claimed to be receiving psychic communications from the long-deceased Marshall Gardner, who kindly endorsed Barton's book.

Far and away the most popular of all such books was *The Hollow Earth* (1964), by Raymond Bernard, the pseudonym of Walter Siegmeister. Siegmeister, a peculiar character, had operated on the fringes of the occult scene since the 1930s, promoting assorted enterprises such as a South American utopian colony (which the U.S. Post Office concluded did not exist) and publishing his bizarre notions about gender (which he believed to be unhealthy) and the male sex (a mutation which ought to be eliminated). Even so, *The Hollow Earth* contributed little new to the inner-earth legends and, in fact, quoted at length from nineteenth-century texts on the subject; the rest of the book focused on Ray Palmer's ruminations, as well as speculations about the conspiracy to hide the truth about the hollow earth, flying saucers, and pole holes. Yet in the inexplicable ways of the marketplace, the book sold robustly, saw multiple printings, and introduced many readers to the subject.

Shaver's version of the inner earth dominated *Secret of the Ages*, a 1974 book by Brinsley le Poer Trench (later Lord Clancarty). According to Trench, an occult-infused saucer enthusiast, evil inner-earthers regularly kidnap surface people and brainwash them into becoming their agents. Now, he said, the "ground work has … been prepared for takeover of this planet by those who live inside it." Small-circulation periodicals such as Richard Toronto's *Shaverton*, Mary Martin's *The Hollow Hassle*, and, later, Dennis G. Crenshaw's *The Hollow Earth Insider* have carried Shaver material and other inner-earth speculation into the present. In the 1980s the "Dark Side" school of ufological extremism, which married far-right political conspiracy theories to paranoia-drenched UFO tall tales, incorporated deros and the hollow earth into its complex mythology.

Nazis inside the earth

Some hollow earth believers show evidence of not just fascination with but open sympathy for Nazi Germany. The chief figure in the Nazi hollow earth movement was a Toronto man named Ernst Zundel, who wrote under the name Christof Friedrich. Zundel operated a clearinghouse for Nazi materials and contended, as have many fellow neo-Nazis, that the Holocaust never took place. In *UFOs—Nazi Secret Weapons?* (1976), he wrote that when World War II ended, Hitler and his Last Battalion boarded a submarine and escaped to Argentina; they then established a base for advanced saucer-shaped aircraft inside the hole at the South Pole. When the Allies learned what had happened, they dispatched Adm. Richard E. Byrd and a "scientific expedition"—in fact (or anyway in Zundel's account) an army—to attack the Nazi base, but they were no match for the superior Nazi weapons.

To Zundel the Nazis were "outer earth representatives of the 'inner earth.'" This in his view accounted for their racial superiority. In 1978, with the publication of his *Secret Nazi Polar Expeditions*, Zundel solicited funds for his own polar expedition, for which he planned to charter an airliner with a large swastika painted on its fuselage. The swastika not only would bear witness to Zundel's ideological loyalties but also let the inner-earthers know that their visitors were friendly.

Around the same time an expedition to the opposite pole, the northern one, was being planned by Tawani Shoush of Houston, Missouri. Shoush, a retired Marine Corps pilot and head of the International Society for a Complete Earth, wanted to fly a dirigible through the pole, where he and his companions would meet the "Nordic" inner-earthers and possibly join them permanently in their realm. "The hollow earth is better than our own world," he told *Chicago Tribune* columnist Bob Greene (October 31, 1978). Though he denied harboring Nazi sympathies, his stationery prominently featured a swastika. Neither Zundel's nor Shoush's expedition ever got off the ground, literally or figuratively.

An openly pro-Nazi, virulently anti-Semitic work, Norma Cox's self-published *Kingdoms within Earth* (1985) held that an international Zionist conspiracy has concealed the truth about the hollow earth as part of its plot to—what else?—

enslave the human race. In this and other homemade books, as well as in a newsletter titled *Secrets*, the unabashedly racist Cox, an elderly Arkansas woman, warned that "here in the United States the White Christian is targeted for extinction," and soon Jesus himself will do open battle with the demonic inner-earthers and their surface-dwelling allies. In the meantime, she noted, "it appears that Deros have all but taken charge of the world."

Comparable themes figured in literature published by Cosmic Awareness Communications of Olympia, Washington. The organization claimed to have its information from spirit beings who channel through the group's representatives.

Further Reading:

Beckley, Timothy Green, ed. *The Smoky God and Other Inner-Earth Mysteries.* New Brunswick, NJ: Inner Light Publications, 1993.

Bernard, Raymond [pseud. of Walter Siegmeister]. *The Hollow Earth: The Greatest Geographical Discovery in History.* New York: Fieldcrest Publishing, 1964.

Clark, Jerome. *Hidden Realms, Lost Continents, and Beings from Other Worlds.* Detroit, MI: Visible Ink Press, 2010.

Collins, Paul. *Banvard's Folly: Thirteen Tales of Renowned Obscurity, Famous Anonymity, and Rotten Luck.* New York: Picador USA, 2001.

Corrales, Scott. "The Realms Below: Where Fact Meets Fiction." *Strange Magazine* 15 (spring 1995): 6–11,54–55.

Cox, Norma. *Kingdoms Within Earth.* Marshall, AR: The Author, 1985.

Crabb, Riley. *The Reality of the Underground.* Vista, CA: Borderland Sciences Research Associates, 1960.

Crenshaw, Dennis. "Special Report on the Shaver Mystery." *Hollow Earth Insider* 3,6 (1996): 10–20.

Fitch, Theodore. *Our Paradise Inside the Earth.* Council Bluffs, IA: The Author, 1960.

Friedrich, Christof [pseud. of Ernst Zundel]. *UFOs—Nazi Secret Weapons?* Toronto, Ontario: Samisdat, 1976.

———. *Secret Nazi Polar Expeditions.* Toronto, Ontario: Samisdat, 1978.

Kafton-Minkel, Walter. *Subterranean Worlds: 100,000 Years of Dragons, Dwarves, the Dead, Lost Races and UFOs from Inside the Earth.* Port Townsend, WA: Loompanics Unlimited, 1989.

Kossy, Donna. *Kooks: A Guide to the Outer Limits of Human Belief.* Los Angeles: Feral House, 1994.

Martin, Mary J., and Tim R. Swartz, eds., with bonus material by Sean Casteel. *The Best of the Hollow Earth Hassle.* New Brunswick, NJ: Global Communications, 2008.

Michell, John. *Eccentric Lives and Peculiar Notions.* San Diego, CA: Harcourt Brace Jovanovich, 1984.

Norman, Eric [pseud. of Brad Steiger]. *The Under-People.* New York: Award Books, 1969.

Standish, David. *Hollow Earth: The Long and Curious History of Imagining Strange Lands, Fantastical Creatures, Advanced Civilizations, and Marvelous Machines Below the Earth's Surface.* Cambridge, MA: Da Capo Press, 2006.

Trench, Brinsley le Poer. *Secret of the Ages: UFOs from Inside the Earth.* London: Souvenir Press, 1974.

Walton, Bruce A., ed. *A Guide to the Inner Earth.* Jane Lew, WV: New Age Books, 1983.

X, Michael [pseud. of Michael Barton]. *Rainbow City and the Inner Earth People.* Los Angeles: Futura, 1960.

Jacko

On June 30, 1884, it is recorded, a strange creature was captured near the village of Yale in south-central British Columbia. As he glimpsed it from a passing British Columbia Express train, engineer Ned Austin's immediate thought was that it was someone lying dangerously near the tracks. He brought the train to a near-immediate standstill.

Suddenly the "man" stood up and uttered a barking sound, then scrambled up one of the bluffs along the Fraser River. Crew members chased the "demented Indian"—which is what they thought the figure to be—until finally they trapped it on a rocky ledge. The conductor, R. J. Craig, climbed to a point about forty feet above it and dropped a rock on its head, knocking it unconscious. The pursuers were then able to tie it up and bring it to town, where it was harbored at the jail.

According to the *British Colonist* (a Victoria newspaper) for July 4, the creature, quickly dubbed Jacko, turned out to be "something of the gorilla type standing about 4 feet 7 inches in height and weighing 127 pounds. He has long, black, strong hair and resembles a human being with one exception, his entire body, excepting his hands (or paws) and feet, are [sic] covered with glossy hair about one inch long. His forearm is much longer than a man's forearm, and he possesses extraordinary strength." The captive subsisted on berries and fresh milk. Noting that some locals had reported seeing a "curious creature" in the past two years, the *Colonist* asked, "Who can unravel the mystery that now surrounds Jacko? Does he belong to a species hitherto unknown in this part of the country?"

The July 9 issue carried a letter from J. B. Goop of Nanaimo, former superintendent of the Lytton Indian Mission and apparently a Catholic priest or monk. Intrigued by the Jacko story, Goop offered some information which "may throw additional light upon this strange event." Perhaps, he suggested, the Jacko encounter may "confirm some mysterious rumors that were current amongst the entire tribe in that locality during our residence":

> On three different occasions in successive years, and in entirely different points of observation, the most startling reports were circulated far and wide, that when camping out for purposes of hunting, fishing, gathering wood and berries, certain of our Indians had been visited in the dead of night by something that seemed half-man half-beast, which had come

into the tents whilst [the campers were] sleeping or prowled around their encampment, producing the greatest consternation and amazement. The idea prevailed that certain wild men of the woods were at large in the less frequented parts of the country.... We, at the time, laughed at their fears and pooh-poohed the matter.

In the 1950s, after Sasquatch/Bigfoot reports in the Pacific Northwest became the focus of popular interest and speculation, newspaperman Brian McKelvie searched for earlier press accounts and found the Jacko story. He pointed it out to John Green and René Dahinden, who were just embarking on what would be lifelong careers as Sasquatch hunters. He told them that this was the only surviving record of the incident; other area papers, which could have confirmed the story, had been lost in a fire. In 1958 Green interviewed an elderly Yale man, August Castle, who claimed to remember the incident, though his parents had not taken him to the jail to see Jacko. Green also received a letter from Adela Bastin, who reported that her mother remembered the stories from Yale people.

The Jacko tale first appeared between book covers in Ivan T. Sanderson's *Abominable Snowmen: Legend Come to Life* (1961). Sanderson wrote, "Now, whatever you may think of the press, you cannot just write off anything and everything reported by it that you don't like, don't believe in, and don't want." The article was, he declared, "excellent ... factual ... hardly being at all speculative." Thereafter hardly a book on Sasquatch failed to mention Jacko. In 1973 Dahinden and coauthor Don Hunter reported that, according to the grandson of a man who had been a judge in Yale in 1884, Jacko "was shipped east by rail in a cage, on the way to an English sideshow." No more was heard of him, and locals assumed that he had died in transit.

> The late primatologist John Napier thought "the description [of Jacko] would fit an adult chimpanzee or even a juvenile male or adult female gorilla...."

The late primatologist John Napier thought "the description [of Jacko] would fit an adult chimpanzee or even a juvenile male or adult female gorilla, but unless it was an escapee from a circus it is difficult to imagine what an African ape was doing swanning about in the middle of British Columbia. At that time chimpanzees were still fairly rare creatures in captivity."

Meanwhile, in his continuing effort to get to the bottom of the matter, Green learned that microfilms of contemporary British Columbia newspapers did exist, not in the British Columbia archives, where McKelvie had looked, but at the University of British Columbia. In the July 9, 1884, issue of the *Mainland Guardian*, published in New Westminster, he found a story datelined two days earlier, from a reporter passing through Yale. "The 'What Is It' is the subject of conversation in town," he wrote. "How the story originated, and by whom, is hard for one to conjecture. Absurdity is written on the face of it. The fact of the matter is, that no such animal was caught, and how the *Colonist* was duped in such a manner, and by such a story, is strange." Two days later another paper, the *British Columbian*, reported that the Jacko story had sent some 200 persons scurrying to the jail, where the "only wild man visible was [keeper] Mr. Murphy ... who completely exhausted his patience" answering questions about the nonexistent beast.

Another telling item, recovered decades later, was reprinted in the *Colonist* the following August 24. The source, cited as the *British Columbian,* had received a letter from a reader from Chilliwhack, asserting that Jacko was now on exhibition in Centerville. "We suppose there is a good point in the joke," the editor sniffed, "but we are really not able to discover it, and we are afraid our readers might be equally unfortunate." The implication seems to be that the *Colonist* realized it had been the victim of a prank but was too embarrassed to own up to it in an open retraction; thus, it took an item from another paper which made it clear that the joke was stale and should be left to die.

Though Green now was satisfied that Jacko was a piece of fiction, those unwilling to abandon the tale of a captured Sasquatch could take heart from Russ Kinne's argument that rival newspapers were simply trying to discredit the *Colonist.* Green noted, however, that the *Colonist* did not dispute its critics. To all appearances, it was as much a victim of the joke as its readers.

A few defenders have trumpeted the decades-old testimony of elderly Yale citizens. In the absence of more compelling evidence, it seems likely that these individuals were dimly recalling the excitement, not the creature itself, that the Jacko story stirred up. Comparably dubious is a speculation proposed by the late physical anthropologist and Sasquatch proponent Grover Krantz, who contended that P. T. Barnum may have exhibited Jacko as "Jo-Jo the Dog-Faced Boy." Cryptozoology scholar George M. Eberhart counters that "it is fairly well established that Jo-Jo was a Russian man, Fedor (or Theodore) Jeftichew, born in 1868 and afflicted with hypertrichosis, which caused him to have long, silky facial hair."

The one uncontested fact of the matter is that newspapers on the Western frontier often published fantastic reports of questionable authenticity. To every available appearance, Jacko existed only in print.

Further Reading:

Coleman, Loren. *Bigfoot! The True Story of Apes in America.* New York: Paraview Pocket Books, 2003.

Eberhart, George M. "Jacko." In *Mysterious Creatures: A Guide to Cryptozoology.* Volume One: A–M, 255. Santa Barbara, CA: ABC-CLIO, 2002.

Green, John. *On the Track of the Sasquatch.* Agassiz, British Columbia: Cheam Publishing, 1968.

Green, John, and Sabina W. Sanderson. "Alas, Poor Jacko." *Pursuit* (January 1975): 18–19.

Hunter, Don, and René Dahinden. *Sasquatch.* Toronto, Ontario: McClelland and Stewart, 1973.

Kinne, Russ. "Jacko Reconsidered." *Pursuit* (April 1976): 43.

Napier, John. *Bigfoot: The Yeti and Sasquatch in Myth and Reality.* New York: E. P. Dutton and Company, 1973.

Sanderson, Ivan T. *Abominable Snowman: Legend Come to Life.* Philadelphia, PA: Chilton Books, 1961.

Martian Mummies and Others

If we are to credit an account from the French newspaper *Le Pays* for June 17, 1864, scientists have had physical proof of visitation from other worlds for nearly a century and a half.

Two geologists, identified only as Paxton and Davis, working near "Pic James, Arrapahaya province, U.S.A.," broke into an egg-shaped rock and discovered cavities inside. As they explored them, they found a white metallic jar covered with engraved hieroglyphics. Under the floor of this cavity was another hollowed-out space containing a jar looking much like the first. This one, however, had something inside it: a thirty-nine-inch mummified body "covered with a calciferous mass."

Paxton and Davis carefully removed the mummy from the container. Examination revealed that it had no hair on its head or face. Its skin was wrinkled. It could have been the remains of a human child except for the unsettling detail that a "trunk" grew out of the middle of its forehead.

An identical story was published in *La Capital*, a Rosario, Argentina, newspaper, on October 13, 1877. This time the discovery, again credited to Paxton and Davis, occurred near the Carcarañá River, near whose banks the egg-shaped object lay half-buried. The body and related artifacts were put on display in a local tavern and subsequently lost.

When the Argentine story was rediscovered a century later, at least two expeditions were sent to the site to investigate. Neither uncovered anything of interest. Sometime later ufologist Fabio Picasso happened upon the earlier French story, cited in a book by ancient-astronaut theorist Robert Charroux. Clearly the *La Capital* account was a plagiarism of the first, which itself was dubious. Many nineteenth-century newspapers routinely carried outrageous yarns, often set in some distant place inaccessible to a doubting reader who might seek verification.

Another tall tale set in South America describes a discovery allegedly made in 1878, just a year after its Argentinian counterpart. One "A. Seraro, Chemist" wrote to the *South Pacific Times* of Callao, Peru, to report that he had found a huge aerolite (meteorite). As he dug through several layers of mineral in his excavation, he uncovered the body of a humanoid creature some four and a half feet tall. Alongside it was a hieroglyph-covered silver plate. The aerolite, he learned from his translation of the alien language, was a ship from Mars.

The story came to the attention of the *New York Times*, which reprinted it with this sardonic commentary in its August 17 issue:

> Undoubtedly, the Peruvians mean well, and tell the best lies they can invent. Indeed, it can be readily perceived that the heart of the inventor of the aerolite story was in the right place, and that his faults were those of the head. The truth is that the Peruvians have never been systematically taught how to lie. Very probably, if they had our educational advantages, they would lie with intelligence and effect, and it is hardly fair for us ... to despise the Peruvians for what is their misfortune, rather than their fault.

A tale with some overlapping details saw print in the *Missouri Democrat* of St. Louis on October 19, 1865. (The account was widely reprinted in newspapers throughout the country in the following weeks.) It was credited to a fur trapper named James Lumley, who was staying at a local hotel for a few days. While there, he related his alleged experience "in the mountains about seventy-five and one hundred miles above the Great Falls" in what would be the state of Montana.

[H]e saw a bright, luminous, fast-moving object through the air. After five seconds or so, it burst into pieces in the fashion of a skyrocket.

One evening after sunset in September 1864, as he happened to be gazing eastward, he saw a bright, luminous, fast-moving object through the air. After five seconds or so, it burst into pieces in the fashion of a skyrocket. "A few minutes later," the *Democrat* recounted, "he heard a heavy explosion, which jarred the earth very perceptibly, and this was shortly after followed by a rushing sound, like a tornado sweeping through the forest. A strong wind sprang up about the same time, but suddenly subsided. The air was also filled with a peculiar odor of a sulphurous character."

Though this was certainly unusual, Lumley made little of it. The next day, however, the events came to mind when he discovered, two miles from his camp, a path cut through the woods:

> [For] several rods [a rod measures 16.5 feet] wide-giant trees [were] uprooted or broken off near the ground, the tops of hills shaved off and the earth plowed up in many places. Great and widespread havoc was everywhere visible. Following up this track of desolation, he soon ascertained the cause of it in the shape of an immense stone driven into the side of a mountain. An examination of this stone, or so much of it as was visible, showed that it was divided into compartments, that in various places it was carved with curious hieroglyphics. More than this, Mr. Lumley also discovered fragments of a substance resembling glass, and here and there dark stains, as though caused by a liquid. He is confident that the hieroglyphics are the work of human hands, and that the stone itself, although but a fragment of an immense body, must have been used for some purpose by animated beings.

The newspaper added, "Strange as the story appears, Mr. Lumley relates with so much sincerity that we are forced to accept it as true." Beyond Lumley's testimony and the newspaper story, there is no other record of the alleged event or of any kind of extraordinary meteoritic fall in the upper Rocky Mountain west in 1864.

Eighteen ninety-seven was a big year for Martians. The *Houston Daily Post*, May 2, 1897, wrote "An aerolite fell in Belgium, injuring a man who was working in the fields. It weighed thirty pounds, one side being smooth and covered with what resembled hieroglyphics cut by means of an instrument. Some people think it may be a message from Mars."

A second 1897 story linking "hieroglyphics" and the fall of a meteorite concerned someone identified as "Prof. Jeremiah McDonald" (sic) of Binghamton, New York. (The correct spelling is MacDonald. Unlike some characters who figure in nineteenth-century marvel stories, he was not a fictitious person but a Binghamton physician and, later, author of a book on astrology.) As the *New York Times* told the story the next day, MacDonald had been walking home in the early hours of November 13, when a blinding light startled him. Almost at the same time, something plowed into the ground near his residence. When dug up, the object proved to be "a mass of some foreign substance ... fused by intense heat." After cold water was poured on it, it cooled down sufficiently to be handled. When it was broken open, a sulphurous odor wafted upwards. "Prof. Whitney of the High School" pronounced it unlike any meteorite he had ever seen. The *Times* went on:

> Inside was found what might have been a piece of metal on which were a number of curious marks that some think to be characters. Several persons have advanced the opinion that this is a message from another planet, probably Mars. The marks bear some resemblance to Egyptian writing, in the minds of some. Prof. McDonald [sic] is among those who believe the mysterious ball was meant as a means of communication with another world.

On the eighteenth, the paper ran an interview with "Prof. Wiggins" of Ottawa, Ontario, linking Martian communicators with the meteorite. He expressed the opinion that Martians had been shooting message-bearing missiles to the earth for thousands of years. As evidence he cited the traditions of "ancient Jews and other nations" concerning sacred works that fell from the heavens. "As the earliest important records were preserved in stone," he reasoned, "it seems probable that the idea originated with certain aerolites like that of Binghamton."

The most notorious story of a Martian incursion came along in the spring of 1897, in the midst of a great turn-of-the-century, still-unexplained wave of mysterious airships (examined at length in the final chapter of my *Hidden Realms, Lost Continents, and Beings from Other Worlds*). In a dispatch out of tiny Aurora in north Texas, the *Dallas Morning News* of April 19 related that at 6 A.M. on the seventeenth, an airship collided with a windmill and "went to pieces with a terrific explosion." In the wreckage searchers came upon the "badly disfigured" body of a small being thought to be a "native of the planet Mars." Indecipherable "hiero-

(Continued on page 399)

Devil's Sea

During the Bermuda Triangle fad of the 1970s, Charles Berlitz, Ivan T. Sanderson, and other writers put forth a parallel claim. According to them, this fabled region of lost planes and ships off Florida had a counterpart off the eastern or southeastern coast of Japan (specifically, around the island of Miyake), site of the "devil's sea." There, vanishings allegedly happened so suddenly that affected craft usually were unable to sound a distress call.

As with the Bermuda Triangle, speculation held that space-time, magnetic, or gravitational anomalies—or else extraterrestrial kidnappers, or even, as in a theory proposed by Sanderson, an intelligent, Earth-dwelling, underwater race—were responsible for the disappearances. It was also claimed that the Japanese government viewed the situation with alarm.

After a period of celebrity status in tabloid newspapers, pulp magazines, and sensationalistic books, the devil's sea fell victim to the first real research into the legend, which was conducted by Arizona State University librarian Larry Kusche. Kusche traced the story back to September 27 and 30, 1952, *New York Times* stories about an unusual oceanic disaster: the sinking of two Japanese ships via tidal wave from an underwater volcano. A January 15, 1955, *Times* report of another ship disaster used the term "devil's sea" and called it the "mystery graveyard of nine ships in the last five years."

In the early 1970s, Kusche corresponded with officials from Japan and nearby islands. None had ever heard the term "devil's sea," and all insisted the sinkings were in no way mysterious or unexplainable. The absence of radio messages in some events from the early 1950s could be attributed to the simple fact that many smaller fishing vessels did not have radios, owing to their owners' poverty.

Writing in 1975, Kusche concluded, "The story is based on nothing more than the loss of a few fishing boats 20 years ago in a 750-mile stretch of ocean over a period of five years. The tale has been reported so many times that it has come to be accepted as fact."

Berlitz's book-length treatment *The Dragon's Triangle* was published in 1989 to little attention.

Further Reading:

Bigham, Barbara J. "The Devil's Sea ... Another Bermuda Triangle?" *Fate* 28,7 (July 1975): 32–39.

Binder, Otto O. "Devil's Sea: Flying Saucer Death Trap." *Saga* (March 1970): 22–25, 68–74.

Drake, Rufus. "The Deadly Mystery of Japan's 'Bermuda Triangle.'" *Saga* (April 1976): 20-23, 54–57.

Kusche, Larry. *The Bermuda Triangle Mystery—Solved*. Buffalo, NY: Prometheus Books, 1986.

———. "The Bermuda Triangle and Other Hoaxes." *Fate* 28,10 (October 1975): 48–56.

Nichols, Elizabeth. *The Devil's Sea*. New York: Award Books, 1975.

Sanderson, Ivan T. *Invisible Residents: A Disquisition upon Certain Matters Maritime, and the Possibility of Intelligent Life under the Waters of This Earth*. New York: World Publishing Company, 1970.

(Continued from page 397)

glyphics" covered pieces of paper were found on or near the body. According to the account:

> The ship was too badly wrecked to form any conclusion as to its construction or its motive power. It was built of an unknown metal, resembling somewhat a mixture of aluminum and silver, and it must have weighed several tons. The town is full of people today who are viewing the wreck and gathering specimens of the strange metal from the debris. The pilot's funeral will take place at noon tomorrow.

No other contemporary document attests to this fantastic event, which ought to have alerted any reader, then or now, to the story's factlessness. In fact (or in fable anyway) just the day before, the *Morning News* had asked its readers to believe that residents of Kaufman County had observed an airship that looked like a "Chinese flying dragon ... a monster breathing red fire through its nostrils.... The legs were the propellers." Elsewhere in the issue we learn that at Farmersville "eye witnesses" saw "three men in the ship and ... heard them singing 'Nearer My God to Thee' and ... distributing temperance tracts"; at Waxahachie an airship was "operated by a woman" at the controls of something "resembling a sewing machine."

In the mid-1960s, ufologists looking for evidence of early UFO sightings stumbled upon the Aurora yarn. An investigator for astronomer and Project Blue Book consultant J. Allen Hynek learned the obvious quickly: that the story wasn't true and may have been concocted to revive the fortunes of a dying town. Over the next several years, however, insufficiently critical-minded souls descended on Aurora, shovels in hand, determined to dig up the body of the dead Martian. The legend was even the subject of a 1985 Grade-Z motion picture, *The Aurora Encounter*.

Two weeks after the *Morning News* dispatch, the *Houston Daily Post* published a long letter from John Leander of El Campo. Leander claimed to have his account from a local man identified only as "Mr. Oleson," a former boatswain in the Danish navy.

In September 1862, Leander wrote, Oleson had been among those cast adrift in the Indian Ocean when the brig *Christine* hit an uncharted island. As the storm raged, he and a handful of survivors awaited their inevitable doom on the barren rocky surface. Suddenly they witnessed an "immense ship" in the sky, clearly in trouble. It crashed into a cliff a few hundred yards away. Then, in Leander's words:

> Speechless with fear, they crept toward the wreck. It seemed a vessel as large as a modern battleship, but the machinery was so crushed that they could form no idea as to how the power was applied to the immense wings or sails, for they could plainly discern the fact that it was propelled by four huge wings. Strange implements and articles of furniture could be seen jumbled in an almost shapeless mass. They found in metal boxes covered with strange characters what they afterwards discovered to be very whole-

The airship looked like a Chinese flying, fire-breathing dragon, according to alleged eyewitnesses in Kaufman County, Texas, in 1897.

some and palatable food which, with the water in the rocks, saved them from immediate death.

But their horror was intensified when they found the bodies of more than a dozen men dressed in garments of strange fashion and texture. The bodies were a dark bronze color, but the strangest feature of all was the immense size of the men. They had no means of measuring their bodies, but estimated them to be more than 12 feet high. Their hair and beards were also long and as soft as the hair of an infant.

They found tools of almost every kind but they were so large that few of them could be used. They were stupefied with fright and one man, driven insane, jumped from the cliff into the boiling waves and was seen no more.

The others fled in horror from the fearful sight, and it was two days before hunger could drive them back to the wreck. After eating heartily of the strange food, they summoned courage to drag the gigantic bodies to the cliff and tumble them over.

Then with feverish haste they built a raft of the wreck, erected sails and gladly quit the horrible island. The sea had become as smooth as a lake and the experienced mariners made rapid progress. They tried as best they could to steer for Vergulen island, but fortunately in about sixty hours fell in with a Russian vessel headed for Australia. Three more of the old man's companions succumbed to their injuries and the awful mental strain and died before reaching port.

Fortunately as a partial confirmation of the truth of his story, Mr. Oleson took from one of the bodies a finger ring of immense size. It is made of a compo, the names of which are unknown to anyone who has ever examined it. The ring was taken from a thumb of the owner and measures 2 ¼ inches in diameter.

Anyone familiar with nineteenth-century adventure fiction will recognize all the elements here, starting with the wrecking of a ship in a storm and the marooning of its surviving crew on an unlocatable island. As Herman Melville said of Queequeg's fictional island home in *Moby-Dick*, "It is not down on any map; true places never are." Of course we also have the amazing coincidence of a spaceship crash at the same improbable spot, not to mention subsequent madness, suicide, and escape in a raft made up of parts of the alien wreckage so conveniently provided. The final detail owes much to period science fiction (for example, the pterodactyl freed at Queen's Hall in London after scientists scoff at Professor Challenger's claims of surviving dinosaurs in Conan Doyle's famous *The Lost World* [1912]), in which proof is produced and the sneerers silenced.

Further Reading:

Bullard, Thomas E., ed. *The Airship File: A Collection of Texts Concerning Phantom Airships and Other UFOs, Gathered from Newspapers and Periodicals Mostly during the Hundred Years Prior to Kenneth Arnold's Sighting.* Bloomington, IN: The Author, 1982.

Chariton, Wallace O. *The Great Texas Airship Mystery.* Plano, TX: Wordware Publishing, 1991.

Clark, Jerome. *Hidden Realms, Lost Continents, and Beings from Other Worlds.* Detroit, MI: Visible Ink Press, 2010.

Doyle, Sir Arthur Conan. *The Lost World.* London: Hodder and Stoughton, 1912.

Picasso, Fabio. "Infrequent Types of South American Humanoids." *Strange Magazine* Pt. I. 8 (fall 1991): 21–23,44. Pt. II. 9 (spring/summer 1992): 34–35, 55.

Watson, Nigel. "Down to Earth." *Magonia* 43 (July 1992): 3–11.

Mono Grande

The mystery of the *mono grande* (Spanish for "big monkey") is one of primatology's most intriguing unanswered questions. The only recognized primates in the Americas are small, long-tailed monkeys; yet occasional reports from the northern end of South America attest to the presence in remote regions of larger, tailless anthropoid apes. In fact, a controversial photograph purports to show the body of one such creature.

The story

Between 1917 and 1920, as the story is told, an expedition led by Swiss oil geologist François de Loys explored the swamps, rivers, and mountains west and southwest of Lake Maracaibo, near the Colombia-Venezuela border. The participants are said to have suffered considerable hardship, and a number died from disease or at the hands of hostile natives. In its last year, what remained of the expedition was camped on the banks of a branch of the Tarra River. Suddenly, two creatures, male and female, stepped from out of the jungle. Loys would claim that at first he thought they were bears, but as they advanced on the camp, he could see that they were apes of some sort, around five feet in height. His account omits the crucial detail of whether they were walking on two or four feet.

The creatures, giving every indication of being furious, broke off branches from nearby trees and wielded them as weapons, meanwhile crying and gesticulating vigorously. Finally they defecated into their hands and hurled the results at the party, who by now had their rifles to their shoulders. In the gunfire that followed, the female was killed, and the wounded male escaped back into the underbrush.

Though no one in the expedition was a zoologist, everyone supposedly understood that the animal was something out of the ordinary. Even the native guides swore they had never seen anything like it. Propping it up with a stick, members sat it on a gasoline crate and took a picture of it at a distance of ten feet. According to Loys, "Its skin was afterward removed, and its skull and jaw were cleaned and preserved." Later, the other remains were lost. Of the original twenty members of the expedition, allegedly no more than four survived.

UNEXPLAINED! Strange Sightings, Incredible Occurrences, and Puzzling Physical Phenomena

The photograph, however, came to light when a friend of Loys's, geologist and amateur anthropologist George Montandon, reviewed Loys's records and other expedition materials. Montandon was looking for information on a South American Indian tribe but considered the picture so important that he laid plans, as he wrote, to "go to the area in question to find the great ape of America." Loys, he noted, had expressed no urgent interest in publishing or otherwise publicizing the photograph. Only at Montandon's insistence was it brought to the world's attention, in 1929, when he reported it in papers that appeared in three French scientific journals. In these Montandon honored the ape's discoverer by offering the formal name *Ameranthropoides loysi* for what he contended was a new animal. That same year Loys told his story publicly for the first time in the popular magazine *Illustrated London News* (June 15).

The skeptical view

Hardly had the ink dried on any of these reports before debunkers were raising questions about Loys's credibility and Montandon's judgment. Leading the attack was the prominent British physical anthropologist Sir Arthur Keith, who strongly implied that Loys had taken a picture of a smaller, tailless animal, the spider monkey, whose existence in the region no one disputed, and tried to peddle it as something more interesting. Keith wrote, "A photograph of the animal from behind would have clinched matters, but the only photograph taken was one of the front—the animal being placed in a sitting position on a box of unknown size and with no standard object in or near the body of the animal to give a clue to the dimensions of its parts."

Nonetheless, other observers would judge the figure to be approximately five feet tall, calculating the size from the crate on which it sat (others of its kind are twenty inches high). How accurate these measurements are has always been a subject of dispute. *If* accurate, the animal was an extraordinary spider monkey indeed; the largest known spider monkey was three feet, seven inches.

In later years at least three persons, one of them an anthropologist, another a wildlife education specialist, have said they remember seeing a second Loys photograph. In this one an adult male is shown standing on either side of the animal. If such a photograph exists, it would make possible a more certain estimate of the animal's size. Unfortunately, no one has been able to produce the photograph or even to determine where it appeared, if anywhere. In this regard, it sits in the same limbo where the notorious "Thunderbird photograph"—discussed elsewhere in this book—may reside.

Keith also sneered at Loys's claim that the animal had thrown feces at the party, as if the idea were too silly to be entertained, though spider monkeys and some apes do such things in confrontations with enemies. He also viewed as suspicious the explorer's assertion that he had lost all evidence but the photograph.

A supposedly unknown ape—thought mistakenly by some to be a mono grande—photographed by François de Loys somewhere in the region of Colombia or Venezuela.

Keith's dismissal has remained for many the last word on the subject. In 1951, for example, *Natural History* reported that Keith had "easily demolished the 'new anthropoid.'" Another critic was a far less conservative figure, the cryptozoologist and anomalist Ivan T. Sanderson, champion of Sasquatch and other exotic creatures. "The original photograph is not just a case of mistaken identity," Sanderson declared, "it is an outright hoax, and an obnoxious one at that, being a deliberate deception." The picture, in his judgment, "is obviously that of a Spider-Monkey."

The nature of the beast

In an extended treatment of the episode, the respected anomalist Michael T. Shoemaker, who argued that the photo depicts an unknown animal, had this to say:

Examination of the photo reveals a strange, but logical, mixture of characteristics from different genera. The flat nose, with the nostrils widely separated and flared outwards, is characteristic of New World monkeys.... Other characteristics that strongly suggest a spider-monkey are the round ridges surrounding the eye sockets, the long hair, and the extremely long fingers and toes. On the other hand, many of its characteristics contradict such an identification.... Compared to other anthropoid apes, the creature's body is like a gibbon's, but its limbs and reduced thumbs are most like those of an orangutan.... The most extraordinary characteristics lie in the shape of the head. Spider-monkeys have a distinctly triangular face, with a pronounced prognathism (jutting of the jaw beyond the upper part of the face). The creature's face is oval, with its lower half much heavier, and with more powerful jaws, than a spider-monkey's. The creature also has little or no prognathism.... Although many New World monkeys tend to have a more prominent forehead than do Old World monkeys, none has a forehead so highly developed as this creature's forehead.

It should be stressed that Loys's is not the only report, real or concocted, of such an animal. The first printed reference appears in a 1553 chronicle by Pedro de Cieza de León, who mentions native accounts and refers to a Spaniard who said "he had seen one of these monsters dead in the woods, and it was the shape and appearance that was told." In *An Essay on the Natural History of Guiana* (1769), Edward Bancroft mentions Indian accounts of creatures "near five feet in height, maintaining an erect position, and having a human form, thinly covered with short, black hair." In 1861, in *The Romance of Natural History*, Philip Gosse pronounced as probable the existence of a "large anthropoid ape, not yet recognized by zoologists," in South America.

In 1876 Charles Barrington Brown, explorer of what was then British Guiana (now Guyana), wrote of what natives called the *Didi*, a "powerful wild man, whose body is covered with hair, and who lives in the forest." He heard it on more than one occasion and on another saw its footprints, or so they were identified to him.

Sighting reports continued into the twentieth century. In 1910 no less than the British Resident Magistrate saw two of them. In 1968 explorer Pino Turolla, while traveling in the area of Marirupa Falls in the jungle-covered mountains of eastern Venezuela, was told of the *mono grande*. The informant, his guide, said that three of the creatures, using branches for clubs, had attacked him and killed his son several years earlier. On his return to the United States, Turolla researched the matter and came upon the Loys photograph; on a subsequent expedition that same year he showed it to his guide, who confirmed that this was what the *mono grande* looked like. Turolla persuaded the guide to take him to the canyon where the fatal attack had taken place, and there, after hearing eerie howling sounds, the explorer saw two fleeing apelike bipeds about five feet tall. He claimed a second, briefer sighting two years later, while on an archaeological expedition on the eastern slope of the Andes in Ecuador.

A later published sighting came from Guyana in 1987. The witness, mycologist Gary Samuels, was doing field work for the New York Botanical Garden—in this instance gathering fungi from the forest floor—when he heard footsteps. When he looked up, expecting to see a Guyanese forester, he was startled to observe a five-foot-tall biped ape "bellowing an occasional 'hoo' sound."

The question of whether an anthropoid ape lives in South America remains an open one. There is, however, good reason to doubt the authenticity of the Loys photograph.

Unsavory associations

Another dimension of the Loys controversy emerged from the research of cryptozoologists Loren Coleman and Michel Raynal, who were to draw attention to the curious—more to the point, unsavory—role of George Montandon in the affair.

Montandon, a Swiss geologist who worked in France, favored a race-driven view of human evolution. He theorized that different human races come from different human species, with the white race—descendants of ancient *Homo sapiens*—at the top. Africans come from gorillas or chimpanzees, Asians from the orangutan, and American Indians from American anthropoids. Montandon saw the *Ameranthropoides loysi* as proof specifically of the last and, by extension, proof of the hypothesis generally.

Swiss geologist George Montandon believed that human races are descended from differing types of apes. Asians, for instance, are, according to him, descended from orangutans like this one, while Africans come from gorillas and chimpanzees.

If Montandon's idea was absurd and pseudoscientific, it was also—and more disturbingly—an expression of deeply rooted racial and ethnic hatreds. Montandon was fiercely anti-Semitic, once suggesting that "cutting off the nose of the Jewish females" would help reduce the Jewish population. He also boasted that Hitler had stolen his racial theories from him. During the German occupation of France (1940–1944) he served as an "ethno-racial" authority assigned to determine whether individuals had Jewish or Aryan features; if the former, they were sent directly to death camps. Intensely and understandably hated, Montandon was killed by French partisans in 1944.

Coleman and Raynal observe that Montandon's one paper on primatology (amid a slew of racist writings) dealt with the *Ameranthropoides loysi*, sure evidence of how important he took the alleged finding to be. According to them, "It should be clear that George Montandon belonged to the 'race' (!) of 'mad scientists' like Mengele or Lyssenko ... that this discovery for him demonstrated the polygenic [various] origin of humans, and therefore humans' classification in unrelated types, some of them deserving to be exterminated (in Montandon's worldview) as bringing alien genes."

The hoax exposed

In 2007, Raynal's further research uncovered documentation proving, essentially conclusively, that the photograph was faked. As early as 1946, in a book on apes and monkeys, physical anthropologist Earnest Hooton—an advocate of racial hierarchy himself, albeit not a sociopathic bigot like Montandon—wrote that in 1927 American petroleum engineer James Durlacher spoke with men who had been in Loys's expedition. They told him the creature in the picture was only a spider monkey.

In a letter to a Caracas newspaper in 1962, a friend of Loys, a physician named Enrique Tejera, called him a prankster given to tricks and jokes. He confirmed that the animal was indeed a spider monkey. Raynal subsequently found a 1960 book by French naturalist and medical doctor Raymond Fiasson, who wrote that Tejera had told him the same. The picture was taken near a small Venezuelan town, not in the depths of the jungle, suggesting that the melodramatic stories about the expedition's often fatal peril were also an invention.

It appears that the controversy is now closed. It also appears that Loys's hoax, even with the skepticism it evoked in some quarters, managed to be among the most enduring in the history of both cryptozoology and primatology.

Further Reading:

"An Alleged Anthropoid Ape Existing in America." *Nature* 123 (June 15, 1929): 924.

Bancroft, Edward. *An Essay on the Natural History of Guiana in South America.* London: T. Becket and P.A. DeHondt, 1769.

Camara, I., and G.H.H. Tate. "Letters: The 'Ape' That Wasn't an Ape." *Natural History* 60,6 (June 1951): 289.

Coleman, Loren, and Patrick Huyghe. *The Field Guide to Bigfoot, Yeti, and Other Mystery Primates Worldwide.* New York: Avon Books, 1999.

Coleman, Loren, and Michel Raynal. "De Loys's Photograph: A Tool of Racism." *The Anomalist* 4 (1996): 84–93.

Gosse, Phillip. *The Romance of Natural History.* London: James Nisbet and Co., 1861.

Heuvelmans, Bernard. *On the Track of Unknown Animals.* New York: Hill and Wang, 1958.

Keith, Sir Arthur. "The Alleged Discovery of an Anthropoid Ape in South America." *Man* 29 (August 1929): 135–36.

Picasso, Fabio. "More on the Mono Grande Mystery." *Strange Magazine* 9 (1992): 41, 53.

Shoemaker, Michael T. "The Mystery of the Mono Grande." *Strange Magazine* 7 (1991): 2–5, 56–60.

Shoemaker, Michael T., Hax [pseudonym], and Loren Coleman and Michel Raynal. "Letters to the Editors." *The Anomalist* 5 (1997): 143–53.

Shuker, Karl. "Alien Zoo: A Third Ameranthropoides Loysi Photo Witness." *Fortean Times* 112 (1998): 16.

Noah's Ark

The Book of Genesis, in chapters six through eight, tells the story of Noah, his family, and their escape from the Great Flood in an ark loaded with animals. At the conclusion of forty days and forty nights, the ark came to rest "upon the mountains of Ararat." Traditional and Bible literalists place this event in 2,345 B.C.E. (the Genesis account was written some 1,300 years later), though geologists and archaeologists, citing the paucity of scientific evidence, doubt that any such massive worldwide flood ever took place.

If the flood did not happen, Noah and his ark did not exist, and the Bible is not inerrant. In the view of most scholars, the story should be read as one of the many tales from all over the world of an immense flood and its chosen survivors. These stories do not prove that a universal deluge occurred; they seem to have arisen in response to devastating local floods that encompassed, if not the whole world, at least the world their victims occupied.

To fundamentalists such an interpretation is unacceptable, and so for a long time hopeful seekers have searched for the remains of Noah's ark on Mount Ararat. There *is* a Mount Ararat; actually, to be more specific, there are two of them: Great Ararat (16,900 feet high) and Little Ararat (12,900). Connecting the two is a rock saddle between 7,000 and 8,000 feet high. These mountains lie in extreme eastern Turkey, along the border of Iran and Armenia.

In fact, Ararat is an ancient name for Armenia and, later, for a small northern district of that nation. The name was not attached to the mountain until around the eleventh century. Other sources, in any case, place the final resting place of the ark elsewhere. The Koran mentions Mount Judi, associated with a mountain (subsequently renamed Judi after the Koran's account) to the south of Ararat. The first-century historian Flavius Josephus put the remains in what is now called Haran, a Turkish city near the Syrian border. Other ancient chroniclers had their own favored sites, most in Turkey but others in Greece, Armenia, and Iran.

Sightings and searches

In short, historical claims for an ark on Ararat, even with their long historical pedigree, are shaky indeed. Nonetheless, eventually Jews and Christians who gave thought to the subject came to believe that the ark's remains were still on Ararat. The pseudonymous travel writer Sir John Mandeville contended, straight-facedly, that on a clear day one could actually look up and see the ark. Around 1670, a Dutchman named Jan Struys, captured and enslaved by bandits in Armenia, met a hermit—or so he would claim later—on Ararat. Struys, believed by his captors to possess magical healing powers, treated the old man, who in gratitude handed him "a piece of hard wood of a dark color" and a sparkling stone, both of which "he told me he had taken from under the Ark."

In the nineteenth century a number of would-be discoverers climbed the mountain without finding anything—until 1876, when James Bryce of Oxford University came upon a four-foot-long stick near the peak of Great Ararat. He declared it to be a piece of the ark. On August 10, 1883, the *Chicago Tribune* published this colorful, but apparently entirely fictitious, tale:

> A paper at Constantinople announces the discovery of Noah's Ark. It appears that some Turkish commissioners appointed to investigate the avalanches on Mt. Ararat suddenly came on a gigantic structure of very dark wood, protruding from the glacier. They made inquiries of the local folk. These had seen it for six years, but had been afraid to approach it, because a spirit of fierce aspect had been seen looking out of the upper windows. The Turkish Commissioners, however, are bold men, not deterred by such trifles, and they determined to reach it.

> Situated as it was among the fastnesses of one of the glens of Mt. Ararat, it was a work of enormous difficulty, and it was only after incredible hardships that they succeeded. The Ark was in a good state of preservation.... They recognized it at once.

> There was an English-speaking man among them, who had presumably read his Bible, and he saw it was made of gopher wood, the ancient timber of the scriptures, which, as everyone knows, grows only on the plains of the Euphrates. Effecting an entrance into the structure, which was painted brown, they found that the Admiralty requirements for the conveyance of horses had been carried out, and the interior was divided into partitions 15 feet high.

> Into only three of these could they get, the others being full of ice, and how far the Ark extended into the glacier they could not tell. If, however, on being uncovered, it turns out to be 300 cubits long (the dimensions cited in Genesis), it will go hard with disbelievers.

In 1892, Archdeacon John Joseph Nouri, of the Chaldean Church, reported that he had found the ark and even entered it. While there, he took the opportunity to measure it, finding—unsurprisingly—that it was 300 cubits long.

In the following decades a number of expeditions were launched, typically with great hoopla and bold expectations. Most ended in disappointment, and a few others returned claiming sightings. A 1952 expedition led by wealthy French

(Continued on page 411)

David Lang Disappearance

On the afternoon of September 23, 1880, David Lang of Sumner County, Tennessee, was crossing a field near his home. His wife, Chanel, was watching him from the porch while her children, George and Sarah, played in the front yard. A Gallatin lawyer, "Judge" August Peck, and his brother-in-law were approaching in a buggy. Suddenly, Mrs. Lang screamed, and the two visitors gaped in disbelief. David Lang had just vanished in front of their eyes.

Extensive searches in the days ahead failed to uncover a trace of him. Nonetheless, an irregular circle fifteen feet in diameter marked the spot of his disappearance for years afterwards. Nothing could grow there, and even insects avoided it. Once the children ventured into the circle and heard their father's tormented voice echoing from another dimension.

This is the substance of an enduring "true mystery" legend that attained its widest popularity in the 1950s and 1960s, owing largely to the story in the July 1953 issue of *Fate*. Titled "How Lost Was My Father?," the piece was supposedly a firsthand account of the event by Sarah Lang, who related it in a 1931 interview with magazine writer Stuart Palmer. It further claimed that in April 1929 Sarah received a message via automatic writing. The message, in her father's handwriting, said, "Together now. Together now and forever ... after many years.... God bless you." To Sarah these words meant

"Mother and Father are together now in the World Beyond, after the nightmare years of separation."

Hershel G. Payne, a Nashville librarian who spent years trying to validate the story, found no archival evidence that a Lang family or an August Peck had ever lived in the area. Eventually he concluded that the tale's genesis was in a journalistic hoax, engineered by notorious traveling salesman Joe M. Mulholland (or Mulhatten in some accounts), who in the late nineteenth and early twentieth centuries contributed far-fetched yarns to various papers under the pseudonym Orange Blossom. In Payne's view, Mulholland probably had based his tale on a 1909 science fiction story, "The Difficulty of Crossing a Field," by Ambrose Bierce. One later chronicler, Jay Robert Nash, added to the confusion by suggesting that Bierce's story (set in Selma, Alabama, and concerning a "planter named Williamson") was the true one. In fact, there is no more reason to believe the Williamson story— which never pretended to be authentic— than its Lang variant.

Palmer's *Fate* account, credited to Lang's daughter, contains what are represented as samples of the victim's handwriting, automatic writing, and signatures by Sarah and a notary public. Investigator Robert Schadewald showed these to Minneapolis handwriting expert Ann B. Hooten, who studied them and declared all "were authored by one individual"—

(Continued from previous page)

presumably Palmer. Sarah Lang, in other words, was as much a figment of a hoaxer's imagination as was her father.

In 1999 a prominent composer wrote an opera, commissioned by Carey Perloff and the American Conservatory Theater in San Francisco. Titled *The Difficulty of Crossing a Field,* it was—obviously—a retelling of Bierce's story. The opera debuted in March 2002 in San Francisco. Warmly reviewed everywhere it has been performed since, *Difficulty* is now something of a contemporary classic. Fittingly, the composer's name happens to be David Lang. Ironically, reviewers mention Bierce, but few have caught the irony of the composer's identity.

Further Reading:

Edwards, Frank. *Stranger Than Science.* New York: Lyle Stuart, 1959.

"Fortean Corrigenda: The Disappearance of David Lang." *Fortean Times* 18 (1976): 6–7.

Nash, Jay Robert. *Among the Missing.* New York: Simon and Schuster, 1978.

Nickell, Joe, with John F. Fischer. *Secrets of the Supernatural: Investigating the World's Occult Mysteries.* Buffalo, NY: Prometheus Books, 1988.

Palmer, Stuart. "How Lost Was My Father?" *Fate* 6,7 (July 1953): 75–85.

Schadewald, Robert. "David Lang Vanishes ... Forever." *Fate* 30,12 (December 1977): 54–60.

Wilkins, Harold T. *Strange Mysteries of Time and Space.* New York: Citadel Press, 1958.

(Continued from page 409)

industrialist Fernand Navarra produced samples of wood that, when first tested, were dated at 5,000 years. A later, more accurate test resulted in a disappointing finding; the wood was from 800 C.E. and probably from a monks' shrine built on the side of the mountain. A 1960 *Life* photograph of a ship-shaped depression on the mountain sent an expedition racing for an on-site look—at what turned out to be a natural formation, created by a recent landslide.

In the years since then, there have been other expeditions and other claims, none especially noteworthy. In the late twentieth and early twenty-first centuries, allegations that satellite photographs picked up a mysterious, shiplike structure on Ararat excited researchers, but ended in so ambiguous a muddle that the British magazine *Fortean Times* compared it to the search for a crashed UFO. Most of the funding and personnel for these ventures have come from fundamentalist sources, who reason that if Genesis can be shown to be accurate about Noah, its account of creation can be trusted, too. Unfortunately, the inflated pronouncements of "arkeologists," as they are called, have proven to be neither accurate nor trustworthy.

Critics have no trouble pointing out the many flaws in arkeological thought. Scientists Charles J. Cazeau and Stuart D. Scott Jr. remarked, "If the ark had come to rest near the summit of Ararat 5,000 years ago, it likely would have shifted by

An illustration of Noah's Ark resting atop Mount Ararat.

glacial movement to lower elevations long ago. To at least some extent, the ark would have broken up, the wood strewn about on the lower slopes of the mountain, easily accessible even to those who are not mountain climbers." In addition, outright hoaxes have served to undercut the credibility of the quest.

Charles Fort, the great anomaly collector and satirist, had this to say about Nouri's account, in words that apply to all of the arkeological quests:

I accept that anybody who is convinced that there are relics upon Mt. Ararat, has only to climb up Mt. Ararat, and he must find something that can be said to be part of Noah's Ark, petrified perhaps. If someone else should be convinced that a mistake has been made, and that the mountain is really Pike's Peak, he has only to climb Pike's Peak and prove that the most virtuous of all lands was once the Holy Land.

Further Reading:

Balsiger, Dave, and Charles Sellier, Jr. *In Search of Noah's Ark*. Los Angeles: Sunn Classic Books, 1976.

Cazeau, Charles J., and Stuart D. Scott Jr. *Exploring the Unknown: Great Mysteries Reexamined*. New York: Plenum Press, 1979.

Fasold, David. *The Discovery of Noah's Ark*. London: Sidgwick and Jackson, 1990.

Fort, Charles. *The Books of Charles Fort*. New York: Henry Holt and Company, 1941.

Hitching, Francis. *The Mysterious World: An Atlas of the Unexplained*. New York: Holt, Rinehart and Winston, 1978.

Michell, John, and Robert J. M. Rickard. *Phenomena: A Book of Wonders*. New York: Pantheon Books, 1977.

"More on Noah's Ark." *INFO Journal* 2,2 (Spring 1970): 32.

Simmons, Robin. "Forbidden Arkeology." *Fortean Times* 120 (1999): 34–39.

Stein, Gordon. "Noah's Ark: Where Is It?" *Fate* 47,2 (February 1988): 40–46.

Wilkins, Harold T. "Is Noah's Ark on Ararat?" *Fate* 3,7 (November 1950): 60–66.

Paluxy Tracks

Did dinosaurs and human beings coexist? No, according to paleontologists, who maintain that dinosaurs and people missed each other by more than sixty million years. Nonetheless, evidence that seemed to indicate the contrary has intrigued creationists—Christian fundamentalists who reject evolution and who hold to a literal interpretation of the Book of Genesis—and secular theorists attracted to unorthodox readings of prehistory.

The story begins in 1909, with the accidental discovery, by a local teenager, of three-toed footprints in a tributary of the Paluxy River near Glen Rose, Texas, southwest of Fort Worth. Eventually they were attributed to meat-eating, bipedal dinosaurs known as theropods. In 1910, however, two young brothers fishing in the river came upon something seemingly different: not only the familiar three-toed tracks embedded in limestone but "giant man tracks" in their company. Fifteen to eighteen inches long, they quickly became known to local people, who regarded them as curiosities, apparently unaware of the radical implications of such a discovery.

By the 1930s, a Glen Rose man, Jim Ryals, was removing dinosaur and "giant man" tracks and peddling them to tourists. George Adams, another local, carved phony tracks of both kinds. Some of these "man" tracks, though amateurishly done, would survive to fool would-be truth-seekers decades later.

Around this time Roland Bird, field explorer for the American Museum of Natural History, examined tracks of both theropod and sauropod dinosaurs in the Paluxy's limestone bed. (Sauropod tracks were new to science, and Bird's discovery received wide publicity.) He also heard rumors of man tracks, and on one occasion Jim Ryals showed him what Bird called a "mystery track," mostly indistinct but "about 15 inches long, with a curious elongated heel." Bird could only speculate that some "hitherto unknown dinosaur or reptile" had made it.

Though Bird rejected any notion that these tracks demanded a revolutionary revision of conventional paleontology, others who came later were not so cautious. Some saw the tracks as a blow to a hated doctrine: evolution.

The first of these was Clifford Burdick who, intrigued by Bird's remarks, made a quick visit to Paluxy. A founder of the creationist Deluge Society, Burdick subsequently wrote an article for the July 25, 1950, issue of *Signs of the Times,* a Seventh Day Adventist publication, wherein he declared that the tracks amounted to a clear refutation of evolution. A popular and influential creationist book, John Whitcomb and Henry M. Morris's *The Genesis Flood* (1961), hailed the discovery, and soon it was being featured prominently in anti-Darwinian literature.

After reading A. E. Wilder-Smith's *Man's Origin, Man's Destiny* (1965), Baptist minister and filmmaker Stanley Taylor led several expeditions to Paluxy over a four-year period. In articles published by the Bible-Science Association, he argued that the tracks were of human origin, but it was his 1972 film, *Footprints in Stone,* that had the most impact on popular perceptions, especially in fundamentalist circles, though the claims also began showing up in Fortean literature.

Conservative Christian scientists leading the assault on Darwinism and its descendants were now certain that the discovery "suggests that simple and complex types of life were consistent in time past or during geologic ages," Clifford Burdick wrote in *Footprints in the Sands of Time* (1975). "This does not harmonize with the hypothesis that complex types of life evolved from lower or more simple forms." Moreover, the tracks not only cast doubt on science's view that the earth is of great age, the creationists asserted, but

At the American Museum of Natural History is this display of an apatosaurus skeleton next to a reproduction of dinosaur tracks from Paluxy.

constitute evidence for a Great Flood that creationists think occurred around 4,000 B.C.E. In the Flood humans and dinosaurs perished together. The tracks also showed, as Genesis indicates, that giants had once walked the planet.

Still, even some creationists were unconvinced. A 1970 study at the Paluxy site, conducted by creation scientists from Loma Linda University, concluded that the tracks were of dinosaurs; other alleged tracks were not that at all, merely the effects of erosion on rock. Ten years later, Tim Bartholomew and Glen J. Kuban, two young science students of creationist disposition, visited Paluxy, studied the tracks, and dismissed the human-origin belief. Some of the tracks were, in their judgment, "some type of unusual dinosaur tracks with elongate 'heels.'"

Evolutionary scientists, who till then had done no more than ridicule the creationist claims, launched a serious, if belated, study of the "human" prints. In the early 1980s four of them traveled to Glen Rose and two other Texas sites and examined every example cited in the anti-evolution literature. Some clearly had been carved and were not tracks at all, as even some creationists had deduced. Others, the scientists thought, were the product of erosion and also not tracks; either that, or they were dinosaur prints in which for various reasons the toe marks had not been preserved.

In 1984 Kuban made a remarkable discovery: colorations that followed the pattern of dinosaurian digits. In other words, sediments different from those in the rest of the track had filled in the toe marks and later hardened to rock.

At first other dinosaur specialists were reluctant to endorse Kuban's findings, since they violated a long-held conviction that bipedal dinosaurs nearly always walked on their toes. The Paluxy tracks suggested that these dinosaurs sometimes pressed the full weight of the soles of their feet on the ground. Subsequently, after other paleontologists found the same colorations in similar tracks near Clayton, New Mexico, they embraced Kuban's interpretation. Kuban and a colleague, Ronnie Hastings, invited leading creation proponents to the site and persuaded them that these were dinosaur, not human, prints. A creationist movie on Paluxy, *Footprints in Stone*, was soon withdrawn.

Even so, some creationist writers and evangelists continue to portray the tracks as human. One of them, Carl Baugh, has produced yet more "evidence" he claims to have uncovered at the site, including a hammer and a human finger. Kuban observes, "The hammer … is encased in a concretion (found loose rather than *in situ*), and thus may be unrelated to the age of the host rock…. The alleged human finger is inconsistent with preservational features of Cretaceous fossils in Texas, and shows a number of anatomic problems. Moreover, Baugh himself has acknowledged that it was found *loose* on a gravel bed. Thus, even if it were a real fossil finger, since it is not reliably linked to an ancient formation, it is of no anti-evolutionary value." Baugh, who has been accused (even by fellow creationists) of scientific incompetence and worse, claims degrees from unaccredited and even nonexistent institutions of higher learning. Kuban states flatly that he "has no valid degrees whatsoever."

The Paluxy prints reached their largest audience, by far, when on February 25, 1996, NBC broadcast a special hosted by the late Charlton Heston and titled *The Mysterious Origins of Man*. Baugh and his associate Don Patton dominated an uncritical treatment of Paluxy. Kuban took note of the irony of it all: that while the show "implied that the Glen Rose objects prove that humans lived with the dinosaurs many millions of years ago … Baugh, Patton, and other strict creationists … use the same objects to argue that both humans and dinosaurs lived together in the recent past."

Further Reading:

Burdick, Clifford. *Footprints in the Sands of Time: A Defense Statement*. Caldwell, Ohio: Bible Science Association, 1975.

Corliss, William R., ed. *Ancient Man: A Handbook of Puzzling Artifacts*. Glen Arm, MD: Sourcebook Project, 1978.

Kitcher, Philip. *Abusing Science: The Case against Creationism*. Cambridge, MA: MIT Press, 1982.

Kuban, Glen J. "The Taylor Site 'Man Tracks.'" *Origins Research*. 9,1 (spring/summer 1986): 2–10.

Patterson, John W. "Dinosaurs and Men: The Case for Coexistence." *Pursuit* 18.3 (Third Quarter 1985): 98–102.

Schadewald, Robert J. Lois A. Schadewald, ed. *Worlds of Their Own: A Brief History of Misguided Ideas: Creationism, Flat-Earthism, Energy Scams, and the Velikovsky Affair*. Minneapolis, MN: The Author, 2008.

Schafersman, Steven. "Raiders of the Lost Tracks: The Best Little Footprints in Texas." *Skeptical Inquirer* 7,3 (Spring 1983): 2–6.

Steiger, Brad. *Worlds before Our Own*. New York: Berkley-Putnam, 1978.

Wilford, John Noble. "Fossils of 'Man Tracks' Shown to Be Dinosaurian." *New York Times* (June 17, 1986).

Stomach Snakes and Other Gastrointestinal Creatures

Usually it's a snake or at least a reptile, but it can also be an amphibian or a small mammal, too. The category name "stomach snake" covers most of it, however, as in the following instance.

In the summer of 1893, a Luverne, Minnesota, man named Ole Eiveson (or Eivenson; the newspaper account spells the name both ways), suffering a stomach ailment local doctors were unable to treat, wrote a physician he had known in his native Norway to ask if he had any suggestions. The doctor replied that the problem was obvious: a snake lived inside him. He offered a prescription that may strike modern readers as worse than the disease: as much strychnine as could be put on the tip of a table knife, to be ingested with as much hot water as the sufferer could drink. Yes, the poison could do in as many as fifty human beings if not swallowed right, but done properly, it *would* eliminate the parasitic serpent without also dispatching the sufferer to an agonizing death.

Immediately following the taking of the medicine, the man began vomiting spectacularly. In the course of that unpleasantness, the snake poked its head out of the man's mouth. The sight of it caused his wife—surely understandably—to faint dead away. The man grabbed the snake and yanked it out of his throat, quickly clamping his mouth shut so that the creature could not crawl back into the comfort of its suddenly lost home.

When the *Luverne News* story was reprinted in an Iowa paper published just down the road, the *Le Mars Sentinel* editor found the tale pretty hilarious. He was led to wonder what his counterpart in Luverne "ate before he wrote it." Readers who didn't know better may have thought this literally stomach-churning horror story was the unique creation of a bored small-town newspaperman. It may have been a creation, but it certainly wasn't a unique one.

Keep your mouth shut

For many centuries, since at least the time of ancient Egypt, Assyria, and Babylonia, where the belief is mentioned in surviving manuscripts, a widespread tradition has held that snakes and other small creatures may enter someone's body in an unguarded moment. The victim may drink water out of a pond or stream, perhaps swallowing snake or frog eggs which are hatched within the stomach, where they grow to adulthood sustaining themselves on the food and liquids consumed by the human host. The victim knows only of persistent discomfort, and sometimes the sensation of unexplained movement through the gastrointestinal system. Or a fully grown snake may crawl through the victim's open mouth, typically, if he or she is sleeping outside, sometimes in a drunken stupor. Other, less fashionable speculations tied the presence of alien creatures inside the body to spontaneous generation or to the machinations of witches.

Many medical authorities, or what passed as authorities in the long, tangled history of pre-modern medicine, embraced the notion. So did such eminent scientists as Carl Linnaeus and Georges Louis Buffon. Even in the nineteenth century accounts appeared in medical journals. In 1813, for example, the *Edinburgh Medical and Surgical Journal* chronicled an alleged incident in Dunfermline. An overweight young woman complained of a variety of ailments, among them vomiting, stomach discomfort, and constipation. When her doctor prescribed her a laxative, she was able at last to move her bowels. The unsettling result was the subsequent observation of a lizard in the chamber pot. The creature fled under a chest of drawers, but the woman forced it out with a poker and tossed it into the fire, where it expired with a shrill squeak.

[A]s early as the sixth century some scholars had been skeptical, pegging the causes to delusion or hoax....

Though as early as the sixth century some scholars had been skeptical, pegging the causes to delusion or hoax, the concerted medical attack on stomach snakes and related beliefs did not begin until the mid–1800s. A German general practitioner, identified only as Dr. Sander, studied the case of Henriette Pfennig, who regularly vomited frogs in the presence of appropriately horrified onlookers. Dr. Sander, who entertained doubts about this, dissected several of these frogs, determining that the creatures had freshly ingested insects in their systems—in short, evidence that they had lived and eaten outside like normal animals. Further experimentation led the doctor to the conclusion that no frog could long survive within the high temperature of the human body.

Later in the same decade, the noted Göttingen physiologist Arnold Adolph Berthold surveyed the vast literature of gastrointestinal animals. He established that the creatures could not survive in the body's heat, and like Sander, he expressed certainty that all stories suggesting the contrary were false. Fifteen years later another medical scientist, the American J. C. Dalton, proved that any creature that got into a human stomach would soon be consumed by gastric juices.

Other investigators over the centuries had cured stomach-snake sufferers by collecting ordinary specimens, then distracting patients' attention or rendering them unconscious. After being shown the snake allegedly removed from their systems, the patients felt a whole lot better and resumed their lives minus mysterious internal discomforts. On some occasions the internal agonies were traced to more conventional ailments. In a number of cases, if we may judge from the description of the creature, tapeworms were the culprits.

Still, such things show up in surprising cultural contexts. Nathaniel Hawthorne borrowed the "bosom serpent" for allegorical use in a disturbing short story published in 1843, remarking in a footnote, "The physical fact, to which it is here attempted to give a moral significance, has been known to occur in more than one instance."

Stomach critters in the American press

Anyone who expects modern journalistic standards in the nineteenth-century press soon learns otherwise. Many aired a range of outlandishly suspect stories offering the sorts of claims one might have encountered in the *Weekly World News*, which was in its day the wildest and woolliest of the supermarket tabloids. Stomach snakes and comparable yarns were a staple, probably because they combined two elements—the weird and the gruesome—forever beloved of readers looking for fright-inducing (or gross-out) thrills. Though they usually cited specific names and places, one telling feature they had in common: an absence of any actual journalistic investigation and documentation. The "reporters" merely wrote down what somebody told them, and that was mostly it. One suspects that most or all of the stories would have shrunk under concentrated scrutiny. Still, they retain their capacity to unsettle the imagination even now. Some examples:

Hardwicke, Massachusetts, July 10, 1822: "Eleanor Smith, 15 years of age, threw up from her stomach a live green snake, nine or ten inches in length, which she had probably taken in three years since while drinking at a brook. During that time she had been confined to her bed, and had become much emaciated. The snake was perfectly lively, running about the house, up on chairs, tables, etc. She is now free from pain, and is apparently on the recovery" (*Ohio Repository*, Canton, August 22, reprinted from *New York American*).

Schenectady, New York, February 4, 1828: "Mr. George Sanders, a respectable industrious mechanic, residing in the vicinity of this city, ejected a *snake* from his stomach nine inches long, and about in the proportion of a common adder, but not resembling in color any snake heretofore seen in this country. The back a light brown, the belly red and green, extending in two strips lengthways, and the eyes white.... Mr. Sanders has been troubled for some more than a year with unusual pain in his stomach.... At breakfast, after swallowing a piece of meat, he felt such a nauseous sickness, that he left the house and commenced a severe vomiting, in the course of which he brought up a living reptile. It expired immediately" (*Sandusky Clarion*, Ohio, March 15, reprinted from *Schenectady Cabinet*).

Sometime in 1858, Michigan: "For the past seventeen years the sufferer [a Michigan man identified only as Beach] has been satisfied there was a living animal in his stomach. If he drank liquor the animal would seem to become drunk. This he judged from the fact that it remained perfectly quiet until the effects of the spirits wore off. At times, when he partook of food offensive to the animal, it would become agitated, and roll about with a motion which could be felt by placing the hand upon the stomach.… A German doctor … recommended the process of starving the intruder out.… The patient succeeded in inducing the animal to come up into his throat, but for fear of strangulation he swallowed vinegar, and drove it back. For four months means were tried to relieve the man's stomach of the unwelcome guest, and finally, a few days ago, he passed an entire snake, measuring just three feet in length. It was somewhat decomposed, and had evidently lost four or five inches of its tail" (*Janesville Morning Gazette*, Wisconsin, November 8, reprinted from *Sandusky Register*, Ohio).

Pennsylvania and New York, 1871: "Hattie M. Cole, aged 10 years, of Buckingham, Wayne county, Pa., is, has been for a long time troubled with a living creature in her stomach. What it is no one can tell for a certainty, but physicians in Oswego, N.Y., where she has been taken recently for treatment, think there is no doubt of its being a snake. By putting the finger on the stomach, where the creature can be distinctly seen to lie, it quickly changes its position, and even when the finger is within an inch or two of the stomach it will as quickly move away. All these changes produce pain to the girl. She recently got hold of the creature with her hand in her throat, and had to let go to save herself from strangling. It then returned to her stomach. A medical electrician operated on the girl at Oswego with his battery, but was obliged to desist, as it caused the snake to squirm and throw itself about so as to cause the subject the most intense agony" (*Daily Alta California*, September 1).

> "**B**y putting the finger on the stomach, where the creature can be distinctly seen to lie, it quickly changes its position.…"

Sedalia, Missouri, December 1883: "Edward Longmore is a young man about 19 years of age.… He was formerly employed by Lafferty Bros., butchers, and while in their employ he was frequently riding around in the country after stock. At such times when he was thirsty he would drink water from springs and ravines.… Over two years ago he began to experience a choking sensation and to feel the presence of something which seemed to be alive, moving about from one position to another.… Meantime, the patient grew worse, suffering terrible pain, and was a few weeks ago confined to his bed and became well nigh helpless.… On Thursday, almost a fortnight ago, he passed, according to his own statement and that of his mother, the vertebrae of something resembling the bone framework of a lizard or fish, about three inches in length, and it is supposed that with the flesh on it would have been as large as the middle finger on a man's hand. The skeleton had nothing on it except some muscles along the spinal column and on the clavicle. On Sunday following, the young man passed the head of the animal, which showed the eye sockets, nasal organs and fins, as large as the finger nail of a grown person. He is also said to have passed on Monday a number of fish-like eggs. These were the last of the remains of the piscatorial or reptilian family" (*Brooklyn Eagle*, January 6, 1884).

Detroit, Michigan, August 6, 1886: "Ten years ago, when but 8 years of age, Mrs. Henry Jameson … swallowed a tiny water snake. From that date to the present she has been in poor health.… A couple of months ago a Detroit physician, who was consulted, decided that something more than dyspepsia was troubling the young woman.... Mrs. Jameson was relieved of a green water snake about two feet long and half an inch in circumference. For ten years this repulsive reptile has been making itself at home in its strange quarters, causing its victim the most terrible physical agony. Mrs. Jameson says that for years she has been forced to eat ravenously in order to satisfy the needs of the strange boarder. The snake was especially fond of iced tea.... She experienced a constant gnawing in the stomach and while drinking water the snake invariably rose to her throat. On several occasions she almost choked to death. While the reptile was dying it would coil itself up and then uncoil with great force, causing the patient intense agony. Mrs. Jameson is severely prostrated" (*St. Paul Daily Globe*, Minnesota, August 8).

Cambridge, Massachusetts, September 1886: "Mrs. Mary Powers ... ejected from her stomach Monday night a winged and living bat which she swallowed while drinking water seven years ago.... Ushering the reporter into the parlor, she left the room and returned in a few moments, carrying in her hand a glass preserve jar. At the bottom of the jar a black object appeared to be moving about.... An examination ... revealed the body of a bat with hooked wings and other appendages peculiar to that animal. It was black on all sides, and the lower part of the body was covered with a thick film of dark hair. The body was about three inches long, and its extended wings measured over seven inches across from tip to tip. The most peculiar feature of the animal was the head. It was about one inch in length and shaped some [sic] like that of a lizard. From its lower jaw several tufts of long dark hair hung in clotted masses. The eyes and nostrils were well marked. The head was topped with two extremely long ears. It weighed from two to three ounces, and possibly more" (*Freeborn County Standard*, Albert Lea, Minnesota, September 29, reprinted from the *Boston Globe*).

Dayton, Ohio, July 1887: "Snake 21 inches long was ejected from the stomach of Michael Wheatley, a Dayton fireman. It had troubled him for five years. It is supposed to have entered his stomach when he was drinking from a spring" (*Coshocton Semi-Weekly Age*, July 16).

Olean, New York, July 23, 1888: "Little Lina Lewis, the 6-year-old daughter of Dr. S. E. Lewis[,] for six months past has been in poor health and complained of feeling something in her stomach. At times she said she felt as if there was a snake in her throat.... Monday the child was taken with a violent fit of vomiting, and finally the people in the room were horrified to see her expel a large red angle worm, which was as lively as though it had just come from mother earth and at once began wriggling about on the floor as though someone was pursuing it for fish bait. It was captured and is now preserved in alcohol at the office of Dr. Richards. The worm ... measured seven inches in length. The family now remember that when Lina was about two years old she was making mud pies and playing in the dirt with some other children one day, and several of them ran into the house and told Mrs. Lewis that Lina had swallowed an angle-worm. The statement was thought nothing of at the time, and was considered a childish story. The worm has reposed in the child's stomach for four years" (*Olean Democrat*, July 26).

Near Trenton, Ohio, August 1889: Farmer Henry Wood drew "a good-sized live snake from his stomach that had been troubling him for years. The snake has become a pet in the family, and is preserved in a large glass jar. Three times a day now, when Mr. Wood comes to his meals, the reptile will twist and writhe in the jar, and nothing will quiet it until Mr. Wood removes the covering. It will then crawl out to a dish of milk set on the table, which it drinks almost like a kitten. It will then crawl back into the jar and curl up apparently satisfied.... Mr. Wood thinks he drank the snake some seven or eight years ago from a small brook, as ever since that time he has had an uneasiness in his stomach" (*Ohio Democrat*, New Philadelphia, August 15, reprinted from *Zanesville Signal*).

Columbus, Ohio, August 9, 1890: "Mrs. Anna Nickel ... has complained of a peculiar sensation in the stomach, as if something having life was moving about. This continued for six months. A number of prominent physicians in Columbus and elsewhere have been consulted, but none gave the woman relief. Saturday evening she complained of a tickling sensation in her throat, and called Dr. Vogt, who formed the opinion that the sensation was caused by the presence of an insect. After swallowing a powerful emetic, Mrs. Nickel was relieved by the expulsion of a live frog from her stomach. It was about two inches long, almost white, and the hind legs were missing. The physician gave it as his opinion that the woman, while drinking water, had swallowed the egg, which was hatched by the warmth of the stomach" (*Indiana County Gazette*, Pennsylvania, August 14).

//"The snake has become a pet in the family, and is preserved in a large glass jar."

Salem Township, Ohio, circa late May/early June 1891: "For nearly two months an 18-year-old son of D. N. Strayer ... was decidedly unwell. His stomach was in a constant state of rebellion.... Remedies without number were tried in vain.... In the night he was suffering very much. He could not eat his supper, was exceedingly restless and had a high fever until daylight.... When he began vomiting Dr. S. G. Good ... was called. Before he reached the house, the young man vomited what looks like a 'horse hair snake.' It is, however, a different semi-reptile. Its length is ten inches. It is brown in color, as large as a wrapping cord used by druggists and is gorgon-eyed—that is, it has a single in the center of the head" (*Mansfield Evening News*, June 4).

Watertown, Wisconsin, September 30, 1891: "An extraordinary incident happened in the life of Charles White, the veteran St. Paul railway conductor, this morning. For a long time he has been in bad health, complaining of stomach troubles, and for several months his friends have feared that nothing would cure him.... A short time before he was to take his train from Watertown to Milwaukee, he was seized with a severe attack of coughing and vomiting, accompanied by violent cramps in the stomach. Slime and foam poured from his mouth, and at last, after an unusually severe paroxysm of vomiting, his stomach ejected a hideous snake, about fifteen inches long, that squirmed and wriggled on the floor. It was promptly killed and afterwards placed in a bottle. As soon as the stomach was relieved of its horrible tenant Mr. White felt better, and was able to come to town, bringing the reptile with him to submit to the judgment of the medical fraternity.... The snake seems to be the common variety known as garter snakes, and the possibility is that he swallowed it when it was very small, and he was a soldier drinking out of a southern spring or creek" (*Milwaukee Journal*, September 30).

Corning, New York, June 11, 1897: "Dr. John Stenger ... made a curious discovery recently while treating a patient for what he believed to be an affection [sic] caused by cancer of the stomach. For some time past Dr. Stenger has been attending Mrs. James Holliday of Stony Brook, Pa., at last decided that Mrs. Holliday's symptoms were so very serious that an operation would be necessary to save her. Friday last the doctor performed the operation, but found no cancer, much to his surprise. He was almost dumbfounded when he found a small water snake crawling through the upper entrance to Mrs. Holliday's stomach.... Mrs. Holliday is recovering from the strain of the operation and has manifested a desire to see the reptile that has caused her so much annoyance for months past. She accounts for the presence of the snake in her stomach from the fact that the family water supply is obtained from an open spring and probably she swallowed the snake when drinking water taken from the spring in the evening" (*Hornellsville Weekly Tribune*, June 18).

St. Louis, Missouri, July 1898: "A snake ten inches long and an inch in circumference has been removed from the stomach of Lena Novosic, 16 years old, by Dr. R. M. Hughes of the city dispensary staff.... Several days ago ... Dr. Hughes ... examined her and soon discovered her ailment. He gave her medicines and told her to come again for final treatment. The girl did so and Dr. Hughes gave her a large glass of medicine. The girl drank it and after a few minutes felt a creeping sensation in her stomach. A few minutes later she felt something in her throat and it almost gagged her. Dr. Hughes was watching her carefully, and with some instruments grabbed the head of the snake and pulled it out of the girl's throat.... The snake ... is one of the largest ever extracted from a human throat" (*Dubuque Daily Herald*, Iowa, July 17).

Buffalo, New York, April 1899: "By means of the X ray a large snake has been found in the stomach of an invalid whose case has baffled doctors for ten years. Mrs. Henry Young, living near Oil City, Pa., has just returned from a Buffalo hospital, where she went to secure treatment for a case of chronic stomach trouble. After one examination with the X ray machine the Buffalo physician informed Mrs. Young and her husband that her stomach contained a live snake several feet long, and they could do nothing for her" (*Dubuque Daily Herald*, Iowa, April 15).

Huntingdon, New York, October 1901: "It is claimed that a woman, named Mrs. P. Charron, who has been under medical treatment for the last three years for stomach trouble, took a violent spell of coughing about a week ago, and in a spasm vomited a lizard, measuring five inches long, which turned out to be a frisky specimen, and is now disporting itself in an aquarium, placed on exhibition in the window of a local drug store" (*Lowville Journal and Republican*, October 31).

Kalamazoo, Michigan, July 25, 1905: "A stomach pump Tuesday saved the life of Frederica Fritch … when the instrument coaxed from her stomach a little garden snake about six inches long. While camping at Gull Lake last Wednesday, Miss Fritch drank from a spring and swallowed the reptile with the water" (*Quincy Daily Journal*, Illinois, July 27).

Shelbyville, Illinois, 1914: "William R. Austin, aged 70, … died today of a complication of diseases, said by specialists who conducted a post-mortem to have been caused by a small snake which lived in his stomach more than three years. Austin coughed up the snake last February and since that time had been rapidly on the decline. He is supposed to have drank [sic] in the snake in water from a spring in a field where he was accustomed to drink when doing work on his farm" (*Chillicothe Constitution*, Missouri, June 2).

Clinton County, New York, 1921: "One of the most singular cases ever to be brought to the attention of the Clinton County Medical Society was introduced yesterday by Dr. J. H. La Rocque, who had on exhibition a snake which is averred to have been vomited by a young woman in this city. The snake was something over 11 inches long and is believed to have been swallowed by the young woman while taking a drink when she was a child some years ago and had grown to the size it was when it was ejected from the stomach of the girl, who is now about twenty years of age…. The young woman has been an acute sufferer with stomach trouble for years…. Since the occurrence mentioned above the girl has been in the best of health…. [Dr. La Rocque] procured affidavits from the girl and her mother, who was present at the time of her curious experience" (*Canton Commercial Advertiser*, November 29, reprinted from *Plattsburgh Sentinel*, November 25).

Distress and delusion

The truth behind stories like these is lost to us. We can be certain, however, that these incidents, if they are based in any reality at all, could not have happened as reported—not because they allege extraordinary anomalies but because they are physiological impossibilities. It also bears noting that not all newspapers reported them so credulously. In the occasional instance, we get some sense of what may really have been going on.

When it reported the Clinton County event recounted above, the upstate New York newspaper took the trouble to contact two authorities at the New York Zoo. "Both of these are experts on the subject of snakes," it stated, "and both claim that it would be absolutely impossible for a snake to live in the stomach of a human being and state their reasons, saying that air is as essential to a snake as to any animal."

In February 1891 a number of newspapers around the country told the sad story of a Syracuse, New York, man named James O'Grady. The dying man, now weeks bedridden, told the press that a few months earlier, while drinking from a stream, he felt some foreign object go down his throat. After that, he suffered terrible stomach agony which kept him from being able to eat most food. He could feel something moving inside him. On occasion, when he consumed a glass of wine, a snake would crawl up his throat and stick its head outside O'Grady's mouth—a horrifying sight which his wife claimed to have witnessed.

After his death the following November, an autopsy uncovered nothing in his system beyond intestinal gas. The distress was real, in other words, but its believed cause was delusional. In those cases that aren't outright hoaxes, one suspects that explanations like this account for the longstanding, though now rarely heard, tradition of stomach snakes.

Further Reading:

Bondeson, Jan. *A Cabinet of Medical Curiosities*. Ithaca, NY: Cornell University Press, 1997.

Hawthorne, Nathaniel. "Egotism; or, The Bosom-Serpent." In *Tales and Sketches*, 781–94. New York: Library of America, 1982.

Thunderbird Photograph

In April 1890 two riders sighted an enormous flying creature—which Indians would have recognized immediately as a thunderbird—alighting on the Arizona desert. The beast had the body of a serpent, immense wings, two clawed feet, and an alligator's face with saucer-sized eyes. The men got as close to it as their terrified horses would allow. They proceeded on foot, rifles in hand, but the creature saw them and flew away, only to land again not far away. This time it came down on one of its wings and so was unable to escape as the men pumped bullets into it.

When measured, the wings were found to span an incredible 160 feet. The body, ninety-two and a half feet long, was smooth and featherless, more like a bat's than a bird's. The men cut off a portion of the wing and brought it with them to Tombstone.

That, at least, is how the *Tombstone Epitaph* told the story in its April 26, 1890, issue. That was the extent of its coverage; there was no follow-up article. The story was revived in a 1930 book, Horace Bell's *On the Old West Coast,* in which the author embellished, tongue-in-cheek, on the legend: "This flying amphibious monster was seen several times from 1881 to 1886." Thirty-three years later, in a dubiously credible feature in the men's action magazine *Saga,* Jack Pearl wrote that in 1886 the *Epitaph* had "published a photograph of a huge bird nailed to a wall. The newspaper said it had been shot by two prospectors and hauled into town by wagon. Lined up in front of the bird were six grown men with their arms outstretched, fingertip to fingertip. The creatures measured about 36 feet from wingtip to wingtip."

Pearl further alleged that in 1889, after being mocked in a Tombstone saloon, one of the prospectors challenged his harassers to go after the bird themselves. "There's plenty more of 'em nesting in the tops of them mountains," he is supposed to have said. The drunks set out into the desert, but when one went into the bushes to relieve himself, his companions heard him screaming, "It's got me!" They ran to investigate and found his footsteps had vanished in the middle of a clearing. All they could hear was his anguished voice coming from above them and finally fading out. (The second half of this story is clearly borrowed from another nineteenth-century yarn [sometimes set in 1889], the Oliver Lerch disappearance [see page 372], in which a young man is snatched up by an unseen something, his footsteps suddenly ending and his screaming voice exclaiming, "It's got me!")

Writing in a letter to the editor of *Fate* a few months after Pearl's story had appeared, regular correspondent H. M. Cranmer of Renova, Pennsylvania, mentioned the photograph without claiming to have seen it personally. He did, however, add the detail that "a group of actors dressed as professors were photographed under the bird, with one of them saying, 'Shucks, there is no such bird, never was, and never will be.'" In a follow-up letter in 1966, he stated flatly, "The photo was copied in many papers."

The fall 1969 issue of *Old West* revived the 1890 tale, citing the original *Epitaph* piece. In response, a reader named Harry F. McClure wrote the magazine to aver that as a boy in Lordsburg, New Mexico, he had seen the two cowboys who saw the creature. Their experience had generated considerable comment at the time, he said, but it was not true that the creature was a bird—it was featherless, for one thing—and it had been neither captured nor killed. No one had ever spoken of a photograph, to his recollection.

Ivan T. Sanderson, a biologist and writer on Fortean phenomena, now declared that he once possessed a photocopy of the picture but had lent it to two associates, who lost it. Soon others began to "remember" that they, too, had seen it somewhere. The editors of *Fate* thought they may have published the picture in an early issue (the magazine started in 1948), but a search through every issue indicated otherwise. Responding to numerous letters from inquirers, the *Epitaph* conducted a thorough search which uncovered no such photograph in any issue of the newspaper. An extended survey of other Arizona and California newspapers of the period produced similarly negative results.

Still, as late as 1990, the late writer John A. Keel insisted, "I *know* I saw it. And not only that—I compared notes with a lot of other people who saw it.… It was either in one of the tabloids or one of the men's magazines.… It looked like a pterodactyl or something.… The guys were all wearing cowboy boots and cowboy hats, and they were all kind of scrungy, like they had been out riding on the range." That same year, Canadian researcher W. Ritchie Benedict thought he remembered seeing Sanderson displaying the photograph on a Canadian television show. "As I recall," he wrote, "the creature had a very pointed head and its eyes were closed."

In a review of the episode, Mark A. Hall observed:

The simple description of the photo—the six men posed to show the size of the dead bird—seems to create a vivid mental image in the minds of many, causing people who have always been particularly curious and eclectic in their knowledge to think it somehow familiar, even when they are unlikely to have ever seen it. Enough people have independently confessed to this reaction that I suspect it has contributed to the mistaken ideas about this photograph. People may think they have seen it when they truly have not.

Those disinclined to take such a prosaic view could take heart from an alternate interpretation offered by Charles Wiedemann:

If we consider the concept of parallel universes or separate realities, it is conceivable that a shift or switch has occurred between two realities. Where, previously, certain publications in "our" reality portrayed the thunderbird (whereas publications in the parallel reality excluded it), *now* the situation has become reversed. In "our" universe all thunderbird pictures have gone out of existence, and the situation is exactly as if they had never existed in the first place.

During the 1990s the search for the thunderbird photo became something of an obsession among Forteans. A discussion of the matter stretched over a number of issues of the late Mark Chorvinsky's *Strange Magazine*. Readers thought they had seen the picture either in a turn-of-the-century book of Old West photographs or in a men's magazine such as *Saga* (though a thorough search of that periodical uncovered nothing except the reference in Jack Pearl's story).

Two contributors produced illustrations based on what they believed to be their memories of the photo. One showed a pterosaur-like creature nailed right side up against a shack wall,

A thunderbird totem pole from the American Northwest.

with three armed men in the foreground. The other depicted a huge crane-like bird held upside down by a dozen or so unarmed men behind it, with another twenty or so individuals standing behind them. Shown both illustrations, an authority on Old West photography at the Bancroft Library in California recognized neither, nor did anyone else at the institution.

If we are to believe him, and there is no reason to do so, Derek Barnes discovered a early 1860s-era pterosaur photograph in 1998, while shopping at a junk store in small-town Arkansas. It was pressed between the pages of a "70s cheesy paranormal book." The supposed creature lies on the ground surrounded by seven or eight musket-bearing, blue-uniformed men, apparently Union soldiers. Though the photo gives at least the outward appearance of a period piece, it manages to betray its modern origin in another way: the soldiers are too old and too hefty for the skinny, scrawny men who fought the Civil War.

When *Fortean Times* ran the photo with skeptical commentary, reader Rosemary Pardoe wrote in to remark, "As one of many people who are positive they remember seeing the Thunderbird photograph in their childhood ... I have to say that the Civil War Thunderbird photograph is (as you suspect) pretty certainly a rather jolly hoax."

(Continued on page 431)

Atmospheric Life Forms

On July 17, 1818, what witnesses described as an "incredible number" of bubbles of various sizes rained down from the sky in the early evening. They fell on an area of Denmark, continuing for at least a couple of hours. Witnesses who caught them reported that they dissolved on contact, leaving yellow spots on the hands and emitting a strong sulphur smell.

Occasional reports of generally comparable phenomena inspired a notion that became briefly popular in the mid-twentieth century during the early years of the UFO controversy. According to some, flying saucers, as they were then called, were neither delusions nor spacecraft but "space animals"—life forms existing in the upper atmosphere. The idea was even entertained for a time by individuals in the Air Force's first UFO project, Sign, after it was suggested to them by John Philip Bessor, a Pennsylvania man interested in psychic phenomena. Bessor thought flying saucers were "of a highly attenuated (ectoplasmic?) substance, capable of materialization and dematerialization, whose propellent is a form of telekinetic energy." He even suspected these creatures were eating people; as evidence he pointed to reported falls from the sky of flesh and blood.

Bessor, however, was not the first to engage in speculation of this sort. In a science fiction story published in the November 1913 issue of *The Strand,* Sir Arthur Conan Doyle imagined "The Horror of the Heights," atmospheric monsters that attacked and killed pilots. In a nonfiction context, Charles Fort took note of reports of "unknown, luminous things" seen in the sky that may describe "living things that occasionally come from somewhere else."

In later years space animals were championed by no less than Kenneth Arnold, whose June 24, 1947, sighting over Mount Rainier, Washington, marked the onset of the UFO age. In Arnold's view, expressed in a 1959 interview, UFOs may be "living organisms ... in the atmosphere.... They have the power to change their density and appearance." Other champions of space animals were Countess Zoe Wassilko-Serecki, biologist Ivan T. Sanderson, and occultist/saucer-contactee Trevor James Constable. Constable claimed to have photographed "critters," as he called them, using infrared film.

But if one rejected Constable's pictures as inconclusive, there was no compelling evidence, logical or material, for space animals. The closest thing to such evidence, as already noted, came in the form of a small number of accounts in which witnesses reported seeing ostensibly organic substances come out of the sky and plop in front of them. In a 1957 article Civilian Saucer Intelligence of New York offered this speculation: "Only rarely do [the atmospheric creatures] descend low enough to be seen from the ground. When (by mischance or illness) one falls to the ground and is killed, there is found a lump of soapy jelly, which soon disappears."

Further Reading:

Bessor, John Philip. "Are the Saucers Space Animals?" *Fate* 8,12 (December 1955): 6–12.

Constable, Trevor James. *The Cosmic Pulse of Life: The Revolutionary Biological Power behind UFOs*. Santa Ana, CA: Merlin Press, 1976.

Gaddis, Vincent H. *Mysterious Fires and Lights*. New York: Dell, 1978.

James, Trevor [pseud. of Trevor James Constable]. *They Live in the Sky*. Los Angeles: New Age Publishing Company, 1958.

Laprade, Armand, ed. *Shapes in the Sky*. Marshall, AR: Would-You-Believe Publications, 1985.

Wassilko-Serecki, Zoe. "Startling Theory on UFOs." *American Astrology* 23 (September 1955): 2–5.

"Who 'Discovered' Space Animals?" *CSI News Letter* (December 15, 1957): 31.

(*Continued from page 429*)

At his Frontiers of Zoology website, on May 9, 2011, Dale A. Drinnon posted a separate photo, purporting to show a large, pterosaur-like creature in the foreground, with five gun-bearing men, dressed in late-nineteenth-century Western garb behind it. He compares it with another photo, showing nine men, five recognizable from the earlier picture, but this time the figure in the foreground is the body of an outlaw, California train-robber John Sontag, killed in a gunfight with a posse (evidently the men depicted) in June 1893. Drinnon, who thinks this is what Keel saw, speculates that the pterosaur was inserted into the picture long ago in a gag postcard.

Further Reading:

Bell, Horace. *On the Old West Coast*. New York: William Morrow and Company, 1930.

"Benedict Hot on Thunderbird Photo Trail." *Strange Magazine* 6 (1990): 44.

Benedict, W. Ritchie. "Strange World: Thunderbird Photograph Investigation." *Strange Magazine* 11 (1993): 39.

Chorvinsky, Mark. "Cryptozoo Conversation with John A. Keel." *Strange Magazine* 5 (1990): 35–40.

Cranmer, H. M. "Report from the Readers: Thunderbird Sightings." *Fate* 16,9 (September 1963): 116–17.

———. "Report from the Readers: Bird Call." *Fate* 19,3 (March 1966): 131–32.

Hall, Mark A. *Thunderbirds! The Living Legend of Giant Birds*. Bloomington, MN: Mark A. Hall Publications and Research, 1988.

———. "Thunderbirds Are Go." *Fortean Times* 105 (1997): 34–38.

"Is This a Pterodactyl?" *Fortean Times* 134 (2000): 21.

Keel, John A. "Beyond the Known." *Fate* 48,1 (January 1995): 28,31.

McClure, Harry F. "Monster Bird." *Old West* (summer 1970): 84.

Pardoe, Rosemary. Letters. *Fortean Times* 137 (2000): 52.

Parrish, J. K. "Our Country's Mysterious Monsters." *Old West* (fall 1969): 25,37–38.

"The Search for the Thunderbird Photo (Continues)." *Strange Magazine* 12 (fall/winter 1993): 38–39; 15 (spring 1995): 44–45; 16 (fall 1995): 40–41; 18 (summer 1997): 34–35; 19 (spring 1998): 26–28.

Wiedemann, Charles. "Jumping Carefully to Conclusions." *Pursuit* 9,2 (April 1976): 44–45.

Winters, Wayne. "Report from the Readers: Situation Normal: All Fowled Up." *Fate* 19,8 (August 1966): 128–29.

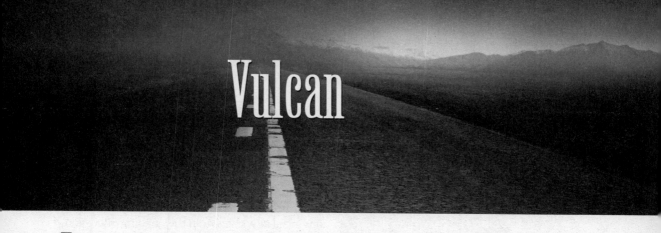

Vulcan

In 1846, Urbain Jean Joseph Le Verrier, of the Paris Observatory, was one of two astronomers to predict where an eighth planet would be discovered. When seen (or at least recognized for what it was) soon afterward, Le Verrier's calculations proved substantially correct. The planet was less than one degree of arc from the position Le Verrier had assigned it. The French astronomer had inferred Neptune's existence from disturbances in the orbit of Uranus.

Le Verrier, whose egotism was both gigantic and legendary, wanted the new planet named after him and fought to diminish recognition for the British astronomer John Adams, who many thought deserved to be named co-discoverer.

Le Verrier's sense of tarnished honor, coupled with a desire for unambiguous acclaim, undoubtedly had much to do with a peculiar episode that began a few years later. Le Verrier now focused his attention on the opposite end of the solar system, toward Mercury, which like Uranus had its own orbital irregularities. Though relativity theory would eventually provide a satisfactory explanation for the problem, in his time the only cause Le Verrier could imagine was an intra-Mercury planet—in other words, a world in orbit between Mercury and the sun.

On December 12, 1859, Le Verrier received a letter from a country doctor and astronomy buff named Edmond Lescarbault. Lescarbault made an extraordinary claim: that on March 26 he had seen a round black spot—a planet in transit—cross the upper part of the sun's face, moving along an upward-slanting path. Over the hour and a quarter it was in view, it crossed less than one fourth of the sun's diameter.

Le Verrier immediately enlisted an associate to serve as witness, then headed straight to the village of Orgeres, where Lescarbault lived. Once there, Le Verrier knocked on his door, refused to identify himself, and spoke rudely to the physician, calling him "the man who pretends to have seen an intra-Mercurial planet." He demanded to know how Lescarbault could have come to such an absurd conclusion. Thoroughly intimidated by this bellicose stranger, the physician recounted his observation in detail. At the end Le Verrier revealed who he was, congratulated him warmly, and on his return to Paris saw to it that Lescarbault would be decorated with the Legion of Honor.

Within days the new discovery had the astronomical world abuzz. Le Verrier, perhaps having attained a degree of modesty after the unpleasant events surround-

A statue of Urbain Jean Joseph Le Verrier can be seen at the Observatoire de Paris in France.

ing Neptune's detection, suggested the planet be named Vulcan. By January, excited discussions about the discovery were appearing in the astronomical journals. Le Verrier calculated its size (about one-seventeenth that of Mercury, he thought) and suggested that it transited the sun's face in early April and early October. He also cited twenty earlier observations of what he could now confidently identify as Vulcan. Le Verrier's death, in 1877, removed one of Vulcan's most convinced advocates from the ongoing discussion.

From the beginning there were skeptics. One was a Brazilian astronomer who reported that at the same time Lescarbault was observing the sun's face, he too had been doing so, only with a far more powerful telescope (presumably, both men were using optical filters). He had seen nothing out of the ordinary.

Over the next few decades astronomers watched for Vulcan during the periods Le Verrier believed it would be in sight. The results were mostly disappointing, erroneous observations (usually of sunspots), and some sightings of anomalous objects that, whatever they may have been, clearly were not Vulcan. By the end of the century, skepticism was nearly universal. In 1899, Asaph Hall, discoverer of the moons of Mars, remarked that the planet no longer figured in the discourse of "rational astronomy."

Still, some of the sightings that played a role in the controversy were and are puzzling. A few would be called UFO reports were they to be made today. Among the more interesting were those that indicated that the objects being seen were much closer to the witnesses than they thought. If so, this would explain why—as in the case of Lescarbault's sightings—astronomers elsewhere did not see the same things.

Aside from Lescarbault's, the most publicized such instance concerned two sightings, independent observations by Lewis Swift (in Wyoming) and another by James Craig Watson (in Colorado)—but apparently no one else. The sightings took place during a total eclipse on July 29, 1878. Watson wrote to the U.S. Naval Observatory:

I have the honor to report that at the time of totality I observed a star of the four and a half magnitude in R. A. 8h. 26m. dec. 18° north, which is, I feel, an intra-Mercurial planet. I observed with a power of forty-five, and did not have time to change the power so as to enlarge the disk. There is no known star in the position observed, and I did not see any elongation, such as ought to exist in the case of a comet very near the sun.... The appearance of the object observed was that of a ruddy star of the four and a half magnitude. The method which I adopted prevents the possibility of error from wrong circle readings; besides I had memorized the Washington chart of the region, and no such star was marked thereon. By comparison with the neighboring stars on Argelander's scale, the magnitude of the planet would be in the fifth, although my direct estimate at the time of the observation was four and a half, as stated.

Swift described his sighting thus:

About one minute after totality two stars caught my eye about three degrees, by estimation, southwest of the sun. I saw them twice and attempted a third observation, but a small cloud obscured the locality. The stars were both of the fifth magnitude, and but one is on the chart of the heavens. This star I recognized as Theta in Cancer. The two stars were about eight minutes apart. There is no such configuration of stars in the constellation of Cancer. I have no doubt that the unknown star is an intra-Mercurial planet, and am also inclined to believe that there may be more than one such planet.

A furious exchange erupted in the astronomical press, and the two were accused of having made the most elementary of errors: they had mistaken two well known stars for two unknown objects. The two observers would have none of it. "I have never made a more valid observation," Swift wrote in *Nature*, "nor one more free from doubt."

Further Reading:

Campbell, W. W. "The Closing of a Famous Astronomical Problem." *Popular Science Monthly* 74 (1909): 494–503.

Corliss, William R., ed. *Mysterious Universe: A Handbook of Astronomical Anomalies*. Glen Arm, MD: Sourcebook Project, 1979.

———, ed. *The Sun and Solar System Debris: A Catalog of Astronomical Anomalies*. Glen Arm, MD: Sourcebook Project, 1986.

"The Discovery of Vulcan." *New York Times* (August 8, 1878).

Fort, Charles. *The Books of Charles Fort*. New York: Henry Holt and Company, 1941.

Gould, Rupert T. *Oddities: A Book of Unexplained Facts*. London: Philip Allan, 1928.

Grossinger, Richard. *The Night Sky*. Los Angeles: Jeremy P. Tarcher, 1981.

Hall, Asaph. "Plus Probans Quam Necesse Est." *Popular Astronomy* 7 (1899): 13.

Hricenak, David. "Phantom Planets and Free-Worlds." *INFO Journal* 8,5 (March/June 1981): 5–6.

"The Planet Vulcan." *Indiana Progress*, Pennsylvania (October 3, 1878).

Swift, Lewis. "The Intra-Mercurial Planet Question." *Nature* 21 (1880): 299.

Wahhoo

Strange sounds awoke A. A. Adams of Reno—a city in west-central Nevada not far from the California border—just before dawn on August 29, 1879. Some large animal treading slowly on his front porch, he deduced as he heard its claws clicking on the boards. After listening for some moments, he decided to get out of bed and investigate.

Quickly dressing himself, he stepped out into a cloudless night to observe what he first took to be a big bulldog. On hearing Adams, the animal turned around and stared at him through two brilliantly luminous eyes, so intense that they resembled glowing coals. Besides a strikingly long, slender neck, the creature also had a snout that resembled a pig's more than a dog's. After gazing at him for a minute or so, it casually retreated to a fence, which it climbed with its front paws in the fashion of a cat. There it reposed as it continued staring at the bewildered, uneasy Adams.

The witness hit upon the idea of spraying the creature with a garden hose, an action sure to hasten its departure. Ten minutes of dowsing later, the beast was still there, still glaring. Now Adams decided to retrieve a firearm. After loading it, he decided it would be better just to lock the door and retire under the covers, where he lay for some time before falling asleep.

When he inspected the porch the next morning, he found no trace of anything out of the ordinary. The next night he and a friend sat up late waiting for a reappearance, to no avail.

What was the creature? The *Reno Evening Gazette* (September 4), which recounted the tale paraphrased above, provided an answer in the form of a couple of questions: "Could it have been one of those ferocious hybrids called wahhoos, which are said to prowl at night in the neighborhood of Halleck and Deeth [in northeastern Nevada]?... What is a wahhoo?"

A follow-up article the next day, however, allows as how Adams's encounter was something less than originally alleged:

A GAZETTE reporter has been credibly informed that the mysterious animal which promenaded the porch of A. A. Adams' house one night last week was not a wahhoo, but a skunk. It is true that the animal appeared in the manner originally described, and retained its post of observation on the fence for a long time. But a friend of Mr. Adams states that he knew the nature of the animal he had to deal with, and refrained from shooting it because he did not wish to draw out the skunk's powers of defense. It is a relief to know that it was not a wahhoo.

But the *Gazette* was by no means finished with wahhoos. In its September 11 issue it noted the sighting of a "strange looking animal" on a road near Peavine just four days earlier. It had the general appearance of a coyote but was too big to be one, and it was too small to be a bear. "It was running on the side of a hill with wonderful speed," the paper related, "and disappeared in a moment. Could the beast have been the Wahhoo?"

The next day, in a long article, the newspaper acknowledged that some readers thought they were getting their legs pulled. It insisted that if the wahhoo was unknown to naturalists, it wasn't the only so far uncatalogued animal out there; "it may yet be found that this strange beast will possess a high scientific interest."

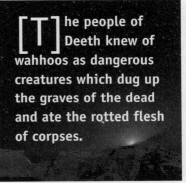

[T]he people of Deeth knew of wahhoos as dangerous creatures which dug up the graves of the dead and ate the rotted flesh of corpses.

Consider, for example, the testimony of Richard Smith, a Wells Fargo agent living in Reno. While hunting near Halleck, Smith and his brother H. R. Smith heard much about the wahhoo. They didn't see one, but they were given the dressed hide of one. The brother took it with him when he returned to Los Angeles. Richard Smith, who spoke with a young man who had shot a number of wahhoos, found that their left legs were noticeably shorter than their right legs. The young man explained that Wahhoos lived on hillsides and the uneven length of the legs apparently was an adaptation which allowed them to traverse them with greater convenience.

Meantime, the people of Deeth knew of wahhoos as dangerous creatures which dug up the graves of the dead and ate the rotted flesh of corpses. Hunters had killed some, finding them to be larger than coyotes though with short legs. Their paws were oversized, with strong projecting claws which enabled them to dig efficiently. In the *Gazette*'s account, "The body is long and slender, the tail of medium length and usually curved over the back, and the jaws provided with formidable teeth."

Central Pacific Railroad express messenger Daniel Roberts provided further details. He informed the paper that wahhoos were widely known in Montana. He himself had seen one in Idaho in the summer of 1867. He and a companion, at the conclusion of a long ride via horseback, were approaching a station in Beaver canyon when he heard a braying sound. His friend explained that it was the cry of a wahhoo. Soon thereafter, the creature came into view sitting upon the edge of a cliff above them. It would cease its howling when it stood up and walked along the cliff, and would resume it intermittently as it stopped and sat on its haunches. Roberts and a fellow rail employee later saw two wahhoos in a rural area around Summit Station. Wahhoos live in wilderness areas far from human habitation, Roberts related, and that is why they are rarely seen.

The *Gazette's* edition of September 20 carried a one-paragraph item of what befell two hunters from Eureka when they headed up to Deeth in search of wahhoos. A day or two into the venture, one of them saw a specimen sitting on a hillside. When he fired at the animal, his rifle blew up, throwing him to the ground in a dazed state with cuts and burns. The hunter recovered sufficiently to decide that he needed to return home forthwith. The wahhoo was unharmed.

Another wahhoo hunt had been announced in a letter published three days earlier from someone identified only as "Subscriber" from Wadsworth:

ED. GAZETTE—Report was brought to town yesterday that a wahhoo had been seen in the mountains west of town. The night before, the people of Jones' ranch had been aroused by the wahhoo's long-drawn howl, which was likened to a shrill fog-whistle. They saw the mountains illumined as with an electric light.

This they found was owing to the glare of the creature's eyeballs. It sat upon a neighboring cliff, and so brilliant was the light emitted that none could gaze upon the creature, even for an instant.

This report, backed by authority, so excited our nimrods that a hunt was organized immediately. Jake Lewis, J. W. Holbrook, Wm. Pierson and others started this morning, and brilliant work is looked for before the close of day.

Anticipating that a lengthened hunt might prove necessary, the party laid in provisions, of which the following is a summary: Whiskey, 200 rounds ammunition, demijohn [wicker-encased bottle], 1 piece bacon, limes, 1 bottle whiskey, 1 box cigars, 50 rounds additional whiskey, more whiskey.

The result of the chase is awaited with breathless anxiety. A special reporter accompanied the party, and full particulars will be given on their return.

The anonymous correspondent caught the spirit of the occasion. There was never a wahhoo outside the pages of the Reno newspaper. In those days (albeit no longer) Nevada hosted a county named Wahhoo. "Wahhoo"—or, as it's usually spelled now, "wahoo"—was and remains a cry of celebration, usually shouted or yodeled at sporting events. Wahoo is the name of a small town in Nebraska. It is the title of a cowboy-themed novelty song, popular in the heyday of Western swing, written by Cliff Friend. It is not attached, however, to any animal, whether a biological one or a genuinely legendary one. That wahhoo lived and died in the pages of the *Reno Gazette* in September 1879. It was a newspaper hoax, and probably an inside joke, whose true underlying humor is lost to all who did not live in the area in the period in question.

The hoaxer or hoaxers borrowed at least one element from American folklore. The sidehill dodger—one of many names by which it is known—is an imaginary creature whose legs are shorter on one side than on the other, enabling it to move quickly around hills.

Further Reading:

Dorson, Richard M. *Man and Beast in American Comic Legend*. Bloomington: Indiana University Press, 1982.

Heinselman, Craig. "Wahhoo, It's a Whoahaw!" *BioFortean Review* 4 (November 2006). http://www.strangeark.com/bfr/articles/wahhoo.html.

INDEX

Note: (ill.) indicates photos and illustrations.

UNEXPLAINED! Strange Sightings, Incredible Occurrences, and Puzzling Physical Phenomena

UNEXPLAINED! Strange Sightings, Incredible Occurrences, and Puzzling Physical Phenomena

N

UNEXPLAINED! Strange Sightings, Incredible Occurrences, and Puzzling Physical Phenomena